THE SYMPOSIUM

OF

PLATO

EDITED

WITH INTRODUCTION, CRITICAL NOTES
AND COMMENTARY

BY

R. G. BURY, M.A.

FORMERLY SCHOLAR OF TRINITY COLLEGE, CAMBRIDGE
LATE LECTURER IN CLASSICS, BRYN MAWR COLLEGE, U.S.A.
EDITOR OF "THE PHILEBUS" OF PLATO

CAMBRIDGE:

W. HEFFER AND SONS
LONDON: SIMPKIN, MARSHALL AND CO. LTD.
1909

Cambridge: Sage
PRINTED BY JOHN CLAY, M.A.
AT THE UNIVERSITY PRESS.

PREFACE

PLATO'S *Symposium* is undeniably one of the masterpieces of classical literature. The subtlest and most brilliant of Greek artists in prose has left us no finer, no more fascinating specimen of his skill than this dialogue in which, with the throbbing pulse of life for his theme, he matches that theme by the dramatic verve and vigour of his style. The interest of the book is not merely literary or philosophical: it appeals also to the wider circle of the students of culture and of life and of the "criticism of life" by its richness of suggestion and by its vividness of portraiture. To mention one point alone,—nowhere else, not even in the *Phaedo*, does the personality of Socrates shine before us so full and clear, " in form and gesture so express and admirable," as in the pages of the *Symposium*. To miss reading it is to miss the enjoyment of a veritable ἑστίαμα λόγων, blended and seasoned with curious art.

In the preparation of this edition I have been indebted mainly to the labours of continental scholars, for the sufficient, if surprising, reason that no English commentary has existed heretofore. It was, indeed, this singular fact, together with the recent publication of an interesting Papyrus fragment of the text, which chiefly moved me to attempt a commentary myself. On many of the interesting questions connected with the literary form and philosophical substance of the dialogue much more might have been said, but I have thought it best to keep both the Introduction and the Notes within a moderate compass. In the framing of the text, although I have ventured on several innovations of my own, I have been more conservative than the majority of the foreign critics, a considerable selection of whose "restorations" will be found in the Critical Notes in addition to the evidence of the leading MSS. and of the Papyrus: in all doubtful cases I have cited also the opinion of Schanz and of the Oxford editor, Prof. Burnet, whose admirable recension has been before me constantly and has aided me much. For expository material I must acknowledge in special my indebtedness to the useful and scholarly edition of A. Hug.

To gild with comment the refined gold of Plato's work is at the best a temerarious task; but if my book helps a single reader more justly to appraise the gold it will not have been wrought wholly in vain.

R. G. B.

October 4, 1909.

CONTENTS

INTRODUCTION

§ i. Summary of the Argument.

I. *The Preface:* 172 A—174 A.

Apollodorus, in reply to the enquiry of some friends, explains the occasion on which the supper-party at Agathon's was held, when Socrates and others delivered Discourses on Eros. The matter is fresh in his memory and, as a φιλόλογος himself, he is quite ready to repeat the whole story as he had it from Aristodemus,—an eye-witness and an intimate disciple of Socrates,—just as he had repeated it a few days before to his friend Glaucon.

II. *Aristodemus's Prologue:* 174 A—178 A.

Aristodemus meeting Socrates smartly attired expresses his surprise at so unusual a circumstance. Socrates explains that being invited to dine with Agathon he feels bound to go "in finery to the fine"; and he presses Aristodemus, although uninvited, to accompany him. On the road Socrates, immersed in thought, lags behind, and Aristodemus arrives at Agathon's alone. Not till they are half-way through the meal does Socrates appear; and Agathon rallies him on his devotion to σοφία. The proposal of Pausanias to restrict the potations, in view of yesterday's banquet, and that of Eryximachus to dismiss the flute-girl and amuse themselves by λόγοι, are unanimously agreed to. Then Eryximachus propounds an idea of Phaedrus, that Eros is the best possible theme for encomia, and suggests that each of the party in turn, commencing with Phaedrus, should now deliver an encomium on Eros. This suggestion is applauded by Socrates. Of the encomia the most noteworthy were the following :—

III. *The Discourse of Phaedrus:* 178 A—180 B.

Prologue: Eros is a great and wondrous god.

(*a*) He is wondrous in origin, being *eldest* of gods and unbegotten —witness what Homer and others say of him.

(*b*) He is the supreme *benefactor* of mankind, (1) as inspiring a high sense of honour in private, civic and military life; (2) as inspiring self-sacrifice, which wins divine favour (*e.g.* Alcestis and Achilles, contrasted with the cowardly Orpheus).

Epilogue: Thus Eros is most ancient, venerable, and beneficent.

IV. *The Discourse of Pausanias:* 180 c—185 c.

Prologue: Eros being not single but dual, we must begin by defining which Eros is to be our theme.

(*a*) The dual nature of Eros follows from the dual nature of Aphrodite: as there is an Aphrodite Urania and an Aphrodite Pandemos, so there is Eros Uranios and Eros Pandemos.

(*b*) From the principle that no action is in the abstract good or bad but derives its moral quality solely from the manner of its execution it follows that Eros is bad or good according to the kind of love-making to which it prompts.

(*c*) The *general characteristics* (1) of Eros Pandemos are that it is directed to women as well as boys, to the body rather than the soul, to unscrupulous satisfaction of lust; (2) whereas Eros Uranios shuns females and seeks only such males as are noble and nearly mature both in mind and body. It is the followers of Eros Pandemos who have brought paederastia into disrepute.

(*d*) *The varying νόμοι concerning Eros* may be classified thus:—

(1) In all Greek states except Athens the νόμος is *simple*, either (a) approving paederastia, as in Elis and Boeotia; or (β) condemning it, as in Ionia and states subject to barbarian rule, where it is held to foster a dangerous spirit of independence (*e.g.* Harmodius and Aristogiton).

(2) At Athens the νόμος is *complex.* (a) Eros is approved, and its excesses condoned, when directed towards superior youths approaching manhood. (β) It appears to be condemned, in so far as parents forbid their boys to hold converse with "erastae." The explanation of this ambiguous attitude must be sought in the principle laid down above,

that the moral quality of an act depends upon the conditions of its performance. The Athenian νόμος provides a test for distinguishing between good and bad forms of Eros: the test of time shows whether or not the right motive (desire for ἀρετή) actuates both the lover and his object. This motive alone justifies all erotic pursuits and surrenders, even mutual deception: hence we conclude that καλὸν ἀρετῆς ἕνεκα χαρίζεσθαι.

Epilogue: This Eros Uranios, which inspires zeal for ἀρετή, possesses the highest value alike for the individual and for the State.

V. *The first Interlude:* 185 c—e.

It was the turn of Aristophanes next; but being seized with a hiccough he called upon Eryximachus either to cure him or to speak in his stead. So Eryximachus, having first prescribed a number of remedies, spoke next.

VI. *The Discourse of Eryximachus:* 185 e—188 e.

Prologue: Pausanias was right in asserting the dual nature of Eros; but he failed to observe that the god's sway extends over the entire universe.

(*a*) The body, with its healthy and diseased appetites, exhibits the duality of Eros; and *medicine* is "the science of bodily erotics in regard to replenishment and depletion." It is the object of "the Art" of Asclepios to produce the Eros which is harmony between the opposite elements—the hot and the cold, the wet and the dry, etc. Eros is, likewise, the patron-god of *gymnastics* and *husbandry.*

(*b*) Similarly with *music.* The "discordant concord" of Heraclitus hints at the power of music to harmonize sounds previously in discord, and divergent times. Thus music is "the science of Erotics in regard to harmony and rhythm." It is less in the pure theory than in applied music (metrical compositions and their educational use) that the dual nature of Eros comes to light; when it does, the Eros Pandemos must be carefully guarded against.

(*c*) Again, in the spheres of *meteorology* and *astronomy* we see the effects of the orderly Eros in a wholesome temperate climate, of the disorderly Eros in blights and pestilences; for astronomy is "the science of Erotics in regard to stellar motions and the seasons of the year."

(*d*) Lastly, in *religion,* it is the disorderly Eros which produces the impiety which it is the function of divination to cure; and religion may be defined as "the science of human Erotics in regard to piety."

Epilogue: To Eros, as a whole, belongs great power; to the virtuous Eros great influence in effecting human concord and happiness.—If my eulogy is incomplete, it is for you, Aristophanes, to supplement it, if you choose.

VII. *The second Interlude:* 189 A—C.

Aristophanes explains that he is now cured of his hiccough, as a result of sneezing according to Eryximachus' prescription. He makes a jocular allusion to Eryximachus' discourse, to which the latter retorts, and after some further banter Aristophanes proceeds to deliver his encomium.

VIII. *The Discourse of Aristophanes:* 189 C—193 D.

Prologue: Men have failed to pay due honour to Eros, the most "philanthropic" of gods, who blesses us by his *healing* power, as I shall show.

(*a*) *Man's original nature* was different from what it now is. It had three sexes—male, female, androgynous; all globular in shape and with double limbs and organs; derived respectively from sun, earth and moon.

(*b*) *Man's woes* were due to the pride of these primal men which stirred them to attempt to carry Heaven by assault. In punishment Zeus sliced them each in two, and then handed them to Apollo to stitch up their wounds. But, because they then kept dying of hunger, owing to the yearning of each for his other-half, Zeus devised for them the present mode of reproduction, altering the position of the sex-organs accordingly. Thus Eros aims at restoring the primal unity and healing the cleft in man's nature.

(*c*) Each of us is a split-half of an original male, female, or androgynon; and the other-halves we seek in love are determined accordingly. Courage is the mark of boy-loving men and of man-loving boys, as both derived from the primal male. In the intense passion of Eros it is not merely sexual intercourse that is sought but a permanent fusing into one (as by the brazing of an Hephaestus); for Love is "*the pursuit of wholeness.*"

(*d*) As it was impiety that caused our "dioikismos" and bisection, so in piety towards the god Eros lies the hope of meeting with our proper halves and regaining our pristine wholeness.

Epilogue: Let us, then, laud Eros as the giver both of present blessings and of bright hopes of *healing* and restoration in the future.

IX. *The third Interlude:* 193 D—194 E.

Some conversation ensues between Aristophanes, Eryximachus, Socrates, and Agathon. Upon Socrates attempting to entangle Agathon in an argument, Phaedrus intervenes and bids Agathon proceed without further delay to offer his meed of praise to the god.

X. *The Discourse of Agathon:* 194 E—197 E.

Prologue: The method of previous speakers needs amendment. The correct method, which I shall adopt, is to laud first the character of Eros, and secondly his gifts to men.

(A) The *attributes* of Eros are (1) supreme felicity, (due to) (2) supreme beauty and (3) goodness.

(2) Eros is most *beautiful*, since he is (*a*) the youngest of gods (all tales to the contrary being false), witness his aversion to old-age; (*b*) most tender, witness his choosing soft souls for his abode; (*c*) supple, witness his power to steal unnoticed in and out of souls; (*d*) symmetrical, because comely as all allow; (*e*) fair-of-skin, for he feeds on flowers amid sweet scents.

(3) Eros is supremely *good*, since he is (*a*) most just, having no lot in violence or injustice; (*b*) most temperate, for he is the master of pleasure since no pleasure is greater than love; (*c*) most courageous, as holding sway over Ares, the most courageous of the gods; (*d*) most wise, being expert (*a*) in both musical and creative poesy, and (*β*) in the practical arts, as instructor of Zeus, Apollo and Athene in their respective crafts (he, too, inspired the gods with love of beauty and de-throned Necessity).

(B) The *blessings* conferred by Eros are, like his attributes, beauty and goodness. He produces peace and pleasantness in all spheres of life: he is the object of universal admiration, the author of all delights, best guide and captain for gods and men alike, whose praises it behoves all to chant in unison.

Epilogue: Such is my tribute of eulogy, not wholly serious nor wholly playful.

XI. *The fourth Interlude:* 198 A—199 C.

Agathon "brought down the house" with his peroration; and Socrates remarked to Eryximachus that its eloquence left him in despair —petrified by the Gorgon of Agathon's brilliant Gorgianisms. "Now," he said, "I must retract my rash tongue-pledge to join in a eulogy of Eros, since I perceive that I was quite astray in my ideas about the encomiastic art: for I supposed that truth came first, ornamental compliment second, whereas the contrary is evidently the fact. Such an encomium is quite beyond my poor powers; but if you care for an unvarnished speech about Eros, that I am ready to make." Phaedrus and the rest bidding him proceed in his own fashion, Socrates began by the following conversation with Agathon.

XII. *Socrates' preliminary Discussion with Agathon:*
199 c—201 D.

(1) "Your exordium on Method was admirable, Agathon. But tell me further, is Eros a relative notion, like 'father' or 'brother'?" "Certainly it is."

(2) "Next, you agree that if Eros desires its object it must lack it; and if a man wishes for some good he already possesses, what he really desires is what he lacks, *viz.* the future possession of that good." "True."

(3) "Again, if Eros is (as you said) love for beauty, Eros must lack beauty, and therefore goodness too, and be neither beautiful nor good." "I cannot gainsay you."

XIII. *The Discourse of Socrates (Diotima):* 201 D—212 c.

Prologue: I will now repeat the discourse on Eros which I once heard from my instructress in Erotics, Diotima the prophetess—assuming the conclusions formulated just now, and treating first of the character and secondly of the effects of Eros, according to Agathon's own method.

A. [*The nature of Eros,* 201 E—204 c.]

(1) Diotima showed me that Eros, although (as we have seen) neither beautiful nor good, is not therefore ugly and bad but rather *a mean* between these contraries.

(2) She argued also that Eros is not a god, since godhead involves the possession of just those goods which Eros desires and lacks. But neither is he a mortal, but stands midway between the two, being *a great daemon*; and the function of the daemonian is to mediate between gods and men.

(3) As to origin, Eros is son of Poros and Penia, and partakes of the nature of both parents—the fertile vigour of the one, the wastrel neediness of the other. As he is a mean between the mortal and the immortal, so he is a mean between the wise and the unwise, *i.e.* a wisdom-lover (*philosopher*). The notion that Eros is a beautiful god is due to a confusion between subjective Eros and the object loved.

B. [*The effects, or utility, of Eros*, 204 D—212 A.]

(1) [The object or end of Eros.]

What does Eros as "love of the beautiful" precisely imply? In the case of the good, its acquisition is a means to happiness as end. But Eros is not used in this generic sense of "desire for happiness," so much as in a narrower specific sense. And if we say that Eros is "the desire for the good," we must expand this definition into "*the desire for the everlasting possession of the good.*"

(2) [The method or mode of action of Eros.]

Eros works by means of generation, both physical and psychical, in the beautiful.

(*a*) Generation, being an immortal thing, requires harmony with the divine, *i.e.* beauty; without which the process is hindered. And generation is sought because it is, for mortals, the nearest approach to immortality. It is in the desire for immortality that we must find the explanation of all the sexual passion and love of offspring which we see in the animal world, since it is only by the way of leaving a successor to take its place that the mortal creature, in this world of flux, can secure a kind of perpetuity.

(*b*) But the soul has its offspring as well as the body. Laws, inventions and noble deeds, which spring from love of fame, have for their motive the same passion for immortality. The lover seeks a beautiful soul in order to generate therein offspring which shall live for ever; and the bonds of such soul-marriages are stronger than any carnal ties.

(*c*) After this elementary prelude, we reach the highest stage of the Mysteries of Love. The right method in Erotic procedure is to pass in upward course from love of bodily beauty to love of soul beauty, thence to the beauty of the sciences, until finally one science is reached which corresponds to the Absolute, Ideal Beauty, in which all finite things of beauty partake. To gain the vision of this is the goal of Love's endeavour, and to live in its presence were life indeed. There, if anywhere, with truth for the issue of his soul, might the lover hope to attain to immortality.

Epilogue : Believing that for the gaining of this boon Eros is man's best helper, I myself praise Eros and practise Erotics above all things and I urge others to do likewise. Such is my "encomium," Phaedrus, if you choose to call it so.

XIV. *The fifth Interlude :* 212 c—215 a.

Applause followed. Then suddenly, when Aristophanes was on the point of making an observation, a loud knocking was heard at the door. Presently Alcibiades, leaning on a flute-girl, appeared. " I am come to crown Agathon," he cried, " if you will admit a drunken reveller." Being heartily welcomed, he took the seat next Agathon, where Socrates had made room for him. And as soon as he perceived Socrates, he began playfully to abuse him. Then, taking some of the ribbands with which he had bedecked Agathon, he crowned "the marvellous head of Socrates, the invincible in words."

Next Alcibiades insisted on all the company drinking along with him. And, when Eryximachus protested against bare drinking without song or speech and explained to him what the previous order of procedure had been, Alcibiades replied, "In the presence of Socrates I dare not eulogize anyone else, so that if I am to deliver an encomium like the rest, Socrates must be my theme."

XV. *Alcibiades' eulogy of Socrates :* 215 a—222 c.

Prologue : My eulogy will take the form of parables—aiming not at mockery but at truth. Socrates resembles (*a*) Silenus-statuettes which serve as caskets for sacred images ; (*b*) the Satyr Marsyas.

I. In *form* he resembles both (*a*) the Sileni, and (*b*) the Satyr.

II. (*In character*) he resembles (*b*) *the Satyr*, being (1) a mocker, (2) a flute-player. As to (2) he excels Marsyas, since his words alone, without an instrument, fascinate all, old and young. Me he charms far more than even Pericles could, filling me with shame and self-contempt, and driving me to my wit's end.

III. He resembles (*a*) *the Sileni* in the contrast between his exterior and interior. (*a*) *Externally* he adopts an erotic attitude towards beautiful youths : (β) but *internally* he despises beauty and wealth, as I know from experience. For I tried to bribe him with my beauty, but all my many attempts came to nothing. Private conversations, gymnastics together, a supper-party *à deux*, even a night on the same couch—all was of no use. Against my battery of charms he was armed (by his *temperance*) in "complete steel"; and I charge him now before you with the crime of ὕβρις. His *hardihood* was shown in the Potidaea campaign, where none could stand the cold like him. His *valour* was displayed in the battle where he saved my life, and in the retreat from Delium. Especially amazing is his unique *originality*, which makes it impossible to find anyone else like him—except Satyrs and Sileni.

IV. His *speeches* too, I forgot to say, are like the Silenus-statuettes, in outward seeming ridiculous, but in inner content supremely rational and full of images of virtue and wisdom.

Epilogue: Such is my eulogy, half praise, half blame. Let my experience, and that of many another, be a warning to you, Agathon: court Socrates less as an "erastes" than as an "anterastes"!

XVI. *Concluding Scene: 222 c—end.*

The company laughed at the erotic candour of Alcibiades. Then ensued some banter between Socrates and Alcibiades as rival "erastae" of Agathon, which was interrupted by the entrance of a band of revellers who filled the room with uproar. Some of the guests left, and Aristodemus himself fell asleep. On awaking, about dawn, he found only three of the party still present and awake—Agathon, Aristophanes, and Socrates: Socrates was trying to convince the others that the scientific tragedy-writer must be capable also of writing comedy. Presently Aristophanes, and then Agathon, dozed off; whereupon Socrates, still "shadowed" by Aristodemus, departed.

§ ii. The Framework of the Dialogue.

(A) *The Method of Narration and the Preface.*

The Platonic dialogues, viewed from the point of view of literary form, may be divided into two chief classes. To the first class belong those in which the story of the discussion is told *directly* by one of the protagonists; to the second class belong those in which the story is told *indirectly* or at second-hand,—a mode of narration which involves the further characteristic that dialogues of this class are necessarily prefaced (and concluded) by some explanatory paragraphs. This second class, moreover, falls into two subdivisions, according as the narrator is or is not represented as being himself present at the discussion. It is to the latter of these subdivisions, in which the narrator is *not* an eye-witness but reports the matter only at second-hand, that the *Symposium* (together with the *Theaetetus* and *Parmenides*) belongs.

It is noteworthy also that, with the exception of the *Phaedo* and *Parmenides*, ours is the only dialogue in which the narrating witness is not Socrates himself. The reason for this is obvious : eulogy of Socrates being one of the main purposes of the dialogue, it would be unfitting to put the story into his mouth, and make him the trumpeter of his own praises. Instead of doing so, Plato selects as the sources of the narrative persons of such a character as to produce the effect of verisimilitude. The way in which Aristodemus, the primary source, and Apollodorus, the secondary source, are described is evidently intended to produce the impression that in them we have reliable witnesses. Apollodorus[1], " the fanatic," is put before us not only as a worshipper of Socrates, imbued with a passionate interest in philosophical discourses such as are here to be related, but also as an intimate disciple who had "companied with" Socrates for the space of nearly three years past and during that time had made it his peculiar task to study the every act and word of the Master (172 E). Moreover, the story of the special occasion in question he had diligently conned (οὐκ ἀμελέτητος, 172 A, 173 C).

Aristodemus[2], the primary source and actual narrator, is spoken of by Apollodorus as "an old disciple" and one of the most intimate with the Master in earlier years, and in his own narrative he represents himself as following Socrates with dog-like fidelity, and showing the closest familiarity with his ways and habits—a man so single-hearted, so engrossed in matters of fact, as to be constitutionally incapable of tampering with the truth. As the "minute biographer," Aristodemus is the prototype of all later Boswells.

Further, the impression of veracity made by the character of the

---

[1] Apollodorus appears also in *Phaedo* 59 A, B as one of those present with Socrates " on the day when he drank the poison in the prison"; as characteristically exhibiting most marked symptoms of grief [this statement would support the epithet μαλακός as well as μανικός in *Symp.* 173 D]; and as a native of Athens (τῶν ἐπιχωρίων). In *Apol.* 34 A he is one of those present at the trial of Socrates; and (in 38 B) one of those who offered to go bail to the extent of 30 minae. Pfleiderer takes Apollodorus to represent Plato himself, by a piece of ironical " Selbstobjektivierung," a notion which had already occurred to me.

[2] For Aristodemus, see also Xen. *Mem.* I. 4. 2 where Socrates converses περὶ τοῦ δαιμονίου πρὸς Ἀριστόδημον τὸν μικρὸν ἐπικαλούμενον, καταμαθὼν αὐτὸν οὔτε θύοντα τοῖς θεοῖς οὔτε μαντικῇ χρώμενον, ἀλλὰ καὶ τῶν ποιούντων ταῦτα καταγελῶντα.

narrators is enhanced by the express statement that in regard to some
points at least (ἔνια 173 B) the account of Aristodemus was confirmed
by Socrates. The points in question are probably (as Hug observes)
those which specially concern the picture drawn of Socrates himself.
At any rate, it is in regard to these that we have the detailed
testimony of Alcibiades, emphasized by repeated asseverations (214 E,
215 A, etc.), and endorsed by the silence of Socrates.

In addition to the evidence it contains for the dates of the
narration and of the banquet[1], and the vivid picture in miniature
which it presents of a certain group of Socratics in whom an ardent
admiration for the Master was blended with a limited capacity for
understanding the deeper side of his practice and doctrine—as if to
go barefoot and to rail at filthy lucre were the sum and substance
of Socraticism,—there are two further points in the Preface which
deserve attention.

Apollodorus, although asked only for the λόγοι spoken at the
banquet (172 B, 173 E), proceeds to give a full account of the ac-
companying incidents as well (ἐξ ἀρχῆς...διηγήσασθαι 174 A). This
may be taken to indicate that for estimating the effect of the dialogue
as a whole we are meant to pay regard not only to the series of
encomia but also to the framework of incident and conversation in
which they are set.

Glaucon, in asking Apollodorus for the desired information concerning the "erotic discourses," states (172 B) that he has already
heard an account of them from "another man" (ἄλλος τις), which
account was unsatisfactory (οὐδὲν σαφές), and that the authority
quoted by this unnamed informant was "Phoenix, son of Philippos."
To this Apollodorus adds the fact (173 B) that this Phoenix was
indebted to the same source as himself, namely Aristodemus. What
precisely these statements signify it is not easy to determine, since
the identity of Phoenix, as well as that of the anonymous informant
(ἄλλος τις), is unknown to us. But it seems reasonable to infer that
there was already in existence, when Plato wrote, at least one other
account of a banquet at which Socrates, Alcibiades and Agathon
figured, and that it is Plato's intention to discredit it. That such
is the intention is shown not only by the phrase οὐδὲν εἶχε σαφὲς λέγειν,
but also by the statement that the evidence of ἄλλος τις was one
degree further off from the primary source (Aristodemus) than is that
of Apollodorus. Further, the assumption of some such controversial

[1] With regard to this evidence, see *Introd.* § viii.

intention throws light on the emphasis laid on the veracity of the narrative—to which attention has been drawn above—and gives it a more definite motive. It is as if the author means us to read into his preface something to this effect: "Socrates has been misrepresented: it is my task to clear his reputation by putting the facts in their true light."

If this, then, be a right reading of the hints thus given, what is the distorted account which Plato thus discredits, and who its author? Unfortunately this must remain a matter of conjecture. The most obvious suggestion to make is that the author in question is Xenophon, and the account alluded to his *Symposium*. But Xenophon's *Symposium* is most probably a later work than Plato's; and it is a further objection that the persons represented by Xenophon as present at the banquet are not—with the exception of Socrates—the persons mentioned by Glaucon.

We are obliged, therefore, to look further afield for the author whose identity is thus shrouded. The best suggestion I can offer is that Polycrates the rhetor is the writer intended. In favour of this we may adduce the fact that Polycrates is ὁ κατήγορος whose calumnies Xenophon aims at refuting in his *Memorabilia*[1]. It is by no means improbable à *priori* that Polycrates in his attacks on Socrates described, amongst other incidents, a banqueting-scene in which Socrates and Alcibiades were pictured in an odious light. And if we take the *Banquet* of Xenophon to be a genuine work, the very fact that Xenophon thought it necessary to supplement his *Memorabilia* by such a work might be construed as showing that the author of the slanders he is at such pains to refute had already libelled Socrates in connexion with a similar scene. But unless, by some happy chance, further light

---

[1] See Cobet, *Nov. Lect.* pp. 662 ff.; Gomperz, *G. T.* II. pp. 63, 118. Gomperz (II. 343) supposes the *Gorgias* to be a counterblast to Polycrates' indictment of Socrates, and Alcibiades' eulogy in *Sympos.* to have the same motive: "Plato had a definite motive for placing such praise in the mouth of Alcibiades—we refer to the pamphlet of Polycrates....This writer had spoken of Socrates as the teacher of Alcibiades—in what tone and with what intention can easily be guessed....Plato himself had touched on the subject (of the *liaison* between the two men), harmlessly enough, in his youthful works, as, for example, in the introduction to the 'Protagoras.'...But after the appearance of Polycrates' libel, he may well have thought it advisable to speak a word of enlightenment on the subject; which is exactly what he does, with a plainness that could not be surpassed, in the present encomium" (*op. cit.* 394–5). Gomperz, however, does not bring this hypothesis into connexion with the passage in the Preface of *Symp.* discussed above. There may be an allusion to the same matter in *Protag.* 347 c (cp. Xen. *Symp.* VII. 1).

should be shed upon the history of Polycrates' literary activity, it is
hardly possible to get beyond the region of conjectural speculation, or
to hope for a definitive solution of this obscure literary problem.

(B) *The Prologue of Aristodemus.*

In the Prologue, with which Aristodemus's narrative opens, special
attention may be drawn to the following points :—

(a) It is significant that the first person to appear on the scene is
Socrates. We are led at once to admire his good humour and ready
wit as shown in the playful tone of his conversation (1) with Aristodemus (174 A, B), in which he makes jesting quotations from Homer
and indulges in a pun on the name of Agathon (cp. the pun he makes
on Gorgias, 198 c); and (2) with Agathon (175 c—E). These amiable
traits in the character of Socrates are further illustrated in other parts
of the dialogue.

(b) Socrates on the way becomes lost in thought and fails to put
in an appearance till the banquet is already far advanced (174 D, 175 c).
Aristodemus explains to Agathon (175 B) that this is no exceptional
occurrence (ἔθος τι τοῦτ᾽ ἔχει). That this incident is intended to be
specially emphasized as typical of Socrates' habits becomes clear when
we notice how Alcibiades in his speech (220 c) describes a similar
incident as taking place in one of the campaigns in which he served.
The corroboration thus effected is one of many examples of the literary
care and ingenuity with which Plato in this dialogue interweaves
incident with speech. Another example occurs a little further on
(176 c) where Eryximachus, discussing the question "to drink or not
to drink," describes Socrates as ἱκανὸς ἀμφότερα : this statement, too,
we find amplified and confirmed by Alcibiades (220 A). Both these
matters illustrate that entire subordination of flesh to spirit in which
Socrates was unique.

(c) Agathon (175 c ff.) expresses a desire to share in the "witty
invention" which Socrates had discovered on his way : Socrates with
his usual mock-modesty disclaims for himself the possession of σοφία,
except of a poor kind, but congratulates Agathon on the fine and
abundant σοφία he has just been displaying so conspicuously : and the
conversational banter concludes with Agathon's remark—"Presently,
with the Wine-god as umpire, you and I will fight out our wisdom-
match." Here, at this early stage, we have struck for us one of the
key-notes of the dialogue. For one main motive of the dialogue as a
whole is to exhibit the σοφία of Socrates, his intellectual as well as

moral supremacy. And we find, in the sequel, that this is done largely by pitting him against Agathon, over the wine-bowl. In this we have the reason for the juxtaposition of the two speeches, matched, as it were, one against the other. His speech is, in itself, one sufficient proof of the superiority of Socrates over his rival. But there are also other proofs: there is the masterly criticism and confutation to which Socrates subjects the belauded poet; there is the express statement, confirmed by expressive action, of Alcibiades, in which is asserted the superiority of Socrates not merely to Agathon but to all others who make claim to σοφία (213 E, 215 c ff.); and finally the Wine-god himself bestows on Socrates the palm when, in the concluding scene, we see him alone pursuing discussion with unflagging zeal and with a clearness of head undimmed by long and deep potations while his rival drowses and succumbs to sleep. Thus the διαδικασία περὶ τῆς σοφίας runs through the book, and always, from beginning to end, νικᾷ ὁ Σωκράτης.

To this we may add one minor point. Agathon, in this preliminary play of wit, applies to Socrates the epithet ὑβριστής, "a mocker." And this, too, is a trait upon which Alcibiades, in the sequel, lays much stress. ὕβρις is one of the most striking characteristics of the Satyr-Socrates (216 E, 219 c).

(d) Another example of the literary interweaving—or the method of "responsions," as we might term it,—which is so marked a feature of the dialogue, is to be found in the statement of Socrates concerning the character of his own knowledge. His speciality in the way of science is, he announces, "erotics," and this is his only speciality (177 D). Accordingly, when we find Socrates in the sequel delivering a discourse on this subject we are evidently intended by Plato to feel that his views are to be taken seriously as those of one who professed to be an expert in this subject if in nothing else. And this intention is emphasized when we come to the later passage (the "responsion") in 198 D where Socrates again refers to his conviction that concerning "erotics" he knew the truth (εἰδὼς τὴν ἀλήθειαν). It is hardly necessary to add that "erotics," construed in the Socratic sense, constitutes by no means an insignificant department of knowledge (φαύλη τις σοφία 175 E), as Socrates modestly implies, inasmuch as it is practically coextensive with a theory of education and involves an insight into the origin, nature and destiny of the human soul.

(e) In 177 B we have an interesting parallel between Plato's language and that of Isocrates. In Hel. 210 B (τῶν μὲν γὰρ τοὺς βομβυλίους καὶ τοὺς ἅλας καὶ τὰ τοιαῦτα βουληθέντων ἐπαινεῖν κ.τ.λ.) Isocrates scoffs at the eulogists of "bees and salt and such-like trumpery," and his language is echoed in the allusion (put in the mouth of Eryximachus quoting Phaedrus) to a βιβλίον ἀνδρὸς σοφοῦ ἐν ᾧ ἐνῆσαν ἅλες ἔπαινον θαυμάσιον ἔχοντες πρὸς ὠφέλειαν (177 B). This eulogist of salt is commonly supposed to be Polycrates, since encomia on similar paltry subjects—mice, χύτραι, ψῆφοι—are ascribed to him[1]. Dümmler, however[2], takes the reference to be to Antisthenes (*Protreptikos*), on the strength of the statement in Pollux VI. 16. 98: βομβύλιος δὲ τὸ στενὸν ἔκπωμα καὶ βομβοῦν ἐν τῇ πόσει, ὡς Ἀντισθένης ἐν προτρεπτικῷ. And for ἅλες as eulogized in the same work he quotes also *Rep.* 372 B ff. (ὄψον ἕξουσιν ἅλας). It may be added that a further allusion to the βομβύλιος, as στενὸν ἔκπωμα, may be discovered in the mention of ἔκπωμα μέγα in *Sympos.* 213 E. Since Antisthenes seems to have devoted a good deal of attention to the subject of μέθη[3], one is inclined to suppose that his views are alluded to in *Sympos.* (176, 213–14); and another allusion to him may be found in the mention of the χρηστοὶ σοφισταί who eulogized Heracles (177 B), since Heracles was, notoriously, the patron-saint of the Cynics[4]. However much they might differ on other points, Plato and Isocrates were agreed in so far as both found the Cynic leader an objectionable person.

(*f*) A significant indication is given us at the conclusion of the Prologue that the account of the speeches which follows is not an exhaustive account, but only a *selection*. And it is a selection that has been sifted twice. For Apollodorus states (178 A) that neither did Aristodemus remember *all* the views put forward by *every* speaker, nor did he (Apollodorus) remember all that Aristodemus had related. This statement is further confirmed by the later statement (180 c) that Aristodemus passed over the discourses of several speakers who followed next after Phaedrus. We are to infer, therefore, that there was a good deal of speechifying at the banquet which was not ἀξιομνημόνευτον. But why Plato is at pains to emphasize this point is

---

[1] So Hug (*Sympos. ad loc.*) following Sauppe and Blass: also Jebb, *Att. Or.* II. 99. I may note here an inconsistency as to the date of Polycrates' "Accusation" in Jebb, *Att. Or.* I. 150–51 compared with *ib.* XLV: in the latter place it is set in 393 B.C.

[2] In this Dümmler (*Akad.* p. 66) follows Winckelmann (*Antisth. fr.* p. 21). Polycrates, however, may be alluded to as well as Antisthenes, as the terms of the reference are wide (ἄλλα τοιαῦτα συχνά); moreover, a close relation may have existed between these two writers.

[3] See Dümmler, *Antisthenica*, pp. 17 ff.

[4] See Gomperz, *G. T.* II. p. 151; Dümmler, *Akad.* p. 66.

not wholly clear. It may, of course, be merely a literary device
meant to enhance the verisimilitude of the account, since the speeches
actually related might be thought insufficient to occupy the length of
time supposed to elapse between the end of the δεῖπνον and the hour
of Alcibiades' arrival—which would probably not be early. It is
possible, however, that we should look for a deeper reason. If so,
may not the intention be to brush aside and discredit other speeches
stated by another author¹ (ἄλλος τις, 172 B) to have been delivered on
this occasion?

(C) The Interludes.

The *first Interlude*, worthy of the name, occurs between the second
and third encomia (185 C—E), and it is noticeable, first, for the
reference to the "isology" of the rhetorical sophists; secondly, for
the device by which the natural order of speakers is changed (Eryximachus taking the place of Aristophanes); and thirdly, for the alleged
cause which renders such a change necessary, namely the hiccough
(λύγξ) of Aristophanes. As regards the significance of this last matter
considerable diversity of opinion exists among the commentators. Of
the ancients, Olympiodorus (*vit. Plat.* 3) supposed that Plato here
ἐκωμῴδησε Ἀριστοφάνη when he εἰσάγει αὐτὸν μεταξὺ λυγγὶ περιπεσόντα
καὶ μὴ δυνάμενον πληρῶσαι τὸν ὕμνον : and similarly Athenaeus (187 c)
writes τὸν μὲν ὑπὸ τῆς λυγγὸς ὀχλούμενον...κωμῳδεῖν ἤθελε καὶ διασύρειν :
and Aristides (*or.* 46, II. p. 287), ἀλλ᾽ οἶμαι λύζειν αὐτὸν ἔδει, ἵνα εἰς
ἀπληστίαν σκωφθῇ. Of the moderns, some have followed the ancients
in supposing that the incident is meant to satirize Aristophanes and
his intemperate habits (so Stallbaum, Rückert, Steinhart); while some
(Stephens, Sydenham, Wolf, Schwegler) take the object of the ridicule
to be not so much the habits of the poet as his speech with its
"indelicate ingredients." On the other hand, Schleiermacher held the
view that Eryximachus with his "physiological and medical notion of
love" is here being satirized; while Ast—whose view is shared in the
main by Hommel, van Prinsterer and Rettig—argued that the real
object of the ridicule is Pausanias, by whose speech Aristophanes
implies that he has been "fed up" to the point of loathing. This
view Rettig thinks is supported by the phrase Παυσανίου παυσαμένου,
which he takes to indicate Apollodorus' ridicule,—by the allusion made
by Aristophanes to Pausanias' speech in 189 c,—and by his mention
of Pausanias again in 193 B; and he construes the hint of another

¹ See above, § ii. A, *ad fin.*

possible cause (ἢ ὑπό τινος ἄλλου, 185 c) as "affording the key to the hidden meaning of the word πλησμονή." This view, however, is open to the objections (urged by Rückert against Ast) that, first, it makes Aristophanes guilty of excessive rudeness in feigning a hiccough to show his disgust ("aliud est in convivio iocari, aliud in scena," *e.g. Nub.* 906 ff., *Ach.* 585 ff., the places cited by Rettig); and that, further, there is no plain sign that the hiccough was feigned, but on the contrary the whole incident is stated by Aristodemus as matter-of-fact. It seems safe, therefore, to conclude that the most obvious view—that of the ancients—is nearest to the truth. The incident shows up Aristophanes in a ludicrous light, and at the same time it gives further occasion to Eryximachus to air his medical lore; so that we can read in it the intention of satirizing gently both these personages. But to construe it as aimed at Pausanias is far-fetched and improbable : he is already disposed of in the satirical reference to sophistical "isology"; and to discover a fresh allusion to him in the "other cause" of the hiccough is to discover a mare's nest, for—as the Scholiast *ad loc.* informs us—other physical causes of this symptom were as a matter of fact recognized by the medical profession, and it is only polite on the part of Aristodemus to leave the matter open.

The *second Interlude* (189 A—c) and the *third* (193 D—194 E) call for no special remark.

The *fourth Interlude* (198 A—199 c), which follows on the speech of Agathon, is linked to the third both by a remark which Socrates addresses to Eryximachus, and also, at the close, by his appeal to Phaedrus (cp. 199 B with 194 D). Here, in even a greater degree than in the previous Interludes, Socrates is the central figure of interest, and this position he continues to hold throughout the rest of the dialogue. This Interlude, indeed, may be regarded as one of the cardinal points of the structure, in which the First Act, as we may term it, passes on into the Second; and in the Second Act we reach at length the theoretical climax, in the doctrine of Socrates-Diotima. To this climax the present Interlude, wherein is laid before us Socrates' confession of rhetorical faith, serves as prologue.

The *fifth Interlude* (212 c—215 A) is by far the longest and, as regards the action of the piece, the most important. For it introduces a new actor, and he a protagonist, in the person of Alcibiades. The contrast is striking between the prophetess in her soaring flights to the heavenly places of the spirit and the tipsy reveller with his lewd train who takes her place in claiming the attention of the audience. The comic relief which, in the earlier scenes, had been supplied by Aristophanes, as γελωτοποιός, is now supplied by Alcibiades. We should notice also how a link with the Second Act is furnished here, at the commencement of the Third Act, by the mention of an attempt by Aristophanes to reply to an observation made by Socrates in the course of his speech. But apart from this, the rest of the speakers and banqueters are left out of account except only Agathon, Socrates and Eryximachus. The action of the last of these here is parallel to his action at the commencement of the First Act where he had taken the lead in fixing the rules for the conduct of the symposium. As regards Agathon and Socrates, the most important incident in this Interlude is the decision concerning their contest in σοφία which is pronounced by Alcibiades, when, acting the not inappropriate part of Dionysus, he awards the crown to Socrates,—an incident to the significance of which we have already (§ ii. B, C) drawn attention.

Of the *Epilogue* or concluding scene (222 c—end) it is unnecessary to say much. The persons that figure most largely in it are the three central characters, Alcibiades, Agathon and Socrates; while towards the close the rest of the characters receive, as it were, a farewell notice. When the curtain finally falls, it falls significantly on the solitary figure of Socrates, the incarnation of the Eros-daemon, behind whom in his shadow stands the form of his erastes, the "shadow"-biographer Aristodemus.

§ iii. The First Five Speeches.

1. *Phaedrus*, son of Pythocles, belonged to the Attic deme Myrrhinus. Lysias describes him as "impoverished" in circumstances, but respectable. In the *Protagoras* he is represented as a disciple of Hippias; while in the *Phaedrus*—named after him—his chief characteristic is his ardent interest in erotic oratory (λόγοι ἐρωτικοί), a specimen of which, by Lysias, he has learnt almost completely by heart. It is, then, in accordance with this character that we find Phaedrus, in the *Symposium*, made responsible for the theme of the series of speeches (viz. ἔπαινος Ἔρωτος, 177 D), and entitled πατὴρ τοῦ λόγου. We may gather also from certain indications contained both in the *Phaedrus* and in the *Symposium* that Phaedrus was neither physically strong nor mentally vigorous[1]. The ostensibly prominent

---

[1] See *Phaedr.* 227 A, *Symp.* 176 C, 223 B, and, generally, his cultivation of medical friends. Also the probable word-play in the deme-name Μυρρινούσιος, *Symp.* 176 D, *Phaedr.* 244 A.

position assigned to such a man in the *Symposium* is more natural if we assume that it is due to the desire to make him a link between this dialogue and the *Phaedrus*[1].

Phaedrus's *speech*, although not without merit in point of simplicity of style and arrangement, is poor in substance. The moral standpoint is in no respect raised above the level of the average citizen; the speaker pays little regard to consistency, and the method of argument, with its want of logical coherence, savours much of the sophists. As examples of this self-contradiction we may point to the statement that Achilles, as younger than Patroclus, must be παιδικά not ἐραστής, whereas Alcestis, though younger than Admetus, is treated as the ἐρῶσα, not the ἐρωμένη; we may point also to the other inconsequence, that the self-sacrifice of Achilles, the παιδικά, is cited in support of the contention that οἱ ἐρῶντες μόνοι are capable of such self-sacrifice. The arbitrary handling of the Orpheus myth is another striking illustration of the sophistic manner.

What is, however, most characteristic of the speech of Phaedrus is its richness of mythological allusion. Lacking, it would seem, in native force of intellect, Phaedrus relies upon authority and tradition. He quotes Hesiod and Homer, Acusilaos and Parmenides: he builds his argument, such as it is, on the sayings of "them of old time," and on the legendary histories of the son of Oeagrus and the daughter of Pelias; and when he can confute Aeschylus on a point of mythology his joy is great. As a lover of religious tradition, we may credit Phaedrus with a capacity for genuine religious feeling; certainly, in his rôle as high-priest of Eros, on the present occasion, he shows a strict regard for ritual propriety when he rebukes Socrates for interrupting the service of speech-offerings to the god (194 D)[2].

In point of *literary style* we may notice the following features :—

(a) *Rhetorical ornamentation:* chiasmus (178 D), paronomasia (179 C), special compound verbs (ἀγασθέντες 179 C, ὑπεραγασθέντες 180 A; ἀποθανεῖν 179 E, ὑπεραποθανεῖν, ἐπαποθανεῖν 180 A);

---

[1] Cf. P. Crain, p. 7: Vera causa, cur Plato sermonis in Symposio Phaedrum parentem praedicaverit, haec mihi videtur esse: rediens ad eas cogitationes quas in Phaedro dialogo instituerat, eundem quoque auctorem colloquii reduxit.

[2] Hug sums up the position of Phaedrus thus (p. xlvi): "Phädros stellt den gewöhnlichen athenischen Bürger dar, den eine rastlose Neugierde zu den rhetorischen und philosophischen Kreisen hindrängt, der da und dort etwas aufschnappt und sich aneignet, jedoch ohne tieferes Verständnis, aber mit desto grösserem Selbstbewusstsein." Cp. Jowett (*Plato* I. p. 528): "The discourse of Phaedrus is half-mythical, half-ethical; and he himself...is half-sophist, half-enthusiast."

(b) *Monotony of expression* (οὔτε...οὔτε 178 c (4), 178 D (2); οὔτως...ὡς 178 D (2), οὔτω...ὥστε 179 A, C, τοσοῦτον...ὥστε 179 C; καὶ μὴν...γε 179 A, B; οὔτω καὶ 179 D, τοιγάρτοι διὰ ταῦτα 179 D, ὅθεν δὴ καὶ 180 A);

(c) *Anacolutha*: 177 A (οὐ δεινὸν κτλ.), 179 A (καὶ μὴν...οὔτω κακός).

2. Of *Pausanias*, of the deme Κεραμῆς, little is known beyond what we are told in this dialogue[1] and in Xenophon's *Symposium*, where also he appears as notorious for his love for the tragedian Agathon. Xenophon represents Pausanias as a vigorous champion of παιδεραστία[2], and Plato here assigns to him a similar rôle, although he paints the fashion of the man in less crude colours.

The *speech* of Pausanias is a composition of considerable ability. Although, like Phaedrus, he starts by grounding his conception of the dual Eros on mythological tradition, yet when this conception is once stated the distinction is maintained and its consequences followed out with no little power of exposition. The manner in which the laws regarding παιδεραστία in the various states are distinguished, and in special treatment of the complex Athenian νόμος, display the cleverness of a first-rate pleader. The general impression, in fact, given us by the speech is that it forms an exceedingly smart piece of special pleading in favour of the proposition καλὸν ἐρασταῖς χαρί-ζεσθαι. The nakedness of this proposition is cloked by the device of distinguishing between a noble and a base Eros, and by the addition of the saving clause ἀρετῆς ἕνεκα[3]. None the less, it would seem that the speaker's main interest is in the χαρίζεσθαι, rather than in the accruing ἀρετή, and that he is fundamentally a sensualist, however refined and specious may be the form in which he gives expression to his sensualism.

Pausanias is a lawyer-like person in his style of argumentation; and, appropriately enough, much of his speech is concerned with νόμοι.

---

[1] He is also mentioned in *Protag.* 315 D.

[2] Xen. *Symp.* VIII. 32 ἀπολογούμενος ὑπὲρ τῶν ἀκρασίᾳ συγκυλινδουμένων.

[3] We must, of course, bear in mind that, as Jowett puts it (*Plato*, vol. I. p. 529), "the value which he attributes to such loves as motives to virtue and philosophy, (though) at variance with modern and Christian notions, is in accordance with Hellenic sentiment." Nor does the Platonic Socrates, in the sequel, fail to take account of them. For some judicious observations on the general question of the Gk. attitude to paederastia, see Jowett, *op. cit.* pp. 534 ff.; Gomperz, *Gk. Thinkers* (E. Tr.) II. pp. 380 ff.; for Eros in Gk. religion, see Miss J. E. Harrison, *Prolegom.* pp. 630 ff.; for Plato's and Xenophon's theories of Love, see I. Bruns, *Vorträge* etc., pp. 118 ff.; P. Crain, pp. 23 ff.

The term is noteworthy, since it inevitably suggests that antithesis νόμος)(φύσις which was so widely debated among the sophists and thinkers of the close of the fifth century. Is the moral standard fixed by nature (φύσει) or merely by convention (νόμῳ)? This was one form of the question; and closely connected with this was the other form: Is knowledge absolute or relative? Pausanias poses as a conventionalist, and a relativist, a champion of law as against nature (πᾶσα πρᾶξις αὐτὴ ἐφ' ἑαυτῆς οὔτε καλὴ οὔτε αἰσχρά); and this is of itself sufficient to show that, in Plato's eyes, he is a specimen of the results of sophistic teaching.

Nor is it only in his adoption of this principle of moral indifference, as we might call it, and in his capacity τὸν ἥττω λόγον κρείττω ποιεῖν, that Pausanias stands before us as a downright sophist; his argumentation also is chargeable with the sophistical vices of inconsistency and self-contradiction[1]. For example, with what right, we may ask, does Pausanias condemn the νόμοι of other states than Athens regarding παιδεραστία, while laying down τὸ νόμιμον as the standard of morality? For such a distinction necessarily involves reference to another, superior, standard; whereas, by his own hypothesis, no such standard exists. Again, the section on the καλὴ ἀπάτη (181 Ε f.) stands out in curious contradiction with the section immediately preceding, in which fidelity and sincerity (τὸ βέβαιον) are put forward as the necessary conditions of a love that is fair (καλός) and irreproachable (οὐκ ἐπονείδιστος).

In *literary style* the speech of Pausanias displays, in a much higher degree than that of Phaedrus, the tricks and ornaments proper to the sophistical schools of rhetoric. Thus we find :—

Paronomasia: ἔργα ἐργαζομένῳ 182 Ε; δουλείας δουλεύειν 183 Α; πράττειν τὴν πρᾶξιν 181 Α, cp. 183 Β.

Alliteration: ἐθέλοντες δουλείας δουλεύειν οἵας οὐδ' ἂν δοῦλος οὐδείς (λ, δ, ο, ου).

Rhythmic correspondence of clauses and periods (εὐρυθμία, ἰσόκωλα): This is an important feature of Greek rhetoric[2], the invention of which is ascribed to Thrasymachus; and it is especially characteristic of the style of Isocrates[3]. The following examples (as formulated by Hug)

---

[1] So Jowett (*Plato* I. p. 529) writes: "(The speech of Pausanias) is at once hyperlogical in form and also extremely confused and pedantic."

[2] Cp. Ar. *Rhet.* III. 9, 1409ᵃ 25 λέξις κατεστραμμένη καὶ ὁμοία ταῖς τῶν ἀρχαίων ποιητῶν ἀντιστρόφοις.

[3] A good example occurs in *Helena* 17·
  τοῦ μὲν ἐπίπονον καὶ φιλοκίνδυνον τὸν βίον κατέστησε
  τῆς δὲ περίβλεπτον καὶ περιμάχητον τὴν φύσιν ἐποίησε.

will serve to indicate the extent to which Pausanias makes use of these artifices :—

I. {
1. πᾶσα γὰρ πρᾶξις ὧδ᾽ ἔχει·
2. αὐτὴ ἐφ᾽ ἑαυτῆς,
3. οὔτε καλὴ οὔτ᾽ αἰσχρά.
}

II. {
4. οἷον ὃ νῦν ἡμεῖς ποιοῦμεν,
5. ἢ πίνειν ἢ ᾁδειν ἢ διαλέγεσθαι,
6. οὐκ ἔστι τούτων αὐτὸ καλὸν οὐδέν,
}

III. {
7. ἀλλ᾽ ἐν τῇ πράξει,
8. ὡς ἂν πραχθῇ,
9. τοιοῦτον ἀπέβη·
}

IV. {
10. καλῶς μὲν γὰρ πραττόμενον καὶ ὀρθῶς καλὸν γίγνεται,
11. μὴ ὀρθῶς δὲ αἰσχρόν,
12. οὕτω καὶ τὸ ἐρᾶν καὶ ὁ Ἔρως οὐ πᾶς ἐστὶ καλὸς οὐδὲ ἄξιος ἐγκωμιάζεσθαι,
13. ἀλλὰ ὁ καλῶς προτρέπων ἐρᾶν. [180 E ad fin.—181 A.]
}

Here we have four περίοδοι of which the first three are τρίκωλοι, the fourth τετράκωλος : in the three τρίκωλοι, the κῶλα of each are approximately equal ; while in the τετράκωλος, long and short κῶλα alternate. Other instances of strophic correspondence are 184 D—E, 185 A ff. (see Hug ad loc.).

3. *Eryximachus*, son of Akumenus, is like his father a physician and a member of the Asclepiad guild (186 E); he is also a special friend of Phaedrus (177 A). Alcibiades alludes to Akumenus as "the most temperate sire" of Eryximachus, and he is mentioned also by Xenophon as an authority on diet. The same "temperance" (σωφροσύνη) is a marked characteristic of Eryximachus in our dialogue : he is the champion of moderation in drinking (176 B ff., 214 B), and when, near the close, the revellers enter and the fun waxes fast and furious, Eryximachus, together with his comrade Phaedrus, is the first to make his escape (223 B). Another characteristic of the man is his *pedantic* manner. He is incapable of laying aside his professional solemnity even for a moment, and he seizes every possible occasion to air his medicinal lore, now with a lecture on μέθη (176 D), presently with another on λύγξ (185 D, E).

Scientific pedantry is, similarly, the characteristic of Eryximachus's *speech*. He starts with a conception of Eros as a cosmic principle, from the standpoint of natural philosophy[1]. This conception he applies and developes with equal rigour in the spheres of medicine, music, astronomy and religion, so that definitions of a precisely parallel kind for each of these departments are evolved. The dogmatic manner appears also in his treatment of the dictum of Heraclitus (187 A), which corresponds to the treatment of Aeschylus by his friend Phaedrus. He resembles Phaedrus also in his fondness for displaying erudition : he knows his Empedocles and his Hippocrates[2], as well as the experts in musical theory.

The theory of the duality of Eros Eryximachus takes over from Pausanias, but he naturally finds a difficulty in applying this concept to other spheres, such as that of music, and in attempting to elude the difficulty he falls into the sophistical vices of ambiguity and inconsistency. *E.g.* in 187 D the reference of δεῖ χαρίζεσθαι is obscure ; and, in the same context, the substitutions of ἡ Οὐρανία Μοῦσα for ᾿Αφροδίτη Οὐρανία and of Πολυμνία for ᾿Αφροδίτη Πάνδημος are arbitrary[3].

As regards *literary style* there is little to notice in the speech, beyond its plainness and lack of ornament. The monotony of expression (seen, *e.g.*, in the recurrence of such formulae as ἔστι δὴ 187 B, ἔστι γὰρ 187 C, ἔστι δὲ 187 D) marks it as the product of a pedantic, would-be scientific mind, in which literary taste is but slightly developed and the ruling interest is the schematization of physical doctrines.

4. *Aristophanes.* The greatest of Greek comic poets, the author of the *Clouds*, was a pronounced anti-Socratic. None the less, Plato

---

[1] Cf. Eurip. *fr.* 839 τὴν ᾿Αφροδίτην οὐχ ὁρᾷς ὅση θεός; | ἢν οὐδ᾿ ἂν εἴποις, οὐδὲ μετρήσειας ἂν | ὅση πέφυκε κἀφ᾿ ὅσον διέρχεται. | ...ἐρᾷ μὲν ὄμβρου γαῖ᾿,...ἐρᾷ δ᾿ ὁ σεμνὸς οὐρανὸς κτλ.

[2] Pfleiderer (*Sokr. u. Plato*, pp. 551 ff.) broaches the theory that Eryx.'s speech is intended as a parody of (Pseudo-) Hippocr. περὶ διαίτης, and that the real author of that work was Eryx. himself. There are, certainly, a number of similarities, but hardly sufficient to prove the case. Obviously, it is a parody of the style of some one or more medical writers, but more than that cannot safely be said: some Hippocratean parallels in matters of detail will be found in the notes. See also my remarks on the next speech (Aristophanes'). Teuffel drew attention to the etymological significance of the name (ἐρυξί-μαχος); this, however, cannot be an invention of Plato's, although it may partly account for the introduction of the λύγξ incident.

[3] The doctrine of Love as a harmony of opposites, which plays so large a part in Eryx.'s discourse, may be illustrated from Spenser ("Hymn to Love"):

"Ayre hated earth and water hated fyre,
 Till Love relented their rebellious yre.
 He then them tooke, and, tempering goodly well
 Their contrary dislikes with loved meanes,
 Did place them all in order," etc.

paints him here in no dark colours, but does justice to his mastery of
language, his fertility of imagination, his surprising wit, his hearty
joviality. In contrast to the puritanism of the pragmatical doctor,
Aristophanes appears as a man of strength to mingle strong drink,
who jokes about his "baptism" by liquor (176 B), and turns the
scientific axioms of the "man of art" to ridicule (189 A). His rôle is,
in fact, throughout that of a γελωτοποιός (189 A), and he supplies the
comic business of the piece with admirable gusto[1]. Yet the part he
plays is by no means that of a vulgar buffoon : he is poet as well as
jester,—a poet of the first magnitude, as is clearly indicated by the
speech which Plato here puts in his mouth.

That *speech* is a masterpiece of grotesque fantasy worthy of
Rabelais himself. The picture drawn of the globular four-legged
men is intensely comic, and the serious manner in which the king
of gods and men ponders the problem of their punishment shows a
very pretty wit. Their sexual troubles, too, are expounded with
characteristic frankness. And it is with the development of the sex
problem that we arrive at the heart of this comedy in miniature,—
the definition of Eros as "the craving for wholeness" (τοῦ ὅλου
ἐπιθυμία 192 E).

This thought, which is the final outcome of the speech, is not
without depth and beauty[2]. It suggests that in Love there is something deeper and more ultimate than merely a passion for sensual
gratification ; it implies that sexual intercourse is something less than
an end in itself. But Aristophanes, while suggesting these more
profound reflexions, can provide no solid ground for their support ;
he bases them on the most portentous of comic absurdities. Here,
as so often elsewhere in the genuine creations of the poet, we find
it difficult to determine where παιδιά ends and σπουδή begins[3]. How
far, we ask ourselves, are the suggestions of an idealistic attitude
towards the problems of life seriously meant ? Does the cloke of
cynicism and buffoonery hide a sincere moralist ? Or is it not rather
the case that the mockery is the man, and the rest but a momentary

---

[1] Cp. Plut. Q. Conv. VII. 7. 710 c Πλάτων δὲ τὸν τ' Ἀριστοφάνους λόγον περὶ τοῦ
ἔρωτος ὡς κωμῳδίαν ἐμβέβληκεν εἰς τὸ συμπόσιον.

[2] Cp. Zeller (n. on 192 c ff. ἀλλ' ἄλλο τι, κτλ.) "Diese Stelle, in welcher der
ernsthafte Grundgedanke unserer Stelle am Deutlichsten zu Tage kommt, gehört
wohl zu dem Tiefsten, was von alten Schriftstellern über die Liebe gesagt ist."

[3] See Jevons, Hist. of Gk. Lit. pp. 258 ff. for some judicious criticisms of the
view that "behind the grinning mask of comedy is the serious face of a great
political teacher."

disguise? Certainly, the view maintained by Rettig that the chief purpose of Aristophanes is to impugn παιδεραστία, and to preach up legitimate matrimony as the only true form of love and the sole road to happiness, is a view that is wholly untenable. And while we may acknowledge with Horn (*Platonstud.* p. 261) that the speech of Aristophanes marks a great advance upon the previous λόγοι, in so far as it recognizes the difficulty of the problem presented by the phenomena of Eros and looks below the surface for a solution,—yet how far we are intended to ascribe this sagacity on the part of the speaker to superior reasoning power rather than to a lucky inspiration (θείᾳ μοίρᾳ) is by no means clear.

In connexion with this question as to the design of the speech there is one point which seems to have been generally overlooked by the expositors,—the topical character, as we might term it, of its main substance. This appears, obviously enough, in the jesting reference (193 B) to the love-affairs of Pausanias and Agathon; and obvious enough too are the allusions to Eryximachus and his much-vaunted "art" in the mention made, both at the beginning (189 D) and at the end (193 D), of the healing power of Love, the good "physician." But in addition to these topical allusions which *sautent aux yeux*, we are justified, I think, in regarding the great bulk of the discourse as being neither more nor less than a caricature of the physiological opinions held and taught by the medical profession of the day. The Hippocratean tract περὶ φύσιος ἀνθρώπου is sufficient evidence that there raged in medical circles a controversy concerning the unity or multiplicity of man's nature: the author of the tract was himself an anti-unity man and assailed with equal vigour the views of all opponents, whether the unity they stood for was αἷμα or χολή or φλέγμα—ἐν γάρ τι εἶναί φασιν, ὅτι ἕκαστος αὐτέων βούλεται ὀνόμασας, καὶ τοῦτο ἓν ἐὸν μεταλλάσσειν τὴν ἰδέην καὶ τὴν δύναμιν. To this controversy Aristophanes, we may suppose, alludes when he speaks of man's ἀρχαία φύσις, which was a unity until by the machinations of Zeus it became a duality. But with this theory of primeval unity of nature the poet combines a theory of sex-characteristics. And, here again, even more definitely, we can discover traces of allusion to current physiological doctrines. Aristophanes derives the different varieties of sex-characters from the bisection of the three primitive ὅλα, viz. φίλανδροι women and φιλογύναικες men from the ἀνδρόγυνον, φιλογύναικες women (ἑταιρίστριαι) from the original θῆλυ, and φίλανδροι men from the original ἄρρεν. Thus we see that Aristophanes analyses existing sex-characters, classifies them under two heads for each sex, and explains them by reference to a three-fold original. If we turn now to Hippocrates περὶ διαίτης (cc. 28 f.) we find there also a theory of "the evolution of sex." Premising that the female principle is akin to water and the male to fire, the writer proceeds thus: "If the bodies secreted by both parents are male (ἄρσενα)...they become men (ἄνδρες) brilliant in soul and strong in body, unless damaged by after regiment (i.e. by lack of ξηρῶν καὶ θερμῶν σίτων, etc.). If, however, the body secreted by the male parent is male and that by the female female, and the male element proves the stronger...then men are produced, less brilliant (λαμπροί), indeed, than the preceding class, yet justly deserving of the name of 'manly' (ἀνδρεῖοι). And again, if the male parent secretes a female body and the female a male body, and the latter proves the stronger, the male element deteriorates and the men so produced are 'effeminates' (ἀνδρόγυνοι). Similarly with the generation of women. When both parents alike secrete female elements, the most feminine and comely women (θηλυκώτατα καὶ εὐφυέστατα) are produced. If the woman secretes a female, the man a male body, and the former proves the stronger, the women so produced are bolder (θρασύτεραι) but modest (κόσμιαι). While if, lastly, the female element prevails, when the female element comes from the male parent and the male element from the female, then the women so produced are more audacious (τολμηρότεραι) than the last class and are termed 'masculine' (ἀνδρεῖαι)."

Here we find the sex-characters arranged under three heads for each sex, and explained by reference to four originals, two from each parent. Obviously, this theory is more complicated than the one which Aristophanes puts forward, but in its main lines it is very similar. According to both the best class of men is derived from a dual male element, and the best class of women from a dual female element (although the poet is less complimentary than the physician in his description of this class). The similarity between the two is less close in regard to the intermediate classes; for while Aristophanes derives from his ἀνδρόγυνον but one inferior class of men and one of women, Hippocrates derives from various combinations of his mixed (θῆλυ + ἄρσεν) secretions two inferior classes of both sexes. Yet here, too, under the difference lies a consentience in principle, since both theorists derive all their inferior sex-characters from a mixed type.

We may imagine, then, that Aristophanes, having before his mind some such physiological theory as this, proceeded to adapt it to his purpose somehow as follows. Suppose we take the male element latent, as the Hippocrateans tell us, in each sex, combine them, and magnify them into a concrete personality, the result will be a Double-man. A similar imaginative treatment of the female elements will yield us a Double-wife. While, if—discarding the perplexing minutiae of the physiological combinations assumed by the doctors—we take a female element from one parent and blend it with a male element from the other, and magnify it according to our receipt, we shall thereby arrive at the Man-wife as our third primeval personality. Such a treatment of a serious scientific theory would have all the effect of a caricature ; and it is natural to suppose that in choosing to treat the matter in this way Aristophanes intended to satirize the theories of generation and of sex-evolution which were argued so solemnly and so elaborately by the confrères of Eryximachus. √

If in this regard the topical character of the speech be granted, one can discern an added point in the short preliminary conversation between Aristophanes and Eryximachus by which it is prefaced. The latter gives a warning (189 A—B) that he will be on the watch for any ludicrous statement that may be made; to which the former replies : " I am not afraid lest I should say what is ludicrous (γελοῖα) but rather what is absurd (καταγέλαστα)." In view of what follows, we may construe this to mean that Aristophanes regards as καταγέλαστα theories such as those of Eryximachus and his fellow-Asclepiads. Moreover, this view of the relation in which Aristophanes' speech stands to the treatises of the medical doctrinaires—of whom Eryximachus is a type—helps to throw light on the relative position of the speeches, and on the incident by which that position is secured and emphasized. For unless we can discover some leading line of connexion between the two which necessitates the priority of the medico's exposition, the motive for the alteration in the order of the speeches must remain obscure.

It may be added that the allusions in 189 E (see notes ad loc.) to the evolutionary theories of Empedocles confirm the supposition that Aristophanes is directly aiming the shafts of his wit at current medical doctrines ; the more so as Empedocles shares with Hippocrates the view that the male element is hot, the female cold, and that the offspring is produced by a combination of elements derived from both parents. Other references to Empedocles may be discerned in the mention of Hephaestus (192 D) who, as personified Fire, is one of Empedocles' "four roots," and in the mention of Zeus (190 C), another of the "roots"; and the fact that these two deities play opposite parts, the one as bisector, the other as unifier, is in accordance with Empedoclean doctrine. Also the statement that the moon "partakes of both sun and earth" (190 B) is, in part at least, Empedoclean.

In point of *style and diction*, the speech of Aristophanes stands out as an admirable piece of simple Attic prose, free at once from the awkwardness and monotony which render the speeches of Phaedrus and Eryximachus tedious and from the over-elaboration and artificial ornamentation which mar the discourses of Pausanias and Agathon. In spite of occasional poetic colouring—as, *e.g.*, in the finely-painted scene between Hephaestus and the lovers (192 c ff.)—the speech as a whole remains on the level of pure, easy-flowing, rhythmical prose, in which lucidity is combined with variety and vivacity of expression.

5. *Agathon*, the tragic poet, if born in 448 B.C., would be a little over thirty at the date of the Symposium (416). He was the παιδικά of Pausanias (193 B), and a man of remarkable beauty as well as of reputed effeminacy[1]. He appears in the dialogue as not only a person of wealth, position and popularity, but a man of refinement, education and social tact. The banquet itself is given by him to a select company of his friends in honour of his recent victory in the tragic contest, and throughout the dialogue he is, formally at least, the central figure— both as host and as victor, and, what is more, as the embodiment of external κάλλος alike in his person (εἶδος) and in his speech (λόγοι). His graceful politeness to his guests never varies, even when Socrates sharply criticises his oration, or when Alcibiades transfers the wreath from his head to that of Socrates (213 E); he himself shares in the admiration for Socrates, welcomes him most warmly and displays the

---

[1] Ar. *Thesm.* 191-2   σὺ δ' εὐπρόσωπος, λευκὸς, ἐξυρημένος,
                 γυναικόφωνος, ἁπαλὸς, εὐπρεπὴς ἰδεῖν.
ib. 200 ff.   καὶ μὴν σύ γ', ὦ κατάπυγον, εὐρύπρωκτος εἶ
              οὐ τοῖς λόγοισιν, ἀλλὰ τοῖς παθήμασιν, κτλ

And Mnesilochus' comments on Agathon's speech and womanish appearance in 130 ff.   ὡς ἡδὺ τὸ μέλος, ὦ πότνιαι Γενετυλλίδες,
                       καὶ θηλυδριῶδες καὶ κατεγλωττισμένον, κτλ.

In estimating the value of Aristophanes' abuse of his contemporary—in the case of Agathon as in the case of Euripides—we must make due allowance for Ar.'s comic style. As Jevons well observes (*Hist. of Gk. Lit.* p. 274): "In polemics, as in other things, the standard of decency is a shifting one. Terms which one age would hesitate to apply to the most abandoned villain are in another century of such frequent use as practically to be meaningless....The charges of immorality which Ar. brings against Eur. and his plays are simply Ar.'s way of saying that on various points he totally disagrees with Eur." Probably the same holds good of his treatment of Agathon.

utmost jubilation when Socrates promises to eulogize him (223 A). Finally, his consideration is shown in the social καρτερία with which he sticks to his post, drinking and talking, till all his guests, except Socrates, have either left or succumbed to drowsiness (223 D).

In his *speech* Agathon claims that he will improve on the *method* of his predecessors. In his attention to method he is probably taking a leaf out of the book of Gorgias, his rhetorical master and model. Besides the initial distinction between the nature and effects of Eros, another mark of formal method is his practice of recapitulation : at the close of each section of his discourse he summarises the results[1]. In his portrait of the nature of Eros—his youth, beauty, suppleness of form and delicacy of complexion—Agathon does little more than formulate the conventional traits of the god as depicted in poetry and art. His attempts to deduce these attributes are mere παιδιά (197 E), pieces of sophistical word-play. Somewhat deeper goes his explanation of the working of Eros upon the soul, as well as the body ; but the thought that Eros aims at the beautiful (197 B) is his most fruitful deliverance and the only one which Socrates, later on, takes up and developes[2].

We may observe, further, how Agathon, like Phaedrus, indulges in mythological references, and how—like most of his predecessors (cp. 180 D, 185 E)—he makes a point of criticising and correcting the views of others (194 E, 195 B). Cp. Isocr. *Busir.* 222 B, 230 A.

In *style and diction* the speech of Agathon gives abundant evidence of the influence of the school of Gorgias, especially in the preface (194 E—195 A) and in the 2nd part (197 C—E). Thus we find repeated instances of :—

---

[1] See 195 E, 196 C, D, 197 C; and cp. Gorg. *Hel.* (*e.g.*) 15 καὶ ὅτι μὲν...οὐκ ἠδίκησεν ἀλλ' ἠτύχησεν, εἴρηται· τὴν δὲ τετάρτην αἰτίαν τῷ τετάρτῳ λόγῳ διέξειμι. Cp. Blass, *att. Bered.* p. 77.

[2] Jowett is somewhat flattering when he writes (*Plato* I. p. 531) : " The speech of Agathon is conceived in a higher strain (*sc.* than Aristophanes'), and receives the real if half-ironical approval of Socrates. It is the speech of the tragic poet and a sort of poem, like tragedy, moving among the gods of Olympus, and not among the elder or Orphic deities....The speech may be compared with that speech of Socrates in the Phaedrus (239 A, B) in which he describes himself as talking dithyrambs.... The rhetoric of Agathon elevates the soul to 'sunlit heights'." One suspects that "the approval of Socrates" is more ironical than real. Agathon's speech belongs to the class condemned by Alcidamas, *de Soph.* 12 οἱ τοῖς ὀνόμασιν ἀκριβῶς ἐξειργασ-μένοι καὶ μᾶλλον ποιήμασιν ἢ λόγοις ἐοικότες : cp. *ib.* 14 ἀνάγκη...τὰ μὲν ὑποκρίσει καὶ ῥαψῳδίᾳ παραπλήσια δοκεῖν εἶναι.

Short parallel Kola[1] with homoeoteleuton : *e.g.* 194 E ἔ|γὼ δὲ δὴ | βούλομαι | πρῶτον μὲν εἰπεῖν | ὡς χρή με εἰπεῖν | ἔπειτα εἰπεῖν : 197 D ἀλλοτριότητος μὲν κενοῖ, οἰκειότητος δὲ πληροῖ.

Homoeoteleuton and assonance : *e.g.* τῶν ἀγαθῶν ὧν ὁ θεὸς αὐτοῖς αἴτιος (194 E); τρόπος ὀρθὸς παντός...περὶ παντός...οἷος <ὧν> οἴων αἴτιος ὤν (195 A); πάντων θεῶν εὐδαιμόνων ὄντων (195 A).

These rhetorical artifices are especially pronounced in the concluding section, as is indicated by the sarcastic comment of Socrates (198 B τὸ δ' ἐπὶ τελευτῆς, κτλ.) ; in fact, the whole of this section is, as Hug puts it, a "förmliche Monodie." Another feature of A.'s style is his fondness for quotation, especially from the poets (196 C, E, 196 A, 197 B), and his tendency to break into verse himself—ἐπέρχεται δέ μοί τι καὶ ἔμμετρον εἰπεῖν (197 c). He has no clear idea of the limits of a prose style, as distinguished from verse ; and the verses he produces are marked by the same Gorgianic features of assonance and alliteration. In fine, we can hardly describe the general impression made on us by the style of Agathon better than by adapting the Pauline phrase—"Though he speak with the tongues of men and of angels, he is become as sounding brass or a tinkling cymbal[2]."

§ iv. SOCRATES AND DIOTIMA.

To *Socrates* it falls to deliver the last of the encomia on Eros. This is no mere accident, but artistically contrived in order to indicate the relative importance of his encomium as the climax of the series. In form and content, as well as in extent, it holds the highest place, although to its speaker is assigned the ἐσχάτη κλίνη.

(A) *The substance and form of Socrates' λόγοι.*

(*a*) The encomium proper is preceded by a *preliminary dialectical discussion with Agathon*, the object of which is to clear the ground of some popular misconceptions of the nature of Eros. The notion of Eros, it is shown, is equivalent to that of Desire (ἔρως = τὸ ἐπιθυμοῦν)

---

[1] Distinguish this from the more Isocratean style of the speech of Pausanias with its more developed ἴσα and εὐρυθμία of periods. Cp. Aristoph. *frag.* 300 καὶ κατ' Ἀγάθων' ἀντίθετον ἐξυρημένον, "shaved Agathon's shorn antithesis."

[2] Horn summarises thus (*Platonstud.* p. 264): "Die ganze Rede mit ihrem anspruchsvollen Eingang, ihrem nichtigen Inhalt, ihren wolklingenden Phrasen und Sophismen und insbesondere mit dem grossen Schlussfeuerwerke von Antithesen und Assonanzen ist demnach nichts anderes als ein mit grosser Geschicklichkeit entworfenes Musterstück der...gorgianisch-sophistischen Rhetorik." See also the rhythmic analysis (of 195 D ff.) worked out by Blass, *Rhythmen*, pp. 76 ff.

—a quality, not a person. And the object of this Desire is the beautiful (τὸ καλόν), as had been asserted by Agathon (201 A—B). That Socrates refuses to embark on an eulogistic description of Eros without this preliminary analysis of the meaning of the name serves, at the start, to differentiate his treatment of the theme from that of all the preceding speakers: it is, in fact, an object-lesson in method, an assertion of the Platonic principle that dialectic must form the basis of rhetoric, and that argument founded on untested assumptions is valueless.

(b) *The speech proper* begins with a mythological derivation of Eros, in which his conflicting attributes as a δαίμων—a being midway between gods and men—are accounted for by his parentage. Eros is at once poor, with the poverty of Desire which lacks its object, and rich, with the vigour with which Desire strives after its object. And in all its features the Eros of Socrates and Diotima stands in marked contrast to the Eros of conventional poetry and art, the divine Eros of Agathon.

Eros is defined as Desire and as Daemon; and, in the next place, its potency[1] is shown to lie in the striving after the everlasting possession of happiness. But Eros implies also propagation in the sphere of beauty. It is the impulse towards immortality—the impulse displayed alike by animals and by men, the ground of parental love towards both physical and mental (φιλοτιμία) offspring.

But when we arrive at this point, the question suggests itself as to how, more precisely, these different determinations of Eros are related to one another. What is the link between Eros defined as "the desire for the abiding possession of the good" and Eros defined as "the desire for procreation in the beautiful"? The former conception involves a desire for abiding existence, in other words for immortality, inasmuch as the existence of the possessor is a necessary condition of possession; while the latter also involves a similar desire, inasmuch as procreation is the one means by which racial immortality can be secured. Thus the link between the two conceptions of Eros is to be found in the implicit notion common to both that Eros is the striving after immortality or self-perpetuation. But there is another point to be borne in mind in order to grasp clearly the connexion of the argument. The beautiful includes the good (τἀγαθὰ καλά 201 c); so that the desire for the good is already, implicitly, a desire for the beautiful (and *vice versa*).

---

[1] *I.e.* its generic notion (εἶναι, τὸ κεφάλαιον 205 D) as distinguished from the specific limitation (καλεῖσθαι 205 C, 206 B) to sex-love. See W. Gilbert in *Philologus* LXVIII. 1, pp. 52 ff.

Thus the main results of the argument so far are these : Eros is the
striving after the lasting possession of the Good, and thereby after
immortality ; but immortality can be secured only through procreation
(τόκος), and the act of procreation requires as its condition the presence
of Beauty. We are, therefore, led on to an examination of the nature
of Beauty, and it is shown that beauty is manifested in a variety of
forms, physical, moral and mental—beauty of body, of soul, of arts and
sciences, culminating in the arch-science and the Idea of absolute
Beauty. Accordingly the Erastes must proceed in upward course[1]
from grade to grade of these various forms of beauty till he finally
reaches the summit, the Idea. On the level of each grade, moreover,
he is moved by the erotic impulse not merely to apprehend the καλόν
presented and to appreciate it, but also to reproduce it in another :
there are two moments in each such experience, that of "conception"
(κύησις) or inward apprehension, and that of "delivery" (τόκος) or
outward reproduction.

The emphasis here laid on the notion of reproduction and delivery
(τίκτειν, γεννᾶν), as applied to the intellectual sphere, deserves special
notice. The work of the intelligence, according to the Socratic method,
is not carried on in solitary silence but requires the presence of a
second mind, an interlocutor, an answerer of questions. For the
correct method of testing hypotheses and searching out truth is the
conversational method, "dialectic," in which mind cooperates with
mind. The practical illustration of this is to be seen in Socrates
himself, the pursuer of beautiful youths who delights in converse with
them and, warmed by the stimulus of their beauty, λόγους τοιούτους
τίκτει οἵτινες ποιήσουσι βελτίους τοὺς νέους (210 c).

(c)   As the conception of Eros as a striving after the Ideal pursued
not in isolation but in spiritual fellowship (κοινωνία) constitutes the core
of the Socratic exposition, so the form of that exposition is so contrived
as to give appropriate expression to this central conception. It commences with a piece of dialectic—the conversation between Socrates
and Agathon. Agathon is the embodiment of that κάλλος which here
stimulates the ἐραστής in his search for truth : it is in Agathon's soul
(ἐν καλῷ) that Socrates deposits the fruits of his pregnant mind. In
much, too, of the exposition of Diotima the semblance, at least, of
intellectual κοινωνία is retained, illustrating the speaker's principle of
philosophic co-operation. Thus the speech as a whole may be regarded

[1] It is interesting to observe how Emerson makes use of this Platonic "anabasis"
when he writes :—"There is a climbing scale of culture...up to the ineffable
mysteries of the intellect."

simply as a Platonic dialogue in miniature, which differs from the average dialogue mainly in the fact that the chief speaker and guiding spirit is not Socrates but another, and that other a woman. If asked for a reason why Socrates here is not the questioner but the answerer, a sufficient motive may be found in the desire to represent him as a man of social tact. Socrates begins by exposing the ignorance of Agathon : next he makes the amend honourable by explaining that he had formerly shared that ignorance, until instructed by Diotima[1].

(B) Diotima and her philosophy.

(1) *Diotima.* Diotima is a fictitious personage. Plato, no doubt purposely, avoids putting his exposition of Eros into the mouth of any historical person : to do so would be to imply that the theory conveyed is not original but derived. It is only for purposes of literary art that Diotima here supplants the Platonic Socrates : she is presented, by a fiction, as his instructor, whereas in facts he merely gives utterance to his own thoughts. These thoughts, however, and this theory are, by means of this fiction, represented as partaking of the nature of divine revelation ; since in Diotima of Mantinea we find a combination of two significant names. The description γυνὴ Μαντινική inevitably implies the "mantic" art, which deals with the converse between men and gods of which τὸ δαιμόνιον, and therefore the Eros-daemon, is the mediating agent (202 E); while the name Διοτίμα, "She that has honour from Zeus," suggests the possession of highest wisdom and authority. This is made clear by the rôle assigned to Zeus and his servants in the *Phaedrus*: ὁ μὲν δὴ μέγας ἡγεμὼν ἐν οὐρανῷ Ζεὺς...πρῶτος πορεύεται, κτλ. (246 E) ; οἱ μὲν δὴ οὖν Διὸς δῖόν τινα εἶναι ζητοῦσι τὴν ψυχὴν τὸν ὑφ᾿ αὑτῶν ἐρώμενον· σκοποῦσιν οὖν εἰ φιλόσοφός τε καὶ ἡγεμονικὸς τὴν φύσιν καὶ...πᾶν ποιοῦσιν ὅπως τοιοῦτος ἔσται, κτλ. (252 E ff.). The characteristics of Zeus, namely guiding power (ἡγεμονία) and wisdom (σοφία), attach also to his ὀπαδοί: consistently with this Diotima is σοφή (201 D), and "hegemonic" as pointing out the ὀρθὴ ὁδός to her pupil, and guiding him along it in a masterful manner (210 A ff., 211 B ff.)[2].

---

[1] Cp. Jowett (*Plato* I. p. 527): "As at a banquet good manners would not allow him (Socr.) to win a victory either over his host or any of the guests, the superiority which he gains over Agathon is ingeniously represented as having been already gained over himself by her. The artifice has the further advantage of maintaining his accustomed profession of ignorance (cp. Menex. 236 fol.)."

[2] Gomperz's suggestion (*G.T.* II. p. 396) that "the chief object of this etherealized affection" which Plato had in mind when "in the teaching (of Diotima) he

In the person of Diotima, "the wise woman," Plato offers us—in Mr Stewart's phrase—"a study in the prophetic temperament[1]"; she represents, that is to say, the mystical element in Platonism, and her discourse is a blend of allegory, philosophy, and myth. As a whole it is philosophical: the allegory we find in the imaginative account of the parentage and nature of Eros, as son of Poros and Penia; the mythical element appears in the concluding portion, in so far as it "sets forth in impassioned imaginative language the Transcendental Idea of the Soul[2]." And as in the allegory the setting is derived from current religious tradition, so in the myth the language is suggested by the enthusiastic cult of the Orphics. It may be well to examine somewhat more closely the doctrine of the prophetess on these various sides.

(2) *Diotima's allegory.* The first point to notice is the artistic motive for introducing an allegory. It is intended to balance at once the traditional derivations of the God Eros in the earlier speeches, and the grotesque myth of Aristophanes. Socrates can match his rivals in imagination and inventive fancy. It also serves the purpose of putting into a concrete picture those characteristic features of the love-impulse which are subsequently developed in an abstract form. And, thirdly, the concrete picture of Eros thus presented allows us to study more clearly the features in which Socrates, as described by Alcibiades, resembles Eros and embodies the ideal of the philosophic character.

In the allegory the qualities which characterise Eros are fancifully deduced from an origin which is related in the authoritative manner of an ancient theogony. The parents of Eros are Poros and Penia. Poros is clearly intended to be regarded as a God (203 B οἱ θεοί, οἵ τε ἄλλοι καὶ ὁ...Πόρος): he attends the celestial banquet and drinks nectar like the rest. The nature of Penia is less clearly stated: she cannot be a divine being according to the description of the divine nature as εὐδαίμων and possessing τἀγαθὰ καὶ καλά given in the context preceding (202 c ff.); and the list of the qualities which she hands down to her son Eros shows that she is in all respects the very antithesis of Poros. We must conclude, therefore, that as Poros is the source of the divine side of the nature of Eros, so Penia is the source of the anti-divine side; and from the description of Eros as δαίμων, combined with the definition of τὸ δαιμόνιον as μεταξὺ θεοῦ τε καὶ θνητοῦ (202 E), we are justified

gave utterance to his own deepest feeling and most intimate experience" was Dion of Syracuse would supply, if admitted, a further significance to the name *Diotima*.

[1] J. A. Stewart, *The Myths of Plato*, p. 428.

[2] J. A. Stewart, *loc. cit.*

in identifying this anti-divine side with mortality, and in regarding
ἡ Πενία as a personification of ἡ θνητὴ φύσις[1]. It is interesting here to
notice that Penia had already been personified by Aristophanes in his
Plutus, and personified as one member of an antithesis[2].
In the description of Poros, the father of Eros, it is significant that
he is stated to be the son of Μῆτις. The idea of Plenty (Πόρος) had
already been personified by Alcman, whether or not the Scholiast
ad loc. is correct in identifying that Poros with the Hesiodic Chaos.
And the idea of Wisdom (Μῆτις) also had played a part, as a personified
being, in the speculations of the theogonists. For it seems, at least,
probable that the Orphic theologians had already in Plato's time
evolved the equation Phanes = Ericapaeus = Metis[3], and that here as
elsewhere in the language of Diotima there lie allusions to the doctrines
of that school of mystics.

Of the incidental details of the allegory, such as "the garden of
Zeus" where the intercourse between Penia and Poros took place
and the intoxication of Poros which led up to that intercourse, the
Neoplatonic commentators, as is their wont, have much to say. But
we may more discreetly follow Zeller and Stallbaum in regarding such
details as merely put in for purposes of literary effect, to fill up and
round off the story. Poros could never have fallen a victim to the
charms of Penia, since she had none; nor could Penia ever have hoped
to win over Poros by persuasion or force, he being endowed with the
strength and wisdom of a god. Obviously, therefore, the god must be
tricked and his senses blinded—as in the case of the sleeping Samson
or of the intoxicated Noah—that the woman might work her will upon
him. Nor need we look for any mystical significance in ὁ τοῦ Διὸς
κῆπος. The celestial banquet would naturally be held in the halls of
the King of the gods; that a king's palace should have a park or
garden attached is not extraordinary; nor is it more strange that one

---

[1] So Plotinus is not far astray when he equates πενία with ὕλη, matter, potency
(*Enn.* III. p. 299 F).

[2] Cp. Plato's Πόρος)(Πενία with Ar.'s Πλοῦτος)(Πενία: also the description of
πτωχεία as intermediate between πλοῦτος and πενία in *Plut.* 552 with the description
of Eros as intermediate between πόρος and πενία in *Symp.* 203 E (οὔτε ἀπορεῖ Ἔρως
οὔτε πλουτεῖ). Cp. also *Plut.* 80 ff. (Πλοῦτος...αὐχμῶν βαδίξεις) with *Symp.* 203 C
(Ἔρως αὐχμηρός). The date of the *Plutus* is probably 388 B.C.

Such pairs of opposites were common in earlier speculation. Cp. Spenser,
"Hymn in Honour of Love":—

"When thy great mother Venus first thee bare,
Begot of Plentie and of Penurie."

[3] Plato's mention of a *single* parent of Poros is in accordance with the Orphic
notion of Phanes-Metis as bisexed.

of the banqueters, when overcome with the potent wine of the gods, should seek retirement in a secluded corner of the garden to sleep off the effects of his revels.

More important than these details is the statement that the celestial banquet was held in celebration of the birth of Aphrodite, so that the begetting of Eros synchronized with the birthday of that goddess. The narrative itself explains the reason of this synchronism : it is intended to account for the fact that Eros is the "attendant and minister" of Aphrodite. Plotinus identifies Aphrodite with "the soul," or more definitely with "the soul of Zeus" (Zeus himself being ὁ νοῦς), but it seems clear from Plato's language that she is rather the personification of beauty (Ἀφροδίτης καλῆς οὔσης 203 c).

As regards the list of opposite qualities which Eros derives from his parents, given in 203 c—E, there are two points which should be especially observed. In the first place, all these qualities, as so derived, are to be regarded not as merely accidental but inborn (φύσει) and forming part of the essential nature of Eros. And secondly, each of these characteristics of Eros, both on the side of his wealth and on the side of his poverty, has its counterpart—as will be shown presently[1]—in the characteristics of Socrates, the historical embodiment of Eros.

Lastly, we should notice the emphasis laid on the fluctuating character of Eros, whose existence is a continual ebb and flow, from plenitude to vacuity, from birth to death. By this is symbolised the experience of the φιλόκαλος and the φιλόσοφος, who by a law of their nature are incapable of remaining satisfied for long with the temporal objects of their desire and are moved by a divine discontent to seek continually for new sources of gratification. This law of love, by which τὸ ποριζόμενον ἀεὶ ὑπεκρεῖ, is parallel to the law of mortal existence by which τὰ μὲν (ἀεὶ) γίγνεται, τὰ δὲ ἀπόλλυται (207 D ff.)—a law which controls not merely the physical life but also the mental life (ἐπιθυμίαι, ἐπιστῆμαι, etc.)[2]. Accordingly, the Eros-daemon is neither mortal nor immortal in nature (πέφυκεν 203 E), neither wise nor foolish, but a combination of these opposites—σοφὸς-ἀμαθής and θνητὸς-ἀθάνατος— and it is in virtue of this combination that the most characteristic title of Eros is φιλόσοφος (which implies also φιλ-αθανασία).

(3) *Diotima's Philosophy.* The philosophic interest of the

---

[1] See § vi. 3.

[2] For an expansion in English of this thought see Spenser's "Two Cantos of Mutabilitie" (*F. Q.* VII.).

remainder of Diotima's discourse (from 204 A to its end) lies mainly in the relations it affirms to exist between Eros and certain leading concepts, *viz.* the Good, Beauty and Immortality.

(a) *The Problem of Immortality.* Enough has been said already as to determination of these various concepts as expounded in the earlier part of the discourse (up to 209 E). But the concluding section, in which "*the final mysteries*" (τὰ τέλεα καὶ ἐποπτικά) are set forth, calls for further investigation. We have already learnt that Eros is "the desire for procreation in the sphere of the beautiful with a view to achieving immortality"; and we have found also that, so far, all the efforts of Eros to achieve this end have been crowned with very imperfect success. Neither by way of the body, nor by way of the mind, can "the mortal nature" succeed, through procreation, in attaining anything better than a posthumous permanence and an immortality by proxy. We have to enquire, therefore, whether any better result can be reached when Eros pursues the ὀρθὴ ὁδός under the guidance of the inspired παιδαγωγός. The process that goes on during this educational progress is similar in the main to what has been already described. *Beauty* is discovered under various forms, and the vision of beauty leads to *procreation*; and procreation is followed by a search for fresh beauty. But there are two new points to observe in the description of the process. First, the systematic method and regularity of procedure, by which it advances from the more material to the less material objects in graduated ascent. And secondly, the part played throughout this progress by the activity of the *intellect* (νοῦς), which discerns the one in the many and performs acts of identification (210 B) and generalisation (210 C). Thus, the whole process is, in a word, a system of intellectual training in the art of dialectic, in so far as it concerns τὸ καλόν. And the end to which it leads is the vision of and converse with Ideal Beauty, followed by the procreation of veritable virtue. It is to be observed that this is expressly stated to be not only the final stage in the progress of Eros but the most perfect state attainable on earth by man (τὸ τέλος 211 B, ἐνταῦθα τοῦ βίου βιωτὸν ἀνθρώπῳ 211 D, τεκόντι...ὑπάρχει θεοφιλεῖ γενέσθαι 212 A). But the question remains, does the attainment of this state convey also personal immortality? It must be granted that this question is answered by Plato, as Horn points out, somewhat ambiguously, "To the man who beholds the Beautiful and thereby is delivered of true ἀρετή it is given to become θεοφιλής and to become ἀθάνατος—to him εἴπερ τῳ ἄλλῳ ἀνθρώπων": but in this last *if*-clause there still lies a possible ground for doubt[1]. We cannot gain full assurance on the point from this sentence taken by itself; we must supplement it either by other indications derived from other parts of Diotima's argument, or by statements made by Plato outside the *Symposium*. Now it may be taken as certain—from passages in the *Phaedrus*, *Phaedo* and *Republic* —that personal immortality was a doctrine held and taught by Plato. It is natural, therefore, to expect that this doctrine will be also taught in the *Symposium*; or, at least, that the teaching of the *Symposium* will not contravene this doctrine. And this is, I believe, the case, in spite of a certain oracular obscurity which veils the clearness of the teaching. When we recal the statement that the generic Eros, as inherent in the individual, aims at the " everlasting possession " of the good as its τέλος, and when we are told that the ἐρωτικὸς-φιλόσοφος at the end of his progress arrives at the "possession" (κτῆμα) of that specific form of Good which is Beauty, and finds in it his τέλος, and when emphasis is laid on the everlastingness (ἀεὶ ὄν) of that possession, then it is reasonable to suppose that the ἀθανασία of the ἐρωτικός who has reached this goal and achieved this possession is implied. It is to be noticed, further, that the phrase here used is no longer μετέχει τοῦ ἀθανάτου nor ἀθανατώτερός ἐστι but ἀθάνατος ἐγένετο. Nor does the language of the clause εἴπερ τῳ ἄλλῳ necessarily convey any real doubt: "he, if any man" may be simply an equivalent for "he above all," "he most certainly[2]." The point of this saving clause may rather be this. The complete philosopher achieves his vision of eternal Beauty by means of νοῦς (or αὐτὴ ἡ ψυχή), as the proper organ ῷ ὁρατὸν τὸ καλόν (212 A): it is in virtue of the possession of that immortal object that he himself is immortalised: and accordingly immortality accrues to him not *qua* ἄνθρωπος so much as *qua* νοητικὸς or λογικός. In other words, while in so far as he is an ἄνθρωπος, a ζῷον, a ὅλον compounded of two diverse

---

[1] See F. Horn, *Platonstud.* pp. 276 ff. Horn also criticises the phrase ἀθάνατος γενέσθαι: "die Unsterblichkeit im eigentlichen Sinne des Wortes...kann nicht erworben werden. Der Mensch kann nur unsterblich *sein* oder es *nicht sein*, er kann aber nicht unsterblich *werden*." But what Plato means by ἀθάν. γενέσθαι is to regain the life of the soul in its divine purity—the result of right education, as a κάθαρσις or μελέτη θανάτου. See J. Adam, *R. T. G.* pp. 383 ff.

It seems quite certain that Plato—whether or not in earnest with his various attempts to prove it—did believe in personal immortality, and would assent to the dictum of Sir Thos. Browne, " There is surely a piece of divinity in us, something that was before the elements, and owes no homage unto the sun."

[2] See my note *ad loc.* It is to be noticed that similar expressions are used in a similar context in *Phaedr.* 253 A (ἐφαπτόμενοι (θεοῦ)...καθ' ὅσον δυνατὸν θεοῦ ἀνθρώπῳ μετασχεῖν): *Tim.* 90 B, C. Cp. θεῖος ὤν 209 B, θεῖον καλόν 211 E, θεοφιλεῖ 212 A. That the Idea (τἀγαθόν) is οἰκεῖον to the Soul seems implied by 205 E.

elements body and soul, the philosopher is not entirely ἀθάνατος but still subject to the sway of sad mortality, yet in so far as he is a philosopher, a purely rational soul, grasping eternal objects, he is immortal. If we choose to press the meaning of the clauses in question, such would seem to be their most probable significance[1].

Another criticism of this passage suggested by Horn is this. If it be true that the philosopher, or ἐρωτικός, does at this final stage attain to immortality, this does not involve the truth of the doctrine of immortality in general, but rather implies that men as such are not immortal and that immortality is the exceptional endowment of a few. Here again we must recal the distinction between ἄνθρωπος and pure ψυχή and νοῦς. The soul as immortal is concerned with the objects of immortal life[2]. In so far as it has drunk of the waters of Lethe and forgotten those objects, in so far as it is engrossed in the world of sense, it has practically lost its hold on immortality, and no longer possesses any guarantee of its own permanence. Although it may remain, in a latent way, in age-long identity, it cannot be self-consciously immortal when divorced from a perception of the eternally self-identical objects. If we may assume that Plato looked at the question from this point of view it becomes intelligible that he might refuse to predicate immortality of a soul that seems so entirely "of the earth, earthy" that the noëtic element in it remains wholly in abeyance.

All that has been said, however, does not alter the fact that individual and personal immortality, in our ordinary sense, is nowhere directly proved nor even expressly stated in a clear and definite way in the *Symposium.* All that is clearly shown is the fact of posthumous survival and influence. That Plato regarded this athanasia of personal δύναμις as an athanasia of personal οὐσία, and identified "Fortwirken" with "Fortleben," has been suggested by Horn, as an explanation of the "ganz neue Begriff der Unsterblichkeit" which, as he contends, is propounded in this dialogue. But it is certainly a rash proceeding to

[1] For this notion of immortality by "communion" or "participation" in the divine life as Platonic, see the passages cited in the last note, also *Theaet.* 176 A. Cp. also the Orphic idea of the mystic as ἔνθεος, "God-possessed." This idea of supersession of personality by divinity ("not I but Christ that dwelleth in me") is a regular feature of all mystic religion.

[2] In other words, ἀθανασία may be used not simply of quantity but of quality of existence. This is probably the case in 212 A: "immortality" is rather "eternal life" than "everlastingness," as connoting "heavenliness" or the kind of life that is proper to divinities. So, as the "spark divine" in man is the νοῦς, ἀθανασία is practically equivalent to pure νόησις. On the other hand, in the earlier parts of the discourse the word denotes only duration (ἀθάνατον εἶναι = ἀεὶ εἶναι).

go thus to the *Sophist*—an evidently late dialogue—for an elucidation of the problem. A sufficient elucidation, as has been suggested, lies much nearer to hand, in the doctrine of the *Phaedo* and *Phaedrus*. It is merely perverse to attempt to isolate the doctrine of the *Symposium* from that of its natural fellows, or to assume that the teaching of Diotima is intended to be a complete exposition of the subject of immortality. "Plato," we do well to remember, "is not bound to say all he knows in every dialogue"; and if, in the *Symposium*, he treats the subject from the point of view of the facts and possibilities of our earthly life, this must not be taken to imply that he has forgotten or surrendered the other point of view in which the soul is naturally immortal and possesses pre-existence as well as after-existence.

(*b*) *The Problem of Beauty.* A further point of interest in the latter section of this discourse is the different value attached to τὸ καλόν in the highest grade of love's progress as compared with the lower grades. In the latter it appeared as merely a means to τόκος and thereby to ἀθανασία; whereas in the former it seems to constitute in itself the final end. Horn, who notices this apparent reversal of the relations between these two concepts, explains it as due to the fact that in the highest grade Eros is supplanted by Dialectic, or "the philosophic impulse," which alone gives cognition of the Idea. But if this be so, how are we to account for the use of the term τεκόντι in the concluding sentence, where the attainment of ἀθανασία is described as having for its pre-condition not merely τὸ ὁρᾶν but τὸ τεκεῖν? This is precisely parallel to the language elsewhere used of the action of Eros in the lower grades, and precludes the supposition that Eros ceases to be operant on the highest grade. The truth is rather that, in this final stage, the Eros that is operant is the Eros of pure νοῦς—enthusiastic and prolific intellection, "the passion of the reason." And the fact that τὸ καλόν in this stage is no longer subordinated to ἀθανασία as means to end of desire is to be explained by the fact that this ultimate κάλλος being Ideal is ἀθάνατον in itself, so that he who gains it thereby gains ἀθανασία.

That there are difficulties and obscurities of detail in this exposition of the concepts we have been considering may be freely admitted. But the line of doctrine, in its general trend, is clear enough, and quite in harmony with the main features of Platonic doctrine as expounded in other dialogues of the same (middle) period. Nor must the interpreter of the dialogue lose sight of the fact that he is dealing here not with the precise phrases of a professor of formal logic but with the inspired utterances of a prophetess, not with the dialectic of a *Parmenides* but with the hierophantic dogmata of the *Symposium*.

(c) *Eros as Philosophy.* The fact that Socrates himself is evidently presented in the dialogue as at once the exemplar of Philosophy and the living embodiment of Eros might be sufficient to indicate that the most essential result of the Socratic discussion of Eros is to show its ultimate identity with "the philosophic impulse." Since, however, this identification has been sometimes denied, it may be well to indicate more particularly how far this leading idea as to the nature of Eros influences the whole trend of the discussion. We notice, to begin with, the stress laid on the midway condition of Eros, as son of Poros and Penia, between wisdom and ignorance, in virtue of which he is essentially a philosopher (φρονήσεως ἐπιθυμητής...φιλοσοφεῖ 203 Dff.). We notice next how the children of the soul (λόγοι περὶ ἀρετῆς) are pronounced superior in beauty to the children of the body (209 c), and σοφία, we know, is one form of ἀρετή. Then, in the concluding section (210 A ff.) we find it expressly stated that κάλλος attaches to ἐπιστῆμαι (210 c), and that φιλοσοφία itself is the sphere in which the production of καλοὶ λόγοι is occasioned by the sight of τὸ πολὺ πέλαγος τοῦ καλοῦ. Thus it is clearly implied throughout the discussion that σοφία, as the highest division of ἀρετή (being the specific ἀρετή of νοῦς), is the highest and most essential form of τὸ ἀγαθόν for man; whence it follows that, if Eros be defined as "the craving for the good," this implies in the first place the "craving for σοφία," which is but another way of stating "the philosophic impulse," or in a word φιλοσοφία.

It must not be supposed, however, that in virtue of this identification the love-impulse (Eros) is narrowed and devitalised. For φιλοσοφία is not merely a matter of book-study, it is also a method of life and a system of education. In reaching the ultimate goal, which is the union of the finite with the infinite in the comprehension of the Idea, the man who is driven by the spirit of Eros passes through all the possible grades of experience in which Beauty plays a part; and from social and intellectual intercourse and study of every kind he enriches his soul. He does not begin and end with what is abstract and spiritual—with pure intellection; nor does he begin and end with the lust after sensual beauty: like the Eros-daemon who is his genius, the true Erastes is οὔτε θηρίον οὔτε θεός, and his life is an anabasis from the concrete and the particular beauties of sense to the larger and more spiritual beauties of the mind.

Thus in its actual manifestation in life the Eros-impulse is far-reaching. And, as already noticed, it is essentially propagative. The philosopher is not only a student, he is also, by the necessity of his nature, a teacher. This is a point of much importance in the eyes of Plato, the Head of the Academy: philosophy must be cultivated in a *school* of philosophy.

The significance of Eros, as thus conceived, has been finely expressed by Jowett (*Plato* I. p. 532): "(Diotima) has taught him (Socr.) that love is another aspect of philosophy. The same want in the human soul which is satisfied in the vulgar by the procreation of children, may become the highest aspiration of intellectual desire. As the Christian might speak of hungering and thirsting after righteousness; or of divine loves under the figure of human (cp. Eph. v. 32); as the mediaeval saint might speak of the 'fruitio Dei'; as Dante saw all things contained in his love of Beatrice, so Plato would have us absorb all other loves and desires in the love of knowledge. Here is the beginning of Neoplatonism, or rather, perhaps, a proof (of which there are many) that the so-called mysticism of the East was not strange to the Greek of the fifth century before Christ. The first tumult of the affections was not wholly subdued; there were longings of a creature 'moving about in worlds not realised,' which no art could satisfy. To most men reason and passion appear to be antagonistic both in idea and fact. The union of the greatest comprehension of knowledge and the burning intensity of love is a contradiction in nature, which may have existed in a far-off primeval age in the mind of some Hebrew prophet or other Eastern sage, but has now become an imagination only. Yet this 'passion of the reason' is the theme of the Symposium of Plato[1]."

(*d*) *Eros as Religion*. We thus see how to "the prophetic temperament" passion becomes blended with reason, and cognition with emotion. We have seen also how this passion of the intellect is regarded as essentially expansive and propagative. We have next to notice more particularly the point already suggested in the words quoted from Jowett—how, namely, this blend of passion and reason is accompanied by the further quality of religious emotion and awe. We are already prepared for finding our theme pass definitely into the atmosphere of religion not only by the fact that the instructress is herself a religious person bearing a significant name, but also by the semi-divine origin and by the mediatorial rôle ascribed to Eros. When we come, then, to "the greater mysteries" we find the passion of the

---

[1] See also J. Adam, *Religious Teachers of Greece*, pp. 396 f.

intellect passing into a still higher feeling of the kind described by the Psalmist as "thirst for God." This change of atmosphere results from the new vision of the goal of Eros, no longer identified with any earthly object but with the celestial and divine Idea (αὐτοκαλόν). Thus the pursuit of beauty becomes in the truest sense a religious exercise, the efforts spent on beauty become genuine devotions, and the honours paid to beauty veritable oblations. By thus carrying up with her to the highest region of spiritual emotion both erotic passion and intellectual aspiration, Diotima justifies her character as a prophetess of the most high Zeus; while at the same time we find, in this theological passage of the Socratic λόγοι, the doctrine necessary at once to balance and to correct the passages in the previous λόγοι which had magnified Eros as an object of religious worship, a great and beneficent deity.

This side of Diotima's philosophising, which brings into full light what we may call as we please either the erotic aspect of religion or the religious aspect of Eros, might be illustrated abundantly both from the writers of romantic love-poetry and from the religious mystics. To a few such illustrations from obvious English sources I here confine myself. Sir Thos. Browne is platonizing when he writes (*Rel. Med.*) "All that is truly amiable is of God, or as it were a divided piece of him that retains a reflex or shadow of himself." Very similar is the thought expressed by Emerson in the words, "Into every beautiful object there enters something immeasurable and divine"; and again, "all high beauty has a moral element in it." Emerson, too, supplies us with a description that might fitly be applied to the Socratic λόγοι of the *Symposium*, and indeed to Plato generally in his prophetic moods, when he defines "what is best in literature" to be "the affirming, prophesying, spermatic words of man-making poets." To Sir Thos. Browne we may turn again, if we desire an illustration of that mental phase, so vividly portrayed by Diotima, in which enjoyment of the things eternal is mingled with contempt of things temporal. "If any have been so happy"—so runs the twice-repeated sentence—"as truly to understand Christian annihilation, ecstasies, exolution, lique-faction, transformation, the kiss of the spouse, gustation of God, and ingression into the divine shadow, they have already had an handsome anticipation of heaven; the glory of the world is surely over, and the earth in ashes with them" (*Hydriotaphia, ad fin.*). A similar phase of feeling is eloquently voiced by Spenser more than once in his "Hymns." Read, for instance, the concluding stanzas of the "Hymne of Heavenly Love" which tell of the fruits of devotion to the "loving Lord ":—

> "Then shalt thou feele thy spirit so possest,
> And ravisht with devouring great desire
> Of his deare self...
> That in no earthly thing thou shalt delight,
> But in his sweet and amiable sight.
>
> "Thenceforth all worlds desire will in thee dye,
> And all earthes glorie, on which men do gaze,
> Seeme durt and drosse in thy pure-sighted eye,
> Compar'd to that celestiall beauties blaze,...
>
> "Then shall thy ravisht soule inspired bee
> With heavenly thoughts farre above humane skil,
> And thy bright radiant eyes shall plainely see
> Th' Idee of his pure glorie present still
> Before thy face, that all thy spirits shall fill
> With sweete enragement of celestiall love,
> Kindled through sight of those faire things above."

From Plato, too, Spenser borrows the idea of the soul's "anabasis" through lower grades of beauty to "the most faire, whereto they all do strive," which he celebrates in his "Hymne of Heavenly Beautie." A few lines of quotation must here suffice :

> "Beginning then below, with th' easie vew
> Of this base world, subject to fleshly eye,
> From thence to mount aloft, by order dew,
> To contemplation of th' immortall sky....
>
> "Thence gathering plumes of perfect speculation,
> To impe the wings of thy high flying mynd,
> Mount up aloft through heavenly contemplation,
> From this darke world, whose damps the soule do blynd,
> And, like the native brood of Eagles kynd,
> On that bright Sunne of Glorie fixe thine eyes,
> Clear'd from grosse mists of fraile infirmities."

These few "modern instances" may be sufficient to indicate in brief how the doctrines of Plato, and of the *Symposium* in special, have permeated the mind of Europe.

The doctrine of love in its highest grades is delivered, as we have seen, by the prophetess in language savouring of "the mysteries," language appropriate to express a mystical revelation.

On the mind of a sympathetic reader, sensitive to literary *nuances*, Plato produces something of the effect of the mystic φέγγος by his τὸ πολὺ πέλαγος τοῦ καλοῦ and his ἐξαίφνης κατόψεταί τι θαυμαστὸν κτλ. Such phrases stir and transport one as "in the Spirit on the Lord's day" to heavenly places "which eye hath not seen nor ear heard" ;

they awake in us emotions similar to those which the first reading of
Homer evoked in Keats :

> " Then felt I like some watcher of the skies
> When a new planet swims into his ken;
> Or like stout Cortes when with eagle eyes
> He stared at the Pacific…Silent, upon a peak in Darien."

§ v. ALCIBIADES AND HIS SPEECH.

Alcibiades was about 34 years old at this time (416 B.C.), and at the
height of his reputation[1]. The most brilliant party-leader in Athens,
he was a man of great intellectual ability and of remarkable personal
beauty, of which he was not a little vain. It was, ostensibly at least,
because of his beauty that Socrates posed as his "erastes"; while
Alcibiades, on his side, attempted to inflame the supposed passion of
Socrates and displayed jealousy whenever his "erastes" showed a
tendency to woo the favour of rival beauties such as Agathon. Other
indications of Alcibiades' character and position which are given in the
dialogue show him to us as a man of wealth, an important and popular
figure in the smart society of his day, full of ambition for social and
political distinction, and not a little influenced, even against his better
judgment, by the force of public opinion and the *on dit* of his set.
With extraordinary *naïveté* and frankness he exposes his own moral
infirmity, and proves how applicable to his case is the confession of the
Latin poet, "video meliora proboque, deteriora sequor." He is guilt-
less, as he says, of pudency, nor would ever have known the meaning
of the word "shame" (αἰσχύνη) had it not been for Socrates.

Yet, totally lacking in virtue though he be, the Alcibiades of the
Symposium is a delightful, even an attractive and lovable person.
Although actually a very son of Belial, we feel that potentially he is
little short of a hero and a saint. And that because he possesses the
capacity for both understanding and loving Socrates; and to love
Socrates is to love the Ideal. Nominally it is Socrates who is the
lover of Alcibiades, but as the story develops we see that the converse
is more near the truth : Alcibiades is possessed with a consuming
passion, an intense and persistent infatuation for Socrates. And in

---

[1] "The character of Alcibiades, who is the same strange contrast of great
powers and great vices which meets us in history, is drawn to the life" (Jowett,
Plato I. p. 526).

the virtue of this "eros" we find something that more than outweighs his many vices: it acts as the charity that "covers a multitude of sins."

The *speech* of Alcibiades, in spite of its resemblance in tone to a satyric drama composed under the influence of the Wine-god, fulfils a serious purpose—the purpose of vindicating the memory of Socrates from slanderous aspersions and setting in the right light his relations with Alcibiades[1]. And as a means to this end, the general theme of the dialogue, Eros, is cleverly taken up and employed, as will be shown in a later section[2].

In regard to *style and diction* the following points may be noticed. In the *disposition and arrangement* there is a certain amount of confusion and incoherence. Alcibiades starts with a double parable, but fails—as he confesses—to work out his comparisons with full precision and with logical exactitude. This failure is only in keeping with his rôle as a devotee of Dionysus.

Frequency of similes: 216 A ὥσπερ ἀπὸ τῶν Σειρήνων: 217A τὸ τοῦ δηχθέντος...πάθος: 218 B κεκοινωνήκατε...βακχείας.

Elliptical expressions: 215 A, C; 216 B, D, E; 220 C, D; 221 D; 222 B.

Anacolutha: 217 E; 218 A.

§ vi. The Order and Connexion of the Speeches.

Disregarding the introductory and concluding scenes and looking at the rest of the dialogue as a whole, we see that it falls most naturally into three main divisions, *three Acts* as we might call them. In the First Act are comprised all the first five discourses; the Second, and central, Act contains the whole of the deliverances of Socrates; the Third Act consists of Alcibiades' encomium of Socrates[3]. We have to consider, accordingly, how each of these Acts is related to the others; and further, in regard to the first, we have to investigate the relative significance of each of its five sub-divisions or scenes.

1. *The first five speeches and their relative significance.*

Plato's own opinion of the earlier speeches appears clearly enough in the criticism which he puts in the mouth of Socrates (198 D ff.).

---

[1] See *Introd.* § ii. (A) *ad fin.*; and Gomperz, *G. T.* II. pp. 394 ff.

[2] See *Introd.* § vi. 3, where some details of the way in which Alcib. echoes the language of the earlier speakers will be found.

[3] Rettig and von Sybel make the First Act conclude with Arist.'s speech, and the Second Act begin with Agathon's: but that this is a perverse arrangement is well shown by F. Horn, *Platonst.* p. 254 (op. Zeller, *Symp.*).

Although that criticism is aimed primarily at the discourse of Agathon, it obviously applies, in the main, to the whole series of which his discourse formed the climax. Instead of endeavouring to ascertain and state the truth about the object of their encomia—such is the gist of Socrates' criticism—the previous speakers had heaped up their praises regardless of their applicability to that object (198 E *ad init.*). What they considered was not facts but appearances (ὅπως ἐγκωμιάζειν δόξει); consequently they described both the nature of Eros and the effects of his activity in such terms as to make him *appear*—in the eyes of the unsophisticated—supremely good and beautiful, drawing upon every possible source (198 E—199 A).

It thus seems clear that Plato intends us to regard all the first five ✓ speeches as on the same level, in so far as all alike possess the common defect of aiming at appearance only (δόξα), not at reality (ἀλήθεια), in virtue of which no one of them can claim to rank as a scientific contribution (ἐπιστήμη) to the discussion.

The relative order of the first five speeches. The question as to the principle upon which the order and arrangement of these speeches depends is an interesting one and has given rise to some controversy.

(*a*) It has been suggested (*e.g.* by Rötscher) that the speeches are arranged in the order of ascending importance, beginning with that of Phaedrus, which is generally admitted to be the slightest and most ✓ superficial, and proceeding gradually upwards till the culminating point is reached in the speech of Agathon[1]. This view, however, is untenable in the face of the obvious fact that Agathon's speech is in no real sense the best or most important of the series; rather, from the point of view of Socrates, it is the worst. The fact that each speaker commences his oration by a critique of his predecessor might seem, at first sight, to lend some colour to the view that each was actually making some improvement, some advance; but this preliminary critique is plainly nothing more than a rhetorical trick of method[2].

(*b*) Steinhart[3] would arrange the speeches in pairs, distinguishing each pair from the others according to the special spheres of the activity of Eros with which they deal. Phaedrus and Pausanias deal with the

---

[1] Cp. Susemihl, *Genet. Entwick. d. plat. Phil.* p. 407: "So bildet denn der Vortrag des Sokrates den eigentlichen theoretischen Mittelpunkt des Werkes, die übrigen aber mit dem Alkibiades eine aufsteigende Stufenreihe."

[2] Observe also how, in 193 E, Eryx. characterizes the first four speeches as πολλὰ καὶ παντοδαπά, "motley and heterogeneous."

[3] Similarly Deinhardt, *Über Inhalt von Pl. Symp.*

ethical sphere; Eryximachus and Aristophanes with the physical; Agathon and Socrates with the higher spiritual sphere.

This scheme, however, is no less artificial, although it contains some elements of truth; and a sufficient ground for rejecting it lies in the fact that the speech of Socrates cannot be classed along with the other five[1].

(c) Hug's view is that the speeches are arranged from the aesthetic, rather than the logical, point of view, in groups of two each. The second speech in each of the groups is, he holds, richer in content than the first; and the groups themselves are arranged with a view to contrast and variety. But here again, little seems gained by the device of pair-grouping; and the development within the groups is obscure. Hug, however, is no doubt correct in recognizing that the arrangement of the speeches is governed mainly, if not entirely, by artistic considerations, and with a view to literary effect; and that an artistic effect depends largely upon the presence of variety and of contrast is beyond dispute.

(d) Any satisfactory explanation of the order in which the speeches are arranged must be based upon the internal indications supplied by the dialogue itself.

The first inference to be drawn from such indications is this: the speech of Socrates must be left to stand by itself, and cannot be grouped with any one of the first five speeches[2]. This is made quite evident by the tone of the whole interlude (198 A—199 c) which divides Agathon's discourse from that of Socrates, and in special by the definite expression οὐ γὰρ ἔτι ἐγκωμιάζω τοῦτον τὸν τρόπον...ἀλλὰ τά

---

[1] Cp. Jowett (Plato I. p. 527): "The speeches have been said to follow each other in pairs....But these and similar distinctions are not found in Plato; they are the points of view of his critics, and seem to impede rather than to assist us in understanding him." This is sensibly observed; still, Jowett is inclined to dismiss the matter too lightly. I may add that, while from the artistic point of view it is absurd to class together the speeches of Arist. and Eryx., there is a certain connexion of thought between the two, in their common relation to physiological theories, and so far we may allow that Steinhart points in the right direction (see § iii. 4, above).

[2] Cp. Jowett (Plato I. p. 256): "The successive speeches...contribute in various degrees to the final result; they are all designed to prepare the way for Socrates, who gathers up the threads anew, and skims the highest points of each of them. But they are not to be regarded as the stages of an idea, rising above one another to a climax. They are fanciful, partly facetious, performances....All of them are rhetorical and poetical rather than dialectical, but glimpses of truth appear in them." This is well said.

γε ἀληθῆ...ἐθέλω εἰπεῖν κατ' ἐμαυτόν, οὐ πρὸς τοὺς ὑμετέρους λόγους (199 A—B): these last words should finally settle the matter.

We are thus left with five speeches, not six; and this of itself might be enough to show that a division into pair-groups is not feasible. And when we further examine the internal indications, the arbitrary character of any such grouping becomes yet more obvious. For although the first two speeches possess a good deal in common, and were, apparently, confounded together by Xenophon, the method of grouping them in one pair tends to obscure the great difference between them in point of substance, style, and general ability of statement, and to obscure also the fact that a number of other discourses intervened between these two (μετὰ δὲ Φαῖδρον ἄλλους τινας εἶναι 180 c). The express mention of this last fact is a land-mark not to be ignored.

Moreover, while this distinction is marked between the first speech and the second, there are internal indications which point to a special connexion between the third and the second. Eryximachus starts from the same assumption (the duality of Eros) as Pausanias; and, moreover, he expressly states that his speech is intended to supplement that of Pausanias (186 A ad init.). Furthermore, we find Aristophanes classing together these two (189 c).

As regards the fourth discourse (Aristophanes'), we are forbidden by similar internal indications to class it along with any of the preceding discourses. Although much of its point lies in its allusiveness to Eryximachus' theories, Aristophanes himself expressly emphasizes the difference between his speech and the others (189 c, 193 D); and indeed it is evident to the most cursory inspection. Nor is it possible, without reducing the group-system to the level of an unmeaning artifice, to pair the speech of Aristophanes with that of Agathon, which follows next in order. The only ground for such a grouping would be the purely fortuitous and external fact that both the speakers are professional poets : in style and substance the two speeches lie leagues apart, while not even an incidental connexion of any kind is hinted at in the text.

The reason for the position of the fifth discourse (Agathon's) is not hard to discover. Once the general plan of the dialogue, as consisting of three Acts, with the discourse of Socrates for the central Act, was fixed in the author's mind, it was inevitable, on artistic grounds, that Agathon's oration should be set in the closest juxtaposition with that of Socrates,—in other words, at the close of the first Act. This disposition is already pointed to in the introductory incident, where Agathon promises to engage in a match " concerning wisdom " with

Socrates (175 E); and we have another indication of it at the very opening of the dialogue, where Glaucon in speaking of the banqueters mentions these three names only—Agathon, Socrates, Alcibiades (172 A). If then, for the purpose of the dialogue as a whole, Agathon is the most important of the first five speakers, it is essential that his discourse should form the climax of the series, and stand side by side with that of Socrates his rival, to point the contrast.

This gives us one fixed point. Another fixed point is the first speech : once Phaedrus has been designated πατὴρ τοῦ λόγου, the primary inventor of the theme[1], the task of initiating the series can scarcely fall to other hands than his. Why the three intermediate discourses are placed in their present order is not so clear. Considerations of variety and contrast count for something, and it may be noticed that the principle of alternating longer and shorter speeches is observed[2]. Similarity in method of treatment counts for something too ; and from this point of view we can see that the order Phaedrus—Pausanias—Eryximachus is more natural than the order Phaedrus—Eryximachus—Pausanias ; since the middle speech of Pausanias has some points in common with both the others, whereas the speech of Eryximachus has practically nothing in common with that of Phaedrus. Granting, then, that on grounds at once of continuity and of variety of extent these three speeches may most artistically be set in their present order, and granting, further, that the proper place for Agathon's speech is the last of the series, the only vacant place left for the speech of Aristophanes is the fourth. Although it is a speech *sui generis*, possessing nothing in common with that of Agathon, yet the mere fact of the juxtaposition of the two famous poets is aesthetically pleasing; while a delightful variation is secured by the interposition of a splendid grotesque which, alike in style and in substance, affords so signal a contrast both to the following and to the preceding speeches[3]. More-

---

[1] That he is so designated may be due, as Crain thinks, to the desire to connect this dialogue with the *Phaedrus*.

[2] The comparative lengths of the speeches, counted by pages of the Oxford text, are roughly these: Phaedrus 3 pp.; Paus. $6\frac{1}{2}$; Eryx. $3\frac{3}{4}$; Arist. 6; Agathon 4; Socr. (a) 3, (b) $14\frac{1}{2}$; Alc. $9\frac{1}{2}$. Thus, in round numbers, the total of the first five speeches comes to 23 pp., which very nearly balances the 24 pp. occupied by Socr. (b) and Alcib.

[3] Jowett explains (*Plato* I. p. 530) that the transposition of the speeches of Arist. and Eryx. is made " partly to avoid monotony, partly for the sake of making Aristophanes ' the cause of wit in others,' and also in order to bring the comic and tragic poet into juxtaposition, as if by accident." No doubt these considerations count for something, but, as I have already tried to show, there is another and a deeper reason for the transposition (see § iii. 4).

over, as is elsewhere shown, Aristophanes handles his theme with special reference to the medical theorists of whom Eryximachus is a type. The first five speakers are all actual historical personages, not mere lay figures. None the less, we must recognize the probability that Plato is not literally true, in all details, to historical facts but, choosing his characters with a view to scenic effect, adapts their personalities to suit the requirements of his literary purpose. That is to say, we probably ought to regard these persons less as individuals than as types, and their speeches less as characteristic utterances of the individual speakers than as the expressions of well-marked tendencies in current opinion. The view proposed by Sydenham, approved by Schleiermacher, and developed by Rückert[1], that under the disguise of the personages named other and more important persons were aimed at by Plato probably goes too far. It is true that some of the traits of Gorgias are reproduced in Agathon, and some of those of Isocrates in Pausanias; but where is the *alter ego* of Aristophanes to be found? Nor, in fact, was Plato at any time much concerned to attack individuals as such: the objects of his satire were rather the false tendencies and the tricks of style which belonged to certain sets and schools of rhetors and writers. And here in the *Symposium* his purpose seems to be to exhibit the general results of sophistic teaching in various contemporary circles *at Athens*; which purpose would be obscured were we to identify any of the characters of the dialogue with non-Attic personages.

The five intellectual types of which Plato here presents us with studied portraits are distinct, yet all the five are merely species of one and the same genus, inasmuch as all represent various phases of ungrounded opinion (δόξα), and inasmuch as all alike, in contrast to the philosopher Socrates, are men of *unphilosophic* mind[2].

2.   *The relation of the speech of Socrates to the first five speeches.*

The speech of Socrates, as we have seen, stands in contrast not only to the speech of Agathon but also to the whole series of which

---

[1] Rückert makes the following identifications: Phaedrus = Tisias; Pausanias = Protagoras or Xenophon; Eryximachus = Hippias; Aristophanes = Prodicus; Agathon = Gorgias.   Jowett (*Plato* I. p. 529) says of Pausanias: "his speech might have been composed by a pupil of Lysias or of Prodicus, although there is no hint given that Plato is specially referring to them."   Sydenham supposed that Phaedrus stands for Lysias.

[2] So Real, *Verhältnis*, etc., p. 31: "Alle diese fünf Reden eine breite Basis, fast auf demselben Niveau stehend, bilden sollen für die später folgenden Reden des Sokrates und Alkibiades."

Agathon's speech forms the climax and conclusion; since all of them alike are tainted with the same vice of sophistry. We have now to examine this contrast in detail.

(a) *Socrates* v. *Phaedrus.* Phaedrus had declared Eros to be μέγας θεὸς καὶ θαυμαστός (178 A): Socrates, on the contrary, argues that Eros is no θεός but a δαίμων (202 c ff.). Phaedrus had relied for his proofs on ancient tradition (τεκμήριον δὲ τούτου κτλ., 178 B; ὁμολογεῖται, 178 c): Socrates bases his argument on dialectic, and on the conclusions of pure reason (Diotima being Reason personified). Phaedrus had ascribed the noble acts of Alcestis and Achilles to the working of sensual Eros (179 B ff.): Socrates ascribes the same acts to a more deeply seated desire—that for everlasting fame (ὑπὲρ ἀρετῆς ἀθανάτου κτλ., 208 D)[1]:

(b) *Socrates* v. *Pausanias.* Pausanias had distinguished two kinds of Eros—Uranios and Pandemos (180 D—E): Socrates, on the other hand, treats Eros as a unity which comprises in its single nature opposite qualities (202 B, 203 c ff.); further, he shows that an apparent duality in the nature of Eros is to be explained as due to a confusion between Eros as genus (= Desire) and Eros in the specific sense of sex-passion (205 B ff.).

Pausanias had argued that sensual Eros, of the higher kind, is a thing of value in social and political life as a source of ἀρετή and ἀνδρεία (182 B—c, 184 D—E, 185 B)[2]: Socrates shows that the production of ἀρετή in the sphere of politics and law is due to an Eros which aims at begetting offspring of the soul for the purpose of securing an immortality of fame (209 A ff., 209 D)[3]. And Socrates shows further that for the true Eros τὸ ἐν τοῖς ἐπιτηδεύμασι καὶ τοῖς νόμοις καλόν (210 c) is not the τέλος. Lastly, the connexion between Eros (in the form of παιδεραστία) with φιλοσοφία which had been merely hinted at by Pausanias in 182 c, and superficially treated in 182 D—E, is explained at length by Socrates.

[1] This is the point noticed by Jowett (*Plato* I. p. 531): "From Phaedrus he (Socr.) takes the thought that love is stronger than death."

[2] Cp. Jowett (*Plato* I. p. 531): "From Pausanias (Socr. takes the thought) that the true love is akin to intellect and political activity."

[3] Gomperz (*G. T.* II. p. 396), à *propos* of his view that Plato is thinking of his παιδικά Dion in *Symp.*, writes: "they were busy with projects of political and social regeneration, which the philosopher hoped he might one day realise by the aid of the prince. On this view there is point and pertinence in that otherwise irrelevant mention of legislative achievement among the fruits of the love-bond." The suggestion is interesting, but the relevance does not depend upon its being true: Plato, in any cause, taught politics.

(c) *Socrates* v. *Eryximachus.* Eryximachus, following Pausanias, had adopted the assumption of the duality of Eros: this Socrates denies (202 B).

Eryximachus had extended the sphere of influence of Eros so as to include the whole of nature (the objects of medicine, music, astronomy, religion): Socrates shows that the Eros-instinct affects animals as well as men (207 A)—as equally included under the head of θνητά (207 D),—and he ascribes to the Eros-daemon the mediation between gods and men and the control of the whole sphere of religion; but he confines his treatment in the main to the narrower subject of Eros proper as concerned with humanity[1].

(d) *Socrates* v. *Aristophanes.* Aristophanes had defined Eros as "the desire and pursuit of wholeness" (τοῦ ὅλου τῇ ἐπιθυμίᾳ καὶ διώξει ἔρως ὄνομα 192 E: cp. 192 B ὅταν...ἐντύχῃ τῷ αὑτοῦ ἡμίσει): Socrates corrects this by showing that wholeness, or one's other half, is only sought when it is good (οὔτε ἡμίσεος εἶναι τὸν ἔρωτα οὔτε ὅλου ἐὰν μὴ... ἀγαθὸν ὄν 205 E[2]). Both, however, agree in maintaining the negative position that Eros is not simply the desire for ἡ τῶν ἀφροδισίων συνουσία (192 C).

(e) *Socrates* v. *Agathon.* The strictly dialectical part of Socrates' speech (199 C—201 C), which takes the form of a cross-questioning of Agathon, consists, in the main, of a hostile critique and refutation of his speech. But in some few particulars Socrates indicates his agreement with statements made by Agathon. We may, therefore, summarize thus:—

(1) *Points of Agreement*: Socrates approves (199 C) of the rule of method laid down by Agathon (195 A) and of the distinction it implies (201 D *ad fin.*). Agathon stated the object of Eros to be the beautiful (197 B): Socrates adopts and developes this statement (201 A). Agathon ascribed ἀνδρεία to Eros (196 C—D): so does Socrates (203 D[3]).

---

[1] It is hardly correct to say with Jowett (*Plato* I. p. 531) that "from Eryximachus Socrates takes the thought that love is a universal phenomenon and the great power of nature": this statement requires limitation.

[2] It may be observed, however, that while the Platonic Socrates is here simply in contradiction to Arist., the idea of a "fall" from a primeval state of perfection which underlies the myth of Arist. is very similar to the view put forth by Plato in the *Phaedrus* and elsewhere that the earthly life of the soul involves a "fall" from its pristine state of purity in a super-terrestrial sphere. And in both Eros is the impulse towards restoration: to achieve communion with the Idea is to regain τὸ οἰκεῖον, τὸ ὅλον, ἡ ἀρχαία φύσις (193 D).

[3] Another "glimpse of truth" which appears in A.'s speech is thus indicated by

(2) *Points of Difference*: Agathon's Eros is κάλλιστος καὶ ἄριστος (197 c): Socrates makes out Eros to be οὔτε καλὸς οὔτε ἀγαθός (201 E). In particular Socrates denies that Eros is σοφός (203 E f.), or ἀπαλός (203 c), as Agathon (196 E f., 195 c, D) had affirmed. Agathon had assumed Eros to be θεός (194 E, *et passim*): this Socrates corrects (202 B ff., E).

Agathon, like the rest, in his lavish laudations had confused Eros with the object of love (τὸ ἐρώμενον, τὸ ἐραστόν); whereas Socrates points out that Eros is to be identified rather with the subject (τὸ ἐρῶν, τὸ ἐπιθυμοῦν, 204 c).

3. *The relation of Alcibiades' speech to the rest.*

(a) The speech of Alcibiades is related to that of Socrates "as Praxis to Theory[1]." Its main purpose is to present to us a vivid portrait of *Socrates* as the perfect exemplar of Eros (ὁ τελέως ἐρωτικός); and thus to compel us to acknowledge that in the living Socrates we have before us both a complete φιλόσοφος—even as Eros is φιλοσοφῶν διὰ παντὸς τοῦ βίου (203 D),—and a δαιμόνιος ἀνήρ—even as Eros is a δαίμων. In addition to this main purpose, the speech serves the secondary purpose of vindicating the master against the charge of indulging in impure relations with his disciples (see § ii. A *ad fin.*).

But the language of Alcibiades echoes not only that of Socrates, in part, but also, in part, that of the earlier encomiasts of Eros. And this is due to the fact that Socrates—the Eros of Alcibiades—plays a double rôle; he is both ὁ ἐρώμενος and ὁ ἐρῶν. This ambiguity of the Socratic nature is already implied in the comparisons with satyrs and Sileni made by Alcibiades, which point to a character that is ἐραστός, however ἐνδεής in outward appearance. We may therefore tabulate the more detailed points of inter-relation as follows:—

(a) The Eros of the ἐραστής (as exhibiting ἔνδεια), Socrates' encomium.	Socrates as ἐραστής (his outward appearance of ἔνδεια) in Alcibiades' encomium.
203 D ἐπίβουλός ἐστι τοῖς καλοῖς καὶ τοῖς ἀγαθοῖς...ἀεί τινας πλέκων μηχανάς.	213 ο διεμηχανήσω ὅπως παρὰ τῷ καλλίστῳ...κατακείσῃ.
203 ο φύσει ἐραστὴς ὢν περὶ τὸ καλόν.	216 D Σωκράτης ἐρωτικῶς διάκειται τῶν καλῶν.

Jowett (*Plato* I. p. 526): "When Agathon says that no man 'can be wronged of his own free will,' he is alluding playfully to a serious problem of Greek philosophy (cp. Arist. Nic. Ethics, v. 9)": see *Symp.* 190 c *ad init.* But, so far as I see, no reference is made to this point by Socrates.

[1] Hug, p. lxvii.

203 D ἀνυπόδητος καὶ ἄοικος, χαμαιπετὴς
ἀεὶ ὢν καὶ ἄστρωτος...ὑπαίθριος κοιμώμενος.

203 D φρονήσεως ἐπιθυμητής.

203 D δεινὸς γόης καὶ φαρμακεὺς καὶ σοφιστής...πόριμος...ὅταν εὐπορήσῃ.

209 B εὐθὺς εὐπορεῖ λόγων περὶ ἀρετῆς.

220 B ἀνυπόδητος...ἐπορεύετο.

220 D εἱστήκει μέχρι ἕως ἐγένετο (with the
context).

220 C ἐξ ἑωθινοῦ φροντίζων τι ἔστηκε (cp.
174 D ff.).

215 C ff. κηλεῖ τοὺς ἀνθρώπους (κατέχει,
ἐκπλήττει), κτλ.   223 A εὐπόρως καὶ
πιθανὸν λόγον ηὗρεν.

It will be noticed that in this list the passages which find
responsions in the language of Alcibiades are all drawn from the
discourse of Socrates. This is due to the fact that it is his discourse
alone, of the earlier encomia, which treats Ἔρως on the side of its
ἔνδεια. The previous speakers had, as we have seen, regarded Ἔρως as
altogether lovely, *i.e.* as τὸ ἐρώμενον. Accordingly, it is to the next list
of parallels that we must look for the passages where Alcibiades echoes
their sentiments.

(β) Ἔρως-ἐρώμενος as κάλλιστος καὶ
ἄριστος in the earlier encomia.

(1) *Courage.*

178 E (Phaedrus) στρατόπεδον ἐραστῶν
...μαχόμενοί γ' ἂν νικῷεν, κτλ.

197 D (Agathon) ἐν πόνῳ ἐν φόβῳ...
παραστάτης τε καὶ σωτὴρ ἄριστος.

203 D (Socrates) ἀνδρεῖος ὢν καὶ ἴτης καὶ
σύντονος.

(2) *Temperance.*

196 C (Agathon) ὁ Ἔρως διαφερόντως ἂν
σωφρονοῖ.

(3) *Complete virtue.*

196 D περὶ μὲν οὖν δικαιοσύνης καὶ σωφροσύνης καὶ ἀνδρείας τοῦ θεοῦ εἴρηται,
περὶ δὲ σοφίας λείπεται.

(4) *Admirableness.*

180 B (Phaedrus) οἱ θεοὶ...μᾶλλον θαυμά-
ζουσιν καὶ ἄγανται...ὅταν ὁ ἐρώμενος
(*e.g.* Achilles) τὸν ἐραστὴν ἀγαπᾷ, κτλ.

197 D (Agathon) θεατὸς σοφοῖς, ἀγαστὸς
θεοῖς.

210 E (Socrates) κατόψεταί τι θαυμαστὸν
τὴν φύσιν καλόν.

(5) *Inspiration of a sense of honour.*

178 D (Phaedrus) (ὁ ἔρως ἐμποιεῖ) τὴν
ἐπὶ μὲν τοῖς αἰσχροῖς αἰσχύνην.

Socrates as the embodiment of Ἔρως-
ἐρώμενος in Alcibiades' encomium.

220 E ὅτι...φυγῇ ἀνεχώρει τὸ στρατόπεδον,
κτλ.

220 E συνδιέσωσε...αὐτὸν ἐμέ.

221 B μάλα ἐρρωμένως ἀμυνεῖται.

219 E τοῖς πόνοις...ἐμοῦ περιῆν, κτλ.

220 E ἐκέλευον σοι διδόναι τἀριστεῖα.

216 D πόσης οἴεσθε γέμει...σωφροσύνης;

219 D ἀγάμενον...σωφροσύνην καὶ ἀνδρείαν
...εἰς φρόνησιν καὶ εἰς καρτερίαν.

219 D ἀγάμενον τὴν τούτου φύσιν, κτλ.

221 C Socr., as οὐδενὶ ὅμοιος, is superior
to Achilles.

220 E ἄξιον ἦν θεάσασθαι Σωκράτη.

216 E τὰ ἐντὸς ἀγάλματα...εἶδον...πάγκαλα
καὶ θαυμαστά.

216 B ἐγὼ δὲ τοῦτον μόνον αἰσχύνομαι.

(6) *Indifference to personal beauty.*

210 B (Socrates) ἑνὸς δὲ (τὸ κάλλος) καταφρονήσαντα, κτλ. (cp. 210 D, 211 E).

219 C ἐμοῦ...κατεφρόνησεν καὶ κατεγέλασεν τῆς ἐμῆς ὥρας.

(7) *Fruitfulness.*

210 C (Socrates) τίκτειν λόγους...οἵτινες ποιήσουσι βελτίους τοὺς νέους (cp. 210 D).

212 A τίκτειν οὐκ εἴδωλα ἀρετῆς...ἀλλ᾽ ἀληθῆ.

209 B εὐπορεῖ λόγων περὶ ἀρετῆς καὶ οἷον χρὴ εἶναι τὸν ἄνδρα τὸν ἀγαθόν (cp. 185 B πολλὴν ἐπεμέλειαν...πρὸς ἀρετήν).

210 D καλοὺς λόγους...τίκτῃ...ἐν φιλοσοφίᾳ ἀφθόνῳ.

222 A (τοὺς λόγους αὐτοῦ εὑρήσει) θειοτάτους καὶ πλεῖστα ἀγάλματα ἀρετῆς ἐν αὐτοῖς ἔχοντας καὶ...τείνοντας...ἐπὶ πᾶν ὅσον προσήκει σκοπεῖν τῷ μέλλοντι καλῷ κἀγαθῷ ἔσεσθαι (cp. 218 D ὡς ὅτι βέλτιστον γενέσθαι).

218 A δηχθεὶς ὑπὸ τῶν ἐν φιλοσοφίᾳ λόγων.

(8) *Range of Influence.*

186 B (Eryximachus) ἐπὶ πᾶν ὁ θεὸς τείνει.

210 D (Socrates) ἐπὶ τὸ πολὺ πέλαγος ...τοῦ καλοῦ.

222 A (τοὺς λόγους αὐτοῦ εὑρήσει) ἐπὶ πλεῖστον τείνοντας, μᾶλλον δὲ ἐπὶ πᾶν, κτλ.

The foregoing lists contain, I believe, most if not all of the passages in which Alcibiades, describing Socrates, uses phrases which definitely echo the language or repeat the thought of the earlier encomiasts. When one considers the number of these "responsions" and the natural way in which they are introduced, one is struck at once both with the elaborate technique of Plato and, still more, with the higher art which so skilfully conceals that technique. For all its appearance of spontaneity, a careful analysis and comparison prove that the encomium by Alcibiades is a very carefully wrought piece of work in which every phrase has its significance, every turn of expression its bearing on the literary effect of the dialogue as a whole. Moreover, as we are now to see, the list of parallels already given by no means exhausts the "responsions" offered by Alcibiades.

(b) The speech of Alcibiades, although primarily concerned with Socrates, is also, in a secondary degree, concerned with *Alcibiades himself.* And Alcibiades, like Socrates, plays a double part : he is at once the παιδικά of Socrates the ἐραστής, and the ἐραστής of Socrates the ἐρώμενος. In his rôle of ἐραστής Alcibiades exhibits a spirit very similar to that described in the earlier speeches, in which every display of erotic passion is regarded as excusable if not actually commendable. We may call attention to the following echoes :—

218 A πᾶν ἐτόλμα δρᾶν τε καὶ λέγειν.

219 E ἠπόρουν δὴ καταδεδουλωμένος.

218 D ἐμοὶ μὲν γὰρ οὐδέν ἐστι πρεσβύτερον τοῦ ὡς ὅτι βέλτιστον ἐμὲ γενέσθαι. τούτου δὲ οἶμαί μοι συλλήπτορα οὐδένα κυριώτερον εἶναι σοῦ. ἐγὼ δὴ τοιούτῳ ἀνδρί... ἂν μὴ χαριζόμενος αἰσχυνοίμην τοὺς φρονίμους.

218 D εἴπερ...τις ἔστ' ἐν ἐμοὶ δύναμις δι' ἧς ἂν σὺ γένοιο ἀμείνων.

222 B οὓς οὗτος ἐξαπατῶν ὡς ἐραστὴς παιδικὰ...μὴ ἐξαπατᾶσθαι ὑπὸ τούτου.

217 C ὥσπερ ἐραστὴς παιδικοῖς ἐπιβουλεύων ...D αὖθις δ' ἐπιβουλεύσας.

219 B ταῦτα...ἀφεὶς ὥσπερ βέλη.

219 B ὑπὸ τὸν τρίβωνα κατακλινεὶς τὸν τουτουί, περιβαλὼν τὼ χεῖρε...κατεκείμην τὴν νύκτα ὅλην.

215 D ἐκπεπληγμένοι ἐσμὲν καὶ κατεχόμεθα.

219 D οὔθ'...εἶχον (ὅπως) ἀποστερηθείην τῆς τούτου συνουσίας.

221 A παρακελεύομαί τε αὐτοῖν θαρρεῖν, καὶ ἔλεγον ὅτι οὐκ ἀπολείψω αὐτώ.

182 E (Pausanias) θαυμαστὰ ἔργα ἐργαζομένῳ...ποιεῖν οἷάπερ οἱ ἐρασταὶ πρὸς τὰ παιδικά, κτλ.

184 C (Paus.) ἐάν τις ἐθέλῃ τινὰ θεραπεύειν ἡγούμενος δι' ἐκεῖνον ἀμείνων ἔσεσθαι... αὕτη αὖ ἡ ἐθελοδουλεία οὐκ αἰσχρά.

184 E τότε δή...συμπίπτει τὸ καλὸν εἶναι παιδικὰ ἐραστῇ χαρίσασθαι.

185 B πᾶν πάντως γε καλὸν ἀρετῆς ἕνεκα χαρίζεσθαι.

184 D ὁ μὲν δυνάμενος εἰς...ἀρετὴν συμβάλλεσθαι.

184 E ἐπὶ τούτῳ καὶ ἐξαπατηθῆναι οὐδὲν αἰσχρόν.

185 B καλὴ ἡ ἀπάτη.

203 D (Socrates) ἐπίβουλός ἐστι (ὁ Ἔρως) τοῖς καλοῖς καὶ ἀγαθοῖς.

203 D (Socr.) θηρευτὴς δεινός.

191 E ff. (Aristoph.) χαίρουσι συγκατακείμενοι καὶ συμπεπλεγμένοι τοῖς ἀνδράσι... οὐ γὰρ ὑπ' ἀναισχυντίας τοῦτο δρῶσιν ἀλλ' ὑπὸ θάρρους...ἀποβαίνουσιν εἰς τὰ πολιτικὰ ἄνδρες οἱ τοιοῦτοι.

192 B (Aristoph.) θαυμαστὰ ἐκπλήττονται φιλίᾳ...καὶ ἔρωτι, οὐκ ἐθέλοντες...χωρίζεσθαι ἀλλήλων οὐδὲ σμικρὸν χρόνον.

179 A (Phaedrus) ἐγκαταλιπεῖν γε τὰ παιδικὰ ἢ μὴ βοηθῆσαι κινδυνεύοντι, οὐδεὶς οὕτω κακός, κτλ.

Since in this list echoes are found of the only two earlier encomiasts who were not represented in the former lists (viz. Pausanias and Aristophanes), it will be seen that the speech of Alcibiades contains references, more or less frequent, to sentiments and sayings expressed by every one of the previous speakers. It is chiefly in his description of himself that Alcibiades echoes the language of the first five speakers, and in his description of Socrates that he echoes the language of Socrates. The general impression made on the mind of the reader who attends to the significance of the facts might be summed up briefly in the form of a proportion: as Alcibiades is to Socrates in point of practical excellence and truth, so are the first five speeches to the discourse of Socrates-Diotima in point of theoretical truth and excellence. But while this is, broadly speaking, true of the inner nature (φύσις, τὰ ἔνδον) of Socrates as contrasted with that of Alcibiades, we must bear in mind that in his outward appearance (σχῆμα) Socrates is " conformed to this world " and, posing as an *erastes* of a similar type to Alcibiades himself, serves to illustrate the theories and sentiments of the earlier speeches.

Lastly, attention may be drawn to one other parallel in Alcibiades' discourse which appears to have passed unnoticed hitherto. It can scarcely be a mere coincidence that Alcibiades' progress in erotics—in other words, " the temptation of saint " Socrates—is marked by a series of stages (συνουσία, συγγυμνασία, συνδειπνεῖν, 217 A ff.) until it reaches its climax in συγκεῖσθαι, and that a similar ἄνοδος by gradual stages (210 A ff., 211 c ff.) up to the final communion with Ideal Beauty had been described as the characteristic method of the true *erastes*. It seems reasonable to suppose that the method of *false* love is designedly represented as thus in detail contrasting with, and as it were caricaturing, the method of *true* love: for thereby an added emphasis is laid upon the latter.

§ vii. THE DIALOGUE AS A WHOLE : ITS SCOPE AND DESIGN.

No small degree of attention has been paid by the expositors of our dialogue to the question regarding its main purport—" de universi operis consilio." It is plausibly argued that there must be some one leading thought, some fundamental idea, which serves to knit together its various parts and to furnish it with that " unity " which should belong to it as an artistic whole. But wherein this leading idea consists has been matter of controversy. Some, like Stallbaum, are content to adopt the simplest and most obvious view that Eros is the central idea, and that the design of the whole is to establish a doctrine of Eros. Others, again, have supposed that Plato was mainly concerned to furnish his readers with another specimen of the right method of handling philosophical problems. But although either of these views, or both combined, might be thought to supply an adequate account of the design and scope of the dialogue if it had ended with the speech of Socrates, they are evidently inadequate when applied to the dialogue as it stands, with the addition of the Alcibiades scenes. In fact, this last part of the dialogue—the Third Act, as we have called it—might be construed as suggesting an entirely different *motif*,—namely, laudation of Socrates in general, or perhaps rather (as Wolf argued) a defence of Socrates against the more specific charge of unchastity.

That this is one purpose of the dialogue is beyond dispute: many indications testify, as has been shown, that Plato intended here to offer an *apologiam pro vita Socratis*. Yet it would be a mistake to argue from this that the main design of the dialogue as a whole lies in this apologetic. Rather it is necessary to combine the leading idea of this last Act with those of the earlier Acts in such a way as to reduce them, as it were, to a common denominator. And when we do this, we find—as I agree with Rückert in believing—that the dominant factor common to all three Acts is nothing else than the personality of Socrates,—Socrates as the ideal both of philosophy and of love,   Ʋ Socrates as at once the type of temperance and the master of magic. Our study of the framework as well as of the speeches has shown us how both the figure of Socrates and his theory dominate the dialogue, and that to throw these into bolder relief constitutes the main value of all the other theories and figures. This point has been rightly emphasized by Rückert (p. 252): "utique ad Socratem animus advertitur; quasi sol in medio positus, quem omnes circummeant, cuius luce omnia collustrantur, vimque accipiunt vitalem, Socrates proponitur, et Socrates quidem philosophus, sapiens, temperans. Quem iuxta multi plane evanescunt, ceteri vix obscure comparent, ipse Agatho, splendidissimum licet sidus ex omnibus, ut coram sole luna pallescit."

It seems clear, therefore, that the explanation of the " Hauptzweck " of our dialogue which was given long ago by Schleiermacher is the right one—" propositum est Platoni in Convivio ut philosophum qualem in vita se exhiberet, viva imagine depingeret": it is in the portrait of the ideal Socrates that the main object of the dialogue is to be sought.

The theory of Teichmüller and Wilamowitz as to the occasion on which the dialogue was produced has no direct bearing on the question of design. They suppose that it was written specially for recital at a banquet in Plato's Academy; and, further, that it was intended to provide the friends and pupils of Plato with a model of what such a banquet ought to be. But it would be absurd to estimate the design of a work of literary art by the temporary purpose which it subserved; nor can we easily suppose that Plato's main interest lay in either imagining or recording gastronomic successes as such. Equally unproven, though more suggestive, is the idea of Gomperz that this dialogue περὶ ἔρωτος was inspired by an affection for Dion.

§ viii. The Date.

We must begin by drawing a distinction between (a) the date of the actual Banquet, (b) that of Apollodorus' narrative, and (c) that of the composition of the dialogue by Plato.

(a) That the date of the Banquet is B.C. 416 (Ol. 90. 4) is asserted by Athenaeus (v. 217 A): ὁ μὲν γὰρ (sc. Ἀγάθων) ἐπὶ ἄρχοντος Εὐφήμου στεφανοῦται Ληναίοις. It is true, as Sauppe and others have pointed out, that the description in 175 E (ἐν μάρτυσι...τρισμυρίοις, cp. 223 B n.), would suit the Great Dionysia better than the Lenaea; but this discrepancy need not shake our confidence in the date assigned by Athenaeus. The year 416 agrees with the mention of Agathon as νέος (175 B), and of Alcibiades as at the height of his influence (216 B) before the ill-fated Sicilian expedition.

(b) The date of the prefatory scene may be approximately fixed from the following indications: (1) It was a considerable number of years after the actual Banquet (οὐ νεωστί 172 C, παίδων ὄντων ἡμῶν ἔτι 173 A); (2) several years (πολλὰ ἔτη 172 C) after Agathon's departure from Athens; (3) within three years of the commencement of Apollodorus' close association with Socrates (172 C); (4) before the death of Socrates (as shown by the pres. tense συνδιατρίβω 172 C); (5) before the death of Agathon (as shown by the perf. ἐπιδεδήμηκεν 172 C). It seems probable that Agathon left Athens about 408, at the latest, and resided till 399 at the court of Archelaus of Macedon[1]. Hence any date before 399 will satisfy the two last data. And since the two first data demand a date as far removed as possible from the years 416 and 408, we can hardly go far wrong if we date the dramatic setting circ. 400 B.C.

(c) We come now to the more important question of *the date of composition*. The *external* evidence available is but slight. A posterior limit is afforded by two references in Aristotle (*Pol.* II. 4. 1262^b 12 : *de An.* II. 415^a 26), a possible allusion by Aeschines (*in Timarch.* 345 B.C.), and a probable comic allusion by Alexis in his *Phaedrus* (ap. Athen. XIII. 562 A)—a work which probably cannot be dated before 370 at the earliest.

The *internal* evidence is more extensive but somewhat indefinite. It is commonly assumed[2] that in 193 A (διῳκίσθημεν...Λακεδαιμονίων)

---

[1] Fritzsche's view that Ar. *Ran.* 72 implies the previous death (*i.e. ante* 405) of A. is refuted by Rettig, *Symp.* pp. 59 ff.

[2] See *e.g.* Zeller, *Plato* (E.T.) p. 139 *n.*; Teichmüller, *Litt. Fehd.* II. 262.

INTRODUCTION lxvii

we have a definite reference to the διοικισμός of Mantinea in 385 B.C. But even if this be granted—as I think it must, in spite of the contradiction of Wilamowitz—it by no means follows that the dialogue must be dated 385—4. We find Isocrates (*Panegyr.* 126) mentioning the same event five years later. All that it affords us is a prior limit. Little weight can be given to Dümmler's view that the previous death of Gorgias (circ. 380) is implied by the allusion to him in 198 c (Γοργίου κεφαλὴν κτλ.)[1]. Nor can we lay much stress on the conclusions drawn (by Rückert and others) from the absence of reference to the re-establishment of Mantinea in 370, or to the exploits of the Theban "Sacred Band" at Leuctra (371), which (as Hug thinks) might naturally have been alluded to in 178 E.

The evidence of date afforded by "stylometric" observations is not of a convincing character. M. Lutoslawski, it is true, dogmatically asserts that the *Symposium* stands between the *Cratylus* and *Phaedo* in the "First Platonic Group"; but his arguments, when examined, prove to be of the most flimsy character. Beyond affording a confirmation of the general impression that our dialogue stands somewhere in the "middle" period, the labours of the stylometrists give us little assistance. If we choose to date it in 390 they cannot refute us, nor yet if we date it 10 or 15 years later. The question as to whether the *Symposium* preceded the *Phaedrus* or followed it is one of special interest in view of the number of points at which the two writings touch each other. The evidence on the whole seems in favour of the priority of the *Phaedrus*[2]; but, even if this be granted, little light is shed on the date of composition of the *Symp.*, since that of the *Phaedrus* eludes precise determination.

Equally difficult is it to draw any certain conclusions from the relation in which our dialogue stands to the *Symposium* of Xenophon. That there are many points of connexion, many close parallels, between

---

[1] See Dümmler, *Akademica*, p. 40; and the refutation by Vahlen, *op. Acad.* I. 482 ff.

[2] So I hold with Schleierm., Zeller, I. Bruns, Hahn and others; against Lutosl., Gomperz and Raeder. It is monstrous to assert, as Lutosl. does, "that the date of the *Phaedrus* as written about 379 B.C. is now quite as well confirmed as the date of the *Symp.* about 385 B.C." I agree rather with the view which makes *Phaedr.* P.'s first publication after he opened his Academy, *i.e. circ.* 388-6 (a view recently supported in England by E. S. Thompson, *Meno* xliii ff., and Gifford, *Euthyd.* 20 ff.). The foll. are some of the parallels: *Ph.* 232 E = *Symp.* 181 E, 183 E; 234 A = 183 E; 234 B = 183 c; 250 c = 209 E; 251 D (240 c) = 215 E, 218 A; 251 A = 215 B, 222 A; 252 A = 189 D; 266 A = 180 E; 267 A (273 A) = 200 A; 272 A = 198 D; 276 A = 222 A; 276 E = 209 B; 278 D = 203 E; 279 B = 216 D, 215 B.

the two works is obvious, but which of the two is prior in date is a problem which has called forth prolonged controversy[1]. This is not the place to investigate the problem : I can only state my firm opinion that the Xenophontic *Sympos.* (whether genuine or not) is the later work. But attempts to fix its date are little better than guess-work : Roquette puts it *circ.* 380—76 ; Schanz, after 371 ; K. Lincke (*Neue Jahrb.* 1897), after 350.

It will be seen that the available evidence is not sufficient to justify us in dogmatizing about the precise date of composition of our dialogue. The most we can say is that *circ.* 383—5 seems on the whole the most probable period.

§ ix. The Text.

(1) *Ancient authorities.* The chief manuscripts which contain the text of the *Symposium* are :—

B = codex Bodleianus (or Clarkianus or Oxoniensis) ; Bekker's 𝔄.

T = codex Venetus append. class. 4, cod. 1 : Bekker's t ("omnium librorum secundae familiae fons " Schanz).

[1] Among those who claim priority for Xenophon are Böckh, Ast, Delbrück, Rettig, Teichmüller, Hug, Dümmler, Pfleiderer ; on the other side are C. F. Hermann, I. Bruns, Schenkl, Gomperz. Beside the broader resemblances set forth by Hug, the foll. refs. to echoes may be of interest:—

Xen.	Plat.		Xen.	Plat.
i. 1	=178 A, 197 E		iv. 53	=219 B
ii. 23	=213 E, 214 A		v. 1, 7	=218 E (175 E)
ii. 26 (iv. 24)	=185 C, 198 C		viii. 1	=218 B (187 D)
iv. 14	=183 A, 184 B, 179 A		,, 8	=219 D
,, 15	=178 E, 179 B, 182 C		,, 13	=184 B
,, 16	=178 E		,, 21	=214 C
,, 17	=181 E, 183 E		,, 23	=183 A (203 B), 172 C
,, 19 (v. 7)	=215 A (216 D, 221 D)		,, 24	=217 E, 222 C
,, 23	=181 D		,, 31	=179 E
,, 25	=193 D		,, 38	=209 E
,, 28	=217 E		,, 32 (iv. 16)	=178 E
,, 47—8	=188 D		,, 34	=182 B
,, 48	=188 D		,, 35	=179 A
,, 50	=189 A, 197 E			

The last three parallels are specially interesting, since Xen. ascribes to Pausan. some of the sentiments which Pl. gives to Phaedrus. Possibly (as Hug, Teichm. and others suppose) both writers are indebted to an actual *apologia* of the real Pausan., which Pl. is handling more freely, Xen. more exactly (cp. I. Bruns, *Vorträge,* p. 152).

W = codex Vindobonensis 54, Suppl. phil. Gr. 7 : Stallbaum's
    Vind. I.

To these we have now to add, as a new authority,

O.-P. = Oxyrhynchus Papyrus (no. 843 in Grenfell and Hunt's
    collection).

Since this last authority for the text was not forthcoming until
after the publication of the latest critical text of the *Symposium*, I add
the description of it given by the editors :—

"The part covered is from 200 B [beginning with the word βου-
λοι[το] after which 40 lines are lost, the next words being αν ενδεια at
the end of 200 E] to the end, comprised in 31 columns, of which four
(xix—xxii) are missing entirely, while two others (i and xviii) are
represented by small fragments ; but the remainder is in a very fair
state of preservation....The small and well-formed but somewhat heavy
writing exemplifies a common type of book hand, and probably dates
from about the year 200 A.D....The corrector's ink does not differ
markedly in colour from that of the text, and in the case of minor
insertions the two hands are at times difficult to distinguish. But as
they are certainly not separated by any wide interval of time the
question has no great practical importance....The text, as so often with
papyri, is of an eclectic character, showing a decided affinity with
no single MS. Compared with the three principal witnesses for the
Symposium it agrees now with B against TW, now with the two latter
as against the former, rarely with T against BW[1] or with W against
BT[2]. Similarly in a passage cited by Stobaeus some agreements with
his readings against the consensus of BTW are counterbalanced by
a number of variations from Stobaeus' text[3]. A few coincidences
occur with variants peculiar to the inferior MSS., the more noticeable
being those with Vindob. 21 alone or in combination with Venet. 184[4]
and Parisin. 1642 alone or with Vat. 229[5]. Of the readings for which
there is no other authority, including several variations in the order of
the words, the majority, if unobjectionable, are unconvincing. The
more valuable contributions, some of which are plainly superior
to anything found in other MSS., are : l. 92 [201 D] επ, l. 112 [202 A]
the omission of καί (so Stallbaum), l. 239 [204 B] αν ειη, where BTW
have a meaningless ἄν, l. 368 [206 C] καλω as conjectured by Badham

[1] See crit. notes on 202 A, 203 A, 205 B, 206 B, 207 D, 211 C.
[2] See crit. notes on 203 B, 211 D, 213 B, 219 E, 220 C (*bis*).
[3] See crit. notes on 202 C—203 A.
[4] See crit. notes on 201 A (*ad fin.*), 218 D, 220 A, 220 B, 223 C.
[5] See crit. notes on 206 B (*ad init.*), 208 A, 223 C.

for τῷ κ., l. 471 [208 B] μετεχει as restored by Stephanus (μετέχειν
MSS.), l. 517 [209 A] τεκειν confirming a conjecture of Hug (κυεῖν MSS.),
l. 529 [209 B] επιθυμη as conjectured by Stephanus (ἐπιθυμεῖ MSS.),
l. 577 [210 A] και συ omitted by MSS., l. 699 [212 A] θεοφιλει (-ῇ BTW),
l. 770 [213 B] κατιδε[ν (?) (καθίζειν MSS), l. 898 [218 D] μοι (probably)
with Vind. 21 (μου BTW), l. 1142 [222 D] διαβαλει as conjectured by
Hirschig (διαβάλῃ BTW).   On the other hand in many cases the
papyrus once more proves the antiquity of readings which modern
criticism rejects or suspects."

It may be added that the editors of the papyrus in citing W have
made use of a new collation of that MS. by Prof. H. Schöne of Basel
"which often supplements and sometimes corrects the report of
Burnet."   And in this edition I have followed the report of W in
their apparatus, where available, while relying elsewhere upon that
given by Burnet.

(2) *Modern criticism.*   Much attention has been paid by Continental critics during the last century to the text of the *Symposium*,
and for the most part they have proceeded on the assumption that the
text is largely vitiated by interpolations[1].   Even Schanz and Hug,
who may be regarded as moderate and cautious critics in comparison
with such extremists as Jahn and Badham, have gone to unnecessary
lengths in their use of the obelus.   Hug, while admitting that we must
take into account the freedom and variety of Plato's style and that it
is folly to rob a writer of his individuality by pruning away any and
every expression which is in strict logic superfluous, and while admitting also that regard must be paid to the characteristic differences
of the various speeches in our dialogue, which forbid our taking any
one speech as the norm with which others should be squared,—yet
maintains that in the speeches, and especially in those of Pausanias
and Socrates, he can detect a number of unquestionable glosses.   No
doubt there are some cases in these speeches in which it is not un-
reasonable to suspect interpolation, but even Hug and Schanz have,
I believe, greatly exaggerated the number of such cases; and I agree
with the editor of the Oxford text in regarding the certain instances
of corruption or interpolation as extremely few.   Consequently, in the
text here printed I have diverged but seldom from the ancient tradition, and such changes as I have made have been more often in the

---

[1] *E.g.* O. Jahn, Hirschig, Badham, Cobet, Naber, Hartmann.   On the other
hand, sensible protests have been made by Teuffel and Vahlen; and Rettig's text
is, if anything, ultra-conservative.

direction of verbal alteration than of omission. I have, however, recorded in the textual notes a selection of the proposed alterations, futile though I consider most of them to be.

§ x. BIBLIOGRAPHY.

The main authorities which I have cited or consulted are[1]:—

i. *Texts:* Bekker (1826), the Zurich ed. (Baiter, Orelli and Winckelmann, 1839), C. F. Hermann (1851), O. Jahn (1864), Jahn-Usener (1875), C. Badham (1866), M. Schanz (1881), J. Burnet (1901). Critical essays or notes by Bast (1794), Voegelin, Naber, Teuffel, M. Vermehren (1870), J. J. Hartmann (1898).

ii. *Annotated Editions:* J. F. Fischer (1776), F. A. Wolf (1782), P. A. Reynders (1825), L. I. Rückert (1829), A. Hommel (1834), G. Stallbaum (2nd ed. 1836), G. F. Rettig (2 vols. 1875—6), A. Hug (2nd ed. 1884).

iii. *Treatises on the subject-matter:* M. H. L. Hartmann (*Chronol. Symp. Pl.* 1798), G. Schwanitz (*Observ. in Pl. Conv.* 1842), M. Lindemann (*De Phaedri orat.* 1853, *De Agath. or.* 1871), J. H. Deinhardt (*Ueber den Inhalt u. s. w. von Pl. Symp.* 1865), M. Koch (*Die Rede d. Sokr. u. das Problem der Erotik,* 1886), W. Resl (*Verhältnis der 5 erster in Pl. Symp. Reden u. s. w.* 1886), C. Boetticher (*Eros u. Erkenntnis bei Pl.* 1894), C. Schirlitz (*Beiträge z. Erklärung d. Rede d. Sokr. u.s.w.* 1890), P. Crain (*De ratione quae inter Pl. Phaedr. et Symp. intercedat,* 1906).

Other more general works consulted are: Teichmüller (*Litt. Fehden,* 1881), F. Horn (*Platonstudien,* 1893), W. Lutoslawski (*Plato's Logic,* 1897), T. Gomperz (*Greek Thinkers,* E.T. II. 1905), H. Raeder (*Platons Philos. Entwickelung,* 1905), J. Adam (*Religious Teachers of Greece,* 1908).

iv. *Translations:* E. Zeller (1857), A. Jung (2nd ed. 1900), B. Jowett, J. A. Stewart (selections, in *The Myths of Plato,* 1905).

---

[1] *Abbreviations* used are—Bdhm. = Badham; Bt. = Burnet; Jn. = Jahn; J.-U. = Jahn-Usener; Sz. = Schanz; Verm. = Vermehren; Voeg. = Voegelin.

ΠΛΑΤΩΝΟΣ ΣΥΜΠΟΣΙΟΝ

[Η ΠΕΡΙ ΑΓΑΘΟΥ · ΗΘΙΚΟΣ]

St. III.
p.

I. Δοκῶ μοι περὶ ὧν πυνθάνεσθε οὐκ ἀμελέτητος εἶναι. καὶ 172
γὰρ ἐτύγχανον πρῴην εἰς ἄστυ οἴκοθεν ἀνιὼν Φαληρόθεν· τῶν οὖν
γνωρίμων τις ὄπισθεν κατιδών με πόρρωθεν ἐκάλεσε, καὶ παίζων
ἅμα τῇ κλήσει, Ὦ Φαληρεύς, ἔφη, οὗτος ['Απολλόδωρος], οὐ περιμενεῖς; κἀγὼ ἐπιστὰς περιέμεινα. καὶ ὅς, 'Απολλόδωρε, ἔφη, καὶ

172 A ⟨νῦν⟩ οὐκ Methodius vulg. Φαληρόθεν del. Naber Ꙉ: ὁ vulg.
'Απολλόδωρος secl. Bdhm. J.-U. οὐ ⟨σὺ⟩ Sauppe περιμενεῖς vulg. Sz.:
περιμενεις B: περιμένεις TW, Bt. ⟨Ꙉ⟩ 'Απολλόδωρε Sz. 'Απολλόδωρε...
ἐζήτουν om. Coisl.

---

172 A **Δοκῶ μοι κτλ.** The speaker, Apollodorus (see *Introd.* § II. A), is
replying to certain unnamed ἑταῖροι who had been questioning him concerning
the incidents and speeches which took place at Agathon's banquet. The plural
πυνθάνεσθε (and ὑμῖν, ὑμεῖς 173 C, D *infra*) indicates that there were several
ἑταῖροι present: the traditional heading of the dialogue, ΕΤΑΙΡΟΣ, is due to
the fact that all but one are κωφὰ πρόσωπα.

οὐκ ἀμελέτητος. μελέτη and μελετᾶν are regular terms for the "conning
over" of a speech or "part": cp. *Phaedr.* 228 B.

καὶ γὰρ ἐτύγχανον. These words explain the preceding statement δοκῶ...
οὐκ ἀμελέτητος εἶναι, and serve to introduce not only the sentence immediately
following but the whole of the succeeding passage down to 173 B where the
initial statement is resumed by the words ὥστε...οὐκ ἀμελετήτως ἔχω.

Φαληρόθεν. Phalerum, the old port of Athens, was about 20 stadia
(2½ miles) distant from the city on the S.E.

καὶ παίζων...περιμενεῖς; Where does the joke come in?

(1) Ast, Hommel, Stallbaum and Jowett look for it in the word Φαληρεύς,
which they take to be a play on φαλαρὸς ("bald-headed," so Jowett) or
φαλαρίς ("bald-coot") in allusion to the bald crown or the peculiar gait of
Apollodorus. But what evidence is there to show that A. either was bald or
walked like a coot?

(2) Another suggestion of Hommel's is to write (with the vulgate) ὁ
'Απολλόδωρος and assume an etymological allusion to the opportuneness of
the meeting (as "Apollo-given"). This also is far-fetched.

(3) Schütz, followed by Wolf and Hug, finds the παιδιά in the playfully

B. P.   1

μὴν καὶ ἔναγχός σε ἐζήτουν βουλόμενος διαπυθέσθαι τὴν Ἀγά-
B θωνος ξυνουσίαν καὶ Σωκράτους καὶ Ἀλκιβιάδου καὶ τῶν ἄλλων
τῶν τότε ἐν τῷ συνδείπνῳ παραγενομένων, περὶ τῶν ἐρωτικῶν
λόγων τίνες ἦσαν. ἄλλος γάρ τίς μοι διηγεῖτο ἀκηκοὼς Φοίνικος
τοῦ Φιλίππου, ἔφη δὲ καὶ σὲ εἰδέναι. ἀλλὰ γὰρ οὐδὲν εἶχε σαφὲς
λέγειν. σὺ οὖν μοι διήγησαι· δικαιότατος γὰρ εἶ τοὺς τοῦ ἑταίρου
λόγους ἀπαγγέλλειν. πρότερον δέ μοι, ἦ δ' ὅς, εἰπέ, σὺ αὐτὸς
C παρεγένου τῇ συνουσίᾳ ταύτῃ ἢ οὔ; κἀγὼ εἶπον ὅτι Παντάπασιν

172 B ἐν τῷ συνδείπνῳ secl. Baiter J.-U.   συνδειπνεῖν T : συνδείπνῳ W (εἶν above)

---

official style of the address, in which the person is designated by the name of
his deme, this being the regular practice in legal and formal proceedings (cp.
Gorg. 495 D Καλλικλῆς ἔφη Ἀχαρνεύς...Σωκράτης...ὁ Ἀλωπεκῆθεν : Ar. *Nub.*
134); but (as Stallb. objected) the order of the words in that case should be
rather ὦ οὗτος Ἀ. ὁ Φαληρεύς. Hug also finds παιδιά in the hendecasyllabic
rhythm (ὦ Φαλ. οὗτος Ἀπ.), and the poetic combination ὦ οὗτος (Soph. *O. C.*
1627, *Aj.* 89).

(4) Rettig, reading ὁ Φαληρεύς, omits (with Badham) the proper name
Ἀπολλόδωρος as an adscript. This seems, on the whole, the best and simplest
solution. Glaucon, at a distance behind, feigns ignorance of the identity of
"the Phalerian," and shouts after Apollodorus "Ho there! you Phalerian,
halt," in a "stop thief!" tone. It is plausible to suppose also that a certain
contempt is conveyed in the description Φαληρεύς ("Wapping-ite"): port-
towns are often places of unsavoury repute: cp. *Phaedr.* 243 C ἐν ναύταις που
τεθραμμένον : Juv. *Sat.* VIII. 174 "permixtum nautis et furibus ac fugitivis."
For the summons to halt cp. Ar. *Plut.* 440 οὗτος, τί δρᾷς; ὦ δειλότατον σὺ
θηρίον, | οὐ περιμενεῖς; *Thesm.* 689 ποῖ ποῖ σὺ φεύγεις; οὗτος, οὗτος, οὐ μενεῖς;
also *Eq.* 240, 1354. These passages support the future περιμενεῖς rather than
the present: "futurum est fortius imperantis; praesens modeste cohortantis
aut lenius postulantis" (Stallb.). For the future as a lively imperative cp.
175 A, 212 D.

172 B ἐν τῷ συνδείπνῳ. Similarly in Aristoph. *Gerytades* (*frag.* 204 ἐν
τοῖσι συνδείπνοις ἐπαινῶν Αἰσχύλον) σύνδειπνον is used for the more precise
συμπόσιον : and a lost play of Sophocles bore the title Ἀχαιῶν σύλλογος ἢ
σύνδειπνον ἢ σύνδειπνοι (see *fragg.* 146 ff., Dindf.).

τίνες ἦσαν. For phrases of this kind, "satis libere subjecta orationi," see
Vahlen, *Op. Acad.* II. 393.

Φοίνικος τοῦ Φιλίππου. Nothing is known of this man. See *Introd.* § II. A.

δικαιότατος γὰρ κτλ. τοῦ ἑταίρου is almost equivalent to ἑταίρου γε ὄντος,
giving the reason why Apollodorus is δικαιότατος.

παρεγένου τῇ συνουσίᾳ. Cp. Hom. *Od.* XVII. 173 καί σφιν παρεγίγνετο
δαιτί: and the exordium of the *Phaedo* (57 A) αὐτὸς, ὦ Φ., παρεγένου Σωκράτει
...ἢ ἄλλου του ἤκουσας;

Παντάπασιν ἔοικέ σοι κτλ. "It is quite evident that his narration was of

ἔοικέ σοι οὐδὲν διηγεῖσθαι σαφὲς ὁ διηγούμενος, εἰ νεωστὶ ἡγεῖ τὴν
συνουσίαν γεγονέναι ταύτην ἣν ἐρωτᾷς, ὥστε καὶ ἐμὲ παραγενέσθαι. Ἔγωγε δή, <ἔφη>. Πόθεν, ἦν δ' ἐγώ, ὦ Γλαύκων; οὐκ
οἶσθ' ὅτι πολλῶν ἐτῶν Ἀγάθων ἐνθάδε οὐκ ἐπιδεδήμηκεν, ἀφ' οὗ
δ' ἐγὼ Σωκράτει συνδιατρίβω καὶ ἐπιμελὲς πεποίημαι ἑκάστης
ἡμέρας εἰδέναι ὅ τι ἂν λέγῃ ἢ πράττῃ, οὐδέπω τρία ἔτη ἐστίν;
πρὸ τοῦ δὲ περιτρέχων ὅπῃ τύχοιμι καὶ οἰόμενος τὶ ποιεῖν ἀθλιώ- 173
τερος ἢ ὁτουοῦν, οὐχ ἧττον ἢ σὺ νυνί, οἰόμενος δεῖν πάντα μᾶλλον
πράττειν ἢ φιλοσοφεῖν. καὶ ὅς, Μὴ σκῶπτ', ἔφη, ἀλλ' εἰπέ μοι
πότε ἐγένετο ἡ συνουσία αὕτη. κἀγὼ εἶπον ὅτι Παίδων ὄντων
ἡμῶν ἔτι, ὅτε τῇ πρώτῃ τραγῳδίᾳ ἐνίκησεν Ἀγάθων, τῇ ὑστεραίᾳ
ᾗ τὰ ἐπινίκια ἔθυεν αὐτός τε καὶ οἱ χορευταί. Πάνυ, ἔφη, ἄρα

172 C κἀμὲ Athenaeus, Sz. ἐγώ γε δή, ἔφη Bt.: ἐγώ γε δή BTW : ἐγὼ
γὰρ ἔφη(ν) Athen.: ἔγωγε γὰρ, ἔφη Voeg.: ἔγωγ', ἔφη Bdhm. ὦ Λύκων
Athen. ἐνθάδε om. Athen. 173 A ᾗ Tb: ἦν pr. B: ἢ Wt νῦν TW
ἔτι ὄντων ἡμῶν Athen. πρώτῃ om. Athen.: τὸ πρῶτον Usener ᾗ om.
Priscian: ἢ ᾗ T: ᾗ Sz. τἀπινίκια Cobet

the vaguest kind." διηγεῖσθαι is here the infin. of διηγεῖτο. The emphatic
repetition of οὐδὲν σαφές is a ground for suspecting that the reference is to a
published account in which the facts were distorted.

172 C Πόθεν...ὦ Γλαύκων; "What makes you think so, Glaucon?" There
is an implicit negation in the question put thus: cp. *Gorg.* 471 D, *Menex.* 235 C.
This Glaucon is perhaps the same as the father of Charmides (*Charm.* 154 A,
etc.), but probably not the same as the Glaucon of the *Republic*, though
Böckh and Munk would identify the two.

πολλῶν ἐτῶν κτλ. For the bearing of this passage on the dramatic date of
this prologue, see *Introd.* § VIII.

ἐπιμελὲς πεποίημαι...εἰδέναι. The nearest Platonic parallel for this construction is *Ep.* vii. 334 A πολλοῖς...ὑμνεῖν ταῦτα ἐπιμελές.

173 A περιτρέχων ὅπῃ τύχοιμι, *i.e.* with no fixed principle of conduct,—
"like a wave of the sea, driven with the wind and tossed." Cp. *Tim.* 43 B
ἀτάκτως ὅπῃ τύχοι προιέναι: Seneca *de vita beata* I. 2 "quamdiu quidem
passim vagamur non ducem secuti...conteretur vita inter errores brevis," etc.

οἰόμενος τὶ ποιεῖν. For τι, *magnum quid*, cp. 219 C, *Phaedr.* 242 E, etc.

Παίδων ὄντων ἡμῶν ἔτι. *Sc.* Apollodorus and Glaucon. Plato, too, born
about 427 B.C., was a παῖς at the date of Agathon's victory (416 B.C.).

τῇ πρώτῃ τραγῳδίᾳ. "Respicit Plato ad tetralogias" (Reynders).

τῇ ὑστεραίᾳ ᾗ. For this (compendious) construction cp. Thuc. I. 60
τεσσαρακοστῇ ἡμέρᾳ ὕστερον...ᾗ Ποτίδαια ἀπέστη (with Shilleto's note);
Lys. XIX. 22.

τὰ ἐπινίκια ἔθυεν. "Made a sacrificial feast in honour of his victory." On
this occasion it was the author himself who provided the feast and offered the
sacrifice. Sometimes however it was the Choregus (*e.g.* Ar. *Ach.* 886), and

πάλαι, ὡς ἔοικεν. ἀλλὰ τίς σοι διηγεῖτο; ἢ αὐτὸς Σωκράτης; Οὐ
B μὰ τὸν Δία, ἦν δ' ἐγώ, ἀλλ' ὅσπερ Φοίνικι· Ἀριστόδημος ἦν τις,
Κυδαθηναιεύς, σμικρός, ἀνυπόδητος ἀεί· παρεγεγόνει δ' ἐν τῇ
συνουσίᾳ, Σωκράτους ἐραστὴς ὢν ἐν τοῖς μάλιστα τῶν τότε, ὡς
ἐμοὶ δοκεῖ. οὐ μέντοι ἀλλὰ καὶ Σωκράτη γε ἔνια ἤδη ἀνηρόμην
ὧν ἐκείνου ἤκουσα, καί μοι ὡμολόγει καθάπερ ἐκεῖνος διηγεῖτο. Τί
οὖν, ἔφη, οὐ διηγήσω μοι; πάντως δὲ ἡ ὁδὸς ἡ εἰς ἄστυ ἐπιτηδεία
πορευομένοις καὶ λέγειν καὶ ἀκούειν.
C Οὕτω δὴ ἰόντες ἅμα τοὺς λόγους περὶ αὐτῶν ἐποιούμεθα, ὥστε,
ὅπερ ἀρχόμενος εἶπον, οὐκ ἀμελετήτως ἔχω. εἰ οὖν δεῖ καὶ ὑμῖν
διηγήσασθαι, ταῦτα χρὴ ποιεῖν. καὶ γὰρ ἔγωγε καὶ ἄλλως, ὅταν
μέν τινας περὶ φιλοσοφίας λόγους ἢ αὐτὸς ποιῶμαι ἢ ἄλλων

173 A τί TW   B ἄλλοσπερ BT   ἀνυπόδητός τ' Ast
παραγεγόνει BT   καὶ om. T   διηγήσῃ W : διηγῇ σὺ vulg.   δὲ
om. al.: γε J.-U.: γὰρ Susemihl   C δεῖ: δοκεῖ Hirschig

sometimes the friends of the successful competitor (e.g. Xen. Symp. I. 4).
Similarly at Rome it was customary for the *dux gregis* to entertain his troupe
after a victory (see Plaut. *Rud.* 1417 ff.).

173 B Ἀριστόδημος. See *Introd.* § II. A.

Κυδαθηναιεύς. Schol. Κυδαθήναιον· δῆμος ἐν ἄστει τῆς Πανδιονίδος φυλῆς.
καλεῖται δὲ καὶ Κύδαθον. The poet Aristophanes also belonged to this deme.

ἀνυπόδητος. In this peculiarity A. imitated Socrates, see 174 A, 220 B,
Ar. *Nub.* 103 τοὺς ἀνυποδήτους λέγεις· | ὧν ὁ κακοδαίμων Σωκράτης καὶ
Χαιρεφῶν, *ibid.* 362. It is a peculiarity which would appeal to disciples
with a *penchant* for the simple life, such as those of the Cynic persuasion.

ἐραστὴς. "An admirer." Cp. the application of ἑταῖρος in 172 B *supra*.

ἐκείνου...ἐκεῖνος. Both pronouns refer to the same person, Aristodemus.
The statement here made is not without significance, see *Introd.* § II. A.

Τί οὖν...οὐ διηγήσω. "Haec interrogatio alacritatem quandam animi et
aviditatem sciendi indicat" (Stallb.). Cp. *Meno* 92 D (with E. S. Thompson's
note, where a full list of the Platonic exx. is given).

πάντως δὲ κτλ. "For to be sure," confirming the preceding clause with a
new argument. A good parallel is *Laws* I. 625 A πάντως δ' ἤ γε ἐκ Κνωσοῦ
ὁδὸς εἰς τὸ τοῦ Διὸς ἄντρον καὶ ἱερόν, ὡς ἀκούομεν, ἱκανή.

173 C ὅπερ ἀρχόμενος εἶπον. See 172 A *ad init.*

εἰ οὖν δεῖ...χρὴ. The comma is better placed before ταῦτα, with Usener
and Burnet, than after it, with Hug and earlier editors. A similar turn of
expression is Soph. *Trach.* 749 εἰ χρὴ μαθεῖν σε, πάντα δὴ φωνεῖν χρεών.

αὐτὸς ποιῶμαι. Here Apollodorus seems to claim to be no mere disciple,
but himself an exponent of philosophy. So far as it goes this might indicate
that Apollodorus represents the real author, Plato. For A.'s delight in
philosophic λόγοι, cp. what is said of Phaedrus in *Phaedr.* 228 B, where Socr.
too is called ὁ νοσῶν περὶ λόγων.

ἀκούω, χωρὶς τοῦ οἴεσθαι ὠφελεῖσθαι ὑπερφυῶς ὡς χαίρω· ὅταν
δὲ ἄλλους τινάς, ἄλλως τε καὶ τοὺς ὑμετέρους τοὺς τῶν πλουσίων
καὶ χρηματιστικῶν, αὐτός τε ἄχθομαι ὑμᾶς τε τοὺς ἑταίρους ἐλεῶ,
ὅτι οἴεσθε τὶ ποιεῖν// οὐδὲν ποιοῦντες. καὶ ἴσως αὖ ὑμεῖς ἐμὲ D
ἡγεῖσθε κακοδαίμονα εἶναι, καὶ οἴομαι ὑμᾶς ἀληθῆ οἴεσθαι· ἐγὼ
μέντοι ὑμᾶς οὐκ οἴομαι ἀλλ᾽ εὖ οἶδα.
ΕΤΑΙ. Ἀεὶ ὅμοιος εἶ, ὦ Ἀπολλόδωρε· ἀεὶ γὰρ σαυτόν τε
κακηγορεῖς καὶ τοὺς ἄλλους, καὶ δοκεῖς μοι ἀτεχνῶς πάντας
ἀθλίους ἡγεῖσθαι πλὴν Σωκράτους, ἀπὸ σαυτοῦ ἀρξάμενος. καὶ

173 C χρηματιστῶν vulg.   D ἡγεῖσθε Coisl. : ἡγεῖσθαι BT

ὑπερφυῶς ὡς χαίρω. This may be explained as a mixture of two constructions, viz. (1) ὑπερφυές ἐστιν ὡς χαίρω, (2) ὑπερφυῶς χαίρω: it is found
also in *Gorg.* 496 c, *Phaedo* 66 A, *Theaet.* 155 c (but in all these places some
codd. and edd. omit ὡς).

χρηματιστικῶν. For this word in the masc., "money-makers," cp. *Rep.*
581 c ὅ γε χρηματιστικὸς πρὸς τὸ κερδαίνειν τὴν τοῦ τιμᾶσθαι ἡδονὴν ἢ τὴν τοῦ
μανθάνειν οὐδενὸς ἀξίαν φήσει εἶναι, εἰ μὴ εἴ τι αὐτῶν ἀργύριον ποιεῖ : also
Phaedr. 248 D. In *Meno* 78 c (ἀγαθὰ...χρυσίον λέγω καὶ ἀργύριον κτᾶσθαι) we
have an expression of the sentiments of a χρηματιστικός. For Apollodorus'
sentiment, cp. Isocr. *c. Soph.* 291 D λέγουσι μὲν ὡς οὐδὲν δέονται χρημάτων,
ἀργυρίδιον καὶ χρυσίδιον τὸν πλοῦτον ἀποκαλοῦντες (where the ref. is probably
to Antisthenes): cp. also what Alcib. says of Socr., 216 E, 219 E. The gloss-
hunting critics, strangely enough (as Vahlen remarks), have left the words
ὑμᾶς τοὺς ἑταίρους unscathed.

173 D ἀληθῆ οἴεσθαι. οἴεσθαι here is substituted for ἡγεῖσθαι, and the
following οὐκ οἴομαι is in antithesis, not to the οἴομαι preceding, but to
ἡγεῖσθε. Apollodorus, conscious of his inferiority to Socrates, his ideal, is
willing to admit that he is not as yet wholly εὐδαίμων.

ἀλλ᾽ εὖ οἶδα. *Sc.* ὅτι κακοδαίμονές ἐστε. For this exposure of the true
condition of "the children of this world" who are εὐδαίμονες in their own
conceit, and despise others, one may cite *Apoc.* iii. 17 "Thou sayest, I am
rich and increased with goods and have need of nothing; and knowest not
that thou art wretched and miserable and poor and blind and naked."

Ἀεὶ ὅμοιος εἶ. "Semper tibi hac in re constas" (Stallb.) : "you are quite
incorrigible." So below we have ἀεὶ τοιοῦτος εἶ. Cp. *Charm.* 170 A ἀλλ᾽ ἐγὼ
κινδυνεύω ἀεὶ ὅμοιος εἶναι.

ἀτεχνῶς πάντας. This seems to be the sole instance in Plato of this
combination "all without exception"; but cp. *Rep.* 432 A δι᾽ ὅλης ἀτεχνῶς
τέταται.

ἀθλίους. Here a synonym for κακοδαίμονας, the word used above. Cp.
Meno 78 A τοὺς δὲ ἀθλίους οὐ κακοδαίμονας; Οἶμαι ἔγωγε...τί γὰρ ἄλλο ἐστὶν
ἄθλιον εἶναι ἢ ἐπιθυμεῖν τε τῶν κακῶν καὶ κτᾶσθαι;

πλὴν Σωκράτους. "Save Socrates only": notice the emphasis on these
words, repeated twice. We may discern, perhaps, in this an allusion, by way

ὁπόθεν ποτὲ ταύτην τὴν ἐπωνυμίαν ἔλαβες τὸ μανικὸς καλεῖσθαι, οὐκ οἶδα ἔγωγε· ἐν μὲν γὰρ τοῖς λόγοις ἀεὶ τοιοῦτος εἶ· σαυτῷ τε καὶ τοῖς ἄλλοις ἀγριαίνεις πλὴν Σωκράτους.

E   ΑΠΟΛ. Ὦ φίλτατε, καὶ δῆλόν γε δὴ ὅτι οὕτω διανοούμενος καὶ περὶ ἐμαυτοῦ καὶ περὶ ὑμῶν μαίνομαι καὶ παράπαίω;

ΕΤΑΙ. Οὐκ ἄξιον περὶ τούτων, Ἀπολλόδωρε, νῦν ἐρίζειν· ἀλλ᾽ ὅπερ ἐδεόμεθά σου, μὴ ἄλλως ποιήσῃς, ἀλλὰ διήγησαι τίνες ἦσαν οἱ λόγοι.

ΑΠΟΛ. Ἦσαν τοίνυν ἐκεῖνοι τοιοίδε τινές—μᾶλλον δ᾽

173 D μαλακος TW : μαλακὸς B, Naber.   οὐκ : εὖ Bast   μὲν γὰρ : μέν γε Bdhm. Sz. : μέντ᾽ ἄρα Mdvg.   E ⟨ὦ⟩ Ἀπολλόδωρε Method. Sz.

---

of antithesis, to the κατηγορία Σωκράτους of the sophist Polycrates (see *Introd.* § II. A).

τὸ μανικὸς καλεῖσθαι. There can be little doubt (*pace* Naber) that μανικός, not μαλακός, is the true reading: it is supported by the words μαίνομαι καὶ παραπαίω in Apollodorus's reply. Stallbaum supposes an ellipse of some such phrase as δοκεῖς δὲ λαβεῖν αὐτόθεν before ἐν μὲν γὰρ κτλ., and (with Wolf) explains μανικός as referring to the vehemence and excess of Apollodorus both in praise and blame: cp. *Polit.* 307 B, and *Apol.* 21 A where Chaerephon (termed μανικός in *Charm.* 153 B) is described as σφοδρὸς ἐφ᾽ ὅ τι ὁρμήσειεν. But the connexion of the sentence ἐν μὲν γὰρ κτλ. with the preceding clause is better brought out by Hug; he supplies (after οὐκ οἶδα) "so ganz ohne Grund wirds wohl nicht sein," so that the line of thought is— "Though I do not know exactly why you got the nickname 'fanatic'—yet in your speeches at any rate you do something to justify the title." For a similar use of μὲν γὰρ cp. *Polit.* 264 C ἐν μὲν γὰρ ταῖς κρήναις τάχ᾽ ἂν ἴσως εἴης ᾐσθημένος. For μανικός cp. also *Meno* 91 C where Anytus regards παρὰ σοφιστὰς ἐλθεῖν as a sign of μανία: and *Acts* xxvi. 24 Μαίνῃ Παῦλε· τὰ πολλά σε γράμματα εἰς μανίαν περιτρέπει.

ἀγριαίνεις. "Rage like a wild beast," "snarl and snap." Cp. *Rep.* 493 B (θρέμμα μέγα) ἡμεροῦταί τε καὶ ἀγριαίνει.

173 E Ὦ φίλτατε κτλ. Ironical—"Why, my very dear Sir, it is surely quite obvious that in holding this view about myself and others I display madness and eccentricity!"

παραπαίω. Ἃ ἅπαξ εἰρημένον in Plato. For the musical metaphor cp. Ophelia's "I see that sovereign and most noble reason, Like sweet bells jangled, out of tune and harsh."

Οὐκ ἄξιον...ἐρίζειν. "We mustn't quarrel." ἐρίζειν, though here used jocularly, is properly a strong term, cp. *Prot.* 337 B ἀμφισβητεῖν μέν, ἐρίζειν δὲ μή: *Rep.* 454 A οὐκ ἐρίζειν, ἀλλὰ διαλέγεσθαι (see Adam *ad loc.*).

μᾶλλον δ᾽. Instead of beginning at once with the speech of Phaedrus, Apollodorus proceeds to give an account of the preliminary incidents which led up to the λόγοι. For the significance of this, see *Introd.* § II. A.

ἐξ ἀρχῆς ὑμῖν ὡς ἐκεῖνος διηγεῖτο καὶ ἐγὼ πειράσομαι διηγή- 174
σασθαι.

II. Ἔφη γάρ οἱ Σωκράτη ἐντυχεῖν λελουμένον τε καὶ τὰς
βλαύτας ὑποδεδεμένον, ἃ ἐκεῖνος ὀλιγάκις ἐποίει· καὶ ἐρέσθαι
αὐτὸν ὅποι ἴοι οὕτω καλὸς γεγενημένος. καὶ τὸν εἰπεῖν ὅτι Ἐπὶ
δεῖπνον εἰς Ἀγάθωνος. χθὲς γὰρ αὐτὸν διέφυγον τοῖς ἐπινικίοις,
φοβηθεὶς τὸν ὄχλον· ὡμολόγησα δ' εἰς τήμερον παρέσεσθαι. ταῦτα
δὴ ἐκαλλωπισάμην, ἵνα καλὸς παρὰ καλὸν ἴω. ἀλλὰ σύ, ἦ δ' ὅς,
πῶς ἔχεις πρὸς τὸ ἐθέλειν ἂν ἰέναι ἄκλητος ἐπὶ δεῖπνον ; κἀγώ, B

174 A   ἃ: ὃ Hertlein   ⟨ἐ⟩ ἐρέσθαι Voeg. Sz.   τήμερον: τὴν
σήμερον vulg.   B   ἐθέλειν ἂν secl. Cobet Jn.   ἂν ἰέναι Steph.: ἀνιέναι BT

ἐξ ἀρχῆς...πειράσομαι διηγήσασθαι. The same formula occurs in *Phaedo*
59 C, *Euthyd.* 272 D, *Epist.* vii. 324 B.

174 A Ἔφη γάρ. *Sc.* ὁ Ἀριστόδημος. The whole narrative of the dialogue
from this point on is dependent upon this initial ἔφη and therefore written in
or. obliqua. οἱ (*sibi*)=Ἀριστοδήμῳ.

λελουμένον. For the practice of bathing and anointing before meals see
Hom. *Od.* VI. 96—7, Xen. *Symp.* I. 7: Ar. *Plut.* 614 εὐωχεῖσθαι...λουσάμενος,
λιπαρὸς χωρῶν ἐκ βαλανείου. The comic poets were fond of gibing at Socrates
and philosophers in general as "unwashed," *e.g.* Ar. *Av.* 1554 ἄλουτος οὗ
ψυχαγωγεῖ Σωκράτης : id. *Nub.* 835 ff. : Aristophon *ap.* Mein. III. 360 ff.
Aristotle, however, was a champion of the bath, Athen. 178 F ἀπρεπὲς γὰρ
ἦν, φησὶν Ἀριστοτέλης (*fr.* 165), ἥκειν εἰς τὸ συμπόσιον σὺν ἱδρῶτι πολλῷ
καὶ κονιορτῷ.

τὰς βλαύτας. Schol. βλαύτας· ὑποδήματα. οἱ δὲ βλαντία, σανδάλια ἰσχνά.
For Socrates' habit of going barefoot, see 220 B *infra*, *Phaedr.* 229 A, Xen.
Mem. I. 6. 2, and the note on ἀνυπόδητος, 173 B *supra*.

ταῦτα δὴ ἐκαλλωπισάμην. ταῦτα is better taken (with Hug and Hommel)
as accus. of "internal object" than (with Stallb.) as accus. of "remoter
object," equiv. to διὰ ταῦτα (cp. *Prot.* 310 E). Elsewhere in Plato καλλωπί-
ζεσθαι means to "plume oneself," "swagger," *e.g. Rep.* 605 D. Observe the
word-play: "I have put on my finery, because he is such a fine man"
(Jowett): cp. the proverb ὅμοιος ὁμοίῳ (195 B).

παρὰ καλόν. *Sc.* Ἀγάθωνα—"to Agathon's (house)"; equiv. to εἰς Ἀγάθωνος above. For "the handsome Agathon," see *Prot.* 315 D—E (τὴν ἰδέαν
πάνυ καλός), Ar. *Thesm.* 191 ff.

πῶς ἔχεις πρός κτλ. Cp. 176 B πῶς ἔχει πρὸς τὸ ἐρρῶσθαι πίνειν ; *Prot.*
352 B, *Parm.* 131 E. Cobet's excision of ἐθέλειν ἄν is wanton : cp. (with Ast)
Phaedo 62 C τὸ τοὺς φιλοσόφους ῥᾳδίως ἂν ἐθέλειν ἀποθνήσκειν.

174 B ἄκλητος. The jester (γελωτοποιός) who frequents feasts as an
uninvited guest seems to have been a stock character in Epicharmus; and
in Xen. *Symp.* Philippus is a person of this type. Araros the comic poet
was, apparently, the first to dub them παράσιτοι. Cp. also Archil. 78. 3 οὐδὲ

ἔφη, εἶπον ὅτι Οὕτως ὅπως ἂν σὺ κελεύῃς. Ἕπου τοίνυν, ἔφη,
ἵνα καὶ τὴν παροιμίαν διαφθείρωμεν μεταβάλλοντες, ὡς ἄρα καὶ

174 B   μεταβάλλοντες B, Athen., Sz.: μεταβαλόντες T, Bt.

μὴν κληθεὶς (ὑφ' ἡμῶν) ἦλθες, οἷα δὴ φίλος; and Plut. Q. Conv. VII. 6. 1, p.
707 B τὸ δὲ τῶν ἐπικλήτων ἔθος, οὓς νῦν "σκιὰς" καλοῦσιν, οὐ κεκλημένους αὐτούς,
ἀλλ' ὑπὸ τῶν κεκλημένων ἐπὶ τὸ δεῖπνον ἀγομένους, ἐζητεῖτο πόθεν ἔσχε τὴν
ἀρχήν. ἐδόκει δ' ἀπὸ Σωκράτους Ἀριστόδημον ἀναπείσαντος οὐ κεκλημένον εἰς
Ἀγάθωνος ἰέναι σὺν αὐτῷ καὶ παθόντα "τι γελοῖον" (see 174 c, with note). In
Lat. vocare is similarly used of "inviting" (aliquem ad cenam Ter. And. 2. 6.
22), and invocatus = ἄκλητος in Plaut. Capt. 1. 1. 2 ("invocatus soleo esse in
convivio").

διαφθείρωμεν μεταβάλλοντες. διαφθείρω is sometimes used of "spoiling" or
"stultifying" a statement or argument, e.g. Gorg. 495 A, Prot. 338 D. And
μεταβάλλειν of linguistic alteration (transposition, etc.), as in Cratyl. 404 c
(Φερσεφόνη for Φερρέφαττα).

ὡς ἄρα κτλ. The force of ἄρα is to indicate that the proverb, when
amended, "still, after all" holds good. Two forms of the proverb are extant,
viz. (1) αὐτόματοι δ' ἀγαθοὶ δειλῶν ἐπὶ δαῖτας ἴασι (see Schol. ad h. l., Athen.
IV. 27); and (2) αὐτόματοι δ' ἀγαθοὶ ἀγαθῶν ἐπὶ δαῖτας ἴασι. The latter form is
vouched for by the poeta anon. quoted by Athen. I. 8 A (Bergk P. L. G. p. 704),
ἀγαθὸς πρὸς ἀγαθοὺς ἄνδρας εἱστιασάμενος ἧκον: Bacchyl. fr. 33 (22 Blass)
αὐτόματοι δ' ἀγαθῶν δαῖτας εὐόχθους ἐπέρχονται δίκαιοι φῶτες [cp. Zenob. II. 19
αὐτόματοι δ' ἀγαθοὶ ἀγαθῶν κτέ.· οὕτως ὁ Βακχυλίδης ἐχρήσατο τῇ παροιμίᾳ, ὡς
Ἡρακλέους ἐπιφοιτήσαντος ἐπὶ τὴν οἰκίαν Κήυκος τοῦ Τραχινίου καὶ οὕτως
εἰπόντος]: Cratinus fr. 111 (Mein.) οἶδ' αὖθ' ἡμεῖς, ὡς ὁ παλαιὸς | λόγος, αὐτο-
μάτους ἀγαθοὺς ἰέναι | κομψῶν ἐπὶ δαῖτα θεατῶν: also a number of post-Platonic
passages cited by Hug, such as Plut. Q. Conv. VII. 6 ad fin. According to the
Scholiast (1) is the original form, which was altered (μεταλλάξας) to (2) by
Cratinus and Eupolis; and this is the view adopted by Stallbaum, Rettig and
others. But Hug's elaborate investigation of the matter proves convincingly,
I think, that the Scholiast is wrong and that the form with ἀγαθοὶ ἀγαθῶν
was the original, of which the form with ἀγαθοὶ δειλῶν is a parody by Eupolis
(or Cratinus). This view, first suggested by Schleiermacher, is also supported
by Bergk (ad Bacchyl. fr. 33): "Schol. Plat. Symp. 174 B a vero aberrat cum
dicit a principio δειλῶν ἐπὶ δαῖτας fuisse, quamquam fidem habuerunt cum
alii tum Müller Dor. II. 481: neque enim par fuit Herculem tam gravi
opprobrio hospitem laedere. Eupolis primus, ut videtur, ludibundus δειλῶν
substituit. Locum difficilem Platonis, qui falso criminatur Homerum cor-
rupisse proverbium quod ille omnino non respexit, nemodum probabiliter
expedivit. Alia varietas, quam nostri homines commenti sunt, δειλοὶ δειλῶν,
omni auctoritate destituta est." The main difficulty in the way of accepting
this view lies in the words διαφθείρωμεν μεταβάλλοντες. For even if (with most
modern editors) we accept Lachmann's brilliant conjecture Ἀγαθων'(ι), the
change thus involved is so slight that it could hardly be called a διαφθορά,
nor could the alteration involved in the Homeric account be spoken of as a

"'Αγάθων' ἐπὶ δαῖτας ἴασιν αὐτόματοι ἀγαθοί." "Ομηρος μὲν γὰρ κινδυνεύει οὐ μόνον διαφθεῖραι ἀλλὰ καὶ ὑβρίσαι εἰς ταύτην τὴν παροιμίαν· π᾿ήσας γὰρ τὸν Ἀγαμέμνονα διαφερόντως ἀγαθὸν C ἄνδρα τὰ πολεμικά, τὸν δὲ Μενέλεων "μαλθακὸν αἰχμητήν," θυσίαν ποιουμένου καὶ ἑστιῶντος τοῦ Ἀγαμέμνονος ἄκλητον ἐποίησεν ἐλθόντα τὸν Μενέλεων ἐπὶ τὴν θοίνην, χείρω ὄντα ἐπὶ τὴν τοῦ

174 B　'Αγάθων' Lachmann : ἀγαθῶν BT　　　διαφερόντως + ἄνδρα + καὶ ἑστιῶντος om. Athen.

---

double one (διαφθεῖραι καὶ ὑβρίσαι). The former objection, if it stood alone, might be obviated by the device of inserting μή before διαφθείρωμεν : but in view of the passage as a whole this device is inadmissible. We seem forced to conclude that, whatever the original form of the proverb may have been (and as to this Hug's view is probably right), the form which Plato had here in mind was the form (1) given by Eupolis : and if Plato knew this form to be only a parody of the original (2), we must suppose further that the serious way in which he deals with it, as if it really were a "wise saw," is only a piece of his fun—a playful display of Socratic irony. (Cp. Teuffel, *Rhein. Mus.* XXIX. pp. 141—2.)

'Αγάθων'...ἀγαθοί.　For the dative cp. *Prot.* 321 c ἀποροῦντι δὲ αὐτῷ ἔρχεται Προμηθεύς.　Similar exx. of paronomasia occur in 185 c, 198 c, *Gorg.* 513 B (δῆμος and Demus, son of Pyrilampes), *Rep.* 614 B (ἄλκιμος, Alcinous) : cp. Riddell *Digest* § 323.　Teuffel (*loc. cit.*) prefers to retain ἀγαθῶν, partly because of the plur. δαῖτας, partly to avoid the elision of the *iota*; but neither of these objections is serious, and as to δαῖτας, the feast in question lasted at least two days, which might in itself suffice to justify the plural.　Jowett's transl. implies that he retains ἀγαθῶν and supposes (1) to have been the original form of the proverb "demolished" by Socr. and Homer.

"Ομηρος μὲν γάρ.　The antithesis—ἡμεῖς δὲ μόνον διαφθείρομεν, or the like— is easily supplied from the context : for μὲν γάρ, elliptical, cp. 176 c, and 173 D *supra*.　The suggestion that Homer wilfully distorted a proverb which in his day was non-existent is, as Hug observes, obviously jocose.

ὑβρίσαι.　The word may retain a flavour of its juridical sense—"liable to a criminal prosecution for assault and battery" : and if so, διαφθείρα too may hint at the crime of "seduction."　Homer is chargeable not only with seducing but with committing a criminal assault upon the virgin soundness of the proverb.

174 C　μαλθακὸν αἰχμητήν.　"A craven spearman." *Il.* XVII. 587 οἷον δὴ Μενέλαον ὑπετρέσας, ὃς τὸ πάρος περ | μαλθακὸς αἰχμητής.　μαλθακός, as a variant for μαλακός, is used by P. also in 195 D, *Phaedr.* 239 C.　Both forms, Μενέλεως and Μενέλαος, are found in Attic prose; the latter, *e.g.*, in *Euthyd.* 288 C.　In Athenaeus v. 3, 188 B we have a criticism of this treatment of Menelaus.

ἄκλητον ἐποίησεν ἐλθόντα.　See *Il.* II. 408 αὐτόματος δέ οἱ ἦλθε βοὴν ἀγαθὸς Μενέλαος : cp. Athen. v. 178 A.　Thus the ὕβρις with which Homer is charged

ἀμείνονος. ταῦτ' ἀκούσας εἰπεῖν ἔφη Ἴσως μέντοι κινδυνεύσω καὶ ἐγὼ οὐχ ὡς σὺ λέγεις, ὦ Σώκρατες, ἀλλὰ καθ' Ὅμηρον φαῦλος ὢν ἐπὶ σοφοῦ ἀνδρὸς ἰέναι θοίνην ἄκλητος. ὅρα οὖν ἄγων με τί ἀπο-
D λογήσῃ, ὡς ἐγὼ μὲν οὐχ ὁμολογήσω ἄκλητος ἥκειν, ἀλλ' ὑπὸ σοῦ κεκλημένος. "Σύν τε δύ'," ἔφη, "ἐρχομένω πρὸ ὁ τοῦ." βουλευσόμεθα ὅ τι ἐροῦμεν. ἀλλὰ ἴωμεν. Τοιαῦτ' ἄττα σφᾶς ἔφη διαλεχθέντας ἰέναι. τὸν οὖν Σωκράτη ἑαυτῷ πως προσέχοντα τὸν νοῦν κατὰ τὴν ὁδὸν πορεύεσθαι ὑπολειπόμενον, καὶ περιμένοντος οὗ κελεύειν προϊέναι εἰς τὸ πρόσθεν. ἐπειδὴ δὲ γενέσθαι ἐπὶ τῇ οἰκίᾳ τῇ Ἀγάθωνος, ἀνεῳγμένην κατα-
E λαμβάνειν τὴν θύραν, καί τι ἔφη αὐτόθι γελοῖον παθεῖν. οἱ μὲν γὰρ εὐθὺς παῖδά τινα ἔνδοθεν ἀπαντήσαντα ἄγειν οὗ κατέκειντο οἱ ἄλλοι, καὶ καταλαμβάνειν ἤδη μέλλοντας δειπνεῖν· εὐθὺς δ' οὖν

174 C ὅρα...τί Bdhm.: ἄρα...τι B: ἄρα...τι T (τί W)   ἀγαγὼν Creuzer
D ὁ τοῦ Gottleber (Hom. K 224): ὁδοῦ BTW: om. Hermog.   ἀλλὰ ἴωμεν
T: ἀλλ' ἐῶμεν B   πορευόμενον ὑπολείπεσθαι Rohde Sz.   δὲ ⟨ἐ⟩ Cobet Sz.:
δ' ἐ Baiter J.-U.   E οἱ Photius, b: οἰ BT: τὸν W   ⟨τῶν⟩ ἔνδοθεν
Porson Sz. J.·U. Bt.: τῶν ἔνδον Photius, Jn.

consists in making not an ἀγαθός but a μαλθακός (=δειλός) come ἄκλητος ἀγαθῶν ἐπὶ δαῖτας.

ἐπὶ σοφοῦ ἀνδρός. σοφός, "accomplished," was "a fashionable epithet of praise in Plato's time, especially applied to poets" (see *Rep.* 331 E, 489 B, with Adam's *notes*).

ὅρα οὖν κτλ. This correction of the traditional ἄρα...τι is certain. Cp. 189 A ὅρα τί ποιεῖς: *Phaedo* 86 D ὅρα οὖν...τί φήσομεν. For the dangers of violating etiquette on such occasions, see Ar. *Av.* 983 ff. αὐτὰρ ἐπὴν ἄκλητος ἰὼν ἄνθρωπος ἀλαζὼν | λυπῇ θύοντας καὶ σπλαγχνεύειν ἐπιθυμῇ, | δὴ τότε χρὴ τύπτειν αὐτὸν πλευρῶν τὸ μεταξύ.

174 D Σύν τε δύ' κτλ. See *Il.* x. 224 (Diomedes loq.) σύν τε δύ' ἐρχομένω καί τε πρὸ ὁ τοῦ ἐνόησεν | ὅππως κέρδος ἔῃ. The same verses are quoted more exactly in *Prot.* 348 c: cp. also Arist. *Pol.* III. 1287ᵇ 13; Cic. *ad fam.* IX. 7. For cxx. of how Plato "variis modis multis affert aliena," see Vahlen *Op. Acad.* I. pp. 476 ff.

ἐπειδὴ δὲ γενέσθαι. The infin. in place of the indic. is due to assimilation: cp. *Rep.* 614 B ἔφη δέ, ἐπειδὴ οὗ ἐκβῆναι τὴν ψυχήν, πορεύεσθαι: see Goodwin *G. M. T.* § 755.

174 E καί τι...γελοῖον παθεῖν. It was an awkward situation in smart society. Cp. Plut. *Conv.* 6 p. 628 ἔλαθε γὰρ κατὰ τὴν ὁδὸν ὑπολειφθεὶς ὁ Σωκράτης, ὁ δὲ παρεισῆλθεν, ἀτεχνῶς σκιὰ προβαδίζουσα σώματος ἐξόπισθε τὸ φῶς ἔχοντος.

οἱ (*sibi*) goes with ἀπαντήσαντα. Porson's insertion (from Photius) of τῶν before ἔνδοθεν is no improvement: ἔνδοθεν is to be taken with ἀπαντήσαντα, and there is no indication that there were any ἔξωθεν παῖδες.

ὡς ἰδεῖν τὸν Ἀγάθωνα, Ὦ, φάναι, Ἀριστόδημε, εἰς καλὸν ἥκεις
ὅπως συνδειπνήσῃς· εἰ δ' ἄλλου τινὸς ἕνεκα ἦλθες, εἰς αὖθις ἀνα-
βαλοῦ, ὡς καὶ χθὲς ζητῶν σε ἵνα καλέσαιμι, οὐχ οἷός τ' ἦ ἰδεῖν.
ἀλλὰ Σωκράτη ἡμῖν πῶς οὐκ ἄγεις; καὶ ἐγώ, ἔφη, μεταστρεφό-
μενος οὐδαμοῦ ὁρῶ Σωκράτη ἑπόμενον· εἶπον οὖν ὅτι καὶ αὐτὸς
μετὰ Σωκράτους ἥκοιμι, κληθεὶς ὑπ' ἐκείνου δεῦρ' ἐπὶ δεῖπνον.
Καλῶς γ', ἔφη, ποιῶν σύ· ἀλλὰ ποῦ ἔστιν οὗτος; Ὄπισθεν ἐμοῦ 175
ἄρτι εἰσῄει· ἀλλὰ θαυμάζω καὶ αὐτὸς ποῦ ἂν εἴη. Οὐ σκέψῃ,
ἔφη, παῖ, φάναι τὸν Ἀγάθωνα, καὶ εἰσάξεις Σωκράτη; σὺ δ', ἦ δ'
ὅς, Ἀριστόδημε, παρ' Ἐρυξίμαχον κατακλίνου.
III. Καὶ ἓ μὲν ἔφη ἀπονίζειν τὸν παῖδα, ἵνα κατακέοιτο·
ἄλλον δέ τινα τῶν παίδων ἥκειν ἀγγέλλοντα ὅτι Σωκράτης οὗτος
ἀναχωρήσας ἐν τῷ τῶν γειτόνων προθύρῳ ἕστηκε καὶ οὗ καλοῦν-
τος οὐκ ἐθέλει εἰσιέναι. Ἄτοπόν γ', ἔφη, λέγεις· οὔκουν καλεῖς
αὐτὸν καὶ μὴ ἀφήσεις; καὶ ὃς ἔφη εἰπεῖν Μηδαμῶς, ἀλλ' ἐᾶτε

174 E ὣ T : ᾧ B	συνδειπνήσεις Laur. xiv. 85, Bekk. Sz.	τ' ἦ T :
τε B	ἔφην T	οὐδαμῇ TW	ἥκοιμι Tb: ἥκοι μη B	γ' T: om. B
175 A εἰσῄειν Cobet	ὅπου Hirschig	ἒ μὲν Bast: ἒ Steph.: ἐμὲ BT
ἔφην T	ἵνα ⟨που⟩ vulg.: ὅπου Tmg.	ἔν τῳ Steph. J.-U.: ἔν του Mdvg.
καὶ οὗ BT: κἀμοῦ W, Bt.: καὶ σοῦ t	καλοῖς Tmg. W: κάλει rec. b
αὐτὸν : αὖθις Herwerden	ἀφήσῃς T

εἰς καλὸν ἥκεις. "Soyez le bienvenu!" For the construction see Goodwin,
§ 317.

χθὲς ζητῶν σε κτλ. Hug regards this as a piece of polite mendacity on the
part of Agathon. Are we, then, to construe Alcibiades' statement, χθὲς μὲν
οὐχ οἷός τε κτλ. (212 E) as a similar exhibition of "Salonweltlichkeit"?

175 A παρ' Ἐ. κατακλίνου. Usually each κλίνη held two, but in 175 c
it is said that Agathon had a couch to himself, while in 213 A we find three
on the same couch.

ἀπονίζειν τὸν παῖδα. The article indicates that a special slave was set
apart for this duty. For the custom of foot-washing see Plut. Phoc. 20;
Petron. Sat. 31; Evang. Luc. vii. 44; Joann. xiii. 5. For the hand-washing
see Ar. frag. 427 φέρε, παῖ, ταχέως κατὰ χειρὸς ὕδωρ, | παράπεμπε τὸ χειρό-
μακτρον.

Σωκράτης οὗτος κτλ. The ipsissima verba of the παῖς are here repeated,
hence the use of οὗτος and of the def. article with προθύρῳ: in the corrections
proposed by Madvig and Herwerden this point is overlooked. For πρόθυρον,
"porch," i.e. the space between the house-door (αὐλεία) and the street, see
Smith D. A. I. 661ᵇ.

οὔκουν καλεῖς κτλ. καλεῖς is of course future, not pres. as Rückert wrongly
supposed. For the constr. see Goodwin G. M. T. § 299.

B αὐτόν. ἔθος γάρ τι τοῦτ' ἔχει· ἐνίοτε ἀποστὰς ὅποι ἂν τύχῃ
ἕστηκεν. ἥξει δὲ αὐτίκα, ὡς ἐγὼ οἶμαι. μὴ οὖν κινεῖτε, ἀλλ'
ἐᾶτε. 'Αλλ' οὕτω χρὴ ποιεῖν, εἰ σοὶ δοκεῖ, ἔφη φάναι τὸν 'Αγα-
θωνα. ἀλλ' ἡμᾶς, ὦ παῖδες, τοὺς ἄλλους ἑστιᾶτε. πάντως παρατίθετε ὅ τι ἂν βούλησθε, ἐπειδάν τις ὑμῖν μὴ ἐφεστήκῃ—ὃ ἐγὼ
οὐδεπώποτε ἐποίησα· νῦν οὖν, νομίζοντες καὶ ἐμὲ ὑφ' ὑμῶν κεκλῆ-
C σθαι ἐπὶ δεῖπνον καὶ τούσδε τοὺς ἄλλους, θεραπεύετε, ἵνα ὑμᾶς
ἐπαινῶμεν.

Μετὰ ταῦτα ἔφη σφᾶς μὲν δειπνεῖν, τὸν δὲ Σωκράτη οὐκ

175 B τοῦτο T Priscian: τοιοῦτον W   ἐνίοτε...ἕστηκεν del. Voeg.
ἔφη T: om. B   ἐπειδάν τις...μὴ BT: ἐπεί τις...οὐ μὴ L. Schmidt: ἐπεί
οὐ δή τις...μὴ Hug: ἐπεὶ δή τις...οὐ μὴ Sz.: ἐπεὶ καὶ τίσις...μὴ (ἐφεστήκοι)
Verm.: εἴ γ' ὁ ταμίας...μὴ Usener: ἐπειδὰν αὐτὸς...μὴ cj. Bt.: εἴγε ἀνάγκη τις...
μὴ coniciebam   ἐφεστήκῃ T: ἐφεστήκη W: ἐφεστήκει B: "latet ἐφέστηκεν"
Usener

---

175 B πάντως παρατίθετε. For the use of πάντως with imper., cp. Xen.
Cyrop. VIII. 3. 27 πάντως τοίνυν...δείξόν μοι: *id. Oecon.* XII. 11, III. 12. For
παρατίθημι of "putting on the table," cp. *Rep.* 372 C τραγήματά που παρα-
θήσομεν αὐτοῖς κτλ. Reynders adopts the reading πάντας, καὶ παρατίθετε.
ἐπειδάν...μὴ ἐφεστήκῃ. These words are difficult. They should naturally
mean (as Stallb. puts it) "si quando nemo vobis est propositus"; and so
Stallb. proposes to construe them, taking the clause as dependent on and
limiting ὅ τι ἂν βούλησθε. This, however, is, as Hug argues, almost certainly
wrong. If we retain the text of the MSS. we can only explain the phrase by
assuming an ellipse—"serve up what dishes you like (as you usually do)
whenever no one is in command." So Zeller renders "tragt uns getrost auf,
was ihr wollt, wie ihr es gewohnt seid, wenn man euch nicht unter Aufsicht
nimmt," etc.; and Rieckher (*Rhein. Mus.* XXXIII. p. 307) "Machet es wie ihr
es immer macht, wenn man euch nicht beaufsichtigt (und das habe ich ja
noch nie gethan), und setzt uns vor was ihr möget." Most of the emendations
offered (see *crit. n.*) are based on the assumption that the clause in question
qualifies the leading clause (πάντως παρατίθετε): none of them are convincing,
and the construction οὐ μή...ἐφεστήκῃ (the pres.-perf.) assumed by Schanz
and Hug lacks support. If compelled to resort to conjecture, the best device
might be to read εἴ γε μή for ἐπειδάν, cut out the μή after ὑμῖν, and change
the mood of the verb to ἐφέστηκεν—following in part the suggestions of
Usener. The ordinary text does not admit of Jowett's rendering, "serve up
whatever you please, for there is no one to give you orders; hitherto I have
never left you to yourselves." As regards the force of ὃ...ἐποίησα, L. Schmidt
explains the clause to mean "nunquam autem rem ita ut nunc institui,"
implying that the concession to the slaves was unusual: Teuffel, on the
contrary, sees in it a piece of ostentation on the part of Agathon, boasting
of his humanity. The former is clearly wrong.

εἰσιέναι. τὸν οὖν Ἀγάθωνα πολλάκις κελεύειν μεταπέμψασθαι
τὸν Σωκράτη, ἓ δὲ οὐκ ἐᾶν. ἥκειν οὖν αὐτὸν οὐ πολὺν χρόνον,
ὡς εἰώθει, διατρίψαντα, ἀλλὰ μάλιστα σφᾶς μεσοῦν δειπνοῦντας.
τὸν οὖν Ἀγάθωνα—τυγχάνειν γὰρ ἔσχατον κατακείμενον μόνον— ╱
Δεῦρ᾽, ἔφη φάναι, Σώκρατες, παρ᾽ ἐμὲ κατάκεισο, ἵνα καὶ τοῦ D
σοφοῦ ἁπτόμενός σου ἀπολαύσω, ὅ σοι προσέστη ἐν τοῖς προθύ-

175 C   ἓ δὲ BW: *** δὲ T (τὸν δὲ fuisse videtur): αὐτὸν δὲ vulg.: ἵ δὲ
cj. Bekk.   οὐκ ἐᾶν B: οὐκαν T   D ἁπτόμενός σου TW: om. B, J.-U. Sz.
προσέστη T: πρόσεστιν B

---

175 C πολλάκις κελεύειν.   This is an ex. of the pres. infin. representing
an impf. indic.: "He said, ἐδειπνοῦμεν, ὁ δὲ Σ. οὐκ εἰσῄει· ὁ οὖν Ἀ. ἐκέλευεν·
ἐγὼ δὲ οὐκ εἴων" (Goodwin *G. M. T.* § 119, where see parallels). The accus. ἓ,
of the speaker, is here used in preference to the more regular nomin. (αὐτός)
in order to balance the accus. τὸν Ἀγάθωνα: cp. *Gorg.* 474 B ἐγὼ οἶμαι καὶ ἐμὲ
καὶ σέ...ἡγεῖσθαι, and below 175 E.

ὡς εἰώθει.   To be taken closely with οὐ π. χρ.: we should rather say
"contrary to his usual custom," the sense being "he arrived unusually soon
for him." For a striking instance of Socrates' ἔθος see 220 c, where πολὺν
χρόνον διέτριψεν.

μάλιστα...δειπνοῦντας.   For μάλιστα of approximate measurement, cp.
Parm. 127 B περὶ ἔτη μάλιστα πέντε καὶ ἑξήκοντα: *Tim.* 21 B, *Crito* 43 A.
Nowhere else in Plato is μεσοῦν joined with a participle, nor does L. and S.
supply any parallel.

ἔσχατον...μόνον.   Agathon occupied the last κλίνη on the right: this was
the "lowest seat" at the table, and commonly taken, in politeness, by the
host. The seat of honour (προνομή) was the left-hand place on the κλίνη
furthest to the left. Thus if four κλῖναι are placed in a row, numbered
A—D, and each seating two persons, the person who occupies A¹ is termed
πρῶτος, and the occupant of D² ἔσχατος: as thus

A¹   A²   B¹   B²·   C¹   C²   D¹   D²

At this "Banquet" Phaedrus as occupying A¹ is described as πρῶτος in 177 D:
see also the discussion between Socrates and Alcibiades in 222 E. Cp. Theophr.
Char. 21 ὁ δὲ μικροφιλότιμος τοιοῦτός τις οἷος σπουδάσαι ἐπὶ δεῖπνον κληθεὶς παρ᾽
αὐτὸν τὸν καλέσαντα δειπνῆσαι: Stob. *Flor.* XIII. 36 Διονύσιος...ἀτιμάζων αὐτὸν...
κατέκλινεν αὐτὸν ἐν τῇ ἐσχάτῃ χώρᾳ.

175 D τοῦ σοφοῦ...ἀπολαύσω.   τοῦ σοφοῦ is neut., being the antecedent of
ὅ, not in agreement with σου: "that I may enjoy the piece of wisdom which
occurred to you." The omission of ἁπτόμενός σου by B is probably accidental:
without the words (as Teuffel observes) Socr.'s remark (ἐὰν ἅπτ.) would be less
natural.

ροις. δῆλον γὰρ ὅτι εὗρες αὐτὸ καὶ ἔχεις· οὐ γὰρ ἂν προαπέστης.
καὶ τὸν Σωκράτη καθίζεσθαι καὶ εἰπεῖν ὅτι Εὖ ἂν ἔχοι, φάναι, ὦ
Ἀγάθων, εἰ τοιοῦτον εἴη ἡ σοφία ὥστ' ἐκ τοῦ πληρεστέρου εἰς τὸ
κενώτερον ῥεῖν ἡμῶν, ἐὰν ἁπτώμεθα ἀλλήλων, ὥσπερ τὸ ἐν ταῖς
κύλιξιν ὕδωρ τὸ διὰ τοῦ ἐρίου ῥέον ἐκ τῆς πληρεστέρας εἰς τὴν
Ε κενωτέραν. εἰ γὰρ οὕτως ἔχει καὶ ἡ σοφία, πολλοῦ τιμῶμαι τὴν
παρὰ σοὶ κατάκλισιν· οἶμαι γάρ με παρὰ σοῦ πολλῆς καὶ καλῆς
σοφίας πληρωθήσεσθαι. ἡ μὲν γὰρ ἐμὴ φαύλη τις ἂν εἴη καὶ
ἀμφισβητήσιμος, ὥσπερ ὄναρ οὖσα, ἡ δὲ σὴ λαμπρά|τε καὶ πολλὴν
ἐπίδοσιν ἔχουσα, ἥ γε παρὰ σοῦ νέου ὄντος οὕτω σφόδρα ἐξέλαμψε
καὶ ἐκφανὴς ἐγένετο πρῴην ἐν μάρτυσι τῶν Ἑλλήνων πλέον ἢ
τρισμυρίοις. Ὑβριστὴς εἶ, ἔφη, ὦ Σώκρατες, ὁ Ἀγάθων. καὶ
ταῦτα μὲν καὶ ὀλίγον ὕστερον διαδικασόμεθα ἐγώ τε καὶ σὺ

175 D τὸ ΒΤ: τὸν corr. Coisl., J.-U. Sz.   ἐρίου: ὀργάνου Cornarius:
ὑλιστηρίου vel ἠθηνίου Fischer   ἐκ τῆς...κενωτέραν del. Voeg. Naber
Ε τιμῶμαι Τ: τιμῶμεν Β: τιμῶ μὲν Stallb.   με del. Usener   καὶ Β:
ἢ καὶ ΤW   ἤ γε Τ: εἴ γε Β   καὶ: ἀλλὰ vulg.

οὐ γὰρ ἂν προαπέστης. The protasis is suppressed: Stallbaum supplies
εἰ μὴ εὗρες αὐτό: while Hug explains the phrase as a conflate of two thoughts,
viz. (1) οὐκ ἂν ἀπέστης εἰ μὴ εὗρες, and (2) οὐ προαπέστης πρὶν εὑρεῖν.

εἰς τὸ κενώτερον. Ficinus renders "ut in vacuum hominem ex pleniore
ipso contactu proflueret," and many edd. adopt τόν in preference to τό (so
too Jowett's transl.).

ὥσπερ τὸ...ὕδωρ κτλ. Editors from Rückert down generally accept the
explanation of this passage offered by Geel. Two cups, one empty the other
full, are placed in contact: a woollen thread, with one end inserted in the full
cup, the other hanging into the empty cup, serves by the law of capillarity to
convey the fluid from the one to the other.

175 Ε φαύλη...καὶ ἀμφισβητήσιμος. "Meagre" in quantity and "question-
able" in quality, in antithesis to πολλή in quantity and καλή in quality.

πολλὴν ἐπίδοσιν ἔχουσα. Hug supposes an astral allusion—"like a quickly-
rising star." This, however, is not necessarily conveyed by the term ἐπίδοσις,
for which cp. Theaet. 146 Β ἡ νεότης εἰς πᾶν ἐπίδοσιν ἔχει, and the intrans. use
of ἐπιδιδόναι, Prot. 318 A, Theaet. 150 D, etc.

οὕτω σφόδρα κτλ. Notice the ironical tone—exaggeration coupled with
a purple patch of poetic diction: "shone out with such dazzling splendour
before the eyes of three myriads of Greek spectators."

Ὑβριστὴς εἶ. "What a scoffer you are!" Observe that ὕβρις is one of the
main charges laid against Socr. by Alcibiades also (219 c, etc.); cp. Introd.
§ II. Β.

ταῦτα...διαδικασόμεθα. "We will formally plead our claims in regard to
these heads." "Technically diadicasia denotes the proceedings in a contest
for preference between two or more rival parties either as to the possession

περὶ τῆς σοφίας, δικαστῇ χρώμενοι τῷ Διονύσῳ· νῦν δὲ πρὸς τὸ δεῖπνον πρῶτα τρέπου.

IV.   Μετὰ ταῦτα, ἔφη, κατακλινέντος τοῦ Σωκράτους καὶ 176 δειπνήσαντος καὶ τῶν ἄλλων, σπονδάς τε σφᾶς ποιήσασθαι καὶ ᾄσαντας τὸν θεὸν καὶ τἆλλα τὰ νομιζόμενα τρέπεσθαι πρὸς τὸν πότον· τὸν οὖν Παυσανίαν ἔφη λόγου τοιούτου τινὸς κατάρχειν.

Εἶεν, ἄνδρες, φάναι, τίνα τρόπον ῥᾷστα πιόμεθα; ἐγὼ μὲν οὖν λέγω ὑμῖν ὅτι τῷ ὄντι πάνυ χαλεπῶς ἔχω ὑπὸ τοῦ χθὲς πότου καὶ

175 E   περὶ τῆς σοφίας del. Hirschig   176 A   ⟨ὡς⟩ καὶ τῶν Rohde καὶ τἆλλα : κατὰ Ast : καὶ...νομιζόμενα post ποιήσασθαι transp. Steinhart ἄνδρες : ὦνδρες Sauppe Sz.   ῥᾷστα BT : ἥδιστα γρ. t

---

of property or as to exemption from personal or pecuniary liabilities....The essential difference between *diadicasia* and the ordinary δίκαι is, that all claimants are similarly situated with respect to the subject of dispute, and no longer classified as plaintiffs and defendants" (Smith, *D. A.* I. 620ᵇ).

περὶ τῆς σοφίας, added loosely as an afterthought, serves to define ταῦτα: Teuffel, as against Jahn, rightly defends the words; and they serve to strike one of the keynotes of the dialogue.

δικαστῇ...τῷ Διονύσῳ.   Dionysus is an appropriate choice since it was under his auspices that Agathon (πρῴην) had engaged in an ἀγών and won a prize for poetic σοφία.   There may also lie in the words (as Wolf and Rettig suppose) a jocular allusion to the σοφία which is *ars bibendi*, wherein also Agathon was δυνατώτατος (176 c).   Compare also the pastoral pipe-contests of Theocritus, and Theognis 993 ff. εἰ...ἄθλον... | σοί τ' εἴη καὶ ἐμοὶ σοφίης πέρι θηρισάντοιν, | γνοίης χ' ὅσσον ὄνων κρέσσονες ἡμίονοι. Cp. *Introd.* § II. B.

176 A   σπονδάς...νομιζόμενα.   Plato spares us the details of the ritual proper to such occasions.   From other sources we may gather that it included (1) a libation of unmixed wine to ἀγαθὸς δαίμων (Ar. *Eq.* 105, etc.) ; (2) the clearing, or removal, of the tables (Xen. *Symp.* II. 1); (3) the fetching, by the παῖδες, of a second supply of water for the hands (Ar. *Vesp.* 1217 etc.); (4) the distribution of wreaths among the guests (Theogn. 1001, Ar. *Acharn.* 1145); (5) the pouring out of three libations, viz. (a) to Zeus Olympios and the Olympian gods, (b) to the Heroes, and (c) to Zeus Soter (Schol. *ad Phileb.* 66 D; Aesch. *Suppl.* 27, etc.); (6) the singing of a *Te Deum* (ᾄδειν τὸν θεόν, παιανίζειν Xen. *Symp.* II. 1, Alcman *fr.* 24 B, etc.): see Hug's exhaustive *note*. Rückert wrongly makes τἆλλα τὰ νομιζόμενα depend on ᾄσαντας: supply (as Reynders) ποιησαμένους.   For καὶ τἆλλα, cp. (with Vahlen) *Euthyd.* 294 c, *Rep.* 400 D: for τὰ νομιζόμενα, *quae moris sunt*, cp. *II. Alc.* 151 B.

τίνα τρόπον ῥᾷστα.   Schol. ῥᾷστα· τὸ ἥδιστα ἐνταῦθα σημαίνει.   Cp. *Od.* IV. 565 τῇ περ (sc. in Elysium) ῥηίστη βιοτή: and the combination ῥᾷστα καὶ ἥδιστα, Xen. *Mem.* II. 1. 9.   (See also Vahlen *Op. Acad.* II. 212 ff. *ad Phaedo* 81 c).

πάνυ χαλεπῶς ἔχω.   The notion is "I was roughly handled in my bout with the wine-god yesterday": cp. *Theaet.* 142 B χαλεπῶς ἔχει ὑπὸ τραυμάτων τινῶν.

δέομαι ἀναψυχῆς τινός, οἶμαι δὲ καὶ ὑμῶν τοὺς πολλούς—παρῆστε
B γὰρ χθές· σκοπεῖσθε οὖν, τίνι τρόπῳ ἂν ὡς ῥᾷστα πίνοιμεν. τὸν
οὖν Ἀριστοφάνη εἰπεῖν, Τοῦτο μέντοι εὖ λέγεις, ὦ Παυσανία, τὸ
παντὶ τρόπῳ παρασκευάσασθαι ῥαστώνην τινὰ τῆς πόσεως· καὶ
γὰρ αὐτός εἰμι τῶν χθὲς βεβαπτισμένων. ἀκούσαντα οὖν αὐτῶν
ἔφη Ἐρυξίμαχον τὸν Ἀκουμενοῦ Ἦ καλῶς, φάναι, λέγετε. καὶ
ἔτι ἑνὸς δέομαι ὑμῶν ἀκοῦσαι, πῶς ἔχει πρὸς τὸ ἐρρῶσθαι πίνειν
Ἀγάθων. Οὐδαμῶς, φάναι, οὐδ᾽ αὐτὸς ἔρρωμαι. Ἕρμαιον ἂν εἴη
C ἡμῖν, ἦ δ᾽ ὅς, ὡς ἔοικεν, ἐμοί τε καὶ Ἀριστοδήμῳ καὶ Φαίδρῳ καὶ
τοῖσδε, εἰ ὑμεῖς οἱ δυνατώτατοι πίνειν νῦν ἀπειρήκατε· ἡμεῖς μὲν
γὰρ ἀεὶ ἀδύνατοι. Σωκράτη δ᾽ ἐξαιρῶ λόγου· ἱκανὸς γὰρ καὶ
ἀμφότερα, ὥστ᾽ ἐξαρκέσει αὐτῷ ὁπότερ᾽ ἂν ποιῶμεν. ἐπειδὴ οὖν
μοι δοκεῖ οὐδεὶς τῶν παρόντων προθύμως ἔχειν πρὸς τὸ πολὺν
πίνειν οἶνον, ἴσως ἂν ἐγὼ περὶ τοῦ μεθύσκεσθαι οἷόν ἐστι τἀληθῆ
λέγων ἧττον ἂν εἴην ἀηδής. ἐμοὶ γὰρ δὴ τοῦτό γε οἶμαι κατά-
D δηλον γεγονέναι ἐκ τῆς ἰατρικῆς, ὅτι χαλεπὸν τοῖς ἀνθρώποις ἡ
μέθη ἐστί· καὶ οὔτε αὐτὸς ἑκὼν εἶναι πόρρω ἐθελήσαιμι ἂν πιεῖν

176 A παρῆστε BTW : παρῆτε in mg. rec. b   B παρασκευάσασθαι TW :
παρασκευάζεσθαι B   αὐτῶν T : αὐτὸν B   Ἐρυξίμαχον T : τὸν Ἐρυξίμαχον B
ἀκουμενοῦ W : ἀκουμένου BT   καὶ : καίτοι Rohde   ἐρρῶσθαι secl. Cobet
πίνειν, Ἀγάθωνος Vahlen   C ἐξαιρῶ Heindorf : ἐξαίρω BT   ἀηδής T : ἀηλης B

---

176 B **βεβαπτισμένων**: "soaked," "drenched." Cp. Lucian *Bacch.* 7 καρη-
καὶ βεβαπτισμένῳ : and the use of βεβρεγμένος, Eubul. *Incert.* 5 ; μέθῃ βαροῦντι
βρεχθείς Eur. *El.* 326 : Sen. *Ep.* 83 mersus vino et madens ; Hor. *C.* IV. 5. 39
dicimus...sicci...dicimus uvidi.   A similar "baptism" is described in Evenos
2. 5—6, εἰ δὲ πολὺς πνεύσειεν (sc. ὁ Βάκχος) ἀπέστραπται μὲν ἔρωτας, | βαπτίζει
δ᾽ ὕπνῳ γείτονι τοῦ θανάτου : of which we find an echo in Clem. Alex. *Paed.*
II. ii. 27² (Stählin) ὑπὸ μέθης βαπτιζόμενος εἰς ὕπνον. There may be an
underlying allusion to Eupolis' play Βάπται (cp. Bergk *P. L. G.* II. p. 268).
176 C **ἐξαιρῶ λόγου**: "I leave out of account": cp. *Phaedr.* 242 B, *Rep.*
394 B, 492 E.   For Socrates as inconvincible "with wine and wassail," see
Alcibiades' description, 220 A.
περὶ τοῦ μεθύσκεσθαι. A favourite subject of discussion with moralists,
e.g. Theognis 473 ff., 500 ff. ; *Laws* I. 677 D ff., Xen. *Symp.* II. ; and the treatise
περὶ μέθης of Antisthenes.
ἧττον...ἀηδής. "Less likely to bore you," sc. than if you were in the mood
for wine-bibbing.   Compare (with Wolf) Hor. *Sat.* II. ii. 1 ff. quae virtus et
quanta, boni, sit vivere parvo...discite non inter lances mensasque nitentes.
176 D **χαλεπὸν...ἡ μέθη.** Similarly in 180 B we have neut. adj. with
masc. subst. (θειότερον...ἐραστής).   For the sentiment cp. Ar. *Vesp.* 1253
κακὸν τὸ πίνειν· κτλ. : Theogn. 211 οἶνόν τοι πίνειν πουλὺν κακόν : Xen.

οὔτε ἄλλῳ συμβουλεύσαιμι, ἄλλως τε καὶ κραιπαλῶντα ἔτι ἐκ τῆς
προτεραίας. Ἀλλὰ μήν, ἔφη φάναι ὑπολαβόντα Φαῖδρον τὸν
Μυρρινούσιον, ἔγωγέ σοι εἴωθα πείθεσθαι ἄλλως τε καὶ ἅττ᾽ ἂν
περὶ ἰατρικῆς λέγῃς· νῦν δ᾽, ἂν εὖ βουλεύωνται, καὶ οἱ λοιποί.
ταῦτα δὴ ἀκούσαντας συγχωρεῖν πάντας μὴ διὰ μέθης ποιήσασθαι E
τὴν ἐν τῷ παρόντι συνουσίαν, ἀλλ᾽ οὕτω πίνοντας πρὸς ἡδονήν.

V　Ἐπειδὴ τοίνυν, φάναι τὸν Ἐρυξίμαχον, τοῦτο μὲν δέδοκται, πίνειν ὅσον ἂν ἕκαστος βούληται, ἐπάναγκες δὲ μηδὲν εἶναι,
τὸ μετὰ τοῦτο εἰσηγοῦμαι τὴν μὲν ἄρτι εἰσελθοῦσαν αὐλητρίδα
χαίρειν ἐᾶν, αὐλοῦσαν ἑαυτῇ ἢ ἂν βούληται ταῖς γυναιξὶ ταῖς
ἔνδον, ἡμᾶς δὲ διὰ λόγων ἀλλήλοις συνεῖναι τὸ τήμερον· καὶ

176 D κραιπαλῶντα T: κραιπαλοῦντα B: κραιπαλῶντι Hirschig　　φαῖδρον
T: φαιδρων B　　μυρινούσιον T　　λέγεις T　　ἂν TW: αὖ B　　βουλεύωνται corr. Coisl. Bast: βούλωνται BTW: βούλονται vulg.: (αὖ) βούλοιντ᾽ ἂν
Thiersch: (αὖ) βούλονται Ast: (αὖ) ἂν βούλωνται Kreyenbühl　　E αὐλητρίδα T: αὐλιτρίδα B　　ἢ ἂν: ἡὰν B: ἐὰν T

Symp. ΙΙ. 26 ἦν μὲν ἀθρόον τὸ ποτὸν ἐγχεώμεθα, ταχὺ ἡμῖν καὶ τὰ σώματα καὶ
αἱ γνῶμαι σφαλοῦνται κτλ.　For the pedantic reference to ἡ ἰατρική, cp. 186 A.
κραιπαλῶντα.　Tim. Lex. Plat. explains by ἔτι ἀπὸ τῆς μέθης βαρυνόμενον.
For the accus., in place of dat. (in appos. to ἄλλῳ), cp. 188 D ἡμῖν...δυνα-
μένους: Rep. 414 A, etc.
νῦν δ᾽...οἱ λοιποί.　With οἱ λοιποί we must supply σοὶ πείσονται, as Stallb.
and Winckelmann observed.　Rettig alone, of later editors, retains the reading
νῦν δ᾽ αὖ εὖ βούλονται, with Wolf's rendering, "nunc bene est, quod item
reliquos id velle video"; but, as Hug remarks, that εὖ βούλονται can mean
"bene est quod volunt" lacks proof.
176 E οὕτω...πρὸς ἡδονήν.　οὕτως is frequently used thus in combination
with adverbs (esp. ῥαδίως, εἰκῇ, ἀπλῶς, and the like; see Blaydes on Ar. Vesp.
461) where it has "a diminishing power" (L. and S.), e.g. 180 C infra, Gorg.
503 D; cp. the force of sic in such phrases as "incentes sic temere" (Hor.
C. II. xi. 14).
τοῦτο μὲν κτλ.　The antithesis to the μέν-clause lies, not in the clause
ἐπάναγκες δὲ μ. εἶναι, but in τὸ μετὰ τοῦτο κτλ.　Cp. Arist. Pol. 1278[b] 6 ἐπεὶ
δὲ ταῦτα διώρισται, τὸ μετὰ ταῦτα σκεπτέον πότερον κτλ.
ἐπάναγκες.　Cp. Theogn. 472 πᾶν γὰρ ἀναγκαῖον χρῆμ᾽ ἀνιηρὸν ἔφυ· | τῷ
πίνειν δ᾽ ἐθέλοντι παρασταδὸν οἰνοχοείτω—where a similar relaxation of com-
pulsory rules is advocated.
εἰσηγοῦμαι.　"I propose," suadeo: cp. Crito 48 A; Xen. Mem. ΙΙ. 7. 10.
τὴν...αὐλητρίδα.　It was the fashion at convivia to provide pipers, dancers,
jesters, jugglers et hoc genus omne to amuse the guests.　Cp. Xen. Symp. ΙΙ. 1,
Rep. 373 A κλῖναί τε...καὶ ἑταῖραι καὶ πέμματα (with Adam's note); Ar. Ach.
1090 ff.; also Protag. 347 C, D (see next page).
ταῖς ἔνδον.　Sc. ἐν τῷ γυναικείῳ.

B. P.　　　　　　　　　　　　　　　　　　　　　　　　　　　　2

177 δι' οἴων λόγων, εἰ βούλεσθε, ἐθέλω ὑμῖν εἰσηγήσασθαι. Φάναι δὴ πάντας καὶ βούλεσθαι καὶ κελεύειν αὐτὸν εἰσηγεῖσθαι. εἰπεῖν οὖν τὸν Ἐρυξίμαχον ὅτι Ἡ μέν μοι ἀρχὴ τοῦ λόγου ἐστὶ κατὰ τὴν Εὐριπίδου Μελανίππην· οὐ γὰρ ἐμὸς ὁ μῦθος, ἀλλὰ Φαίδρου τοῦδε, ὃν μέλλω λέγειν. ⌡ Φαῖδρος γὰρ ἑκάστοτε πρός με ἀγανακτῶν λέγει Οὐ δεινόν, φησίν, ὦ Ἐρυξίμαχε, ἄλλοις μέν τισι θεῶν ὕμνους καὶ παιῶνας εἶναι ὑπὸ τῶν ποιητῶν πεποιημένους, τῷ δὲ

177 A καὶ ante βουλ. secl. Hermann Sz.: καὶ βούλεσθαι del. Voeg.
παιανας W : παίονας BT : παιᾶνας bt

δι' οἴων λόγων. For an appreciation of the συνουσία διὰ λόγων, cp. Theogn. 493 ff. ὑμεῖς δ' εὖ μυθεῖσθε παρὰ κρητῆρι μένοντες... | ἐς τὸ μέσον φωνεῦντες ὁμῶς ἑνὶ καὶ συνάπασιν· | χοὖτως συμπόσιον γίνεται οὐκ ἄχαρι. Simplic. in Epict. 33. 6, p. 266 καλῶς εἴρηται ὅτι ἡ χωρὶς λόγων τράπεζα φάτνης οὐδὲν διαφέρει which is probably a reminiscence of Protag. 347 C, D καὶ γὰρ οὗτοι (sc. οἱ φαῦλοι καὶ ἀγοραῖοι), διὰ τὸ μὴ δύνασθαι ἀλλήλοις δι' ἑαυτῶν συνεῖναι ἐν τῷ πότῳ μηδὲ διὰ τῆς ἑαυτῶν φωνῆς καὶ τῶν λόγων τῶν ἑαυτῶν ὑπὸ ἀπαιδευσίας, τιμίας ποιοῦσι τὰς αὐλητρίδας κτλ. Cp. Phaedr. 276 D.

177 A Φάναι δὴ κτλ. It is tempting to excise (with Hermann, Teuffel and Hug) the first καί and to construe φάναι closely with βούλεσθαι, as balancing κελεύειν εἰσηγεῖσθαι, πάντας being the subject of both the leading infinn., φάναι and κελεύειν: cp. 177 E ξυνέφασάν τε καὶ ἐκέλευον : Euthyd. 274 c ὅ τε οὖν Κτήσιππος συνέφη...καὶ οἱ ἄλλοι, καὶ ἐκέλευον...ἐπιδείξασθαι κτλ. If the first καί be retained, it seems most natural to take κελεύειν as dependent on φάναι: Stallb., however, puts a comma after βούλεσθαι, as if making κελεύειν parallel to φάναι: and so too, apparently, Zeller.

κατὰ τὴν Μελανίππην. Euripides wrote two plays of this name, M. ἡ σοφή and M. δεσμῶτις. The reference here is to the former (Frag. 488 Nauck), οὐκ ἐμὸς ὁ μῦθος ἀλλ' ἐμῆς μητρὸς πάρα, κτλ. Melanippe, a daughter of Aeolus, bore two sons to Poseidon; they were suckled by a cow, and brought to their grandfather Aeolus as βουγενῆ τέρατα : when he proposed to burn them, Melanippe appeared and tried to dissuade him, arguing ὅτι οὐδὲν τέρας ἐστίν. According to another account, M. was a daughter of Cheiron, seduced by Aeolus, and finally metamorphosed into a mare. Cp. Apol. 20 E οὐ γὰρ ἐμὸν ἐρῶ τὸν λόγον, κτλ.: Hor. Sat. II. ii. 2 nec meus hic sermo est sed quae praecepit Ofellus.

Οὐ δεινόν κτλ. With this passage, cp. Isocr. IX. 5—8, and X. 12 with its scornful reference to encomiasts of "humble-bees, salt-diets, and the like" (see Introd. § II. B (e)).

ὕμνους καὶ παιῶνας. Properly speaking ὕμνοι are odes set for the lyre, παιῶνες odes set for the flute and sung esp. in honour of Apollo. "The paean is a hymn (1) of supplication or propitiation during the pain or danger; (2) a thanksgiving after it is past" (see Smith, D. A. II. 307 s.v.).

Ἔρωτι, τηλικούτῳ ὄντι καὶ τοσούτῳ θεῷ, μηδὲ ἕνα πώποτε τοσού- B
των γεγονότων ποιητῶν πεποιηκέναι μηδὲν ἐγκώμιον; εἰ δὲ βούλει
αὖ σκέψασθαι τοὺς χρηστοὺς σοφιστάς, Ἡρακλέους μὲν καὶ
ἄλλων ἐπαίνους καταλογάδην ξυγγράφειν, ὥσπερ ὁ βέλτιστος
Πρόδικος· καὶ τοῦτο μὲν ἧττον καὶ θαυμαστόν, ἀλλ' ἔγωγε ἤδη
τινὶ ἐνέτυχον βιβλίῳ ἀνδρὸς σοφοῦ, ἐν ᾧ ἐνῆσαν ἄλες ἔπαινον
θαυμάσιον ἔχοντες πρὸς ὠφέλειαν, καὶ ἄλλα τοιαῦτα συχνὰ ἴδοις
ἂν ἐγκεκωμιασμένα· τὸ οὖν τοιούτων μὲν πέρι πολλὴν σπουδὴν C
ποιήσασθαι, Ἔρωτα δὲ μηδένα πω ἀνθρώπων τετολμηκέναι εἰς
ταυτηνὶ τὴν ἡμέραν ἀξίως ὑμνῆσαι· ἀλλ' οὕτως ἠμέληται τοσοῦτος
θεός. ταῦτα δή μοι δοκεῖ εὖ λέγειν Φαῖδρος. ἐγὼ οὖν ἐπιθυμῶ

177 B μηδὲν : μηδὲ Valckenaer		καὶ ante τοῦτο del. Thiersch		καὶ
ἧττον θαυμαστόν Wolf Thiersch		καὶ ante θαυμαστόν om. Steph. Bast.
ἀνδρὸς σοφοῦ T : om. B, Sz.		ὠφελίαν T : ὠφέλειαν B		C ⟨πολλοὺς⟩
πολλὴν Hirschig		ἀξίως T : ἀξιῶ B		⟨ὅτι⟩ οὕτως Wyttenbach
ἠμελῆσθαι τοσοῦτον θεόν Steph.		λέγειν : ψέγειν cj. Bdhm.

τηλικούτῳ. "A god so venerable": Phaedrus holds Eros to be the most
ancient of deities, see 178 B. The complaint was not entirely well-grounded,
since before this date (416 B.C.) hymns to Eros of a eulogistic character had
already been published by Sophocles (*Antig.* 781 ff.), and Euripides (*Hippol.*
525 ff.), and possibly others.

177 B εἰ δὲ βούλει. This phrase serves to introduce a fresh point, marking
the transition from poets to "sophists"; cp. 209 D, 220 D (εἰ δὲ βούλεσθε),
Lach. 188 C, etc.: but to add an infin., as here (σκέψασθαι), is unusual.

τοὺς χρηστοὺς σοφιστάς. "The worthy sophists"; considering that
Phaedrus is the speaker, we must suppose that the adj. is seriously meant,
not ironical.

καταλογάδην ξυγγράφειν. "Writing in prose," *oratione soluta.* Cp. Isocr.
II. 7 καὶ τῶν μετὰ μέτρου ποιημάτων καὶ τῶν καταλογάδην συγγραμμάτων: *Lysis*
204 D, *Laws* 811 E, 975 D.

ὥσπερ...Πρόδικος. This alludes to Prodicus's celebrated parable "The
Choice of Heracles," for which see Xen. *Mem.* II. i. 21 ff. For Prodicus of
Ceos, see Zeller *Presocr. Phil.* vol. II. pp. 416 ff., 473 (E. T.); Gomperz
Gr. Thinkers (E. T.) I. pp. 425 ff.

ἧττον καὶ. For the unusual position of καὶ after the comparative, cp. Xen.
Cyr. I. vi. 38 ταῦτα γὰρ μᾶλλον καὶ ἐξαπατᾶν δύναται.

ἐνῆσαν ἄλες. Logically, of course, the subject ought to be ἔπαινος, not
ἄλες. The same βιβλίον is alluded to in Isocr. x. 12 τῶν...τοὺς βομβυλιοὺς
καὶ τοὺς ἅλας καὶ τὰ τοιαῦτα βουληθέντων ἐπαινεῖν: its authorship is now
generally ascribed (as by Sauppe, Blass, Hug) to the rhetor Polycrates: see
further *Introd.* § II. B (e).

177 C τὸ οὖν...ὑμνῆσαι. The infin. may be explained (with Ast) as an ex.
of the infin. "indignantis," cp. Ar. *Nub.* 819 τὸ Δία νομίζειν ὄντα τηλικουτονί.

2—2

ἅμα μὲν τούτῳ ἔρανον εἰσενεγκεῖν καὶ χαρίσασθαι, ἅμα δ' ἐν τῷ
παρόντι πρέπον μοι δοκεῖ εἶναι ἡμῖν τοῖς παροῦσι κοσμῆσαι τὸν
θεόν. εἰ οὖν ξυνδοκεῖ καὶ ὑμῖν, γένοιτ' ἂν ἡμῖν ἐν λόγοις ἱκανὴ
διατριβή· δοκεῖ γάρ μοι χρῆναι ἕκαστον ἡμῶν λόγον εἰπεῖν ἔπαινον
Ἔρωτος ἐπὶ δεξιὰ ὡς ἂν δύνηται κάλλιστον, ἄρχειν δὲ Φαῖδρον
πρῶτον, ἐπειδὴ καὶ πρῶτος κατάκειται καὶ ἔστιν ἅμα πατὴρ τοῦ
λόγου. Οὐδείς σοι, ὦ Ἐρυξίμαχε, φάναι τὸν Σωκράτη, ἐναντία
ψηφιεῖται. οὔτε γὰρ ἄν που ἐγὼ ἀποφήσαιμι, ὃς οὐδέν φημι ἄλλο
E ἐπίστασθαι ἢ τὰ ἐρωτικά, οὔτε που Ἀγάθων καὶ Παυσανίας, οὐδὲ
μὴν Ἀριστοφάνης, ᾧ περὶ Διόνυσον καὶ Ἀφροδίτην πᾶσα ἡ δια-

177 C τουτωὶ Bdhm.   καὶ χαρίσασθαι del. Hartmann   D ⟨περὶ⟩
Ἔρωτος Hirschig   κάλλιστα W   ἄρχειν : λέγειν Hirschig   δὲ πρῶτον
Φαῖδρον vulg.   E ἀφροδίτη T   ἡ om. T

ἔρανον εἰσενεγκεῖν. *Symbolum dare*: cp. *Laws* 915 E, 927 C ὡς ἔρανον εἰσ-
φέροντα ἑαυτῷ—the only other instances of ἔρανος in Plato. For a defence of
the text against Hartmann, who excises καὶ χαρίσασθαι, see Vahlen *Op. Acad.*
II. 296.   This passage is echoed in Aristid. *Or.* t. I. p. 18.

177 D δοκεῖ γάρ μοι. "My sentence is," an official formula : cf. Dem. I. 2,
IV. 17.   Hence the point of Socrates' phrase ἐναντία ψηφιεῖται, four lines below.
λόγον...ἔπαινον. Cp. 214 B, *Phaedr.* 260 B συντιθεὶς λόγον ἔπαινον κατὰ
τοῦ ὄνου.
ἐπὶ δεξιά. "From left to right": cp. *Rep.* 420 E (with Adam's *note*);
Theaet. 175 E. Critias 2. 7 καὶ προπόσεις ὀρέγειν ἐπιδέξια.
κάλλιστον. Notice that, in Eryximachus' view, the first requisite is
κάλλος, and contrast the view of Socrates in 198 D ff.
πατὴρ τοῦ λόγου. *I.e.* εἰσηγητὴς τοῦ λ., as Plutarch explains (*Plat. Q.*
1000 F) : the same phrase recurs in *Phaedr.* 257 B, cp. *Theaet.* 164 E ὁ πατὴρ
τοῦ μύθου : *Lys.* 214 A πατέρες τῆς σοφίας καὶ ἡγεμόνες.
τὰ ἐρωτικά. The objects or principles with which ἡ ἐρωτικὴ τέχνη (*Phaedr.*
257 A) is concerned ; cp. 186 C, 212 B, *Lysis* 204 B. This passage is alluded to
by Themist. *Or.* XIII. p. 161, Max. Tyr. *diss.* XXIV. p. 288 : for its significance
here, see *Introd.* § II. B.
οὔτε που...καὶ. καὶ is used rather than οὔτε because Pausanias and Agathon
formed "ein Liebespaar" (Hug).
177 E περὶ Διόνυσον καὶ Ἀφροδίτην. There are many points of mutual
connexion between Eros, Dionysus and Aphrodite. Thus, Dionysus is the
patron-god of the theatre, as shown by the phrases οἱ περὶ τὸν Δ. τεχνῖται,
"actors" (Arist. *Probl.* XXX. 10), and Διονυσοκόλακες, "stage-lackeys" (Arist.
Rhet. III. 1205ᵃ 23); and on the comic stage erotic scenes were frequent.
Moreover, Dionysus was sometimes represented (as by Praxilla of Sicyon,
c. 450 B.C.) to be a son of Aphrodite; and in Aristoph. *fr. incert.* 490 (Df.)
οἶνος is termed Ἀφροδίτης γάλα. For the traditional inter-connexion of
"Wein, Weib und Gesang," we may also compare Solon 26 ἔργα δὲ Κυπρο-

τριβή, οὐδὲ ἄλλος οὐδεὶς τουτωνὶ ὧν ἐγὼ ὁρῶ. καίτοι οὐκ ἐξ ἴσου γίγνεται ἡμῖν τοῖς ὑστάτοις κατακειμένοις· ἀλλ᾽ ἐὰν οἱ πρόσθεν ἱκανῶς καὶ καλῶς εἴπωσιν, ἐξαρκέσει ἡμῖν. ἀλλὰ τύχῃ ἀγαθῇ καταρχέτω Φαῖδρος καὶ ἐγκωμιαζέτω τὸν Ἔρωτα. ταῦτα δὴ καὶ οἱ ἄλλοι πάντες ἄρα ξυνέφασάν τε καὶ ἐκέλευον ἅπερ ὁ Σωκράτης.

πάντων μὲν οὖν ἃ ἕκαστος εἶπεν, οὔτε πάνυ ὁ ᾽Αριστόδημος ἐμέ- 178 μνητο οὔτ᾽ αὖ ἐγὼ ἃ ἐκεῖνος ἔλεγε πάντα· ἃ δὲ μάλιστα καὶ ὧν ἔδοξέ μοι ἀξιομνημόνευτον, τούτων ὑμῖν ἐρῶ ἑκάστου τὸν λόγον.

VI. Πρῶτον μὲν γάρ, ὥσπερ λέγω, ἔφη Φαῖδρον ἀρξάμενον ἐνθένδε ποθὲν λέγειν, ὅτι μέγας θεὸς εἴη ὁ Ἔρως καὶ θαυμαστὸς ἐν

177 E καὶ καλῶς del. Naber ἡμῖν : ὑμῖν J.-U. ταῦτα : ταὐτὰ Usener ἄρα : ἅμα Wyttenbach 178 A ἃ BT : ὅσα mg. t ἀξιομνημόνευτον ⟨εἶναι⟩ TW : ἀξιομνημονεύτων b : ἀξιομνημόνευτα εἶναι vulg.: ἄξια μνημονεύειν cj. Liebhold ἕκαστα Bdhm. τὸν λόγον secl. Bdhm.

γενοῦς νῦν μοι φίλα καὶ Διονύσου | καὶ Μουσέων, ἃ τίθησ᾽ ἀνδράσιν εὐφροσύνας. Echoes of this phrase are to be found in Aristaen. I. ep. 3, p. 11; Plut. amat. 750 A; Lucian Symp. p. 444.

ἡμῖν τοῖς ὑστάτοις. ὕστατος here is equivalent to ἔσχατος as used in 175 C (where see note), i.e. placed on the extreme right.

ἐξαρκέσει ἡμῖν. "We shall be content," i.e. we shall not be called upon to speak: for the impers. ἐξαρκεῖ c. dat. cp. 176 C, 192 B, 210 C.

τύχῃ ἀγαθῇ. "In Gottes Namen" (Wolf); cp. Phileb. 57 E, Tim. 26 E.

πάντες ἄρα. For the position of ἄρα cp. Prot. 319 A ἦ καλόν, ἦν δ᾽ ἐγώ, τέχνημα ἄρα κέκτησαι : Rep. 358 C πολὺ γὰρ ἀμείνων ἄρα κτλ.

178 A ἀξιομνημόνευτον. We should expect rather the plural. We must suppose that the sentence is slightly confused, the original idea being to put ἃ δὲ μάλιστα ἔδοξέ μοι ἀξιομνημόνευτα (ταῦτα ἐρῶ), which was altered owing to the insertion, as an afterthought, of καὶ ὧν : then, instead of proceeding ὧν ἔδοξέ μοι ἄξιον τὸ μεμνῆσθαι (or μεμνῆσθαι τοῦ λόγου), the word originally in mind was put down, but in the sing.: but it is tempting to restore either ἀξιομνημόνευτ᾽ εἶναι (supposing εἶναι to be corrupted from a compendium), or ἄξιον μνημονεύειν. Prot. 343 A (ῥήματα βραχέα ἀξιομνημόνευτα) is the only other instance of the word in Plato: there may be an echo of the present passage in Xen. Symp. I. 1 ἐμοὶ δοκεῖ τῶν καλῶν κἀγαθῶν ἀνδρῶν ἔργα...ἀξιομνημόνευτα εἶναι. For the significance of the statement here made by Apollod., see Introd. § II. B (g).

Πρῶτον μὲν γάρ κτλ. For the discourse of Phaedrus (178 A—180 B) see Introd. § I. (analysis), § III. (1).

ὥσπερ λέγω. "As has been stated": the present tense (186 E, 193 A, etc.) is commoner than the past tense (εἶπον 173 C, 182 D, etc.) in this formula. The reference is to 177 D.

ἐνθένδε ποθὲν. "Roughly at this point," hinc fere : the combination recurs 199 C, Phaedr. 229 B, Euthyd. 275 E; so ἐντεῦθέν ποθεν Phaedr. 270 A, Rep. 524 C.

ἀνθρώποις τε καὶ θεοῖς, πολλαχῇ μὲν καὶ ἄλλῃ, οὐχ ἥκιστα δὲ
κατὰ τὴν γένεσιν. τὸ γὰρ ἐν τοῖς πρεσβύτατον εἶναι τὸν θεὸν
B τίμιον, ἢ δ᾽ ὅς· τεκμήριον δὲ τούτου· γονῆς γὰρ Ἔρωτος οὔτ᾽ εἰσὶν
οὔτε λέγονται ὑπ᾽ οὐδενὸς οὔτε ἰδιώτου οὔτε ποιητοῦ, ἀλλ᾽ Ἡσίοδος
πρῶτον μὲν Χάος φησὶ γενέσθαι,

αὐτὰρ ἔπειτα
Γαῖ᾽ εὐρύστερνος, πάντων ἔδος ἀσφαλὲς αἰεί,
ἠδ᾽ Ἔρος.

178 A ἄλλοι Stobaeus   πρεσβύτατον BW, Stob.: πρεσβυτάτοις T
τὸν θεὸν W: τῶν θεῶν BT   B ἦ δ᾽ ὅς del. Bast: ὄνειδος Creuzer   τεκμήριον δέ· τούτου (Ἔρωτος deleto) Naber   γοναὶ Stob., vulg.   Ἔρωτος:
Χάους cj. Bdhm.   Ἡσίοδος ⟨ὃς⟩ Heindorf   γαῖ...Ἔρος secl. Herm.

κατὰ τὴν γένεσιν. "In respect of his origin."
ἐν τοῖς πρεσβύτατον. For the doctrine of the antiquity of Eros, cp. Xen.
Symp. VIII. 1 τῷ μὲν χρόνῳ ἰσήλικος τοῖς ἀειγενέσι θεοῖς...Ἔρωτος : Ar. Av. 700
πρότερον δ᾽ οὐκ ἦν γένος ἀθανάτων, πρὶν Ἔρως συνέμιξεν ἅπαντα. Agathon,
in 195 A, expressly contradicts Phaedrus on this point. Bast excised ἦ δ᾽ ὅς
on the ground that "in fine periodi Platonicae non magis usurpatur quam
inquit Latinorum."
178 B τεκμήριον δὲ...γάρ. Cp. Critias 110 E, Apol. 40 C: Xen. Symp. IV.
17 τεκμήριον δέ· θαλλοφόρους γὰρ...ἐκλέγονται.
γονῆς...οὔτε λέγονται. This is a rash statement on the part of Phaedrus ;
for Alcaeus (fr. 13 Bgk.) makes Eros son of Zephyros and Iris ; Simonides
(fr. 43), son of Ares and Aphrodite; Euripides (Hippol. 534), son of Zeus ;
Sappho (fr. 132), of Gê and Uranos ; Ibycus (fr. 31), of Chaos ; see also the
statements in 199 D, 203 ff. infra. On the other hand ignorance or doubt as
to the parentage of Eros is expressed in Theocr. Id. XIII. 1, 2 οὐχ ἁμῖν τὸν
Ἔρωτα μόνοις ἔτεχ᾽...ᾧτινι τοῦτο θεῶν ποκα τέκνον ἔγεντο; Anth. Pal. v. 176.
7—8 πατρὸς δ᾽ οὐκέτ᾽ ἔχω φράζειν τίνος· οὔτε γὰρ Αἰθήρ, | οὐ Χθών φησι τεκεῖν
τὸν θρασύν, οὐ Πέλαγος. For the usual Greek assumption that the poets are
religious teachers, cp. Ar. Ran. 1054 τοῖς μὲν γὰρ παιδαρίοισιν | ἔστι διδά-
σκαλος ὅστις φράζει, τοῖς ἡβῶσιν δὲ ποιηταί : and see Adam, R. T. G. pp. 9 ff.
ἰδιώτου. For this distinction between the prose-writer and the poet, cp.
Phaedr. 258 D ; Laws 890 A ; Rep. 366 E. The term ἰδιώτης may be taken as
a survival of the time when the poet alone had his work "published "—at
religious festivals, theatrical shows, κῶμοι, etc.
Ἡσίοδος κτλ. The reference is to Theog. 116 ff. ἤτοι μὲν πρώτιστα Χάος
γένετ᾽, αὐτὰρ κτλ. Cp. Ar. Av. 693 ff. Χάος ἦν καὶ Νὺξ κτλ. The order of the
text I have adopted, in the passage following, is that proposed by Schanz,
except that he reads ὁμολογεῖ ⟨ὅς⟩ φησι, while Burnet, accepting the transposition, prints σύμφησι instead of ὁμολογεῖ φησι. Hug and others eject the
clause φησι...Ἔρωτα as a marginal prose paraphrase of the words of Hesiod ;
since, as it stands in the traditional order, the clause is obviously tautologous :
but tautology is in itself no objection, but rather characteristic of Ph.'s style

Ἡσιόδῳ δὲ καὶ Ἀκουσίλεως ὁμολογεῖ [φησὶ μετὰ τὸ Χάος δύο τούτω γενέσθαι, Γῆν τε καὶ Ἔρωτα]. Παρμενίδης δὲ τὴν Γένεσιν λέγει

πρώτιστον μὲν Ἔρωτα θεῶν μητίσατο πάντων·

οὕτω πολλαχόθεν ὁμολογεῖται ὁ Ἔρως ἐν τοῖς πρεσβύτατος εἶναι. C

178 B Ἡσιόδῳ...ὁμολογεῖ (quae in BT post πάντων extant) transposui, auctorr. Wolf Sz. Bt.   ὁμολογεῖ BT: ξύμφησιν Stob.: σύμφησιν Bt. φησὶ...Ἔρωτα secl. Hommel Jn. Hug: φησὶ...πάντων secl. Ast Turr. J.-U. φησὶ om. Stob.: ⟨ὃς⟩ φησὶ Schanz   Παρμενίδης...πάντων om. Stob., Heyne Wunder   τὴν Γένεσιν λέγει secl. Jn.: τὴν γένεσιν secl. Rettig C πρεσβυτάτοις Stob.

(see Teuffel in *Rhein. Mus.* XXIX. p. 133); and there is force in Hermann's remark "aegre intelligo quomodo aliquis clarissimis poetae verbis (paraphrasin) addendam existimaverit, multoque verisimilius videtur Hesiodi locum...postmodo adscriptum...irrepsisse." I bracket the clause as a gloss on ὁμολογεῖ. The clause Παρμενίδης...πάντων is rightly defended by Hug, against Voegelin and others, on the grounds that (1) οὕτω πολλαχόθεν in the following sentence is more appropriate after three than after two instances, and (2) Agathon in 195 C, when alluding to Phaedrus's speech, expressly mentions Ἡσίοδος καὶ Παρμενίδης. The authority of Hesiod is similarly cited by Plut. *amat.* 756 E.

Ἀκουσίλεως. Acusilaus of Argos, the "logographer," about B.C. 475 (?), wrote in the Ionic dialect several books of Genealogies, largely based on Hesiod (see the fragg. in A. Kordt, *De Acusilao*, 1903). But the reputed work of A., extant in the time of Hadrian, was probably a forgery: a collector of myths is not, properly speaking, a "logographer" at all (see Jevons, *Gk. Lit.* p. 299). Cp. Clem. Alex. VI. ii. 26. 7 τὰ δὲ Ἡσιόδου μετήλλαξαν εἰς πεζὸν λόγον καὶ ὡς ἴδια ἐξένεγκαν Εὔμηλός τε καὶ Ἀκουσίλαος οἱ ἱστοριογράφοι. Hug, retaining the order of the MSS., would explain the fact that A. is put last as due to his being an ἰδιώτης, the others ποιηταί.

Παρμενίδης. See Parmen. *frag.* 132 (Karsten), R. and P. 101 A ; Arist. *Met.* I. 4. 984[b] 25 ; Plut. *amat.* 756 F. It is to be presumed that the famous Eleate relegated this theogony to his "Way of Opinion." Cp. Spenser's lines (*H. to Love*), "Or who alive can perfectly declare The wondrous cradle of thine infancie... For ere this worlds still moving mightie masse Out of great Chaos ugly prison crept... Love... Gan reare his head, by Clotho being waked."

τὴν Γένεσιν...μητίσατο. Hermann and Hug follow Stallbaum in supplying Γένεσις as the subject of μητίσατο: cp. *Phaedo* 94 D οὐ λέγει τὸν Ὀδυσσέα στῆθος δὲ πλήξας κραδίην ἠνίπαπε μύθῳ. For the personification of γένεσις, cp. Hom. *Il.* XIV. 201 Ὠκεανόν τε θεῶν γένεσιν καὶ μητέρα Τηθύν (cited by Plato in *Theaet.* 180 D, *Crat.* 402 B). Plutarch (*loc. cit.*) differs by making Ἀφροδίτη the subject of μητίσατο. It is, of course, possible that another (suppressed) subject is intended; since we do not know what the context was in the original.

πρεσβύτατος δὲ ὢν μεγίστων ἀγαθῶν ἡμῖν αἴτιός ἐστιν. οὐ γὰρ
ἔγωγ' ἔχω εἰπεῖν ὅ τι μεῖζόν ἐστιν ἀγαθὸν εὐθὺς νέῳ ὄντι ἢ
ἐραστὴς χρηστὸς καὶ ἐραστῇ παιδικά. ὃ γὰρ χρὴ ἀνθρώποις
ἡγεῖσθαι παντὸς τοῦ βίου τοῖς μέλλουσι καλῶς βιώσεσθαι, τοῦτο
οὔτε συγγένεια οἷά τε ἐμποιεῖν οὕτω καλῶς οὔτε τιμαὶ οὔτε
D πλοῦτος οὔτ' ἄλλο οὐδὲν ὡς ἔρως. λέγω δὲ δὴ τί τοῦτο; τὴν ἐπὶ
μὲν τοῖς αἰσχροῖς αἰσχύνην, ἐπὶ δὲ τοῖς καλοῖς φιλοτιμίαν· οὐ
γὰρ ἔστιν ἄνευ τούτων οὔτε πόλιν οὔτε ἰδιώτην μεγάλα καὶ καλὰ
ἔργα ἐξεργάζεσθαι. φημὶ τοίνυν ἐγὼ ἄνδρα ὅστις ἐρᾷ, εἴ τι
αἰσχρὸν ποιῶν κατάδηλος γίγνοιτο ἢ πάσχων ὑπό του δι' ἀναν-

---

178 C πρεσβύτατος δὲ ὤν : πρὸς δὲ τούτῳ τῶν Bast ⟨μέγιστός τε καὶ⟩
μεγίστων Bdhm. αἴτιος ἡμῖν Stob. ⟨ἢ⟩ παιδικά Hommel Jn. εὐγένεια
Wyttenbach καλῶς ⟨οὔτε κάλλος⟩ vulg.: οὕτως οὔτε κάλλος Reynd. Jacobs

---

178 C πρεσβύτατος δὲ ὤν κτλ. The partic. gives the impression of a
causal connexion—as if beneficence must be in direct proportion to antiquity!
μεγίστων...αἴτιος. Cp. 197 c infra; Ar. Plut. 469 ἀγαθῶν ἁπάντων αἰτίαν.
εὐθὺς νέῳ ὄντι. "From his earliest youth": this properly applies only to
the παιδικά. With παιδικά supply χρηστά. For a similar estimate of the
value of φίλοι, see Lys. 211 E, Xen. Mem. II. 4. 1 ff.
ἀνθρώποις...βίου. For ἡγεῖσθαι c. dat. of person and gen. of thing, cp.
Hom. Od. XXIII. 134 ἡμῖν ἡγείσθω ὀρχηθμοῖο: Xen. Cyr. VIII. 7. 1 τοῦ χόρου
ἡγήσατο Πέρσαις. It would be easy, however, by inserting διά after the
termin. -αι, to restore a favourite Platonic phrase διὰ παντὸς τοῦ βίου (cp.
203 D, Phil. 39 E).
συγγένεια. "Kindred," implying nobility of kin: for the concrete use cp.
Gorg. 472 B, Laws 730 B, 874 A, etc., and esp. Rep. 491 C κάλλος καὶ πλοῦτος
καὶ ἰσχὺς σώματος καὶ ξυγγένεια ἐρρωμένη ἐν πόλει. Taking συγγένεια here in a
similar sense, we can dispense with Wyttenbach's plausible conj., εὐγένεια
(for which cp. Euthyd. 279 B, Ar. Rhet. II. 15, Soph. Antig. 38), which
Reynders adopts.
178 D αἰσχύνην...φιλοτιμίαν. Cp. Lys. XIV. 2, and 42 (in Alcib.) ἐπὶ μὲν
τοῖς καλοῖς αἰσχύνεσθαι, ἐπὶ δὲ τοῖς κακοῖς φιλοτιμεῖσθαι, "taking glory for
shame and shame for glory." Remembering that Phaedrus was a professed
admirer of Lysias, we may, perhaps, recognize here a verbal echo. For a
discussion of αἰσχύνη (not distinguished from αἰδώς) see Arist. Eth. Nic. IV.
ix. 1128ᵇ 10, and Rhet. II. vi. 1383ᵇ 12.
οὔτε πόλιν οὔτε ἰδιώτην. Notice that in the subsequent treatment of these
two heads the order is reversed (to secure rhetorical "Chiasmus").
εἴ τι αἰσχρὸν κτλ. Cp. Xen. Cyneg. XII. 20 ὅταν μὲν γάρ τις ὁρᾶται ὑπὸ τοῦ
ἐρωμένου ἅπας ἑαυτοῦ ἐστι βελτίων καὶ οὔτε λέγει οὔτε ποιεῖ αἰσχρὰ οὐδὲ κακά,
ἵνα μὴ ὀφθῇ ὑπ' ἐκείνων. Also 194 c infra.
ἢ πάσχων κτλ. Cp. "It hath been said by them of old time, An eye for an
eye, and a tooth for a tooth." Ordinary Greek ethics approved of retaliation:

δρίαν μὴ ἀμυνόμενος, οὔτ᾽ ἂν ὑπὸ πατρὸς ὀφθέντα οὕτως ἀλγῆσαι
οὔτε ὑπὸ ἑταίρων οὔτε ὑπ᾽ ἄλλου οὐδενὸς ὡς ὑπὸ παιδικῶν.
ταὐτὸν δὲ τοῦτο καὶ τὸν ἐρώμενον ὁρῶμεν, ὅτι διαφερόντως τοὺς Ε
ἐραστὰς αἰσχύνεται, ὅταν ὀφθῇ ἐν αἰσχρῷ τινὶ ὤν. εἰ οὖν μηχανή
τις γένοιτο ὥστε πόλιν γενέσθαι ἢ στρατόπεδον ἐραστῶν τε καὶ
παιδικῶν, οὐκ ἔστιν ὅπως ἂν ἄμεινον οἰκήσειαν τὴν ἑαυτῶν [ἢ]
ἀπεχόμενοι πάντων τῶν αἰσχρῶν καὶ φιλοτιμούμενοι πρὸς ἀλλή-
λους· καὶ μαχόμενοί γ᾽ ἂν μετ᾽ ἀλλήλων οἱ τοιοῦτοι νικῷεν ἂν 179
ὀλίγοι ὄντες, ὡς ἔπος εἰπεῖν, πάντας ἀνθρώπους. ἐρῶν γὰρ ἀνὴρ

178 E   τὸν ἐραστὴν Hirschig   ἢ στρατόπεδον secl. J.-U.   ⟨ἐξ⟩ ἐραστῶν
Hirschig   ἑαυτῶν ⟨πόλιν⟩ Hirschig   ἢ seclusi, auctorr. Rückert Jn.
Bdhm. Sz. Naber: καὶ J.-U.   καὶ ⟨ἐπὶ τοῖς καλοῖς⟩ φ. Ast   179 A   γ᾽ ἂν
BT: γ᾽ αὖ Verm. J.-U.: δ᾽ γ᾽ ἂν W

---

cp. Xen. *Cyrop.* VIII. 7. 7; see Dobbs, *Philos. and Popular Morals,* etc. p. 39.
For another incentive to courage, see *Rep.* 467 B.

178 E   ταὐτὸν δὲ τοῦτο. "In exactly similar fashion," adverbial accus.:
so ταὐτὰ ταῦτα *Meno* 90 E.

τοὺς ἐραστάς. The plural is due to the fact that it was usual for a number
of ἐρασταί to pay court to the same παιδικά (cp. *Charm.* 154 A).

εἰ οὖν μηχανή τις κτλ. Here Ph. passes on to his second head,—the benefits
derived from Eros in civic and national life (πόλιν, 178 D *supra*). For the
phrase cp. *Laws* 640 B εἰ δ᾽ ἦν τις μηχανή κτλ.: *Parm.* 132 D, *Phileb.* 16 A.

στρατόπεδον ἐραστῶν. It is noteworthy that Xen. (*Symp.* VIII. 32) puts a
similar statement in the mouth of Pausanias—Παυσανίας γε...εἴρηκεν ὡς καὶ
στράτευμα ἀλκιμώτατον ἂν γένοιτο ἐκ παιδικῶν τε καὶ ἐραστῶν (cp. *Introd.*
§ VIII. ad fin.). Cp. also Xen. *Cyrop.* VII. 1. 30 οὐκ ἔστιν ἰσχυροτέρα φάλαγξ
ἢ ὅταν ἐκ φίλων συμμάχων ἠθροισμένη ᾖ. This principle was exemplified in the
famous ἱερὸς λόχος of the Thebans, organized by Gorgidas (or Epaminondas),
which fought first at Leuctra, 371 B.C., see Athen. XIII. 561 F, 602 A. A
Roman analogy is afforded by Scipio's φίλων ἴλη. The parallel in Xenophon
is of itself sufficient to refute Jahn's athetesis of ἢ στρατόπεδον.

οὐκ ἔστιν ὅπως ἂν κτλ. Hug, retaining ἢ before ἀπεχόμενοι, would supply,
with the participles, from the context "welche Gefühle allein durch den Eros
in wirksamer Weise erregt werden." This, however, is exceedingly awkward;
and his further remark that οὐκ ἄμεινον οἰκήσειαν ἂν ἢ ἀπεχόμενοι is equivalent
to ἄριστ᾽ ἂν οἰκ. ἀπεχ. does nothing to lessen the difficulty. By ejecting ἢ, as
a very natural interpolation after the comparative by a copyist careless of
the sense, we obtain the meaning required—"it would be impossible for
them to secure a better constitution of their city, since thus they would
abstain" etc.

179 A   μαχόμενοι κτλ. Cp. *Rep.* 471 D ἄριστ᾽ ἂν μάχοιντο τῷ ἥκιστα
ἀπολείπειν ἀλλήλους...ἄμαχοι ἂν εἶεν: Xen. *Symp.* VIII. 32 ff.

ὑπὸ παιδικῶν ὀφθῆναι ἢ λιπὼν τάξιν ἢ ὅπλα ἀποβαλὼν ἧττον ἂν
δή που δέξαιτο ἢ ὑπὸ πάντων τῶν ἄλλων, καὶ πρὸ τούτου τεθνάναι
ἂν πολλάκις ἔλοιτο· καὶ μὴν ἐγκαταλιπεῖν γε τὰ παιδικὰ ἢ μὴ
βοηθῆσαι κινδυνεύοντι, οὐδεὶς οὕτω κακὸς ὅντινα οὐκ ἂν αὐτὸς ὁ
"Ερως ἔνθεον ποιήσειε πρὸς ἀρετήν, ὥσθ᾿ ὅμοιον εἶναι τῷ ἀρίστῳ
B φύσει· καὶ ἀτεχνῶς, ὃ ἔφη "Ομηρος, " μένος ἐμπνεῦσαι" ἐνίοις τῶν
ἡρώων τὸν θεόν, τοῦτο ὁ "Ερως τοῖς ἐρῶσι παρέχει γιγνόμενον
παρ᾿ αὐτοῦ.

VII. Καὶ μὴν ὑπεραποθνήσκειν γε μόνοι ἐθέλουσιν οἱ ἐρῶντες, οὐ μόνον ὅτι ἄνδρες, ἀλλὰ καὶ αἱ γυναῖκες. τούτου δὲ καὶ ἡ

---

179 A μὴν B: μὴ T　　　hiatum ante οὐδεὶς notav. J.-U.　　B ⟨πᾶσι⟩
παρέχει Orelli　　οὐ μόνον ὅτι: οὐ μόνον οἱ Steph. Sz.: οὐχ ὅτι Fischer J.-U.
αἱ B: om. T　　τούτου: δοκεῖ Verm.

λιπὼν τάξιν ἢ ὅπλα ἀποβαλών.　"The principal military offences at Athens
were dealt with by one law. A citizen was liable to indictment, and, if con-
victed, to disfranchisement for (1) Failure to join the army—ἀστρατείας:
(2) Cowardice in battle—δειλίας: (3) Desertion of his post—λιποταξίου:
(4) Desertion from the army—λιποστρατίου. Of these terms, λιποταξίου was
that used in the widest sense, and might include any of the others" (Smith,
D. A. I. 212ᵇ). Cp. Rep. 468 A, Laws 943 D ff., and the compounds ῥίψασπις
(Laws 944 B, C; Ar. Vesp. 19), ἀσπιδαποβλής (Vesp. 592). The conduct of the
ideal ἐραστής on such an occasion is shown in 220 E infra.

κινδυνεύοντι.　For the sing. dat. referring to παιδικοῖς, cp. Phaedr. 239 A,
and 184 D infra. After κινδυνεύοντι we should expect the sentence to conclude
with οὐδεὶς τολμῴη ἂν or the like: the fact that a new ending is substituted
may be regarded (with Ast) as due to the agitation (real or pretended) of the
speaker "vom furor eroticus ergriffen."

ἔνθεον πρὸς ἀρετήν.　For ἔνθεος, "god-inhabited," "inspired," cp. Ion 533 E
ἔνθεοι ὄντες καὶ κατεχόμενοι: ibid. 534 B and below, 180 B.　φύσει, denoting
"natural" temper, is here opposed to this supervenient grace. For the
thought cp. Spenser (H. to Love), "(The lover) dreads no danger, nor mis-
fortune feares...Thou cariest him to that which he hath eyde Through seas,
through flames, through thousand swords and speares."

179 B "Ομηρος. See Il. x. 482 τῷ δ᾿ ἔμπνευσε μένος γλαυκῶπις 'Αθήνη:
ib. xv. 262, Od. ix. 381. Cp. the (Lacedaemonian) term εἰσπνήλας for ἐραστής:
also Xen. Symp. iv. 15.

ὑπεραποθνήσκειν.　Cp. Isocr. Hel. 217 C ἧς ἕνεκα πολλοὶ τῶν ἡμιθέων ἀποθνήσκειν ἠθέλησαν.

οὐ μόνον ὅτι.　This expression may be defended by Thuc. iv. 85. 3 καὶ γὰρ
οὐ μόνον ὅτι αὐτοὶ ἀνθίστασθε, ἀλλὰ καὶ οἷς ἂν ἐπίω, ἧσσόν τις ἐμοὶ πρόσεισιν:
Arist. Pol. vii. 11. 1331ᵃ 11 οὐχ ὅτι τείχη μόνον περιβλητέον (with Newman's
note): Xen. Mem. ii. 9. 8. Jahn's οὐχ ὅτι would give, as Teuffel argues, the

Πελίου θυγάτηρ Ἄλκηστις ἱκανὴν μαρτυρίαν παρέχεται ὑπὲρ τοῦδε τοῦ λόγου εἰς τοὺς Ἕλληνας, ἐθελήσασα μόνη ὑπὲρ τοῦ αὐτῆς ἀνδρὸς ἀποθανεῖν, ὄντων αὐτῷ πατρός τε καὶ μητρός· οὓς C ἐκείνη τοσοῦτον ὑπερεβάλετο τῇ φιλίᾳ διὰ τὸν ἔρωτα, ὥστε ἀποδεῖξαι αὐτοὺς ἀλλοτρίους ὄντας τῷ υἱεῖ καὶ ὀνόματι μόνον προσήκοντας· καὶ τοῦτ' ἐργασαμένη τὸ ἔργον οὕτω καλὸν ἔδοξεν ἐργάσασθαι οὐ μόνον ἀνθρώποις ἀλλὰ καὶ θεοῖς, ὥστε πολλῶν πολλὰ καὶ καλὰ ἐργασαμένων εὐαριθμήτοις δή τισιν ἔδοσαν τοῦτο γέρας οἱ θεοί, ἐξ Ἅιδου ἀνεῖναι πάλιν τὴν ψυχήν, ἀλλὰ τὴν ἐκείνης ἀνεῖσαν ἀγασθέντες τῷ ἔργῳ· οὕτω καὶ θεοὶ τὴν περὶ τὸν ἔρωτα D

179 B παρέχεσθαι Verm. ὑπέρ...Ἕλληνας secl. Bdhm.: ὑπέρ... λόγου secl. Wolf Sz., post Ἕλληνας posuit Bast: ὑπὲρ τοῦδε del. et τοῦ λόγου post τούτου δὲ posuit Steph.: ὑπὲρ τοῦδε del. Wyttenbach Winckelmann C κατεργασαμένων Methodius δὴ τοῦτο TW τὸ γέρας vulg. ἀνιέναι Hommel ἀλλ' αὐτὴν ἐκείνην Earle τῷ ἔργῳ secl. Baiter: τῷ...θεοὶ secl. Bdhm.

---

wrong sense "I do not say men do so, cela va sans dire." We may explain οὐ μόνον ὅτι as elliptical for οὐ μόνον (λέγω) ὅτι.

ἄνδρες...αἱ γυναῖκες. The addition of the article serves to signalize the second case as the more striking: cp. I. Alcib. 105 B ἐν Ἕλλησιν...ἐν τοῖς βαρβάροις: Phileb. 45 E, ib. 64 C; Vahlen on Arist. Poet. IV. 1449ᵃ 1.

Ἄλκηστις. Besides Euripides, Phrynichus (438 B.C.) and later Antiphanes (354 B.C.) made Alcestis the theme of a tragedy: see also the Skolion by Praxilla in Bergk P. L. G. III. § 1293.

ὑπὲρ τοῦδε τοῦ λόγου. "In support of my argument."

εἰς τοὺς Ἕλληνας. Cp. Protag. 312 A εἰς τοὺς Ἕλληνας σαυτὸν σοφιστὴν παρέχων: Gorg. 526 B: Thuc. I. 33. 2.

ἐθελήσασα μόνη κτλ. Cp. Eur. Alc. 15 ff. πάντας δ' ἐλέγξας...Οὐχ εὗρε πλὴν γυναικὸς ἥτις ἤθελε | θανεῖν πρὸ κείνου.

179 C οὓς ἐκείνη κτλ. See Eur. Alc. 683 ff. where the appeal of Admetus is thus answered by his father Pheres: οὐ γὰρ πατρῷον τόνδ' ἐδεξάμην νόμον | παίδων προθνήσκειν πατέρας οὐδ' Ἑλληνικόν.

ἀλλοτρίους. Admetus might have described his ἀλλότριοι προσήκοντες as "a little more than kin and less than kind."

εὐαριθμήτοις. A grandiose synonym for ὀλίγοις.

ἔδοσαν τοῦτο γέρας...ἀγασθέντες. Cp. Phaedr. 259 B ὃ γέρας παρὰ θεῶν ἔχουσιν ἀνθρώποις διδόναι, τάχ' ἂν δοῖεν ἀγασθέντες. ἄγαμαι can take either the genitive (Rep. 426 D, etc.) or the accus. (Symp. 219 D, etc.). This passage is alluded to by Plut. amat. 762 A λέγοντες ἐξ ᾅδου τοῖς ἐρωτικοῖς ἄνοδον εἰς φῶς ὑπάρχειν.

οὕτω...τιμῶσιν. Cp. Xen. Symp. VIII. 28 ἀλλὰ καὶ θεοὶ καὶ ἥρωες τὴν τῆς ψυχῆς φιλίαν περὶ πλείονος...ποιοῦνται.

σπουδήν τε καὶ ἀρετὴν μάλιστα τιμῶσιν. Ὀρφέα δὲ τὸν Οἰάγρου
ἀτελῆ ἀπέπεμψαν ἐξ "Αιδου, φάσμα δείξαντες τῆς γυναικὸς ἐφ᾽
ἣν ἧκεν, αὐτὴν δὲ οὐ δόντες, ὅτι μαλθακίζεσθαι ἐδόκει, ἅτε ὢν
κιθαρῳδός, καὶ οὐ τολμᾶν ἕνεκα τοῦ ἔρωτος ἀποθνήσκειν ὥσπερ
Ἄλκηστις, ἀλλὰ διαμηχανᾶσθαι ζῶν εἰσιέναι εἰς "Αιδου. τοιγάρτοι διὰ ταῦτα δίκην αὐτῷ ἐπέθεσαν, καὶ ἐποίησαν τὸν θάνατον
E αὐτοῦ ὑπὸ γυναικῶν γενέσθαι, οὐχ ὥσπερ Ἀχιλλέα τὸν τῆς Θέτι-
δος υἱὸν ἐτίμησαν καὶ εἰς μακάρων νήσους ἀπέπεμψαν, ὅτι πεπυ-
σμένος παρὰ τῆς μητρὸς ὡς ἀποθανοῖτο ἀποκτείνας "Εκτορα, μὴ
ἀποκτείνας δὲ τοῦτον οἴκαδ᾽ ἐλθὼν γηραιὸς τελευτήσοι, ἐτόλμησεν

179 D μάλιστα τιμῶσιν secl. Bdhm.   φάντασμα TW   τολμῶν Naber
διαμηχανήσασθαι W, vulg.   ζῆν ἰέναι T   ἐποίησαν ἔργον γενέσθαι γυναικῶν
Naber   E καὶ...ἀπέπεμψαν damnat Naber   ἀποθάνοιτο T : ἀποθάνοι B
ἀποκτείνας δὲ τοῦτον B : ποιήσας δὲ τοῦτο T   οἴκαδ᾽ T : οἴκαδε δ᾽ B

179 D **Ὀρφέα.** For the legend of Orpheus and his wife Eurydice, see
Paus. IX. 30, Virg. *Georg.* IV. 454 ff., Ovid *Met.* X. 1 ff. Phaedrus modifies
the usual story (1) by making Eurydice a φάσμα, and Orpheus consequently
ἀτελής (cp. Stesichorus' treatment of the Helen-legend, followed also by
Euripides in his *Helena*, and *Phaedr.* 243 B): (2) by making O.'s descent
an act of μαλακία rather than of τόλμα (as Hermesianax 2. 7, Ov. *Met.* X. 13
ad Styga Taenaria *est ausus* descendere porta): (3) by representing O.'s death
to be a penalty for this cowardice rather than for his irreverence to Dionysus
(as Aeschylus *Bassarai*, etc.). For Orpheus and Orphism in general, see
Miss J. Harrison *Proleg.* pp. 455 ff.

ἅτε ὢν κιθαρῳδός. As if the "soft Lydian airs" of the cithara conduced to
effeminacy. For the cithara, as distinguished from the λύρα, see *Rep.*
399 D—E (with Adam's *note*). It is worth noticing that Spenser (*H. to
Love*) cites Orpheus as an instance of ἔνθεος τόλμα—"Orpheus daring to
provoke the yre Of damned fiends, to get his love retyre."

τοιγάρτοι διὰ ταῦτα. Cp. Isocr. VII. 52, Andoc. I. 108, Dem. XXIII. 203;
an example of the rhetorical trick of amplitude. Phaedrus, as Hug observes,
is blind to the obvious corollary that Eros sometimes fails to implant τόλμα.
179 E **οὐχ ὥσπερ.** "Whereas, on the contrary": cp. *Gorg.* 522 A, 189 C
infra.

εἰς μακάρων νήσους. Cp. Pind. *Ol.* II. 78 ff., *Skolion* ap. Bgk. *P. L. G.* III. 1290.
Achilles, after death, is variously located, by Homer (*Od.* XI. 467 ff.) in Hades,
by Ibycus (*fr.* 37) in Elysium, by Arctinus and others in Leuke ("white-
island"), for which see Pind. *Nem.* IV. 49, and Rohde *Psyche* II. 369 ff. For
the situation of the μ. νῆσοι, see Strabo I. 3: cp. Adam *R. T. G.* 135 f.

ὡς ἀποθανοῖτο. See Hom. *Il.* XVIII. 96 αὐτίκα γάρ τοι ἔπειτα μεθ᾽ "Εκτορα
πότμος ἑτοῖμος : *ibid.* IX. 410 ff.; *Apol.* 28 C, D.

οἴκαδ᾽...τελευτήσοι. This clause is echoed, as Wolf observed, by Aeschines
I. 145 ἐπανελθὼν οἴκαδε γηραιὸς...ἀποθανεῖται.

ἐλέσθαι βοηθήσας τῷ ἐραστῇ Πατρόκλῳ καὶ τιμωρήσας οὐ μόνον
ὑπεραποθανεῖν ἀλλὰ καὶ ἐπαποθανεῖν τετελευτηκότι· ὅθεν δὴ καὶ 180
ὑπεραγασθέντες οἱ θεοὶ διαφερόντως αὐτὸν ἐτίμησαν, ὅτι τὸν
ἐραστὴν οὕτω περὶ πολλοῦ ἐποιεῖτο. Αἰσχύλος δὲ φλυαρεῖ φάσ-
κων Ἀχιλλέα Πατρόκλου ἐρᾶν, ὃς ἦν καλλίων οὐ μόνον Πατρόκλου
ἀλλ᾽ ἄρα καὶ τῶν ἡρώων ἁπάντων, καὶ ἔτι ἀγένειος, ἔπειτα νεώ-
τερος πολύ, ὥς φησιν Ὅμηρος. ἀλλὰ γὰρ τῷ ὄντι μάλιστα μὲν
ταύτην τὴν ἀρετὴν οἱ θεοὶ τιμῶσι τὴν περὶ τὸν ἔρωτα, μᾶλλον B
μέντοι θαυμάζουσι καὶ ἄγανται καὶ εὖ ποιοῦσιν, ὅταν ὁ ἐρώμενος
τὸν ἐραστὴν ἀγαπᾷ, ἢ ὅταν ὁ ἐραστὴς τὰ παιδικά. θειότερον γὰρ
ἐραστὴς παιδικῶν· ἔνθεος γάρ ἐστι. διὰ ταῦτα καὶ τὸν Ἀχιλλέα

179 E βοηθῆσαι W   Πατρόκλῳ del. Naber   180 A Αἰσχύλος...
Ὅμηρος del. Valckenaer   ἀλλ᾽ ἄρα W : ἀλλὰ ἄρα T : ἀλλὰ B : ἀλλ᾽ ἅμα Bt.
καὶ...ἀγένειος post πολύ transp. Petersen   B ἐραστὴς...ἐστι secl. Bdhm.

βοηθήσας. Cp. Arist. Rhet. I. 3. 1359ᵃ 3 οἷον Ἀχιλλέα ἐπαινοῦσιν ὅτι ἐβοή-
θησε τῷ ἑταίρῳ Πατρόκλῳ εἰδὼς ὅτι δεῖ αὐτὸν ἀποθανεῖν ἐξὸν ζῆν. Isocrates (in
Panegyr. 53) lauds the Athenians for a similar nobility of conduct.
180 A ἐπαποθανεῖν. This and 208 D are the only classical instances cited
of this compound ; nor does there seem to be another class. instance of ὑπερα-
γασθῆναι.
Αἰσχύλος δὲ φλυαρεῖ. The reference is to Aesch. Myrmidons (fr. 135,
136 N.). Sophocles, too, wrote an Ἀχιλλέως Ἐρασταί: cp. also Xen. Symp.
VIII. 31. Achilles, like Asclepius and others, was worshipped in some places
(e.g. Epirus) as a god, in others (e.g. Elis) as a hero.
ἀλλ᾽ ἄρα καὶ. "Ἄρα h. l. stare potest, valet: nimirum" (Wyttenbach):
for ἄρα affirmative in a universal statement, cp. 177 E, Rep. 595 A. To alter
to ἅμα, as Burnet, is unnecessary.
καλλίων. For the beauty of Achilles, see Il. II. 673. Ov. Trist. II. 411
refers to Sophocles' play—"nec nocet auctori mollem qui fecit Achillem":
cp. Lucian dial. mort. 18. 1.
ἀγένειος. The hero is so represented in art; and the Schol. ad Il. I. 131
applies to him the epithet γυναικοπρόσωπος. Similarly Apollo, in Callim. H.
II. 36 f. οὔποτε Φοίβου | θηλείησ᾽ οὐδ᾽ ὅσσον ἐπὶ χνόος ἦλθε παρειαῖς.
νεώτερος. See Il. XI. 786 γενεῇ μὲν ὑπέρτερός ἐστιν Ἀχιλλεύς | πρεσβύτερος
δὲ σύ (sc. Πάτροκλος) ἐσσι: and Schol. ad Il. XXIII. 94. For the relative ages
of παιδικά and ἐραστής, see 181 B ff. infra; Xen. Anab. II. 6. 28 αὐτὸς δὲ (sc.
Meno) παιδικὰ εἶχε Θαρύπαν ἀγένειος ὢν γενειῶντα (mentioned as an enormity);
Ov. Met. X. 83 ff.
μάλιστα μὲν...μᾶλλον μέντοι. This savours of a Hibernicism: cp. Gorg.
509 B μέγιστον τῶν κακῶν...καὶ ἔτι τούτου μεῖζον.
180 B θαυμάζουσι. Cp. Rep. 551 A ἐπαινοῦσί τε καὶ θαυμάζουσι καὶ εἰς
τὰς ἀρχὰς ἄγουσι: Xen. Symp. IV. 44.
θειότερον...ἔνθεος. Cp. 179 A, 209 B ad init.; Schol. ad Eur. Hippol. 144

τῆς Ἀλκήστιδος μᾶλλον ἐτίμησαν, εἰς᾿μακάρων νήσους ἀποπέμψαντες.

Οὕτω δὴ ἔγωγέ φημι Ἔρωτα θεῶν καὶ πρεσβύτατον καὶ τιμιώτατον καὶ κυριώτατον εἶναι εἰς ἀρετῆς καὶ εὐδαιμονίας κτῆσιν ἀνθρώποις καὶ ζῶσι καὶ τελευτήσασιν.

C VIII. Φαῖδρον μὲν τοιοῦτόν τινα λόγον ἔφη εἰπεῖν, μετὰ δὲ Φαῖδρον ἄλλους τινὰς εἶναι, ὧν οὐ πάνυ διεμνημόνευεν· οὓς παρεὶς τὸν Παυσανίου λόγον διηγεῖτο. εἰπεῖν δ᾿ αὐτὸν ὅτι Οὐ καλῶς μοι δοκεῖ, ὦ Φαῖδρε, προβεβλῆσθαι ἡμῖν ὁ λόγος, τὸ ἁπλῶς οὕτως παρηγγέλθαι ἐγκωμιάζειν Ἔρωτα. εἰ μὲν γὰρ εἷς ἦν ὁ Ἔρως, καλῶς ἂν εἶχε, νῦν δὲ οὐ γάρ ἐστιν εἷς· μὴ ὄντος δὲ ἑνός, D ὀρθότερόν ἐστι πρότερον προρρηθῆναι ὁποῖον δεῖ ἐπαινεῖν. ἐγὼ οὖν πειράσομαι τοῦτο ἐπανορθώσασθαι, πρῶτον μὲν Ἔρωτα φράσαι ὃν δεῖ ἐπαινεῖν, ἔπειτα ἐπαινέσαι ἀξίως τοῦ θεοῦ. πάντες γὰρ

180 B τῆς Ἀλκήστιδος del. Schütz Bdhm.   καὶ post θεῶν om. T
καὶ τιμιώτατον om. T (add. in mg. t)   κυριώτερον T   C εἶναι del.
Hirschig: εἰπεῖν postea idem cj.   D ὁποῖον: ὁπότερον Herm.

ἔνθεοι λέγονται οἱ ὑπὸ φάσματός τινος ἀφαιρεθέντες τὸν νοῦν, καὶ ὑπ᾿ ἐκείνου τοῦ θεοῦ τοῦ φασματοποιοῦ κατεχόμενοι καὶ τὰ δοκοῦντα ἐκείνῳ ποιοῦντες. See Rohde *Psyche* II. 19 ff.

Οὕτω δὴ κτλ. In this epilogue καὶ πρεσβ. καὶ τιμ. summarize the first part of the speech; καὶ κυριώτατον κτλ., the second part. Cp. Isocr. *Hel.* 218 D κάλλους...μετέσχεν ὃ σεμνότατον καὶ τιμιώτατον καὶ θειότατον τῶν ὄντων ἐστίν.

180 C ἄλλους τινὰς εἶναι. The construction here has been misunderstood: Hirschig proposed to write εἰπεῖν for εἶναι, while Hug bids us supply λέγοντας. Evidently both suppose that ἄλλοι τινές mean persons, but it seems better to take them to be λόγοι and to construe μετὰ Φαῖδρον as a compendium for μετὰ τὸν Φαίδρου λόγον. By this means we secure the word required, λόγους, as the antecedent to ὧν: for διαμνημονεύειν would be less naturally used of a person than of a speech (cp. 178 A πάντων...ἐμέμνητο). For the brachylogy, cp. Thuc. I. 71. 2 ἀρχαιότροπα ὑμῶν τὰ ἐπιτηδεύματα πρὸς αὐτούς ἐστιν (with Shilleto's *n.*).

τὸ...ἐγκωμιάζειν Ἔρωτα. This clause is best taken, with Stallb. and Hug, as nomin. in epexegetic apposition to προβεβλῆσθαι ὁ λόγος. Equally improbable are Rückert's view that the clause is accus. ("quatenus sic simpliciter" etc.), and Hommel's that it is exclamatory.

ἁπλῶς οὕτως. Cp. 176 E.

νῦν δὲ οὐ γάρ. We may assume the ellipse of οὐ καλῶς ἔχει after νῦν δέ: cp. *Theaet.* 143 E, *Apol.* 38 B, etc.

προρρηθῆναι. Hommel renders by "prius praefari," Hug by "edicere." In favour of Hommel's view cp. προυρρήθη 198 E, τούτων προρρηθέντων *Laws* 823 D; *Rep.* 504 A.

ἴσμεν ὅτι οὐκ ἔστιν ἄνευ Ἔρωτος Ἀφροδίτη. μιᾶς μὲν οὖν οὔσης εἶς ἂν ἦν Ἔρως· ἐπεὶ δὲ δὴ δύο ἐστόν, δύο ἀνάγκη καὶ Ἔρωτε εἶναι. πῶς δ' οὐ δύο τὼ θεά; ἡ μέν γέ που πρεσβυτέρα καὶ ἀμήτωρ Οὐρανοῦ θυγάτηρ, ἣν δὴ καὶ Οὐρανίαν ἐπονομάζομεν· ἡ δὲ νεωτέρα Διὸς καὶ Διώνης, ἣν δὴ Πάνδημον καλοῦμεν. ἀναγ- E καῖον δὴ καὶ Ἔρωτα τὸν μὲν τῇ ἑτέρᾳ συνεργὸν Πάνδημον ὀρθῶς καλεῖσθαι, τὸν δὲ Οὐράνιον. ἐπαινεῖν μὲν οὖν δεῖ πάντας θεούς, ἃ δ' οὖν ἑκάτερός εἴληχε πειρατέον εἰπεῖν. πᾶσα γὰρ πρᾶξις ὧδ' ἔχει· αὐτὴ ἐφ' ἑαυτῆς [πραττομένη] οὔτε καλὴ οὔτε αἰσχρά. οἷον 181

180 D   ἄνευ Ἔρως Ἀφροδίτης. Ἀφροδίτης δὲ μιᾶς Graser   ⟨ἧς⟩ μιᾶς
Rückert   οὖν om. Stob. Bekk.   δὲ δὴ BW: δὲ T, Stob.   ἔρωτας Stob.
τὰ θεά Stob.: τὼ θεώ Cobet   διώνης T: διόνης B   E ἐπαινεῖν...
θεούς del. Orelli J.-U.   δεῖ πάντας θεούς: οὐ δεῖ πάντα· Bast: οὐ δεῖ πάντα
γ' ὁμοίως· Vermehren: hiatum ante ἃ notavit Sz.   δ' οὖν: οὖν Orelli: δ'
Ast   ⟨πράττειν⟩ πειρατέον Kreyenbühl   ὡδὶ Stob.   πραττομένη BT,
Stob. Gell.: om. Proclus Steph. Sz.: ταττομένη Bernays: ἐξεταζομένη Liebhold.

---

180 D   οὐκ ἔστιν...Ἀφροδίτη. Cp. Hes. Theog. 201 τῇ δ' Ἔρος ὡμάρτησε
καὶ Ἵμερος ἔσπετο καλὸς | γεινομένη τὰ πρῶτα θεῶν τ' εἰς φῦλον ἰούσῃ: Orph.
H. 55. 1 Οὐρανίη πολύυμνε, φιλομμειδὴς Ἀφροδίτη... (8) μῆτερ ἐρώτων.
μιᾶς οὔσης. Cp. Xen. Symp. VIII. 9 εἰ μὲν οὖν μία ἐστὶν Ἀφρ. ἢ διτταί κτλ.
τὼ θεά. Plato uses both θεός (181 C, Rep. 327 A, etc.) and θεά (Rep. 388 A,
391 C, etc.) for "goddess," and θεά here serves to preclude confusion with
Ἔρως. For the notion of a dual Aphrodite cp. Xen. l. c., Apuleius apol. 12,
Plotin. Enn. III. 5. 293 B. For Aphrodite Urania, with a temple in Athens,
see Hdt. I. 105, 131, etc.; Paus. I. 14. 6. See also Cic. N. D. III. 23; Pind. fr. 87.
Πάνδημον. For the temple in honour of A. Pandemos, see Paus. I. 22. 3.
It is doubtful whether the title originally attached to her as the common
deity of the deme, or as the patroness of the ἑταῖραι. But whatever its origin,
the recognized use of the title at the close of the 5th century was to indicate
Venus meretrix.
180 E   καὶ Ἔρωτα κτλ.   The notion of a duality, or plurality, in Eros is
also hinted at in Eurip. fr. 550 ἑνὸς δ' Ἔρωτος ὄντος οὐ μί' ἡδονή· | οἱ μὲν
κακῶν ἐρῶσιν, οἱ δὲ τῶν καλῶν: fr. adesp. 151 δισσὰ πνεύματα πνεῖς Ἔρως.
Cp. Phaedr. 266 A.
ἐπαινεῖν...θεούς.   This is merely a formal saving clause, to avert possible
Nemesis, and although it involves the speaker in something like self-
contradiction, there is no good reason to suspect corruption in the text (if
correction be required, the easiest would be εὐφημεῖν, cp. Epin. 992 D εὐφημεῖν
πάντας θεοὺς κτλ.).   The laudation of base gods would sound less strange in
ancient than in modern ears; and Eryximachus uses very similar language
in 188 D (cp. 195 A).
181 A   αὐτὴ ἐφ' ἑαυτῆς κτλ.   Gellius XVII. 20 ignores πραττομένη in his
rendering ("Omne," inquit, "omnino factum sic sese habet: neque turpe est,

ὃ νῦν ἡμεῖς ποιοῦμεν, ἢ πίνειν ἢ ᾄδειν ἢ διαλέγεσθαι, οὐκ ἔστι τούτων αὐτὸ καλὸν οὐδέν, ἀλλ' ἐν τῇ πράξει, ὡς ἂν πραχθῇ, τοιοῦτον ἀπέβη· καλῶς μὲν γὰρ πραττόμενον καὶ ὀρθῶς καλὸν γίγνεται, μὴ ὀρθῶς δὲ αἰσχρόν. οὕτω δὴ καὶ τὸ ἐρᾶν καὶ ὁ Ἔρως οὐ πᾶς ἐστὶ καλὸς οὐδὲ ἄξιος ἐγκωμιάζεσθαι, ἀλλ' ὁ καλῶς προτρέπων ἐρᾶν.

IX. Ὁ μὲν οὖν τῆς Πανδήμου Ἀφροδίτης ὡς ἀληθῶς πάνδη-
B μός ἐστι καὶ ἐξεργάζεται ὅ τι ἂν τύχῃ· καὶ οὗτός ἐστιν ὃν οἱ φαῦλοι τῶν ἀνθρώπων ἐρῶσιν. ἐρῶσι δὲ οἱ τοιοῦτοι πρῶτον μὲν οὐχ ἧττον γυναικῶν ἢ παίδων, ἔπειτα ὧν καὶ ἐρῶσι τῶν σωμάτων μᾶλλον ἢ τῶν ψυχῶν, ἔπειτα ὡς ἂν δύνωνται ἀνοητοτάτων, πρὸς τὸ διαπράξασθαι μόνον βλέποντες, ἀμελοῦντες δὲ τοῦ καλῶς ἢ μή. ὅθεν δὴ ξυμβαίνει αὐτοῖς, ὅ τι ἂν τύχωσι, τοῦτο πράττειν, ὁμοίως μὲν ἀγαθόν, ὁμοίως δὲ τοὐναντίον. ἔστι γὰρ καὶ ἀπὸ τῆς θεοῦ
C νεωτέρας τε οὔσης πολὺ ἢ τῆς ἑτέρας, καὶ μετεχούσης ἐν τῇ γενέσει καὶ θήλεος καὶ ἄρρενος. ὁ δὲ τῆς Οὐρανίας πρῶτον μὲν οὐ μετεχούσης θήλεος ἀλλ' ἄρρενος μόνον, [καὶ ἔστιν οὗτος ὁ τῶν

181 A   αὐτὸ ⟨καθ' αὑτὸ⟩ t   τῇ om. Stob.   καλὸς B: καλῶς T
B   ἀνοητοτάτως W   ἀπὸ τῆς: ἀπὸ secl. Sz.   Hug: τοιαύτης J.-U.
C   καὶ...ἔρως secl. Schütz Teuffel Hug Sz. Bdhm. J.-U.

---

quantum in eo est, neque honestum, uelut est quas nunc facimus ipsi res, bibere cantare disserere. nihil namque horum ipsum ex se honestum est; quali cum fieret modo factum est, tale extitit," etc.): Proclus also (*in Alcib. I.* p. 215) omits it. It must certainly, I think, be ejected, since it only serves to confuse the argument; none of the alternatives proposed are at all probable; while Rettig's attempt to justify its retention by the device of setting a comma before it is merely absurd. For the language cp. *Meno* 88 c πάντα τὰ κατὰ τὴν ψυχὴν αὐτὰ μὲν καθ' αὑτὰ οὔτε ὠφέλιμα οὔτε βλαβερά ἐστιν: *Phaedr.* 258 c, D. See also *Eryx.* 397 E; Arist. *Pol.* 1333ᵃ 9, for the moral indifference of πράξεις καθ' αὑτάς.

ὅ τι ἂν τύχῃ. "At random"; so ὅ τι ἂν τύχωσι 181 B *infra*: *Prot.* 353 A οἱ ὅ τι ἂν τύχωσι τοῦτο λέγουσι.

181 B ὧν καὶ ἐρῶσι. "In the actual objects of their passion": the full statement would be ἐρῶσι τῶν σωμάτων ἐκείνων (sc. παίδων ἢ γυναικῶν) ὧν ἐρῶσι μᾶλλον ἢ τῶν ψ.

τὸ διαπράξασθαι. A polite euphemism for the sexual act: cp. 182 c, *Phaedr.* 256 c; Lysias I. 33.

ἔστι γὰρ...ἄρρενος. Observe that the reasons are put in chiastic order.

181 C καὶ ἔστιν...Ἔρως. This clause is obviously open to suspicion as (1) anticipating the sense of ὅθεν δὴ κτλ., and (2) standing in partial contradiction to the later statement (181 D *ad init.*) οὐ γὰρ ἐρῶσι παίδων.

παίδων ἔρως·] ἔπειτα πρεσβυτέρας, ὕβρεως ἀμοίρου· ὅθεν δὴ ἐπὶ τὸ ἄρρεν τρέπονται οἱ ἐκ τούτου τοῦ ἔρωτος ἔπιπνοι, τὸ φύσει ἐρρωμενέστερον καὶ νοῦν μᾶλλον ἔχον ἀγαπῶντες. καί τις ἂν γνοίη καὶ ἐν αὐτῇ τῇ παιδεραστίᾳ τοὺς εἰλικρινῶς ὑπὸ τούτου τοῦ ἔρωτος ὡρμημένους· οὐ γὰρ ἐρῶσι παίδων, ἀλλ' D ἐπειδὰν ἤδη ἄρχωνται νοῦν ἴσχειν, τοῦτο δὲ πλησιάζει τῷ γενειάσκειν. παρεσκευασμένοι γάρ, οἶμαι, εἰσὶν οἱ ἐντεῦθεν ἀρχόμενοι ἐρᾶν ὡς τὸν βίον ἅπαντα ξυνεσόμενοι καὶ κοινῇ συμβιωσόμενοι, ἀλλ' οὐκ ἐξαπατήσαντες, ἐν ἀφροσύνῃ λαβόντες ὡς νέον, καταγελάσαντες οἰχήσεσθαι ἐπ' ἄλλον ἀποτρέχοντες. χρῆν δὲ καὶ νόμον εἶναι μὴ ἐρᾶν παίδων, ἵνα μὴ εἰς ἄδηλον πολλὴ σπουδὴ ἀνηλίσκετο· τὸ γὰρ τῶν παίδων τέλος ἄδηλον οἷ τελευτᾷ E

181 C παίδων in παιδεραστῶν mutato post ἀγαπῶντες trs. Verm.   πρεσβυτέρας ⟨οὔσης καὶ⟩ Christ   ἀμοίρου libri : ἄμοιρος Ficinus Bast Bdhm. :   ὕβρεως ἀμοίρου addub. Sz.   D ἀλλ' ⟨ἢ⟩ Steph. Hug   οἴχεσθαι Herwerden   παῖδας Markland   E τέλος secl. Bdhm.

ὕβρεως ἀμοίρου. For ὕβρις as especially associated with juvenile "lustihead," cp. *Euthyd.* 273 B ὑβριστὴς διὰ τὸ νέος εἶναι: Lysias XXIV. 16 ὑβρίζειν εἰκὸς... τοὺς ἔτι νέους καὶ νέαις ταῖς διανοίαις χρωμένους: Soph. *fr.* 705 ὕβρις δέ τοι...ἐν νέοις ἀνθεῖ τε καὶ φθίνει πάλιν.

ἔπιπνοι. "Driven by the spirit": the only other exx. of the word in Plato are *Cratyl.* 428 C and *Meno* 99 D φαῖμεν ἂν θείους τε εἶναι καὶ ἐνθουσιάζειν, ἐπίπνους ὄντας καὶ κατεχομένους ἐκ τοῦ θεοῦ (cp. 179 A n., 180 B n.).

181 D τοῦτο δὲ. *Sc.* τὸ νοῦν ἴσχειν. This is in contradiction to the statements of Phaedrus, 178 C (εὐθὺς νέῳ ὄντι), 180 A (ἔτι ἀγένειος ἦν). For γενειάσκειν (*pubescere*), cp. Solon 27. 5—6 τῇ τριτάτῃ δὲ γένειον ἀεξομένων ἔτι γυίων | λαχνοῦται, χροιῆς ἄνθος ἀμειβομένης. Cp. Spenser *F. Q.* II. xii. 79 "And on his tender lips the downy heare Did now but freshly spring, and silken blossoms beare": Hor. *C.* IV. 10. 2 (*pluma*).

παρεσκευασμένοι κτλ. For the change of construction from ὡς with fut. partic. to (fut.) infin., cp. *Charm.* 164 D, *Rep.* 383 A ποιεῖν ὡς μήτε...ὄντας... μήτε...παράγειν. The clause ἐν ἀφροσύνῃ...νέον is best taken closely with the preceding participle, and καταγελάσαντες...ἀποτρέχοντες closely together. For ἐξαπατήσαντες cp. 184 E, 185 A : Theogn. 254 ἀλλ' ὥσπερ μικρὸν παῖδα λόγοις μ' ἀπατᾷς. This ἀπάτη and καταγελᾶν are forms of the ὕβρις mentioned above, 181 C: cp. 219 C, 222 A.

μὴ ἐρᾶν παίδων. παῖς, as here used, is Theognis' μικρὸς παῖς, the παιδάριον of 210 B *infra*.

181 E ἄδηλον οἷ τελευτᾷ. Cp. *Phaedr.* 232 E τῶν μὲν ἐρώντων πολλοὶ πρότερον τοῦ σώματος ἐπεθύμησαν ἢ τὸν τρόπον ἔγνωσαν κτλ. : Theogn. 1075 ff. πρήγματος ἀπρήκτου χαλεπώτατόν ἐστι τελευτὴν | γνῶναι...ὀρφνη γὰρ τέταται : Alcid. *Odyss.* 5 πᾶσά τε ἀπορία ἦν ποῖ ποτε προβήσοιτο ἠ...τελευτή. A similar

κακίας καὶ ἀρετῆς ψυχῆς τε πέρι καὶ σώματος. οἱ μὲν οὖν
ἀγαθοὶ τὸν νόμον τοῦτον αὐτοὶ αὑτοῖς ἑκόντες τίθενται, χρῆν δὲ
καὶ τούτους τοὺς πανδήμους ἐραστὰς προσαναγκάζειν τὸ τοιοῦτον,
ὥσπερ καὶ τῶν - ἐλευθέρων - γυναικῶν προσαναγκάζομεν αὐτοὺς
182 καθ' ὅσον δυνάμεθα μὴ ἐρᾶν. οὗτοι γάρ εἰσιν οἱ καὶ τὸ ὄνειδος
πεποιηκότες, ὥστε τινὰς τολμᾶν λέγειν ὡς αἰσχρὸν χαρίζεσθαι
ἐρασταῖς· λέγουσι δὲ εἰς τούτους ἀποβλέποντες, ὁρῶντες αὐτῶν
τὴν ἀκαιρίαν καὶ ἀδικίαν, ἐπεὶ οὐ δή που κοσμίως γε καὶ νομίμως
ὁτιοῦν πραττόμενον ψόγον ἂν δικαίως φέροι.
Καὶ δὴ καὶ ὁ περὶ τὸν ἔρωτα νόμος ἐν μὲν ταῖς ἄλλαις πόλεσι

181 E κακίας ἤ edd. Stobaei, Hommel   χρῆν W: χρην B: χρὴ T
τῶν τοιοῦτον W   182 A τινὰ vulg.   ἀκαιρίαν : ἀκοσμίαν Liebhold
γε : τε vulg.   ὁτιοῦν ⟨πρᾶγμα⟩ mg. t, Bt.

sentiment occurs in the Clown's song in *Twelfth-Night*: " What's to come is
still unsure...Youth's a stuff will not endure."

κακίας καὶ ἀρετῆς. Possibly these genitives are to be construed (with
Rückert) as dependent on the preceding adverb οἷ: cp. Soph. *O. T.* 413 οὐ
βλέπεις ἵν' εἶ κακοῦ (Madv. *Gr. Synt.* § 50 B). Hug, however, takes them to
be governed by πέρι, comparing for the separation of prepos. from case *Apol.*
19 c, Soph. *Aj.* 793.

τούτους...ἐραστὰς. For οὗτος contemptuous cp. *Apol.* 17 B, *Rep.* 492 D οὗτοι
οἱ παιδευταί τε καὶ σοφισταί (" οὗτοι is the contemptuous *isti*" Adam).

τὸ τοιοῦτον. Sc. μὴ ἐρᾶν παίδων (D *ad fin.*). For the db. accus. with
-αναγκάζω, cp. *Rep.* 473 A τοῦτο μὴ ἀνάγκαζέ με: *Phaedr.* 242 B. Hommel,
perversely, construes τὸ τοιοῦτον as an adverbial accus., " ganz in der Weise
wie " etc.

τῶν ἐλευθέρων γυναικῶν. For the legal penalties (by a γραφὴ μοιχείας or
ὕβρεως or a δίκη βιαίων) for rape and adultery, see Lysias I. 26, 30, 49. One
of the lesser penalties was that alluded to by Catullus XV. 18 f., Quem...Per-
current raphanique mugilesque.

182 A χαρίζεσθαι ἐρασταῖς. χαρίζεσθαι, *obsequi*, " to grant favours "—the
converse of διαπράξασθαι—is a *vox propria* in this connexion: cp. Schol. ad
Phaedr. 227 C τὸ χαριστέον ἐστίν...τὸ πρὸς ἀφροδίσιον ἑαυτὸν συνουσίαν ἐπιδιδόναι τινί. For the sentiment here disputed, see Xen. *Symp.* VIII. 19 ff. ;
Mem. I. 2. 29 ; and the paradox in *Phaedr.* 233 E ἴσως προσήκει οὐ τοῖς σφόδρα
δεομένοις χαρίζεσθαι. Aeschines I. 136 agrees with Pausanias.

τὴν ἀκαιρίαν. " Impropriety " or " tactlessness " : for exx. of such ἀκαιρία,
see 181 D, *Phaedr.* 231 D ff.

ὁ...νόμος. νόμος here includes both " law " proper and " public sentiment "
or " custom " (" die Anschauungen des Volkes," Hug) which are distinguished
in Dem. *de Cor.* 114: cp. Thuc. VI. 18. 7 : but in Thuc. VI. 16. 2 νόμος is
" custom."

νοῆσαι ῥᾴδιος, ἁπλῶς γὰρ ὥρισται· ὁ δ' ἐνθάδε [καὶ ἐν Λακεδαί-
μονι] ποικίλος. ἐν Ἤλιδι μὲν γὰρ καὶ ἐν Βοιωτοῖς, καὶ οὗ μὴ B
σοφοὶ λέγειν, ἁπλῶς νενομοθέτηται καλὸν τὸ χαρίζεσθαι ἐρασταῖς,
καὶ οὐκ ἄν τις εἴποι οὔτε νέος οὔτε παλαιὸς ὡς αἰσχρόν, ἵνα, οἶμαι,
μὴ πράγματ' ἔχωσι λόγῳ πειρώμενοι πείθειν τοὺς νέους, ἅτε
ἀδύνατοι λέγειν· τῆς δὲ Ἰωνίας καὶ ἄλλοθι πολλαχοῦ αἰσχρὸν
νενόμισται, ὅσοι ὑπὸ βαρβάροις οἰκοῦσι. τοῖς γὰρ βαρβάροις
διὰ τὰς τυραννίδας αἰσχρὸν τοῦτό γε καὶ ἥ γε φιλοσοφία καὶ ἡ

182 A   ⟨ὁ⟩ ἐν Hirschig   καὶ ἐν Λακεδαίμονι secl. Winckelmann Hug
Sz. J.-U.: fort. post γὰρ transpon. (cf. Teuffel)   ὁ supra ἐν Λακεδαίμονι
add. T   B οὗ T: οὐ B   τὸ BT: del. t   τοῖς δὲ Ἰωνίας Ast:
τῇ δὲ Ἰωνίᾳ Thiersch   πολλαχοῦ καὶ ἄλλοθι cj. Steph.   ⟨καὶ⟩ ὅσοι
Rückert   γε (post τοῦτό): τε Herm. Sz.

182 A   καὶ ἐν Λακεδαίμονι. I follow Winckelmann and others (see *crit. n.*)
in bracketing these words: possibly they should be transposed to a place in
the next clause, either after γὰρ or after Βοιωτοῖς (in suggesting this I find
myself anticipated by an anonymous critic, *ap.* Teuffel, *Rhein. Mus.* XXIX.
p. 145). That Laconia was a hot-bed of paederasty might be inferred *à priori*
from its military-oligarchical constitution, and is betokened by the verb λακω-
νίζειν used as a synonym for παιδικοῖς χρῆσθαι (Ar. *frag.* 322), and the adj.
κυσολάκων for παιδεραστής. It is certainly unlikely that a ποικίλος νόμος
would be ascribed to the Laconians, and unlikely too that they would be
classed apart from the μὴ σοφοὶ λέγειν. Moreover, in 182 D ff. it is ὁ ἐνθάδε
⟨ἡμέτερος⟩ νόμος which is treated as ποικίλος, and no mention is made there
of a similar Laconian νόμος. For Laconian *mores*, Stallb. cites Xen. *Rep.
Lac.* II. 13; Plut. *Lac. Inst.* p. 237 B; Aelian *V. H.* III. 10. 12. In Xen. *Symp.*
VIII. 35 the Lacedaemonians are lauded—θεὰν γὰρ οὐ τὴν Ἀναίδειαν ἀλλὰ τὴν
Αἰδῶ νομίζουσι (which ought, perhaps, to be construed as implying that they
are slighted here).

182 B   ἐν Ἤλιδι κτλ. Cp. Xen. *Symp.* VIII. 34, *Rep. Lac. l.c.*, Athen. XIII. 2.
The Cretan ἁρπαγμὸς παιδων (*Laws* VIII. 836) points to a similar state of things.

τῆς δὲ Ἰωνίας. The genitive is taken by Hug as dependent on πολλαχοῦ,
by Stallb. as dependent on ὅσοι, "vel potius ex demonstrativo ante ὅσοι
intelligendo." Hug quotes Xen. *Hell.* IV. 4. 16 πολλαχόσε καὶ τῆς Ἀρκαδίας
ἐμβαλόντες.

ὅσοι...οἰκοῦσι. The grammar is loose—"per synesin additur ὅσοι perinde
ac si praecessisset 'apud Ionas autem et multos alios'" (Stallb.). The
language is most appropriate to a time after the Peace of Antalcidas (387 B.C.),
when the Greeks of Asia Minor were again reduced to subjection to the
Great King (see Bury, *Hist. Gr.* p. 552); cp. *Cratyl.* 409 E οἱ ὑπὸ τοῖς βαρβάροις οἰκοῦντες: *Laws* 693 A.

τοῦτό γε καὶ κτλ. Strictly we should supply, with τοῦτο, τὸ χαρίζεσθαι
ἐρασταῖς, but the notion latent is probably the more general one τὸ ἐρᾶν
⟨παίδων⟩. The palaestrae (gymnasia) were recognized as the chief seats of

3—2

C φιλογυμναστία· οὐ γάρ, οἶμαι, συμφέρει τοῖς ἄρχουσι φρονήματα
μεγάλα ἐγγίγνεσθαι τῶν ἀρχομένων, οὐδὲ φιλίας ἰσχυρὰς καὶ
κοινωνίας, ὃ δὴ μάλιστα φιλεῖ τά τε ἄλλα πάντα καὶ ὁ ἔρως
ἐμποιεῖν. ἔργῳ δὲ τοῦτο ἔμαθον καὶ οἱ ἐνθάδε τύραννοι· ὁ γὰρ
Ἀριστογείτονος ἔρως καὶ ἡ Ἁρμοδίου φιλία βέβαιος γενομένη
κατέλυσέν αὐτῶν τὴν ἀρχήν. οὕτως οὐ μὲν αἰσχρὸν ἐτέθη χαρί-

182 C	γίγνεσθαι Jn.		τοῖς ἀρχομένοις ex emend. Vindob. 21 : τῷ
ἀρχομένῳ Rohde: τῶν ἀρχομένων (ταῖς ψυχαῖς) Bdhm.			μάλιστα post καὶ
trs. Ast	ἄλλα: καλά J.-U.		πάντα: ταῦτα Schleierm. καὶ ὁ: καὶ secl.
Bdhm. Sz.	οὖ Tb: ον B		

φιλοσοφία and παιδεραστία as well as of φιλογυμναστία. Cp. (for παιδεραστία)
Ar. Nub. 973 ff., 980 αὐτὸς ἑαυτὸν προαγωγεύων τοῖς ὀφθαλμοῖς: Laws 636 B :
Xen. Cyrop. II. 3. 21: Cic. Tusc. IV. 33. 70 in Graecorum gymnasiis…isti
liberi et concessi sunt amores. Bene ergo Ennius: flagiti principium est
nudare inter cives corpora: Plut. amat. 751 F ff. The gymnasia also served,
at Athens, as headquarters of political clubs, cp. Athen. XIII. 602.

182 C φρονήματα…ἐγγίγνεσθαι. For φρον. μεγάλα cp. 190 B. For ἐγγίγνεσθαι cp. Xen. Rep. Lac. v. 6 ὥστ' ἐκεῖ ἥκιστα μὲν ὕβριν…ἐγγίγνεσθαι: and
184 A infra. The genitive τῶν ἀρχομένων, in place of the more natural dative,
may be explained, with Stallb., as due to "a confusion of two constructions,"
the gen. being dependent on φρον. μεγ. and the dat. after the verb omitted.
For the thought, cp. (with Jowett) Arist. Pol. v. 11. 15.

ὃ δὴ…ἐμποιεῖν. The neut. sing., which is acc. after ἐμποιεῖν, serves to grasp
under one general head the preceding plurals. For this common use of φιλεῖ,
solet, cp. 188 B infra, Phileb. 37 B. Hug, excising the καὶ after πάντα, construes τὰ ἄλλα πάντα as a second object, parallel to ὅ. But no change is
needed: the phrase means "prae ceteris omnibus maxime amor," as Stallb.
renders, cp. the usage of ἄλλος τε καί, τά τε ἄλλα καί in 220 A, Apol. 36 A, etc.

ὁ γὰρ Ἀριστογείτονος κτλ. For the exploits of these tyrannicides, who
slew the Pisistratids in 514 B.C., see Bury H. G. p. 205. Aristogeiton was the
ἐραστής of Harmodius, and popular sentiment invested the pair, in later days,
with a halo of glory as the patron-saints and martyrs of Love and Liberty.
Cp. Skolia 9 (Bgk. P. L. G. III. p. 646) ἐν μύρτου κλαδὶ τὸ ξίφος φορήσω, |
ὥσπερ Ἁρμόδιος καὶ Ἀριστογείτων, | ὅτε τὸν τύραννον κατανέτην | ἰσονόμους τ'
Ἀθήνας ἐποιησάτην: Ar. Ach. 980, Lys. 632. The exploit was also com-
memorated by Antenor's bronzes and a group by Critias and Nesiotes (reproduced in Bury H. G. p. 209).

ἐτέθη. As aor. pass. of τίθεσθαι, this is equiv. to ἐνομίσθη (cp. two
ll. below). It is plain that θεμένων must here be taken to include both rulers
and subjects. For πλεονεξία, "arrogant greed," as opposed to ἡ τοῦ ἴσου τιμή,
see Rep. 359 C. For the theory implied in the following passage, that ἔρως
and ἀνδρεία go together (as Phaedrus also had contended, 178 D ff.), cp.
Bacon, Essay x. (Of Love): "I know not how, but Martiall men are given to
Love: I think it is but as they are given to Wine; for perils commonly aske
to be paid in pleasures."

ζεσθαι ἐρασταῖς, κακίᾳ τῶν θεμένων κεῖται, τῶν μὲν ἀρχόντων
πλεονεξίᾳ, τῶν δὲ ἀρχομένων ἀνανδρίᾳ· οὗ δὲ καλὸν ἁπλῶς ἐνο- D
μίσθη, διὰ τὴν τῶν θεμένων τῆς ψυχῆς ἀργίαν. ἐνθάδε δὲ πολὺ
τούτων κάλλιον νενομοθέτηται, καὶ ὅπερ εἶπον, οὐ ῥᾴδιον κατανοῆσαι.

Χ. Ἐνθυμηθέντι γὰρ ὅτι λέγεται κάλλιον τὸ φανερῶς ἐρᾶν
τοῦ λάθρᾳ, καὶ μάλιστα 'τῶν γενναιοτάτων καὶ ἀρίστων, κἂν
αἰσχίους ἄλλων ὦσι, καὶ ὅτι αὖ ἡ παρακέλευσις τῷ ἐρῶντι παρὰ
πάντων θαυμαστή, οὐχ ὥς τι αἰσχρὸν ποιοῦντι, καὶ ἑλόντι τε
καλὸν δοκεῖ εἶναι καὶ μὴ ἑλόντι αἰσχρόν, καὶ πρὸς τὸ ἐπιχειρεῖν E
ἑλεῖν ἐξουσίαν ὁ νόμος δέδωκε τῷ ἐραστῇ θαυμαστὰ ἔργα ἐργαζομένῳ ἐπαινεῖσθαι, ἃ εἴ τις τολμῴη ποιεῖν ἄλλ' ὁτιοῦν διώκων
καὶ βουλόμενος διαπράξασθαι πλὴν τοῦτο [φιλοσοφίας], τὰ μέ- 183
γιστα καρποῖτ' ἂν ὀνείδη· εἰ γὰρ ἢ χρήματα βουλόμενος παρά

182 D οὐ δὲ Τ: οὐ δὲ Β   δὲ Β: om. TW   κατανοῆσαι ἐνθ. γ' ὅτι
Bdhm.   ἐνεθυμήθην in mg. W   τε Τ: om. Β   E πρὸς τῷ Ast
ἃ εἰ TW: αἰεὶ Β: γρ. καὶ αἰεὶ W   183 A φιλοσοφίας secl. Schleierm. Bekk.
Hug Sz. Bdhm. Bt.: φιλίας, τοῦτο deleto, Herm.: φίλοις ὀφθείς cj. Bdhm.:
alii alia   εἰ BT: ἢ W

182 D Ἐνθυμηθέντι γὰρ κτλ.   The construction is grammatically incomplete: one would expect δόξειεν ἄν, or the like, to govern the dative. It is
not till we get to 183 c (ταύτῃ μὲν οὖν κτλ.) that we find the sense resumed.
παρὰ πάντων.   Jowett's "all the world" is misleading: the treatment is
here confined to Athenian νόμος.
182 E πρὸς τὸ ἐπιχειρεῖν κτλ.   "Quod attinet ad amasii capiendi conatum"
(Stallb.).
ἐξουσίαν...ἐπαινεῖσθαι.   Here, as often, the main idea is put in the
participle.   Again Jowett misleads, in rendering ὁ νόμος "the custom of
mankind."
θαυμαστὰ ἔργα.   "θαυμαστὰ vel θαυμάσια ποιεῖν vel ἐργάζεσθαι est sich
wunderlich geberden...quod dicitur de iis qui vel propter dolorem et indigna-
tionem vel ob ingentem laetitiam vel etiam prae vehementi aliqua cupiditate
insolito more se gerunt" (Stallb.).   Cp. 213 D, Apol. 35 A, Theaet. 151 A.
183 A πλὴν τοῦτο [φιλοσοφίας].   φιλοσοφίας is most probably corrupt: if
retained, it would be better to construe it as genit. of object ("the reproaches
levelled against philosophy") than as genit. of subject or origin (as Ast,
Stallb., Kreyenbühl), for which we should expect rather φιλοσόφων.   The
simplest and best remedy is, with Schleiermacher, to eject φιλοσοφίας as a
gloss on the misreading τούτου.   For ὄνειδος, cp. Rep. 347 B τὸ φιλότιμόν τε
καὶ φιλάργυρον εἶναι ὄνειδος λέγεται.   For καρποῦσθαι, in malam partem, cp.
Rep. 579 C; Eur. Hipp. 1427 κ. πένθη.   In their translations, Jowett follows
Ast, but Zeller adopts Schl.'s excision.

τοῦ λαβεῖν ἢ ἀρχὴν ἄρξαι ἤ τιν' ἄλλην δύναμιν ἐθέλοι ποιεῖν
οἷάπερ οἱ ἐρασταὶ πρὸς τὰ παιδικά, ἱκετείας τε καὶ ἀντιβολήσεις
ἐν ταῖς δεήσεσι ποιούμενοι, καὶ ὅρκους ὀμνύντες, καὶ κοιμήσεις ἐπὶ
θύραις, καὶ ἐθέλοντες δουλείας δουλεύειν οἵας οὐδ' ἂν δοῦλος οὐδείς,
ἐμποδίζοιτο ἂν μὴ πράττειν οὕτω τὴν πρᾶξιν καὶ ὑπὸ φίλων καὶ
B ὑπὸ ἐχθρῶν, τῶν μὲν ὀνειδιζόντων κολακείας καὶ ἀνελευθερίας,
τῶν δὲ νουθετούντων καὶ αἰσχυνομένων ὑπὲρ αὐτῶν· τῷ δ' ἐρῶντι
πάντα ταῦτα ποιοῦντι χάρις ἔπεστι, καὶ δέδοται ὑπὸ τοῦ νόμου
ἄνευ ὀνείδους πράττειν, ὡς πάγκαλόν τι πρᾶγμα διαπραττομένου·
ὃ δὲ δεινότατον, ὥς γε λέγουσιν οἱ πολλοί, ὅτι καὶ ὀμνύντι μόνῳ
συγγνώμη παρὰ θεῶν ἐκβάντι τῶν ὅρκων—ἀφροδίσιον γὰρ ὅρκον

183 A ἄρξαι secl. Verm. Hug Sz.   ἤ τιν': δή τιν' Bdhm.   ἄλλην
δύναμιν secl. Bdhm.   ἐθέλει T   καὶ...ὀμνύντες del. Voeg. J.-U.: ὀμνύντες
secl. Hertz Hug Sz.   καὶ κοιμ....θύραις secl. Wolf Jn.: post ποιούμενοι
transp. Rückert   ἐθέλοντὰς vulg.: ἐθέλονταὶ (δ. δουλεύοντες) Ast   B αὐτῶν:
αὐτοῦ Orelli Sz.   ταῦτα πάντα T   ἔπεστι T: επεται B: ἔπεται J.-U. Sz.
διαπραττομένῳ vulg.   μόνον Stob.   τῶν ὅρκων T: τῶν ὅρκον B: τὸν ὅρκον
al., J.-U.   ὅρκον ⟨κύριον⟩ scripsi: ὅρκον ⟨ὅρκον⟩ Hertz Hug

κοιμήσεις ἐπὶ θύραις.   Cp. 203 D; Ov. A. A. II. 238 frigidus et nuda saepe
iacebis humo: Hor. C. III. 10. 2 asperas | porrectum ante fores, etc. For the
other love-symptoms cp. also Xen. Cyrop. v. 1. 12.

183 B αἰσχυνψμένων ὑπὲρ αὐτῶν.   For this construction cp. Euthyd. 305 A,
Charm. 175 D. With the whole of this passage cp. Xen. Symp. IV. 15, VIII.
12 ff.: Isocr. Hel. 219 B μόνους αὐτοὺς (sc. τοὺς καλοὺς) ὥσπερ τοὺς θεοὺς οὐκ
ἀπαγορεύομεν θεραπεύοντες, ἀλλ' ἥδιον δουλεύομεν τοῖς τοιούτοις ἢ τῶν ἄλλων
ἄρχομεν...καὶ τοὺς μὲν ὑπ' ἄλλῃ τινι δυνάμει γιγνομένους λοιδοροῦμεν καὶ κόλακας
ἀποκαλοῦμεν, τοὺς δὲ τῷ κάλλει λατρεύοντες φιλοκάλους καὶ φιλοπόνους εἶναι
νομίζομεν (with which cp. also 184 C infra).

τῷ δ' ἐρῶντι...διαπραττομένου.   For the gen. absolute after a dative, cp.
Laws 839 B ἡμῖν τις παραστὰς ἀνήρ...λοιδορήσειεν ἂν ὡς ἀνόητα...τιθέντων:
Phileb. 44 c is a less certain case. For the sense of the passage, cp. Bacon,
Essay x. (Of Love): "It is a strange thing to note the excesse of this passion;
and how it braves the nature and value of things; by this, that the speaking
in a perpetuall hyperbole is comely in nothing but in Love."

ὥς γε λέγουσιν κτλ.   These words qualify the following, not the preceding,
clause: Pausanias himself censures perjury in 183 E. For ὥς γε, cp. Rep.
352 D, 432 B.

ἀφροδίσιον γὰρ ὅρκον κτλ.   This proverbial expression is found in two
forms,—ἀφροδίσιος ὅρκος οὐ δάκνει (Hesych.) and ἀφρ. ὅρκος οὐκ ἐμποίνιμος
(Suid.). The Scholiast quotes Hesiod (fr. 5 G.) ἐκ τοῦδ' ὅρκον ἔθηκεν ἀμείνονα
(ἀπήμονα G. Hermann) ἀνθρώποισι | νοσφιδίων ἔργων πέρι Κύπριδος. Cp.
Soph. fr. 694 ὅρκους δὲ μοιχῶν εἰς τέφραν ἐγὼ γράφω: Callim. Epigr. 27 (Anth.
Pal. v. 5. 3) ἀλλὰ λέγουσιν ἀληθέα, τοὺς ἐν ἔρωτι | ὅρκους μὴ δύνειν οὔατ' ἐς

<κύριον> οὗ φασιν εἶναι—οὕτω καὶ οἱ θεοὶ καὶ οἱ ἄνθρωποι πᾶσαν ἐξουσίαν πεποιήκασι τῷ ἐρῶντι, ὡς ὁ νόμος φησὶν ὁ ἐνθάδε· C ταύτῃ μὲν οὖν οἰηθείη ἄν τις πάγκαλον νομίζεσθαι ἐν τῇδε τῇ πόλει καὶ τὸ ἐρᾶν καὶ τὸ φίλους γίγνεσθαι τοῖς ἐρασταῖς. ἐπειδὰν δὲ παιδαγωγοὺς ἐπιστήσαντες οἱ πατέρες τοῖς ἐρωμένοις μὴ ἐῶσι διαλέγεσθαι τοῖς ἐρασταῖς, καὶ τῷ παιδαγωγῷ ταῦτα προστεταγμένα ᾖ, ἡλικιῶται δὲ καὶ ἑταῖροι ὀνειδίζωσιν, ἐάν τι ὁρῶσι τοιοῦτο γιγνόμενον, καὶ τοὺς ὀνειδίζοντας αὖ οἱ πρεσβύτεροι μὴ διακω- D λύωσι μηδὲ λοιδορῶσιν ὡς οὐκ ὀρθῶς λέγοντας, εἰς δὲ ταῦτά τις αὖ βλέψας ἡγήσαιτ᾽ ἂν πάλιν αἴσχιστον τὸ τοιοῦτον ἐνθάδε νομίζεσθαι. τὸ δέ, οἶμαι, ὧδ᾽ ἔχει· οὐχ ἁπλοῦν ἐστίν, ὅπερ ἐξ ἀρχῆς

183 B εἶναι BT Stob. Cyril.: δάκνειν Teuffel: εἶναι ἐμποίνιμον Osann Jn. Sz. καὶ θεοὶ καὶ ἄνθρωποι W. Cyril. vulg. C πεποιήκασι πᾶσαν Cyril. διαλ. τοὺς ἐραστὰς Orelli καὶ...ᾖ secl. Jn.: καὶ...προστεταγμένα secl. Hug Sz. ᾖ TW: οἱ B: ᾖ οἱ al. ἑταῖροι Heindorf: ἕτεροι BT D οὐχ ἁπλοῦν: ἁπλοῦν Bast: οὐχ ἁπλῶς Ast

---

ἀθανάτων: Aristaen. II. 20: Ov. A. A. I. 633 Iuppiter ex alto periuria ridet amantum: Tibull. I. 4. 21 ff. nec iurare time: Veneris periuria venti | irrita... ferunt, etc. As to the text, the parallels quoted lead us to expect a fuller expression. Hertz's ὅρκον (ὅρκον), adopted by Hug, is ingenious but rather weak in sense. I prefer to insert κύριον (abbreviated κōν) after ὅρκον. For κύριος, "valid," cp. Laws 926 D: Ep. vi. 323 C, and see L. and S. s.v. II. 2: οὐ κύριος is equiv. to ἄκυρος, irritus. To Jahn's insertion ⟨ἐμποίνιμον⟩ Teuffel rightly objects that it smacks but little of the proverbial manner.

καὶ οἱ θεοὶ καὶ οἱ ἄνθρωποι. This seems to balance the statement made by Phaedrus, 179 C—D.

183 C τοῖς ἐρωμένοις. From this dative (governed by ἐπιστήσαντες), we must supply an acc. (τοὺς ἐρωμένους) to act as subject to διαλέγεσθαι. For the general sense of the passage, cp. Phaedr. 255 A ἐάν...ὑπὸ ξυμφοιτητῶν ἤ τινων ἄλλων διαβεβλημένος ᾖ, λεγόντων ὡς αἰσχρὸν ἐρῶντι πλησιάζειν: ibid. 234 B.

καὶ...προστεταγμένα ᾖ. Hug, after Jahn and others, condemns this clause on the grounds that (1) ᾖ is wanting in B; (2) the change of number, from παιδαγωγούς to παιδαγωγῷ, is awkward; (3) the clause contains nothing new. But there is point in the change from plur. to sing. as serving to individualize the parents' action; and the clause does add to the statement in the context the further idea that the paedagogi are appointed not only as a general safeguard, but with special instructions to ward off this particular danger. ταῦτα, the subject of προστ. ᾖ, represents (as Stallb. notes) μὴ ἐῶσι διαλέγεσθαι τοῖς ἐρασταῖς.

183 D τὸ δέ...ἔχει. For this formula, introducing the solution of a problem, cp. 198 D; Theaet. 166 A.

οὐχ ἁπλοῦν ἐστίν. Stallbaum, ejecting οὐχ with Bast, renders ἁπλοῦν by

ἐλέχθη οὔτε καλὸν εἶναι αὐτὸ καθ᾿ αὑτὸ οὔτε αἰσχρόν, ἀλλὰ καλῶς
μὲν πραττόμενον καλόν, αἰσχρῶς δὲ αἰσχρόν. αἰσχρῶς μὲν οὖν
ἐστι πονηρῷ τε καὶ πονηρῶς χαρίζεσθαι, καλῶς δὲ χρηστῷ τε καὶ
E καλῶς. πονηρὸς δ᾿ ἐστὶν ἐκεῖνος ὁ ἐραστὴς ὁ πάνδημος, ὁ τοῦ
σώματος μᾶλλον ἢ τῆς ψυχῆς ἐρῶν· καὶ γὰρ οὐδὲ μόνιμός ἐστιν,
ἅτε οὐ μονίμου ἐρῶν πράγματος. ἅμα γὰρ τῷ τοῦ σώματος
ἄνθει λήγοντι, οὗπερ ἤρα, "οἴχεται ἀποπτάμενος," πολλοὺς λόγους
καὶ ὑποσχέσεις καταισχύνας· ὁ δὲ τοῦ ἤθους χρηστοῦ ὄντος
ἐραστὴς διὰ βίου μένει, ἅτε μονίμῳ συντακείς. τούτους δὴ βού-

183 D εἶναι del. Steph. Ast ⟨οὐδὲν⟩ οὔτε Bdhm. αἰσχρῶς μὲν : αἰσχρὸν
μὲν Steph. καλῶς δὲ Par. 1810 : καλὸν δὲ BT καὶ καλῶς : καὶ χρηστῶς
Sauppe Sz. E ἐρῶν η τῆς ψυχῆς T ἅτε οὐ B : ἅτε οὐδὲ T

"verum simpliciter," citing *Phaedo* 62 A, *Phaedr.* 244 A, *Protag.* 331 B. Retaining οὐχ, we cannot take the foll. accus. and infin. as the subject (with
Wolf), but must supply τὸ χαρίζεσθαι (with Hug) from the context.

αἰσχρῶς μὲν…καλῶς δὲ. With each adverb, *sc.* χαρίζεσθαι: cp. *Rep.* 339 c
τὸ δὲ ὀρθῶς…τὸ δὲ μὴ ὀρθῶς (*sc.* τιθέναι).

183 E τῷ τοῦ σώματος ἄνθει λ. Youth "is like the flower of the field, so
soon passeth it away, and it is gone." Cp. Mimn. 2. 7 μίνυνθα δὲ γίγνεται ἥβης
καρπός: Theogn. 1305 παιδείας πολυηράτου ἄνθος | ὠκύτερον σταδίου: Ségur's
refrain "Ah! le Temps fait passer l'Amour": Spenser (*H. to Beautie*) "For
that same goodly hew of white and red, With which the cheeks are sprinckled,
shal decay, And those sweete rosy leaves, so fairely spred Upon the lips, shall
fade and fall away" etc.: *Rep.* 601 B οὐκοῦν ἔοικεν τοῖς τῶν ὡραίων προσώποις…
ὅταν αὐτὰ τὸ ἄνθος προλίπῃ: Xen. *Symp.* VIII. 14 τὸ μὲν τῆς ὥρας ἄνθος ταχὺ
δήπου παρακμάζει, κτλ.: Tyrt. 10. 28 ὄφρ᾿ ἐρατῆς ἥβης ἀγλαὸν ἄνθος ἔχῃ:
Mimnerm. 1. 4. So Emerson (*On Beauty*) "The radiance of the human
form…is only a burst of beauty for a few years or a few months, at the
perfection of youth, and in most rapidly declines. But we remain lovers
of it, only transferring our interest to interior excellence."

οἴχεται ἀποπτάμενος. A reminiscence of *Il.* II. 71. For the thought, cp.
181 D *supra*: Xen. *Symp.* l.c. ἀπολείποντος δὲ τούτου (*sc.* τοῦ τῆς ὥρας ἄνθους),
ἀνάγκη καὶ τὴν φιλίαν συναπομαραίνεσθαι. Cp. also *Phaedr.* 232 E, 234 A.

συντακείς. "Fused into one" by the flame of love. Cp. 192 D, Eur.
fr. 964 πᾶσα γὰρ ἀγαθὴ γυνὴ | ἥτις ἀνδρὶ συντέτηκε σωφρονεῖν ἐπίσταται:
id. Supp. 1029.

τούτους δή. With the text as it stands in the MSS., τούτους refers to the
ἐρασταί only, who are divided into two classes, the good (τοῖς μὲν) and the bad
(τοὺς δὲ). But in the next clause τοῖς μὲν refers to the ἐρασταί en bloc, and
τοῖς δὲ to the ἐρώμενοι. This is extremely awkward; and it is a further
objection to the clause that the statement it contains is premature, and
would fit in better below (184 D—E). I therefore follow Voegelin and Hug
in obelizing. For the language, cp. Theogn. 1299 ff. ὦ παῖ, μέχρι τίνος με
προφεύξεαι; ὥς σε διώκων | δίζημ᾿…ἀλλ᾿ ἐπίμεινον, ἐμοὶ δὲ δίδου χάριν.

λεται ὁ ἡμέτερος νόμος εὖ καὶ καλῶς βασανίζειν [,καὶ τοῖς μὲν 184
χαρίσασθαι, τοὺς δὲ διαφεύγειν]. διὰ ταῦτα οὖν τοῖς μὲν διώκειν
παρακελεύεται, τοῖς δὲ φεύγειν, ἀγωνοθετῶν καὶ βασανίζων ποτέρων ποτέ ἐστιν ὁ ἐρῶν καὶ ποτέρων ὁ ἐρώμενος. οὕτω δὴ ὑπὸ
ταύτης τῆς αἰτίας πρῶτον μὲν τὸ ἁλίσκεσθαι ταχὺ αἰσχρὸν νενόμισται, ἵνα χρόνος ἐγγένηται, ὃς δὴ δοκεῖ τὰ πολλὰ καλῶς βασανίζειν, ἔπειτα τὸ ὑπὸ χρημάτων καὶ ὑπὸ πολιτικῶν δυνάμεων
ἁλῶναι αἰσχρόν, ἐάν τε κακῶς πάσχων πτήξῃ καὶ μὴ καρτερήσῃ, Β
ἄν τ' εὐεργετούμενος εἰς χρήματα ἢ εἰς διαπράξεις πολιτικὰς μὴ
καταφρονήσῃ· οὐδὲν γὰρ δοκεῖ τούτων οὔτε βέβαιον οὔτε μόνιμον
εἶναι, χωρὶς τοῦ μηδὲ πεφυκέναι ἀπ' αὐτῶν γενναίαν φιλίαν. μία
δὴ λείπεται τῷ ἡμετέρῳ νόμῳ ὁδός, εἰ μέλλει καλῶς χαριεῖσθαι
ἐραστῇ παιδικά. ἔστι γὰρ ἡμῖν νόμος, ὥσπερ ἐπὶ τοῖς ἐρασταῖς ἦν
δουλεύειν ἐθέλοντα ἡντινοῦν δουλείαν παιδικοῖς μὴ κολακείαν εἶναι C

184 A καὶ...διαφεύγειν secl. Bdhm. Sz.   διαφυγεῖν Hirschig   διὰ...
ἐρώμενος del. Schütz Ast   καὶ ποτέρων del. Bast : καὶ...ἐρώμενος secl. J.-U.
δὴ ΒΤ : δὴ καὶ W   ὑπὸ...αἰτίας del. Baiter   τὸ ⟨ἢ⟩ Hirschig   καὶ ὑπὸ :
ἢ ὑπὸ Hirschig   Β αἰσχρόν del. Hirschig   ἀντευεργετούμενος Τ   εἰς
χρ....πολιτικὰς secl. Hirschig J.-U. Hug Sz.   μόνιμον : νόμιμον Wolf   ἔστι :
ὡς J.-U.: ὥσπερ Bdhm.: ἔστι...νόμος om. Verm. Sz. Hug   ὥσπερ Τ: ὅσπερ
Β Stob. Jn.: ὥσπερ γὰρ Verm. Sz.: ὡς γὰρ Hug: del. Bdhm.   ἐθέλοντα ΒΤ:
ἐθέλοντας vel ἐθελοντὰς Stob. Sz.: ἐθελοντὴν Bast: ἐθέλοντι Bdhm.

184 A ἵνα χρόνος κτλ. For the touchstone of time, cp. Simon. fr. 175
οὐκ ἔστιν μείζων βάσανος χρόνου οὐδενὸς ἔργου | ὃς καὶ ὑπὸ στέρνοις ἀνδρὸς
ἔδειξε νόον : Soph. O. T. 614 χρόνος δίκαιον ἄνδρα δείκνυσιν μόνος : Eur.
Hippol. 1051 μηνυτὴν χρόνον. On the signif. of βάσανος, see Vahlen Op. Acad.
ΙΙ. 7 ff.: cp. Gorg. 486 D, Rep. 413 E; Clem. Al. Strom. I. 291 D.
τὸ ὑπὸ χρημάτων...ἁλῶναι. Cp. 185 A πλούτου ἕνεκα χαρισάμενος : 216 D
μέλει αὐτῷ οὐδὲν...εἴ τις πλούσιος : Ar. Plut. 153 ff. καὶ τούς γε παῖδας...δρᾶν...
τἀργυρίου χάριν. As against the deletion of the second αἰσχρόν by Hirschig,
see the parallels collected by Vahlen Op. Acad. ΙΙ. 359. For πολιτ. δυνάμεων,
cp. Xen. Mem. IV. 2. 35; this may be a hit at Alcibiades, cp. 216 B.
184 B εἰς χρήματα...πολιτικὰς The reasons for which Hug, after Hirschig
and others, rejects these words—as (1) superfluous for the sense, and (2)
spoiling the responsion of the clauses ἐάν τε καρτερήσῃ and ἄν τε...καταφρο-
νήσῃ—are not convincing. This is the only ex. of διάπραξις, actio, cited by
L. and S.
ἔστι γὰρ κτλ. Hug, objecting to the "ganz unerträgliche Anakoluthie,"
follows Vermehren in excising the clause ἔστι...νόμος, as a gloss on the
following νενόμισται, and writing ὡς γὰρ for ὥσπερ. This is too rash. For
the sense, cp. 183 B and the passage from Isocr. Hel. 219 B there quoted.
ἦν...εἶναι. For simple ἦν (ἔστι) with accus. and infin. cp. Phaedo 72 D
ἀλλ' ἔστι τῷ ὄντι...τὰς τῶν τεθνεώτων ψυχὰς εἶναι. For ἐθέλων as adj. ("volun-

μηδὲ ἐπονείδιστον, οὕτω δὴ καὶ ἄλλη μία μόνον δουλεία ἑκούσιος
λείπεται οὐκ ἐπονείδιστος· αὕτη δέ ἐστιν ἡ περὶ τὴν ἀρετήν.

XI. Νενόμισται γὰρ δὴ ἡμῖν, ἐάν τις ἐθέλῃ τινὰ θεραπεύειν
ἡγούμενος δι' ἐκεῖνον ἀμείνων ἔσεσθαι ἢ κατὰ σοφίαν τινὰ ἢ κατὰ
ἄλλο ὁτιοῦν μέρος ἀρετῆς, αὕτη αὖ ἡ ἐθελοδουλεία οὐκ αἰσχρὰ
εἶναι οὐδὲ κολακεία. δεῖ δὴ τὼ νόμω τούτω ξυμβαλεῖν εἰς ταὐτό,
D τόν τε περὶ τὴν παιδεραστίαν καὶ τὸν περὶ τὴν φιλοσοφίαν τε καὶ
τὴν ἄλλην ἀρετήν, εἰ μέλλει ξυμβῆναι καλὸν γενέσθαι τὸ ἐραστῇ
παιδικὰ χαρίσασθαι. ὅταν γὰρ εἰς τὸ αὐτὸ ἔλθωσιν ἐραστής τε
καὶ παιδικά, νόμον ἔχων ἑκάτερος, ὁ μὲν χαρισαμένοις παιδικοῖς
ὑπηρετῶν ὁτιοῦν δικαίως ἂν ὑπηρετεῖν, ὁ δὲ τῷ ποιοῦντι αὐτὸν
σοφόν τε καὶ ἀγαθὸν δικαίως αὖ ὁτιοῦν ἂν ὑπουργῶν ⟨ὑπουργεῖν⟩,

184 C μία μόνον T: μία μῶν B: μόνη μία Stob.: μία μόνη vulg., Bt.: μία
νόμῳ Ficinus: μία παιδικῶν Verm.: μία ἐρωμένῳ Usener: μία νέων Hug: ἡμῖν
νόμῳ Kreyenbühl: μία ⟨τῶν ἐρωμένων τῷ ἡμετέρῳ νό⟩μῳ Sz: μία τῷ ἐρωμένῳ
Steinhart: μῶν δουλεία secl. Bdhm.: μῶν...ἑκούσιος fort. delenda   τίς τινα
θέλῃ Stob.   ἐκεῖνον T, Stob.: ἐκεῖνο B   τινὰ del. Hirschig   εἶναι: ἐστιν
Stob.   τὼ νόμω τούτω apographa: τῷ νόμῳ τούτῳ BT   D τὴν σοφίαν
Hirschig   τὸ T: τῷ BW   χαρισαμένοις secl. J.-U.: ⟨τοῖς⟩ χαρ. Hirschig:
χαρ. ⟨τοῖς⟩ Baiter   ἂν T: οὖν B   ὑπηρετῶν Bast   αὐτὸν Sauppe
⟨ὑπουργῶν⟩ δικαίως Rettig: δικαίως ⟨ὑπουργῶν⟩ Sz.   ἂν T: αὖ B   ὑπουργῶν
⟨ὑπουργεῖν⟩ Baiter Vahlen: ὑπουργῶν BTW: ὑπουργεῖν vulg., J.-U.: ⟨ὑπουργεῖν⟩
ὑπουργῶν Bt.

tarily") in prose, cp. Xen. *Anab.* VI. 2. 6; Lys. XIX. 6: in poetry the use is
common, *e.g.* Soph. *O. T.* 649.

184 C οὕτω δὴ κτλ. In this clause the method of action permissible to
παιδικά is presented as parallel to that permissible to ἐρασταί. That there is
some corruption in the text is indicated by the divergence of the MSS. in regard
to the words after ἄλλη: but of the many emendations suggested (see *crit. n.*)
none is convincing. Perhaps the safest plan is to bracket μῶν...ἑκούσιος, as
an adscript meant to suggest a subject for λείπεται, and to supply ὁδός as
subject from the preceding context.

σοφίαν...μέρος ἀρετῆς. Cp. *Protag.* 329 E, *Rep.* 427 E (with Adam's *n.*):
"the nearest approach to the doctrine before Plato is in Xen. *Mem.* III.
9. 1—5." How many μέρη ἀρετῆς are assumed here by Pausanias is, of course,
left indefinite. (See also 196 B *n.*)

184 D ὅταν γὰρ κτλ. Notice the balance and rhythm of the clauses in
this sentence—(a¹) ὅταν...ἑκάτερος, (b¹) ὁ μὲν...ὑπηρετῶν, (b²) ὁ δὲ...ὑπουργῶν,
(c¹) ὁ μὲν...ξυμβάλλεσθαι, (c²) ὁ δὲ...κτᾶσθαι, (a²) τότε δὴ...ἐνταῦθα, (a³) ξυμπίπτει...οὐδαμοῦ.

ὑπηρετεῖν...ὑπουργεῖν. Both words are used in an erotic sense. So ὑπουργία
is used *in re venerea*, Amphis Ἰαλ. That ὑπουργῶν ⟨ὑπουργεῖν⟩ is the best
restoration is shown by Vahlen *Op. Acad.* I. 499 ff.: cp. 193 C.

καὶ ὁ μὲν δυνάμενος εἰς φρόνησιν καὶ τὴν ἄλλην ἀρετὴν ξυμβάλ
λεσθαι, ὁ δὲ δεόμενος εἰς παίδευσιν καὶ τὴν ἄλλην σοφίαν κτᾶσθαι, **E**
τότε δὴ τούτων ξυνιόντων εἰς ταὐτὸν τῶν νόμων μοναχοῦ ἐνταῦθα
ξυμπίπτει τὸ καλὸν εἶναι παιδικὰ ἐραστῇ χαρίσασθαι, ἄλλοθι δὲ
οὐδαμοῦ. ἐπὶ τούτῳ καὶ ἐξαπατηθῆναι οὐδὲν αἰσχρόν· ἐπὶ δὲ
τοῖς ἄλλοις πᾶσι καὶ ἐξαπατωμένῳ αἰσχύνην φέρει καὶ μή.
εἰ γάρ τις ἐραστῇ ὡς πλουσίῳ πλούτου ἕνεκα χαρισάμενος ἐξαπα- 185
τηθείη καὶ μὴ λάβοι χρήματα, ἀναφανέντος τοῦ ἐραστοῦ πένητος,
οὐδὲν ἧττον αἰσχρόν· δοκεῖ γὰρ ὁ τοιοῦτος τό γε αὑτοῦ ἐπιδεῖξαι,
ὅτι ἕνεκα χρημάτων ὁτιοῦν ἂν ὁτῳοῦν ὑπηρετοῖ, τοῦτο δὲ οὐ καλόν.
κατὰ τὸν αὐτὸν δὴ λόγον κἂν εἴ τις ὡς ἀγαθῷ χαρισάμενος καὶ
αὐτὸς ὡς ἀμείνων ἐσόμενος διὰ τὴν φιλίαν ἐραστοῦ ἐξαπατηθείη,

184 D ξυμβάλλεσθαι T: ξυμβαλέσθαι B   **E** εἰς del. Schütz J.‑U.   κτᾶσθαι:
ἵστασθαι Sz.: κτᾶσθαί τι cj. Hug   τότε δὲ Wolf   τῶν νόμων del. Bast
185 **A** ὡς πλουσίῳ secl. Cobet   καὶ…χρήματα del. Cobet   κἂν: καὶ
Hirschig   χαρισόμενος cj. Steph.   διὰ…ἐραστοῦ secl. Hug   τοῦ ἐραστοῦ
apogr. Coisl. 155

184 **E** εἰς παίδευσιν…κτᾶσθαι. If the text is right we must suppose that
κτᾶσθαι is here equiv. to ὥστε κτᾶσθαι, appended to the main verb ξυμβάλ
λεσθαι which is to be supplied with εἰς παίδευσιν κτλ. (so Vahlen). Of the
corrections suggested (see *crit. n.*) Schanz's is the neatest, but spoils the
sense-balance with ξυμβάλλεσθαι. The corruption is, perhaps, to be sought
elsewhere : the expression τὴν ἄλλην σοφίαν is open to suspicion, since σοφίαν
as here used after ἄλλην stands as a generic subst. whereas σοφία has just
been termed (184 c) μέρος ἀρετῆς : moreover, we should expect that σοφία
should itself constitute the κτῆμα of the recipient, just as φρόνησις is itself
the contribution of ὁ ξυμβαλλόμενος. On these grounds, I venture to suggest
that another fem. subst., such as διδαχήν, may have fallen out after ἄλλην
(ἐκπαίδευσιν for εἰς π. is just possible).

ἐπὶ τούτῳ. "In this case," *i.e.* in the quest for ἀρετή, in contrast to "the
other cases" where lucre or position is coveted (184 A).

εἰ γάρ τις κτλ. Observe the effort after rhythm, with strophe and anti-
strophe. For the thought, see 184 A and cp. Isocr. *Hel.* 219 c τῶν ἐχόντων τὸ
κάλλος τοὺς μὲν μισθαρνήσαντας…ἀτιμάζομεν.

185 **A** καὶ μὴ λάβοι χρήματα. In defence of the text here, against the
excisions of Cobet and Hug, see Vahlen, *Op. Acad.* II. 366: cp. *Hipp. Min.*
372 E σὺ οὖν χάρισαι καὶ μὴ φθονήσῃς ἰάσασθαι τὴν ψυχήν μου: Thuc. II. 13. 1
μὴ τοὺς ἀγροὺς αὐτοῦ παραλίπῃ καὶ μὴ δῃώσῃ.

διὰ τὴν φιλίαν ἐραστοῦ. This phrase also is rejected by Hug (followed by
Hirzel) on the grounds that (1) "an der correspondierenden Stelle nichts
steht," (2) we should expect rather διὰ τὸν ἔρωτα τοῦ ἐραστοῦ (cp. 182 c).
The latter objection falls if, with Rückert, we take ἐραστοῦ as object. gen.
("suam caritatem erga amatorem"). φιλία ἐραστοῦ here is, I take it, equiv.
to the compound φιλεραστία (213 D, cp. 192 B).

44 ΠΛΑΤΩΝΟΣ [185 A

B ἀναφανέντος ἐκείνου κακοῦ καὶ οὐ κεκτημένου ἀρετήν, ὅμως καλὴ
ἡ ἀπάτη· δοκεῖ γὰρ αὖ καὶ οὗτος τὸ καθ᾽ αὑτὸν δεδηλωκέναι, ὅτι
ἀρετῆς γ᾽ ἔνεκα καὶ τοῦ βελτίων γενέσθαι πᾶν ἂν παντὶ προθυμη-
θείη, τοῦτο δὲ αὖ πάντων κάλλιστον· οὕτω πάντως γε καλὸν
ἀρετῆς ἔνεκα χαρίζεσθαι.

Οὗτός ἐστιν ὁ τῆς οὐρανίας θεοῦ ἔρως καὶ οὐράνιος καὶ
πολλοῦ ἄξιος καὶ πόλει καὶ ἰδιώταις, πολλὴν ἐπιμέλειαν ἀναγ-
C κάζων ποιεῖσθαι πρὸς ἀρετὴν τόν τε ἐρῶντα αὐτὸν αὐτοῦ καὶ τὸν
ἐρώμενον· οἱ δ᾽ ἕτεροι πάντες τῆς ἑτέρας, τῆς πανδήμου. ταῦτά
σοι, ἔφη, ὡς ἐκ τοῦ παραχρῆμα, ὦ Φαῖδρε, περὶ Ἔρωτος συμβάλλομαι.

Παυσανίου δὲ παυσαμένου, διδάσκουσι γάρ με ἴσα λέγειν
οὑτωσὶ οἱ σοφοί, ἔφη ὁ Ἀριστόδημος δεῖν μὲν Ἀριστοφάνη λέγειν,
τυχεῖν δὲ αὐτῷ τινὰ ἢ ὑπὸ πλησμονῆς ἢ ὑπό τινος ἄλλου λύγγα

185 B καὶ οὐ...ἀρετὴν secl. Hug   ἡ om. pr. T   ⟨πᾶν⟩ πάντως Stob., Bt.
ἀρετῆς γ᾽ ἔνεκα T : ἔνεκα ἀρετῆς Stob.   C ἔρωτα Stob.   αὐτοῦ ⟨τε⟩ Ast
τοῦ ἐρωμένου Bast Ast   συμβάλλομαι T, Method.: συμβάλλομεν B   οὑτωσὶ
om. Hermog.

185 B καλὴ ἡ ἀπάτη. Sc. τῷ ἐξαπατωμένῳ.
δοκεῖ γὰρ αὖ καὶ οὗτος. This corresponds to δοκεῖ γὰρ ὁ τοιοῦτος κτλ. in
185 A.
185 C ἐκ τοῦ παραχρῆμα. For the sense subito s. ex tempore, cp. Crat.
399 D, Critias 107 E. On extempore, as opposed to premeditated orations,
see Alcidamas de Soph. 3 εἰπεῖν ἐκ τοῦ παραυτίκα κτλ.
συμβάλλομαι. "This is my contribution," with allusion to the literary
ἔρανος mentioned in 177 C.
ἴσα λέγειν. This alludes to the ἴσα σχήματα (including sound-echoes etc.,
as well as "isokolia") of the rhetorical τεχνῖται (see Spengel, rhet. Gr. II.
pp. 436—7). We may render (after Jowett): "When Pausanias had come
to a pause—a pretty piece of 'isology' I have been taught by the professors—"
etc. The title οἱ σοφοί is variously applied in Plato to the Orphics (Rep.
583 B), to poets (Rep. 489 B), and, as here, to linguistic craftsmen. For σοφία
as applied to etymological "puns," cp. Crat. 396 C, D, and the use of σοφί-
ζεσθαι (in connexion with the etymology of οὐρανός) in Rep. 509 D (see
Adam's n. ad loc.). For a rhetorical repetition of the same word (παύω),
see Gorg. Hel. 2 τὴν μὲν κακῶς ἀκούουσαν παῦσαι τῆς αἰτίας, τοὺς δὲ μεμφο-
μένους...παῦσαι τῆς ἀμαθίας.
λύγγα. The Scholiast has a long note here: τὸ τοῦ λυγμοῦ σύμπτωμα
ἐπιγίνεται τῷ στομάχῳ διὰ πλήρωσιν ἢ κένωσιν ἢ ψῦξιν, ἐνίοτε δὲ καὶ διὰ δῆξιν
δριμέων ὑγρῶν καὶ φαρμακωδῶν ταῖς ποιότησιν...ὅταν δὲ ὑπὸ πληρώσεως λυγμὸς
γένηται, ἔμετος τούτοις ἅμα καὶ τῶν ἄκρων τρῖψις καὶ πνεύματος κατοχή. The
hiccough of Aristophanes is part of the comic relief in the piece (see Introd.
§ II. c). For πλησμονή, as a cause of disorder, cp. 186 C n., Hippocr. de diaet.
III. 72 ff.

ἐπιπεπτωκυῖαν καὶ οὐχ οἶόν τε εἶναι λέγειν, ἀλλ' εἰπεῖν αὐτόν—
ἐν τῇ κάτω γὰρ αὐτοῦ τὸν ἰατρὸν Ἐρυξίμαχον κατακεῖσθαι—Ὦ D
Ἐρυξίμαχε, δίκαιος εἰ ἢ παῦσαί με τῆς λυγγὸς ἢ λέγειν ὑπὲρ ἐμοῦ,
ἕως ἂν ἐγὼ παύσωμαι. καὶ τὸν Ἐρυξίμαχον εἰπεῖν Ἀλλὰ ποιήσω
ἀμφότερα ταῦτα· ἐγὼ μὲν γὰρ ἐρῶ ἐν τῷ σῷ μέρει, σὺ δ' ἐπειδὰν
παύσῃ, ἐν τῷ ἐμῷ. ἐν ᾧ δ' ἂν ἐγὼ λέγω, ἐὰν μέν σοι ἐθέλῃ
ἀπνευστὶ ἔχοντι πολὺν χρόνον παύεσθαι ἡ λύγξ· εἰ δὲ μή, ὕδατι
ἀνακογχυλίασον. εἰ δ' ἄρα πάνυ ἰσχυρά ἐστιν, ἀναλαβών τι Ε
τοιοῦτον οἴῳ κνήσαις ἂν τὴν ῥῖνα, πτάρε· καὶ ἐὰν τοῦτο ποιήσῃς
ἅπαξ ἢ δίς, καὶ εἰ πάνυ ἰσχυρά ἐστι, παύσεται. Οὐκ ἂν φθάνοις
λέγων, φάναι τὸν Ἀριστοφάνη· ἐγὼ δὲ ταῦτα ποιήσω.

XII. Εἰπεῖν δὴ τὸν Ἐρυξίμαχον, Δοκεῖ τοίνυν μοι ἀναγκαῖον
εἶναι, ἐπειδὴ Παυσανίας ὁρμήσας ἐπὶ τὸν λόγον καλῶς οὐχ ἱκανῶς 186
ἀπετέλεσε, δεῖν ἐμὲ πειρᾶσθαι τέλος ἐπιθεῖναι τῷ λόγῳ. τὸ μὲν
γὰρ διπλοῦν εἶναι τὸν Ἔρωτα δοκεῖ μοι καλῶς διελέσθαι· ὅτι δὲ

185 C λέγειν om. W   D ἐν τῇ κάτω : ἐγγυτάτω Steph.   τὸν ἰατρὸν T:
τῶν ἰατρῶν B   ⟨οὐ⟩ πολὺν Sauppe   παύσασθαι Stob.   E ἀναλαβών :
λαβών Stob.   οἴῳ : ὅτῳ Cobet   κνήσαις Wyttenbach : κνήσαιο Luzac :
κινήσαις BT, Stob. Athen.   πταρὼν Stob.   φᾶναι B : εἰπεῖν TW
ἀναγκαῖον εἶναι del. Sz.   οὐχ ἱκανῶς : οὐχὶ καλῶς olim Sz.   186 A δεῖν
om. Method. Sz.: δεῖν ἐμὲ del. Hirschig

ἐν τῇ κάτω αὐτοῦ. *Sc.* κλίνῃ—referring to what might jocosely be termed
the *clinical* position of the worthy doctor. Cp. *n.* on ἔσχατον κατακείμενον,
175 C.

185 D ἐν τῷ σῷ μέρει. Cp. *Meno* 92 E ἀλλὰ σὺ δὴ ἐν τῷ μέρει αὐτοῦ εἰπέ.
ἐὰν μέν σοι κτλ. We have here a case of "aposiopesis" or suppressed
apodosis; cp. *Protag.* 311 D; Hom. *Il.* I. 135 ff.: see Goodwin *G. M. T.* § 482.

ἀνακογχυλίασον. Schol. ἀνακογχυλιάσαι· τὸ κλύσαι τὴν φάρυγγα, ὃ λέγομεν
ἀναγαργαρίσαι. With Eryximachus's treatment of λύγξ, cp. Hippocr. *de diaet.*
III. 75 ff. γίνεται δὲ καὶ τοιάδε πλησμονή· ἐς τὴν ὑστεραίην τὸν σῖτον ἐρυγ-
γάνεται κτλ.

185 E πτάρε. Cp. Hippocr. *Aphor.* VI. 13 ὑπὸ λυγμοῦ ἐχομένῳ πταρμοὶ
ἐπιγενόμενοι λύουσι τὸν λυγμόν : Arist. *Probl.* 33.

Οὐκ ἂν φθάνοις λέγων. A familiar idiom: "the sooner you speak the better"
(see Goodwin *G. M. T.* § 894): more rarely of 1st person, 214 E *infra*.

οὐχ ἱκανῶς. Schanz's οὐχὶ καλῶς is ingenious but needless : for a similar
variety in antithesis Vahlen cites *Theaet.* 187 E κρεῖττον γάρ που σμικρὸν
εὖ ἢ πολὺ μὴ ἱκανῶς περᾶναι. For δεῖν redundant cp. *Alc. II.* 144 D, 146 B,
Rep. 535 A, *Laws* 731 D, E : Schanz in *nov. comm.* p. 83 regards both ἀναγκαῖον
εἶναι and δεῖν ἐμέ as interpolations by copyists who failed to see the force of
δοκεῖ=*aptum videtur*; but in his text he excises only δεῖν : against this, see
Teuffel, *Rh. Mus.* XXIX. p. 140.

οὐ μόνον ἐστὶν ἐπὶ ταῖς ψυχαῖς τῶν ἀνθρώπων πρὸς τοὺς καλοὺς
ἀλλὰ καὶ πρὸς ἄλλα πολλὰ καὶ ἐν τοῖς ἄλλοις, τοῖς τε σώμασι
τῶν πάντων ζώων καὶ τοῖς ἐν τῇ γῇ φυομένοις καὶ ὡς ἔπος εἰπεῖν
ἐν πᾶσι τοῖς οὖσι, καθεωρακέναι μοι δοκῶ ἐκ τῆς ἰατρικῆς, τῆς
B ἡμετέρας τέχνης, ὡς μέγας καὶ θαυμαστὸς καὶ ἐπὶ πᾶν ὁ θεὸς
τείνει καὶ κατ᾽ ἀνθρώπινα καὶ κατὰ θεῖα πράγματα. ἄρξομαι δὲ
ἀπὸ τῆς ἰατρικῆς λέγων, ἵνα καὶ πρεσβεύωμεν τὴν τέχνην. ἡ γὰρ
φύσις τῶν σωμάτων τὸν διπλοῦν Ἔρωτα τοῦτον ἔχει. τὸ γὰρ
ὑγιὲς τοῦ σώματος καὶ τὸ νοσοῦν ὁμολογουμένως ἕτερόν τε καὶ
ἀνόμοιόν ἐστι, τὸ δὲ ἀνόμοιον ἀνομοίων ἐπιθυμεῖ καὶ ἐρᾷ. ἄλλος
μὲν οὖν ὁ ἐπὶ τῷ ὑγιεινῷ ἔρως, ἄλλος δὲ ὁ ἐπὶ τῷ νοσώδει. ἔστι
δή, ὥσπερ ἄρτι Παυσανίας ἔλεγε τοῖς μὲν ἀγαθοῖς καλὸν χαρί-
C ζεσθαι τῶν ἀνθρώπων, τοῖς δὲ ἀκολάστοις αἰσχρόν, οὕτω καὶ ἐν

186 A πάντων τῶν Hirschig   δοκῶ ⟨γνοὺς⟩ Herwerden   τῆς ἰατρικῆς
secl. Hirschig   ὡς ⟨καὶ⟩ Ficinus Steph.   B κατὰ τἀνθρώπινα Stob.
κατὰ τὰ θεῖα Stob.   καὶ om. Stob.   πρεσβεύω μου Bdhm.   ἡ γὰρ
ἦ τε γὰρ Sauppe: καὶ γὰρ J.-U.   ἔχει T: ἔχῃ B   ὁμολογοῦμεν ὡς TW,
Stob.   τε: τι Stob., Thiersch   ὑγιεινῷ ἔρως T: ὑγιεῖνοερος B   ἔστι
δή: ἔτι δὲ Bdhm.   τῶν ἀνθρώπων del. Thiersch

---

186 A τῆς ἰατρικῆς. Eryx. speaks, as a member of the Asclepiad guild,
of "*our* art": for his glorification of "the art," see also 176 D, 196 A, and
Agathon's allusion in 196 D. Cp. *Theaet.* 161 E τὸ δὲ δὴ ἐμόν τε καὶ τῆς ἐμῆς
τέχνης τῆς μαιευτικῆς κτλ., where also Naber excises τῆς μ. (cp. Vahlen *Op.
Ac.* II. 273).

ὡς μέγας κτλ. This ὡς-clause serves to repeat in another form the initial
ὅτι-clause, thus making two object-clauses to one main clause in the sentence,
for which cp. 211 E *infra, Apol.* 20 C.

186 B ἐπὶ πᾶν...τείνει. Cp. 222 B ἐπὶ πλεῖστον τείνοντες (λόγους): we might
render " of universal scope."

πρεσβεύωμεν. For the sense, "venerate," cp. 188 C, and πρεσβύτερον 218 D :
Crito 46 C τοὺς αὐτοὺς πρεσβεύω καὶ τιμῶ : *Rep.* 591 C.

τὸ δὲ ἀνόμοιον κτλ. "Things dissimilar in themselves crave dissimilar
objects": *e.g.* the appetites of the sound body differ from those of the sick
body. Cp. Hippocr. *de nat. hom.* 9 ὁκόσα πλησμονὴ τίκτει νουσήματα, κένωσις
ἰῆται, ὁκόσα δὲ ἀπὸ κενώσιος γένεται νουσήματα, πλησμονὴ ἰῆται...τὸ δὲ ξύμπαν
γνῶναι, δεῖ τὸν ἰητρὸν ἐναντίον ἵστασθαι τοῖσι καθεστεῶσι καὶ νουσήμασι καὶ
εἴδεσι κτλ.

ὁ ἐπὶ τῷ ὑγιεινῷ ἔρως. "The craving felt by the sound body": cp. ἐπὶ ταῖς
ψυχαῖς, 186 A. In the doctor's parable, τὸ ὑγιεινόν corresponds to the good,
τὸ νοσῶδες to the bad ἐραστής.

ἔστι δή. This is, as Hug observes, a favourite opening with Eryx.: cp.
ἔστι γάρ, 186 C; ἔστι δέ, 186 D, 187 A.

αὐτοῖς τοῖς σώμασι τοῖς μὲν ἀγαθοῖς ἑκάστου τοῦ σώματος καὶ
ὑγιεινοῖς καλὸν χαρίζεσθαι καὶ δεῖ, καὶ τοῦτό ἐστιν ᾧ ὄνομα τὸ
ἰατρικόν, τοῖς δὲ κακοῖς καὶ νοσώδεσιν αἰσχρόν τε καὶ δεῖ ἀχαρι-
στεῖν, εἰ μέλλει τις τεχνικὸς εἶναι. ἔστι γὰρ ἰατρική, ὡς ἐν κεφαλαίῳ εἰπεῖν, ἐπιστήμη τῶν τοῦ σώματος ἐρωτικῶν πρὸς πλησμονὴν καὶ κένωσιν, καὶ ὁ διαγιγνώσκων ἐν τούτοις τὸν καλόν τε
καὶ αἰσχρὸν ἔρωτα, οὗτός ἐστιν ὁ ἰατρικώτατος, καὶ ὁ μεταβάλλειν D
ποιῶν, ὥστε ἀντὶ τοῦ ἑτέρου ἔρωτος τὸν ἕτερον κτᾶσθαι, καὶ οἷς
μὴ ἔνεστιν ἔρως, δεῖ δ᾽ ἐγγενέσθαι, ἐπιστάμενος ἐμποιῆσαι καὶ
ἐνόντα ἐξελεῖν, ἀγαθὸς ἂν εἴη δημιουργός. δεῖ γὰρ δὴ τὰ ἔχθιστα

186 C αὐτοῖς: αὖ Rohde   καὶ δεῖ, καὶ: καὶ δὴ καὶ Naber   τὸν ante
καλόν delend. cj. Usener   D κτᾶσθαι B: κτήσασθαι T: fort. ἵστασθαι
ἔρως secl. J.-U.   καὶ...ἐξελεῖν secl. Sz.   ἐνόντα ⟨οἷς μὴ δεῖ⟩ Herw.

186 C ἔστι γὰρ ἰατρική κτλ.   Cp. (with Poschenrieder) Hippocr. de flat. I.
p. 570 K.   πάλιν αὖ πλησμονὴν ἰῆται κένωσις· κένωσιν δὲ πλησμονή...τὰ ἐναντία τῶν ἐναντίων ἐστὶν ἰήματα.   ἰητρικὴ γάρ ἐστι πρόσθεσις καὶ ἀφαίρεσις,
ἀφαίρεσις μὲν τῶν ὑπερβαλλόντων, πρόσθεσις δὲ τῶν ἐλλιπόντων· ὁ δὲ κάλλιστα
τοῦτο ποιέων ἄριστος ἰητρός.   Also Phileb. 32 A, 35 A for "repletion" and
"depletion" in connexion with bodily φύσις: and Tim. 82 A γῆς πυρὸς ὕδατος
τε καὶ ἀέρος...ἡ παρὰ φύσιν πλεονεξία καὶ ἔνδεια...στάσεις καὶ νόσους παρέχει.

ὁ διαγιγνώσκων κτλ.   In this passage there is a distinction implied between
pure and applied ἰατρική, between medicine as a science (ἐπιστήμη) and as an
art (τέχνη).   διαγιγνώσκω is here used almost in the technical sense of
making a medical diagnosis (cp. Hippocr. de nat. hom. 9 τὴν διάγνωσιν...
ποιέεσθαι): possibly earlier "Asclepiads" than Hippocrates may have ear-
marked διάγνωσις as a medical term.   Cf. the distinction between κατὰ
γνώμην and κατὰ χειρουργίην in Hippocr. de morbis I. 6.

186 D ὁ μεταβάλλειν ποιῶν κτλ.   Cp. Hippocr. de morbo sacro, p. 396 L.
ὅστις δὲ ἐπίσταται ἐν ἀνθρώποισι τὴν τοιαύτην μεταβολὴν καὶ δύναται ὑγρὸν καὶ
ξηρὸν ποιέειν καὶ θερμὸν καὶ ψυχρὸν ὑπὸ διαίτης τὸν ἄνθρωπον, οὗτος καὶ ταύτην
τὴν νοῦσον ἰῷτο ἄν: id. de nat. hom. 9 τὴν θεραπείην χρὴ ποιέεσθαι...τῇ τῶν
διαιτημάτων μεταβολῇ κτλ.   In later Greek δημιουργός becomes the vox propria
for a medical "practitioner," as δημοσιεύειν for "to practise": similarly χειρο-
τέχνης, Hippocr. περὶ παθῶν 1.

ὥστε...κτᾶσθαι.   Supply as subject τὰ σώματα.

καὶ ἐνόντα ἐξελεῖν.   Schanz would excise these words; but though they
present a rather awkward case of brachylogy, they are otherwise unobjectionable.   Herwerden's proposal (see crit. n.), though supplying the right sense,
is needless; while Lehrs is obviously blundering when he construes ἐνόντα as
neut. plural, "und wieder auch das Vorhandene fortzubringen."   Hommel
gives the meaning rightly, "und die einwohnende (Neigung), die nicht ein-
wohnen darf, heraus zu treiben."

δεῖ γὰρ δή.   "For he must, as a matter of fact"—an appeal to recognized

ὄντα ἐν τῷ σώματι φίλα οἷόν τ᾽ εἶναι ποιεῖν καὶ ἐρᾶν ἀλλήλων.
ἔστι δὲ ἔχθιστα᾽᾽τὰ ἐναντιώτατα, ψυχρὸν θερμῷ, πικρὸν γλυκεῖ,
E ξηρὸν ὑγρῷ, πάντα τὰ τοιαῦτα· τούτοις ἐπιστηθεὶς ἔρωτα ἐμποιῆσαι καὶ ὁμόνοιαν ὁ ἡμέτερος πρόγονος Ἀσκληπιός, ὥς φασιν οἵδε
οἱ ποιηταὶ καὶ ἐγὼ πείθομαι, συνέστησε τὴν ἡμετέραν τέχνην.
ἥ τε οὖν ἰατρική, ὥσπερ λέγω, πᾶσα διὰ τοῦ θεοῦ τούτου κυβερ-
187 νᾶται, ὡσαύτως δὲ καὶ γυμναστικὴ καὶ γεωργία· μουσικὴ δὲ καὶ

186 D φίλια Hirschig   πικρὸν γλυκεῖ del. Thiersch Hug   ⟨καὶ⟩ πάντα
Wolf   E τοῦ θεοῦ secl. Bdhm.   187 A καὶ γεωργία del. Sauppe Jn.

---

axioms of "the Art." Hippocrates based his medical theory on the assumption of two pairs of opposite and primary qualities, ψυχρόν)(θερμόν, and
ξηρόν)(ὑγρόν. By the permutations and combinations of these he sought to
account for all varieties of physical health and disease: see e.g. Hippocr. de
morb. I. 2; de affect. 1. Cp. Lys. 215 E: Theo. Smyrn. Math. p. 15 Bull.
καὶ τοῦτο τὸ μέγιστον ἔργον θεοῦ κατὰ μουσικήν τε καὶ ἰατρικὴν, τὰ ἐχθρὰ φίλα
ποιεῖν: also Tim. 82 A for the "hot" and "cold" in health and disease.

πικρὸν γλυκεῖ. Ast's excision of these words (approved by Stallb., Hug,
and others) is, at first sight, plausible, inasmuch as these opposites of taste
seem hardly on a par with the other two pairs of primary opposites. But in
Lysis 215 E the same three pairs are mentioned, with ὀξύ)(ἀμβλύ as a fourth,
as exx. of the law of ἐπιθυμία τῶν ἐναντίων. Moreover, it is obvious that the
question of savours is of special importance in medical science: cp. Theaet.
166 E τῷ...ἀσθενοῦντι πικρὰ φαίνεται ἃ ἐσθίει καὶ ἔστι: Hippocr. περὶ διαίτης II.
56 τὰ γλυκέα...καὶ τὰ πικρά...θερμαίνειν πέφυκε, καὶ ὅσα ξηρά ἐστι καὶ ὅσα
ὑγρά: id. de nat. hom. 2, 6: and the connexion between πικρότης and χολή
brought out in Tim. 83 A ff. Further, as Hommel observed, πάντα τὰ τοιαῦτα
after only two exx. is unusual.

186 E ὁ ἡμέτερος πρόγονος Ἀ. Asclepius in Homer is not more than
ἰητὴρ ἀμύμων: in Pindar (Pyth. III.) and later poets he is the son of Apollo
and Coronis. The earliest seats of his worship seem to have been Thessaly
and Boeotia, and his cult, as a "chthonic" and "mantic" deity, may have
its roots in a primitive ophiolatry (see Rohde, Psyche I. 141 ff.). Cp. Orph.
Fr. 272 διὸ καὶ οἱ θεολόγοι τὴν μὲν εἰς Ἀσκληπιὸν ἀναφέρουσιν ὑγίειαν τὴν
ἰατρικὴν πᾶσαν τῶν παρὰ φύσιν κτλ. Also Orph. H. 67, addressed to A. as
Ἰητὴρ πάντων, Ἀσκληπιέ, δέσποτα παιάν κτλ. The Asclepiadae were a
recognized medical guild, with hereditary traditions; their most famous
schools were at Cos and Cnidus, for which see the account in Gomperz G. T.
(E. tr.) vol. I. pp. 275 ff.: cp. Phaedr. 270 c (with Thompson's note).

οἵδε οἱ ποιηταί. The "deictic" οἵδε points to the presence of Aristophanes
and Agathon.

187 A γυμναστική. The curative value of physical training is said to
have been emphasized especially by Iccos of Tarentum and Herodicus of
Selymbria, both 5th century experts in dieting. For the latter as an ad-
vocate of walking exercise see Phaedr. 227 D (with Schol. ad loc.); cp. Rep.

παντὶ κατάδηλος τῷ καὶ σμικρὸν προσέχοντι τὸν νοῦν ὅτι κατὰ
ταὐτὰ ἔχει τούτοις, ὥσπερ ἴσως καὶ Ἡράκλειτος βούλεται λέγειν,
ἐπεὶ τοῖς γε ῥήμασιν οὐ καλῶς λέγει. τὸ ἓν γάρ φησι " διαφερόμενον αὐτὸ ὑαὑτῷ ξυμφέρεσθαι, ὥσπερ ἁρμονίαν τόξου τε καὶ
λύρας." ἔστι δὲ πολλὴ ἀλογία ἁρμονίαν φάναι διαφέρεσθαι ἢ ἐκ
διαφερομένων ἔτι εἶναι. ἀλλ' ἴσως τόδε ἐβούλετο λέγειν, ὅτι ἐκ
διαφερομένων πρότερον τοῦ ὀξέος καὶ βαρέος, ἔπειτα ὕστερον B

187 A ἔχοντι νοῦν Hirschig   ταὐτὰ T: ταῦτα B   ἓν: ὂν vel
πᾶν Ast   τόξου...λύρας: τοῦ ὄξεος τε καὶ βαρέος Bast Gladisch   λύρας:
νεύρας Bergk

---

406 A : for the former, as an example of abstinence, see *Laws* 839 E. That
Plato himself recognizes the connexion between ἰατρική and γυμναστική is
shown by such passages as *Gorg.* 452 A ff., 464 B ff., *Soph.* 228 E, *Polit.* 295 C.

καὶ γεωργία. The appositeness of γεωργία is not so evident as that of
γυμναστική, but the use of the word here is defended by 186 A (τοῖς ἐν τῇ γῇ
φυομένοις) and by other exx. of a similar collocation, such as *Lach.* 198 D, *Laws*
889 D (cp. also *Protag.* 334 A f.). The art which deals with φυτά is regarded
as analogous to that which deals with ζῷα, involving a similar command of
the permutations and combinations, the attractions and repulsions (τὰ ἐρωτικά), of the fundamental qualities.

τὸ ἓν γάρ φησι κτλ. The words of Heraclitus (*Fr.* 45) are given in *Hippol.*
refut. haer. IX. 9 thus: οὐ ξυνίασιν ὅκως διαφερόμενον ἑωντῷ ὁμολογέει· παλίντροπος ἁρμονίη ὅκωσπερ τόξου καὶ λύρης : cp. Plut. *de Is.* 45 παλίντονος γὰρ
ἁρμονίη κόσμου ὅκωσπερ λύρης καὶ τόξου καθ᾽ Ἡράκλειτον : *Soph.* 242 E. Probably, as Burnet holds, the original word used by H. was παλίντονος, not
παλίντροπος, and ἁρμονίη combines the original sense of "structure" with
the musical sense "octave," the point of the simile being (see Campbell,
Theaet. p. 244) "as the arrow leaves the string the hands are pulling opposite
ways to each other, and to the different parts of the bow (cf. Plato, *Rep.*
4. 439); and the sweet note of the lyre is due to a similar tension and retention.
The secret of the universe is the same." That is to say, the world, both as a
whole and in its parts, is maintained by the equilibrium resultant from
opposite tensions. For more detailed discussion of the theory see Burnet,
Early Gk. Phil. pp. 158 ff., Zeller, *Pre-Socr.* (E. T.) vol. II. pp. 33 ff. The
τόξον H. had in mind is probably, as Bernays suggested, the Scythian bow—
the φόρμιγξ ἄχορδος of Arist. *Rhet.* III. 1412^b 35 (see the woodcut in Smith,
D. A. s.v. "arcus").

ἀλλ᾽ ἴσως κτλ. Eryximachus argues that H.'s dictum is defensible only if
we understand the opposites to be not co-existent : the discordant cannot *be*
simultaneously concordant, though it may be capable of becoming so in
lapse of time (πρότερον...ὕστερον). For τὸ ὀξὺ καὶ βαρύ as matter for ἁρμονία
cp. Heraclit. *Fr.* 43 (R. and P. § 27) οὐ γὰρ ἂν εἶναι ἁρμονίαν μὴ ὄντος ὀξέος
καὶ βαρέος, οὐδὲ τὰ ζῷα ἄνευ θηλέος καὶ ἄρρενος, ἐναντίων ὄντων : *Soph.* 253 A ;
Phileb. 17 C, 26 A ; *Laws* 665 B.

ὁμολογησάντων γέγονεν ὑπὸ τῆς μουσικῆς τέχνης. οὐ γὰρ δή που
ἐκ διαφερομένων γε ἔτι τοῦ ὀξέος καὶ βαρέος ἁρμονία ἂν εἴη· ἡ
γὰρ ἁρμονία συμφωνία ἐστί, συμφωνία δὲ ὁμολογία τις. ὁμολογίαν δὲ ἐκ διαφερομένων, ἕως ἂν διαφέρωνται, ἀδύνατον εἶναι. διαφερόμενον δὲ αὖ καὶ μὴ ὁμολογεῖν ἀδυνατοῦν <δυνατὸν> ἁρμόσαι,
C ὥσπερ γε καὶ ὁ ῥυθμὸς ἐκ τοῦ ταχέος καὶ βραδέος ἐκ διενηνεγμένων
πρότερον, ὕστερον δὲ ὁμολογησάντων γέγονε. τὴν δὲ ὁμολογίαν
πᾶσι τούτοις, ὥσπερ ἐκεῖ ἡ ἰατρική, ἐνταῦθα ἡ μουσικὴ ἐντίθησιν,
ἔρωτα καὶ ὁμόνοιαν ἀλλήλων ἐμποιήσασα· καὶ ἔστιν αὖ μουσικὴ
περὶ ἁρμονίαν καὶ ῥυθμὸν ἐρωτικῶν ἐπιστήμη. καὶ ἐν μέν γε
αὐτῇ τῇ συστάσει ἁρμονίας τε καὶ ῥυθμοῦ οὐδὲν χαλεπὸν τὰ

187 B τέχνης ⟨ἡ ἁρμονία⟩ vulg.   δὲ αὖ : δὲ δὴ Sz. : δὴ οὖν Rohde   ὁμολογεῖν
scripsi : ὁμολογοῦν codd., edd.   ἀδυνατοῦν (δυνατὸν) scripsi : ἀδύνατον
codd.: δυνατὸν Susem.   C ἐκ post βραδέος om. edd. recc. cum Vindob. 21
ὁμόνοιαν : ἁρμονίαν Wolf   ἀλλήλοις T   ⟨τῶν⟩ περὶ Ast

187 B ὁμολογησάντων κτλ. Cp. Theo. Smyrn. math. p. 15 καὶ οἱ Πυθα-
γορικοὶ δέ, οἷς πολλαχῇ ἕπεται Πλάτων, τὴν μουσικήν φασιν ἐναντίων συναρ-
μογὴν καὶ τῶν πολλῶν ἕνωσιν καὶ τῶν δίχα φρονούντων συμφρόνησιν, οὐ γὰρ
ῥυθμῶν μόνον καὶ μέλους συντακτικήν, ἀλλ᾽ ἁπλῶς παντὸς συστήματος· τέλος
γὰρ αὐτῆς τὸ ἑνοῦν τε καὶ συναρμόζειν. For the Pythagorean ἁρμονία see
Philolaus, fr. 4. 3 (R. and P. § 56) τὰ δὲ ἀνόμοια...ἀνάγκα τᾷ τοιαύτᾳ ἁρμονίᾳ
συγκεκλεῖσθαι κτλ. The same notion of a cosmic ἁρμονία or ὁμολογία appears
in Orph. fr. 139 τὴν Ἀφροδίτην...τάξιν καὶ ἁρμονίαν καὶ κοινωνίαν πᾶσι τοῖς
ἐγκοσμίοις...(ὁ δημιουργὸς) φιλίας ἐστὶν αἴτιος τοῖς δημιουργήμασιν καὶ ὁμολογίας.
συμφωνία. Cp. Crat. 405 D περὶ τὴν ἐν τῇ ᾠδῇ ἁρμονίαν, ἡ δὴ συμφωνία
καλεῖται : Rep. 430 E, 398 D, E with Adam's notes : "in its musical application
συμφωνία is used both of consonance in the octave or double octave and also
of other musical intervals" : " ἁρμονία 'reconciles' ὀξύ and βαρύ by a proper
arrangement of notes of higher and lower pitch. In the wider sense, therefore, any ὁμολογία of ὀξύ and βαρύ is a ἁρμονία, but in practice the word was
used specifically of certain scales or modes."

διαφερόμενον δὲ αὖ κτλ. With the MS. text the sequence of thought is dis-
jointed and obscure ; αὖ seems out of place, and the next clause (ὥσπερ γε
καὶ κτλ.) seems to imply that the possibility rather than the impossibility of
harmonizing opposites is stated in the present clause (cp. Susemihl, Philol.
Anz. VII. 412). Hence, rather than alter αὖ with Schanz, I prefer to read
διαφερόμενον δὲ αὖ καὶ μὴ ὁμολογεῖν ἀδυνατοῦν (or ἀδύνατον) ⟨δυνατὸν⟩ ἁρμόσαι :
this gives a proper antithesis to the clause preceding.

187 C ὁμόνοιαν. It is possible that this word may contain an allusion
to Antiphon's work περὶ ὁμονοίας, for which see Dümmler, Akad. p. 79.

αὐτῇ τῇ συστάσει ἁρμονίας. "In the constitution of harmony per se" :
ἐν αὐτῇ τῇ ἁρμονίᾳ might have sufficed, but the addition of συστάσει serves
to emphasize the fact that ἁρμονία is a synthesis—ὁμολογία—of a plurality of

ἐρωτικὰ διαγιγνώσκειν, οὐδὲ ὁ διπλοῦς ἔρως ἐνταῦθά πω ἔστιν·
ἀλλ' ἐπειδὰν δέῃ πρὸς τοὺς ἀνθρώπους καταχρῆσθαι ῥυθμῷ τε D
καὶ ἁρμονίᾳ ἢ ποιοῦντα, ὃ δὴ μελοποιίαν καλοῦσιν, ἢ χρώμενον
ὀρθῶς τοῖς πεποιημένοις μέλεσί τε καὶ μέτροις, ὃ δὴ παιδεία
ἐκλήθη, ἐνταῦθα δὴ καὶ χαλεπὸν καὶ ἀγαθοῦ δημιουργοῦ δεῖ.
πάλιν γὰρ ἥκει ὁ αὐτὸς λόγος, ὅτι τοῖς μὲν κοσμίοις τῶν ἀνθρώπων, καὶ ὡς ἂν κοσμιώτεροι γίγνοιντο οἱ μήπω ὄντες, δεῖ χαρίζεσθαι καὶ φυλάττειν τὸν τούτων ἔρωτα, καὶ οὗτός ἐστιν ὁ καλός,
ὁ οὐράνιος, ὁ τῆς Οὐρανίας μούσης Ἔρως· ὁ δὲ Πολυμνίας ὁ πάν- E
δημος, ὃν δεῖ εὐλαβούμενον προσφέρειν οἷς ἂν προσφέρῃ, ὅπως ἂν
τὴν μὲν ἡδονὴν αὐτοῦ καρπώσηται, ἀκολασίαν δὲ μηδεμίαν ἐμ-
ποιήσῃ, ὥσπερ ἐν τῇ ἡμετέρᾳ τέχνῃ μέγα ἔργον ταῖς περὶ τὴν
ὀψοποιικὴν τέχνην ἐπιθυμίαις καλῶς χρῆσθαι, ὥστ' ἄνευ νόσου
τὴν ἡδονὴν καρπώσασθαι. καὶ ἐν μουσικῇ δὴ καὶ ἐν ἰατρικῇ καὶ
ἐν τοῖς ἄλλοις πᾶσι καὶ τοῖς ἀνθρωπείοις καὶ τοῖς θείοις, καθ' ᾗ
ὅσον παρείκει, φυλακτέον ἑκάτερον τὸν Ἔρωτα· ἔνεστον γάρ.

187 C οὐδὲ...ἔστιν del. Schütz   πω Bdhm. Mdvg.: πῶς BT   D μέτροις
BT: ῥυθμοῖς W   τούτων BT: τοιούτων W   μούσης del. Sauppe   E ἔργον
ταῖς Tb: ἐργῶντες B   παρείκει W rec. t: παρήκει BT   ἐν ἐστὸν W

elements: cp. Laws 812 C τὰς τῶν ἁρμονιῶν συστάσεις: Epin. 991 E ἁρμονίας
σύστασιν ἅπασαν. For ῥυθμός, see Adam's note on Rep. 398 D: "The elements
of music are ῥυθμός and ἁρμονία. The former 'reconciles' ταχύ and βραδύ by
arranging a proper sequence of short and long notes and syllables": also
Laws 665 A τῇ δὲ τῆς κινήσεως τάξει ῥυθμὸς ὄνομα εἴη, τῇ δὲ αὖ τῆς φωνῆς...
ἁρμονία, κτλ., Phileb. 17 D (with my note).
Eryximachus analyses Music into Theory (αὐτὴ ἡ σύστασις) and Practice
(καταχρῆσθαι ῥ.), the latter being further subdivided into μελοποιία and παιδεία.
187 D παιδεία ἐκλήθη. For "education" as "the right use of melody
and verse," compare what Plato has to say about the psychological effects
of music and its place in education in Rep. II., III., Laws II., VIII. Of course
παιδεία in the ordinary sense includes also gymnastic; cp. Rep. II. 376 E,
Laws 659 D: in dancing to music (ὀρχηστικὴ Laws 816 A) we have a combination of both. It is worth noticing that in the Pythagorean quadrivium
μουσική had a place beside ἀριθμητική, γεωμετρία and σφαιρική or ἀστρονομία:
see Adam's Republic vol. II. pp. 163 ff.
πάλιν...ὁ αὐτὸς λόγος. Pausanias was the author of the λόγος, cp. 186 B
supra.
187 E Πολυμνίας. "The Muse of the sublime hymn" here replaces
Aphrodite, being selected out of the Nine probably, as Ast supposes, because
the first part of her name is congruous with the character of Aphr. πάνδημος.
προσφέρῃ...καρπώσηται...ἐμποιήσῃ. Supply as subject the indef. τις.
καθ' ὅσον παρείκει. "So far as possible." Cp. Rep. 374 E, Laws 734 B.

188   XIII.   Ἐπεὶ καὶ ἡ τῶν ὡρῶν τοῦ ἐνιαυτοῦ σύστασις μεστή
ἐστιν ἀμφοτέρων τούτων, καὶ ἐπειδὰν μὲν πρὸς ἄλληλα τοῦ
κοσμίου τύχῃ ἔρωτος ἃ νῦν δὴ ἐγὼ ἔλεγον, τά τε θερμὰ καὶ τὰ
ψυχρὰ καὶ ξηρὰ καὶ ὑγρά, καὶ ἁρμονίαν καὶ κρᾶσιν λάβῃ σώ-
φρονα, ἥκει φέροντα εὐετηρίαν τε καὶ ὑγίειαν ἀνθρώποις καὶ τοῖς
ἄλλοις ζώοις τε καὶ φυτοῖς, καὶ οὐδὲν ἠδίκησεν· ὅταν δὲ ὁ μετὰ
τῆς ὕβρεως Ἔρως ἐγκρατέστερος περὶ τὰς τοῦ ἐνιαυτοῦ ὥρας
B γένηται, διέφθειρέν τε πολλὰ καὶ ἠδίκησεν. οἵ τε γὰρ λοιμοὶ
φιλοῦσι γίγνεσθαι ἐκ τῶν τοιούτων καὶ ἄλλ᾽ ἀνόμοια πολλὰ νοσή-
ματα καὶ τοῖς θηρίοις καὶ τοῖς φυτοῖς· καὶ γὰρ πάχναι καὶ
χάλαζαι καὶ ἐρυσῖβαι ἐκ πλεονεξίας καὶ ἀκοσμίας περὶ ἄλληλα
τῶν τοιούτων γίγνεται ἐρωτικῶν, ὧν ἐπιστήμη περὶ ἄστρων τε

188 A κοσμίου Bt, Stob.: κόσμου T   ἐγὼ ἔλεγον BT: λέγω Stob.: ἔλεγον
Wolf   τὰ ξηρὰ Stob.   ⟨καὶ⟩ περὶ Stob.   B διέφθειρεν T: διέφθειρε Stob.:
διαφθείρει B   ἀνόμοια BT: ἀνόμοια καὶ Stob.: ὅμοια Schütz Bdhm.: ἂν
ὅμοια Orelli: αὖ ὅμοια Hermann: δὴ ὅμοια Sauppe: ἅττ᾽ ὅμοια Ast Jn.: ἄνομα
Sommer: ἀλλόκοτα Rohde: παντοῖα Winckelmann: ἀνήνυτα Stallb.   γίγνεται
del. Sauppe: γίγνονται Canter: fort. γίγνεται.   ἐρωτικῶν οὖν ἐπιστήμη κτλ.
ὧν...καλεῖται del. Schütz   τε: γε Christ

---

188 A   ἡ τῶν ὡρῶν...σύστασις.   For the influence of the seasons on health
see Hippocr. de nat. hom. 7 ὡς γὰρ ὁ ἐνιαυτὸς μετέχει μὲν πᾶς πάντων καὶ τῶν
θερμῶν καὶ τῶν ψυχρῶν καὶ τῶν ξηρῶν καὶ τῶν ὑγρῶν κτλ.: cp. Phileb. 26 B.

ἃ νῦν δὴ...ἔλεγον.   See above, 186 D.

οὐδὲν ἠδίκησεν κτλ.   For these aorists, following presents, see Goodwin
G. M. T. § 155.

188 B   ἀνόμοια...νοσήματα.   "Divers diseases": the adj. is similarly used
in Arist. Poet. 24. 1459ᵇ 30 ἐπεισοδιοῦν ἀνομοίοις ἐπεισοδίοις, "relieving the
story with varying episodes" (Butcher): cp. id. H. An. IV. 1. 523ᵇ 12:
Hippocr. de flat. 3 δοκέει μὲν οὖν τὰ νουσήματα οὐδὲν ἀλλήλοισιν ἐοικέναι διὰ
τὴν ἀλλοιότητα καὶ ἀνομοιότητα τῶν τόπων.

πάχναι...καὶ ἐρυσῖβαι.   Timaeus defines thus: ἐρυσίβη μιλτώδης δρόσος·
πάχνη δὲ δρόσος χιονώδης.   Roman religion had a goddess Robigo.   Ruhnken
(ad Tim. p. 122) cites Orph. de lap. 15, v. 91 καὶ αἰθερίην ἐρυσίβην, | ἥτε κατου-
ρανόθεν πταμένη ποτὶ καρπὸν ἐρυθρή, | ἀμφὶ περὶ σταχύεσσι περισμύχουσα
κάθηται.

τῶν τοιούτων γίγνεται κτλ.   There are two difficulties in this passage:
(1) the singular verb after the plural subjects is harsh; to explain it we
must assume a mental unification of the subjects, of which similar but easier
instances occur in Rep. 363 A, 618 D, Laws 925 E.   We might evade this
difficulty by removing the colon at φυτοῖς, marking καὶ γὰρ...ἐρυσῖβαι as
parenthetic, and thus construing ἄλλα...νοσήματα as the direct subject of
γίγνεται.   (2) We should naturally expect τοιούτων to have the same reference

φορὰς καὶ ἐνιαυτῶν ὥρας ἀστρονομία καλεῖται. ἔτι τοίνυν καὶ αἱ θυσίαι πᾶσαι καὶ οἷς μαντικὴ ἐπιστατεῖ—ταῦτα δ᾽ ἐστὶν ἡ περὶ θεούς τε καὶ ἀνθρώπους πρὸς ἀλλήλους κοινωνία—οὐ περὶ ἄλλο C τί ἐστιν ἢ περὶ Ἔρωτος φυλακήν τε καὶ ἴασιν. πᾶσα γὰρ [ἡ] ἀσέβεια φιλεῖ γίγνεσθαι, ἐὰν μή τις τῷ κοσμίῳ Ἔρωτι χαρίζηται μηδὲ τιμᾷ τε αὐτὸν καὶ πρεσβεύῃ ἐν παντὶ ἔργῳ, ἀλλὰ [περὶ] τὸν ἕτερον, καὶ περὶ γονέας καὶ ζῶντας καὶ τετελευτηκότας καὶ περὶ θεούς· ἃ δὴ προστέτακται τῇ μαντικῇ ἐπισκοπεῖν τοὺς Ἔρωτας καὶ ἰατρεύειν, καὶ ἔστιν αὖ ἡ μαντικὴ φιλίας θεῶν καὶ ἀνθρώπων δημιουργὸς τῷ ἐπίστασθαι τὰ κατὰ ἀνθρώπους ἐρωτικά, ὅσα D τείνει πρὸς θέμιν καὶ εὐσέβειαν.

188 B   φορὰς W, Stob.: φορας B: φορᾶς T   καὶ...ὥρας del. Bast.
ὥρας: ὅρους Creuzer   αἱ T, Stob.: om. B   πᾶσαι B Stob.: ἅπασαι T
⟨ἡ⟩ μαντικὴ Fischer   ἐπιστατεῖ ⟨τέχνη⟩ Stob.   ταῦτα...κοινωνία del. Schütz
C   ἀσεβεία Stob.: ἡ ἀσεβεία BT   μή τις: μήτε ἐν Stob.   ⟨μὲν⟩ ἐν Pflugk
τὸν Stob.: περὶ τὸν BT: περιττῶς τὸν Koch: θεραπεύῃ Winckelm.: περιττότερον
τὸν Pflugk: fort. πῃ τὸν   ⟨περὶ⟩ ἃ Verm.   προτέτακται Stob.   ἔρωτας
BT: ἐρῶντας Stob., Bt.: ἐρωτῶντας cj. Verm.: τοὺς ἔρωτας secl. Herm. Hug Sz.
D   εὐσέβειαν Stob.: ἀσέβειαν BT

here as τῶν τοιούτων has above (*viz.* to the combinations of elements in which the bad Eros predominates), whereas it seemingly stands in agreement with ἐρωτικῶν: this being so, what does ἐρωτικῶν precisely mean? For it cannot well retain, in this connexion, its proper meaning as genitive of τὰ ἐρωτικά "the laws of affinity" (186 c, 187 c). Ought we, then, to put a stop after γίγνεται and begin a new sentence with ἐρωτικῶν οὖν ἐπιστήμη κτλ.?

ἀστρονομία. The term as here used includes what we should rather call "meteorology": cp. *Rep.* 527 D τρίτον θῶμεν ἀστρονομίαν;...τὸ γὰρ περὶ ὥρας εὐαισθητοτέρως ἔχειν καὶ μηνῶν καὶ ἐνιαυτῶν...ναυτιλίᾳ προσήκει. For "astronomy" as a regular part of the school curriculum see *n.* on παιδεία 187 D, and cp. *Theaet.* 145 C, D; *Protag.* 318 E.

ἡ περὶ θεούς...κοινωνία. Simpler would have been ἡ θεῶν...κοινωνία, but, as Hug remarks, "Eryximachus liebt das unbestimmte περί c. accus."

188 C ἀσέβεια. "Undutifulness," *impietas.* Reverence to parents and country was a matter of religious obligation; cp. Xen. *Mem.* II. 2. 13 ἐὰν δέ τις γονέας μὴ θεραπεύῃ, τούτῳ δίκην τε ἐπιτίθησι (ἡ πόλις) κτλ.; *ib.* IV. 4. 20; *Rep.* 615 C.

[περὶ] τὸν ἕτερον. Perhaps an original πῃ was mistaken for a compendium of περί: for the combination ἀλλά πῃ, cp. *Theaet.* 191 B ἀλλά πῃ δυνατόν.

ἃ δὴ...ἰατρεύειν. The infinitives may be taken as epexegetic of ἃ (so Stallb., Zeller), or ἃ may be construed separately as accus. of respect ("qua in caussa" Ast; "in welcher Beziehung" Hommel). There is no need to eject or emend τοὺς Ἔρωτας: the phrase used 4 ll. above, περὶ Ἔρωτος φυλακήν τε καὶ ἴασιν, supports Ἔρωτας here.

Οὕτω πολλὴν καὶ μεγάλην, μᾶλλον δὲ πᾶσαν δύναμιν ἔχει ξυλλήβδην μὲν ὁ πᾶς Ἔρως, ὁ δὲ περὶ τἀγαθὰ μετὰ σωφροσύνης καὶ δικαιοσύνης ἀποτελούμενος καὶ παρ᾽ ἡμῖν καὶ παρὰ θεοῖς, οὗτος τὴν μεγίστην δύναμιν ἔχει καὶ πᾶσαν ἡμῖν εὐδαιμονίαν παρασκευάζει καὶ ἀλλήλοις δυναμένους ὁμιλεῖν καὶ φίλους εἶναι Ε καὶ τοῖς κρείττοσιν ἡμῶν θεοῖς. ἴσως μὲν οὖν καὶ ἐγὼ τὸν Ἔρωτα ἐπαινῶν πολλὰ παραλείπω, οὐ μέντοι ἑκών γε. ἀλλ᾽ εἴ τι ἐξέλιπον, σὸν ἔργον, ὦ Ἀριστόφανες, ἀναπληρῶσαι· ἢ εἴ πως ἄλλως ἐν νῷ ἔχεις ἐγκωμιάζειν τὸν θεόν, ἐγκωμίαζε, ἐπειδὴ καὶ τῆς λυγγὸς πέπαυσαι.

189 Ἐκδεξάμενον οὖν ἔφη εἰπεῖν τὸν Ἀριστοφάνη ὅτι Καὶ μάλ᾽ ἐπαύσατο, οὐ μέντοι πρίν γε τὸν πταρμὸν προσενεχθῆναι αὐτῇ, ὥστε με θαυμάζειν εἰ τὸ κόσμιον τοῦ σώματος ἐπιθυμεῖ τοιούτων ψόφων καὶ γαργαλισμῶν, οἷον καὶ ὁ πταρμός ἐστι· πάνυ γὰρ εὐθὺς ἐπαύσατο, ἐπειδὴ αὐτῷ τὸν πταρμὸν προσήνεγκα. καὶ τὸν

188 D καὶ παρ᾽ ἡμῖν...θεοῖς secl. Hug   δυναμένοις Stob.   φίλοις
Stob.   Ε καὶ del. Rückert   ἡμῶν θεοῖς secl. J.-U.   189 A ὥστ᾽
ἐμὲ Bekk.

---

188 D Οὕτω πολλὴν. The German translators mostly take οὕτω as qualifying the adjj., "so vielfach und gross" (Zeller, Schleierm.), but Hommel is probably right in taking οὕτω by itself ("hoc modo," "itaque") comparing οὕτω πολλαχόθεν 178 C. Cp. Hippocr. *de flat.* 3 οὗτος (*sc.* ὁ ἀήρ) δὲ μέγιστος ἐν τοῖσι πᾶσι τῶν πάντων δυνάστης ἐστίν· ἄξιον δὲ αὐτοῦ θεήσασθαι τὴν δύναμιν.

καὶ...παρὰ θεοῖς. Hug condemns these words, as implying a slur on the righteousness of the gods. But the phrase is merely a stock formula, like our "heaven and earth," not intended to bear rigid analysis; cp. 186 B, 187 E καὶ τοῖς ἀνθρωπείοις καὶ τοῖς θείοις.

καὶ ἀλλήλοις...θεοῖς. For the accus. δυναμένους after ἡμῖν cp. 176 D. The καὶ after εἶναι is rendered "auch" by Hug, as if ὁμιλεῖν governed ἀλλήλοις and φίλους εἶναι the other datives, but Zeller's rendering, which makes both the infinitives govern both sets of datives, seems more natural.

188 E καὶ ἐγώ, *i.e.* "I as well as Pausanias": see 185 E *ad fin.*

ἐπειδὴ καί. καί implies a suppressed reason—"since (it is your turn) *and* you are cured of your cough."

189 A τὸν πταρμόν. This was one of the remedies prescribed by Eryx. in 185 E, hence the def. article. προσφέρειν is a *vox propria* for medical "applications," cp. 187 E, *Phaedr.* 268 A ; Hippocr. *de flat.* 1 οἷός τ᾽ ἂν προσφέρειν τὰ ξυμφέροντα τῷ σώματι: *id. de affect.* 1 ὅσα δὲ τοὺς χειροτέχνας εἰκὸς ἐπίστασθαι καὶ προσφέρειν καὶ διαχειρίζειν κτλ.

τὸ κόσμιον. This is in ridicule of the theory of medicine stated in 186 C ff and of the use of the term κόσμιος in 187 D, 188 C.

Ἐρυξίμαχον, Ὠγαθέ, φάναι, [Ἀριστόφανες,] ὅρα τί ποιεῖς. γελω-
τοποιεῖς μέλλων λέγειν, καὶ φύλακά με τοῦ λόγου ἀναγκάζεις
γίγνεσθαι τοῦ σεαυτοῦ, ἐάν τι γελοῖον εἴπῃς, ἐξόν σοι ἐν εἰρήνῃ Β
λέγειν. καὶ τὸν Ἀριστοφάνη γελάσαντα εἰπεῖν Εὖ λέγεις, ὦ
Ἐρυξίμαχε, καί μοι ἔστω ἄρρητα τὰ εἰρημένα. ἀλλὰ μή με
φύλαττε, ὡς ἐγὼ φοβοῦμαι περὶ τῶν μελλόντων ῥηθήσεσθαι, οὔ τι
μὴ γελοῖα εἴπω,—τοῦτο μὲν γὰρ ἂν κέρδος εἴη καὶ τῆς ἡμετέρας
μούσης ἐπιχώριον,—ἀλλὰ μὴ καταγέλαστα. Βαλών γε, φάναι, ὦ
Ἀριστόφανες, οἴει ἐκφεύξεσθαι· ἀλλὰ πρόσεχε τὸν νοῦν καὶ οὕτω
λέγε ὡς δώσων λόγον· ἴσως μέντοι, ἂν δόξῃ μοι, ἀφήσω σε.   C
XIV. Καὶ μήν, ὦ Ἐρυξίμαχε, εἰπεῖν τὸν Ἀριστοφάνη, ἄλλη
γέ πη ἐν νῷ ἔχω λέγειν, ἢ ᾗ σύ τε καὶ Παυσανίας εἰπέτην. ἐμοὶ
γὰρ δοκοῦσιν ἄνθρωποι παντάπασι τὴν τοῦ ἔρωτος δύναμιν οὐκ
ᾐσθῆσθαι, ἐπεὶ αἰσθανόμενοί γε μέγιστ' ἂν αὐτοῦ ἱερὰ κατα-

189 A ὠγαθὲ φάναι T: ὠγαθὲ φᾶναι ὠγαθὲ B   Ἀριστόφανες del. Sauppe
Hug   B ὦ om. vulg.   μή γε Bdhm.   ῥηθήσεσθαι T: ἡττηθήσεσθαι
(sed ἥτ extra versum) B: ἤδη ῥηθήσεσθαι Rettig: fort. ἔτι ῥ.   C εἴπετον
Blass   ἄνθρωποι Bekk.: ἄνθρωποι BT: οἱ ἄνθρωποι W, vulg.

[Ἀριστόφανες]. I follow Sauppe and Hug in regarding the proper name
as a gloss on ὠγαθέ: as a rule, ὠγαθέ stands alone.

189 B οὔ τι…εἴπω. In γελοῖα Arist. applies the term used by Eryx. in
a different sense, distinguishing between γελοῖα, *ridicula*, and καταγέλαστα,
deridenda; whereas Eryx. had meant by γελοῖον what A. calls καταγέλαστον,
cp. 199 D, 221 E.

τῆς ἡμετέρας μούσης. This may allude (as Rettig thinks) to Eryximachus's
Οὐρανία μοῦσα and Πολυμνία, and to his phrase ἐν τῇ ἡμετέρᾳ τέχνῃ (187 D, E).

Βαλών γε κτλ. "So you think you are going to get off scot-free!" Suidas
s.v. βαλών explains by πρὸς τοὺς κακόν τι δράσαντας καὶ οἰομένους ἐκφεύγειν.
Cp. *Rep.* 344 D οἷον ἐμβαλὼν λόγον ἐν νῷ ἔχεις ἀπιέναι: *Phaedo* 91 C; Plut.
de s. n. v. 548 B ἀλλ' οὐδ' εἰ βαλὼν, εἶπεν, ἀπηλλάγη, καλῶς εἶχε περιορᾶν τὸ βέλος
ἐγκείμενον.

189 C Καὶ μήν κτλ. This clause has reference to what Eryx. had said,
not in 189 B, but in 188 E (εἴ πως ἄλλως ἐν νῷ ἔχεις κτλ.)—"Yea verily, it *is*
my intention to act as you suggested."

παντάπασι…οὐκ. "To have completely failed to discern." For δύναμις
)(φύσις as a rhetorical category, cp. Isocr. *Hel.* 218 D ῥᾴδιον δὲ γνῶναι τὴν
δύναμιν αὐτοῦ κτλ.

ἐπεὶ αἰσθ. γε κτλ. For ἐπεί…γε cp. *Rep.* 352 C. The following infinitives
(with ἄν) are governed by δοκοῦσιν, repeated in thought from the main clause.
For the sense, cp. Isocr. *Hel.* 221 A ὡς…δυναμένην, ἀναθήμασι καὶ θυσίαις καὶ
τοῖς ἄλλαις προσόδοις ἱλάσκεσθαι καὶ τιμᾶν αὐτὴν χρή.

σκευάσαι καὶ βωμούς, καὶ θυσίας ἂν ποιεῖν μεγίστας, οὐχ ὥσπερ
νῦν τούτων οὐδὲν γίγνεται περὶ αὐτόν, δέον πάντων μάλιστα
D γίγνεσθαι. ἔστι γὰρ θεῶν φιλανθρωπότατος, ἐπίκουρός τε ὢν τῶν
ἀνθρώπων καὶ ἰατρὸς τούτων, ὧν ἰαθέντων μεγίστη εὐδαιμονία ἂν
τῷ ἀνθρωπείῳ γένει εἴη. ἐγὼ οὖν πειράσομαι ὑμῖν εἰσηγήσασθαι
τὴν δύναμιν αὐτοῦ, ὑμεῖς δὲ τῶν ἄλλων διδάσκαλοι ἔσεσθε. δεῖ
δὲ πρῶτον ὑμᾶς μαθεῖν τὴν ἀνθρωπίνην φύσιν καὶ τὰ παθήματα
αὐτῆς. ἡ γὰρ πάλαι ἡμῶν φύσις οὐχ αὐτὴ ἦν ἥπερ νῦν, ἀλλ'
ἀλλοία. πρῶτον μὲν γὰρ τρία ἦν τὰ γένη τὰ τῶν ἀνθρώπων, οὐχ
E ὥσπερ νῦν δύο, ἄρρεν καὶ θῆλυ, ἀλλὰ καὶ τρίτον προσῆν κοινὸν ὂν
ἀμφοτέρων τούτων, οὗ νῦν ὄνομα λοιπόν, αὐτὸ δὲ ἠφάνισται·
ἀνδρόγυνον γὰρ ἓν τότε μὲν ἦν καὶ εἶδος καὶ ὄνομα ἐξ ἀμφοτέρων

189 C καὶ βωμούς del. Blass ποιεῖσθαι Hirschig D εὐδαιμονία ἂν
BTW: ἂν εὐδαιμονία vulg. εἰσηγήσασθαι post αὐτοῦ trs. Blass ἔσεσθαι T
δεῖ δὴ Blass παλαιὰ Blass αὐτὴ B: αὕτη T, Stob.: ἡ αὐτὴ Euseb., Blass
ἀλλὰ ἄλλη Euseb. πρῶτα W τὰ τῶν BT: τῶν W, Euseb. Stob. E δύο
om. Stob. ἀλλὰ καὶ: ἀλλὰ Stob. Eusebii codd. aliquot ον om. Stob.
Euseb. ἓν B: om. T, Euseb. Stob., Sz.

οὐχ ὥσπερ. "Whereas": cp. 179 E.
189 D ἰατρὸς. This term recalls the doctor's speech, esp. 186 B ff.,
188 c ff.; cp. Phaedr. 252 A.
ἐγὼ οὖν πειράσομαι. "Parodie des Pausanias (180 D) und Eryximachos
(186 A)" (Rettig).
εἰσηγήσασθαι. The force of this word is lost if we render it "narrate,"
"relate" with L. and S.: it means "to initiate into": cp. 176 E, Xen. Mem.
II. 7. 10. For the next clause cp. Menex. 240 D ἡγεμόνες καὶ διδάσκαλοι τοῖς
ἄλλοις γενόμενοι.
φύσιν...παθήματα. This is the order of A.'s exposition—περὶ φύσεως
189 D—190 C, περὶ παθημάτων 190 C—193 A. For various views of physio-
logists as to the φύσις ἀνθρώπου, see Hippocrates' tract with this title,
where the theory that man ἔν τι εἶναι (αἷμα, χολή, φλέγμα, etc.) is combated.
Aristotle's exposition is intended, no doubt, as a caricature of the medicos
of his age (see Introd. § iii. 4).
189 E ἀνδρόγυνον κτλ. Suidas ἀνδρόγυνος· ὁ τὰ ἀνδρὸς ποιῶν καὶ τὰ
γυναικῶν πάσχων. Rückert wrongly renders εἶδος by "genus": it means
"forma" (as Stallb.). εἶδος καὶ ὄνομα are taken by Rückert and Hug as
nomin., by Stallb. as accus. of respect, the construction being ἐν γὰρ (sc. τῶν
γενῶν) ἦν τότε ἀνδρόγυνον: the latter way seems the better. Rettig proposes
to insert τό before ἕν, which would give the same sense. If εἶδος καὶ ὄνομα
are construed as accus., it is better to take them closely with ἀνδρόγυνον

κοινὸν τοῦ τε ἄρρενος καὶ θήλεος, νῦν δὲ οὐκ ἔστιν ἀλλ' ἢ ἐν
ὀνείδει ὄνομα κείμενον. ἔπειτα ὅλον ἦν ἑκάστου τοῦ ἀνθρώπου τὸ
εἶδος στρογγύλον, νῶτον καὶ πλευρὰς κύκλῳ ἔχον, χεῖρας δὲ
τέτταρας εἶχε, καὶ σκέλη τὰ ἴσα ταῖς χερσί, καὶ πρόσωπα δύ' ἐπ'
αὐχένι κυκλοτερεῖ, ὅμοια πάντῃ· κεφαλὴν δ' ἐπ' ἀμφοτέροις τοῖς 190
προσώποις ἐναντίοις κειμένοις μίαν, καὶ ὦτα τέτταρα, καὶ αἰδοῖα
δύο, καὶ τἆλλα πάντα ὡς ἀπὸ τούτων ἄν τις εἰκάσειεν. ἐπορεύετο
δὲ καὶ ὀρθὸν ὥσπερ νῦν, ὁποτέρωσε βουληθείη· καὶ ὁπότε ταχὺ
ὁρμήσειε θεῖν, ὥσπερ οἱ κυβιστῶντες καὶ εἰς ὀρθὸν τὰ σκέλη περι-

189 Ε ⟨τοῦ⟩ θήλεος Euseb., Blass   ἐν ὀνείδει Τ: ἐν ὂν εἴδει Β   νῶτόν τε
καὶ Stob., Blass   τὰ σκέλη ἴσα Hirschig: σκέλη ⟨δὲ⟩ Blass   190 Α κειμένοις om. Stob.   ὡς: ὅσα Stob.   ὁποτέρως Stob.   θεῖν Β, Stob.: ἐλθεῖν Τ
καὶ ΒΤ, Stob.: om. al.   ὀρθὸν τὰ: ὀρθὰ ὄντα Stob.: ὀρθὰ Blass

than with ἐξ ἀμφοτ. κτλ. (as Stallb.). For ἀνδρόγυνος, see also Hippocr.
de diaet. 28.
   For the description cp. Emped. 257 ff. (St.) πολλὰ μὲν ἀμφιπρόσωπα καὶ
ἀμφίστερνα φύεσθαι | ...μεμιγμένα τῇ μὲν ἀπ' ἀνδρῶν | τῇ δὲ γυναικοφυῆ, στείροις
ἠσκημένα γυίοις: Lucr. v. 837 ff. portenta...androgynum, interutrasque nec
utrum, utrimque remotum : Ov. Met. IV. 378 nec femina dici | nec puer ut
possint ; neutrumque et utrumque videntur : Livy XXVII. 11. 4. Theophrastus
(Char. 16) mentions Hermaphroditus-statues ; and the Orphic conception of
Eros-Phanes may also be compared.
   νῦν δὲ κτλ. "But now the name exists solely as a term of reproach": cp.
the use in Latin of semivir, Virg. A. IV. 215 ille Paris cum semiviro comitatu :
Livy XXXIII. 28. 7.
   ὅλον ἦν κτλ. Cp. Emped. 265 (St.) οὐλοφυεῖς μὲν πρῶτα τύποι χθονὸς
ἐξανέτελλον. ὅλον is predicate and not merely (as Ast, Schleierm.) a qualifying adj. with τὸ εἶδος. Certainly, as Rettig notes, Zeller's "ganz rund" is
impossible. Rabelais (I. 8) has a reference to this passage—" ung corps
humain ayant deux testes, l'une virée vers l'autre, quatre bras, quatre pieds,
et deux culs; tel que dict Platon, in Symposio, avoir esté l'humaine nature
à son commencement mysticq"—in his description of Gargantua's equipment.
   190 Α κεφαλὴν δ' ἐπ' κτλ. "Quis non Iani meminerit?" (Hommel). The
notion of a similar double-fronted, androgynous being is found in the Talmud,
and Euseb. pr. Evang. XII. 12 quotes our passage as a plagiarism from Moses.
   οἱ κυβιστῶντες. Schol. κυβιστὴρ ὁ ὀρχηστής, καὶ κυβιστᾶν τὸ ὀρχεῖσθαι. Cp.
Il. XVI. 750, and the evolutions of the "tumbler" Hippoclides described in
Hdt. VI. 129: also Xen. Symp. II. 11, VII. 3. The καί before εἰς ὀρθόν reads
awkwardly; if retained, we must render it "actually" (adeo, Wolf), but
possibly ἴσα or ἴσα καὶ may have been the original. Rettig quotes Cic.
de Fin. V. 35 si aut manibus ingrediatur quis aut non ante sed retro fugere,
plane se ipse et hominen ...ens ex homine naturam odisse (videtur).

φερόμενοι κυβιστῶσι κύκλῳ, ὀκτὼ τότε οὖσι τοῖς μέλεσιν ἀπερει-
δόμενοι ταχὺ ἐφέροντο κύκλῳ.| ἦν δὲ διὰ ταῦτα τρία τὰ γένη καὶ
B τοιαῦτα, ὅτι τὸ μὲν ἄρρεν ἦν τοῦ ἡλίου τὴν ἀρχὴν ἔκγονον, τὸ δὲ
θῆλυ τῆς γῆς, τὸ δὲ ἀμφοτέρων μετέχον τῆς σελήνης, ὅτι καὶ ἡ
σελήνη ἀμφοτέρων μετέχει·// περιφερῆ δὲ δὴ ἦν καὶ αὐτὰ καὶ ἡ
πορείᾳ αὐτῶν διὰ τὸ τοῖς γονεῦσιν ὅμοια εἶναι. ἦν οὖν τὴν ἰσχὺν
δεινὰ καὶ τὴν ῥώμην, | καὶ τὰ φρονήματα μεγάλα εἶχον, ἐπεχεί-
ρησαν δὲ τοῖς θεοῖς, καὶ ὃ λέγει "Ομηρος περὶ Ἐφιάλτου τε καὶ
"Ωτου, περὶ ἐκείνων λέγεται, τὸ εἰς τὸν οὐρανὸν ἀνάβασιν ἐπιχει-
C ρεῖν ποιεῖν, ὡς ἐπιθησομένων τοῖς θεοῖς.

XV. Ὁ οὖν Ζεὺς καὶ οἱ ἄλλοι θεοὶ ἐβουλεύοντο ὅ τι χρὴ
αὐτοὺς ποιῆσαι, καὶ ἠπόρουν· οὔτε γὰρ ὅπως ἀποκτείναιεν εἶχον

190 A κυβιστῶσι κύκλῳ del. Sauppe Bdhm Sz. τότε ὀκτὼ T, Stob.
ἀπερειδόμενοι T: ἅπερ εἰδόμεναι B: ἐπερειδόμενοι ej. Steph. B ἀμφότερον T
ὅτι...μετέχει del. Jn. μετεῖχεν Stob., Blass 〈καὶ〉 περιφερῆ Blass δὴ om.
Stob. αὐτῶν del. Blass τε καὶ BT: καὶ W C ὡς...θεοῖς post "Ωτου
transp. Steinhart ὁ γοῦν Stobaei A

190 B ὅτι τὸ μὲν ἄρρεν κτλ. Aristophanes too can pose as an erudite
physicist. His astronomical lore may come partly from Parmenides, partly
from the Pythagoreans. Cp. Arist. de gen. an. I. 2 ἄρρεν γὰρ λέγομεν ζῷον
τὸ εἰς ἄλλο γεννῶν, θῆλυ δὲ τὸ εἰς αὐτό· διὸ καὶ ἐν τῷ ὅλῳ τὴν τῆς γῆς φύσιν ὡς
θῆλυ καὶ μητέρα νομίζουσιν, οὐρανὸν δὲ καὶ ἥλιον...ὡς γεννῶντας καὶ πατέρας
προσαγορεύουσιν. For the moon as bisexed, cp. Orph. Hymn. IX. 4 (θῆλύς τε
καὶ ἄρσην); Macrob. III. 8 Philochorus affirmat Venerem esse lunam et ei
sacrificium facere viros cum veste muliebri, mulieres cum virili, quod eadem
et mas aestimetur et femina. Procl. in Tim. p. 326 c (οὕτω δὴ καὶ σεληνιακὴν
ψυχὴν εἰς ἀνδρὸς κατιέναι φύσιν, καθὰ τὴν Μουσαίου φασί, καὶ ἀπολλωνιακὴν
(ἡλιακὴν Jahn) εἰς γυναικός, καθάπερ ἱστοροῦσι τὴν Σίβυλλαν) shows that
opinion on the matter was not uniform: see also Plutarch, Is. et Os. II.
368 c, 371 F ff. ὅτι...μετέχει. Vögelin and others rightly defend this clause against athe-
tizers like Jahn: it adds to the impression of "komische Gelehrsamkeit."
περιφερῆ. "Globular" rather than "circular" ("kreisformig," Ast,
Schleierm.). For πορεία, incessus, cp. Tim. 45 A, Polit. 266 B.
τὰ φρονήματα μεγάλα εἶχον. They were "high minded" and had "proud
looks"; they did not "refrain their soul and keep it low": "μεγάλα φρονήματα
dicuntur habere qui contra dominos conspirant, cp. 182 c" (Hommel).
ὃ λέγει "Ομηρος. See Od. XI. 305 ff., Il. v. 385 ff. We may compare also
Ps. ii. 2, "The kings of the earth set themselves...against the Lord"; and
the Babel tradition (Gen. xi. 4 ff.; cp. Orig. c. Cels. IV. p. 515 A ff.).
190 C οὔτε γὰρ...εἶχον. This obviously implies, as Hug remarks, moral
rather than physical impossibility—the inexpedience of killing the goose that
lays the golden egg. Supply ἠφάνισαν with κερα ταντες.

καὶ ὥσπερ τοὺς γίγαντας κεραυνώσαντες τὸ γένος ἀφανίσαιεν—αἱ
τιμαὶ γὰρ αὐτοῖς καὶ ἱερὰ τὰ παρὰ τῶν ἀνθρώπων ἠφανίζετο—
οὔθ' ὅπως ἔφεν ἀσελγαίνειν. μόγις δὴ ὁ Ζεὺς ἐννοήσας λέγει
ὅτι Δοκῶ μοι, ἔφη, ἔχειν μηχανήν, ὡς ἂν εἶέν τε ἄνθρωποι καὶ
παύσαιντο τῆς ἀκολασίας ἀσθενέστεροι γενόμενοι. νῦν μὲν γὰρ D
αὐτούς, ἔφη, διατεμῶ δίχα ἕκαστον, καὶ ἅμα μὲν ἀσθενέστεροι
ἔσονται, ἅμα δὲ χρησιμώτεροι ἡμῖν διὰ τὸ πλείους τὸν ἀριθμὸν
γεγονέναι· καὶ βαδιοῦνται ὀρθοὶ ἐπὶ δυοῖν σκελοῖν. ἐὰν δ' ἔτι
δοκῶσιν ἀσελγαίνειν καὶ μὴ 'θέλωσιν ἡσυχίαν ἄγειν, πάλιν αὖ,
ἔφη, τεμῶ δίχα, ὥστ' ἐφ' ἑνὸς πορεύσονται σκέλους ἀσκωλίζοντες.
ταῦτα εἰπὼν ἔτεμνε τοὺς ἀνθρώπους δίχα, ὥσπερ οἱ τὰ ὄα τέμ-

190 C γὰρ ⟨ἂν⟩ Ast ⟨τὰ⟩ ἱερὰ Stob., J.-U. μόλις δὲ Stob. εἴέν τε :
ἰῶνται Stob. ἄνθρωποι Vocg.: ἄνθρωποι BT ἀσθενέστεροι γενόμενοι secl.
Kreyenbühl Sz. D δ' ἔτι Stob., vulg.: δέ τι BT 'θέλωσιν Baiter Bt.:
θέλωσιν B, Stob.: ἐθέλωσιν T ἀσχαλίζοντες Stob. ὄα Timaeus Pollux :
ὠὰ BT, Suidas: ὠὰ Stob. Photius: ὦτα Euseb.

ἠφανίζετο. For the impf. without ἄν, cp. (with Stallb.) *Rep.* 450 D, *Euthyd.*
304 D ; Ar. *Nub.* 1212.

μόγις...ἐννοήσας. Notice the comic touch : the omniscient Zeus has to
cudgel his brains over the business !

ὡς ἂν εἶέν. For this construction after a present, cp. Xen. *Cyrop.* I. 2. 5
(Goodwin *G. M. T.* § 349, cp. § 351).

ἀσθενέστεροι γενόμενοι. Although these words are superfluous, a little legal
verbosity may be excused in a comedian's Zeus.

190 D χρησιμώτεροι. "More lucrative." Zeus, with a sharp eye to "the
loaves and fishes," contrives to kill two birds with one stone. The propagation
of piety by making fissures in men is an idea that tickles, and the discovery
of the benefits—from the Olympian point of view—which result from schisms
of this sort is νόημα γελοιότατον. This passage is alluded to by Musonius *ap.*
Stob. *flor.* LXVII. 20; Julian, *Ep.* LX. p. 448 C.

ἐὰν δ' ἔτι κτλ. The ingenious Deity has still "a rod in pickle": the
process of bisection may be repeated *ad lib.* until the wicked are left literally
with not a leg to stand on.

ἀσκωλίζοντες. Schol. ἀσκωλιάζειν κυρίως μὲν τὸ ἐπὶ τοὺς ἀσκοὺς ἅλλεσθαι
ἀληλιμμένους, ἐφ' οὓς ἐπήδων γελοίου ἕνεκα· τινὲς δὲ καὶ ἐπὶ τῶν συμπεφυκόσι
τοῖς σκέλεσιν ἁλλομένων. ἤδη δὲ τιθέασι καὶ ἐπὶ τοῦ ἄλλεσθαι τὸ νεῦρον (τὸν
ἕτερον cj. Bekk.) τῶν ποδῶν ἀνέχοντα, ἢ ὡς νῦν ἐπὶ σκέλους ἑνὸς βαίνοντα.
ἔστι δὲ καὶ τὸ χωλαίνειν. Hesych. ἀσκωλίζοντες· ἐφ' ἑνὸς ποδὸς ἐφαλλόμενοι.
Cp. Schol. ad Ar. *Plut.* 1130 : Virg. *Georg.* II. 383 inter pocula laeti | mollibus
in pratis unctos saluere per utres. See also Smith *D. A. s.v.* "ascoliasmus."

ὥσπερ οἱ τὰ ὄα κτλ. For ὄα (see *crit. n.*) cp. Pollux VI. 79 ἦν δὲ τρωγάλια
κάρυα μυρτίδες μέσπιλα, ἃ καὶ ὄα καλεῖται : Tim. (Phot., Suid.) ὄα· ἀκροδρύων

Ε νοντες καὶ μέλλοντες ταριχεύειν [, ἢ ὥσπερ οἱ τὰ ᾠὰ ταῖς θριξίν]·
ὅντινα δὲ τέμοι, τὸν Ἀπόλλω ἐκέλευε τό τε πρόσωπον μεταστρέ-
φειν καὶ τὸ τοῦ αὐχένος ἥμισυ πρὸς τὴν τομήν, ἵνα θεώμενος τὴν
αὑτοῦ τμῆσιν κοσμιώτερος εἴη ὁ ἄνθρωπος, καὶ τἆλλα ἰᾶσθαι
ἐκέλευεν. ὁ δὲ τό τε πρόσωπον μετέστρεφε, καὶ συνέλκων πάντα-
χόθεν τὸ δέρμα ἐπὶ τὴν γαστέρα νῦν καλουμένην, ὥσπερ τὰ
σύσπαστα βαλλάντια, ἐν στόμα ποιῶν ἀπέδει κατὰ μέσην τὴν
γαστέρα, ὃ δὴ τὸν ὀμφαλὸν καλοῦσι. καὶ τὰς μὲν ἄλλας ῥυτίδας

190 D τέμνοντες καὶ secl. Kreyenbühl Bt.: καὶ secl. Bdhm. Hug Sz.
Ε ταριχεύσειν Photius Suidas ἢ...θριξίν secl. Sydenham Sz. Bt.   οἱ Τ,
Stob.: om. Β   θριξὶ (διαιροῦντες) Toup   καὶ...ἥμισυ del. Sauppe
καὶ τὸ: κατὰ τὸ Verm.   αὐτοῦ Τ: αὐτοῦ Β, Stob.   τμῆσιν: πρότμησιν
Naber   βαλλάντια Τ: βάλλοντα Β   ἀπέδεσε Stob.   τὸν del. Hommel
τὰς om. Stob.

εἶδος μήλοις μικροῖς ἐμφερές. It is the "sorb-apple" or "service-berry," Lat.
sorbum; for the mode of preserving these cp. Varro de re rust. I. 59 (putant
manere) sorba quidam dissecta et in sole macerata, ut pira, et sorba per se
ubicumque sint posita, in arido facile manere: and for ταριχεύειν in this sense
of "drying," cp. Phot. (Suid.) ταριχεύειν·...σημαίνειν δὲ καὶ τὸ ξηραίνειν.
The clause ἢ ὥσπερ...ταῖς θριξίν is condemned by most edd. It is an
objection to the phrase that, as Rettig notes, we ought naturally to supply
with it not only the appropriate τέμνοντες but also the inappropriate μέλλοντες
ταριχεύειν: this objection however is not insuperable, and if necessary τέμνοντες might be transposed. It is argued on the other hand by Hommel and
Vögelin that a second simile is really required, the sorb-slicing describing
only the mode of operation, whereas the egg-slicing adds the idea of ease
and facility. That ᾠα θριξὶ διαιρεῖν was a proverbial saying is shown by
Plut. amat. 24, p. 770 B οἶσθα τοὺς παιδικοὺς ἔρωτας ⟨εἰς⟩ ἀβεβαιότητα πολλὰ
λέγουσι καὶ σκώπτουσι λέγοντες ὥσπερ ᾠον αὐτῶν τριχὶ διαιρεῖσθαι τὴν φιλίαν.
Rückert supposes "ovorum per crines dissectionem ludi genus fuisse;
fortasse ex ovorum dissectione per crines facta convivae futura praedicere
solebant": Zeller writes "vielleicht ein Gesellschafts- oder Liebesspiel, das
darin bestanden haben könnte, dass zwei Tischgenossen sich in die zwei
Hälften eines hartgesottenen Eies theilten, nachdem es mit einem dem
Einen von ihnen ausgezogenen Haare zerschnitten war, also ein griechisches
Vielliebchen." It is, perhaps, possible that it had some connexion with
(Orphic) magic and divination by ᾠοσκοπία. For the process of bisection,
cp. Phaedr. 265 E.

190 E τὴν αὑτοῦ τμῆσιν. Here τμῆσις denotes, of course, the result rather
than the process: Naber's πρότμησιν, umbilicum, is ingenious but needless.

τἆλλα ἰᾶσθαι. Apollo, as ἀκέσιος and ἰητήρ, very properly plays the part
of surgeon's assistant.

τὰ σύσπαστα βαλλάντια. "Round pouches with strings to draw": see
Smith D. A. I. 565.

τὰς πολλὰς ἐξελέαινε καὶ τὰ στήθη διήρθρου, ἔχων τι τοιοῦτον 191
ὄργανον οἷον οἱ σκυτοτόμοι περὶ τὸν καλάποδα λεαίνοντες τὰς
τῶν σκυτῶν ῥυτίδας· ὀλίγας δὲ κατέλιπε, τὰς περὶ αὐτὴν τὴν
γαστέρα καὶ τὸν ὀμφαλόν, μνημεῖον εἶναι τοῦ παλαιοῦ πάθους.
ἐπειδὴ οὖν ἡ φύσις δίχα ἐτμήθη, ποθοῦν ἕκαστον τὸ ἥμισυ-τὸ
αὑτοῦ ξυνῄει, καὶ περιβάλλοντες τὰς χεῖρας καὶ συμπλεκόμενοι
ἀλλήλοις, ἐπιθυμοῦντες συμφῦναι, ἀπέθνῃσκον ὑπὸ λιμοῦ καὶ τῆς
ἄλλης ἀργίας διὰ τὸ μηδὲν ἐθέλειν χωρὶς ἀλλήλων ποιεῖν. καὶ B
ὁπότε τι ἀποθάνοι τῶν ἡμίσεων, τὸ δὲ λειφθείη, τὸ λειφθὲν ἄλλο
ἐζήτει καὶ συνεπλέκετο, εἴτε γυναικὸς τῆς ὅλης ἐντύχοι ἡμίσει,
ὃ δὴ νῦν γυναῖκα καλοῦμεν, εἴτε ἀνδρός· καὶ οὕτως ἀπώλλυντο.
ἐλεήσας δὲ ὁ Ζεὺς ἄλλην μηχανὴν πορίζεται, καὶ μετατίθησιν
αὐτῶν τὰ αἰδοῖα εἰς τὸ πρόσθεν· τέως γὰρ καὶ ταῦτα ἐκτὸς εἶχον,
καὶ ἐγέννων καὶ ἔτικτον οὐκ εἰς ἀλλήλους ἀλλ᾽ εἰς γῆν, ὥσπερ οἱ C

191 A ὄργανον del. Creuzer   καλάποδα T, Pollux Stob.: καλόποδα B
ἐπειδὴ: ἐπεὶ Stob.   ἡ φύσις (αὐτῶν) vel (ἡμῶν) Ast   ἐπόθουν Verm. J.-U.
ἕκαστοι τῷ ἡμίσει Verm.   τὸ libri: τε Stob. Priscian: τῷ Verm. J.-U.
αὑτοῦ om. Priscian   ξυνῄει T, Stob. Priscian: ξυνεῖναι B, Verm. J.-U.: del.
Rettig   ἀμπλεκόμενοι Stob.   λιμοῦ B: τοῦ λιμοῦ T, Stob.: τῆς λιμοῦ W,
vulg.   B τὸ δὲ T: τόδε B   ξυνεπέπλεκτο Stob.   ἡμισείας Stob.
ἀπώλλοντο T: ἀπύλλυντο B: ἀπώλλυτο Stob.

---

191 A **διήρθρου.** "Shaped out," "moulded"; cp. *Phaedr.* 253 D. Cp.
Aelian, *H. A.* II. 19, v. 39, VI. 3.

τὸν καλάποδα. "The (cobbler's) last": Lat. *forma* (Hor. *Sat.* II. 3. 106),
or *tentipellium.* Suidas (*s.v.* κᾶλα) κᾶλον γὰρ τὸ ξύλον· ἐξ οὗ καὶ καλόπους, ὁ
ξύλινος πούς.

μνημεῖον...πάθους. The residue of the wrinkles was intended to serve as a
memorial "of man's first disobedience...and all our woe." This repeats the
idea already expressed in 190 E *supra* (ἵνα θεώμενος κτλ.).

ἡ φύσις. Creuzer renders this by "nos homines," disapproving of Ficinus'
"natura" and Schleierm.'s "forma": but φύσις is no mere periphrasis but
connotes *original* nature or form.

ποθοῦν ἕκαστον κτλ. To attempt to restore the Bodleian reading ξυνεῖναι,
as several of the later critics do, involves too much alteration; thus Hug
writes τῷ αὑτοῦ ξυνεῖναι, Usener ἐπόθουν...τῷ αὑτοῦ ξυνεῖναι. Notice the
"constructio ad sensum," ποθοῦν...περιβάλλοντες...ἀπέθνῃσκον. There is an
echo of this passage in Philo *de op. mund.* 53 p. 36 M.

τῆς ἄλλης ἀργίας. "General inactivity," implying that the λιμός itself was
due to ἀργία. Cp. *Rep.* 554 A, C (with Adam *ad loc.*).

191 B **εἴτε ἀνδρός.** Abbreviated for εἴτε ἀνδρὸς τοῦ ὅλου ἐντύχοι ἡμίσει.
Notice that the third possibility (εἴτ᾽ ἀνδρογύνου) is omitted.

191 C **ὥσπερ οἱ τέττιγες.** This is not merely a piece of natural history;

τέττιγες· μετέθηκέ τε οὖν οὕτω ⟨ταῦτ'⟩ αὐτῶν εἰς τὸ πρόσθεν
καὶ διὰ τούτων τὴν γένεσιν ἐν ἀλλήλοις ἐποίησε, διὰ τοῦ ἄρρενος
ἐν τῷ θήλει, τῶνδε ἕνεκα, ἵνα ἐν τῇ συμπλοκῇ ἅμα μὲν εἰ ἀνὴρ
γυναικὶ ἐντύχοι, γεννῷεν καὶ γίγνοιτο τὸ γένος, ἅμα δ' εἰ καὶ ἄρρην
ἄρρενι, πλησμονὴ γοῦν γίγνοιτο τῆς συνουσίας καὶ διαπαύοιντο
καὶ ἐπὶ τὰ ἔργα τρέποιντο καὶ τοῦ ἄλλου βίου ἐπιμελοῖντο. ἔστι
D δὴ οὖν ἐκ τόσου ὁ ἔρως ἔμφυτος ἀλλήλων τοῖς ἀνθρώποις καὶ τῆς
ἀρχαίας φύσεως συναγωγεὺς καὶ ἐπιχειρῶν ποιῆσαι ἓν ἐκ δυοῖν
καὶ ἰάσασθαι τὴν φύσιν τὴν ἀνθρωπίνην.

191 C τε: δὲ Ast   οὕτω αὐτῶν: ὁμοῦ πάντων cj. Usener   ⟨ταῦτ'⟩ αὐτῶν
scripsi: αυτῶν B: αὐτῶν T: αὖ Schanz: αὐτὰ vulg.: del. Rückert   αὐτῶν...
πρόσθεν del. Jn. Hug   ἔμπροσθεν Stob.   fort. ⟨τὰ αἰδοῖα⟩ καὶ διὰ   τοῦτο
Stob.   γέννησιν Verm. Sz.   ἐν: νέαν Stob.   διὰ...θήλει del. Jn. Sz.
⟨σῶν⟩ (vel ἔτι) γίγνοιτο Rückert: γένοιτο Stob.: σώζοιτο Susemihl   τὸ γένος
BT, Stob.: γένος J.-U.: τόκος Verm.: ὁ γόνος Hommel   ἄρρεν apogr. Coisl.
155 Stob.   D συναγωγὸς Stob.   ἕνα Stobaei A

it contains also an allusion to the cicada as the symbol of Athenian auto-
chthony: cp. *Polit.* 271 A τὸ μὲν ἐξ ἀλλήλων οὐκ ἦν ἐν τῇ τότε φύσει γεννώμενον,
τὸ δὲ δὴ γηγενὲς εἶναί ποτε γένος λεχθέν κτλ.: Thuc. I. 6, Ar. *Eq.* 1331.   For
the mode of propagation of cicadae, cp. Ael. *H. A.* II. 22 ταῖς ἀφύαις ὁ πηλὸς
γένεσίς ἐστι· δι' ἀλλήλων δὲ οὐ τίκτουσιν οὐδὲ ἐπιγίνονται κτλ.: the female lays
her eggs in the sand, where the young are hatched out by the sun's heat.
Cp. also Plut. *amat.* 767 C.

οὕτω...πρόσθεν.   Hommel explains οὕτω by *hac ratione, qua dixi*; Rückert
by *uti nunc posita sunt*, which seems preferable. αὐτῶν (sc. τὰ αἰδοῖα) by itself
reads rather awkwardly; but, as Vögelin points out, a glossator would certainly have added the missing words. It is, perhaps, just possible that
τὰ αἰδοῖα fell out before καὶ διὰ, owing to similarity of letters; but the
insertion of ταῦτ' is a simpler change.

γίγνοιτο τὸ γένος, i.e. τὸ ἀνθρώπινον γένος, cp. 190 D τὸ γένος...ἄνθρωποι.
There is no reason to tamper with the text: the present tense secures the
notion of continuance without need of supplements such as Rückert's σῶν
or ἔτι. (A neater change would be τείνοιτο.)

ἐπὶ τὰ ἔργα.   In contrast to their former ἀργία (191 B). Cp. Hesiod's title
ἔργα καὶ ἡμέραι. βίος is here practically equiv. to ἡ τοῦ βίου κατασκευή (*Laws*
842 C); and the phrase means "husbandry and other means of subsistence."

ἔστι δὴ οὖν.   Here at last we come to the point of the whole tale—the
function and value of Eros.

ἐκ τόσου.   "From such early times," *tam longo ex tempore*: the only other
ex. in Plato is *Laws* 642 E, but the phrase is common in Hdt., *e.g.* v. 88, VI. 84.

191 D συναγωγεὺς.   "A unifier," in the sense of "restorer." This subst.
is unique in Plato, and rare elsewhere; cp. the use of συναγωγός, *Prot.* 322 C,
Tim. 31 C.

XVI. Ἕκαστος οὖν ἡμῶν ἐστὶν ἀνθρώπου ξύμβολον, ἅτε
τετμημένος ὥσπερ αἱ ψῆτται, ἐξ ἑνὸς δύο. ζητεῖ δὴ ἀεὶ τὸ αὑτοῦ
ἕκαστος ξύμβολον. ὅσοι μὲν οὖν· τῶν ἀνδρῶν τοῦ κοινοῦ τμῆμά
εἰσιν, ὃ δὴ τότε ἀνδρόγυνον ἐκαλεῖτο, φιλογύναικές τ' εἰσὶ καὶ οἱ
πολλοὶ τῶν μοιχῶν ἐκ τούτου τοῦ γένους γεγόνασι, καὶ ὅσαι αὖ Ε
γυναῖκες φίλανδροί τε καὶ μοιχεύτριαι [ἐκ τούτου τοῦ γένους
γίγνονται]. ὅσαι δὲ τῶν γυναικῶν γυναικὸς τμῆμά εἰσιν, οὐ πάνυ
αὗται τοῖς ἀνδράσι τὸν νοῦν προσέχουσιν, ἀλλὰ μᾶλλον πρὸς τὰς
γυναῖκας τετραμμέναι εἰσί, καὶ αἱ ἑταιρίστριαι ἐκ τούτου τοῦ

191 D οὖν: γοῦν cj. Useuer   ἕκαστος TW: ἕκαστον B, Stob.   τμήματος
Stob.   Ε φιλομοιχευτρίαι Stob.   ἐκ...γίγνονται del. Bdhm. Sz.
γυναικῶν W   καὶ αἱ...γίγνονται del. Voeg.   αἱ om. Stob.

ἀνθρώπου ξύμβολον. "But the indenture of a man" (Jowett): σύμβολον
here is the *tessera hospitalis*; the host presents his departing guest with one
half of a broken die (ἀστράγαλος), retaining the other half himself (see Smith
D. A. s.v. "hospitium"). Cp. the use of the word by Empedocles, in his theory
of reproduction stated in Arist. *de gen. an.* I. 18. 772ᵇ 10 Ἐμπεδοκλῆς...φησὶ
ἐν τῷ ἄρρενι καὶ ἐν τῷ θήλει οἷον σύμβολον εἶναι, ὅλον δ' ἀπ' οὐδετέρου ἀπιέναι—
"ad quod decretum philosophi respexit fortasse Aristophanes" (Stallb.).

αἱ ψῆτται. Lat. *rhombi*, a kind of flat-fish (perhaps plaice or turbot):
Schol. ἰχθύδιόν τι τῶν πλατείων ἡ ψῆττα, ἐκ δύο δερμάτων συγκεῖσθαι τὴν ἰδέαν
δοκοῦν, ὅ τινες σανδάλιον καλοῦσιν κτλ.: "genus piscium, quod oculos et nares
in altera tantum parte capitis habet" (Stallb.). Cp. Ar. *Lys.* 115 (where the
Schol. curiously defines ψ. as ὄρνεον τετμημένον κατὰ τὸ μέσον, ὡς οἱ σφῆκες),
Athen. VIII. p. 329.

φιλογύναικές. Cp. Cic. *Tusc.* IV. 11. 25 similiterque ceteri morbi...ut
mulierositas, ut ita appellem eam, quae Graece φιλογυνία dicitur, etc. The
sing. is φιλογύνης (see L. and S.).

191 E φίλανδροί. The word here has the bad sense noted in Hermog.
de id. III. p. 324 W. τὴν γὰρ ἀκολασίαν βούλεται νῦν δήπου σημαίνειν καὶ τὸ
μοιχεύεσθαι. Somewhat different is the force in Soph. *fr.* 1006 N. (Hermog.
Rhet. III. p. 324) καὶ ὁ Σοφοκλῆς δὲ φίλανδρόν που τὴν Ἀταλάντην εἶπε διὰ τὸ
ἀσπάζεσθαι σὺν ἀνδράσιν εἶναι: and Eur. *Androm.* 229; while in Ep. *Titus* ii. 4
φιλανδρία is a virtue.

ἐκ τούτου...γίγνονται. I follow Badham and Hug in rejecting these words
as an adscript derived from the context (a view already suggested by
Hommel). Badham writes, "si altero praedicato opus esse credidisset Plato,
quod aegre adducar ut credam, aliquanto pulcrius orationem variasset quam
γεγόνασι in γίγνονται mutando." The three-fold repetition sounds clumsy.

γυναικὸς τμῆμα, *i.e.* a section of the γυνὴ ὅλη ("Doppelweib") of 191 B.
Similarly below ἄρρενος τμῆμα refers to the ἀνὴρ ὅλος ("Doppelmann"). With
the theory of sex-characters here expounded, cp. Hippocr. *de diaet.* I. 28 ff.

αἱ ἑταιρίστριαι. Timaeus ἑταιρίστριαι· αἱ καλούμεναι τριβάδες. Cp. Clem.
Alex. *Paed.* III. 21, p. 264 P. γυναῖκες ἀνδρίζονται παρὰ φύσιν γαμούμεναί τε
καὶ γαμοῦσαι γυναῖκες: and Ep. *Rom.* i. 26.

γένους γίγνονται. ὅσοι δὲ ἄρρενος τμῆμά εἰσι, τὰ ἄρρενα διώκουσι, καὶ τέως μὲν ἂν παῖδες ὦσιν, ἅτε τεμάχια ὄντα τοῦ ἄρρενος,
192 φιλοῦσι τοὺς ἄνδρας καὶ χαίρουσι συγκατακείμενοι καὶ συμπεπλεγμένοι τοῖς ἀνδράσι, καί εἰσιν οὗτοι βέλτιστοι τῶν παίδων καὶ
μειρακίων, ἅτε ἀνδρειότατοι ὄντες φύσει. φασὶ δὲ δή τινες αὐτοὺς
ἀναισχύντους εἶναι, ψευδόμενοι· οὐ γὰρ ὑπ' ἀναισχυντίας τοῦτο
δρῶσιν ἀλλ' ὑπὸ θάρρους καὶ ἀνδρείας καὶ ἀρρενωπίας, τὸ ὅμοιον
αὐτοῖς ἀσπαζόμενοι. μέγα δὲ τεκμήριον· καὶ γὰρ τελεωθέντες
μόνοι ἀποβαίνουσιν εἰς τὰ πολιτικὰ ἄνδρες οἱ τοιοῦτοι. ἐπειδὰν
B δὲ ἀνδρωθῶσι, παιδεραστοῦσι καὶ πρὸς γάμους καὶ παιδοποιίας οὐ
προσέχουσι τὸν νοῦν φύσει, ἀλλὰ ὑπὸ τοῦ νόμου ἀναγκάζονται·

191 E ⟨ἄρρενες⟩ ἄρρενος Bast   τέως: ἕως Ast Sz.   τεμάχια om. Stob.
192 A οὗτοι ⟨οἱ⟩ Hommel Sz.   τῶν μειρακίων Stob.   δὲ δή: δὴ Stob.
οὔτε γὰρ Stob.   αὐτοῖς vulg.   B φύσει...ἀναγκάζονται del. Hug   ἀλλὰ...
ἀναγκάζονται del. Jn. Sz.

τέως ἄν. "I.q. ἕως ἄν, quamdiu" (Ast). As this use is unique in Plato,
Ast proposed to write ἕως ἄν. In 191 B τέως has its usual force, adhuc.

τεμάχια. "Slices": this recalls the comparison with ψῆτται, τέμαχος being
used esp. of fish.

συγκατακείμενοι. An example of this is Alcibiades: see his own account
in 217 D ff.

192 A ἀνδρειότατοι. An allusion, as Hommel remarks, to the ambiguity
of the word ἀνδρεῖος. Cp. Hippocr. de diaet. I. 28 ἢν μὲν οὖν ἐς ἄρσενα τὰ σώματα
ἀποκριθέντα ἀμφοτέρων τύχῃ...γίνονται οὗτοι ἄνδρες λαμπροὶ τὰς ψυχὰς καὶ τὸ
σῶμα ἰσχυροί.

φασὶ...τινες. Cp. what Pausanias says in 182 A (ὥστε τινὰς τολμᾶν
λέγειν κτλ.).

ἀρρενωπίας. Etym. M. s.v. ἀρρενωπός· ὁ ἄρρενος πρόσωπον ἔχων, κατὰ
συνεκδοχήν. ἤγουν ὁ ἀνδρεῖος καὶ ἰσχυρὸς καὶ δυνάμενος πρὸς ἐχθρὸν ἀντι-
ταχθῆναι. The subst. is ἅπ. λεγ., but the adj. occurs in Laws 802 E τὸ δὴ
μεγαλοπρεπὲς οὖν καὶ τὸ τὴν πρὸς ἀνδρείαν ῥέπον ἀρρενωπὸν φατέον εἶναι.
Rettig regards all these apparently encomiastic terms as ironical.

τελεωθέντες. "When grown up," cp. Rep. 377 B, 466 E.

ἄνδρες is predicative: "Such as these, and they alone, turn out men (i.e.
manly, capable) in public affairs": Ficinus wrongly renders "cum adoleverint,
soli ad civilem administrationem conversi, viri praestantes evadunt"; and
Schleierm. also goes wrong. For the connexion between the paederastic
temper and politics, cp. 182 C, Ar. Nub. 1093, Eq. 333 ff., etc.

ἀνδρωθῶσι. This verb is not found elsewhere in Plato: cp. Hdt. I. 123,
Eur. ⊕H. F. 42.

192 B φύσει...ἀναγκάζονται. Hug, on quite insufficient grounds, expunges
these words. It is true that there was, so far as is known, no law at Athens to
enforce matrimony, though there was such a law at Sparta, according to Stob.
(Serm. 65 p. 410) and Pollux (VIII. 40), by which citizens were liable to a

ἀλλ' ἐξαρκεῖ αὐτοῖς μετ' ἀλλήλων καταζῆν ἀγάμοις. πάντως μὲν οὖν ὁ τοιοῦτος παιδεραστής τε καὶ φιλεραστὴς γίγνεται, ἀεὶ τὸ ξυγγενὲς ἀσπαζόμενος. ὅταν μὲν οὖν καὶ αὐτῷ ἐκείνῳ ἐντύχῃ τῷ αὑτοῦ ἡμίσει καὶ ὁ παιδεραστὴς καὶ ἄλλος πᾶς, τότε καὶ θαυμαστὰ ἐκπλήττονται φιλίᾳ τε καὶ οἰκειότητι καὶ ἔρωτι, οὐκ ἐθέλοντες, ὡς C ἔπος εἰπεῖν, χωρίζεσθαι ἀλλήλων οὐδὲ σμικρὸν χρόνον. καὶ οἱ διατελοῦντες μετ' ἀλλήλων διὰ βίου οὗτοί εἰσιν, οἳ οὐδ' ἂν ἔχοιεν εἰπεῖν ὅ τι βούλονται σφίσι παρ' ἀλλήλων γίγνεσθαι. οὐδενὶ γὰρ ἂν δόξειε τοῦτ' εἶναι ἡ τῶν ἀφροδισίων συνουσία, ὡς ἄρα τούτου ἕνεκα ἕτερος ἑτέρῳ χαίρει ξυνὼν οὕτως ἐπὶ μεγάλης σπουδῆς· ἀλλ' ἄλλο τι βουλομένη ἑκατέρου ἡ ψυχὴ δήλη ἐστίν, ὃ οὐ δύναται D

192 B ἀγάμοις οὖσι· Stob.   μὲν οὖν (post ὅταν): μέντοι Sauppe: μὲν Sz. καὶ om. Stob.   θαυμαστότατ' Bdhm.   C ἐκπλήττονται Τ: ἐκπλήττοντα Β ⟨ἐπὶ⟩ σμικρὸν Stob.   οὐδενὶ Stob., Bt.: οὐδὲν BTW: οὐδὲ rccc., J.-U. ἑτέρῳ: ἑκατέρῳ Stob.   χαίρει Τ: χαίρειν Β   D ἡ ψυχὴ ἑκατέρου Stob.

γραφὴ ἀγαμίου (or ὀψιγαμίου). But, as Hommel notes, νόμος covers not only law but custom; and it appears that "certain disabilities attached, at Athens, to the state of celibacy; those who entered public life, as ῥήτορες or στρατηγοί, were required παιδοποιεῖσθαι κατὰ τοὺς νόμους (Deinarch. c. Demosth. p. 99 § 72)": see Smith D. A. I. 43 a. And it is to be noticed that it is precisely public men who are spoken of in the text. The antithesis φύσει)(νόμῳ derives from the Sophists (Hippias v. Protagoras), see my Philebus p. xxviii n., Adam R. T. G. pp. 279 ff., Gomperz G. T. I. pp. 401 ff.

φιλεραστής. This applies to the ἐρώμενος; cp. the use of φιλεραστία in 213 D. Those who are παιδερασταί in manhood were φιλερασταί in boyhood (φιλοῦσι τοὺς ἄνδρας 191 E), so that the words here are put in chiastic order, as Stallb. observes. Hommel absurdly suggests that π. τε καὶ φιλεραστής may denote "virum qui neque alios vituperet amatores puerorum, et ipse pueros amet." The point is also missed by Rückert's "amicorum amator," and Wolf's "sodalium amator."

αὐτῷ...ἡμίσει. This refers to 191 D, ζητεῖ δὴ ἀεὶ τὸ αὑτοῦ ξύμβολον.

ἄλλος πᾶς. This is a short way of referring comprehensively to the segments of the other ὅλα, viz. the androgynous and the "Doppelweib" (191 D, E).

θαυμαστὰ ἐκπλήττονται κτλ. Cp. 211 D.

192 C ὡς ἔπος εἰπεῖν. This qualifies the negatives in the clause, like paene dixerim: "Barely consenting to be sundered for even a moment."

καὶ οἱ διατελοῦντες κτλ. "It is these who continue in fellowship their life long, although they could not so much as say what gain they expect from one another." Schleierm. misses the force of οὗτοι by making it direct antecedent to οἵ ("diese sind es welche" etc.). For the thought of this passage, cp. 181 D, 183 E, Phaedr. 254 A ff., 255 E ff.

τούτου ἕνεκα, i.e. τῆς τῶν ἀφρ. συνουσίας ἕνεκα.

B. P.   5

εἰπεῖν, ἀλλὰ μαντεύεται ὃ βούλεται καὶ αἰνίττεται. καὶ εἰ αὐτοῖς ἐν τῷ αὐτῷ κατακειμένοις ἐπιστὰς ὁ "Ηφαιστος, ἔχων τὰ ὄργανα, ἔροιτο· Τί ἔσθ' ὃ βούλεσθε, ὦ ἄνθρωποι, ὑμῖν παρ' ἀλλήλων γενέσθαι; καὶ εἰ ἀποροῦντας αὐτοὺς πάλιν ἔροιτο· 'Αρά γε τοῦδε ἐπιθυμεῖτε, ἐν τῷ αὐτῷ γενέσθαι ὅ τι μάλιστα ἀλλήλοις, ὥστε καὶ νύκτα καὶ ἡμέραν μὴ ἀπολείπεσθαι ἀλλήλων; εἰ γὰρ τούτου

E ἐπιθυμεῖτε, ἐθέλω ὑμᾶς συντῆξαι καὶ συμφυσῆσαι εἰς τὸ αὐτό, ὥστε δύ' ὄντας ἕνα γεγονέναι καὶ ἕως τ' ἂν ζῆτε, ὡς ἕνα ὄντα, κοινῇ ἀμφοτέρους ζῆν, καὶ ἐπειδὰν ἀποθάνητε, ἐκεῖ αὖ ἐν "Αιδου ἀντὶ δυοῖν ἕνα εἶναι κοινῇ τεθνεῶτε· ἀλλ' ὁρᾶτε εἰ τούτου ἐρᾶτε καὶ ἐξαρκεῖ ὑμῖν ἂν τούτου τύχητε· ταῦτα ἀκούσας ἴσμεν ὅτι οὐδ' ἂν εἷς ἐξαρνηθείη οὐδ' ἄλλο τι ἂν φανείη βουλόμενος, ἀλλ' ἀτεχνῶς οἴοιτ' ἂν ἀκηκοέναι τοῦτο ὃ πάλαι ἄρα ἐπεθύμει, συνελθὼν καὶ συντακεὶς τῷ ἐρωμένῳ ἐκ δυοῖν εἷς γενέσθαι. τοῦτο γάρ ἐστι τὸ αἴτιον, ὅτι ἡ ἀρχαία φύσις ἡμῶν ἦν αὕτη καὶ ἦμεν ὅλοι· τοῦ

193 ὅλου οὖν τῇ ἐπιθυμίᾳ καὶ διώξει ἔρως ὄνομα. καὶ πρὸ τοῦ, ὥσπερ λέγω, ἓν ἦμεν, νυνὶ δὲ διὰ τὴν ἀδικίαν διῳκίσθημεν ὑπὸ τοῦ θεοῦ,

192 D θέλω Β   E συμφυσῆσαι BTW: συμφῦσαι b t, vulg.   ζῆτε ὡς
T: ζητήσεως Β   ἄλλο ὅτι TW   τοῦτο ὅ: τοῦ οὗ Bdhm.   τούτου γάρ
Ficinus Bast: τούτου ἄρ' Wolf   193 A διῳκίσθημεν: διεσχίσθημεν
Cornarius   ὑπὸ: ἀπὸ Hommel

192 D καὶ εἰ...ἔροιτο. The apodosis to this duplicated protasis is to be found in ἴσμεν ὅτι κτλ. (192 E). For Hephaestus and his tools, see *Od.* VIII. 266 ff., esp. 274 ἐν δ' ἔθετ' ἀκμοθέτῳ μέγαν ἄκμονα, κόπτε τε δεσμοὺς | ἀρρήκτους ἀλύτους ὄφρ' ἔμπεδον αὖθι μένοιεν. He would also have his bellows (φῦσαι), tongs (πύραγρα), and hammer (σφῦρα, ῥαιστήρ): see *Il.* XVIII. 372 ff., 474 ff.

192 E συντῆξαι. Cp. 183 E, *Tim.* 43 A πυκνοῖς γόμφοις ξυντήκοντες: Eur. *fr.* 964 πᾶσα γὰρ ἀγαθὴ γυνή, | ἥ τις ἀνδρὶ συντέτηκε, σωφρονεῖν ἐπίσταται. For τήκειν of the effects of love, cp. Theocr. *id.* I. 66; Xen. *Symp.* VIII. 3.

συμφυσῆσαι. Stallb., Hommel and Jowett retain the vulgate, συμφῦσαι, but the other lection gives a better sense—"to weld together," *conflare*: cp. *Il.* XVIII. 470. There is a ref. to this passage in Arist. *Pol.* II. 4. 1262ᵇ 11 καθάπερ ἐν τοῖς ἐρωτικοῖς λόγοις ἴσμεν λέγοντα τὸν 'Αριστοφάνην ὡς τῶν ἐρώντων διὰ τὸ σφόδρα φιλεῖν ἐπιθυμούντων συμφῦναι καὶ γενέσθαι ἐκ δύο ὄντων ἀμφοτέρους ἕνα (Newman here reads συμφυσῆναι), but the word συμφῦναι is probably due to a reminiscence of 191 A. For the sense, cp. Orph. *Fr.* 139 παρήγαγεν...τὸν "Ερωτα, ἑνοποιὸν ὄντα τῶν ὅλων.

τοῦ ὅλου...ὄνομα. This *definition* sums up the description of Eros given in 191 D ad init.

193 A διῳκίσθημεν κτλ. This is apparently a reference—in spite of the audacious anachronism (cp. *Introd.* § VIII.), to the διοικισμός of Mantinea in

καθάπερ Ἀρκάδες ὑπὸ Λακεδαιμονίων. φόβος οὖν ἔστιν, ἐὰν μὴ κόσμιοι ὦμεν πρὸς τοὺς θεούς, ὅπως μὴ καὶ αὖθις διασχισθησό- μεθα, καὶ περίιμεν ἔχοντες ὥσπερ οἱ ἐν ταῖς στήλαις καταγραφὴν ἐκτετυπωμένοι, διαπεπρισμένοι κατὰ τὰς ῥῖνας, γεγονότες ὥσπερ λίσπαι. ἀλλὰ τούτων ἕνεκα πάντ᾽ ἄνδρα χρὴ ἅπαντα παρακε- λεύεσθαι εὐσεβεῖν περὶ θεούς, ἵνα τὰ μὲν ἐκφύγωμεν, τῶν δὲ Β τύχωμεν, ὡς ὁ Ἔρως ἡμῖν ἡγεμὼν καὶ στρατηγός. ᾧ μηδεὶς ἐναντία πραττέτω—πράττει δ᾽ ἐναντία, ὅστις θεοῖς ἀπεχθάνεται— φίλοι γὰρ γενόμενοι καὶ διαλλαγέντες τῷ θεῷ ἐξευρήσομέν τε καὶ ἐντευξόμεθα τοῖς παιδικοῖς τοῖς ἡμετέροις αὐτῶν, ὃ τῶν νῦν ὀλίγοι ποιοῦσι. καὶ μή μοι ὑπολάβῃ Ἐρυξίμαχος, κωμῳδῶν τὸν λόγον, ὡς Παυσανίαν καὶ Ἀγάθωνα λέγω· ἴσως μὲν γὰρ καὶ οὗτοι τούτων τυγχάνουσιν ὄντες καὶ εἰσὶν ἀμφότεροι τὴν φύσιν ἄρρενες· λέγω C

193 A   διασχισθησόμεθα Τ: διασχησθησώμεθα Β   καταγραφῇ Schneider: κατὰ γραφὴν Ruhnken Sz.   διαπεπρισμένοι Τ: διαπεπρησμένοι Β: δίχα πεπρισμένοι Ruhnken   ἅπαντι Hirschig Sz.   Β ὡς ΒΤ: ἂν recc. vulg., Herm. J.-U.: fort. ὅσων   ἡμιτόμοις αὐτῶν Bast   μοι Β: μου Τ   γὰρ καὶ: γὰρ Wolf   C ἄρρενος Bast: ἄρρενος ἑνός Orelli

<hr/>

385 B.C., for which see Xen. *Hell.* v. 2. 1 ff. ἐκ δὲ τούτου καθῃρέθη μὲν τὸ τεῖχος, διῳκίσθη δὲ ἡ Μαντινεία τετραχῇ καθάπερ τὸ ἀρχαῖον ᾤκουν (i.e. κατὰ κώμας): Isocr. *Pan.* 67 A: Arist. *Pol.* II. 2, § 3.

καταγραφὴν. Many editors divide the word κατὰ γραφήν. Probably whichever reading we adopt the meaning is the same, "in profile," the figures being bas-reliefs (*crusta*). Cp. Plin. xxxv. 34 hic catagrapha invenit, hoc est obliquas imagines.

ὥσπερ λίσπαι. These are διαπεπρισμένοι ἀστράγαλοι (Schol. *ad loc.*, Suidas), like the σύμβολον of 191 D : cp. Ar. *Ran.* 826, Schol. ad Eur. *Med.* 610.

193 B **ὡς ὁ Ἔρως.** The Bodleian's ὡς, though doubtful, is possible. Perhaps the variants arose from an original ὅσων or ἐν ᾧ.

πράττει...ἀπεχθάνεται. This may contain an allusion, as Usener suggests, to some familiar verse such as, *e.g.*, πράττει δ᾽ ἐναντί᾽ ὃς θεοῖς ἀπήχθετο.

μή μοι ὑπολάβῃ. This is one of three cases in Plato of "μή with the (independent) subjunctive implying apprehension coupled with the desire to avert the object of fear,"—the other cases being *Euthyd.* 272 C, *Laws* 861 E (see Goodwin *G. M. T.* § 264).

κωμῳδῶν τὸν λόγον. "Ridiculing my discourse," cp. 189 B : so ἐπικωμῳδῶν, *Apol.* 31 D. As Hug observes, A. is really κωμῳδῶν himself when, in comic contrast to the picture drawn of Agathon in *Thesm.* 31 ff., he here suggests that he is τὴν φύσιν ἄρρην.

193 C **ἀμφότεροι...ἄρρενες.** "H. e. ἄρρενος ἑνός" Stallb. As Wolf (like Stallb.) says, ἄρρενες τὴν φύσιν means "mares origine, τμήματα seu τεμάχια τοῦ ἄρρενος," and implies further, as Rettig notes, "mares natura, geborene Päderasten."

δὲ οὖν ἔγωγε καθ᾽ ἁπάντων καὶ ἀνδρῶν καὶ γυναικῶν, ὅτι οὕτως
ἂν ἡμῶν τὸ γένος εὔδαιμον γένοιτο, εἰ ἐκτελέσαιμεν τὸν ἔρωτα καὶ
τῶν παιδικῶν τῶν αὑτοῦ ἕκαστος τύχοι, εἰς τὴν ἀρχαίαν ἀπελθὼν
φύσιν. εἰ δὲ τοῦτο ἄριστον, ἀναγκαῖον καὶ τῶν νῦν παρόντων τὸ
τούτου ἐγγυτάτω ἄριστον εἶναι· τοῦτο δ᾽ ἐστὶ παιδικῶν τυχεῖν
κατὰ νοῦν αὐτῷ πεφυκότων· οὗ δὴ τὸν αἴτιον θεὸν ὑμνοῦντες
D δικαίως ἂν ὑμνοῖμεν Ἔρωτα, ὃς ἔν τε τῷ παρόντι ἡμᾶς πλεῖστα
ὀνίνησιν εἰς τὸ οἰκεῖον ἄγων, καὶ εἰς τὸ ἔπειτα ἐλπίδας μεγίστας
παρέχεται, ἡμῶν παρεχομένων πρὸς θεοὺς εὐσέβειαν, καταστήσας
ἡμᾶς εἰς τὴν ἀρχαίαν φύσιν καὶ ἰασάμενος μακαρίους καὶ εὐδαίμονας ποιῆσαι.
Οὗτος, ἔφη, ὦ Ἐρυξίμαχε, ὁ ἐμὸς λόγος ἐστὶ περὶ Ἔρωτος,
ἀλλοῖος ἢ ὁ σός. ὥσπερ οὖν ἐδεήθην σου, μὴ κωμῳδήσῃς αὐτόν,
E ἵνα καὶ τῶν λοιπῶν ἀκούσωμεν τί ἕκαστος ἐρεῖ, μᾶλλον δὲ τί
ἑκάτερος· Ἀγάθων γὰρ καὶ Σωκράτης λοιποί.

193 C ἀπελθὼν: ἐπανελθὼν Mehler Naber   τοῦτο δ᾽ Τ: τοῦτον δ᾽ Β
D Ἔρωτα del. Voeg.   τε Τ: om. Β   ἡμῶν...εὐσέβειαν del. Voeg.
ποιήσειν Hirschig   E λοιποὶ ⟨μόνοι⟩ Naber

ἀπελθών. "Returning," "being restored to": so, perhaps, ἀπῆμεν πρὸς τὸ
ἄστυ Rep. 327 Β; cp. πάλιν ἀπιέναι Phaedr. 227 E, etc. Hence Mehler's
ἐπανελθών is superfluous.

ὑμνοῦντες...ὑμνοῖμεν. Cp. 184 D ὑπηρετῶν ὁτιοῦν δικαίως ἂν ὑπηρετεῖν κτλ.:
and Agathon's echo of the word (ἐφυμνοῦντα) in 197 E.

193 D εἰς τὸ οἰκεῖον. Cp. Charm. 163 D ὅτι τὰ οἰκεῖά τε καὶ τὰ αὑτοῦ ἀγαθὰ
καλοίης: Rep. 586 E. Possibly there is an intentional echo in the word of
διῳκίσθημεν, as used in 193 A.

ἐλπίδας μ. παρέχεται. Cp. 179 B μαρτυρίαν παρέχεται: Xen. Symp. IV. 25.
For the aor. infin. (without ἄν) after a verb of "hoping," cp. Phaedo 67 B
(Goodwin G. M. T. § 136). Notice the rhetorical care with which this
peroration echoes (ἰασάμενος...εὐδαίμονας) the exordium (ἰατρὸς...εὐδαιμονία,
189 D); also, in εὐσέβειαν we have an echo of εὐσεβεῖν, 193 A ad fin.: and the
emphasis on ἰασάμενος (with Ἐρυξίμαχε in the next line) should not be
missed.

ἀλλοῖος ἢ ὁ σός. This serves to emphasize, by repetition, the statement
made by A. in 189 C (ἄλλῃ γέ πῃ...λέγειν κτλ.).

ὥσπερ οὖν ἐδεήθην σου. See 189 B, 193 B.

193 E τί ἑκάτερος. A. corrects himself with a precision worthy of
Prodicus, the comparative form being more proper than the superlative
(ἕκαστος) in speaking of two only. Observe that Aristodemus (the narrator)
should have spoken next after Eryx., but is here ignored: to have represented
him as a chief speaker "wäre auch nicht richt passend gewesen" (Zeller).

XVII. Ἀλλὰ πείσομαί σοι, ἔφη φάναι τὸν Ἐρυξίμαχον· καὶ
γάρ μοι ὁ λόγος ἡδέως ἐρρήθη. καὶ εἰ μὴ ξυνῄδη Σωκράτει τε καὶ
Ἀγάθωνι δεινοῖς οὖσι περὶ τὰ ἐρωτικά, πάνυ ἂν ἐφοβούμην μὴ
ἀπορήσωσι λόγων διὰ τὸ πολλὰ καὶ παντοδαπὰ εἰρῆσθαι· νῦν δὲ
ὅμως θαρρῶ. τὸν οὖν Σωκράτη εἰπεῖν Καλῶς γὰρ αὐτὸς ἠγώνισαι, 194
ὦ Ἐρυξίμαχε· εἰ δὲ γένοιο οὗ νῦν ἐγώ εἰμι, μᾶλλον δὲ ἴσως οὐ
ἔσομαι, ἐπειδὰν καὶ Ἀγάθων εἴπῃ εὖ, καὶ μάλ' ἂν φοβοῖο καὶ ἐν

193 E ξυνῄδη Cobet: ξυνῄδειν libri   ἀπορήσωσι T: ἀπορήσω B
194 A ου νῦν B   ἴσως ου B: οὐ ἴσως Sz.: οὐ Jn.   εὖ, καὶ μάλ' distinxi
auctore Vahlen: εὖ καὶ μάλ' BT, Bt.: εὖ μάλ' Hirschig Sz.: καὶ μάλ' Verm.

___

καὶ γάρ...ἐρρήθη. "Indeed I was quite pleased with your discourse": hence,
Eryximachus could "let off" Aristophanes (cp. 189 c ἴσως...ἀφήσω σε). Whatever the esoteric meaning of A.'s discourse may have been, Eryx. apparently
regards it simply as a piece of pleasantry—"er hat sich also offenbar nicht
verstanden, sondern hat sich blos an die lustige Aussenseite derselben
gehalten" (Rettig).

εἰ μὴ ξυνῄδη κτλ. For this construction with ξύνοιδα, cp. *Prot.* 348 B ἵνα
τούτῳ μὲν ταῦτα συνειδῶμεν (with Adam's *note*); *Phaedo* 92 D, *Apol.* 34 B.

πάνυ ἂν ἐφοβούμην. For the imperf. here (in an unfulfilled condition) as a
primary tense, cp. *Theaet.* 143 E (Goodwin *G. M. T.* § 172).

194 A Καλῶς...ἠγώνισαι. This implies that the various encomiasts are
engaged in a rhetorical contest (ἀγών): "your display in the competition was
a fine one."

εἰ δὲ γένοιο κτλ. Cp. Ter. *Andr.* II. 1. 9 tu si hic sis, aliter censeas. For
μᾶλλον δὲ ἴσως (rashly altered by critics) cp. *Rep.* 589 D, Ar. *Vesp.* 1486, and
see Vahlen *Op. Acad.* I. 494 f.

ἐπειδὰν κτλ. Notice the elaborate courtesy, not devoid of irony, with
which S. treats Agathon, who evidently is a man with a taste for flattery.
Since the combination εὖ καὶ μάλα is open to suspicion, the regular forms
being either εὖ μάλα (*Gorg.* 496 c, etc.) or καὶ μάλα (*Phaedr.* 265 A, etc.), I
adopt the punctuation suggested by Vahlen. Other critics have proposed to
eject either the καὶ or the εὖ: it would be equally easy to alter εὖ to σύ, or
transpose to καὶ εὖ. The text, punctuated after εἴπῃ, has been construed
(1) as "plenius dictum pro εὖ μάλα" (Stallb.), the καὶ connecting μάλα with
εὖ (Hommel), or (2) as εὖ μάλα with καὶ, corresponding to the following καὶ,
interjected (so Ast); but neither of these explanations is tenable. In favour
of construing εὖ with εἴπῃ may be cited εὖ ἐροῦντος three ll. below and εὖ ἐρεῖ
198 A: for the order, cp. *Rep.* 613 B ὅσοι ἂν θέωσιν εὖ: *Laws* 805 B, 913 B (see
Vahlen *Op. Acad.* I. 494 ff.): add Thuc. I. 71. 7 πρὸς τάδε βουλεύεσθε εὖ,
καὶ κτλ.

ἐν παντὶ εἴης. "You would be at your wits' end," *in summa consilii inopia*
(Ast). Cp. *Euthyd.* 301 A ἐν παντὶ ἐγενόμην ὑπὸ ἀπορίας: *Rep.* 579 B; Xen.
Hell. v. 4. 29. Cp. the use of παντοῖος εἶναι (γίγνεσθαι).

παντὶ εἴης ὥσπερ ἐγὼ νῦν. Φαρμάττειν βούλει με, ὦ Σώκρατες, εἰπεῖν τὸν Ἀγάθωνα, ἵνα θορυβηθῶ διὰ τὸ οἴεσθαι τὸ θέατρον προσδοκίαν μεγάλην ἔχειν ὡς εὖ ἐροῦντος ἐμοῦ. Ἐπιλήσμων μεντἂν εἴην, ὦ Ἀγάθων, εἰπεῖν τὸν Σωκράτη, εἰ ἰδὼν τὴν σὴν B ἀνδρείαν καὶ μεγαλοφροσύνην ἀναβαίνοντος ἐπὶ τὸν ὀκρίβαντα μετὰ τῶν ὑποκριτῶν, καὶ βλέψαντος ἐναντία τοσούτῳ θεάτρῳ, μέλλοντος ἐπιδείξεσθαι σαυτοῦ λόγους, καὶ οὐδ᾽ ὁπωστιοῦν ἐκπλαγέντος, νῦν οἰηθείην σε θορυβηθήσεσθαι ἕνεκα ἡμῶν ὀλίγων ἀνθρώπων. Τί δέ, ὦ Σώκρατες; τὸν Ἀγάθωνα φάναι, οὐ δή πού

194 B ἀκρίβαντα B   ἐπεδείξασθαι T   θορυβήσεσθαι TW   σὺ δή που cj. Steph.

Φαρμάττειν β. με. "To cast a spell upon me." Extravagant praise was liable to cause nemesis and the evil eye: cp. *Phaedo* 95 B μὴ μέγα λέγε, μή τις ἡμῖν βασκανία περιτρέψῃ τὸν λόγον τὸν μέλλοντα λέγεσθαι (with Stallb. *ad loc.*): Virg. *Ecl.* VII. 27, and the Latin terms *fascinum, mala lingua*. For φαρμάττειν, cp. *Meno* 80 A γοητεύεις με καὶ φαρμάττεις. Both here and in *Meno l. c.* the phrase may be reminiscent of Gorg. *Hel.* 15 οἱ δὲ τῶν λόγων πειθοῖ τινι κακῇ τὴν ψυχὴν ἐφαρμάκευσαν καὶ ἐξεγοήτευσαν.

τὸ θέατρον. "The house,"—rather absurdly applied to the small gathering of banqueters, but A. is still full of his recent triumph in the θέατρον proper and readily takes up the idea that he is again engaged in a literary ἀγών (cp. ἠγωνίσαι, 194 A *n.*).

Ἐπιλήσμων. Cp. Ar. *Nub.* 129 γέρων ὢν κἀπιλήσμων καὶ βραδύς. As Hommel notes, the word is "senum decrepitorum constans epitheton." Socrates applies it to himself also in *Prot.* 334 C, D.

τὴν σὴν...ἀναβαίνοντος. For the construction, cp. Ar. *Ach.* 93 (ἐκκόψειε...) τόν γε σὸν (ὀφθαλμὸν) τοῦ πρέσβεως. See Madv. *Gr. Syntax* § 67.

194 B ἐπὶ τὸν ὀκρίβαντα. It seems to have been usual for the poet, as well as the players and choreutae, to appear before the audience, wearing crowns but not in costume, at the προαγών of the great Dionysia held in the Odeum of Pericles on the 8th of Elaphebolion: see Aesch. III. 67 (Schol.), Ar. *Vesp.* 1109 (Schol.). The ὀκρίβας was apparently a platform (βῆμα, cp. *Ion* 535 E) in the Odeum, and not, as formerly supposed, the λογεῖον or stage in the theatre itself (cp. Smith *D. A.* II. 813 b, 818 b): Schol. ὀκρίβαντα· τὸ λογεῖον, ἐφ᾽ οὗ οἱ τραγῳδοὶ ἠγωνίζοντο. τινὲς δὲ κιλλίβαντα τρισκελῆ φασίν, ἐφ᾽ οὗ ἵστανται οἱ ὑποκριταὶ καὶ τὰ ἐκ μετεώρου λέγουσιν. Another meaning of ὀκρίβας is a painter's "easel."

μέλλοντος ἐπιδείξεσθαι. The force of μέλλοντος is seen when we remember that the ἀνάβασις of the poets took place at the προαγών, before the actual performance of the play. For ἐπιδείκνυσθαι of theatrical displays, cp. Ar. *Ran.* 771 ὅτε δὴ κατῆλθ᾽ Εὐριπίδης, ἐπεδείκνυτο τοῖς λωποδύταις κτλ. With Agathon's self-assurance cp. Isocr. *Paneg.* 43 ὁ μικρὸν ὑπὲρ ἐμαυτοῦ θρασυνάμενος...ποιήσομαι τοὺς λόγους.

με οὕτω θεάτρου μεστὸν ἡγεῖ, ὥστε καὶ ἀγνοεῖν ὅτι νοῦν ἔχοντι
ὀλίγοι ἔμφρονες πολλῶν ἀφρόνων φοβερώτεροι; Οὐ μεντἂν καλῶς C
ποιοίην, φάναι τὸν Σωκράτη, ὦ 'Αγάθων, περὶ σοῦ τι ἐγὼ ἄγροικον
δοξάζων· ἀλλ' εὖ οἶδα, ὅτι εἴ τισιν ἐντύχοις οὓς ἡγοῖο σοφούς,
μᾶλλον ἂν αὐτῶν φροντίζοις ἢ τῶν πολλῶν· ἀλλὰ μὴ οὐχ
οὗτοι ἡμεῖς ὦμεν—ἡμεῖς μὲν γὰρ καὶ ἐκεῖ παρῆμεν καὶ ἦμεν τῶν
πολλῶν—εἰ δὲ ἄλλοις ἐντύχοις σοφοῖς, τάχ' ἂν αἰσχύνοιο αὐτούς,
εἴ τι ἴσως οἴοιο αἰσχρὸν ὂν ποιεῖν· ἢ πῶς λέγεις; 'Αληθῆ λέγεις,
φάναι. Τοὺς δὲ πολλοὺς οὐκ ἂν αἰσχύνοιο, εἴ τι οἴοιο αἰσχρὸν D
ποιεῖν; καὶ τὸν Φαῖδρον ἔφη ὑπολαβόντα εἰπεῖν 'Ω φίλε 'Αγάθων,
ἐὰν ἀποκρίνῃ Σωκράτει, οὐδὲν ἔτι διοίσει αὐτῷ ὅπῃοῦν τῶν ἐνθάδε
ὁτιοῦν γίγνεσθαι, ἐὰν μόνον ἔχῃ ὅτῳ διαλέγηται, ἄλλως τε καὶ
καλῷ. ἐγὼ δὲ ἡδέως μὲν ἀκούω Σωκράτους διαλεγομένου, ἀναγκαῖον δέ μοι ἐπιμεληθῆναι τοῦ ἐγκωμίου τῷ ῎Ερωτι καὶ ἀποδέξασθαι

194 C φάναι τὸν Σωκράτη vulg.   ἄλλοις: ἀλλ' Bdhm.   ἴσως secl. Sz.
Bt.: πως cj. Usener: fort. transp. post τάχ' ἂν   ὂν secl. Wolf: ἂν cj. Bt.
D οἴοιτο B.   γίγνεται Mdvg.

οὕτω θεάτρου μεστόν. This means " theatri applausu inflatum esse "
(Stallb.); rather than "stage-struck," cp. Themist. 26. 311 B; Synes. de
provid. 105 B θεάτρου καὶ ἀγορᾶς ἄπληστος.

194 C πολλῶν ἀφρόνων. As Wolf observes, "ein feines Compliment für das
Parterre in Athen." But such a lofty contempt for the bourgeois of the pit
and gallery is quite in keeping with A.'s position as the artistic aristocrat.
If Aristophanes flatters his public on their σοφία (as ἲh Ran. 1109 ff.), it is
obvious that he does so with his tongue in his cheek. Cp. Laws 659 A,
οὔτε γὰρ παρὰ θεάτρου δεῖ τόν γε ἀληθῆ κριτὴν κρίνειν μανθάνοντα.

περὶ σοῦ τι ἐγώ. " Nota vim pronominum... : de te, viro tanto tamque
insigni, ego, homo vilis " (Hommel). For ἄγροικος, cp. 218 B, Laws 880 A
Theaet. 174 D ἄγροικον δὲ καὶ ἀπαίδευτον...γίγνεσθαι.

μὴ οὐχ...ὦμεν. For Platonic exx. of μή or μὴ οὐ in "cautions assertions or
negations," see Goodwin G. M. T. § 265.

ἄλλοις...σοφοῖς. Not "other wise men" but "others who are wise"
(sc. unlike us).

ἴσως. This word is probably genuine. Possibly, however, it should be
transferred to a place before, or after, τάχ' ἂν (for the combination ἴσως τάχ'
ἄν, cp. Tim. 38 E, Laws 676 C, etc.; Schanz nov. comm. p. 14). The ὂν after
αἰσχρόν is sufficiently confirmed by Rep. 425 C, Phaedo 77 A (see Vahlen,
Op. Acad. I. 496 f. on the whole passage).

194 D οὐδὲν ἔτι διοίσει...γίγνεσθαι. For Socrates as φιλόλογος, see Apol.
38 A, Phaedo 61 E; and for his " cramp-fish " style of dialectic, Laches 187.

ἄλλως τε καὶ καλῷ. For Socrates as φιλόκαλος, cp. 213 C, 216 D: it is a
mark of the ἐρωτικός.

παρ' ἑνὸς ἑκάστου ὑμῶν τὸν λόγον· ἀποδοὺς οὖν ἑκάτερος τῷ θεῷ
E οὕτως ἤδη διαλεγέσθω. Ἀλλὰ καλῶς λέγεις, ὦ Φαῖδρε, φάναι τὸν
Ἀγάθωνα, καὶ οὐδέν με κωλύει λέγειν· Σωκράτει γὰρ καὶ αὖθις
ἔσται πολλάκις διαλέγεσθαι. XVIII. Ἐγὼ δὲ δὴ βούλομαι πρῶτον μὲν εἰπεῖν ὡς χρή με
εἰπεῖν, ἔπειτα εἰπεῖν. δοκοῦσι γάρ μοι πάντες οἱ πρόσθεν εἰρηκότες
οὐ τὸν θεὸν ἐγκωμιάζειν, ἀλλὰ τοὺς ἀνθρώπους εὐδαιμονίζειν τῶν
ἀγαθῶν ὧν ὁ θεὸς αὐτοῖς αἴτιος· ὁποῖος δέ τις αὐτὸς ὢν ταῦτα
195 ἐδωρήσατο, οὐδεὶς εἴρηκεν. εἷς δὲ τρόπος ὀρθὸς παντὸς ἐπαίνου
περὶ παντός, λόγῳ διελθεῖν οἷος ὢν <οἵων> αἴτιος ὢν τυγχάνει
περὶ οὗ ἂν ὁ λόγος ᾖ. οὕτω δὴ τὸν Ἔρωτα καὶ ἡμᾶς δίκαιον
ἐπαινέσαι πρῶτον αὐτὸν οἷός ἐστιν, ἔπειτα τὰς δόσεις.

Φημὶ οὖν ἐγὼ πάντων θεῶν εὐδαιμόνων ὄντων Ἔρωτα, εἰ θέμις
καὶ ἀνεμέσητον εἰπεῖν, εὐδαιμονέστατον εἶναι αὐτῶν, κάλλιστον

194 E ὡς BTW: ᾖ vulg. ἐπαινεῖν, ἔπειτ' ἐπαινεῖν Hirschig   195 A ὀρθὸς
om. T   παντὸς om. Bdhm.   οἷος ὢν ⟨οἵων⟩ scripsi: οἷος οἵων Sz. Bt.:
οἷς οἵων ex emend. T: οἷος ὢν BT: οἷος ὢν vulg., J.-U.: οἷος ὅσων Baiter: οἷος
ὢν ⟨ὅσων⟩ Voeg.: οἷος Bdhm.   αἴτιος: αὐτὸς Bdhm.

ἀποδοὺς οὖν. Cp. Polit. 267 A καλῶς καὶ καθαπερεὶ χρέως ἀπέδωκάς μοι τὸν
λόγον: Rep. 612 B, C; 220 D infra.

194 E πρῶτον μὲν...ἔπειτα εἰπεῖν. Stallbaum, though reading ὡς, punctuates
like Hommel (who keeps the vulgate ᾖ) after the first as well as after the
second εἰπεῖν, as if the meaning were "to speak in the way in which I ought
to speak," which is nonsense. The first εἰπεῖν (=δηλοῦν) is different in force
from the other two (=λόγον ποιεῖσθαι), the sense being "first to state the
proper method I am to adopt in my oration, and secondly to deliver it."
Agathon has imbibed a "worship of machinery"—the machinery of method—
from the fashionable schools of rhetoric.

δοκοῦσι γάρ μοι. Agathon, like the rest (cp. 180 D, 185 E), adopts the
favourite rhetorical device of criticizing the manner or thought of previous
speakers: cp. Isocr. Busir. 222 B, 230 A; Hel. 210 B φησὶ μὲν γὰρ ἐγκώμιον...
τυγχάνει δ' ἀπολογίαν εἰρηκὼς κτλ.: Panegyr. 41 B ff., 44 C.

195 A οἷος ὢν ⟨οἵων⟩. This doubling of relatives is a favourite trick of poets
and rhetors; cp. Soph. Aj. 923 οἷος ὢν οἵως ἔχεις ("mighty and mightily
fallen"), ib. 557, Trach. 995, 1045; Eur. Alc. 144; Gorg. Palam. 22 οἷος ὢν
οἵῳ λοιδορεῖ: id. Hel. 11 ὅσοι δὲ ὅσους περὶ ὅσων καὶ ἔπεισαν καὶ πείσουσι.

εἰ θέμις καὶ ἀνεμέσητον. For excess in laudation as liable to provoke
νέμεσις, see n. on φαρμάττειν, 194 A. For the thought (here and at the end of
A.'s speech) cp. Spenser, H. to Love, "Then would I sing of thine immortall
praise...And thy triumphant name then would I raise Bove all the gods, thee
onely honoring, My guide, my God, my victor, and my king."

ὄντα καὶ ἄριστον. ἔστι δὲ κάλλιστος ὢν τοιόσδε. πρῶτον μὲν νεώτατος θεῶν, ὦ Φαῖδρε. μέγα δὲ τεκμήριον τῷ λόγῳ αὐτὸς Β παρέχεται, φεύγων φυγῇ τὸ γῆρας, ταχὺ ὂν δῆλον ὅτι· θᾶττον γοῦν τοῦ δέοντος ἡμῖν προσέρχεται. ὃ δὴ πέφυκεν Ἔρως μισεῖν καὶ οὐδ᾽ ἐντὸς πολλοῦ πλησιάζειν. μετὰ δὲ νέων ἀεὶ ξύνεστί τε καὶ ἔστιν· ὁ γὰρ παλαιὸς λόγος εὖ ἔχει, ὡς " ὅμοιον ὁμοίῳ ἀεὶ πελάζει." ἐγὼ δὲ Φαίδρῳ πολλὰ ἄλλα ὁμολογῶν τοῦτο οὐχ ὁμολογῶ, ὡς Ἔρως Κρόνου καὶ Ἰαπετοῦ ἀρχαιότερός ἐστιν, ἀλλὰ

195 B τῶν λόγων Stob. ⟨ἐν⟩ φυγῇ Stob. ταχὺ...προσέρχεται del. Heusde ὂν B: οὖν T ἔρωτος B οὐδ᾽ ἐντὸς Stob.: οὐ δόντος B: οὐδ᾽ ὄντος T πλησιάζειν T, Stob.: πλησιάζει B ἔστι ⟨νέος⟩ Sauppe J.-U. Sz.: ἔπεται Winckelmann δεῖ πελάζειν Stob. ἄλλα πολλὰ Hirschig

195 B ὦ Φαῖδρε. Phaedrus is specially addressed because it is his thesis (ἐν τοῖς πρεσβύτατος ὁ Ἔρως 178 A, c) which is here challenged.

μέγα δὲ τεκμήριον. This serves to echo, and reply to, Phaedrus's τεκμήριον δὲ τούτου 178 B (cp. 192 A). For the attributes youth and beauty, cp. Callim. H. II. 36 καὶ μὲν ἀεὶ καλὸς καὶ ἀεὶ νέος (of Phoebus).

φεύγων φυγῇ. A poetical mode of giving emphasis. "φυγῇ φεύγειν nunquam sic legitur ut simplex φεύγειν de victis militibus, sed per translationem, fugientium modo, h. e. omni contentione aliquid defugere atque abhorrere" (Lobeck Parall. II. p. 524). Prose exx. are Epin. 974 B, Epist. viii. 354 c; Lucian adv. indoct. 16.

ταχὺ ὂν...προσέρχεται. Bast, "motus ἀτοπίᾳ sententiae," condemned these words; but the presence of sophistical word-play is no reason for suspicion in A.'s speech. A. argues that Age, in spite of its "lean shrunk shanks," is nimble, only too nimble indeed in its pursuit of men : therefore, à fortiori, the god who can elude its swift pursuit must be still more nimble. For the agility of Eros, cp. Orph. H. 58. 1, 2 (κικλήσκω) Ἔρωτα...εὔδρομον ὁρμῇ.

ἐντὸς πολλοῦ. Cp. Thuc. II. 77 ἐντὸς γὰρ πολλοῦ χωρίου τῆς πόλεως οὐκ ἦν πελάσαι. For the sense (abhorrence of age), cp. Anacr. 14. 5 ἡ δὲ (νῆνις)...τὴν μὲν ἐμὴν κόμην, | λευκὴ γάρ, καταμέμφεται κτλ.

ἀεὶ ξύνεστί τε καὶ ἔστιν. Hug adopts Sauppe's addition ⟨νέος⟩, but this spoils the ring of the clause and it is best to leave it to be mentally supplied: for the ellipse, cp. 213 c γελοῖος ἔστι τε καὶ βούλεται. For μετὰ...σύνεστι, cp. Laws 639 c; Plut. de Is. et Os. 352 A παρ᾽ αὐτῇ καὶ μετ᾽ αὐτῆς ὄντα καὶ συνόντα.

ὅμοιον ὁμοίῳ. The original of this is Hom. Od. XVII. 218 ὡς ἀεὶ τὸν ὁμοῖον ἄγει θεὸς ὡς τὸν ὁμοῖον. Cp. 186 B supra, Lysis 214 A, Rep. 329 A ; Aristaen. Ep. I. 10 : and for a Latin equivalent, Cic. de Senect. 3. 7 pares cum paribus, vetere proverbio, facillime congregantur: so Anglicè, "birds of a feather flock together." Similar in sense is ἧλιξ ἥλικα τέρπει (Arist. Rhet. I. 11. 25).

Φαίδρῳ. The reference is to 178 B. Spenser (H. to Love) combines these opposite views,—"And yet a chyld, renewing still thy yeares, And yet the eldest of the heavenly Peares."

Κρόνου καὶ Ἰαπετοῦ ἀρχαιότερός. A proverbial expression to denote the

C φημὶ νεώτατον αὐτὸν εἶναι θεῶν καὶ ἀεὶ νέον, τὰ δὲ παλαιὰ πράγματα περὶ θεούς, ἃ Ἡσίοδος καὶ Παρμενίδης λέγουσιν, Ἀνάγκῃ
καὶ οὐκ Ἔρωτι γεγονέναι, εἰ ἐκεῖνοι ἀληθῆ ἔλεγον· οὐ γὰρ ἂν
ἐκτομαὶ οὐδὲ δεσμοὶ ἀλλήλων ἐγίγνοντο καὶ ἄλλα πολλὰ καὶ
βιαια, εἰ Ἔρως ἐν αὐτοῖς ἦν, ἀλλὰ φιλία καὶ εἰρήνη, ὥσπερ νῦν,
ἐξ οὗ Ἔρως τῶν θεῶν βασιλεύει. νέος μὲν οὖν ἐστί, πρὸς δὲ τῷ
D νέῳ ἁπαλός· ποιητοῦ δ' ἔστιν ἐνδεὴς οἷος ἦν Ὅμηρος πρὸς τὸ
ἐπιδεῖξαι θεοῦ ἁπαλότητα. Ὅμηρος γὰρ Ἄτην θεόν τέ φησιν
εἶναι καὶ ἁπαλήν—τοὺς γοῦν πόδας αὐτῆς ἁπαλοὺς εἶναι—λέγων

195 C νεώτατόν τε Stob.   πράγματα Τ, Stob.: γράμματα Β   παρμενίδης Τ: παρμενείδης Β: Ἐπιμενίδης Ast   εἰ ἐκεῖνοι om. Stob.   λέγουσιν
Stob.   ἐγένοντο Stob.   D οἷός περ ἦν ὁ Ὅμηρος Stob.   τοὺς...εἶναι
secl. Jn. Sz.: τοὺς...βαίνει secl. Orelli.   ⟨φησιν⟩ εἶναι Stob.

"ne plus ultra" of antiquity : cp. Moeris p. 200 Ἰαπετός· ἀντὶ τοῦ γέρων. καὶ
Τίθωνος καὶ Κρόνος· ἐπὶ τῶν γερόντων : Lucian *dial. deor.* 2. 1 ; Ar. *Nub.* 398,
Plut. 581. Cronus and Iapetus were both Titans, sons of Uranus and Gê
(Hes. *Th.* 507), and imprisoned together in Tartarus (*Il.* VIII. 479). Iapetus
was father of Prometheus, and grandfather of Deucalion, the Greek "Adam":
hence "older than Iapetus" might be rendered "ante-preadamite."
195 C ἃ Ἡσίοδος καὶ Π. λέγουσιν. These were the authorities adduced by
Phaedrus (178 B). Hesiod relates such παλαιὰ πράγματα in *Theog.* 176 ff.,
746 ff. ; but no such accounts by Parmenides are extant. Accordingly, it has
been supposed (*e.g.* by Schleierm.) that A. is mistaken, and Ast proposed to
read Ἐπιμενίδης : but cp. Macrob. *somn. Scip.* I. 2 Parmenides quoque et
Heraclitus de diis fabulati sunt. If P. did relate such matters in the poem of
which portions remain, clearly (as Stallb. observed) it could only have been
in Pt. II. ("The Way of Opinion"). Cp. Ritter and Pr. § 101 D, "Generati
sunt deinceps (*i.e.* post Amorem) ceteri dei, de quibus more antiquiorum
poetarum παλαιὰ πράγματα narravit, v. Plat. *Symp.* 195 c, Cic. *D. Nat.* I. 11";
Zeller, *Presocr.* p. 596 (E. Tr.) ; Krische *Forsch.* p. 111 f. For Ἀνάγκη in
the cosmogonists, cp. Parmen. 84 K., κρατερὴ γὰρ Ἀνάγκη | πείρατος ἐν δεσ-
μοῖσιν ἔχει, τό μιν ἀμφὶς ἐέργει : *id.* 138 ὥς μιν ἄγουσ' ἐπέδησεν Ἀνάγκη :
Emped. 369 ἔστιν Ἀνάγκης χρῆμα κτλ.
εἰ...ἔλεγον. Rettig and Stallb. rightly explain the imperf. as due to the
reference to Phaedrus's mention of H. and P. (178 B).
ἐκτομαὶ οὐδὲ δεσμοί. Cp. *Euthyphro* 5 E ff., *Rep.* 377 E where such tales of
divine immorality are criticized.
195 D ἁπαλός. Cp. Theogn. 1341 αἰαῖ, παιδὸς ἐρῶ ἁπαλόχροος : Archil. 100
θάλλεις ἁπαλὸν χρόα : *Phaedr.* 245 A λαβοῦσα ἁπαλὴν καὶ ἄβατον ψυχήν.
Ὅμηρος γάρ. See *Il.* XIV. 92—3. Schol. πίλναται· προσπελάζει, προσεγ-
γίζει.
τοὺς γοῦν...εἶναι. As Hug observes, the occurrence of καὶ ποσὶ καὶ πάντη
below is sufficient to establish the soundness of these words.

τῆς μένθ' ἁπαλοὶ πόδες· οὐ γὰρ ἐπ' οὔδεος
πίλναται, ἀλλ' ἄρα ἥ γε κατ' ἀνδρῶν κράατα βαίνει.
καλῷ οὖν δοκεῖ μοι τεκμηρίῳ τὴν ἁπαλότητα ἀποφαίνειν, ὅτι οὐκ
ἐπὶ σκληροῦ βαίνει, ἀλλ' ἐπὶ μαλθακοῦ. τῷ αὐτῷ δὴ καὶ ἡμεῖς
χρησώμεθα τεκμηρίῳ περὶ Ἔρωτα ὅτι ἁπαλός. οὐ γὰρ ἐπὶ γῆς Ε
βαίνει οὐδ' ἐπὶ κρανίων, ἅ ἐστιν οὐ πάνυ μαλακά, ἀλλ' ἐν τοῖς
μαλακωτάτοις τῶν ὄντων καὶ βαίνει καὶ οἰκεῖ. ἐν γὰρ ἤθεσι καὶ
ψυχαῖς θεῶν καὶ ἀνθρώπων τὴν οἴκησιν ἵδρυται, καὶ οὐκ αὖ ἐξῆς
ἐν πάσαις ταῖς ψυχαῖς, ἀλλ' ᾗτινι ἂν σκληρὸν ἦθος ἐχούσῃ ἐντύχῃ,
ἀπέρχεται, ᾗ δ' ἂν μαλακόν, οἰκίζεται. ἁπτόμενον οὖν ἀεὶ καὶ ποσὶ
καὶ πάντῃ ἐν μαλακωτάτοις τῶν μαλακωτάτων, ἁπαλώτατον
ἀνάγκη εἶναι. νεώτατος μὲν δή ἐστι καὶ ἁπαλώτατος, πρὸς δὲ 196
τούτοις ὑγρὸς τὸ εἶδος. οὐ γὰρ ἂν οἷός τ' ἦν πάντῃ περιπτύσσεσθαι

195 D τῆς ΒΤ, Stob.: τῇ Aristarchus, Homeri (Τ 92) codd.   οὔδεος ΒΤ,
Stob.: οὔδει W, vulg., Hom. codd.   πίλναται ex πίδναται Τ: πήδναται Β:
πιτνᾶται Stob.   μοι δοκεῖ Stob.   τῷ αὐτῷ TW, Stob.: τὸ αὐτὸ Β   Ε χρη-
σόμεθα Stob., vulg.   καὶ (ante βαίνει) om. Stob.   ἐξῆς Τ: ἐξ ἧς Β   ἐνοι-
κίζεται Naber   ἐν μαλακοῖς τ. μ. Naber   ἁπαλώτατον om. Stob.

---

195 Ε ἤθεσι καὶ ψυχαῖς. "In the tempers and souls": here ἦθος seems
to be co-ordinate with ψυχή, but below (ἦθος ἐχούσῃ, sc. ψυχῇ) subordinate,
i.e. A. uses the word loosely with more attention to sound than sense: cp.
Lys. 222 A κατὰ τὴν ψυχὴν ἢ κατά τι τῆς ψυχῆς ἦθος ἢ τρόπους ἢ εἶδος: 183 Ε
supra, 207 Ε *infra*. Notice also the material way in which ἤθη and ψυχαί are
here conceived: cp. Moschus I. 17 ἐπὶ σπλάχνοις δὲ κάθηται: and the figure in
such a phrase as "the iron entered into his soul."

καὶ ποσὶ καὶ πάντῃ. "With feet and with form entire," "nicht wie Ate
blos mit Füssen" (Wolf): πάντῃ, like ἀεί, is A.'s own extension of the Homeric
statement.

ἐν μαλακωτάτοις τῶν μ. The genitive is governed by ἁπτόμενον, and ἐν
μαλακωτάτοις is parallel to ἐν τοῖς (πρεσβύτατον) 178 A: "the most soft of
softest things."

196 A νεώτατος...ἁπαλώτατος. Cp. *Rep.* 377 A νέῳ καὶ ἁπαλῷ ὁτῳοῦν.

ὑγρὸς τὸ εἶδος. ὑγρός, here opposed to σκληρός, is often used "de rebus
lubricis, lentis, flexibilibus, mollibus" (Stallb.): cp. *Theaet.* 162 B τῷ δὲ δὴ
νεωτέρῳ τε καὶ ὑγροτέρῳ ὄντι (opp. to σκληρῷ ὄντι) προσπαλαίειν: Pind. *Pyth.*
I. 17 (11) ὁ δὲ (αἰετὸς) κνώσσων ὑγρὸν νῶτον αἰωρεῖ: Callistr. *descript.* 3 (of a
bronze of Eros) ὑγρὸς μὲν ἦν ἀμοιρῶν μαλακότητος. Another sense of ὑγρός, in
erotic terminology, is "melting," "languishing," *e.g.* Anth. Plan. 306 ἐπ'
ὄμμασιν ὑγρὰ δεδορκώς: Anacr. xxviii. 21: and in *hymn. Hom.* xviii. 33 ὑγρός
is an epithet of πόθος. "Supple of form" is the best rendering here. Arist.
G. A. I. 7. 3 applies ὑγρότης (τοῦ σώματος) to serpents.—περιπτύσσεσθαι is
ἅπ. λεγ. in Plato, and mainly used in poetry.

οὐδὲ διὰ πάσης ψυχῆς καὶ εἰσιὼν τὸ πρῶτον λανθάνειν καὶ ἐξιών, εἰ σκληρὸς ἦν. συμμέτρου δὲ καὶ ὑγρᾶς ἰδέας μέγα τεκμήριον ἡ εὐσχημοσύνη, ὃ δὴ διαφερόντως ἐκ πάντων ὁμολογουμένως Ἔρως ἔχει· ἀσχημοσύνη γὰρ καὶ Ἔρωτι πρὸς ἀλλήλους ἀεὶ πόλεμος. χρόας δὲ κάλλος ἡ κατ' ἄνθη δίαιτα τοῦ θεοῦ σημαίνει· ἀνανθεῖ γὰρ καὶ B ἀπηνθηκότι καὶ σώματι καὶ ψυχῇ καὶ ἄλλῳ ὁτῳοῦν οὐκ ἐνίζει Ἔρως, οὗ δ' ἂν εὐανθής τε καὶ εὐώδης τόπος ᾖ, ἐνταῦθα καὶ ἵζει καὶ μένει.

196 A καὶ (ante εἰσιὼν) om. W   καὶ ὑγρᾶς secl. Jn. Sz.: καὶ τρυφερᾶς Verm.: καὶ ἁβρᾶς Sehrwald   ἰδέας: οὐσίας Stob.   ἡ κατ': ἡ καὶ τὰ Stob. δίαιτα: δὴ τὰ Stob.   B εὐώδης τε καὶ εὐανθὴς Stob.   ἐνταῦθα ⟨δὲ⟩ Stob., Bt.

συμμέτρου...ἰδέας. "Acute vidit Astius σύμμετρον referendum esse ad περιπτύσσεσθαι. Amor enim, quia potest πάντη περιπτύσσεσθαι, recte σύμμετρος vocatur. Itaque ne hic quidem audiendus est Orellius qui σύμμετρος legendum putabat" (Stallb., so too Rückert and Hommel). Rettig takes σύμμετρος to be merely a synonym for ὑγρός, supposing that the proof of the statement ὑγρὸς τὸ εἶδος, which was first stated negatively, is here being stated positively—"nun hängt συμμετρία mit der εὐσχημοσύνη zusammen und ebenso ὑγρότης mit συμμετρία. Vgl. Legg. VI. 773 A, Phileb. 66 B." On the other hand Hug, supposing that συμμετρία is introduced as a new attribute distinct from ὑγρότης, follows Jahn in ejecting the words καὶ ὑγρᾶς. Rettig's view, adopted also by Teuffel, seems the most reasonable : A., with sophistical looseness, smuggles in the extra term σύμμετρος beside ὑγρός in order to secure the applicability of εὐσχημοσύνη. By συμμετρία, properly used, is meant the perfect proportion of the parts in relation to one another which results in a harmonious whole: see my Phileb. p. 176. For εὐσχημοσύνη, cp. Rep. 400 c ff.

ἐκ πάντων. Cp. Theaet. 171 B ἐξ ἁπάντων ἄρα...ἀμφισβητήσεται, "on all hands, then,...we find it disputed" (so Campbell ad loc., who observes that "this use of ἐξ has been needlessly disputed by Heindorf and others"). Ficinus seems to connect ἐκ π. with διαφ., which is possible but less probable.

χρόας δὲ κάλλος κτλ. Possibly we have here a reminiscence of some passage in poetry : χρόας...ἄνθη admits, as Hug observes, of being scanned as a "catalectic pentapody" (like Eur. Phoen. 294). In the repeated mention in these lines of ἄνθος and its compounds, we may discern an allusion to Agathon's tragedy Ἀνθεύς. Cp. Plato 32 (P. L. G. II. 311) αὐτὸς δ' (sc. ὁ Ἔρως) ἐν καλύκεσσιν ῥόδων πεπεδημένος ὕπνῳ | εὗδεν μειδιόων : Alcman 38 μάργος δ' Ἔρως οἷα παῖς παίσδει...ἄκρ' ἐπ' ἄνθη καβαίνων...τῶ κυπαιρίσκω : Simon. fr. 47 ὁμιλεῖ δ' ἄνθεσιν, (ὧτε) μέλισσα ξανθὸν μέλι μηδομένα : Eros, like Titania, loves "a bank where the wild thyme blows" (εὐώδης τόπος), and might echo the song "where the bee sucks, there suck I," etc. For the negative thought ἀνανθεῖ...οὐκ ἐνίζει, cp. Philo de meretr. merc. II. 264 ἐξώροις γενομέναις ("when past the flower of their age," sc. ταῖς ἑταίραις) οὐδεὶς ἔτι πρόσεισιν, ἀπομωρανθείσης ὥσπερ τινῶν ἀνθῶν τῆς ἀκμῆς. For εὐώδης τόπος, cp. Phaedr. 230 B. The description of Eros lying soft in Soph. Antig. 781 ff. is somewhat similar,

XIX. Περὶ μὲν οὖν κάλλους τοῦ θεοῦ καὶ ταῦθ' ἱκανὰ καὶ ἔτι
πολλὰ λείπεται, περὶ δὲ ἀρετῆς Ἔρωτος μετὰ ταῦτα λεκτέον, τὸ
μὲν μέγιστον ὅτι Ἔρως οὔτ' ἀδικεῖ οὔτ' ἀδικεῖται οὔθ' ὑπὸ θεοῦ
οὔτε θεόν, οὔθ' ὑπ' ἀνθρώπου οὔτε ἄνθρωπον. οὔτε γὰρ αὐτὸς βίᾳ
πάσχει, εἴ τι πάσχει· βία γὰρ Ἔρωτος οὐχ ἅπτεται· οὔτε ποιῶν
ποιεῖ· πᾶς γὰρ ἑκὼν Ἔρωτι πᾶν ὑπηρετεῖ, ἃ δ' ἂν ἑκὼν ἑκόντι C
ὁμολογήσῃ, φασὶν " οἱ πόλεως βασιλῆς νόμοι" δίκαια εἶναι. πρὸς

196 ᴗ ἔτι: ὅτι Stob.   οὔτ' ἀδικεῖ om. Stob.   οὔτε θεῶν Stob.
ἀνθρώπων. οὐδὲ Stob.   C πάνθ' Stob.   ἂν BT, Stob.: ἄν τις vulg.
τῶν πόλεων Stob. (τῶν om. Stobaei A).

(Ἔρως) ὃς ἐν μαλακαῖς παρειαῖς | νεανίδος ἐννυχεύεις: cp. Hor. C. IV. 13. 6 ff.
(Amor) virentis...pulcris excubat in genis. Also the echo of our passage in
Aristaen. Ep. II. 1.
196 B Περὶ μὲν οὖν...περὶ δὲ κτλ. Cp. Isocr. Pan. 47 ο περὶ μὲν οὖν τοῦ
μεγίστου...ταῦτ' εἰπεῖν ἔχομεν. περὶ δὲ τοὺς αὐτοὺς χρόνους κτλ.: Phaedr. 246 A.
περὶ δὲ ἀρετῆς. In drawing out this part of his theme Agathon follows the
customary four-fold division of ἀρετή into δικαιοσύνη, σωφροσύνη, ἀνδρεία,
σοφία. Adam (on Rep. 427 E) writes "There is no evidence to shew that
these four virtues and no others were regarded as the essential elements of
a perfect character before Plato." Yet it certainly seems probable that these
four were commonly recognized as leading ἀρεταί at an earlier date (see the
rest of the evidence cited by Adam), and a peculiarly Platonic tenet would
hardly be put into the mouth of Agathon. Cp. Protag. 329 c ff.; and for a
similar use made of this classification in encomiastic oratory, see Isocr. Hel.
31 ff., Nicocl. 31 ff., 36 ff. (cp. n. on 184 c).
οὔτ' ἀδικεῖ οὔτ' ἀδικεῖται. The maxims "love your enemies, do good to
them which despitefully treat you" formed no part of current Greek ethics:
cp. Meno 71 E αὕτη ἐστὶν ἀνδρὸς ἀρετή,...τοὺς μὲν φίλους εὖ ποιεῖν, τοὺς δ'
ἐχθροὺς κακῶς: Crito 49 B: Xen. Mem. II. 3. 14; and other passages cited by
Adam on Rep. 331 E. See also Dobbs, Philos. etc. pp. 39, 127, 243. Notice
the chiasmus ἀδικεῖ...ἀδικεῖται...ὑπὸ θεοῦ...θεόν.
βίᾳ πάσχει. These words form one notion and are put as a substitute for
ἀδικεῖται, just as ποιεῖ (sc. βίᾳ) below is a substitute for ἀδικεῖ. Cp. Polit. 280 D
τὰς βίᾳ πράξεις. There may be a ref. here to the ἔρωτος ἀνάγκαι of Gorgias
Hel. 19.
πᾶς γὰρ κτλ. With but slight modification this would form an iambic
trimeter. Cp. Gorgias ap. Phileb. 58 A ἡ τοῦ πείθειν πολὺ διαφέρει πασῶν
τεχνῶν· πάντα γὰρ ὑφ' αὑτῇ δοῦλα δι' ἑκόντων ἀλλ' οὐ διὰ βίας, of which our
passage may be a reminiscence.
196 C ἃ δ' ἂν κτλ. The argument is that where mutual consent obtains,
since βία is absent, there can be no ἀδικία. For a different view of δικαιοσύνη
see Arist. Eth. N. v. 9. 1136^b 32 ff. ἕτερον γὰρ τὸ νομικὸν δίκαιον καὶ τὸ πρῶτον
κτλ.: Crito 52 E: Xen. Symp. VIII. 20.
οἱ πόλεως...νόμοι. Apparently a quotation from Alcidamas, a rhetor of the

δὲ τῇ δικαιοσύνῃ σωφροσύνης πλείστης μετέχει. εἶναι γὰρ ὁμολογεῖται σωφροσύνη τὸ κρατεῖν ἡδονῶν καὶ ἐπιθυμιῶν, Ἔρωτος δὲ μηδεμίαν ἡδονὴν κρείττω εἶναι· εἰ δὲ ἥττους, κρατοῖντ᾽ ἂν ὑπὸ Ἔρωτος, ὁ δὲ κρατοῖ, κρατῶν δὲ ἡδονῶν καὶ ἐπιθυμιῶν ὁ Ἔρως διαφερόντως ἂν σωφρονοῖ. καὶ μὴν εἴς γε ἀνδρείαν Ἔρωτι " οὐδ᾽ D Ἄρης ἀνθίσταται." οὐ γὰρ ἔχει Ἔρωτα Ἄρης, ἀλλ᾽ Ἔρως Ἄρη, Ἀφροδίτης, ὡς λόγος· κρείττων δὲ ὁ ἔχων τοῦ ἐχομένου· τοῦ δ᾽ ἀνδρειοτάτου τῶν ἄλλων κρατῶν πάντων ἂν ἀνδρειότατος εἴη. περὶ μὲν οὖν δικαιοσύνης καὶ σωφροσύνης καὶ ἀνδρείας τοῦ θεοῦ εἴρηται, περὶ δὲ σοφίας λείπεται· ὅσον οὖν δυνατόν, πειρατέον μὴ ἐλλείπειν. καὶ πρῶτον μέν, ἵν᾽ αὖ καὶ ἐγὼ τὴν ἡμετέραν τέχνην

196 C πλεῖστον Cobet κρατεῖ Stob., Naber: κρατοίη Bdhm. σωφρονοίη Stob. ἀνδρίαν BT D ἄρην Stob. Ἀφροδίτης del. Naber ἂν om. B ἵν᾽ αὖ T: αὖ B: ἵν᾽ οὖν Stob.

school of Gorgias: see Arist. *Rhet.* III. 1406ᵃ 18 ff. διὸ τὰ Ἀλκιδάμαντος ψυχρὰ φαίνεται· οὐ γὰρ ἡδύσματι χρῆται ἀλλ᾽ ὡς ἐδέσματι τοῖς ἐπιθέτοις, οὕτω πυκνοῖς καὶ μειζόσι καὶ ἐπιδήλοις, οἷον...οὐχὶ νόμους ἀλλὰ τοὺς τῶν πόλεων βασιλεῖς νόμους (see Cope *ad loc.*). Two extant works are ascribed to Alcidamas, viz. an *Odysseus* and a *de Sophistis*: the latter is probably genuine and "seems to justify Aristotle's strictures on his want of taste in the use of epithets" (Cope *loc. cit.*). See further Vahlen, *Alkidamas* etc. pp. 508 ff.; Blass, *Att. Bereds.* II. 328.

εἶναι γὰρ...σωφροσύνη. This definition of "temperance" is common to both scientific and popular morals. Cp. *Rep.* 389 D σωφροσύνης...αὐτοὺς (εἶναι) ἄρχοντας τῶν περὶ πότους καὶ ἀφροδίσια καὶ περὶ ἐδωδὰς ἡδονῶν ("temperance, soberness and chastity"): *ib.* 430 E, *Phaedo* 68 C: Antiphon *fr.* 6 σωφροσύνην δ᾽ ἀνδρός...ὅστις τοῦ θυμοῦ τὰς παραχρῆμα ἡδονὰς ἐμφράσσων κρατεῖν τε καὶ νικᾶν ἠδυνήθη αὐτὸς ἑαυτόν. See Dobbs *op. cit.* pp. 149 ff.; Nägelsbach, *Nachhom. Theol.* pp. 227 ff.

Ἔρωτος δὲ κτλ. The argument is vitiated both by the ambiguity in the use of Eros (as affection and as person) and by the ambiguity in κρατεῖ ἡδονῶν, which in the minor premiss is equivalent to ἐστὶν ἡ κρατίστη ἡδονή. For similar fallacies, see *Euthyd.* 276 D ff.; Arist. *soph. el.* 165ᵇ 32 ff. For ἔρως as a master-passion, cp. *Rep.* 572 E ff. Agathon here again echoes Gorgias (*Hel.* 6 πέφυκε γὰρ οὐ τὸ κρεῖσσον ὑπὸ τοῦ ἥσσονος κωλύεσθαι, ἀλλὰ τὸ ἧσσον ὑπὸ τοῦ κρείσσονος ἄρχεσθαι καὶ ἄγεσθαι κτλ.).

οὐδ᾽ Ἄρης ἀνθίσταται. This comes from Soph. (*Thyestes*) *fr.* 235 N. πρὸς τὴν ἀνάγκην οὐδ᾽ Ἄρης ἀνθίσταται. Cp. Anacreontea 27 A, 13 ἔλαβεν βέλεμνον (sc. Ἔρωτος) Ἄρης.

196 D ὡς λόγος. See Hom. *Od.* VIII. 266 ff., already alluded to in 192 D.

πάντων ἂν...εἴη. Another illegitimate conclusion. By means of a tacit substitution of the notion ἀνδρεία for κράτος, it is assumed that ὁ κρατῶν τοῦ ἀνδρείου must be ἀνδρειότερος.

τιμήσω ὥσπερ Ἐρυξίμαχος τὴν αὐτοῦ, ποιητὴς ὁ θεὸς σοφὸς οὕτως Ε
ὥστε καὶ ἄλλον ποιῆσαι· πᾶς γοῦν ποιητὴς γίγνεται, " κἂν ἄμουσος
ᾖ τὸ πρίν," οὗ ἂν Ἔρως ἅψηται. ᾧ δὴ πρέπει ἡμᾶς μαρτυρίῳ
χρήσασθαι, ὅτι ποιητὴς ὁ Ἔρως ἀγαθὸς ἐν κεφαλαίῳ πᾶσαν ποίησιν
τὴν κατὰ μουσικήν· ἃ γάρ τις ἢ μὴ ἔχει ἢ μὴ οἶδεν, οὔτ᾽ ἂν ἑτέρῳ
δοίη οὔτ᾽ ἂν ἄλλον διδάξειε. καὶ μὲν δὴ τήν γε τῶν ζῴων ποίησιν 197
πάντων τίς ἐναντιώσεται μὴ οὐχὶ Ἔρωτος εἶναι σοφίαν, ᾗ γίγνεταί
τε καὶ φύεται πάντα τὰ ζῷα; ἀλλὰ τὴν τῶν τεχνῶν δημιουργίαν
οὐκ ἴσμεν, ὅτι οὗ μὲν ἂν ὁ θεὸς οὗτος διδάσκαλος γένηται, ἐλλόγιμος
καὶ φανὸς ἀπέβη, οὗ δ᾽ ἂν Ἔρως μὴ ἐφάψηται, σκοτεινός; τοξικήν
γε μὴν καὶ ἰατρικὴν καὶ μαντικὴν Ἀπόλλων ἀνεῦρεν ἐπιθυμίας καὶ

196 E κἂν T: καὶ B   χρήσασθαι Stob., Blass: χρῆσθαι BT, cet.   τὴν...
μουσικήν del. Sauppe Jn.   ἔχῃ T.   197 A μὲν δὴ BT: μὴν δὴ W: μὴν
Stob.   ποίησιν del. Blass   πάντως Stob.   τε om. Stob.   τὰ ζῷα πάντα
Blass οὐκ del. Blass

196 E ὥσπερ Ἐρυξίμαχος. See 186 B.

πᾶς γοῦν κτλ. An allusion to Eurip. (Stheneboea) fr. 663 N. ποιητὴν δ᾽
ἄρα | Ἔρως διδάσκει, κἂν ἄμουσος ᾖ τὸ πρίν. This last phrase had a vogue:
cp. Ar. Vesp. 1074; Menander Com. 4, p. 146; Plut. amat. 17. 762 B, Symp. I.
622 c; Longin. de subl. 39. 2 (quoted with other passages by Nauck). For
the ditties of a love-sick swain, cp. Lysis 204 D. See also Aristid. t. I. Or. IV.
p. 30.

πᾶσαν...μουσικήν. With A.'s bisection of ποίησις cp. the analysis of the
notion by Socrates, 205 B infra.

197 A καὶ μὲν δὴ...γε. Porro etiam, quin etiam. (See Madv. Gr. Synt.
§ 236.)

Ἔρωτος...σοφίαν. σοφίαν is here predicate (against Rückert) and stands
for σοφίας ἔργον. For Eros as "poetic" in this sense, cp. Spenser (H. to Love),
"But if thou be indeede, as men thee call, The worlds great Parent."

τὴν...δημιουργίαν. This branch of ποίησις is really a distinct kind from
the other two, as not involving invention or creation. For "demiurgic arts,"
see Phileb. 55 D ff., and for ἰατρική as an example Phileb. 56 A; cp. 186 c, D
supra. Cp. Isocr. Hel. 219 B (where H. is eulogized as the cause τεχνῶν καὶ
φιλοσοφιῶν καὶ τῶν ἄλλων ὠφελειῶν).

φανὸς. Illustris: Hesych. φανόν· φωτεινὸν καὶ λαμπρόν: cp. Phaedr. 256 D.
For gods as διδάσκαλοι and ἡγεμόνες (197 E), cp. Isocr. Busir. 229 B—C τοὺς
θεοὺς...ἡγοῦμαι...αὐτούς τε πάσας ἔχοντας τὰς ἀρετὰς φῦναι καὶ τοῖς ἄλλοις τῶν
καλλίστων ἐπιτηδευμάτων ἡγεμόνας καὶ διδασκάλους γεγενῆσθαι.

Ἀπόλλων ἀνεῦρεν. For Apollo as the inventor of τοξική, see Hom. Il. II.
827; of μαντική, Il. I. 72; of ἰατρική, 190 E ff. supra. See also h. Hom. Apoll.
131 ff.; and for μαντική in connexion with the cult of A., Rohde Psyche II.
pp. 56 ff.

Β ἔρωτος ἡγεμονεύσαντος, ὥστε καὶ οὗτος Ἔρωτος ἂν εἴη μαθητής, καὶ Μοῦσαι μουσικῆς καὶ "Ηφαιστος χαλκείας καὶ Ἀθηνᾶ ἱστουργίας καὶ Ζεὺς " κυβερνᾶν θεῶν τε καὶ ἀνθρώπων." ὅθεν δὴ καὶ κατεσκευάσθη τῶν θεῶν τὰ πράγματα Ἔρωτος ἐγγενομένου, δῆλον ὅτι κάλλους· αἶσχει γὰρ οὐκ ἔπι Ἔρως· πρὸ τοῦ δέ, ὥσπερ ἐν ἀρχῇ εἶπον, πολλὰ καὶ δεινὰ θεοῖς ἐγίγνετο, ὡς λέγεται, διὰ τὴν τῆς Ἀνάγκης βασιλείαν· ἐπειδὴ δ' ὁ θεὸς οὗτος ἔφυ, ἐκ τοῦ ἐρᾶν τῶν καλῶν πάντ' ἀγαθὰ γέγονε καὶ θεοῖς καὶ ἀνθρώποις.

C Οὕτως ἐμοὶ δοκεῖ, ὦ Φαῖδρε, Ἔρως πρῶτος αὐτὸς ὢν κάλλιστος καὶ ἄριστος μετὰ τοῦτο τοῖς ἄλλοις ἄλλων τοιούτων αἴτιος εἶναι.

197 B καὶ οὗτος del. Blass ⟨τε⟩ χαλκείας Blass καὶ Ζεὺς...ἀνθρώπων om. Stobaei ed. princ. κυβερνᾶν BTW, Stob.: κυβερνήσεως Vindob. 21, vulg.: κυβερνᾶν τὰ cj. Voeg. ἐγγιγνομένου Stob. αἴσχους Ast ἔπι Blass Bt. (ἔπι vel ἔτι Β): ἔπεστιν Τ, Stob.: ἔνι corr. b, Porson J.-U.: ἔνεστιν in mg. rec. b: ἔστιν D, Ast πρώτου δὲ Stob. C πρῶτον Stob.

197 B ἔρωτος...Ἔρωτος. Here, as elsewhere in these λόγοι, there is a play on the double sense of the word as (1) a mental affection (i.q. ἐπιθυμία), and (2) a personal agent.

καὶ Μοῦσαι μουσικῆς. Supply (as Stallb. and Hug) Ἔρωτος ἂν εἶεν μαθηταί. Less probable is the explanation of Ast and Rückert who, regarding ὥστε...μαθητής as parenthetic, supply ἀνεῦρον with Μοῦσαι (and the other nominatives) and take μουσικῆς (and the other genitives) as dependent on ἐπιθυμίας...ἡγεμονεύσαντος mentally repeated. For the double genitive of person and thing, cp. Rep. 599 C τίνας μαθητὰς ἰατρικῆς κατελίπετο.

χαλκείας...ἱστουργίας. For Hephaestus, cp. 192 D n.; and for Athene as patroness of weavers Il. XIV. 178, v. 735; Hes. Op. D. 63.

Ζεὺς κυβερνᾶν. The sudden change of construction from genitive to bare infin., together with the unusual genit. after κυβερνᾶν, are best explained by assuming (with Usener) that we have here another of Agathon's poetical tags. For Zeus as world-pilot, see Il. II. 205, IX. 98: cp. Parmen. fr. 128 M. δαίμων, ἣ πάντα κυβερνᾷ: and below, 197 E ad init., κυβερνήτης is applied to Eros (cp. 186 E).

κατεσκευάσθη κτλ. This sentence is quoted later on (201 A) by Socrates. τὰ πράγματα echoes the παλαιὰ πράγματα of 195 C. κάλλους is object. gen. after Ἔρωτος.

αἶσχει γὰρ κτλ. This repeats the assertion of 196 A—B. Rettig reads αἶσχει...ἔστιν, arguing that ἔστιν, not ἔνι, is required by the ref. in 201 A: but αἶσχει ἔστιν as an equiv. for αἴσχους ἔστιν would be a strange use. The restoration ἔπι is as certain as such things can be.

ἐν ἀρχῇ εἶπον. See 195 C. Notice that here as there A. refuses to make himself responsible for the ascription of violence to the gods, as shown by the saving clause ὡς λέγεται.

197 C ἄλλων τοιούτων. Sc. οἷα κάλλος καὶ ἀρετή: cp. Rep. 372 D.

ἐπέρχεται δέ μοί τι καὶ ἔμμετρον εἰπεῖν, ὅτι οὗτός ἐστιν ὁ ποιῶν
εἰρήνην μὲν ἐν ἀνθρώποις, πελάγει δὲ γαλήνην
νηνεμίαν, ἀνέμων κοίτην ὕπνον τ' ἐνὶ κήδει.

οὗτος δὲ ἡμᾶς ἀλλοτριότητος μὲν κενοῖ, οἰκειότητος δὲ πληροῖ, τὰς D
τοιάσδε ξυνόδους μετ' ἀλλήλων πάσας τιθεὶς ξυνιέναι, ἐν ἑορταῖς,
197 C ἐμμέτρως Hermog. Method.   ἀνέμων BT : τ' ἀνέμων Stob. vulg.:
δ' ἀνέμοις Hermog.   κοίτην BT : κοίτην τ' Stob. : κοίτη Hermog. cod. Monac.:
κοίτῃ θ' Dindorf Jn. : κοίτῃ δ' Herm.   τ' ἐνὶ κήδει Stob. Hermog. : τε νικηδει
B : τε νηκηδῆ T: τε νικήδει W (in mg. γρ. καὶ νηκηδεῖ) : τ' ἐνὶ γήθει Bast:
νηκηδῇ Dindf. Herm. Jn.: λαθικηδῆ Winckelmann : τ' ἐνὶ κήτει Hommel Christ
(ὕπνον τ' ἐνὶ κοίτῃ ἀκηδῆ Bdhm.)   D οὗτος γὰρ Stob.   ἀλλοτριώτατος Stob.

ἐπέρχεται δέ μοί κτλ. Here Agathon breaks out into verse of his own,
whereas hitherto he had contented himself with quoting from others (196 C, E).
Observe the alliterative effect, dear to the school of Gorgias, of the play with
ρ and ν, γ and λ, in the former, and of ν and μ in the latter of the two verses.
νηνεμίαν...κήδει. Both the punctuation and reading of this verse are
doubtful. Rückert, Stallb., and the Zurich edd. print commas after γαλήνην
and ἀνέμων, Hug and Burnet only after ἀνέμων, Hommel after γαλήνην and
κοίτην. It would appear, however, from the Homeric passage (Od. v. 391 =
XII. 168, ἄνεμος μὲν ἐπαύσατο ἠδὲ γαλήνη | ἔπλετο νηνεμίη), of which this is
obviously an echo, that no stop should be placed after γαλήνην, but rather
after νηνεμίαν or ἀνέμων : while the compound word ἀνεμοκοῖται, applied to a
sect (γένος) in Corinth who claimed to be able τοὺς ἀνέμους κοιμίζειν (see
Hesych. and Suid. s.v.; also Welcker Kl. Schr. 3. 63 ; Rohde Psyche II. p. 88 ;
and 202 E n.), makes it probable that ἀνέμων κοίτην are meant to go closely
together. Further, although as Zeller argues it is appropriate enough in
general to describe Love as "is qui non aequoris solum sed etiam humani
pectoris turbas sedat" (cp. Il. XXIV. 128 ff., Catull. 68. 1—8), still the reversion
to human κῆδος after mentioning waves and winds is a little curious, and it is
tempting to adopt Hommel's conjecture ἐνὶ κήτει which, if κῆτος can bear the
sense of "sea-depths" (see L. and S. s.vv. κῆτος, μεγακήτης) would furnish a
more satisfactory disposition of ideas—"peace on land and on sea, repose in
heaven above and in the depths below." Or, if we assumed that an original
ἐνὶ νείκη (=νείκει) was corrupted by haplography to ἐνὶ κη, a fair sense would
be obtained. If the ordinary text be kept, we may notice (with Vögelin) how
the force of the prepos. in ἐν ἀνθρ....ἐνὶ κήδει varies "in the style of the
Sophists." In Theaet. 153 C we have a similar combination, νηνεμίας τε καὶ
γαλήνας, the only other Platonic ex. of νηνεμία being Phaedo 77 E. γαληνός
as an adj. occurs in Ax. 370 D.
197 D ἀλλοτριότητος κτλ. For Eros as the peace-maker, cp. Isocr. Hel.
221 B εὑρήσομεν τοὺς Ἕλληνας δι' αὐτὴν ὁμονοήσαντας καὶ κοινὴν στράτειαν...
ποιησαμένους.
τὰς τοιάσδε ξυνόδους. "Haec δεικτικῶς dicta sunt: quale est hoc convivium
nostrum" (Stallb.).

ἐν χοροῖς, ἐν θυσίαις γιγνόμενος ἡγεμών· πρᾳότητα μὲν πορίζων,
ἀγριότητα δ' ἐξορίζων· φιλόδωρος εὐμενείας, ἄδωρος δυσμενείας·
ἵλεως ἀγανός· θεατὸς σοφοῖς, ἀγαστὸς θεοῖς· ζηλωτὸς ἀμοίροις,
κτητὸς εὐμοίροις· τρυφῆς, ἁβρότητος, χλιδῆς, χαρίτων, ἱμέρου,
πόθου πατήρ· ἐπιμελὴς ἀγαθῶν, ἀμελὴς κακῶν· ἐν πόνῳ, ἐν φόβῳ,

197 D θυσίαις BT: θυσίαισι W: εὐθυμίαις Stob., Jn.: fort. θιάσοις
ἀγανός Usener Bt.: ἀγαθός BT: ἀγαθοῖς Stob., Jn. Sz.: ἵλεως ἀγαθοῖς secl.
Rettig: ἱμερτὸς ἀγαθοῖς Schulthess   τρυφῆς secl. J.-U. Sz.   χλίδῆς T:
χληδης B: χληδῆς W   ἡμέρου B   πόθου om. Stob., secl. Voeg. Sz.
ἀνελὴς B

___

ἐν θυσίαις. For θ. Stob. has εὐθυμίαις, which looks like a gloss on some
word other than θυσίαις. I am inclined to suspect that θιάσοις should be
restored: the word would fit in well between χοροῖς and ἡγεμών, "in festive
bands." The corruption might be due to the loss of the termination, after
which θιάς was mistaken for θυσιάς. Cp. Xen. Symp. VIII. 1 πάντες ἐσμεν τοῦ
θεοῦ τούτου θιασῶται.

ἀγανός. The ἀγαθός of the MSS. cannot stand, and Stobaeus's ἀγαθοῖς
(adopted by most edd. since Wolf) is open to objection both as spoiling the
symmetry and because of the occurrence of ἀγαθῶν just below. We want a
more exquisite word, and Usener's ἀγανός is more appropriate in sense than
such possible alternatives as ἀγανός or ἀγλαός. For Agathon's antitheses, cp.
Clem. Al. Strom. v. 614 D; Athen. v. 11.

τρυφῆς...χλιδῆς. Moeris: χλιδὴ Ἀττικοί, τρυφὴ Ἕλληνες. Hence Hug
omits τρυφῆς as a gloss on χλιδῆς, and (to preserve symmetry) omits πόθου
also.

ἐν πόνῳ κτλ. These words have given rise to much discussion and many
emendations (see crit. n.). Two main lines of interpretation are possible:
either (1) we may suppose that maritime allusions are to be sought in these
words to match those in κυβερνήτης κτλ.; or (2) we may suppose the latter
set of words to be used in a merely metaphorical sense. Badham adopts
line (1); so too Schütz regards the whole figure as borrowed "e re nautica."
Nautis enim saepe timor naufragii, desiderium terrae, labor in difficultate
navigandi, aerumna nauseantibus...accidere solet"; and he takes the following
four substt. (κυβερν. κτλ.) as referring in order to these four conditions. And,
adopting this line, I myself formerly proposed to read (for ἐν πόθῳ, ἐν λόγῳ)
ἐν πόρῳ, ἐν ῥόθῳ. The 2nd line of explanation is adopted (a) by those who
attempt to defend the vulgate, and (b) by some who have recourse to emendation. Thus (a) Stallb. commends Ast's view that λόγος can stand here
because Agathon's speech is full of "merus verborum lusus"; while Hommel
takes the words ἐν πόνῳ etc. as "e re amatoria depromta," expressing the
affections of the lover while seeking the society of his beloved, and connects
(in the reverse order) λόγῳ with κυβερν., πόθῳ with ἐπιβ., φόβῳ with παραστ.,
and πόνῳ with σωτήρ. On the other hand, (b) Rettig—while altering the
second pair to ἐν μόθῳ, ἐν λόχῳ—also disregards the maritime metaphor and

ἐν πότῳ, ἐν λόγῳ κυβερνήτης, ἐπιβάτης, παραστάτης τε καὶ σωτὴρ Ε
ἄριστος, ξυμπάντων τε θεῶν καὶ ἀνθρώπων κόσμος, ἡγεμὼν κάλλιστος καὶ ἄριστος, ᾧ χρὴ ἔπεσθαι πάντα ἄνδρα ἐφυμνοῦντα
197 D ἐν πόνῳ ἐν φόβῳ ἐν πότῳ ἐν λόγῳ scripsi: ἐν πόνῳ ἐν φόβῳ ἐν
πόθῳ ἐν λόγῳ codd.: ἐν φόβῳ ἐν πόθῳ ἐν πόνῳ ἐν μόγῳ Schütz: ἐν πόνῳ ἐν
φόβῳ ἐν μόθῳ ἐν μόγῳ Jn.: ἐν π. ἐν φ. ἐν μόθῳ ἐν λόχῳ Rettig: ἐν π. ἐν φ. ἐν
πόθῳ ἐν νόσῳ Winckelmann: ἐν π. ἐν φ. ἐν πόθῳ ἐν σάλῳ Usener: ἐν πλῷ ἐν
πόνῳ ἐν φόβῳ Bdhm.   Ε ἐπιβάτης del. Bdhm.: ἐπιδώτης Usener   τε καὶ
del. Bdhm.

understands the passage "überhaupt von Kriegsgefahren und dem in solchen
geleisteten Beistand," comparing the allusions to such matters by Phaedrus
(179 A) and Alcibiades (220 D ff.). Here Rettig is, I believe, partly on the
right track; since the clue to the sense (and reading) here is to be looked
for in Alcibiades' eulogy of Socrates. We find πόνῳ echoed there (219 E τοῖς
πόνοις...περιῆν), and φόβῳ also (220 E φυγῇ ἀνεχώρει, 221 A ἐν φόβῳ) and
ἐν λόγῳ may be defended by the allusions to Socrates' λόγοι (215 C ff., 221 D ff.).
Thus the only doubtful phrase is ἐν πόθῳ, which has no parallel in Alcib.'s
speech, and is also objectionable here because of the proximity of πόθου.
In place of it I propose ἐν πότῳ (cp. Phileb. 48 A), of which we find
an echo (in sense if not in sound) in 220 A ἐν τ' αὖ ταῖς εὐωχίαις...καὶ πίνειν...
πάντας ἐκράτει.   For maritime terms in connexion with λόγος, cp. Lach. 194 C
ἀνδράσι φίλοις χειμαζομένοις ἐν λόγῳ καὶ ἀποροῦσι βοήθησον: Parm. 137 A
διανεῦσαι...τοσοῦτον πέλαγος λόγων: Phaedr. 264 A; Phileb. 29 B. So both λόγος
and πότος in Dionys. Chalc. 4. 1 ff. ὕμνους οἰνοχοεῖν...τόνδε...εἰρεσίῃ γλώσσης
ἀποπέμψομεν...τοῦδ' ἐπὶ συμποσίου· δεξιότης τε λόγου | Φαίακος Μουσῶν ἐρέτας
ἐπὶ σέλματα πέμπει: id. 5. 1 ff. καί τινες οἶνον ἄγοντες ἐν εἰρεσίῃ Διονύσου, |
συμποσίου ναῦται καὶ κυλίκων ἐρέται | ⟨μάρναται⟩ περὶ τοῦδε. Cp. also Cic. Tusc.
IV. 5. 9 quaerebam utrum panderem vela orationis statim, an eam...dialecti-
corum remis propellerem.   For παραστάτης, of Eros, cp. ὁ παρ' ἑκάστῳ δαίμων
in later Stoic literature (Rohde Psyche II. 316): Epict. diss. I. 14. 12;
Menander (ap. Mein. Com. IV. 238) ἅπαντι δαίμων ἀνδρὶ συμπαρίσταται | εὐθὺς
γενομένῳ μυσταγωγὸς τοῦ βίου.   For Socrates as σωτήρ, see 220 D ff.: the
term is regularly applied to a ἥρως, e.g. Soph. O. C. 460 (Oedipus); Thuc.
V. 11. 2 (Brasidas); Eur. Heracl. 1032 (Eurystheus): Pind. fr. 132 has the
same combination, σωτὴρ ἄριστος: cp. Spenser, "(Love) the most kind
preserver Of living wights." ἐν πόνῳ might be a reminiscence of Pind.
Nem. X. 78 ταῦροι...ἐν πόνῳ πιστοί: or used, Homerically, of "the toil of
war" (= ἐν μαχαῖς, cp. 220 D).   For κυβερνήτης used metonymously, cp. 197 B
(n. on κυβερνᾶν); so Emerson, "Beauty is the pilot of the young soul."
ἐπιβάτης, in the present context, must mean "a marine," classiarius miles,
and hence, by metonymy, "a comrade" in general.—The general sense of the
passage is this: "in the contests both of war and peace the best guide and
warden, comrade and rescuer is Eros." Cp. also Procl. in I Alc. p. 40.

197 E ξυμπάντων...κόσμος. Cp. Gorg. Hel. 1 κόσμος πόλει μὲν εὐανδρία,
σώματι δὲ κάλλος.

ἡγεμὼν...ἐφυμνοῦντα. The image is that of Eros as coryphaeus leading a

καλῶς, ᾠδῆς μετέχοντα ἣν ᾖδει θέλγων πάντων θεῶν τε καὶ ἀνθρώπων νόημα.

Οὗτος, ἔφη, ὁ παρ᾽ ἐμοῦ λόγος, ὦ Φαῖδρε, τῷ θεῷ ἀνακείσθω, τὰ μὲν παιδιᾶς, τὰ δὲ σπουδῆς μετρίας, καθ᾽ ὅσον ἐγὼ δύναμαι, μετέχων.

198 XX. Εἰπόντος δὲ τοῦ Ἀγάθωνος πάντας ἔφη ὁ Ἀριστόδημος ἀναθορυβῆσαι τοὺς παρόντας, ὡς πρεπόντως τοῦ νεανίσκου εἰρηκότος καὶ αὐτῷ καὶ τῷ θεῷ. τὸν οὖν Σωκράτη εἰπεῖν βλέψαντα εἰς τὸν Ἐρυξίμαχον, Ἆρά σοι δοκῶ, φάναι, ὦ παῖ Ἀκουμενοῦ, ἀδεὲς πάλαι δέος δεδιέναι, ἀλλ᾽ οὐ μαντικῶς ἃ νῦν δὴ ἔλεγον εἰπεῖν, ὅτι Ἀγάθων θαυμαστῶς ἐροῖ, ἐγὼ δ᾽ ἀπορήσοιμι; Τὸ μὲν ἕτερον, φάναι τὸν Ἐρυξίμαχον, μαντικῶς μοι δοκεῖς εἰρηκέναι, ὅτι Ἀγάθων εὖ ἐρεῖ· τὸ δὲ σὲ ἀπορήσειν, οὐκ οἶμαι.

197 E καλῶς BT: καλῆς Stob.: καλῶς καλῆς vulg.: καλῶς τῆς Ast: καλῶς καὶ τῆς Orelli Teuffel: καὶ Mdvg. Sz. δὲ ⟨καὶ⟩ Method. 198 A πρεπόντως b t: πρέποντος BTW ἄρα B ἐροίη Cobet Jn. δοκεῖς μοι T

procession of singers, and singing ("a song of my beloved") himself (ᾠδῆς ἣν ᾖδει). Notice how Agathon repeats the phrase θεῶν τε καὶ ἀνθρώπων (cp. 197 B). For ἡγεμών, cp. Spenser (*H. to Love*) "Thou art his god, thou art his mighty *guide.*" καλῆς is omitted in Ficinus' transl.

νόημα. Here used, poetically, as equivalent to νοῦς: cp. Pind. *Pyth.* VI. 29; Theogn. 435; Emped. 329 St., αἷμα γὰρ ἀνθρώποις περικάρδιόν ἐστι νόημα.

τῷ θεῷ ἀνακείσθω. "Let it be presented as a votive-offering (ἀνάθημα) to the God (*sc.* Eros)."

παιδιᾶς...σπουδῆς. Possibly an echo of Gorg. *Hel. ad fin.* Ἑλένης μὲν ἐγκώμιον, ἐμὸν δὲ παίγνιον. For the antithesis, cp. 216 E; *Laws* 647 D; *Phileb.* 30 E; Ar. *Ran.* 389.

μετρίας. "H.e. κοσμίας" (Stallb.), with, perhaps, a latent play on the other sense of μέτρον, in allusion to the rhythmical style of A.'s oration; cp. 187 D, 205 C, *Phaedr.* 267 A ἐν μέτρῳ λέγειν.

198 A ἀναθορυβῆσαι. Cp. *Protag.* 334 C εἰπόντος οὖν ταῦτα αὐτοῦ οἱ παρόντες ἀνεθορύβησαν ὡς εὖ λέγοι: *Euthyd.* 276 B; Cic. *Sen.* 18. 64 a cuncto consessu plausus multiplex datus.

πρεπόντως...τῷ θεῷ. Cp. *Laws* 699 D εἴρηκας σαυτῷ τε καὶ τῇ πατρίδι πρεπόντως.

ὦ παῖ Ἀκουμενοῦ. Observe the mock-solemnity of this mode of address: cp. 172 A, 214 B. Socrates addresses Eryx. with allusion to his language in 193 E (εἰ μὴ ξυνῄδη κτλ.).

ἀδεὲς...δέος δεδιέναι. Schol. ἀδεὲς δέος· ἐπὶ τῶν τὰ μὴ ἄξια φόβου δεδιότων. ὅμοιον τούτῳ καὶ τὸ ψοφοδεὴς ἄνθρωπος (*Phaedr.* 257 D). Observe how Socr. here, in caricature of Agathon's style (*e.g.* 197 D), combines in one phrase the *figura etymologica* and the figure *oxymoron*: cp. Eur. *I. T.* 216 νύμφαν δύσνυμφον: *ib.* 566 χάριν ἄχαριν: *id. Hel.* 690 γάμον ἄγαμον.

ἃ νῦν δὴ ἔλεγον. The reference is to 194 A.

Καὶ πῶς, ὦ μακάριε, εἰπεῖν τὸν Σωκράτη, οὐ μέλλω ἀπορεῖν Β
καὶ ἐγὼ καὶ ἄλλος ὁστισοῦν, μέλλων λέξειν μετὰ καλὸν οὕτω καὶ
παντοδαπὸν λόγον ῥηθέντα; καὶ τὰ μὲν ἄλλα οὐχ ὁμοίως μὲν
θαυμαστά· τὸ δὲ ἐπὶ τελευτῆς τοῦ κάλλους τῶν ὀνομάτων καὶ
ῥημάτων τίς οὐκ ἂν ἐξεπλάγη ἀκούων; ἐπεὶ ἔγωγε ἐνθυμούμενος
ὅτι αὐτὸς οὐχ οἷός τ᾽ ἔσομαι οὐδ᾽ ἐγγὺς τούτων οὐδὲν καλὸν εἰπεῖν,
ὑπ᾽ αἰσχύνης ὀλίγου ἀποδρὰς ᾠχόμην, εἴ πῃ εἶχον. καὶ γάρ με C
Γοργίου ὁ λόγος ἀνεμίμνησκεν, ὥστε ἀτεχνῶς τὸ τοῦ Ὁμήρου

198 B καὶ παντοδαπὸν οὕτω TW   μὲν om. Vind. 21, vulg. Sz.: (μέν,
θαυμαστὰ δέ· Bdhm.)   ἀκούων om. W

---

198 B οὐ μέλλω κτλ. Notice the change of tense in ἀπορεῖν...λέξειν: Plato
uses pres., fut., and aor. infinitives after μέλλω, of which the last is the rarest
construction. For the sense, cp. Soph. 231 B.

παντοδαπὸν λόγον. There is irony in the epithet. Socr. implies that he
regards it as a motley λόγος, "a thing of shreds and patches." Cp. 193 E,
and 198 E (πάντα λόγον κινοῦντες κτλ.).

οὐχ ὁμοίως μὲν θαυμαστά. The antithesis must be mentally supplied: "the
earlier parts were not equally marvellous (although they were marvellous)."
Stallb. explains differently, "τὰ μὲν ἄλλα accipi potest absolute pro et quod
cetera quidem attinet; quo facto non inepte pergitur sic: οὐχ ὁμοίως μὲν
θαυμαστά, particula μὲν denuo iterata." But the former explanation (adopted
by Rettig and Hug, after Zeller) is the simpler and better.

τὸ δὲ ἐπὶ τελευτῆς κτλ. τό is accus. of respect, going closely with ἐπὶ
τελευτῆς, not with τοῦ κάλλους (as Rückert): "quod autem exitum orationis
tuae attinet" (Stallb., and so Hommel). τοῦ κάλλους is governed by ἐξεπλάγη, as gen. of causative object (cp. Madv. Gr. Synt. § 61 b). ἀκούων, "as
he heard."

τῶν ὀνομάτων καὶ ῥημάτων. Cp. 199 B ὀνόμασι δὲ καὶ θέσει ῥημάτων. ✓
Properly, ὄνομα and ῥῆμα are distinguished as, in logic, the subject and predicate and, in grammar, the noun and verb respectively. But commonly ὄνομα
is used of any single word, and ῥῆμα of a clause, or proposition (e.g. Protag.
341 E); cp. Apol. 17 B; Cratyl. 399 A, 431 B. Both here and below, as
Athenaeus observes (v. 187 C), Πλάτων χλευάζει τε τὰ ἰσόκωλα τὰ Ἀγάθωνος
καὶ τὰ ἀντίθετα. Cp. the criticism of the Sophistic style in Alcid. de Soph. 12
οἱ τοῖς ὀνόμασιν ἀκριβῶς ἐξειργασμένοι καὶ μᾶλλον ποιήμασιν ἢ λόγοις ἐοικότες
καὶ τὸ μὲν αὐτόματον καὶ πλέον ἀληθείας ἀποβεβληκότες: Isocr. c. Soph. 294 D
τοῖς ἐνθυμήμασι πρεπόντως ὅλον τὸν λόγον καταποικίλαι καὶ τοῖς ὀνόμασι εὐρύθ-
μως καὶ μουσικῶς εἰπεῖν.

οὐδ᾽ ἐγγὺς τούτων. Cp. 221 D infra; Rep. 378 D τοὺς ποιητὰς ἐγγὺς τούτων
ἀναγκαστέον λογοποιεῖν.

ὀλίγου. I.e. ὀλίγου δεῖν. Cp. Theaet. 180 D; Euthyd. 279 D.

198 C Γοργίου...ἀνεμίμνησκεν. For Agathon as a "Gorgiast," see Introd.
§ III. 5. Cp. Philostr. de vit. Soph. I. καὶ Ἀγάθων...πολλαχοῦ τῶν ἰαμβείων
γοργιάζει: Xen. Symp. II. 26, IV. 24.

τὸ τοῦ Ὁμήρου. See Od. XI. 632 ἐμὲ δὲ χλωρὸν δέος ᾕρει | μή μοι γοργείην

ἐπεπόνθη· ἐφοβούμην μή μοι τελευτῶν ὁ Ἀγάθων Γοργίου κεφαλὴν
δεινοῦ λέγειν ἐν τῷ λόγῳ ἐπὶ τὸν ἐμὸν λόγον πέμψας αὐτόν με
λίθον τῇ ἀφωνίᾳ ποιήσειε. καὶ ἐνενόησα τότε ἄρα καταγέλαστος
ὤν, ἡνίκα ὑμῖν ὡμολόγουν ἐν τῷ μέρει μεθ' ὑμῶν ἐγκωμιάσεσθαι
D τὸν Ἔρωτα καὶ ἔφην εἶναι δεινὸς τὰ ἐρωτικά, οὐδὲν εἰδὼς ἄρα τοῦ
πράγματος, ὡς ἔδει ἐγκωμιάζειν ὁτιοῦν. ἐγὼ μὲν γὰρ ὑπ' ἀβελ-
τερίας ᾤμην δεῖν τἀληθῆ λέγειν περὶ ἑκάστου τοῦ ἐγκωμιαζομένου,
καὶ τοῦτο μὲν ὑπάρχειν, ἐξ αὐτῶν δὲ τούτων τὰ κάλλιστα ἐκλε-
γομένους ὡς εὐπρεπέστατα τιθέναι· καὶ πάνυ δὴ μέγα ἐφρόνουν ὡς

198 C ἐν τῷ λόγῳ secl. J.-U.: πελώρου Bdhm.   τῇ ἀφωνίᾳ del. Hartmann
D ἀβελτηρίας T   τοῦ (post ἑκάστου) del. Hommel   τοῦτο πρῶτον μὲν Bast

---

κεφαλὴν δεινοῖο πελώρου | ἐξ Ἀίδεω πέμψειεν ἀγαυὴ Περσεφόνεια. Miss
Harrison (Proleg. p. 191) renders γοργείην by "grizzly," with the note
"Homer does not commit himself to a definite Gorgon": his Gorgoneion
is "an underworld bogey, an ἀποτρόπαιον." That "the Gorgon was regarded
as a sort of incarnate evil eye" (ibid. p. 196) appears from Athen. v. 64. 221
κτείνει τὸν ὑπ' αὐτῆς θεωρηθέντα, οὐ τῷ πνεύματι ἀλλὰ τῇ γιγνομένῃ ἀπὸ τῆς
τῶν ὀμμάτων φύσεως φορᾷ καὶ νεκρὸν ποιεῖ. Rohde (Psyche II. 407) points out
that "Hekate selbst wird angerufen als Γοργὼ καὶ Μορμὼ καὶ Μήνη καὶ πολύ-
μορφε: hymn bei Hippol. ref. haer. 4. 35 p. 73 Mill"; and that Γοργώ appears
to be a shorter form for Γοργύρα (Ἀχέροντος γυνή, Apollod.). For the pun
on Gorgias-Gorgon, cp. that on ἀγαθῶν (174 B n.). As against Dümmler's
inference that Gorgias' previous death is here implied, see Vahlen op. Acad.
I. 482 ff.

ἐν τῷ λόγῳ. Cp. 201 A, Gorg. 457 D, Theaet. 169 B. To eject these words
with Hug, or to substitute πελώρου with Badham, would (as Voegelin and
Rettig contend) destroy the antithesis ἐν τῷ λ.)(ἐπὶ τὸν ἐμὸν λ., and spoil
the "Gorgianische Wortspiel." Further, the phrase serves as a parallel to
the Homeric ἐξ Ἀίδεω. Observe, as a feature of the parody, the different
sense in which Socr. uses δεινός: also, how the sentence as a whole forms a
playful retort to Agathon's remark in 194 A (φαρμάττειν βούλει με κτλ.). For
the adverbial use of τελευτῶν, cp. Phaedr. 228 B, C; Gorg. 457 D. (See also
Vahlen, l.c. for a discussion and defence of the text.)

τότε...ἡνίκα. The τότε goes with ὤν which is imperf. partic.: the ref. is to
177 D.

198 D ἐγὼ μὲν κτλ. The μέν here is answered by the δέ in τὸ δὲ ἄρα
below. For ἀβελτερία, cp. Theaet. 174 C, Phil. 48 C (see my note ad loc.).

τοῦτο μὲν ὑπάρχειν. "That this (viz. the statement of the facts) should be
the ground-work": there is no need to insert, with Bast, πρῶτον or μέγιστον
after τοῦτο. For this sense of ὑπάρχειν, cp. Menex. 237 B. For the thought,
cp. Emerson "Veracity first of all and forever. Rien de beau que le vrai."

ἐξ αὐτῶν δὲ τούτων. Rettig's comment on this is "mit Beziehung auf das
collective in τοῦτο gedachte τἀληθῆ." This is misleading, since τοῦτο means

εὖ ἐρῶν, ὡς εἰδὼς τὴν ἀλήθειαν [τοῦ ἐπαινεῖν ὁτιοῦν]. τὸ δὲ ἄρα,
ὡς ἔοικεν, οὐ τοῦτο ἦν τὸ καλῶς ἐπαινεῖν ὁτιοῦν, ἀλλὰ τὸ ὡς μέγιστα **E**
ἀνατιθέναι τῷ πράγματι καὶ ὡς κάλλιστα, ἐάν τε ᾖ οὕτως ἔχοντα
ἐάν τε μή· εἰ δὲ ψευδῆ, οὐδὲν ἄρ' ἦν πρᾶγμα. προυρρήθη γάρ, ὡς
ἔοικεν, ὅπως ἕκαστος ἡμῶν τὸν Ἔρωτα ἐγκωμιάζειν δόξει, οὐχ
ὅπως ἐγκωμιάσεται. διὰ ταῦτα δή, οἶμαι, πάντα λόγον κινοῦντες

198 D τοῦ...ὁτιοῦν secl. Bdhm. Sz.   τούτοις ἦν Bast   **E** δόξει
Steph.: δόξῃ BT

τὸ τἀληθῆ λέγειν, a singular notion, and αὐτὰ ταῦτα here represents simply
τἀληθῆ. In the Socratic theory of rhetoric here stated we have the following
order of treatment proposed: (1) τὸ τἀληθῆ λέγειν, (2) ἡ τῶν καλλίστων ἐκλογή,
(3) ἡ εὐπρεπὴς θέσις. But it is implied that the 2nd and 3rd of these—artistic
selection and arrangement—are valueless, except in so far as they are based
on the 1st requisite : in other words, matter is more important than form.
Cp. Procl. *in Tim.* p. 27 αἱ γὰρ ἀπὸ τῆς οὐσίας εὐφημίαι πασῶν προέχουσεν, ὡς
καὶ ὁ ἐν τῷ Συμποσίῳ Σωκράτης παραδίδωσιν.

ὡς εἰδὼς τὴν ἀλήθειαν. I follow Badham and Hug in bracketing the next
words (τοῦ ἐπαινεῖν ὁτιοῦν) as an erroneous gloss on ἀλήθειαν, with which we
must supply περὶ τοῦ ἔρωτος, as required by δεινὸς τὰ ἐρωτικά above and the
passage there alluded to (175 D). Cp. *Phaedr.* 259 E ἆρ' οὖν οὐχ ὑπάρχειν δεῖ τοῖς
εὖ γε καὶ καλῶς ῥηθησομένοις τὴν τοῦ λέγοντος διάνοιαν εἰδυῖαν τὸ ἀληθὲς ὧν ἂν
ἐρεῖν πέρι μέλλῃ. Rettig defends the traditional text, asking "ist denn ἡ
ἀλήθεια τοῦ ἐπαινεῖν ὁτιοῦν hier nicht identisch mit ἡ ἀλήθεια περὶ Ἔρωτος?"
To this the answer is "no !": for if the tradition be kept we must take τὴν
ἀλήθειαν as equivalent to τὴν ἀληθῆ (or rather ὀρθὴν) μέθοδον, which is a very
unlikely equation, especially so soon after τἀληθῆ in another sense : Stallb.'s
rendering may serve to indicate the difficulty involved,—"utpote *veram
tenens laudationis cujuslibet naturam et rationem*": Jowett's "thinking I
knew the nature of true praise" shirks the difficulty.

τὸ δὲ ἄρα. For τὸ δέ, "but in reality," cp. *Meno* 97 C (with Thompson's
note), *Apol.* 23 A (with Stallb.'s *note*).

198 E **οὐ τοῦτο**, *i.e.* οὐ τὸ τἀληθῆ λέγειν.

τὸ...ἀνατιθέναι. Perhaps an allusion to the term used by Agathon, ἀνακείσθω 197 E. For Socrates' criticism, cp. *Phaedr.* 272 A, *Menex.* 234 C οἱ
οὕτω καλῶς ἐπαινοῦσιν, ὥστε καὶ τὰ προσόντα καὶ τὰ μὴ περὶ ἑκάστου λέγοντες,
κάλλιστά πως τοῖς ὀνόμασι ποικίλλοντες γοητεύουσιν ἡμῶν τὰς ψυχάς: Isocr.
Busir. 222 B δεῖ τοὺς μὲν εὐλογεῖν τινας βουλομένοις πλείω τῶν ὑπαρχόντων
ἀγαθῶν προσόντ' ἀποφαίνειν (which sentiment is, perhaps, referred to here).

προυρρήθη. Cp. 180 D. The reference is to 177 D.

ἐγκωμιάζειν δόξει. The emphasis is on δόξει, implying the regular Platonic
antithesis δόξα)(ἀλήθεια. Cp. Simon. 76 τὸ δοκεῖν καὶ τὰν ἀλάθειαν βιᾶται
(cited in *Rep.* 365 C).

πάντα λόγον κινοῦντες. "Raking up every tale." Cp. *Phileb.* 15 E ; *Theaet.*
163 A ; *Rep.* 450 A.

ἀνατίθετε τῷ Ἔρωτι, καί φατε αὐτὸν τοιοῦτόν τε εἶναι καὶ τοσού-
199 των αἴτιον, ὅπως ἂν φαίνηται ὡς κάλλιστος καὶ ἄριστος, δῆλον ὅτι
τοῖς μὴ γιγνώσκουσιν—οὐ γάρ δή που τοῖς γε εἰδόσι—, καὶ καλῶς γ᾿
ἔχει καὶ σεμνῶς ὁ ἔπαινος. ἀλλὰ γὰρ ἐγὼ οὐκ ᾔδη ἄρα τὸν τρόπον
τοῦ ἐπαίνου, οὐ δ᾿ εἰδὼς ὑμῖν ὡμολόγησα καὶ αὐτὸς ἐν τῷ μέρει
ἐπαινέσεσθαι. "ἡ γλῶσσα" οὖν ὑπέσχετο, "ἡ δὲ φρὴν" οὔ·
χαιρέτω δή. οὐ γὰρ ἔτι ἐγκωμιάζω τοῦτον τὸν τρόπον· οὐ γὰρ
ἂν δυναίμην. οὐ μέντοι ἀλλὰ τά γε ἀληθῆ, εἰ βούλεσθε, ἐθέλω
B εἰπεῖν κατ᾿ ἐμαυτόν, οὐ πρὸς τοὺς ὑμετέρους λόγους, ἵνα μὴ γέλωτα
ὄφλω. ὅρα οὖν, ὦ Φαῖδρε, εἴ τι καὶ τοιούτου λόγου δέῃ, περὶ
Ἔρωτος τἀληθῆ λεγόμενα ἀκούειν, ὀνόμασι δὲ καὶ θέσει ῥημάτων
τοιαύτη ὁποία δἂν τις τύχῃ ἐπελθοῦσα.

198 E τοιούτων τε εἶναι Steph.   199 A δήπου Cobet Bt.: ἄν που T:
που B, Sz.   ἤδη ἄρα T: ᾔδη B   οὐ δ᾿ Sauppe: οὐδ BT   γλῶσσα W:
γλῶττα BT   ἐγκωμιάσω Wolf Jn.   B δέει Bekk. Sz.   περὶ...λεγόμενα
del. Hirschig   ὀνομάσει W Vind. suppl. 7   δἂν J.-U. Sz. Bt.: δὴ ἂν
Stallb.: δ᾿ ἄν B: δ᾿ ἂν T: ἄν apogr. Vat. 1030

___

199 A ὅπως ἂν φαίνηται. φαίνηται here, as δόξει above, is emphatic. A comparison with 195 A shows that Socr. is alluding especially to Agathon's oration.
οὐ γάρ δή που κτλ. Cp. *Gorg.* 459 A οὐ γὰρ δή που ἔν γε τοῖς εἰδόσι τοῦ ἰατροῦ
πιθανώτερος ἔσται: and for οὐ γάρ που... 200 B, *Euthyph.* 13 A.
καὶ καλῶς γ᾿ κτλ. Earlier editors generally print a full stop after εἰδόσι.
Socr. here sarcastically endorses the approval with which Agathon's ἔπαινος
had been received (ὡς πρεπόντως εἰρηκότος κτλ., 198 A).
ἡ γλῶσσα οὖν κτλ. Euripides' line (ἡ γλῶσσ᾿ ὀμώμοχ᾿, ἡ δὲ φρὴν ἀνώμοτος
Hippol. 612) soon became a familiar quotation : see Ar. *Thesm.* 275, *Ran.* 101,
1471 ; *Theaet.* 154 D ; Cic. *de offic.* III. 29. 108 iuravi lingua, mentem iniuratam
gero.
χαιρέτω δή. "I say good-bye to it": cp. *Laws* 636 D τὸ...τοῦ μύθου χαιρέτω:
id. 886 D. Rettig suggests that here the formula may be intended as another
echo of Euripides: cp. *Med.* 1044 οὐκ ἂν δυναίμην· χαιρέτω βουλεύματα | τὰ
πρόσθεν : *Hippol.* 113.
οὐ γὰρ ἔτι κτλ. "I withdraw my offer to eulogize." ἐγκωμιάζω must here
be a "present for future" (see Madv. *Gr. Synt.* § 110. 3), since Socr. has not
yet begun the eulogy.
199 B κατ᾿ ἐμαυτόν, οὐ πρὸς κτλ. "In my own fashion, not entering into
competition with your orations." For κατὰ c. acc. in this sense, cp. *Apol.* 17 B
οὐ κατὰ τούτους εἶναι ῥήτωρ ("not after their pattern"): *Gorg.* 505 D.
γέλωτα ὄφλω. This resumes the notion in καταγέλαστος ὤν, 198 C.
ὦ Φαῖδρε. Socrates, like Agathon (197 E), politely appeals to Ph. as the
πατὴρ λόγου: cp. 194 D.
εἴ τι κτλ. For εἴ τι, *numquid,* cp. *Rep.* 526 E σκοπεῖσθαι δεῖ εἴ τι πρὸς
ἐκεῖνο τείνει κτλ.
ὀνόμασι δὲ κτλ. See 198 B n. Of ὁποία δή Ast cites no instance ; the

Τὸν οὖν Φαῖδρον ἔφη καὶ τοὺς ἄλλους κελεύειν λέγειν, ὅπῃ αὐτὸς οἴοιτο δεῖν εἰπεῖν, ταύτῃ. Ἔτι τοίνυν, φάναι, ὦ Φαῖδρε, πάρες μοι Ἀγάθωνα σμίκρ' ἄττα ἐρέσθαι, ἵνα ἀνομολογησάμενος παρ' αὐτοῦ οὕτως ἤδη λέγω. Ἀλλὰ παρίημι, φάναι τὸν Φαῖδρον, C ἀλλ' ἐρώτα. μετὰ ταῦτα δὴ τὸν Σωκράτη ἔφη ἐνθένδε ποθὲν ἄρξασθαι.

XXI. Καὶ μήν, ὦ φίλε Ἀγάθων, καλῶς μοι ἔδοξας καθηγήσασθαι τοῦ λόγου, λέγων ὅτι πρῶτον μὲν δέοι αὐτὸν ἐπιδεῖξαι ὁποῖός τίς ἐστιν ὁ Ἔρως, ὕστερον δὲ τὰ ἔργα αὐτοῦ. ταύτην τὴν ἀρχὴν πάνυ ἄγαμαι. ἴθι οὖν μοι περὶ Ἔρωτος, ἐπειδὴ καὶ τἆλλα καλῶς καὶ μεγαλοπρεπῶς διῆλθες οἷός ἐστι, καὶ τόδε εἰπέ· D πότερόν ἐστι τοιοῦτος οἷος εἶναί τινος ὁ Ἔρως ἔρως, ἢ οὐδενός; ἐρωτῶ δ' οὐκ εἰ μητρός τινος ἢ πατρός ἐστι—γελοῖον γὰρ ἂν εἴη τὸ

199 C ἀλλ' ἐρώτα Ἀgathóni tribuit B, Naber   D οἷός τ' TW   ἔρως
ἔρως B : ἔρως T

---

force of δή is to heighten the notion of indefiniteness which lies in ὁποία (so Hug).

ἔτι τοίνυν κτλ. ἔτι goes with ἐρέσθαι. Socrates appeals thus to Ph. because Ph. had previously (194 D, E) debarred him from catechizing A.

ἀνομολογησάμενος κτλ. Cf. 200 E, Gorg. 489 A. For οὕτως ἤδη, cp. 194 D. For ἐνθένδε ποθὲν, 178 A.

199 C καθηγήσασθαι. The ref. is to A.'s exordium, 195 A.

ἴθι οὖν. agedum; cp. Gorg. 452 D, Rep. 376 D.

199 D τινος...ἢ οὐδενός. These are objective genitives to be construed with the second ἔρως: "Is Love love for some object or for none?" For the use of the indef. in such phrases, cp. Phileb. 35 B ὅ γ' ἐπιθυμῶν τινὸς ἐπιθυμεῖ.

οὐκ εἰ μητρός τινος κτλ. These words have been variously interpreted: (1) Lehrs and Prantl construe the genitives as subjective ("love felt by a mother"); (2) Ast as objective ("love for a mother"); (3) Rückert, followed by Hommel and Hug, takes them to be genn. of origin; so too Zeller renders "ich meine damit aber nicht, ob er eine Mutter oder einen Vater hat." Of these, (1) seems the least probable in point of sense, and with subjective genitives τινος would be superfluous. It is a serious objection (as Hug admits) to (3) that it compels us to regard the "absurdity" (γελοῖον) of the question as lying in its form rather than its substance. That the "absurdity" lies in the substance of the statement is shown, e.g., by Lys. 221 A ἢ γελοῖον τὸ ἐρώτημα, ὅ τί ποτ' ἔσται τότε ἢ μὴ ἔσται; τίς γὰρ οἶδεν; (cp. Phaedr. 274 c). But if so, recourse must be had to textual alteration : we must strike out either the second ἔρως, with Sommer, or the whole block of words εἰ Ἔρως... πατρός, as Hug (followed by Jowett) suggests. This, however, is a hazardous alternative. On the whole, then, the explanation (2) put forward by Ast seems the most probable. Construing, "I do not ask whether Eros has for its object a father or a mother, since to ask whether Eros is eros for a parent

ἐρώτημα, εἰ Ἔρως ἐστὶν ἔρως μητρὸς ἢ πατρός—ἀλλ' ὥσπερ ἂν εἰ
αὐτὸ τοῦτο πατέρα ἠρώτων, ἆρα ὁ πατήρ ἐστι πατήρ τινος ἢ οὔ;
εἶπες ἂν δή πού μοι, εἰ ἐβούλου καλῶς ἀποκρίνασθαι, ὅτι ἔστιν
υἱέος γε ἢ θυγατρὸς ὁ πατὴρ πατήρ· ἢ οὔ; Πάνυ γε, φάναι τὸν
Ἀγάθωνα. Οὐκοῦν καὶ ἡ μήτηρ ὡσαύτως; Ὁμολογεῖσθαι καὶ
E τοῦτο. Ἔτι τοίνυν, εἰπεῖν τὸν Σωκράτη, ἀπόκριναι ὀλίγῳ πλείω,
ἵνα μᾶλλον καταμάθῃς ὃ βούλομαι. εἰ γὰρ ἐροίμην, τί δέ; ἀδελφός,
αὐτὸ τοῦθ' ὅπερ ἔστιν, ἔστι τινὸς ἀδελφὸς ἢ οὔ; Φάναι εἶναι.
Οὐκοῦν ἀδελφοῦ ἢ ἀδελφῆς; Ὁμολογεῖν. Πειρῶ δή, φάναι, καὶ
τὸν ἔρωτα εἰπεῖν. ὁ Ἔρως ἔρως ἐστὶν οὐδενὸς ἢ τινός; Πάνυ μὲν
200 οὖν ἔστιν. Τοῦτο μὲν τοίνυν, εἰπεῖν τὸν Σωκράτη, φύλαξον παρὰ
σαυτῷ μεμνημένος ὅτου· τοσόνδε δὲ εἰπέ, πότερον ὁ Ἔρως ἐκείνου

199 D εἰ Ἔρως...πατρός secl. Hug   εἰ ὁ Hirschig   ἔρως del. Sommer
ὁμολογεῖσθαι BTW : ὁμολογῆσαι vulg.: ὁμολογεῖν Stallb. Sz.   E ἀδελφός
Cobet Sz.: ἀδελφός libri, Bt.   ἀδελφὸς del. Bdhm.   200 A μεμνημένος
del. Bdhm.   ὅπου Mdvg.

were an absurd question," the point will be taken to lie in the fact that ἔρως,
as properly denoting *sexual* passion, cannot naturally have for its object a
parent. The same interpretation might be kept if we struck out—as perhaps
we ought—the words μητρὸς ἢ πατρός, and construed " the question would be
absurd if (*or* granting that) Eros is (really) ἔρως (*i.e.* sex-love)."

αὐτὸ τοῦτο πατέρα ἠρώτων. Rettig approves Stallbaum's explanation,
" *h. e.* πατέρα, αὐτὸ τοῦτο ὅπερ ἔστιν ut mox loquitur. Vult autem cogitari de
patris notione, qualem mente informatum habemus." But the use of the
neuter in apposition to the masc. is sufficient to indicate that "cogitari de
patris notione"; and it is most natural to regard αὐτὸ τοῦτο as implying a
reference to the previous use of "this very word, πατήρ."

εἶπες ἄν. "You would at once reply." (See Goodwin *G. M. T.* § 414,
Thompson on *Meno* 72 B.)

ἡ μήτηρ ὡσαύτως. *Sc.* ἐστὶν υἱέος γε ἢ θυγατρὸς μήτηρ.

199 E Εἰ γὰρ ἐροίμην. For apodosis we may supply τί ἂν φαίης; or
the like: cp. 204 D, *Prot.* 311 E.

αὐτὸ τοῦθ' ὅπερ ἔστιν. "Notionally," "in its abstract significance."

200 A Τοῦτο μὲν...ὅτου. Rettig, Rückert and Lehrs put a comma before
μεμνημένος, rendering "hoc igitur apud animum serva (*sc.* alicujus esse) atque
cujus sit, memento." Hommel and Hug, on the other hand, follow Ast and
Schleierm. in removing the comma, explaining ὅτου (*sc.* ὁ Ἔρως ἔρως ἐστίν) as
epexegetic of τούτο, and construing φύλαξον μεμνημένος closely together: thus
Schleierm. renders "Dieses nun, habe Socrates gesagt, halte noch bei dir fast
in Gedanken, wovon sie (er) Liebe ist." On this latter view—which is
certainly preferable—we must suppose Socrates to be alluding to the definition
of the object of love (*viz.* κάλλος) previously given by Agathon (in 197 B),
while debarring him from restating it at this point in the discussion.

οὗ ἔστιν ἔρως, ἐπιθυμεῖ αὐτοῦ ἢ οὔ; Πάνυ γε, φάναι.   Πότερον
ἔχων αὐτὸ οὗ ἐπιθυμεῖ τε καὶ ἐρᾷ, εἶτα ἐπιθυμεῖ τε καὶ ἐρᾷ, ἢ οὐκ
ἔχων; Οὐκ ἔχων, ὡς τὸ εἰκός γε, φάναι.   Σκόπει δή, εἰπεῖν τὸν
Σωκράτη, ἀντὶ τοῦ εἰκότος εἰ ἀνάγκη οὕτως, τὸ ἐπιθυμοῦν ἐπιθυμεῖν οὗ ἐνδεές ἐστιν, ἢ μὴ ἐπιθυμεῖν, ἐὰν μὴ ἐνδεὲς ᾖ; ἐμοὶ μὲν
γὰρ θαυμαστῶς δοκεῖ, ὦ Ἀγάθων, ὡς ἀνάγκη εἶναι· σοὶ δὲ πῶς; B
Κἀμοί, φάναι, δοκεῖ.   Καλῶς λέγεις.   ἆρ᾽ οὖν βούλοιτ᾽ ἄν τις
μέγας ὢν μέγας εἶναι, ἢ ἰσχυρὸς ὢν ἰσχυρός; Ἀδύνατον ἐκ τῶν
ὡμολογημένων.   Οὐ γάρ που ἐνδεὴς ἂν εἴη τούτων ὅ γε ὤν.
Ἀληθῆ λέγεις.   Εἰ γὰρ καὶ ἰσχυρὸς ὢν βούλοιτο ἰσχυρὸς εἶναι,
φάναι τὸν Σωκράτη, καὶ ταχὺς ὢν ταχύς, καὶ ὑγιὴς ὢν ὑγιής—
ἴσως γὰρ ἄν τις ταῦτα οἰηθείη καὶ πάντα τὰ τοιαῦτα, τοὺς ὄντας
τε τοιούτους καὶ ἔχοντας ταῦτα τούτων ἅπερ ἔχουσι καὶ ἐπιθυ- C
μεῖν, ἵν᾽ οὖν μὴ ἐξαπατηθῶμεν, τούτου ἕνεκα λέγω· τούτοις γάρ, ὦ
Ἀγάθων, εἰ ἐννοεῖς, ἔχειν μὲν ἔκαστα τούτων ἐν τῷ παρόντι
ἀνάγκη ἃ ἔχουσιν, ἐάν τε βούλωνται ἐάν τε μή, καὶ τούτου γε δή

200 B ὁμολογημένων W : ὁμολογουμένων vulg.   εἰ δ᾽ ἄρα Stallb.   γὰρ
καὶ BT : γὰρ W   ταυτὶ T   C ἔκαστον vulg.

ἐπιθυμεῖ αὐτοῦ.   For αὐτοῦ resuming ἐκείνου, cp. 195 A, Soph. O. T. 248.
Observe that the entire argument here is based on the identification of ἔρως
with ἐπιθυμία (see 205 D): cp. the use of ἐρᾶν in Theogn. 256 πρῆγμα δὲ
τερπνότατον, τοῦ τις ἐρᾷ, τὸ τυχεῖν.   Cp., for the question here discussed,
Lys. 221 D f.

ἀντὶ τοῦ εἰκότος.   Cp. Phaedr. 267 A, 269 D ; see Blass, Att. Bereds. I. 78.

ἐπιθυμεῖν οὗ ἐνδεές ἐστιν.   Cp. Lysis 221 D τό γε ἐπιθυμοῦν, οὗ ἂν ἐνδεὲς ᾖ,
τούτου ἐπιθυμεῖ: Eryx. 405 E αἱ δ᾽ ἐπιθυμίαι πᾶσαι οὐδὲν ἕτερον ἢ ἔνδειαί τινων :
Gorg. 496 D.   A similar theory is implied in Phileb. 35 A ὁ κενούμενος…
ἐπιθυμεῖ τῶν ἐναντίων ἢ πάσχει· κενούμενος γὰρ ἐρᾷ πληροῦσθαί (which also
illustrates the use of ἐρᾶν and ἐπιθυμεῖν as synonyms).   Cp. also Isocr. Hel.
219 A (quoted below, on 200 c).

200 B θαυμαστῶς…ὡς.   For ὡς thus separated from its adverb, cp.
Phaedo 95 A, 99 D, Theaet. 157 D.   Thus Bast's suspicions as to the soundness
of the text were unfounded.

Εἰ γὰρ καὶ κτλ.   In this sentence we have an ex. of anacoluthon : after the
protasis the sentence is interrupted by a parenthesis (ἴσως…λέγω), then the
protasis is resumed in an altered form (ἀλλ᾽ ὅταν τις κτλ.), which leads up
finally to the apodosis in the form εἴποιμεν ἂν αὐτῷ κτλ.   The main purpose
of the whole paragraph is to guard against a possible misunderstanding as to
the nature of βούλησις and ἐπιθυμία which might arise from carelessness in
analyzing the sense of popular phraseology.

ταῦτα οἰηθείη.   ταῦτα and πάντα τὰ τοιαῦτα are accusatives of "remoter
object" with οἰηθείη, "with regard to these and all similar cases."

που τίς ἂν ἐπιθυμήσειεν; ἀλλ᾽ ὅταν τις λέγῃ ὅτι ἐγὼ ὑγιαίνων
βούλομαι καὶ ὑγιαίνειν, καὶ πλουτῶν βούλομαι καὶ πλουτεῖν, καὶ
ἐπιθυμῶ αὐτῶν τούτων ἃ ἔχω, εἴποιμεν ἂν αὐτῷ ὅτι σύ, ὦ ἄνθρωπε,
D πλοῦτον κεκτημένος καὶ ὑγίειαν καὶ ἰσχὺν βούλει καὶ εἰς τὸν
ἔπειτα χρόνον ταῦτα κεκτῆσθαι, ἐπεὶ ἐν τῷ γε νῦν παρόντι,
εἴτε βούλει εἴτε μή, ἔχεις· σκόπει οὖν, ὅταν τοῦτο λέγῃς, ὅτι ἐπιθυμῶ τῶν παρόντων, εἰ ἄλλο τι λέγεις ἢ τόδε, ὅτι βούλομαι τὰ νῦν
παρόντα καὶ εἰς τὸν ἔπειτα χρόνον παρεῖναι. ἄλλο τι ὁμολογοῖ ἄν;
Συμφάναι ἔφη τὸν Ἀγάθωνα. εἰπεῖν δὴ τὸν Σωκράτη, Οὐκοῦν
τοῦτό γ᾽ ἐστὶν ἐκείνου ἐρᾶν, ὃ οὔπω ἕτοιμον αὐτῷ ἐστὶν οὐδὲ ἔχει, τὸ
εἰς τὸν ἔπειτα χρόνον ταῦτα εἶναι αὐτῷ σῳζόμενα καὶ < ἀεὶ >
E παρόντα; Πάνυ γε, φάναι. Καὶ οὗτος ἄρα καὶ ἄλλος πᾶς ὁ ἐπιθυμῶν τοῦ μὴ ἑτοίμου ἐπιθυμεῖ καὶ τοῦ μὴ παρόντος, καὶ ὃ μὴ ἔχει

200 C καὶ πλουτεῖν B: πλουτεῖν T   D ἔχεις T: ἔχῃς B   ὁμολογοῖς b:
ὁμολογοῖ Steph.   οὐκοῦν δὴ pr. T   τὸ...παρόντα secl. Bdhm. Sz.   τὸ T:
τὰ B: τὸ τοῦ cj. Usener   ταῦτα: τοιαῦτα Liebhold   σῳζόμενα secl. Liebhold
καὶ TW, Bt.: μοι B: τὰ νῦν Vindob. 21: τὰ μὴ Sauppe: μὴ Rettig: οἱ Voeg.:
ἤτοι cj. Usener: ἀεὶ Schirlitz: καὶ ἀεὶ scripsi   μοι παρόντα secl. Herm. J.-U.
Hug   E ὁ ἄλλος T

---

200 C βούλομαι...καὶ ἐπιθυμῶ. The point here emphasized is that βούλησις
and ἐπιθυμία, when their sense is investigated, are found to apply only to the
future (εἰς τὸν ἔπειτα χρόνον), not to the present (ἐν τῷ παρόντι). For investigation shows that "I wish for what I have" is really an abbreviated phrase
for "I wish to continue having in the future what I now at present have"
(βούλομαι τὰ νῦν παρόντα παρεῖναι). For the force of βούλησις, cp. Isocr. Hel.
219 A τῶν μὲν γὰρ ἄλλων, ὧν ἂν ἐν χρείᾳ γενώμεθα, τυχεῖν μόνον βουλόμεθα...
τῶν δὲ καλῶν ἔρως ἡμῖν ἐγγίγνεται, τοσούτῳ μείζω τοῦ βούλεσθαι ῥώμην ἔχων,
ὅσῳπερ καὶ τὸ πρᾶγμα κρεῖττον ἐστίν (with which cp. also 205 D infra).

200 D ἄλλο τι ὁμολογοῖ ἄν; For the interrogative ἄλλο τι, ἄλλο τι ἤ, see
Meno 82 c (with Thompson's note); Prot. 353 c (with Adam's note).

Οὐκοῦν τοῦτό γ᾽ ἐστὶν κτλ. The main construction is rightly explained by
Stallb.: "τὸ εἰς τὸν ἔπειτα χρ. κτλ. relativo pronomini per epexegesin ad-
duntur, nec assentior Rückerto interpunctionem post αὐτῷ ἐστὶν inferenti":
τὸ is in the nominative, where we should rather expect τοῦ in apposition to
ἐκείνου, owing to assimilation to ὅ. For the reading of the last words in the
sentence, see crit. n. Rettig reads μὴ παρόντα "in hypothetisch-causalem
Sinne." More attractive is Usener's excision of the words μοι παρόντα,
adopted by Hug. The objection to καὶ, printed by Burnet, is that it fails to
supply an explanation of B's μοι: hence I prefer to read καὶ ἀεὶ, supposing
that an abbreviated καὶ blending with ἀεὶ might account for both variants.

200 E Καὶ οὗτος κτλ. οὗτος represents the typical τις and ἄνθρωπος of
200 c; and ἄλλος πᾶς serves to generalise, cp. 192 B.

καὶ ὃ μὴ ἔστιν αὐτὸς καὶ οὗ ἐνδεής ἐστι, τοιαῦτ᾽ ἄττα ἐστὶν ὧν
ἡ ἐπιθυμία τε καὶ ὁ ἔρως ἐστίν; Πάνυ γ᾽, εἰπεῖν. Ἴθι δή, φάναι
τὸν Σωκράτη, ἀνομολογησώμεθα τὰ εἰρημένα. ἄλλο τι ἔστιν ὁ
Ἔρως πρῶτον μὲν τινῶν, ἔπειτα τούτων ὧν ἂν ἔνδεια παρῇ αὐτῷ;
Ναί, φάναι. Ἐπὶ δὴ τούτοις ἀναμνήσθητι τίνων ἔφησθα ἐν τῷ 201
λόγῳ εἶναι τὸν Ἔρωτα· εἰ δὲ βούλει, ἐγώ σε ἀναμνήσω. οἶμαι
γάρ σε οὑτωσί πως εἰπεῖν, ὅτι τοῖς θεοῖς κατεσκευάσθη τὰ πράγματα δι᾽ ἔρωτα καλῶν· αἰσχρῶν γὰρ οὐκ εἴη ἔρως. οὐχ οὑτωσί
πως ἔλεγες; Εἶπον γάρ, φάναι τὸν Ἀγάθωνα. Καὶ ἐπιεικῶς γ᾽
ἔλεγες, ὦ ἑταῖρε, φάναι τὸν Σωκράτη· καὶ εἰ τοῦτο οὕτως ἔχει,
ἄλλο τι ὁ Ἔρως κάλλους ἂν εἴη ἔρως, αἴσχους δ᾽ οὔ; Ὡμολόγει.
Οὐκοῦν ὡμολόγηται, οὗ ἐνδεής ἐστι καὶ μὴ ἔχει, τούτου ἐρᾶν; Ναί, Β
εἰπεῖν. Ἐνδεὴς ἄρ᾽ ἐστὶ καὶ οὐκ ἔχει ὁ Ἔρως κάλλος. Ἀνάγκη,
φάναι. Τί δέ; τὸ ἐνδεὲς κάλλους καὶ μηδαμῇ κεκτημένον κάλλος
ἆρα λέγεις σὺ καλὸν εἶναι; Οὐ δῆτα. Ἔτι οὖν ὁμολογεῖς Ἔρωτα
καλὸν εἶναι, εἰ ταῦτα οὕτως ἔχει; καὶ τὸν Ἀγάθωνα εἰπεῖν Κινδυνεύω, ὦ Σώκρατες, οὐδὲν εἰδέναι ὧν τότε εἶπον. Καὶ μὴν καλῶς

200 E τε καὶ ΒΤ: καὶ W   ἀνομολογησόμεθα W   ἂν ἔνδεια κτλ. (usque
ad 213 E ὅτι) exstat in Oxyr. Pap. 843   παρην O.-P.   201 A δι᾽ ἔρωτος
O.-P.: δι᾽ ἔρωτα O.-P. corr.   ἔρως ΒΤ O.-P.: ὁ ἔρως W   γ᾽ ἔλεγες scripsi :
γε λέγεις libri, edd.: γε λέγε[ι]ς O.-P.   ἄλλο τι ἢ O.-P. corr., Ven. 184 Vind 21
B ἔχει W : ἔχῃ ΒΤ   του[τ]ου O.-P. corr.: του O.-P.   ω Σωκρατες κινδυ-
νευω O.-P.

ἔνδεια παρῇ. This sounds like a jocular contradiction in terms : in Eros
there is a plentiful lack.

201 A ἔφησθα ἐν τῷ λόγῳ. See 197 B : cp. Isocr. *Hel.* 219 A τῶν δὲ καλῶν
ἔρως ἡμῖν ἐγγίγνεται.

ἐπιεικῶς γ᾽ ἔλεγες. For ἐπιεικῶς, *probe, recte*, cp. *Rep.* 431 E, *Laws* 635 A.
I have ventured to read ἔλεγες for the traditional λέγεις. In the present
context λέγεις seems objectionable because of its ambiguity, since "You say
well" would more naturally be taken to refer to A.'s reply (εἶπον γάρ) than
to his previous statement. This objection is not touched by Rettig's defence
of the tense: "auch das Präsens ist ganz an seinem Platze. Da Agathon
bestätigt, dass er sich so geäussert habe, wie Sokrates angebe, so gilt seine
obige Aeusserung auch jetzt."

201 B οὗ...καὶ μὴ ἔχει. "Sic dictum est ut ὅ apud ἔχει repetendum est"
(Stallb.).

τὸ ἐνδεὲς κάλλους. With reference to this Proclus (*in Tim.* p. 128) comments : ἐνδεὲς κάλλους ἐν συμποσίῳ προσεῖπε τὸ μὴ πρώτως καλὸν ἀλλὰ μετέχον
κάλλους: cp. *ib.* p. 110. For the tautologous form of expression, cp. 185 A *n.*;
Eur. *Ion* 680 αὐτὴ δ᾽ ἄπαις ἦ καὶ λελειμμένη τέκνων : id. *Heracl.* 530, etc.
(see Vahlen *op. Acad.* II. 366).

Κινδυνεύω...εἶπον. εἰδέναι is past, not present, in sense.

Καὶ μὴν...εἶπες. Not "recte dixisti" (Ficinus), but "praeclare dixisti"

C γε εἶπες, φάναι, ὦ 'Αγάθων. ἀλλὰ σμικρὸν ἔτι εἰπέ· τἀγαθὰ οὐ
καὶ καλὰ δοκεῖ σοι εἶναι; Ἔμοιγε. Εἰ ἄρα ὁ Ἔρως τῶν καλῶν
ἐνδεής ἐστι, τὰ δὲ ἀγαθὰ καλά, κἂν τῶν ἀγαθῶν ἐνδεὴς εἴη. Ἐγώ,
φάναι, ὦ Σώκρατες, σοὶ οὐκ ἂν δυναίμην ἀντιλέγειν, ἀλλ᾽ οὕτως
ἐχέτω ὡς σὺ λέγεις. Οὐ μὲν οὖν τῇ ἀληθείᾳ, φάναι, ὦ φιλούμενε
'Αγάθων, δύνασαι ἀντιλέγειν, ἐπεὶ Σωκράτει γε οὐδὲν χαλεπόν.
D XXII. Καὶ σὲ μέν γε ἤδη ἐάσω· τὸν δὲ λόγον τὸν περὶ τοῦ
Ἔρωτος, ὅν ποτ᾽ ἤκουσα γυναικὸς Μαντινικῆς Διοτίμας, ἣ ταῦτά
τε σοφὴ ἦν καὶ ἄλλα πολλά, καὶ 'Αθηναίοις ποτὲ θυσαμένοις πρὸ
τοῦ λοιμοῦ δέκα ἔτη ἀναβολὴν ἐποίησε τῆς νόσου, ἣ δὴ καὶ ἐμὲ τὰ

201 C εἶπας O.-P. Vat. 227	φιλούμενε : φιλε O.-P.	⟨οὐ⟩ δύνασαι
Sauppe D μαντινικῆς BT O.-P.: μαντικῆς W vulg.		μ / Διοτιˉˉνας O.-P.
ἦν : ειναι O.-P.¹ θυσαμένη Steph.	δεκέτη Bdhm. Sz.	της / [ε]ποιησατο
νοσου O.-P.		

(Wolf). What Socr. alludes to is not A.'s foregoing reply, but his oration
(cp. 198 B, 199 C); and the point of his remark is to suggest that formal
beauty of diction does not necessarily involve the more essential beauty
of ἀλήθεια.

201 C τὰ δὲ ἀγαθὰ καλά. For the coincidence of these two concepts, cp.
Prot. 360 B, *Hipp. Maj.* 297 B, C, *Phileb.* 64 E ff. It might be near the truth
to say that τὸ καλόν is neither less nor more than τὸ ἀγαθὸν in its external
aspect, "goodness" as apprehended by the aesthetic faculty, or goodness *qua*
attractive and soul-stirring. See also Plotin. *de pulcr.* p. 46 ; Procl. *in I Alc.*
p. 329.

Ἐγώ...σοί...σύ. The personal pronouns are, by position and repetition,
emphatic. Agathon means to imply that he yields not so much to the force
of argument as to the wordplay of Socrates' invincible dialectic : cp. 216 B
infra : Xen. *Symp.* v. 8.

201 D Καὶ σὲ...ἐάσω. "You I will now release": this is said with
reference to the phrase used in 199 B ἔτι...πάρες μοι 'Αγάθωνα κτλ.

Μαντινικῆς Διοτίμας. Probably both these names are meant to be ety-
mologically significant : the resemblance of the adj. to μαντικὴ is patent (in
fact some MSS. give μαντικῆς, and Ficin. *fatidica muliere*), while as illustrating
the omen of Διοτίμα one might cite Soph. *fr.* 226 N. σοφὸς γὰρ οὐδεὶς πλὴν ὃν
ἂν τιμᾷ θεός. See further *Introd.* § IV. C. Hug quotes an imitative passage
from Dio. Chrys. I. p. 59 R. μῦθον...ὃν ἐγώ ποτε ἤκουσα γυναικὸς Ἠλείας ἢ
'Αρκαδίας ὑπὲρ 'Ηρακλέους διηγουμένης. See also Max. Tyr. *diss.* XXIV. 4,
p. 588 ; Clem. Al. *Strom.* VI. p. 631 B.

πρὸ τοῦ λοιμοῦ κτλ. For the Great Plague at Athens in 430 B.C. see
Thuc. II. 47, Bury *H. G.* p. 407. That the plague had been rife elsewhere for
some time previously is implied by Thuc. *l. c.* For similar instances of the
averting or postponing of impending evils by divine or prophetic agency,
see Hdt. I. 91 τρία γὰρ ἔτεα ἐπανεβάλετο (sc. ὁ Λοξίης) τὴν Σαρδίων ἅλωσιν:

ἐρωτικὰ ἐδίδαξεν,—ὃν οὖν ἐκείνη ἔλεγε λόγον, πειράσομαι ὑμῖν διελθεῖν ἐκ τῶν ὡμολογημένων ἐμοὶ καὶ Ἀγάθωνι, αὐτὸς ἐπ᾽ ἐμαυτοῦ, ὅπως ἂν δύνωμαι. δεῖ δή, ὦ Ἀγάθων, ὥσπερ σὺ διηγήσω, διελθεῖν αὐτὸν πρῶτον, τίς ἐστιν ὁ Ἔρως καὶ ποῖός τις, ἔπειτα τὰ ἔργα αὐτοῦ. δοκεῖ οὖν μοι ῥᾷστον εἶναι οὕτω διελθεῖν, ὥς ποτέ με ἡ ξένη ἀνακρίνουσα διῄει. σχεδὸν γάρ τι καὶ ἐγὼ πρὸς αὐτὴν ἕτερα τοιαῦτα ἔλεγον οἷάπερ νῦν πρὸς ἐμὲ Ἀγάθων, ὡς εἴη ὁ Ἔρως μέγας θεός, εἴη δὲ τῶν καλῶν· ἤλεγχε δή με τούτοις τοῖς λόγοις οἷσπερ ἐγὼ τοῦτον, ὡς οὔτε καλὸς εἴη κατὰ τὸν ἐμὸν λόγον οὔτε ἀγαθός. καὶ ἐγώ, Πῶς λέγεις, ἔφην, ὦ Διοτίμα; αἰσχρὸς ἄρα

201 D λογον εκεινη ελεγεν O.-P.   ἐπ᾽ Coisl. corr. Paris 1642 O.-P., Bast:
ἀπ᾽ BTW   δεῖ δὴ TW O.-P.:   δείλη B   διηγήσω BT O.-P.: δὴ ἡγήσω Sz.
Bt.: καθηγήσω Hirschig: ὑφηγήσω Sauppe: διῄρησαι Usener: ἡγήσω olim
Herm.   E   ποῖός: οποιος O.-P.   ποτ᾽ ἐμὲ vulg.   γάρ: δὲ O.-P.   εφην
λεγεις O.-P.   αισχρο[ν] O.-P.

Athen. XIII. 602 B : Euseb. praep. evang. v. 35, p. 233 B, C : cp. Virg. Aen.
VII. 313 ff., VIII. 398 ff. (where "decem annos" is the interval named). A
specially interesting parallel, as mentioning the same 10 years' interval, is
Laws 642 D ἀκήκοας ὡς Ἐπιμενίδης γέγονεν ἀνὴρ θεῖος...ἐλθὼν δὲ πρὸ τῶν
Περσικῶν δέκα ἔτεσι πρότερον παρ᾽ ὑμᾶς...θυσίας τε ἐθύσατο τινας...καὶ δὴ καὶ
φοβουμένων τὸν Περσικὸν Ἀθηναίων στόλον εἶπεν ὅτι δέκα μὲν ἐτῶν οὐχ
ἥξουσιν κτλ.

αὐτὸς ἐπ᾽ ἐμαυτοῦ. Rückert alone retains the lection ἀπ᾽ ἐμαυτοῦ. Cp.
I Alc. 114 B εἰ μὲν βούλει, ἐρωτῶν με, ὥσπερ ἐγὼ σέ, εἰ δὲ καὶ αὐτὸς ἐπὶ σαυτοῦ
λόγῳ διέξελθε : Soph. 217 C.

ὥσπερ σὺ διηγήσω. I think the traditional text, supported also by the
Papyrus, may stand, taking διηγήσω to imply—with veiled contempt—a
lengthy or meticulous disquisition. Schanz's δὴ ἡγήσω is open to a double
objection, (1) the repeated δὴ is unpleasing, and (2) ἡγήσω is a feeble word to
apply to Agathon's dogmatic exposition (in 195 A) of the rules of method.
Sauppe's ὑφηγήσω is appropriate enough (cp. Gorg. 455 D, Crat. 392 D), but
does not explain the corruption.

201 E διελθεῖν αὐτὸν κτλ. Here Socrates cites almost verbatim the
language used by Agathon in 195 A λόγῳ διελθεῖν...δόσεις. Observe however
the significant addition by Socr. of the words τίς ἐστιν : he requires a statement of the essential notion (τίς ἐστι) as well as of the attributes (ποῖός τις).

εἴη δὲ τῶν καλῶν. The genitive is not masc. nor one of origin (=ἐκ τῶν
καλῶν) as Wolf thought, but as Stallb. rightly notes "καλῶν pendet ex Ἔρως,
quod etiam hic positum est ut p. 196 D": cp. 201 A, 204 D, for similar genn.
of the object.

αἰσχρὸς ἄρα κτλ. Socrates represents himself (ironically) as unversed in
the rules of logic, and habitually confusing contradictory with contrary
notions (οὐ-καλός with αἰσχρός): for the distinction, cp. Soph. 257 B, 257 D ff. ;
Euthyd. 283 B, 285 A ff., Cratyl. 429 B ff.

ὁ Ἔρως ἐστὶ καὶ κακός; καὶ ἦ, Οὐκ εὐφημήσεις; ἔφη· ἢ οἴει, ὅ τι
202 ἂν μὴ καλὸν ᾖ, ἀναγκαῖον αὐτὸ εἶναι αἰσχρόν; Μάλιστά γε.
᾿Η
καὶ ἂν μὴ σοφόν, ἀμαθές; ἢ οὐκ ᾔσθησαι ὅτι ἔστι τι μεταξὺ
σοφίας καὶ ἀμαθίας; Τί τοῦτο; Τὸ ὀρθὰ δοξάζειν [καὶ] ἄνευ τοῦ
ἔχειν λόγον δοῦναι οὐκ οἶσθ᾽, ἔφη, ὅτι οὔτε ἐπίστασθαί ἐστιν·
ἄλογον γὰρ πρᾶγμα πῶς ἂν εἴη ἐπιστήμη; οὔτε ἀμαθία· τὸ γὰρ
τοῦ ὄντος τυγχάνον πῶς ἂν εἴη ἀμαθία; ἔστι δὲ δή που τοιοῦτον
ἡ ὀρθὴ δόξα, μεταξὺ φρονήσεως καὶ ἀμαθίας. Ἀληθῆ, ἦν δ᾽ ἐγώ,
B λέγεις. Μὴ τοίνυν ἀνάγκαζε ὃ μὴ καλόν ἐστιν αἰσχρὸν εἶναι,
μηδὲ ὃ μὴ ἀγαθόν, κακόν. οὕτω δὲ καὶ τὸν Ἔρωτα ἐπειδὴ αὐτὸς
ὁμολογεῖς μὴ εἶναι ἀγαθὸν μηδὲ καλόν, μηδέν τι μᾶλλον οἴου δεῖν
αὐτὸν αἰσχρὸν καὶ κακὸν εἶναι, ἀλλά τι μεταξύ, ἔφη, τούτοιν.
Καὶ μήν, ἦν δ᾽ ἐγώ, ὁμολογεῖταί γε παρὰ πάντων μέγας θεὸς εἶναι.
Τῶν μὴ εἰδότων, ἔφη, πάντων λέγεις, ἢ καὶ τῶν εἰδότων; Ξυμπάντων μὲν οὖν. καὶ ἡ γελάσασα, Καὶ πῶς ἄν, ἔφη, ὦ Σώκρατες,

201 E ἔφη· ἢ : εφην O.-P.¹   202 A ἂν (post καὶ): ⟨ὃ⟩ ἂν Ast Mdvg. Sz.:
ὅ τι ἂν Steph. Hirschig: ὅτι ἂν, deleto καὶ, Reynders: ἂν οἴοιο Hommel   τὸ
ὀρθὰ δοξάζειν T O.-P.: τὸ τὰ ὀρθὰ δ. W: τὸ ὀρθοδοξάζειν B   καὶ om. O.-P.,
del. Stallb. Bdhm. Sz.   τοιουτο O.-P.: τοιοῦτόν τι Hirschig   ἡ ὀρθὴ δόξα del.
Bdhm.   B τουτοιν εφη O.-P.   γε BT O.-P.: μοι W

202 A .Ἡ καὶ ἂν μὴ κτλ. "Η. e. ἄν τι μὴ σοφόν. Nam τι e superiore ὅ τι
facile intelligas" (Stallb.).
    Τὸ ὀρθὰ δοξάζειν κτλ. This distinction between δόξα and ἐπιστήμη is much
insisted on by Plato; see esp. Rep. 477 ff.; Meno 99 A: cp. Isocr. Hel. 209 A.
    For τὸ ἔχειν λόγον δοῦναι as the distinctive mark of ἐπιστήμη, cp. Meno 98 A;
but this definition is criticised unfavourably in Theaet. 201 C ff. (see Zeller,
Plato, pp. 171 ff.). I bracket καὶ before ἄνευ: if retained, we must render
with Rückert (and Hug) "auch ohne Rechenschaft geben zu können." For
this "intensive" use of καί, see Thompson on Meno 71 B. Rettig defends the
Bodleian ὀρθοδοξάζειν thus "ὀρθὰ δοξάζειν ginge auf Einzelnes und Thatsäch-
liches, nicht auf den Begriff als solchen und die geistige Eigenschaft": but
this distinction is imaginary, and there is no other evidence, in Plato or
elsewhere, for the existence of this compound, Aristotle's word (E. N. VII.
8. 4) being ὀρθοδοξέω. Possibly we should write καὶ ⟨ὄντα⟩ ἄ., cp. Rep. 413 A.
    μεταξὺ φρονήσεως κτλ. Cp. Rep. 477 A μεταξύ τι...ἀγνοίας τε καὶ ἐπιστήμης:
ib. 478 D.
    202 B Μὴ τοίνυν ἀνάγκαζε. "I. q. μὴ ἀναγκαῖον νόμιζε, v. Heindorf ad
Euthyd. (sic) p. 432 C" (Stallb.). For this use to denote logical compulsion, cp.
also Cratyl. 432 E μὴ ἀνάγκαζε πάντ᾽ ἔχειν τὰ γράμματα...ἀλλ᾽ ἔα κτλ.: Parmen.
133 C.
    Τῶν μὴ εἰδότων. Sc. παρά: cp. Crat. 408 D, Soph. 243 D, etc. A similar
distinction had been drawn twice by Socr. himself, see 194 B ff., 199 A.

ὁμολογοῖτο μέγας θεὸς εἶναι παρὰ τούτων, οἵ φασιν αὐτὸν οὐδὲ C
θεὸν εἶναι; Τίνες οὗτοι; ἦν δ' ἐγώ. Εἰς μέν, ἔφη, σύ, μία δ' ἐγώ.
κἀγὼ εἶπον, Πῶς τοῦτο, ἔφην, λέγεις; καὶ ἥ, 'Ραδίως, ἔφη.
λέγε
γάρ μοι, οὐ πάντας θεοὺς φῂς εὐδαίμονας εἶναι καὶ καλούς; ἢ
τολμήσαις ἄν τινα μὴ φάναι καλόν τε καὶ εὐδαίμονα θεῶν εἶναι;
Μὰ Δί' οὐκ ἔγωγ', ἔφην. Εὐδαίμονας δὲ δὴ λέγεις οὐ τοὺς τἀγαθὰ
καὶ τὰ καλὰ κεκτημένους; Πάνυ γε. 'Αλλὰ μὴν Ἔρωτά γε ὡμο-
λόγηκας δι' ἔνδειαν τῶν ἀγαθῶν καὶ καλῶν ἐπιθυμεῖν αὐτῶν D
τούτων ὧν ἐνδεής ἐστιν. 'Ωμολόγηκα γάρ. Πῶς δἂν οὖν θεὸς
εἴη ὅ γε τῶν καλῶν καὶ ἀγαθῶν ἄμοιρος; Οὐδαμῶς, ὥς γ' ἔοικεν.
'Ορᾷς οὖν, ἔφη, ὅτι καὶ σὺ Ἔρωτα οὐ θεὸν νομίζεις;
XXIII. Τί οὖν ἄν, ἔφην, εἴη ὁ Ἔρως; θνητός; Ἥκιστά γε.

202 C ἔφην om. O.-P.   καὶ καλούς secl. Bdhm. Sz.   καλόν τε καὶ secl.
Bdhm. Sz.   θεῶν BT O.-P.: θεὸν pr. W   τοὺς τἀγαθὰ BT Stob. O.-P.:
τοὺς ἀγαθοὺς W   τὰ καλὰ B O.-P., J.-U.: καλὰ TW Stob., Sz. Bt.   D τῶν
καλῶν καὶ τῶν ἀγαθῶν Stob.   πῶς δἂν scripsi: πῶς ἂν B Stob. O.-P., J.-U.:
πῶς δ' ἂν TW, Bt.   τῶν TW Stob. O.-P.: γ' ὧν B   ὥστ' ἔοικεν Stob.
τί οὖν; ἔφην· εἴη ἂν ὁ Ἔρως θνητός; cj. Steph.   ὁ ἔρως εἴη Stob.   ἔφην B
Stob., J.-U. Sz. Bt.: ἔφη TW O.-P., Jn.

202 C κἀγὼ εἶπον...ἔφην. We might avoid this tautology (for which cp.
177 A) by reading κἀγώ, Εἶπον πῶς κτλ., construing εἶπον as 1st aor. imper.,
as in *Meno* 71 D. Cp. *Rep.* 338 D ἀλλὰ σαφέστερον εἰπὲ τί λέγεις.

'Ραδίως. *Sc.* τοῦτο λέγω. For tho use of ῥᾳδίως with λέγω and tho like,
often with a bad meaning, of ill-timed lightness, cp. *Meno* 94 E (with
Thompson's *note*), *Rep.* 377 B, 378 A. Here, however, the meaning is probably
ῥᾴδιόν ἐστιν ὃ λέγω (so Rettig), or as Stallb. "sic ut res facilem habet expli-
cationem": cp. *Rep.* 475 E ἀλλὰ πῶς αὐτὸ λέγεις; Οὐδαμῶς, ἦν δ' ἐγώ, ῥᾳδίως
πρός γε ἄλλον· σὲ δὲ οἶμαι κτλ. It would also be possible to suppose that
Diotima, playfully, adapting her reply to the form rather than the sense of
Socr.'s question : "In what way do you speak thus?" "I speak it lightly"
(without compunction): *i.e.* the λέγω may be supplied with ῥᾳδίως may mean
"I say, utter the word," whereas the λέγεις of Socr. meant "do you mean."

εὐδαίμονας εἶναι κτλ. Badham's excision of both καὶ καλούς and καλόν
τε καὶ is plausible: if the words are sound, we must assume the stress in each
clause to be laid on the terms here in question, εὐδαίμονας...εὐδαίμονα.

Εὐδαίμονας δὲ δὴ κτλ. Cp. the phrases used by Agathon in 195 A.
202 D 'Ωμολόγηκα γάρ. Socr. represents himself as having already conceded to Diotima exactly as much as Agathon had conceded to him (cp.
201 E σχεδὸν γάρ τι κτλ.): for A.'s concession of the point here in question,
see 200 A, E.

ἄμοιρος. This word had already been employed by Agathon, 197 D (cp.
181 C); it is a poetical word rarely used by Plato elsewhere, except in *Laws*
(693 E, etc.).

B. P.   7

'Αλλὰ τί μήν; "Ωσπερ τὰ πρότερα ἔφην, μεταξὺ θνητοῦ καὶ
ἀθανάτου. Τί οὖν, ὦ Διοτίμα; Δαίμων μέγας, ὦ Σώκρατες· καὶ
E γὰρ πᾶν τὸ δαιμόνιον μεταξύ ἐστι θεοῦ τε καὶ θνητοῦ.
Τίνα, ἦν
δ' ἐγώ, δύναμιν ἔχον; 'Ερμηνεῦον καὶ διαπορθμεῦον θεοῖς τὰ παρ'
ἀνθρώπων καὶ ἀνθρώποις τὰ παρὰ θεῶν, τῶν μὲν τὰς δεήσεις καὶ
θυσίας, τῶν δὲ τὰς ἐπιτάξεις τε καὶ ἀμοιβὰς [τῶν θυσιῶν], ἐν μέσῳ
δὲ ὂν ἀμφοτέρων συμπληροῖ, ὥστε τὸ πᾶν αὐτὸ αὑτῷ ξυνδεδέσθαι.

202 E τε καὶ BT O.-P.: καὶ W Stob.   τίνα δ' ἦν Stob.   διαπροθ-
μευον O.-P.   θεοῖς τε τὰ Stob.   τῶν θυσιῶν om. Pollux, secl. Sz.   ⟨τὸ⟩ ἐν
μέσῳ δέον Vermehren   εμ μεσω O.-P.: ἐμμέσῳ Lobeck   δὲ ὂν : δὴ ὂν Peipers :
ὁδεῦον cj. anon.   ὂν ⟨τὰ⟩ Bergk   ⟨τὰ ὅλα⟩ συμπληροῖ Reynders: ⟨ἀμφοτέ-
ρους⟩ σ. Bdhm.   τὸ πᾶν ὥστε αὐτὸ Orelli   αὐτὸ om. Stob.

"Ωσπερ τὰ πρότερα. Viz. the exx. of a mean between extremes given in
202 A, B.

Δαίμων μέγας. The epithet serves to point the correction of Socrates'
definition, μέγας θεός (202 B). Cp. Olympiod. in Alcib. I. p. 22 "δαίμονα" δὲ
ὡς μέσον αὐτὸν προσαγορεύει· μέσος γάρ ἐστιν ὁ "Ερως οὐσίας καὶ ἐνεργείας καὶ
ἐρωμένου καὶ ἐραστοῦ· "μέγαν" δέ, ἐπειδὴ ὑπὲρ αἴσθησιν καὶ νοερῶς ἐνεργεῖ.
Procl. in Alcib. I. p. 64 Cr., p. 66. For τὸ δαιμόνιον as μεταξύ, cp. Eur. Troad.
55—6 : Med. 1391: Hel. 1137 ὅ τι θεὸς ἢ μὴ θεὸς ἢ τὸ μέσον κτλ. (see Rohde,
Psyche II. 249 n. 1).

202 E Ερμηνεῦον κτλ. For the term ἑρμηνεύειν to describe the mediating
office of δαίμονες, cp. Epin. 985 B ἑρμηνεύεσθαι (δαίμονας) πρὸς ἀλλήλους τε καὶ
τοὺς...θεοὺς πάντας τε καὶ πάντα.   Hommel bids us take ἑρμηνεῦον with ἀνθρ.
τὰ παρὰ θεῶν (as "eiusdem atque 'Ερμῆς radicis") and διαπορθμεῦον with θεοῖς
τὰ παρ' ἀνθρώπων (the office of the πορθμεύς, Charon, being " animas e terra
ad sedes deorum transvehere ").   This is probably right ; but in any case it is
a mistake to regard the two words as synonymous, as do L. and S. (s. v.
διαπορθμεύω, " to translate from one tongue into another, to interpret ").

ἀμοιβὰς [τῶν θυσιῶν].   ἀμοιβή as a "return-present" (in transactions
between gods and men) is used in Hom. Od. I. 318 σοὶ δ' ἄξιον ἔσται ἀμοιβῆς
⟨sc. τὸ δῶρον⟩: ib. III. 58 ἄλλοισι δίδου χαρίεσσαν ἀμοιβήν...ἀγακλειτῆς ἑκα-
τόμβης: cp. Eur. Or. 467 οἷς...ἀπέδωκ' ἀμοιβὰς οὐ καλάς. Pollux (VI. 187)
when quoting our passage ignores τῶν θυσιῶν. Cp. also Procl. in Alcib. I.
p. 46, 63: Plut. de Is. et Os. 26, p. 361 B ὅ τε Πλάτων ἑρμηνευτικὸν τὸ τοιοῦτον
ὀνομάζει γένος καὶ διακονικὸν ἐν μέσῳ θεῶν καὶ ἀνθρώπων, εὐχὰς μὲν ἐκεῖ καὶ
δεήσεις...ἀναπέμποντας, ἐκεῖθεν δὲ μαντεῖα δεῦρο καὶ δόσεις ἀγαθῶν φέροντας :
Apuleius de deo Socr. 6 hos Graeci nomine δαίμονας nuncupant, inter homines
caelicolasque vectores hinc precum inde donorum, qui ultro citro portant hinc
petitiones inde suppetias, ceu quidam utrisque interpretes et salutigeri. per
hos eosdem, ut Plato in symposio autumat, cuncta denuntiata et magorum
varia miracula omnesque praesagiorum species reguntur : see also Plut. de or.
def. 415 A ; Philo Jud. de somn. p. 586 D (δαίμονες) τὰς τοῦ πατρὸς ἐπικελεύσεις
τοῖς ἐκγόνοις, καὶ τὰς τῶν ἐκγόνων χρείας τῷ πατρὶ διαγγέλλουσι.

ἐν μέσῳ δὲ ὂν.   This calls for no alteration (such as is suggested by

διὰ τούτου καὶ ἡ μαντικὴ πᾶσα χωρεῖ καὶ ἡ τῶν ἱερέων τέχνη τῶν
τε περὶ τὰς θυσίας καὶ τὰς τελετὰς καὶ τὰς ἐπῳδὰς καὶ τὴν 203
μαγγανείαν πᾶσαν καὶ γοητείαν. θεὸς δὲ ἀνθρώπῳ οὐ μίγνυται,
ἀλλὰ διὰ τούτου πᾶσά ἐστιν ἡ ὁμιλία καὶ ἡ διάλεκτος θεοῖς πρὸς
ἀνθρώπους < καὶ πρὸς θεοὺς ἀνθρώποις >, καὶ ἐγρηγορόσι καὶ

202 E ἱερῶν Stob. 203 A τὰς τελετὰς B Stob. O.-P., J.-U.: τελετὰς
TW, Bt. καὶ τὰς ἐπῳδὰς...γοητείαν secl. Hug καὶ τὴν...γοητείαν secl. Voeg.
μαγγανείαν Geel J.-U. Sz.: μαντείαν BT Stob. O.-P.: μαγείαν Bdhm. Bt.
ἀνθρώπους ⟨καὶ πρὸς θεοὺς ἀνθρώποις⟩ Wolf Usener Sz.: ἀ. ⟨καὶ ἀνθρώποις πρὸς
θεοὺς⟩ Heusde: ἀνθρώποις Stobaei P εγληγοροσ[σ]ι O.-P.

Vermehren): with συμπληροῖ sc. ἀμφοτέρους. The μέσον serves as the δεσμός
by which the extremes (here θνητοί and ἀθάνατοι) are united into an organic
whole (ὅλον). Cp. Procl. in Alc. I. pp. 69, 72, 77.

203 A τὰς τελετὰς. "Ritual": cp. Rep. 365 A λύσεις τε καὶ καθαρμοὶ ἀδικη-
μάτων...ἃς δὴ τελετὰς καλοῦσιν: Phaedr. 244 E (with Thompson's note): Laws
738 C θυσίας τελεταῖς συμμίκτους. That καθαρμοί (and τελεταί) included περιθειώ-
σεις, λουτρά, περιρράνσεις appears from Cratyl. 405 A. Rohde (Psyche II. 70 n. 3)
points out that "diese μάντεις entsprechen in allem Wesentlichen den Zaubern
und Medicinmännern der Naturvölker. Wahrsager, Arzt, Zauberer, sind hier
noch eine Person." E.g. Apis in Aesch. Suppl. 260 ff. ; cp. Eur. Heracl. 401,
Phoen. 1255 ff., and the part played by Empedocles. In Hippocr. de morb.
sacr. p. 591 the μάντεις and καθαρταί are witch-doctors, claiming control of
the elements, as rain-makers, etc. (καθαρμοὺς προσφέροντες καὶ ἐπαοιδὰς...
περικαθαίρων καὶ μαγεύων...τε καὶ θύων σελήνην τε καθαιρήσει καὶ ἥλιον ἀφανιεῖ
καὶ χειμῶνα καὶ εὐδίην ποιήσει κτλ.): cp. 197 C n.

τὴν μαγγανείαν πᾶσαν. Geel's correction μαγγανείαν is perhaps slightly
preferable, on the ground of Platonic usage, to Badham's μαγείαν. Cp.
Laws 908 D ἐξ ὧν μάντεις τε κατασκευάζονται πολλοὶ καὶ περὶ πᾶσαν τὴν
μαγγανείαν κεκινημένοι: id. 933 A ἄλλη δὲ (φαρμακεία) ἣ μαγγανείαις τέ τισι καὶ
ἐπῳδαῖς καὶ καταδέσεσι λεγομέναις πείθει κτλ. (cp. 933 C): Gorg. 484 A τὰ
ἡμέτερα γράμματα καὶ μαγγανεύματα καὶ ἐπῳδάς: also [Dem.] XXV. 79 λαβὼν τὰ
φάρμακα καὶ τὰς ἐπῳδας...μαγγανεύει καὶ φενακίζει. Hug objects to γοητείαν,
as elsewhere used by Plato in a bad sense. There is, however, no need to
suppose that any of these terms are intended here to convey more than a
neutral sense ; and to represent ἡ Μαντινική as a disbeliever in any of the
arts of divination or wizardry would be less artistic than pedantic. Moreover,
the language used here is supported by the echo it finds in the description of
Eros below (203 D ad fin.) as δεινὸς γόης καὶ φαρμακεὺς καὶ σοφιστής. Rep.
364 B, C shows Plato's own low opinion of current μαντική, but Socrates was
probably more credulous, see Xen. Mem. I. 1. 9, 4. 15.

θεοῖς πρὸς ἀνθρώπους κτλ. Since the participles can neither be construed
with θεοῖς, because of the sense, nor with ἀνθρώπους, because of the case, it is
necessary to supply some supplement such as that adopted in the text.
Rettig accepts Stallbaum's explanation of the traditional text: " Quum enim

καθεύδουσι· καὶ ὁ μὲν περὶ τὰ τοιαῦτα σοφὸς δαιμόνιος ἀνήρ, ὁ δὲ ἄλλο τι σοφὸς ὢν ἢ περὶ τέχνας ἢ περὶ χειρουργίας τινὰς βάναυσος. οὗτοι δὴ οἱ δαίμονες πολλοί τε καὶ παντοδαποί εἰσιν, εἷς δὲ τούτων ἐστὶ καὶ ὁ Ἔρως.

Πατρὸς δέ, ἦν δ' ἐγώ, τίνος ἐστὶ καὶ μητρός; Μακρότερον μέν,
B ἔφη, διηγήσασθαι· ὅμως δέ σοι ἐρῶ. ὅτε γὰρ ἐγένετο ἡ Ἀφροδίτη, εἱστιῶντο οἱ θεοί, οἵ τε ἄλλοι καὶ ὁ τῆς Μήτιδος υἱὸς Πόρος. ἐπειδὴ δὲ ἐδείπνησαν, προσαιτήσουσα οἷον δὴ εὐωχίας οὔσης ἀφίκετο ἡ Πενία, καὶ ἦν περὶ τὰς θύρας. ὁ οὖν Πόρος μεθυσθεὶς

203 A σοφὸς : ὀφὸς O.-P. : σφοδρὸς Stob.   ὧν om. Stob.   περὶ
β
χειρουργίας Stob. O.-P.: χειρουργίας BTW, J.-U. Bt.   αναυσους O.-P.   πολλοί
τε Stob. O.-P.: πολλοὶ BTW   τουτων· O.-P.   ἐστὶ om. Stob.   τίνος
ἐστὶ καὶ μητρός BW: καὶ μητρὸς τίνος ἐστι T¹ O.-P. (εστιν)   B   εἱστιῶντο
W b t, Hermog., Sz.: ἱστιωντο O.-P.: ἡστιῶντο T, Bt.: ἡστιῶντο B   οἵ τε
ἄλλοι θεοὶ καὶ Hermog.   προσαιτήσουσα T O.-P.: προσαιτῆς οὖσα B: προσαῖτις
οὖσα Euseb. Origen

dicatur ὁμιλεῖν τινι et διαλέγεσθαί τινι, etiam ὁμιλία καὶ διάλεκτος τινι recte dici potuit. Et quum antea…perspicuitatis caussa usus esset praepositione πρὸς addito casu accusativo, nunc ad legitimam constructionem revertens, neglecta grammatica diligentia, dativum post accusativum recte inferri potuit." But at this rate one might justify anything in the way of distorted grammar! Hug marks a lacuna after ἀνθρώπους. For the ref. to divine communications in sleep ("the visions of the head upon the bed"), cp. Pind. *fr.* 131. 3 ff. ; *Rep.* 571 D ff. (with Adam's *notes*) ; Rohde, *Psyche* I. 6 ff.

δαιμόνιος ἀνήρ. Compare the etymological definition (δαίμων = δαήμων) in *Cratyl.* 398 C. For Socrates as an example of the δαιμόνιος ἀνήρ, see 219 B.

περὶ τέχνας…βάναυσος. Cp. *Theaet.* 176 C, *Laws* 644 A ; Arist. *Rhet.* I. 9. 1367ᵃ 31 (ἐλευθέρου σημεῖον) τὸ μηδεμίαν ἐργάζεσθαι βάναυσον τέχνην. The question as to why manual labour is held in contempt is asked in *Rep.* 590 C, and answered in *Rep.* 495 D (see Adam's *notes ad loc.*).

οἱ δαίμονες. Other Platonic passages mentioning these intermediary beings are *Rep.* 392 A, 427 B, 617 D (with Adam's *note*), *Laws* 713 D, 717 B. For later developments see esp. Plutarch (*de defect. orac.*, *de Is. et Os.*, *de daem. Socr.*, etc.). Cp. Rohde, *Psyche* I. 153.

Πατρὸς δέ…τίνος κτλ. These are genitives of origin. Here we have it tacitly assumed that Phaedrus's statement (178 B), that Eros is unbegotten, is untrue.

203 B Πόρος. We find in Alcman *fr.* 16 (with the Schol. ὅτι τὸν Πόρον εἴρηκε τὸν αὐτὸν τῷ ὑπὸ τοῦ Ἡσιόδου μεμυθευμένῳ Χάει) a precedent for this personification of Πόρος. Πενία is personified by Aristophanes in the *Plutus*, *passim*. For Μῆτις, see Hes. *Theog.* 886 Ζεὺς δὲ θεῶν βασιλεὺς πρώτην ἄλοχον θέτο Μῆτιν, | πλεῖστα θεῶν τε ἰδυῖαν ἰδὲ θνητῶν ἀνθρώπων : (μῆτις is, in Epic, the especial attribute of Zeus, as μητίετα): Μῆτις was also an Orphic *alias* of

τοῦ νέκταρος—οἶνος γὰρ οὔπω ἦν—εἰς τὸν τοῦ Διὸς κῆπον εἰσελθών,
βεβαρημένος ηὗδεν. ἡ οὖν Πενία ἐπιβουλεύουσα διὰ τὴν αὑτῆς
ἀπορίαν παιδίον ποιήσασθαι ἐκ τοῦ Πόρου, κατακλίνεταί τε παρ᾽
αὐτῷ καὶ ἐκύησε τὸν Ἔρωτα. διὸ δὴ καὶ τῆς Ἀφροδίτης ἀκό- C
λουθος καὶ θεράπων γέγονεν ὁ Ἔρως, γεννηθεὶς ἐν τοῖς ἐκείνης
γενεθλίοις, καὶ ἅμα φύσει ἐραστὴς ὢν περὶ τὸ καλὸν καὶ τῆς Ἀφροδίτης καλῆς οὔσης. ἅτε οὖν Πόρου καὶ Πενίας υἱὸς ὢν ὁ Ἔρως ἐν
τοιαύτῃ τύχῃ καθέστηκε. πρῶτον μὲν πένης ἀεί ἐστι, καὶ πολλοῦ

203 B ἐξελθών O.-P.	ηὗδεν BTW : εὗδεν O.-P., al.	παιδοποιήσασθαι
Naber J.-U.	C δὴ καὶ BT O.-P.: δὴ W	καὶ θεράπων : καὶ om. Orig.
ἐκείνων Orig.	ἐραστὴς del. Bdhm.	καλὸν καὶ BT O.-P.: καὶ om. W :
fort. καλόν, ὡς	καὶ τῆς...οὔσης del. Bdhm.	πένης TW O.-P.: πενίης B

Eros. For nectar as the primeval substitute for wine, cp. Hom. *Il.* v. 341,
etc., also *Phaedr.* 247 E τοὺς ἵππους...νέκταρ ἐπότισε. The celestial δεῖπνον
was, it appears, followed by a συμπόσιον. Spenser, *H. to Love*, speaks of the
god as "Begot of Plentie and of Penury." See further *Introd.* § IV. c 2.

εἰς τὸν τοῦ Διὸς κῆπον. Cp. Soph. *fr.* (*Ion*) 297 N. ἐν Διὸς κήποις ἀροῦσθαι
μόνον εὐδαίμονας ὄλβους. It is interesting to notice that Origen (*Contra Cels.*
IV. 39) identifies the "garden of Zeus" with Paradise, Poros with Adam,
Penia with the Serpent. With the intoxication and its results we might
compare the O. T. stories of Noah and his sons and of Lot and his daughters.
For the neo-Platonic interpretation of the myth, see Plotinus *Enn.* III. 5. 2,
292 F ff., 298 F : cp. also *Introd.* § IV. c 2. A similar Orphic legend is
mentioned by Porphyry *de antr. nymph.* 16 (*Orphica* p. 180) παρὰ δὲ τῷ
Ὀρφεῖ ὁ Κρόνος μέλιτι ὑπὸ Διὸς ἐνεδρεύεται· πλησθεὶς γὰρ μέλιτος μεθύει καὶ
σκοτοῦται ὡς ὑπὸ οἴνου καὶ ὑπνοῖ, ὡς παρὰ Πλάτωνι ὁ Πόρος τοῦ νέκταρος
πλησθείς, οὔπω γὰρ οἶνος ἦν. Another classical example is the trick played
by Lady Macbeth on Duncan's "spongy officers" ("his two chamberlains
Will I with wine and wassail so convince" etc.).

βεβαρημένος. A later form for the Epic βεβαρηώς (*Od.* III. 139): cp.
Theocr. XVII. 61 βεβαρημένα ὠδίνεσσιν.

παιδίον ποιήσασθαι ἐκ κτλ. So Andoc. IV. 22 υἱὸν ἐξ αὐτῆς πεποίηται: and
παῖδας ποιεῖσθαι in *Crito* 45 D, *Laws* 674 B, 783 D, as equiv. to the cpd.
παιδοποιεῖσθαι (*Rep.* 449 D, *Laws* 784 A, B, E). These parallels are sufficient
to defend the text (see *crit. n.*), without resorting to Rettig's absurd notion
that παιδίον π. is "verecundior" than the cpd.

203 C τῆς Ἀφροδίτης...θεράπων. Cp. *Orph. fr.* 139 τὴν γὰρ Ἀφροδίτην
παρήγαγεν ὁ δημιουργός...καὶ τὸν Ἔρωτα ὀπαδὸν αὐτῆς: Sappho *fr.* 74 (λέγει ἡ
Ἀφροδίτη) σύ τε καλὸς (κἀμὸς Bgk.) θεράπων Ἔρος: Hes. *Theog.* 201 τῇ δ᾽ (sc.
Ἀφροδίτῃ) Ἔρος ὡμάρτησε καὶ Ἵμερος ἕσπετο καλὸς | γεινομένῃ τὰ πρῶτα κτλ.:
Max. Tyr. *diss.* XXIV. p. 297.

ἐραστὴς ὢν περὶ τὸ καλόν. Cp. 204 B, 206 E. For the thought, cp. Sir
T. Browne (*Rel. Med.*) "I am naturally amorous of all that is beautiful."

πρῶτον μὲν κτλ. Here follows a list of the properties which attach to
Eros in virtue of his descent from Penia. Observe that the order is chiastic—
here Penia-Poros, above Poros-Penia.

δεῖ ἁπαλός τε καὶ καλός, οἷον οἱ πολλοὶ οἴονται, ἀλλὰ σκληρὸς D καὶ αὐχμηρὸς καὶ ἀνυπόδητος καὶ ἄοικος, χαμαιπετὴς ἀεὶ ὢν καὶ ἄστρωτος, ἐπὶ θύραις καὶ ἐν ὁδοῖς ὑπαίθριος κοιμώμενος, τὴν τῆς μητρὸς φύσιν ἔχων, ἀεὶ ἐνδείᾳ ξύνοικος. κατὰ δὲ αὖ τὸν πατέρα ἐπίβουλός ἐστι τοῖς καλοῖς καὶ τοῖς ἀγαθοῖς, ἀνδρεῖος ὢν καὶ ἴτης καὶ σύντονος, θηρευτὴς δεινός, ἀεί τινας πλέκων μηχανάς, καὶ

203 D καὶ οἶκος Themistius   ὑπαίθριος BW O.-P., Orig.: ὑπαι-
θρίοις T ⟨ἔστι μὲν οὖν⟩ τὴν cj. Sommer   τοῖς ἀγαθοῖς libri: ἀγαθοῖς O.-P.
δεινὸς om. apogr. Paris. 1810, del. Kreyenbühl   ἀεὶ προσπλέκων Orig.
μηχανὰς: [α]νας βᾶς O.-P. (i.e. αμοιβας O.-P.¹)

οἷον οἱ πολλοὶ οἴονται. This popular opinion had been esp. voiced by Agathon, 195 c ff.; and he had used the term σκληρός in 195 E, 196 A. The properties of Eros are, as observed by Max. Tyr. diss. XXIV. 4. p. 461, ἀτεχνῶς οἷα εἰς αὐτὸν Σωκράτην ἔσκωπτον ἐν Διονυσίοις οἱ κωμῳδοί: cp. Themist. or. 13. p. 161 D ff.

203 D αὐχμηρὸς. This is evidently intended as the contrary of Agathon's epithet ὑγρός, 196 A. Cp. Ar. Plut. 80 ff. (Πλοῦτος) ἀθλίως διακείμενος...αὐχμῶν βαδίζεις; and the echoes in Plut. de fort. p. 98 D, in amat. 759 A.

ἀνυπόδητος...ἄστρωτος. These, too, are characteristics of the Socratic (and Cynic) way of life. For ἀνυπόδητος, see 173 B, 220 B; for χαμαιπετὴς καὶ ἄστρωτος the account given by Alcibiades in 220 B, C. Compare also the description of the Σελλοί ("fakirs") in Il. XVI. 234 ff. Σελλοί, ἀνιπτόποδες, χαμαιεῦναι κτλ. (see Welcker Kl. Schr. 3. 90 f.; Rohde, Psyche I. 122).

ἐπὶ θύραις κτλ. For the θυραυλίαι of ἐρασταί, see 183 A, Anthol. V. 5; and for this phrase as applicable to Socrates, 175 A, 220 C, Ar. Nub. 169 ff. So too Penia was described in 203 B as (οὖσα) περὶ τὰς θύρας. ὑπαίθριος and σύνοικος are words of a poetical flavour: cp. Xen. Symp. VIII. 24 ὁ ἀεὶ σύνοικος ἐμοὶ ἔρως.

ἴτης. "Energetic" ("go-ahead"): Schol. ἴτης· ἴστωρ, ἐπιστήμων, ὡς ἐνταῦθα. λαμβάνεται δὲ καὶ ἐπὶ τοῦ ἰταμοῦ καὶ θρασέος. The Scholiast's ὡς ἐνταῦθα is clearly wrong, and that Plato connected the word with ἰέναι is shown by Protag. 349 E πότερον τοὺς ἀνδρείους θαρραλέους λέγεις ἢ ἄλλο τι; καὶ ἴτας γ᾽, ἔφη, ἐφ᾽ ἃ οἱ πολλοὶ φοβοῦνται ἰέναι. Cp. Prot. 359 C: Callinus I. 9—10 ἀλλά τις ἰθὺς ἴτω | ἔγχος ἀνασχόμενος κτλ. Here, however, the special sense of intellectual progress (μέθοδος, ἄνοδος) may be implied, cp. 210 A (μετίῃ, ἰόντα, ἰέναι), and my note on ἀνδρείαν 212 B (also 205 D).

θηρευτὴς δεινός. "A mighty hunter," a very Nimrod. For the notion of the chase in erotics, cp. the use of ἑλεῖν and διώκειν in 182 E, etc., and of θήρα in Soph. 222 D τῇ τῶν ἐρώντων θήρα (cp. θηρῶμαι in Isocr. Hel. 219 D): for the same notion applied to philosophical enquiry, cp. Phaedo 66 C τὴν τοῦ ὄντος θήραν: Gorg. 500 D, Theaet. 198 A ff. So Emerson (On Beauty), "The sharpest-sighted hunter in the world is Love, for finding what he seeks and only that."

πλέκων μηχανάς. "Weaving plots," "intriguing": cp. Eur. Androm. 66 ποίας μηχανὰς πλέκουσιν αὖ; Orph. H. 55. 3 (Ἀφροδίτῃ) δολοπλόκε: Aelian H. A. III. 30 σοφώτατος ὁ κόκκυξ, καὶ πλέκειν εὐπόρους ἐξ ἀπόρων μηχανὰς δεινότατος.

φρονήσεως ἐπιθυμητὴς καὶ πόριμος, φιλοσοφῶν διὰ παντὸς τοῦ
βίου, δεινὸς γόης καὶ φαρμακεὺς καὶ σοφιστής· καὶ οὔτε ὡς
ἀθάνατος πέφυκεν οὔτε ὡς θνητός, ἀλλὰ τοτὲ μὲν τῆς αὐτῆς ἡμέρας Ε
θάλλει καὶ ζῇ, ὅταν εὐπορήσῃ, τοτὲ δὲ ἀποθνῄσκει, πάλιν δὲ ἀνα-
βιώσκεται διὰ τὴν τοῦ πατρὸς φύσιν, τὸ δὲ ποριζόμενον ἀεὶ
ὑπεκρεῖ· ὥστε οὔτε ἀπορεῖ Ἔρως ποτὲ οὔτε πλουτεῖ, σοφίας τε αὖ
καὶ ἀμαθίας ἐν μέσῳ ἐστίν. ἔχει γὰρ ὧδε. θεῶν οὐδεὶς φιλοσοφεῖ
οὐδ᾽ ἐπιθυμεῖ σοφὸς γενέσθαι—ἔστι γάρ—οὐδ᾽ εἴ τις ἄλλος σοφός, 204
οὐ φιλοσοφεῖ. οὐδ᾽ αὖ οἱ ἀμαθεῖς φιλοσοφοῦσιν οὐδ᾽ ἐπιθυμοῦσι

203 D πόριμος T O.-P. corr.: πορισμος B: φρονιμος O.-P.[1]   φιλοσοφῶν
T: φιλοσόφων B   γόης καὶ: καὶ om. O.-P.   Ε αὐτῆς om. O.-P.   καὶ
ζῇ B O.-P.: τε καὶ ζῇ TW, Orig.   ὅταν εὐπορήσῃ secl. Jn. Hug: ὅταν ἀπορήσῃ
Hommel   πάλιν: παλιν παλιν O.-P. corr., Orig.   αναβιοσκε[ι]ται O.-P.
ποτ᾽ Ἔρως vulg. Hirschig   τε αὖ T, Bt.: τε B, Herm.: δ᾽ αὖ Orig.: αυ O.-P.:
δὲ Sommer Sz.

πόριμος. As son of Πόρος. Agathon, too, had described Eros as (πρᾳότητα)
πορίζων, 197 D.

δεινὸς γόης κτλ. For γόης, see 203 A *n.*; and for Socrates as wizard or
charmer, 215 C ff., *Meno* 80 A ff., Xen. *Mem.* III. 11. 17—18. For σοφιστής,
cp. 177 B, 208 C; *Rep.* 596 D; Xen. *Cyrop.* VI. 1. 41 νῦν τοῦτο πεφιλοσόφηκα
μετὰ τοῦ ἀδίκου σοφιστοῦ τοῦ Ἔρωτος: Maxim. Tyr. XXIV. 9 (=Sappho *fr.*
125) τὸν Ἔρωτα Σωκράτης σοφιστὴν λέγει, Σαπφὼ μυθοπλόκον. The esoteric
meaning of these epithets is thus explained by Hermias *in Plat. Phaedr.*
p. 97: (εἶπε τὸν Ἔρωτα) φιλόσοφον μὲν ὡς τὸ λογικὸν ἡμῶν διεγείροντα ἐπὶ τὰ
καλά· γόητα δὲ ὡς τὸν θυμὸν καταστέλλοντα· φαρμακέα (δὲ) ὡς τὸ ἐπιθυμητικὸν
κηλοῦντα· σοφιστὴν δὲ ὡς τὴν φύσιν ἀπατῶντα καὶ δελεάζοντα—this however
must be taken "with a grain of salt." Cp. also Procl. *in Cratyl.* p. 94, 158
ὅτι οἶδεν ὁ Πλάτων τὸ ὄνομα τὸν σοφιστὴν ἐπὶ σεμνῷ τάττειν πράγματι· τὸν γὰρ
πρὸς ἑαυτὸν τὰ ἄλλα δυνάμενον ἐπιστρέφειν οὕτως καλεῖ, οἷον τὸν Δία (*Min.*
319 C), τὸν Ἅιδην (*Crat.* 403 E), τὸν Ἔρωτα.

203 E θάλλει. Cp. *Cratyl.* 414 A αὐτό γε τὸ θάλλειν τὴν αὔξην μοι δοκεῖ
ἀπεικάζειν τὴν τῶν νέων. For the alternation of life and death in Eros, compare
the case of Polydeuces in Pind. *Nem.* X. 87 ff.

ὅταν εὐπορήσῃ. These words are condemned, on no sufficient grounds, by
Hug and others as "sehr prosaische und abschwächend."

ἀεὶ ὑπεκρεῖ. "Die geistigen Güter werden uns zu Theil nur insofern wir
sie erwerben" (Rettig). The cpd. ὑπεκρεῖν is ἅπ. λεγ. in Plato, but cp. *Euthyd.*
291 B αἱ δ᾽ (ἐπιστῆμαι) ἀεὶ ὑπεξέφυγον.

οὔτε ἀπορεῖ...οὔτε πλουτεῖ. ἀπορία is a quality of the mother of Eros (διὰ
τὴν αὐτῆς ἀπορίαν 203 B), as πλοῦτος of the father. On the other hand πενία
is described as a mean between πλοῦτος and πτωχεία in Ar. *Plut.* 552.

204 A ἔστι γάρ. Sc. σοφός: cp. Simon. 5. 10 θεὸς ἂν μόνος τοῦτ᾽ ἔχοι
γέρας (*sc.* ἐσθλὸν ἔμμεναι). For the midway position of the φιλόσοφος, cp.
Phaedr. 278 D, *Lysis* 218 A; Plotin. *Enn.* VI. 7. 35 ff.

σοφοὶ γενέσθαι· αὐτὸ γάρ τοῦτό ἐστι χαλεπὸν ἀμαθία, τὸ μὴ ὄντα
καλὸν κἀγαθὸν μηδὲ φρόνιμον δοκεῖν αὑτῷ εἶναι ἱκανόν· οὔκουν
ἐπιθυμεῖ ὁ μὴ οἰόμενος ἐνδεὴς εἶναι οὗ ἂν μὴ οἴηται ἐπιδεῖσθαι.

Τίνες οὖν, ἔφην ἐγώ, ὦ Διοτίμα, οἱ φιλοσοφοῦντες, εἰ μήτε
B οἱ σοφοὶ μήτε οἱ ἀμαθεῖς; Δῆλον δή, ἔφη, τοῦτό γε ἤδη καὶ παιδί,
ὅτι οἱ μεταξὺ τούτων ἀμφοτέρων, ὧν αὖ καὶ ὁ Ἔρως. ἔστι γὰρ δὴ
τῶν καλλίστων ἡ σοφία, Ἔρως δ᾽ ἐστὶν ἔρως περὶ τὸ καλόν, ὥστε
ἀναγκαῖον Ἔρωτα φιλόσοφον εἶναι, φιλόσοφον δὲ ὄντα μεταξὺ
εἶναι σοφοῦ καὶ ἀμαθοῦς. αἰτία δ᾽ αὐτῷ καὶ τούτων ἡ γένεσις·
πατρὸς μὲν γὰρ σοφοῦ ἐστι καὶ εὐπόρου, μητρὸς δὲ οὐ σοφῆς καὶ
ἀπόρου. ἡ μὲν οὖν φύσις τοῦ δαίμονος, ὦ φίλε Σώκρατες, αὕτη·
C ὃν δὲ σὺ ᾠήθης Ἔρωτα εἶναι, θαυμαστὸν οὐδὲν ἔπαθες. ᾠήθης δέ,
ὡς ἐμοὶ δοκεῖ τεκμαιρομένῃ ἐξ ὧν σὺ λέγεις, τὸ ἐρώμενον Ἔρωτα
εἶναι, οὐ τὸ ἐρῶν. διὰ ταῦτά σοι, οἶμαι, πάγκαλος ἐφαίνετο ὁ Ἔρως.
καὶ γὰρ ἔστι τὸ ἐραστὸν τὸ τῷ ὄντι καλὸν καὶ ἁβρὸν καὶ τέλεον
καὶ μακαριστόν· τὸ δέ γε ἐρῶν ἄλλην ἰδέαν τοιαύτην ἔχον, οἵαν
ἐγὼ διῆλθον.

204 **A** σοφοὶ γενέσθαι: σοφοις γ. O.-P.   αὐτῷ γὰρ τούτῳ Vindob. 21,
Sydenham   χαλεπὸν del. Hommel Bdhm.: χαλεπη O.-P.   ἀμαθίας cj. Ast
αὐτῷ W b: αὐτῷ T: αυτω O.-P.: αὐτὸ B   ἱκανὸν del. Hirschig   **B** δῆλον
δή TW O.-P., vulg. Sz. Bt.: δηλονότι B: δῆλον Herm. J.-U.: δηλόν ἐστι Rettig
δηλον τοῦτό γ᾽, ἢ δ᾽ ἥ, καὶ Bdhm.   αὖ Ven. 184 Vind. 21, vulg. Bt.: ἂν εἴη
O.-P.: ἂν BTW: δὴ Usener Sz.: del. Rückert: fort. εἶς   μεταξυ O.-P.
C ωθης O.-P.   τεκμαιρομένη B¹   λέγεις: ελεγες O.-P.   ειναι Ερωτα O.-P.
οιομαι O.-P.   τὸ τῷ: τῷ Bdhm.   αβρον O.-P. corr.: αγαθον O.-P.¹
τελειον O.-P.

αὐτὸ γὰρ τοῦτό κτλ. "Precisely herein is ignorance a grievous thing, (viz.)
that" etc. If, with Stallb., we take αὐτὸ τοῦτο as adverbial accus. of respect,
with τὸ μὴ...ἱκανόν as an epexegetic supplement, no emendation is required.
For the neuter χαλεπὸν in appos. to ἀμαθία, cp. 176 D, Phileb. 12 C.

204 **B** Δῆλον δή...καὶ παιδί. Cp. Euthyd. 279 D τοῦτο δὲ κἂν παῖς γνοίη:
ib. 301 B, Lys. 205 C (Schanz nov. comm. p. 72). Observe how sharply Diotima
snubs Socrates, ὥσπερ οἱ τέλεοι σοφισταί (208 C). For my cj. ὧν εἶς, cp. 203 A.

φιλόσοφον εἶναι. Cp. Procl. in Tim. 52 δύο τούτους θεοὺς ὁ Πλάτων φιλοσόφους ἐκάλεσε, τόν τε Ἔρωτα καὶ τὴν Ἀθηνᾶν (Tim. 24 D),...ἣν γὰρ ὁ δημιουργὸς
"καὶ Μῆτις πρῶτος γενέτωρ καὶ Ἔρως πολυτερπής" (Orph. Theog. fr. 8. 11), καὶ
ὡς μὲν Μῆτις τίκτει τὴν Ἀθηνᾶν, ὡς δὲ Ἔρως ἀπογεννᾷ τὴν ἐρωτικὴν σειράν.

204 **C** ἁβρόν. Agathon had (earlier to) had used the subst. ἀβρότης
(197 D), besides the epithets ἁπαλός and ὑγρός (195 C ff.).

μακαριστόν. The only other Platonic exx. are Rep. 465 D, Phaedr. 256 C.
Cp. the use of μακαρίζω in 216 E infra.

XXIV. Καὶ ἐγὼ εἶπον, Εἶεν δή, ὦ ξένη· καλῶς γὰρ λέγεις· τοιοῦτος ὢν ὁ Ἔρως τίνα χρείαν ἔχει τοῖς ἀνθρώποις; Τοῦτο δὴ μετὰ ταῦτ᾽, ἔφη, ὦ Σώκρατες, πειράσομαί σε διδάξαι. ἔστι μὲν D γὰρ δὴ τοιοῦτος καὶ οὕτω γεγονὼς ὁ Ἔρως, ἔστι δὲ τῶν καλῶν, ὡς σὺ φῄς. εἰ δέ τις ἡμᾶς ἔροιτο· τί τῶν καλῶν ἐστιν ὁ Ἔρως, ὦ Σώκρατές τε καὶ Διοτίμα; ὧδε δὲ σαφέστερον ἐρῶ· ὁ ἐρῶν τῶν καλῶν τί ἐρᾷ; καὶ ἐγὼ εἶπον ὅτι Γενέσθαι αὑτῷ. Ἀλλ᾽ ἔτι ποθεῖ, ἔφη, ἡ ἀπόκρισις ἐρώτησιν τοιάνδε· τί ἔσται ἐκείνῳ ᾧ ἂν γένηται τὰ καλά; Οὐ πάνυ ἔφην ἔτι ἔχειν ἐγὼ πρὸς ταύτην τὴν ἐρώτησιν/ προχείρως ἀποκρίνασθαι. Ἀλλ᾽, ἔφη, ὥσπερ ἂν εἴ τις μεταβαλὼν E ἀντὶ τοῦ καλοῦ τῷ ἀγαθῷ χρώμενος πυνθάνοιτο· φέρε, ὦ Σώκρατες, ὅρα· ὁ ἐρῶν τῶν ἀγαθῶν τί ἐρᾷ; Γενέσθαι, ἦν δ᾽ ἐγώ, αὑτῷ. Καὶ τί

204 C ⟨δὲ⟩ ὢν cj. Steph.   δὴ ⟨τὰ⟩ μετὰ Bdhm.   D και ουτω superscr.
O.-P.   σὺ φῄς: σύμφῃς Jn.   τε Β O.-P.: om. TW   ἐρῶ Aldin., edd.:
ἐρῷ b: ἐρᾷ BTW: ερα O.-P.: fort. ὅρα (cf. E infra)   ἔτι ποθεῖ TW O.P.,
Bt.: ἐπιποθεῖ Β, Sz.: ἔτι ἐπιποθεῖ Rückert   τοιανδει O.-P.   E πυνθάνοιτο
secl. Usener   ὅρα scripsi: ἐρᾷ BTW O.-P.: ἐρῶ Aldin. vulg. Bt.: ἔροιτο
Herm. J.-U.: om. Ven. 184, Bast Sz.: εἴ γ᾽ ἐρᾷ Rohde   τῶν ἀγαθῶν· τί
distinxit Winckelmann : τῶν ἀγαθῶν τί; olim Voeg.   αὑτῷ ΒΤ

τίνα χρείαν κτλ.   Here begins the second section of Socrates-Diotima's exposition. For χρεία, "utility,"—equiv. here to the δόσεις of 195 A, the ἔργα of 199 C—cp. *Gorg.* 480 A, etc.

Τοῦτο δὴ μετὰ ταῦτ᾽ κτλ.   "Ebenso 180 D, 186 A, 189 D, 194 E. Also wohl parodisch und spöttisch" (Rettig).

204 D ἔστι δὲ τῶν καλῶν.   This is object. genitive: cp. 201 E, 206 E. As Rettig notes, Diotima herself affects περὶ τὸ καλόν in preference to τοῦ καλοῦ (after ἔρως, etc.); and this may be used as an argument against Jahn-Usener's σύμφῃς.

εἰ δέ τις κτλ.   For the omission of the apodosis, cp. 199 E εἰ γὰρ ἐροίμην κτλ.

σαφέστερον ἐρῶ.   The preceding query had been ambiguously worded, since τῶν καλῶν might be taken either as a partitive gen. dependent on τί, or as an object. gen. with Ἔρως (τί being adverbial accus.): that the latter was the construction intended is now shown by the revised statement of the query—ὁ ἐρῶν...τί ἐρᾷ; I am inclined to suspect that we should read ὅρα (see 204 E *n.*) for ἐρῶ (ἐρᾷ MSS.).

ἔτι ποθεῖ.   If we read ἐπιποθεῖ we must ascribe to the proposition its full force, "craves further"; the other exx. of the cpd. in Plato are *Prot.* 329 D τοῦτ᾽ ἐστὶν ὃ ἔτι ἐπιποθῶ: *Laws* 855 E. The former of these supports Rückert's ἔτι ἐπιποθεῖ.

Οὐ πάνυ...ἔτι.   For οὐ πάνυ, cp. *Meno* 71 C (with Thompson's *note*).

204 E μεταβαλών.   Here the participle "adverbii partes agit," cp. *Gorg.* 480 E, *Phileb.* 51 A. For the ellipse, cp. 204 D, 199 E.

φέρε, ὦ Σ., ὅρα.   Most editors bracket the MSS.' ἐρᾷ: Stallb., after

ἔσται ἐκείνῳ ᾧ ἂν γένηται τἀγαθά; Τοῦτ᾽ εὐπορώτερον, ἦν δ᾽ ἐγώ,
205 ἔχω ἀποκρίνασθαι, ὅτι εὐδαίμων ἔσται. Κτήσει γάρ, ἔφη, ἀγαθῶν
οἱ εὐδαίμονες εὐδαίμονες, καὶ οὐκέτι προσδεῖ ἐρέσθαι, ἵνα τί δὲ
βούλεται εὐδαίμων εἶναι ὁ βουλόμενος, ἀλλὰ τέλος δοκεῖ ἔχειν
ἡ ἀπόκρισις. Ἀληθῆ λέγεις, εἶπον ἐγώ. Ταύτην δὲ τὴν βούλησιν
καὶ τὸν ἔρωτα τοῦτον πότερα κοινὸν οἴει εἶναι πάντων ἀνθρώπων, καὶ πάντας τἀγαθὰ βούλεσθαι αὑτοῖς εἶναι ἀεί, ἢ πῶς
λέγεις; Οὕτως, ἦν δ᾽ ἐγώ· κοινὸν εἶναι πάντων. Τί δὴ οὖν,
B ἔφη, ὦ Σώκρατες, οὐ πάντας ἐρᾶν φαμέν, εἴπερ γε πάντες τῶν
αὐτῶν ἐρῶσι καὶ ἀεί, ἀλλὰ τινὰς φαμεν ἐρᾶν, τοὺς δ᾽ οὔ; Θαυμάζω,
ἦν δ᾽ ἐγώ, καὶ αὐτός. Ἀλλὰ μὴ θαύμαζ᾽, ἔφη· ἀφελόντες γὰρ ἄρα
τοῦ ἔρωτός τι εἶδος ὀνομάζομεν, τὸ τοῦ ὅλου ἐπιτιθέντες ὄνομα,
ἔρωτα, τὰ δὲ ἄλλα ἄλλοις καταχρώμεθα ὀνόμασιν. Ὥσπερ τί; ἦν
δ᾽ ἐγώ. Ὥσπερ τόδε. οἶσθ᾽ ὅτι ποίησίς ἐστί τι πολύ· ἡ γάρ τοι ἐκ

205 A ἀγάθων B   δὲ τὴν B O.-P., J.-U. Sz.: δὴ τὴν TW, Bt.   εἶναι
οἴει W   B αὐτῶν: ἀγαθῶν cj. Naber   γὰρ ἄρα T O.-P., Bt.: γὰρ BW, J.-U.
ἐρῶντος T   ⟨ἔν⟩ τι εἶδος Hirschig   τοι Vind. 21, vulg. Sz. Bt.: τι BTW :
τω O.-P., ᾧ O.-P. mg.

Winckelmann, retains it with the punctuation ἐρᾷ ὁ ἐρῶν τῶν ἀγαθῶν· τί
ἐρᾷ;—a mode of expression which is "vehementius quam ut aptum videri
possit huic loco" (Rettig). Rückert defends the Aldine reading ἐρῶ as a
permissible superfluity "in familiari sermone." I suspect that here, as above,
we should read ὅρα: cp. ὅρα τί ποιεῖς 189 A; *Rep.* 596 c; *Crat.* 385 D φέρε...εἰπέ.

205 A **ἵνα τί.** Sc. γένηται: for this colloquial use see Goodwin *G. M. T.*
§ 331.

τέλος...ἔχειν. Because it is recognized that εὐδαιμονία constitutes in itself
the ethical τέλος or "summum bonum": cp. *Clit.* 410 E ἐμπόδιον τοῦ πρὸς
τέλος ἀρετῆς ἐλθόντα εὐδαίμονα γενέσθαι: Arist. *E. N.* I. 7. 1097ᵃ 33 ἁπλῶς δὴ
τέλειον τὸ καθ᾽ αὑτὸ αἱρετὸν ἀεί...τοιοῦτον δ᾽ ἡ εὐδαιμονία μάλιστ᾽ εἶναι δοκεῖ. Cp.
also 210 E πρὸς τέλος ἤδη ἰὼν κτλ.

πάντας...ἀεί. Here ἀεί goes with βούλεσθαι, not with αὑτοῖς εἶναι (as in
206 A *infra*).

Τί δὴ οὖν κτλ. Diotima here points out an apparent contradiction between
the previous conclusion (κοινὸν πάντων) and common opinion, due to the
ambiguity of the term ἔρως (ἐρᾶν) which is used both in a generic and in a
specific sense.

205 B **Ὥσπερ τί;** "For example—?"

ποίησις. The selection of this term as an ex. of varying connotation is
partly, no doubt, due to the fact that it was one of the matters specially
emphasized by Agathon, 197 A. For πολύ, *multiplex*, cp. *Polit.* 282 A.

ἡ γάρ τοι κτλ. For the definition, cp. *Soph.* 219 B, 265 B ποιητικήν...πᾶσαν
ἔφαμεν εἶναι δύναμιν, ᾗ τις ἂν αἰτία γίγνηται τοῖς μὴ πρότερον οὖσιν ὕστερον
γίγνεσθαι: also *Phileb.* 26 D; Xen. *Mem.* II. 2. 3; Procl. *inst. theol.* p. 74.

τοῦ μὴ ὄντος εἰς τὸ ὂν ἰόντι ὁτῳοῦν αἰτία πᾶσά ἐστι ποίησις, ὥστε
καὶ αἱ ὑπὸ πάσαις ταῖς τέχναις ἐργασίαι ποιήσεις εἰσὶ καὶ οἱ C
τούτων δημιουργοὶ πάντες ποιηταί. Ἀληθῆ λέγεις. Ἀλλ' ὅμως,
ἦ δ' ἥ, οἶσθ' ὅτι οὐ καλοῦνται ποιηταὶ ἀλλ' ἄλλα ἔχουσιν ὀνόματα,
ἀπὸ δὲ πάσης τῆς ποιήσεως ἐν μόριον ἀφορισθὲν τὸ περὶ τὴν μου-
σικὴν καὶ τὰ μέτρα τῷ τοῦ ὅλου ὀνόματι προσαγορεύεται. ποίησις
γὰρ τοῦτο μόνον καλεῖται, καὶ οἱ ἔχοντες τοῦτο τὸ μόριον τῆς
ποιήσεως ποιηταί. Ἀληθῆ λέγεις, ἔφην. Οὕτω τοίνυν καὶ περὶ
τὸν ἔρωτα· τὸ μὲν κεφάλαιόν ἐστι πᾶσα ἡ τῶν ἀγαθῶν ἐπιθυμία D

205 C ἦ δ' ἥ Bekker: η δ η O.-P.: ἤδη BTW   οὐ om. W   ἔχουσιν
TW O.-P., Sz.: ἔξουσιν B, Bt.: ἴσχουσιν Sauppe   μόριον BT O.-P.: μόνον
pr. W   γὰρ τοῦτο: γ. ταυτα O.-P.   εφη[ν] λεγεις O.-P.   D πᾶσα...ευδαι-
μονεῖν del. Bdhm.

205 C αἱ...ἐργασίαι. Cp. *Gorg.* 450 c τῶν μὲν (τεχνῶν) ἐργασία τὸ πολύ ἐστι.
The word denotes manufacturing processes: cp. *n.* on περὶ τέχνας κτλ., 203 A.
For ὑπὸ *c. dat.*, a construction rare in Attic prose, cp. *Phileb.* 58 A: *Hipp.*
Maj. 295 D τά τε ὑπὸ τῇ μουσικῇ καὶ τὰ ὑπὸ ταῖς ἄλλαις τέχναις (ὄργανα): *Rep.*
511 A. Cp. Aristotle's use of ὑπὸ *c. acc.* to denote the subordination of arts,
E. N. I. 1. 1094ᵃ 10 ff. ὅσαι δ' εἰσὶ τῶν τοιούτων ὑπὸ μίαν τινὰ δύναμιν κτλ.

ἐν μόριον. Equivalent to ἐν εἶδος (205 B): for this logical use of the term
cp. *Gorg.* 464 B, *Laws* 696 B. For ἀφορίζω, cp. *Soph.* 257 c, 268 D τῆς ποιήσεως
ἀφωρισμένον ἐν λόγοις...μόριον.

τὸ περὶ...τὰ μέτρα. Cp. 187 D, 196 E.

205 D τὸ μὲν κεφάλαιόν κτλ. Opinions are divided as to the construction
of τὸ κεφάλαιον: it may be construed (1) as nominative and subject, "the
generic concept (*sc.* τοῦ ἔρωτος) is—"; so Hommel, Vermehren, Hug, Prantl,
comparing *Gorg.* 463 A καλῶ δὲ αὐτοῦ (*sc.* τῆς ῥητορικῆς) τὸ κεφάλαιον κολακείαν:
or (2) as adverbial accus. (of respect), "in its generic aspect," cp. *Phileb.* 48 c
ἔστι δὴ πονηρία μέν τις τὸ κεφάλαιον: *Euthyphr.* 8 E. The latter is certainly
the more natural mode of construing here, since no genitive (αὐτοῦ) is added.
But other difficulties remain: what is the subject of ἐστι, if τὸ κεφάλαιον is
adverbial? Should we (*a*) construe with Ficinus (followed by Stallb.[2], Lehrs,
Zeller, Jowett and others) "nam summatim quidem omnis bonorum felicita-
tisque appetitio maximus et insidiator amor est cuique"? Or (*b*) should we
rather, with Stallb.[1] and Prantl, supply ὁ ἔρως as the subject of ἐστι and
construe πᾶσα ἡ...εὐδαιμονεῖν as the predicate? To my mind the latter is
the more natural method. Next arises the question, how are we to deal
with the last part of the sentence, ὁ μέγιστός...παντί? If with most edd.
(except Rückert, Stallb.[2] and Rettig) we regard δολερὸς as corrupt, the best
plan is to excise the whole clause with Hug (and Stallb.[1]), since none of the
corrections of δολερὸς hitherto proposed (see *crit. n.*) are at all convincing.
The chief objection to δολερὸς is, not so much the meaning of the word
itself (which may be defended by 203 D), as rather (to quote Stallb.[2]) "conjunctio superlativi μέγιστος cum δολερός positivo." But even this objection

καὶ τοῦ εὐδαιμονεῖν, ὁ "μέγιστός τε καὶ δολερὸς" ἔρως παντί· ἀλλ'
οἱ μὲν ἄλλῃ τρεπόμενοι πολλαχῇ ἐπ' αὐτόν, ἢ κατὰ χρηματισμὸν
ἢ κατὰ φιλογυμναστίαν ἢ κατὰ φιλοσοφίαν, οὔτ' ἐρᾶν καλοῦνται
οὔτ' ἐρασταί, οἱ δὲ κατὰ ἕν τι εἶδος ἰόντες τε καὶ ἐσπουδακότες τὸ
τοῦ ὅλου ὄνομα ἴσχουσιν, ἔρωτά τε καὶ ἐρᾶν καὶ ἐρασταί. Κινδυνεύεις ἀληθῆ, ἔφην ἐγώ, λέγειν. Καὶ λέγεται μέν γέ τις, ἔφη,
E λόγος, ὡς οἳ ἂν τὸ ἥμισυ ἑαυτῶν ζητῶσιν, οὗτοι ἐρῶσιν· ὁ δ' ἐμὸς
λόγος οὔθ' ἡμίσεός φησιν εἶναι τὸν ἔρωτα οὔθ' ὅλου, ἐὰν μὴ
τυγχάνῃ γέ που, ὦ ἑταῖρε, ἀγαθὸν ὄν· ἐπεὶ αὑτῶν γε καὶ πόδας
καὶ χεῖρας ἐθέλουσιν ἀποτέμνεσθαι οἱ ἄνθρωποι, ἐὰν αὐτοῖς δοκῇ

205 D ὁ...δολερὸς secl. Usener: ὁ...παντί secl. Stallb. (1827) Hug μέγιστός: ὁρμητικός Creuzer δολερὸς: δολερώτατος Stallb. (1852): δεινότατος
Ast: κοινὸς Hommel: ὁλόκληρος Pflugk Mdvg.: ὅλος Bdhm.: ἀθρόος Verm.:
πρῶτος cj. Sz.: τολμηρὸς Creuzer: σφοδρότατος Sydenham: σφοδρὸς Cobet:
μόνος Schirlitz: κερδαλέος Naber πάντῃ Pflugk αὐτόν: αὐτό Voeg. Sz.:
ἀγαθόν Orelli χρηματισμῳ O.-P.¹ εσχον O.-P. ἔρωτά...ἐρασταί secl. Sz.
ἔρως τε Hertlein ἐρασταί: fort. ἐρασταίς κινδυνευουσι O.-P.¹ E τὸ
ἑαυτῶν ἥμισυ Sz.: τὸ ἥμισυ τὸ ἑαυτῶν Sauppe Jn.: ἑαυτῶν secl. Usener ἐπεὶ
T O.-P.: ἐπὶ B

---

is not, I think, insuperable; for if we construe παντί closely with δολερὸς as
"all-ensnaring," we get a superlative idea which balances μέγιστος, while in
sense it is supported by 203 B, D and Sappho's δολοπλόκε Ἀφροδίτα. If,
adopting this explanation, we retain the traditional text, it seems best to
regard the clause ὁ μέγιστός...παντί as an appositional quotation and to
construe, with Prantl, "nämlich jene grösste und für jeden verfängliche
Liebe." Hommel is singular in taking τοῦ εὐδαιμονεῖν (sc. ἡ ἐπιθυμία), as well
as τὸ κεφάλαιον, as subject ("und das Streben nach dem höchsten Gute, d. i.
nach Glückseligkeit, ist die grösste Liebe").

ἔρωτα...ἐρασταί. This sequence is irregular. Usually with ὄνομα ἔχειν the
name is in the nominative, in apposition with the subject, e.g. Laws 956 c
διαιτηταὶ ὄνομα...ἔχοντες (so here ἐρασταί): but the accus. is also possible (in
appos. with ὄνομα), as in Plut. Arist. 2. But the combination of the two
constructions is certainly awkward, and the words may well be, as Schanz
supposes, a gloss.

Καὶ λέγεται κτλ. An allusion to Aristophanes' speech, esp. 192 B, E ff.:
cp. 212 c. For οὔθ' ὅλου, below, cp. 192 E.

205 E ἐπεὶ αὐτῶν γε κτλ. Cp. Xen. Mem. I. 2. 54 ἔλεγε δ' ὅτι καὶ ζῶν ἕκαστος
ἑαυτοῦ, ὃ πάντων μάλιστα φιλεῖ, τοῦ σώματος ὅ τι ἂν ἀχρεῖον ᾖ καὶ ἀνωφελὲς
αὐτός τε ἀφαιρεῖ καὶ ἄλλῳ παρέχει. αὐτοί τέ γε αὑτῶν ὄνυχάς τε καὶ τρίχας καὶ
τύλους ἀφαιροῦσι κτλ.: Ev. Matth. 5. 30 καὶ εἰ ἡ δεξιά σου χεὶρ σκανδαλίζει σε,
ἔκκοψον αὐτήν κτλ.

τὰ ἑαυτῶν πονηρὰ εἶναι. οὐ γὰρ τὸ ἑαυτῶν, οἶμαι, ἕκαστοι ἀσπά- ζονται, εἰ μὴ εἴ τις τὸ μὲν ἀγαθὸν οἰκεῖον καλεῖ καὶ ἑαυτοῦ, τὸ δὲ κακὸν ἀλλότριον· ὡς οὐδέν γε ἄλλο ἐστὶν οὗ ἐρῶσιν ἄνθρωποι 206 ἢ τοῦ ἀγαθοῦ. ἢ σοὶ δοκοῦσιν; Μὰ Δί' οὐκ ἔμοιγε, ἦν δ' ἐγώ. Ἆρ' οὖν, ἦ δ' ἥ, οὕτως ἁπλοῦν ἐστι λέγειν, ὅτι οἱ ἄνθρωποι τοῦ ἀγαθοῦ ἐρῶσιν; Ναί, ἔφην. Τί δέ; οὐ προσθετέον, ἔφη, ὅτι καὶ εἶναι τὸ ἀγαθὸν αὑτοῖς ἐρῶσιν; Προσθετέον. Ἆρ' οὖν, ἔφη, καὶ οὐ μόνον εἶναι, ἀλλὰ καὶ ἀεὶ εἶναι; Καὶ τοῦτο προσθετέον. Ἔστιν ἄρα ξυλλήβδην, ἔφη, ὁ ἔρως τοῦ τὸ ἀγαθὸν αὑτῷ εἶναι ἀεί. Ἀλη- θέστατα, ἔφην ἐγώ, λέγεις.

XXV. Ὅτε δὴ τούτου ὁ ἔρως ἐστὶν ἀεί, ἦ δ' ἥ, τῶν τίνα B τρόπον διωκόντων αὐτὸ καὶ ἐν τίνι πράξει ἡ σπουδὴ καὶ ἡ σύντασις ἔρως ἂν καλοῖτο; τί τοῦτο τυγχάνει ὂν τὸ ἔργον; ἔχεις εἰπεῖν; Οὐ

205 E καλεῖ W : καλῇ BT   206 A ἄνθρωποι Bekk. Sz. Bt.: ἄνθρωποι BT: ανθρωποι O.-P.: οἱ ἄνθρωποι W : del. Baiter   ἢ τἀγαθόν Hirschig ἢ σοὶ...ἀγαθοῦ om. O.-P.¹   ἢ δ' ἥ Bekker: η[δ]η O.-P. corr.: ἤδη BT ὅτι ἄνθρωποι Sauppe Jn.   τοῦ ἀγαθοῦ BW O.-P. corr.: τἀγαθοῦ T, Bt.   προσθε- ταιον O.-P.¹ (bis)   οὖν BT O.-P.: om. W   τοῦ τὸ T O.-P.: τοῦτο B αὑτῷ TW O.-P.: αὐτὸ B   B δὴ: δε O.-P. Paris 1642   τούτου Bast Sz. Bt.: τοῦτο libri, O.-P.   ἀεί om. Vat., Bekk. Sz.: ἄγε Usener   ἦ δ' ἥ Bekk.: ἤδη BT: η δ η O.-P.   τῶν T b O.-P.: τὸν B   αὐτὸν T σύντασις B O.-P.: σύστασις TW

εἰ μὴ εἴ. See Goodwin G. M. T. § 476⁴.
τὸ μὲν ἀγαθὸν οἰκεῖον. Cp. Rep. 586 E εἴπερ τὸ βέλτιστον ἑκάστῳ, τοῦτο καὶ οἰκειότατον (with Adam's note): Charm. 163 C, D ἐμάνθανον τὸν λόγον, ὅτι τὰ οἰκεῖά τε καὶ τὰ αὑτοῦ ἀγαθὰ καλοίης: Arist. E. N. x. 7.
206 A ἢ τοῦ ἀγαθοῦ. For the assumption that τἀγαθὸν is the final end of desire, cp. Phileb. 20 B ff., Gorg. 467 D ff., etc. The statement here is referred to by Proclus in Alcib. I. p. 129.
ἁπλοῦν. Equivalent to ἄνευ προσθέσεως ἀληθές: cp. 183 D; Phaedr. 244 A εἰ μὲν γὰρ ἦν ἁπλοῦν τὸ μανίαν κακὸν εἶναι κτλ. ("true without qualification," Thompson); Prot. 331 C.
206 B ὁ ἔρως ἐστὶν ἀεί. Most edd. follow Bekker in ejecting ἀεί: Rettig, however, rightly keeps it with the note "ἀεί=die gegebene Definition gilt überall und für alle Fälle"; cp. 205 A, B.
αὐτὸ. Sc. τὸ τἀγαθὸν αὑτοῖς εἶναι ἀεί.
ἡ σύντασις. Cp. 203 D (Ἔρως ἐστι) σύντονος: Phileb. 46 D σύντασιν ἀγρίαν ποιεῖ (with my note): Euthyd. 288 D. For the limitation of the notion of Eros here (ἂν καλοῖτο), cp. that in 205 A ff. (καλοῦνται, C, D).
τυγχάνει ὄν. Not "what does it happen to be," but "what in reality is it": see Verrall on Eur. Med. 608: cp. Phaedo 65 D—E.
Οὐ μεντᾶν κτλ. For the suppressed protasis (sc. εἰ τοῦτο εἶχον εἰπεῖν), cp. 175 D.

μεντἃν σέ, ἔφην ἐγώ, ὧ Διοτίμα, ἐθαύμαζον ἐπὶ σοφία καὶ ἐφοίτων
παρὰ σὲ αὐτὰ ταῦτα μαθησόμενος. 'Αλλ' ἐγώ σοι, ἔφη, ἐρῶ. ἔστι
γὰρ τοῦτο τόκος ἐν καλῷ καὶ κατὰ τὸ σῶμα καὶ κατὰ τὴν ψυχήν.
Μαντείας, ἦν δ' ἐγώ, δεῖται ὅ τί ποτε λέγεις, καὶ οὐ μανθάνω.
C 'Αλλ' ἐγώ, ἦ δ' ἥ, σαφέστερον ἐρῶ. κυοῦσι γάρ, ἔφη, ὧ Σώκρατες,
πάντες ἄνθρωποι καὶ κατὰ τὸ σῶμα καὶ κατὰ τὴν ψυχήν, καὶ
ἐπειδὰν ἐν τῇ ἡλικίᾳ γένωνται, τίκτειν ἐπιθυμεῖ ἡμῶν ἡ φύσις.
τίκτειν δὲ ἐν μὲν αἰσχρῷ οὐ δύναται, ἐν δὲ [τῷ] καλῷ. [ἡ γὰρ

206 B ἔφην, ἐγὼ distinxit Ast   καὶ οὐ μανθάνω del. Naber   C ἦ δ' ἥ
Bekk.: ἤδη ΒΤ : δη Ο.-Ρ.   ἄνθρωποι Sauppe Jn.   καὶ κατὰ τὸ TW O.-P.,
Bt.: κατὰ τὸ B   τὴν om. T   ἐν τῇ Bdhm. J.-U. Sz. : ἔν τινι libri, Bt. :
ἐν Naber   τίκτειν δὲ...ἐστίν del. Rettig   καλῷ Bdhm. : καλω Ο.-Ρ. : τῷ
καλῷ libri   ἡ γὰρ...ἐστίν del. Ast Sz. Bt.

ἐφοίτων παρὰ σὲ. φοιτᾶν is the regular word for "attending" lectures or
a school, see *Prot.* 326 C εἰς διδασκάλων...φοιτᾶν : *Rep.* 328 D δεῦρο παρ' ἡμᾶς
φοίτα : *Phaedo* 59 B.

τόκος ἐν καλῷ. The act of procreation appears to be called almost in-
differently (1) τόκος, as here, (2) γέννησις (206 C, E, 209 D), (3) γέννησις καὶ
τόκος (206 E), (4) in passive aspect γένεσις (206 D, 207 D). Similarly with the
verbs: we find τίκτειν (206 C, 210 C, etc.), γεννᾶν (206 D, 207 A, etc.), τίκτειν καὶ
γεννᾶν (206 D, 209 B, C).

Μαντείας...μανθάνω. Notice the play on the stem-sound. Rettig, citing
Eur. *Hippol.* 237 (τάδε μαντείας ἄξια πολλῆς), writes " Witzspiel mit Anklang
an Eur. und Anspielung auf Diotima's Heimath und Beruf" : the latter
allusion is likely enough, but the "Anklang an Eur." is very problematical;
had it been specially intended we should have had ἄξια or πολλῆς echoed
as well.

206 C κυοῦσι. κύησις, "pregnancy," is properly the condition intermediate
between conception (σύλληψις) and delivery (τόκος). Cp. Achill. Tat. I. 10
καὶ νεανίσκος ἔρωτος πρωτοκύμων οὐ δεῖται διδασκαλίας πρὸς τὸν τοκετόν. For
the language and thought of this whole passage, cp. *Theaet.* 150 ff., *Phaedr.*
251 A ff., *Tim.* 91 A : also Max. Tyr. *diss.* XVI. 4, p. 179 κυοῦσι δὲ πᾶσαι μὲν
ψυχαὶ φύσει, ὠδίνουσι δὲ ἔθει, τίκτουσι δὲ λόγῳ κτλ. : Clem. Al. *Strom.* V. 552 B :
Themist. *or.* XXXII. p. 355 D.

ἐν τῇ ἡλικίᾳ γ. I adopt Badham's correction τηι for τινι since the change
involved is very slight and ἔν τινι ἡλικίᾳ is unexampled in Plato: cp. *Gorg.*
484 C ἐν τῇ ἡλικίᾳ : *Rep.* 461 B ; *Phaedr.* 209 B *infra* ; 255 A ; *Meno* 89 B.
Plato also uses ἐν ἡλικίᾳ, e.g. *Rep.* 461 B : *Charm.* 154 A : *Laws* 924 E.

τίκτειν δὲ...καλῷ. There is much to be said for Rettig's view that this
sentence (as well as the next) is a gloss. As he argues, the words " gehören
also ihrem Inhalte nach nicht an die Stelle, an welcher sie stehen, sondern sie
müssten nach dem Satze ἔστι δὲ τοῦτο κτλ. folgen. An dieser Stelle collidiren
sie aber mit den gleichbedeutenden Worten τὰ δὲ ἐν τῷ ἀναρμόστῳ...ἁρμόττον,

ἀνδρὸς καὶ γυναικὸς συνουσία τόκος ἐστίν.] ἔστι δὲ τοῦτο θεῖον τὸ πρᾶγμα, καὶ τοῦτο ἐν θνητῷ ὄντι τῷ ζώῳ ἀθάνατον ἔνεστιν, ἡ κύησις καὶ ἡ γέννησις. τὰ δ᾽ ἐν τῷ ἀναρμόστῳ ἀδύνατον γενέσθαι. ἀνάρμοστον δ᾽ ἐστὶ τὸ αἰσχρὸν παντὶ τῷ θείῳ, τὸ δὲ καλὸν ἁρμόττον. D Μοῖρα οὖν καὶ Εἰλείθυια ἡ Καλλονή ἐστι τῇ γενέσει. διὰ ταῦτα

206 C δὲ: γὰρ Rohde   ἔνεστιν B O.-P.: ἐστιν TW   τὰ B O.-P.: ταῦτα TW   D θείῳ TW: θεῷ B O.-P.   τῇ γενέσει διὰ ταῦτα· ὅταν κτλ. distinxit Schirlitz

für deren Glosse ich sie ansehe. Worauf sollten auch die Worte ἔστι δὲ... πρᾶγμα gehen, wenn ihnen die Worte τίκτειν δὲ...καλῷ unmittelbar vorangingen?" It is just possible, however, to retain the clause as a kind of parenthetic addendum to the preceding sentence, which forestalls, somewhat confusingly, the sentences τὰ δ᾽...ἁρμόττον. The omission of the article before καλῷ, confirmed by the Papyrus, is certainly an improvement. For the thought, cp. Plotin. Enn. III. v. p. 157 B.

[ἡ γὰρ...τόκος ἐστίν.] Most edd. (except Hommel and Stallb.) agree in excising this clause as a meaningless intrusion. Hommel and Stallb. explain the words as intended to introduce the first part of the exposition of τόκος, viz. τόκος κατὰ σῶμα: and Stallb. renders "nam (γάρ=nemlich) viri et mulieris coitus, est ille nihil aliud nisi τόκος." Susemihl's comment is "die Zeugung werde als die wahrhafte Aufhebung der Geschlechtsdifferenz bezeichnet." But, as Rettig shows, none of these attempts to justify the clause are satisfactory. Perhaps it is a gloss on ἡλικία.

ἔστι δὲ τοῦτο κτλ. Cp. Laws 773 E, 721 C γαμεῖν δὲ...διανοηθέντα ὡς ἔστιν ᾗ τὸ ἀνθρώπινον γένος φύσει τινὶ μετείληφεν ἀθανασίας· οὗ καὶ πέφυκεν ἐπιθυμίαν ἴσχειν πᾶς πᾶσαν κτλ.: Cicero Tusc. I. 35 quid procreatio liberorum, quid propagatio nominis...significant, nisi nos futura etiam cogitare?: Clem. Al. Strom. II. p. 421 C ἐπισκευάσας τὴν ἀθανασίαν τοῦ γένους ἡμῶν (sc. διὰ τοῦ γάμου), καὶ οἰονεὶ διαμονήν τινα παισὶ παίδων μεταλαμπαδευομένην.

ἐν τῷ ἀναρμόστῳ. For the connexion of Eros with ἁρμονία, see 187 A ff.; for harmony of the body, cp. Rep. 591 D; and of the soul, Rep. 430 E ff., Phaedo 85 E ff.

206 D Μοῖρα...Εἰλείθυια. Cp. Pind. Ol. VI. 41 τᾷ μὲν ὁ Χρυσοκόμας πραΰμητίν τ᾽ Ἐλείθυιαν παρέστασέν τε Μοίρας: id. Nem. VII. 1 Ἐλείθυια πάρεδρε Μοιρᾶν βαθυφρόνων. Μοῖρα ("the Dispenser") is a birth-goddess also in Hom. Il. XXIV. 209 τῷδ᾽ ὥς ποθι Μοῖρα κραταιή | γιγνομένῳ ἐπένησε λίνῳ. For Eileithyia, see also Il. XII. 270, Hes. Theog. 922; and it is noteworthy that Olen made out Eros to be the son of Eileithyia (see Paus. IX. 27). Libanius (or. V. t. I. p. 231 R.) identifies Eil. with Artemis.

ἡ Καλλονή. Usener was no doubt right in taking καλλονή here as a proper name, in spite of Rettig's objection that "deren Existenz nachzuweisen ihm aber nicht gelungen ist"; for such a personification, in this context, requires no precedent. "Beauty acts the part of our Lady of Travail at the birth." Possibly we ought to insert ἐπὶ after ἐστί(ν) or read ἔτι in place of ἐστι.

ὅταν μὲν καλῷ προσπελάζῃ τὸ κυοῦν, ἵλεών τε γίγνεται καὶ εὐφραινόμενον διαχεῖται καὶ τίκτει τε καὶ γεννᾷ· ὅταν δὲ αἰσχρῷ, σκυθρωπόν τε καὶ λυπούμενον συσπειρᾶται καὶ ἀποτρέπεται καὶ ἀνείλλεται καὶ οὐ γεννᾷ, ἀλλὰ ἴσχον τὸ κύημα χαλεπῶς φέρει. ὅθεν δὴ τῷ κυοῦντί τε καὶ ἤδη σπαργῶντι πολλὴ ἡ πτοίησις γέγονε

206 D   σκυθρωπόν τε ⟨γίγνεται⟩ cj. Usener   συσπειρᾶται TW: ξυ[ν]σπειραται O.-P.: συνσπείρεται B   καὶ ἀποτρέπεται secl. Usener Sz.   ἀνίλλεται O.-P.: ἀνειλλεται B: ἀνείλλεται W: ἀνείλλειται T   σπαργοῦντι W   πτοίησις TW O.-P., Abresch: ποίησις B: πτόησις Bekk. Sz.: πόνησις Sydenham

---

προσπελάζῃ. For this poetical word, cp. Hom. *Od.* IX. 285, and (of sexual converse) Soph. *O. T.* 1101 Πανὸς προσπελασθεῖσα.
ἵλεών. Cp. 197 D.
διαχεῖται. This word may signify both physical and emotional effects: for the former cp. *Laws* 775 C τῶν σωμάτων διακεχυμένων ὑπὸ μέθης: for the latter, Suidas (Hesych.) διαχεῖται· χαίρει, διαχέεται, and the Psalmist's "I am poured out like water."
συσπειρᾶται κτλ. Schol. συσπειρᾶται· συστρέφεται. Suid. κυρίως δὲ ἀνίλλεσθαι τὸ ἀπαξιοῦν. They are realistic terms to express aversion, derived perhaps from the action of a snail in drawing in its horns and rolling itself into a ball. Cp. Plotin. *Enn.* I. VI. 2. 51 ἡ ψυχὴ...πρὸς τὸ αἰσχρὸν προσβαλοῦσα ἀνίλλεται καὶ ἀρνεῖται καὶ ἀνανεύει ἐπ' αὐτοῦ οὐ συμφωνοῦσα καὶ ἀλλοτριουμένη. Usener and Hug may be right in bracketing καὶ ἀποτρέπεται, on which Hug comments "Zwischen dem der Gleichnissprache angehörenden συσπειρᾶται und ἀνίλλεται ist das matte, prosaische ἀποτρέπεται unpassend"; but the extra word helps to add emphasis, if nothing more, and Plotinus too uses three verbs. In ἀνείλλεται Rettig sees an "Anspielung auf ἀνειλείθυια" (cp. Eur. *Ion* 453). Cp. Plut. *de s. n. v.* p. 562 A.
σπαργῶντι. For σπαργᾶν, *lacte turgere*, cp. *Rep.* 460 C: in *Phaedr.* 256 A (σπαργῶν δὲ καὶ ἀπορῶν περιβάλλει τὸν ἐραστὴν καὶ φιλεῖ) σπαργῶν = *Venere tumens*. The Scholiast here has σπαργῶντι· ὁρμῶντι, ὀργῶντι, ταραττομένῳ, ἢ ἀνθοῦντι. λαμβάνεται δὲ καὶ ἐπὶ τῶν μαστῶν πεπληρωμένων γάλακτος. Here the realism of the language and the juxtaposition of κυοῦντι compels us to construe "great with child" (as L. and S.) or "with swelling bosom"—not merely "bursting with desire" or excitement. Cp. σφριγῶ as used in Ar. *Lysistr.* 80.
ἡ πτοίησις. "Sic feliciter emendavit Abresch"—his conj. turning out to have some MS. support. The subst. occurs also in *Prot.* 310 D γιγνώσκων αὐτοῦ τὴν ἀνδρείαν καὶ τὴν πτοίησιν: *Crat.* 404 A τὴν τοῦ σώματος πτοίησιν καὶ μανίαν: and the verb (ἐπτοῆσθαι) in *Rep.* 439 D, *Phaedo* 68 C, 108 A. Cp. Mimnermus 5. 2 πτοιῶμαι δ' ἐσορῶν ἄνθος ὁμηλικίης. It seems a *vox propria* for the condition of the lover "sighing like a furnace": cp. Plotin. *de pulcr.* p. 26 (with Creuzer's *note*).

περὶ τὸ καλὸν διὰ τὸ μεγάλης ὠδῖνος ἀπολύειν τὸν ἔχοντα. ἔστι Ε
γάρ, ὦ Σώκρατες, ἔφη, οὐ τοῦ καλοῦ ὁ ἔρως, ὡς σὺ οἴει. Ἀλλὰ τί
μήν; Τῆς γεννήσεως καὶ τοῦ τόκου ἐν τῷ καλῷ. Εἶεν; ἦν δ' ἐγώ.
Πάνυ μὲν οὖν, ἔφη. τί δὴ οὖν τῆς γεννήσεως; ὅτι ἀειγενές ἐστι
καὶ ἀθάνατον ὡς θνητῷ ἡ γέννησις. ἀθανασίας δὲ ἀναγκαῖον ἐπι- 207
θυμεῖν μετὰ ἀγαθοῦ ἐκ τῶν ὡμολογημένων, εἴπερ τοῦ ἀγαθὸν
ἑαυτῷ εἶναι ἀεὶ ἔρως ἐστίν. ἀναγκαῖον δὴ ἐκ τούτου τοῦ λόγου
καὶ τῆς ἀθανασίας τὸν ἔρωτα εἶναι.

XXVI.   Ταῦτά τε οὖν πάντα ἐδίδασκέ με, ὁπότε περὶ τῶν

206 Ε ἀπολύειν TW O.-P.: ἀπολαύειν B: ἀποπαύειν cj. Naber   ἔχοντα:
ἐρῶντα Voeg.   τίνος μήν Steph.   πάνυ...ἔφη del. Bdhm.   τί...γεννήσεως
vulgo Socrati tribuunt, Diotimae Herm. (Voeg.) reddidit   δὴ ΒΤ O.-P.:
δεῖ W   γεννήσεως: γενεσεως O.-P.   ἀειγενές: αει γενεσις O.-P.   207 A ἀγαθὸν scripsi : ἀγαθοῦ ΒΤ O.-P.: τἀγαθὸν W Vind. Suppl. 7, vulg. Bast ⟨ὁ⟩ ἔρως
Bekk. Sz.

206 Ε ὠδῖνος ἀπολύειν. This is the office of Καλλονή as Εἰλείθυια: cp.
Theaet. 151 A ταύτην...τὴν ὠδῖνα ἐγείρειν τε καὶ ἀποπαύειν ἡ ἐμὴ τέχνη (*sc.* ἡ
μαιευτικὴ) δύναται: *Rep.* 490 B ᾧ πλησιάσας καὶ μιγεὶς τῷ ὄντως ὄντι, γεννήσας
νοῦν καὶ ἀλήθειαν...καὶ οὕτω λήγοι ὠδῖνος: Max. Tyr. *diss.* XVI. 4, p. 179 λόγος
μαιεύεται ψυχὴν κυοῦσαν καὶ ὠδίνων μεστήν.

τὸν ἔχοντα. "*Sc.* ταύτην τὴν ὠδῖνα" (Wolf): but Hommel and Stallb.
supply αὐτό, *i.e.* τὸ καλόν. Cp. *Phaedr.* 252 A τὸν τὸ κάλλος ἔχοντα ἰατρὸν
εὕρηκε μόνον τῶν μεγίστων πόνων,—which settles the question.

τί...γεννήσεως; τί, answered by ὅτι, means "why" or "wherein" rather
than "what" (as in 204 D), and the genitive, like those preceding, is objective.
Supply ἐστὶν ὁ ἔρως.

ἀειγενές. This is practically a re-assertion of the statement in 206 C (θεῶν
τὸ πρᾶγμα κτλ.). Cp. *Laws* 773 Ε ὡς χρὴ τῆς ἀειγενοῦς φύσεως ἀντέχεσθαι τῷ
παῖδας παίδων καταλείποντα κτλ.

207 A εἴπερ τοῦ ἀγαθὸν κτλ. Against Bekker, Dindorf, Ast, Stallb.[1] who
adopted τοῦ τἀγαθὸν Rückert wrote: "etiam vulg. proba est. Construe : εἴπερ
τοῦ ἀγαθοῦ ἔρως ἐστὶν, quibus ἐξηγητικῶς addita sunt verba ἑαυτῷ εἶναι ἀεί. In
quibus supplendum est subj. ὁ ἔρως." To this Stallb.[2] and Rettig assent,
comparing Pind. *Ol.* III. 33 τῶν νιν γλυκὺς ἵμερος ἔσχεν...φυτεῦσαι: Thuc. V.
15. 1 ἐπιθυμίᾳ τῶν ἀνδρῶν τῶν ἐκ τῆς νήσου κομίσασθαι (where Poppo cites for
the epexegetic infin. *Crito* 52 C, Xen. *Cyr.* v. 231). None the less, the MSS.'
text seems—if not "sine ullo sensu" as Wolf put it—at least very awkward
Greek. The obvious allusion to the former definition, ὁ ἔρως ἐστὶ τοῦ τὸ
ἀγαθὸν αὑτῷ εἶναι ἀεί (206 A *ad fin.*), supports Bekker's reading here as the
right one : but if we read τοῦ τἀγαθόν here consistency requires that we also
read μετὰ τἀγαθοῦ in the preceding line, an easy change but supported by no
authority. Hence I content myself with the minimum of alteration, *viz.*
ἀγαθὸν for ἀγαθοῦ.

ἐρωτικῶν λόγους ποιοῖτο, καί ποτε ἤρετο Τί οἴει, ὦ Σώκρατες, αἴτιον
εἶναι τούτου τοῦ ἔρωτος καὶ τῆς ἐπιθυμίας; ἢ οὐκ αἰσθάνει ὡς
δεινῶς διατίθεται πάντα τὰ θηρία, ἐπειδὰν γεννᾶν ἐπιθυμήσῃ, καὶ
B τὰ πεζὰ καὶ τὰ πτηνά, νοσοῦντά τε πάντα καὶ ἐρωτικῶς διατι-
θέμενα, πρῶτον μὲν περὶ τὸ ξυμμιγῆναι ἀλλήλοις, ἔπειτα περὶ τὴν
τροφὴν τοῦ γενομένου, καὶ ἕτοιμά ἐστιν ὑπὲρ τούτων καὶ διαμάχεσθαι τὰ ἀσθενέστατα τοῖς ἰσχυροτάτοις καὶ ὑπεραποθνήσκειν,
καὶ αὐτὰ τῷ λιμῷ παρατεινόμενα ὥστ' ἐκεῖνα ἐκτρέφειν, καὶ ἄλλο
πᾶν ποιοῦντα; τοὺς μὲν γὰρ ἀνθρώπους, ἔφη, οἴοιτ' ἄν τις ἐκ
λογισμοῦ ταῦτα ποιεῖν· τὰ δὲ θηρία τίς αἰτία οὕτως ἐρωτικῶς
C διατίθεσθαι; ἔχεις λέγειν; καὶ ἐγὼ αὖ ἔλεγον ὅτι οὐκ εἰδείην·
ἡ δ' εἶπε, Διανοεῖ οὖν δεινός ποτε γενήσεσθαι τὰ ἐρωτικά, ἐὰν
ταῦτα μὴ ἐννοῇς; 'Αλλὰ διὰ ταῦτά τοι, ὦ Διοτίμα, ὅπερ νῦν δὴ
εἶπον, παρὰ σὲ ἥκω, γνοὺς ὅτι διδασκάλων δέομαι. ἀλλά μοι λέγε

207 A αἰσθάνῃ Bt. ἐπιθυμῶσι O.-P.¹ B ἐστιν del. Bdhm. τούτων
καὶ ΒΤ O.-P.: τούτων W αὐτὰ: αυτω O.-P. τῷ del. Bdhm. παρατει-
νομενω O.-P.¹ ἐρωτικῶς del. Naber C αὖ ἔλεγον b, vulg. Sz. Bt.:
ἀνελεγον Β: ἂν ἔλεγον TW: ελεγον O.-P.

ὡς δεινῶς διατίθεται. "In welchem gewaltsamen Zustande sich die Thiere
befinden" (Schlei.). The phrase is echoed by Alcibiades in 215 E, cp. 207 B,
208 C. For διάθεσις see Phileb. 11 D, with my note.
207 B νοσοῦντα...περί. Cp. Phaedr. 228 B νοσοῦντι περὶ λόγων ἀκοήν:
Soph. fr. 162 (Dindf.) νόσημ' ἔρωτος τοῦτ' ἐφίμερον κακόν (but Nauck fr. 153
reads the verse otherwise).
καὶ διαμάχεσθαι κτλ. This is a correction of Phaedrus's statement
(179 B ff.): cp. 220 D ff. For the fact, cp. Aelian H. A. I. 18, II. 40: Laws
814 B μηδ' ὥσπερ ὄρνιθας περὶ τέκνων μαχομένας...ἐθέλειν ἀποθνήσκειν κτλ.
καὶ αὐτὰ κτλ. "Schleiermacher: um sie nur zu ernähren. Recte. Fallitur
enim Hommel, ὥστε sic usurpari negans ideoque voculam ejectam cupiens.
Conf. De Rep. VIII. p. 549 C al." (Stallb.). As Stallb. explains, αὐτὰ κτλ.
depend on αἰσθάνει, the construction being changed, and αὐτὰ=sponte. For
παρατείνεσθαι, "racked," cp. Lys. 204 C: Ar. fr. 421.
τίς αἰτία κτλ. For αἰτία with the (anarthrous) infin., cp. Phaedo 97 A
αἰτία...γενέσθαι. For the foregoing description of the phenomena connected
with reproduction in the animal-world, cp. (with Rettig) Od. XVI. 216 ff.;
Laws 814 B; Arist. Hist. An. VIII. 1; Cic. de fin. III. 19. 62.
207 C Διανοεῖ. "Do you fancy—?": cp. Laws 755 B μηκέτι...τὴν τηλι-
καύτην ἀρχὴν ὡς ἄρξων διανοηθήτω. Notice the tone of indignant scorn in
which Diotima speaks, cp. 204 B.
δεινὸς τὰ ἐρωτικά. Cp. 193 E, 198 D.
ὅπερ νῦν δὴ εἶπον. See 206 B.

καὶ τούτων τὴν αἰτίαν καὶ τῶν ἄλλων τῶν περὶ τὰ ἐρωτικά. Εἰ τοίνυν, ἔφη, πιστεύεις ἐκείνου εἶναι φύσει τὸν ἔρωτα, οὗ πολλάκις ὡμολογήκαμεν, μὴ θαύμαζε. ἐνταῦθα γὰρ τὸν αὐτὸν ἐκείνῳ D λόγον ἡ θνητὴ φύσις ζητεῖ κατὰ τὸ δυνατὸν ἀεὶ τὸ εἶναι ἀθάνατος. δύναται δὲ ταύτῃ μόνον, τῇ γενέσει, ὅτι ἀεὶ καταλείπει ἕτερον νέον ἀντὶ τοῦ παλαιοῦ, ἐπεὶ καὶ ἐν ᾧ ἓν ἕκαστον τῶν ζῴων ζῆν

207 D 〈κατὰ〉 τὸν αὐτὸν Hirschig	αἰεὶ τὸ εἶναι ἀθάνατος B: ἀεί τε εἶναι καὶ ἀθάνατος T O.-P., Jn. Bt.: τὸ ἀεὶ εἶναι Sz.: τὸ εἶναι ἀεί J.-U.	τῇ γενέσει libri, O.-P.: τῇ γεννήσει Wolf Bdhm. J.-U.: secl. Verm. Sz. Bt.	ὅτι: ὅταν Usener	καταλείπῃ Usener	ἐν...ζῴων del. Ast

οὗ πολλάκις ὡμ. οὗ means ἀθανασίας: πολλάκις refers not only to 206 E f. but also to other conversations such as are implied in 207 A (ἐδίδασκέ με ὁπότε κτλ.).

207 D ἐνταῦθα. "Here," i.e. in the case of τὰ θηρία, as distinguished from that of humans.

τὸν αὐτὸν...λόγον. Adv. accus.; cp. 178 E.

κατὰ τὸ δυνατόν. This implies (cp. 208 A ad fin., B) that only partial immortality, at the best, can attach to ἡ θνητὴ φύσις.

ἀεὶ τὸ εἶναι ἀθάνατος. I retain the reading of B rejected by recent edd. (see crit. n.): ἀεὶ goes with the preceding words, cp. Rep. 618 C τὸν βελτίω ἐκ τῶν δυνατῶν ἀεὶ πανταχοῦ αἱρεῖσθαι: and 206 A, B supra. If, with Burnet, we adopt the reading of T, we must suppose εἶναι to be doing double duty, "both to exist (εἶναι) always and to be (εἶναι) immortal." For the desire of this mortal "to put on immortality," cp. Eur. fr. 808 ὦ φιλόζωοι βροτοί... οὕτως ἔρως βρότοισιν ἔγκειται βίου: Browne Hydriot. c. 5 "Restless inquietude for the diuturnity of our memories unto present considerations seems a vanity almost out of date, and superannuated piece of folly."

δύναται κτλ. This introduces the explanation of the saving phrase κατὰ τὸ δυνατόν. ταύτῃ is adverbial (equiv. to ταύτῃ τῇ μηχανῇ in 208 B ad init.), and τῇ γενέσει, if genuine, is an epexegetic supplement. Possibly we should excise τῇ γενέσει, with Vermehren; or else alter to τῇ γεννήσει. But the use of τῇ γενέσει above (206 D) in the sense of "the process of generation," combined with the emphasis, by repetition of its moods and tenses, laid on γίγνεσθαι in the sequel (207 D—208 A), may make us hesitate to adopt any change; cp. also the passage quoted in the next note.

ἀεὶ καταλείπει κτλ. Cp. Laws 721 C γένος οὖν ἀνθρώπων...τούτῳ τῷ τρόπῳ ἀθάνατον ὄν, τῷ παῖδας παίδων καταλειπόμενον ταὐτὸν καὶ ἓν ὂν ἀεὶ γενέσει τῆς ἀθανασίας μετειληφέναι: ib. 773 E (cited above). On this "conceit" of "a fruitful issue wherein, as in the truest chronicle, they seem to outlive themselves," Sir T. Browne (Rel. Med. § 41) observes "This counterfeit subsisting in our progenies seems to me a mere fallacy" etc.

ἐπεὶ καὶ κτλ. We should expect this first clause to be followed by something like οὐκ ἔστι τὸ αὐτὸ ἀλλὰ νέον ἀεὶ γίγνεται, τὰ δὲ ἀπόλλυσι or οὐδέποτε τὰ αὐτὰ ἔχει ἐν ἑαυτῷ, but, affected by the parenthetic clause οἷον...γένηται, the

καλεῖται καὶ εἶναι τὸ αὐτό, οἷον ἐκ παιδαρίου ὁ αὐτὸς λέγεται ἕως
ἂν πρεσβύτης γένηται· οὗτος μέντοι οὐδέποτε τὰ αὐτὰ ἔχων ἐν
αὑτῷ ὅμως ὁ αὐτὸς καλεῖται, ἀλλὰ νέος ἀεὶ γιγνόμενος, τὰ δὲ
E ἀπολλύς, καὶ κατὰ τὰς τρίχας καὶ σάρκα καὶ ὀστᾶ καὶ αἷμα καὶ
ξύμπαν τὸ σῶμα. καὶ μὴ ὅτι κατὰ τὸ σῶμα, ἀλλὰ καὶ κατὰ τὴν
ψυχὴν οἱ τρόποι, τὰ ἤθη, δόξαι, ἐπιθυμίαι, ἡδοναί, λῦπαι, φόβοι,
τούτων ἕκαστα οὐδέποτε τὰ αὐτὰ πάρεστιν ἑκάστῳ, ἀλλὰ τὰ μὲν
γίγνεται, τὰ δὲ ἀπόλλυται. πολὺ δὲ τούτων ἀτοπώτερον ἔτι, ὅτι
208 καὶ αἱ ἐπιστῆμαι μὴ ὅτι αἱ μὲν γίγνονται, αἱ δὲ ἀπόλλυνται ἡμῖν,
καὶ οὐδέποτε οἱ αὐτοί ἐσμεν οὐδὲ κατὰ τὰς ἐπιστήμας, ἀλλὰ καὶ
μία ἑκάστη τῶν ἐπιστημῶν ταὐτὸν πάσχει. ὃ γὰρ καλεῖται μελε-

207 D τὰ αὐτὰ : ταυτα O.-P. : ταῦτ' Bdhm.　ἀλλὰ νέος : ἀλλοῖος Steph. :
ἀλλὰ νέος τὰ μὲν Sommer : fort. ⟨τὰ μὲν⟩ ἅμα νέος　⟨τὰ μὲν προσλαμβάνων⟩ τὰ
δὲ Wolf : τὰ δὲ ⟨παλαιὰ⟩ Bast　E τρόποι T O.-P. : τόποι B　ἔθη Fischer
ἔτι B O.-P. : ἔστιν TW

---

sentence follows a different course. Cp. the cases of anacoluthon in 177 B,
182 D.

νέος...τὰ δὲ ἀπολλύς. For the omission of τὰ μὲν, cp. *Theaet.* 181 D, *Protag.*
330 A, *Rep.* 451 D. I think it not unlikely that for ἀλλὰ we should read ἅμα :
the processes of growth and decay are synchronous. For the substance of
this passage cp. Heraclitus *fr.* 41 δὶς ἐς τὸν αὐτὸν ποταμὸν οὐκ ἂν ἐμβαίης :
(Heraclitus *ap.*) Plut. *de EI Delph.* c. 18 ὁ χθὲς (ἄνθρωπος) εἰς τὸν σήμερον
τέθνηκεν, ὁ δὲ σήμερον εἰς τὸν αὔριον ἀποθνήσκει.　μένει δ' οὐδείς, οὐδ' ἔστιν εἷς,
ἀλλὰ γιγνόμεθα πολλοὶ περὶ ἓν φάντασμα : Max. Tyr. *diss.* XLI. 4 μεταβολὴν
ὁρᾷς σωμάτων καὶ γενέσεως ἀλλαγήν, ὁδὸν ἄνω καὶ κάτω κατὰ τὸν Ἡράκλειτον
κτλ.: Plut. *cons. ad Apoll.* 10: *Cratyl.* 439 D ff.: see also Rohde *Psyche* II. 148.
The influence of "the flowing philosophers" is noticeable also in Epicharm.
fr. 40. 12 ff. (Lorenz)—

ὧδε νῦν ὅρη
καὶ τὸς ἀνθρώπους· ὁ μὲν γὰρ αὔξεθ', ὁ δέ γα μὰν φθίνει.
ἐν μεταλλαγᾷ δὲ πάντες ἐντὶ πάντα τὸν χρόνον.
ὁ δὲ μεταλλάσσει κατὰ φύσιν κωὔποκ' ἐν τωὐτῷ μένει,
ἅτερον εἴη κα τόδ' ἤδη τοῦ παρεξεστακότος.
καὶ τὺ δὴ κἀγὼ χθὲς ἄλλοι καὶ νὺν ἄλλοι τελέθομες,
καθὶς ἄλλοι κωὔποχ' ωὐτοὶ καττὸν αὐτὸν αὖ λόγον.

Cp. Spenser *F. Q.* VII. 7. 19 And men themselves do change continually, |
From youth to eld from wealth to poverty...Ne doe their bodies only flit and
fly, | But eeke their minds (which they immortall call) | Still change and vary
thoughts, as new occasions fall."

208 A αἱ ἐπιστῆμαι. The word is used here in the popular sense—
"notitiae rerum in sensus cadentium" (Rückert); cp. *Rep.* 476 D ff.

μελετᾶν. See *note* on ἀμελέτητος 172 A *supra.*

ταν, ὡς ἐξιούσης ἐστὶ τῆς ἐπιστήμης· λήθη γὰρ ἐπιστήμης ἔξοδος,
μελέτη δὲ πάλιν καινὴν ἐμποιοῦσα ἀντὶ τῆς ἀπιούσης [μνήμην]
σῴζει τὴν ἐπιστήμην, ὥστε τὴν αὐτὴν δοκεῖν εἶναι.   τούτῳ γὰρ τῷ
τρόπῳ πᾶν τὸ θνητὸν σῴζεται, οὐ τῷ παντάπασι τὸ αὐτὸ ἀεὶ εἶναι
ὥσπερ τὸ θεῖον, ἀλλὰ τῷ τὸ ἀπιὸν καὶ παλαιούμενον ἕτερον νέον Β
ἐγκαταλείπειν οἷον αὐτὸ ἦν.   ταύτῃ τῇ μηχανῇ, ὦ Σώκρατες, ἔφη,
θνητὸν ἀθανασίας μετέχει, καὶ σῶμα καὶ τἆλλα πάντα· ἀδύνατον
δὲ ἄλλῃ.   μὴ οὖν θαύμαζε εἰ τὸ αὑτοῦ ἀποβλάστημα φύσει πᾶν
τιμᾷ· ἀθανασίας γὰρ χάριν παντὶ αὕτη ἡ σπουδὴ καὶ ὁ ἔρως
ἔπεται.

208 A μνήμην secl. Baiter Sz. Bt.: μνημη O.-P.: μνήμη Sauppe Jn.
θνητὸν Τ O.-P.: ὀνητὸν B   οὐ τῷ Τ O.-P.: οὕτω B   τὸ αὐτὸν B O.-P.:
ταὐτὸν Bdhm. J.-U.   B   τῷ τὸ: τῷ Liebhold: τῷ τὸ ἀεὶ Usener   καὶ
παλαιούμενον om. Stob., J.-U.   ἐγκαταλείπειν: ενκαταλιπειν O.-P.: καταλείπειν
Stob.: ἀεὶ καταλείπειν Hirschig Jn.   ταύτῃ...ἄλλῃ om. Stob.   μετέχει
Steph., O.-P.: μετέχειν libri, Voeg.   ἀδύνατον Creuzer Sz. Bt.: δυνατόν,
ἀδύνατον Voeg.· ἀθάνατον libri, O.-P.   ἄπαν Stob.

λήθη γὰρ κτλ. Cp. *Phaedo* 75 D οὐ τοῦτο λήθην λέγομεν...ἐπιστήμης ἀπο-
βολήν; *Phileb.* 33 E ἔστι γὰρ λήθη μνήμης ἔξοδος: *Meno* 81 C; *Laws* 732 C.
For the πηγὴ Λήθης (Μνημοσύνης) in Hades, see Pind. *fr.* 130; Rohde, *Psyche*
II. 209³, 390¹.

[μνήμην]. This word is either interpolated or corrupted (*pace* Rettig who
attempts to defend it by citing *Phileb.* 34 B): ἀπιούσης must refer to the same
subst. as ἐξιούσης above, viz. τῆς ἐπιστήμης, while καινήν must qualify the
same subst. as ἀπιούσης. For later reff. to this doctrine, see Philo Jud.
de nom. mut. p. 1060; Nemes. *de nat. hom.* 13, p. 166.

208 B ἀλλὰ τῷ...οἷον αὐτὸ ἦν. This view is reproduced by Aristotle,
de an. II. 4. 415ᵃ 26 ff. φυσικώτατον γὰρ τῶν ἔργων τοῖς ζῶσιν...τὸ ποιῆσαι
ἕτερον οἷον αὐτό...ἵνα τοῦ ἀεὶ καὶ τοῦ θείου μετέχωσιν...ἐπεὶ οὖν κοινωνεῖν
ἀδυνατεῖ τοῦ ἀεὶ καὶ τοῦ θείου τῇ συνεχείᾳ...κοινωνεῖ ταύτῃ...καὶ διαμένει οὐκ
αὐτὸ ἀλλ᾽ οἷον αὐτό, ἀριθμῷ μὲν οὐχ ἕν, εἴδει δ᾽ ἕν: cp. *id. Pol.* I. 1252ᵃ 26 ff.;
de gen. an. II. 735ᵃ 17 ff.

ταύτῃ τῇ μ. Cp. ταύτῃ, 207 D *ad init.*

ἀδύνατον δὲ ἄλλῃ. Stallb.², retaining the traditional ἀθάνατον, comments:
"haec addita videntur et oppositionis gratia et propter verba extrema καὶ
τἆλλα πάντα: quae ne falso intelligerentur, sane cavendum fuit"—which, as
Hommel points out, is unsatisfactory. Against ἀδύνατον Rückert absurdly
objects that Plato would have written ἄλλη δὲ ἀδύνατον.

παντί...ἔπεται. Since ἔπεσθαι is more naturally used of attendance on a
divinity (cp. 197 E, *Phaedr.* 248 A etc.) perhaps ἔπεστιν ought to be read
(cp. 183 B *crit. n.*). ἡ σπουδὴ serves to recall 206 B.

XXVII. Καὶ ἐγὼ ἀκούσας τὸν λόγον ἐθαύμασά τε καὶ εἶπον
Εἶεν, ἦν δ' ἐγώ, ὦ σοφωτάτη Διοτίμα, ταῦτα ὡς ἀληθῶς οὕτως
C ἔχει; καὶ ἤ, ὥσπερ οἱ τέλεοι σοφισταί, Εὖ ἴσθι, ἔφη, ὦ Σώκρατες·
ἐπεὶ καὶ τῶν ἀνθρώπων εἰ ἐθέλεις εἰς τὴν φιλοτιμίαν βλέψαι,
θαυμάζοις ἂν τῆς ἀλογίας [περὶ] ἃ ἐγὼ εἴρηκα εἰ μὴ ἐννοεῖς, ἐνθυ-
μηθεὶς ὡς δεινῶς διάκεινται ἔρωτι τοῦ ὀνομαστοὶ γενέσθαι " καὶ
κλέος ἐς τὸν ἀεὶ χρόνον ἀθάνατον καταθέσθαι," καὶ ὑπὲρ τούτου
κινδύνους τε κινδυνεύειν ἕτοιμοί εἰσι πάντας ἔτι μᾶλλον ἢ ὑπὲρ τῶν
D παίδων, καὶ χρήματ' ἀναλίσκειν καὶ πόνους πονεῖν οὑστινασοῦν

208 C ἔφη BT O.-P.: om. W   ἐπεὶ B O.-P., Sz.: ἐπεί γε TW, Bt.
ἐθέλοις Steph.   περὶ BT: πέρι Vind. 21, Bast Herm.: περι O.-P.: secl. Ast
Sz.   ἐς B, Sz. Bt.: εἰς TW O.-P.   ἀθάνατον del. Wolf   πάντες W
μᾶλλον om. T

Εἶεν. " Really!": " In irrisione verti potest so?" (Ast).   This is a somewhat rare use; cp. *Rep.* 350 E ἐγὼ δέ σοι, ὥσπερ ταῖς γραῦσιν ταῖς τοὺς μύθους
λεγούσαις, " εἶεν " ἐρῶ: *ib.* 424 E; *Euthyd.* 290 C.   For the doubled " verbum
dicendi " (εἶπον…ἦν), cp. 177 A, 202 C.

208 C ὥσπερ οἱ τέλεοι σοφισταί. We might render " in true professorial
style." The reference may be partly (as Wolf and Hommel suggest) to the
fact that the sophistic, as contrasted with the Socratic, method was that of
didactic monologue (δόλιχον κατατείνουσι τοῦ λόγου *Prot.* 329 A)—the lecture
rather than the conversation. Thus in the sequel (208 C—212 A) Diotima
developes her own doctrine without the aid of further question-and-answer.
Stallb., however, explains the phrase as intended to ridicule the pretended
omniscience of the sophists; Rettig sees in it an indication that what follows
is meant, in part, as a parody of the earlier speeches; and by Ast and
Schleierm. it is taken to refer only to the dogmatic tone of εὖ ἴσθι. For
τέλεος σοφιστής, cp. *Crat.* 403 E (applied to Hades); σοφιστής applied to Eros,
203 D; οἱ χρηστοὶ σοφισταί, 177 B; οἱ σοφοί, 185 C. It is possible also that in
τέλεος there may be a hint at the mystery-element in D.'s speech (cp. 210 A
and πρὸς τέλος 210 E).

εἰ ἐθέλεις κτλ. For φιλοτιμία, cp. 178 D. The thought here recalls Milton's
" Fame is the spur that the clear spirit doth raise " etc.

θαυμάζοις ἂν κτλ. Stallb., defending περὶ, says " ad ἐννοεῖς facillime e
superioribus intelligitur αὐτά." But we may justly complain here, as Badham
does at *Phileb.* 49 A, of " the dunce who inserted περὶ."

καὶ κλέος…καταθέσθαι. " Ex poeta aliquo petita esse ipse verborum
numerus declarat" (Stallb.): but it is just as probable that Diotima herself
is the authoress—rivalling Agathon. Cp. Tyrtaeus 12. 31—2 οὐδέ ποτε κλέος
ἐσθλὸν ἀπόλλυται οὐδ' ὄνομ' αὐτοῦ | ἀλλ' ὑπὸ γῆς περ ἐὼν γίγνεται ἀθάνατος:
Theogn. 245—6 οὐδὲ τότ' οὐδὲ θανὼν ἀπολεῖς κλέος, ἀλλὰ μελήσεις | ἄφθιτον
ἀνθρώποις αἰὲν ἔχων ὄνομα: Simon. 99. 1 ἄσβεστον κλέος…θέντες. For the
thought, see also Cic. *Tusc.* I. p. 303; *Cat. Mai.* 22. 3.

καὶ ὑπεραποθνῄσκειν. ἐπεὶ οἴει σύ, ἔφη, Ἄλκηστιν ὑπὲρ Ἀδμήτου
ἀποθανεῖν ἄν, ἢ Ἀχιλλέα Πατρόκλῳ ἐπαποθανεῖν, ἢ προαποθανεῖν
τὸν ὑμέτερον Κόδρον ὑπὲρ τῆς βασιλείας τῶν παίδων, μὴ οἰομένους
" ἀθάνατον μνήμην ἀρετῆς πέρι " ἑαυτῶν ἔσεσθαι, ἣν νῦν ἡμεῖς
ἔχομεν ; πολλοῦ γε δεῖ, ἔφη, ἀλλ᾽, οἶμαι, ὑπὲρ ἀρετῆς ἀθανάτου
καὶ τοιαύτης δόξης εὐκλεοῦς πάντες πάντα ποιοῦσιν, ὅσῳ ἂν ἀμεί-

208 D ἄν...προαποθανεῖν om. W   βαλειας O.-P.   πέρι Ast Sz. Bt.:
περὶ ΒΤ

---

208 D **ὑπεραποθνῄσκειν.** An obvious allusion to 180 A ff.: Diotima corrects
Phaedrus by showing the motive for self-sacrifice to be not so much personal
ἔρως as ἔρως for immortal fame. The use of the cognate accus. (κινδύνους,
πόνους) is another poetical feature in this passage—reminiscent of Agathon's
style.

Κόδρον. Schol.: πολέμου τοῖς Δωριεῦσιν ὄντος πρὸς Ἀθηναίους, ἔχρησεν
ὁ θεὸς τοῖς Δωριεῦσιν αἱρήσειν τὰς Ἀθήνας, εἰ Κόδρον τὸν βασιλέα μὴ φονεύ-
σουσιν. γνοὺς δὲ τοῦτο ὁ Κόδρος, στείλας ἑαυτὸν εὐτελεῖ σκεύῃ ὡς ξυλιστὴν καὶ
δρέπανον λαβών, ἐπὶ τὸν χάρακα τῶν πολεμίων προῄει. δύο δὲ αὐτῷ ἀπαντη-
σάντων πολεμίων τὸν μὲν ἕνα πατάξας κατέβαλεν, ὑπὸ δὲ τοῦ ἑτέρου ἀγνοηθεὶς
ὅστις ἦν, πληγεὶς ἀπέθανε. This "popular story" is late: "according to the
older tradition Codrus fell in battle" (see Bury *Hist. Gr.* p. 169): the
traditional date of the event is about 1068 B.C. Notice the rare προαποθανεῖν (once each in Hdt., Antiphon, Xen.), and the "sophistic" jingle in
προ-, ἐπ-, ἀποθανεῖν. For later allusions to Codrus, see Cic. *Tusc.* I. 48 ;
Hor. *C.* III. 19. 2.

ἀθάνατον μνήμην κτλ. Cp. Simon. 123 μνῆμα δ᾽ ἀποφθιμένοισι πατὴρ
Μεγάριστος ἔθηκεν | ἀθάνατον θνητοῖς παισὶ χαριζόμενος : *id.* 4. 8 (Λεωνίδας)
ἀρετᾶς λελοιπὼς | κόσμον ἀέναον κλέος τε : *id.* 96. Observe how near ἀθάνατον
...ἔσεσθαι goes to forming a complete hexameter.

ἀρετῆς ἀθανάτου. Cp. Soph. *Philoct.* 1419 ὅσους ποιήσας καὶ διεξελθὼν
πόνους | ἀρετὴν ἔσχον : Pind. *Ol.* VII. 163 ἄνδρα τε πὺξ ἀρετὰν εὑ-
ρόντα : *id. Nem.* X. 2 φλέγεται δ᾽ ἀρεταῖς μυρίαις ἔργων θρασέων ἕνεκεν
("countless monuments" J. B. Bury, see *Append.* A in his ed.): *id. Isthm.*
IV. 17 (with Bury, *App.* F): Thuc. I. 33. 2: *Rep.* 618 B ἐπὶ γένεσι καὶ προγόνων
ἀρεταῖς : Xen. *Cyrop.* VIII. 1. 29 : *Anth. Pal.* VII. 252. These passages show
that ἀρετή can denote not only "excellence" but its result, reward or token,
"renown," "distinction," whether or not embodied in a concrete "monument."
For the thought cp. Spenser *F. Q.* III. iii. 1 "Most sacred fyre, that burnest
mightily In living brests...which men call Love...Whence spring all noble
deedes and never dying fame."

εὐκλεοῦς. Cp. Simon. 95 εὐκλέας αἶα κέκευθε, Λεωνίδα, οἳ μετὰ σεῖο | τῇδ᾽
ἔθανον : *Menex.* 247 D. With the thought of this passage, cp. Sir T. Browne
Hydriot. c. 5 "There is no antidote against the opium of time....But the
iniquity of oblivion blindly scattereth her poppy, and deals with the memory
of men without distinction to merit of perpetuity....In vain do individuals

Ε *νους ὦσι, τοσούτῳ μᾶλλον· τοῦ γὰρ ἀθανάτου ἐρῶσιν.* οἱ μὲν οὖν *ἐγκύμονες, ἔφη, κατὰ τὰ σώματα ὄντες πρὸς τὰς γυναῖκας μᾶλλον τρέπονται καὶ ταύτῃ ἐρωτικοί εἰσι, διὰ παιδογονίας ἀθανασίαν καὶ μνήμην καὶ εὐδαιμονίαν, ὡς οἴονται, αὑτοῖς " εἰς τὸν ἔπειτα χρόνον* 209 *πάντα ποριζόμενοι"· οἱ δὲ κατὰ τὴν ψυχήν—εἰσὶ γὰρ οὖν, ἔφη, οἳ ἐν ταῖς ψυχαῖς κυοῦσιν ἔτι μᾶλλον ἢ ἐν τοῖς σώμασιν, ἃ ψυχῇ προσήκει καὶ κυῆσαι καὶ τεκεῖν· τί οὖν προσήκει; φρόνησίν τε καὶ τὴν ἄλλην ἀρετήν· ὧν δή εἰσι καὶ οἱ ποιηταὶ πάντες γεννή-*

208 Ε *κατὰ τὰ* O.-P., Paris 1812, vulg. Sz.: *κατὰ* BTW, Bt. *οἷόν τε* Vind. 21
209 Α *ἢ* ⟨*αἱ*⟩ *ἐν* Naber *κυησεται* O.-P.[1]: *κυησαιτε* O.-P. corr.: *κυεῖσθαι*
Bdhm. *τεκεῖν* Hug Sz., O.-P.: *κυεῖν* libri: *τίκτειν* Jn.: *γεννᾶν* cj. Teuffel

hope for immortality, or any patent from oblivion, in preservations below the
moone." Also Soph. *Philoct.* 1422 *ἐκ τῶν πόνων τῶνδ' εὐκλεᾶ θέσθαι βίον.*
208 Ε **οἱ μὲν οὖν ἐγκύμονες.** Here first the two kinds of pregnancy, bodily
and mental,—mentioned together in 206 B, C—are definitely separated.
πρὸς τὰς γ. μ. τρέπονται. Cp. 181 C, 191 Ε.
ἀθανασίαν κτλ. Hug points out that by a few slight alterations this can
be turned into an elegiac couplet:—

ἀθάνατον μνήμην κεὐδαιμονίαν σφίσιν αὑτοῖς
εἰς τὸν ἔπειτα χρόνον πάντα ποριζόμενοι.

Hommel had already printed *εἰς...χρόνον* as a half-verse.
209 Α **οἱ δὲ κατὰ τὴν ψυχήν.** *Sc. ἐγκύμονες ὄντες.* In this anacoluthic
period Rettig sees a parody of Phaedrus's style with its "langathmigen,
anakoluthischen und regellosen Perioden."
καὶ κυῆσαι καὶ τεκεῖν. Hug's conjecture, *τεκεῖν* for *κυεῖν*, is fortunate
in finding confirmation in the Papyrus. If *κυεῖν* be read, what is the
point of the distinction of tenses? Schleierm. renders by "erzeugen und
erzeugen zu wollen"; Schulthess, "zeugen und empfangen"; Rettig explains
that "*κυεῖν* geht auf den dauernden, *κυῆσαι* auf den vollendeten Process";
Stallb. "et concepisse (quae est actio semel...perfecta) et conceptum tenere."
But there is certainly not much point here in making any such fine-spun
distinction, unless it be to imply that Diotima is playing the part of a
σοφιστής!
φρόνησιν...ἀρετήν. "Moral wisdom and virtue in general": the phrase is
an echo of that in 184 D. For *φρόνησις*, cp. *Rep.* 427 Ε (with Adam's *note*);
Meno 88 B (with Thompson's *note*).
οἱ ποιηταί. That the poets were ethical teachers and the stage a pulpit—
just as Homer was the Greek Bible—was an axiom in the Hellenic world.
See the appeal to the authority of poets in the *Protagoras* (and Adam's *note*
on 338 Ε); Ar. *Ran.* 1009 (Eurip. loquitur) *βελτίους τε ποιοῦμεν τοὺς ἀνθρώπους ἐν ταῖς πόλεσιν*: *Lysis* 214 Α *οὗτοι γὰρ (sc. οἱ ποιηταὶ) ἡμῖν ὥσπερ πατέρες
τῆς σοφίας εἰσὶ καὶ ἡγεμόνες.* The fact that most kinds of poetry were produced in connexion with, and under the sanction of, religion, had no doubt
something to do with this estimate of it. See further Adam *R. T. G.* pp. 9 ff.

τορες καὶ τῶν δημιουργῶν ὅσοι λέγονται εὑρετικοὶ εἶναι· πολὺ δὲ
μεγίστη, ἔφη, καὶ καλλίστη τῆς φρονήσεως ἡ περὶ τὰς τῶν πόλεών
τε καὶ οἰκήσεων διακοσμήσεις, ᾗ δὴ ὄνομά ἐστι σωφροσύνη τε καὶ
δικαιοσύνη· τούτων αὖ ὅταν τις ἐκ νέου ἐγκύμων ᾖ τὴν ψυχὴν Β
θεῖος ὢν καὶ ἡκούσης τῆς ἡλικίας τίκτειν τε καὶ γεννᾶν ἤδη ἐπιθυμῇ, ζητεῖ δή, οἶμαι, καὶ οὗτος περιιὼν τὸ καλὸν ἐν ᾧ ἂν γεννή-
σειεν· ἐν τῷ γὰρ αἰσχρῷ οὐδέποτε γεννήσει. τά τε οὖν σώματα τὰ
καλὰ μᾶλλον ἢ τὰ αἰσχρὰ ἀσπάζεται ἅτε κυῶν, καὶ ἂν ἐντύχῃ
ψυχῇ καλῇ καὶ γενναίᾳ καὶ εὐφυεῖ, πάνυ δὴ ἀσπάζεται τὸ ξυναμ-

209 A   τὰς libri, O.-P.: τὰ Sommer Bt.   διακοσμήσεις Vind. 21, vulg.
Bast Heindorf J.-U. Sz.: διακόσμησις libri, O.-P., Sommer Bt.   B   αὖ Β
O.-P., J.-U. Sz.: δ' αὖ TW, Bt.   ψυχήν, ⟨τὴν φύσιν⟩ Heusde   θεῖος libri,
O.-P., Sz.: ἤθεος Parmentier Bt.: θεῖος ὢν del. Jn.   ἐπιθυμῇ Steph. J.-U.
Sz.: ἐπιθυμῃ O.-P.: ἐπιθυμεῖ libri, Bt.   δὴ BT O.-P.: δὲ W   περιιὼν Τ
O.-P.: περὶ ὢν B   ἐν ᾧ δὴ γεννήσῃ Bdhm.   ἢ τὰ αἰσχρὰ del. Bdhm.
ἅτε: ὅ γε Usener

δημιουργῶν...εὑρετικοί.   An allusion to 197 A δημιουργίαν...ἀνεῦρεν.
μεγίστη...τῆς φρονήσεως.   Cp. Crat. 391 B ὀρθοτάτη τῆς σκέψεως: Rep. 416 B;
Thuc. I. 2 τῆς γῆς ἡ ἀρίστη: see Madv. Gr. S. § 50 a, R. 3.
σωφροσύνη τε καὶ δικαιοσύνη.   Cp. Phaedo 82 A οἱ τὴν δημοτικήν τε καὶ πολι-
τικὴν ἀρετὴν ἐπιτετηδευκότες, ἣν δὴ καλοῦσι σωφροσύνην τε καὶ δικαιοσύνην, ἐξ
ἔθους τε καὶ μελέτης γεγονυῖαν ἄνευ φιλοσοφίας τε καὶ νοῦ: Meno 73 A.   For
these virtues in the Republic, see Adam on 432 A, 434 C.   Here they combine
to form a description of "ordinary civil virtue."
209 B   τούτων αὖ κτλ.   Here the main statement is resumed.   With
Stephens (followed by Ast, Rückert and Hug) I read ἐπιθυμῇ, whereas
Burnet prints ἐπιθυμεῖ. ζητεῖ δὴ κτλ., with commas after ψυχὴν and ἡλικίας.
Stallb. takes καί as intensive rather than connective, and renders θεῖος ὢν
"quippe divinus." Burnet adopts Parmentier's ἤθεος, but there seems little
point in emphasizing the celibacy of the youth.   If alteration be required,
the best would be ἔνθεος, for which cp. 179 A, 180 B.   But in Meno 99 c ff.
θεῖος, in much the same sense as ἔνθεος, is applied to the very classes here
mentioned—ὀρθῶς ἂν καλοῖμεν θείους τε, οὓς νῦν δὴ ἐλέγομεν χρησμῳδοὺς καὶ
μάντεις καὶ τοὺς ποιητικοὺς ἅπαντας· καὶ τοὺς πολιτικούς...φαῖμεν ἂν θείους τε
εἶναι καὶ ἐνθουσιάζειν κτλ. (see Thompson ad loc.): hence the word may well
be sound here also.   For τῆς ἡλικίας (and θεῖος) cp. 206 C.
ζητεῖ...περιιών.   Cp. Prot. 348 D περιιὼν ζητεῖ ὅτῳ ἐπιδείξηται: Rep. 620 C:
Apol. 23 B.   περιιέναι occurs also in 193 A, 219 E.
ἐν τῷ γὰρ αἰσχρῷ.   A repetition of 206 C: cp. Rep. 402 D, Phaedr. 253 A ff.
καὶ ἂν...εὐφυεῖ.   Notice the iambic rhythm.   For the sense of γενναῖος,
"well-bred" (of a dog, Rep. 375 A), cp. (Eurip. ap.) Gorg. 485 E.   For εὐφυής
also cp. (Eurip. ap.) Gorg. 484 C ff.; Rep. 409 E.   Cp. for the sense Plotin. de
pulcr. 309 (Cr.); Rep. 620 B; Cic. Lael. 14; and esp. Phaedr. 276 E.
τὸ ξυναμφότερον.   Cp. I. Alc. 130 A ψυχὴν ἢ σῶμα ἢ ξυναμφότερον.

φότερον, καὶ πρὸς τοῦτον τὸν ἄνθρωπον εὐθὺς εὐπορεῖ λόγων περὶ
C ἀρετῆς καὶ [περὶ] οἷον χρὴ εἶναι τὸν ἄνδρα τὸν ἀγαθὸν καὶ ἃ ἐπιτη-
δεύειν, καὶ ἐπιχειρεῖ παιδεύειν. ἁπτόμενος γάρ, οἶμαι, τοῦ καλοῦ
καὶ ὁμιλῶν αὐτῷ, ἃ πάλαι ἐκύει, τίκτει καὶ γεννᾷ, καὶ παρὼν καὶ
ἀπὼν μεμνημένος, καὶ τὸ γεννηθὲν συνεκτρέφει κοινῇ μετ᾽ ἐκείνου,
ὥστε πολὺ μείζω κοινωνίαν [τῆς τῶν παίδων] πρὸς ἀλλήλους οἱ
τοιοῦτοι ἴσχουσι καὶ φιλίαν βεβαιοτέραν, ἅτε καλλιόνων καὶ
ἀθανατωτέρων παίδων κεκοινωνηκότες. καὶ πᾶς ἂν δέξαιτο ἑαυτῷ
D τοιούτους παῖδας μᾶλλον γεγονέναι ἢ τοὺς ἀνθρωπίνους, καὶ εἰς
Ὅμηρον ἀποβλέψας καὶ <εἰς> Ἡσίοδον καὶ τοὺς ἄλλους ποιητὰς
τοὺς ἀγαθοὺς ζηλῶν οἷα ἔκγονα ἑαυτῶν καταλείπουσιν, ἃ ἐκείνοις

209 C περὶ secl. Steph. Mdvg. Sz. Bt.: περὶ τοῦ Coisl.: περὶ οἵου Sommer
ἀπὼν καὶ παρὼν T καὶ (ante τὸ) om. Vind. 21, Bast τῆς...παίδων
seclusi τῶν παίδων: ἄλλων παίδων Hug¹: θνητῶν παίδων Schirlitz: τῶν
πολλῶν Rohde: τῶν παιδογόνων Bast: fort. τῶν ⟨γηίνων⟩ παίδων καλλίων
ὧν B παίδων secl. Creuzer J.-U. D εἰς Ἡσιοδον O.-P.: Ἡσίοδον libri,
edd. ζητῶν ὅσα Proclus: ζηλοίη οἷα Ast καταλελοίπασιν Method. Bdhm.

εὐπορεῖ λόγων. Cp. 223 A; Tim. 26 D ἵνα εὐποροῖεν λόγων μετ᾽ ἐμοῦ.
209 C καὶ [περὶ] οἷον κτλ. περὶ is retained by Hommel and Stallb. who
renders "quale sit in quo tractando versari debeat is qui boni viri nomen et
dignitatem obtinere velit," taking οἷον as neut., and by Rettig who regards
the "redundancy and tautology" of the words as due to the "sophistical
character" of the passage.
τοῦ καλοῦ. This is masc., not neuter, as the context shows.
καὶ παρὼν καὶ ἀπὼν. A rhetorical formula; cp. Soph. Antig. 1109 οἵ τ᾽
ὄντες οἵ τ᾽ ἀπόντες: id. El. 305: Crat. 420 A, Laws 635 A. As Hommel
observes, μεμνημένος (sc. αὐτοῦ) can in strictness apply only to ἀπών.
τὸ γεννηθὲν κτλ. Cp. 207 B, Phaedr. 276 E.
τῆς τῶν παίδων. Hug prints τῶν × × × παίδων with the note (after Vermehren)
"es scheint ein Epitheton wie φύσει o. ähnl. ausgefallen zu sein." Stallb.
explains ἡ κοινωνία τῶν παίδων to mean "conjunctio ex liberorum procreatione
oriunda." The simplest remedy is to bracket the words τῆς τῶν παίδων (see
crit. n.).
ἀθανατωτέρων. For this Hibernian comparison cp. Phaedo 99 C.
209 D ζηλῶν οἷα κτλ. I.e. ζηλῶν αὐτοὺς ὅτι τοιαῦτα κτλ., "With envy for
the noble offspring they leave." For οἷος=ὅτι τοιοῦτος, cp. Xen. Cyr. VII. 3. 13
(Madv. Gr. S. § 198 R. 3). Rückert punctuates after Ἡσίοδον, Hommel after
ἀπόβλεψας, and it is evident from Rettig's note,—"Homer kann man nur
bewundern, mit andern Dichtern ist es eher möglich zu wetteifern,"—that
he too mistakes the construction: we must supply αὐτούς (as Stallb.) with
ζηλῶν and construe the accusatives as depending on εἰς: cp. I. Alc. 120 A,
122 B, C. This passage is quoted by Proclus ad Pl. Rep. p. 393.

ἀθάνατον κλέος καὶ μνήμην παρέχεται αὐτὰ τοιαῦτα ὄντα· εἰ δὲ
βούλει, ἔφη, οἵους Λυκοῦργος παῖδας κατελίπετο ἐν Λακεδαίμονι
σωτῆρας τῆς Λακεδαίμονος καὶ ὡς ἔπος εἰπεῖν τῆς Ἑλλάδος.
τίμιος δὲ παρ᾽ ὑμῖν καὶ Σόλων διὰ τὴν τῶν νόμων γέννησιν, καὶ
ἄλλοι ἄλλοθι πολλαχοῦ ἄνδρες, καὶ ἐν Ἕλλησι καὶ ἐν βαρβάροις, Ε
πολλὰ καὶ καλὰ ἀποφηνάμενοι ἔργα, γεννήσαντες παντοίαν ἀρετήν·
ὧν καὶ ἱερὰ πολλὰ ἤδη γέγονε διὰ τοὺς τοιούτους παῖδας, διὰ δὲ
τοὺς ἀνθρωπίνους οὐδενός πω.
XXVIII. Ταῦτα μὲν οὖν τὰ ἐρωτικὰ ἴσως, ὦ Σώκρατες, κἂν
209 D κατελίπετο b O.-P, J.-U. Sz. Bt.: κατελιπεν...τὸ B: κατελείπετο
T: κατέλιπε τοῖς vulg.: κατέλιπεν αὑτοῦ Rettig   ὑμῖν TW vulg.: ἡμῖν B O.-P.
(probab.) ⟨ὁ⟩ Σολων O.-P.   E ἐν Ἕλλησι: Ελλησι O.-P.   ἐν βαρβάροις:
βαρβάροις Clement   πολλά...ἔργα secl. Hartmann   καλὰ: αλλα O.-P. ⟨και⟩
γεννησαντες O.-P.   ⟨οὐδὲν⟩ οὐδενός πω Hirschig

ἀθάνατον κλέος καὶ μνήμην. Cp. 208 D (*note*).

αὐτὰ τοιαῦτα. Rettig says "*sc.* ἀθάνατα"; but the words imply κλέος as well
as ἀθανασία.

εἰ δὲ βούλει. See on 177 D. This is a brachylogy for εἰ δὲ βούλει, ζηλῶν
Λυκοῦργον οἵους παῖδας κτλ.

παῖδας κατελίπετο. For the middle, cp. *Laws* 721 C, *Rep.* 594 C.

σωτῆρας τῆς Λ. "Dadurch, dass sie die revolutionären Bewegungen ein
Ende machten" (Rettig). Agathon had already applied σωτήρ to Eros (197 E).
For Plato's philo-Laconism, see Zeller's *Plato* (E. T.) p. 484. For the
mythical lawgiver "Lycurgus" (vulgarly dated at 885 B.C.), see Bury *H. Gr.*
p. 135. The statement that his laws were the salvation "practically" of
Hellas may be taken to refer to the part played by the Spartans during
the Persian invasions, cp. Pind. *Pyth.* I. 77 ff. See also the parallel passage
in Xen. *Symp.* VIII. 38—9.

τίμιος δὲ κτλ. For this emphatic position of the adj., cp. *Laws* 730 D τίμιος
μὲν δὴ καὶ ὁ μηδὲν ἀδικῶν.

209 E ἄλλοι ἄλλοθι πολλαχοῦ. An echo of 182 B: cp. *Prot.* 326 D. This
passage is alluded to by Clem. Al. *Strom.* I. p. 130. 38 ἔν τε τῷ συμποσίῳ
ἐπαινῶν Πλάτων τοὺς βαρβάρους κτλ.

πολλά...ἔργα. Another rhetorical "tag," as is shown by the parallel
in *Menex.* 239 A πολλὰ...καὶ καλὰ ἔργα ἀπεφήναντο εἰς πάντας ἀνθρώπους:
cp. Phaedrus's expressions in 179 B, D.

παντοίαν ἀρετήν. Cp. *Critias* 112 E κατὰ τὴν τῶν ψυχῶν παντοίαν ἀρετήν:
Eur. *Med.* 845 (ἔρωτας) παντοίας ἀρετὰς ξυνέργους.

ἱερὰ πολλά. For the shrine of Lycurgus, see Hdt. I. 66, Plut. *Lyc.* 31. The
language echoes Aristophanes' μέγιστ᾽ ἂν αὐτοῦ ἱερὰ κατασκευάσαι (189 C); and
it is cited by Clem. Al. *Strom.* I. p. 300 P.

Ταῦτα...κἂν σὺ μυηθείης. Here Diotima passes on to the final section of
her discourse on erotics (see 210 D *n.*). Hug and P. Crain (following
C. F. Hermann and Schwegler) suppose that κἂν σὺ μ. indicates that what
follows is something beyond the ken of the *historical* Socrates, whose view

210 σὺ μυηθείης· τὰ δὲ τέλεα καὶ ἐποπτικά, ὧν ἕνεκα καὶ ταῦτα ἔστιν,
ἐάν τις ὀρθῶς μετίῃ, οὐκ οἶδ᾽ εἰ οἷός τ᾽ ἂν εἴης.   ἐρῶ μὲν οὖν, ἔφη,
ἐγὼ καὶ προθυμίας οὐδὲν ἀπολείψω· πειρῶ δὲ <καὶ σὺ> ἔπεσθαι,

210 A   ἂν post οἶδ᾽ transp. Naber   ἐφην O.-P.   και συ επεσθαι O.-P.:
ἔπεσθαι libri, edd.

they regard as correctly represented in Xen. *Symp.* VIII. 97 ff.   But although
we may admit (with Thompson, *Meno* p. 158) that "we often find Plato
making his ideal Socrates criticise the views the real Socrates held," we are
not hereby justified in assuming such criticism on every possible occasion.
And, in the case before us, another and more probable explanation of the
words lies to hand.   Socrates throughout—with his usual irony—depicts
himself as a mere tiro in the hands of the Mantinean mistress; but he is
still, in spite of his mock-modesty, the ideal philosopher of Alcibiades'
encomium.   As it was a part of his irony that he had already (201 E) put
himself on the level of Agathon and the rest of the unphilosophic, so the
contemptuous κἂν σὺ here serves to keep up the same ironical fiction,—*i.e.*
it applies neither to the ideal nor to the real (historical) Socrates, but to
the hypothetical Socrates—the disguise assumed by the ideal Socrates when
he played the part of pupil (cp. Rettig's *note*, and F. Horn *Platonstud.* p. 248).
The attitude of Socr. may be illustrated by the words of S. Paul (1 *Cor.* iv. 6)
ταῦτα δέ, ἀδελφοί, μετεσχημάτισα εἰς ἐμαυτὸν καὶ Ἀπολλὼ δι᾽ ὑμᾶς, ἵνα ἐν ὑμῖν
μάθητε κτλ.   For μυηθείης, see next note.

210 A   τὰ δὲ...ἐποπτικά.   Cp. *Phaedr.* 250 C εὐδαίμονα φάσματα μυούμενοί
τε καὶ ἐποπτεύοντες: *ib.* 249 C τελέους ἀεὶ τελετὰς τελούμενος.   On the former
passage Thompson comments, "μυούμενοι and ἐποπτεύοντες are not to be
distinguished here, except in so far as the latter word defines the sense of
the former.   Properly speaking μύησις is the generic term for the entire
process, including the ἐποπτεία, or state of the epopt or adept, who after
due previous lustrations and the like is admitted into the adytum to behold
the αὐτοπτικὰ ἀγάλματα (Iambl. Myst. II. 10. 53)": "the distinction between
the two words (μύησις and ἐποπτεία), as if they implied, the one an earlier,
the other a more advanced stage of imitation, was a later refinement."   According to Theo Smyrnaeus (*Math.* p. 18) there were five grades of initiation,
viz. καθαρμός, ἡ τῆς τελετῆς παράδοσις, ἐποπτεία, ἀνάδεσις καὶ στεμμάτων
ἐπίθεσις, ἡ θεοφιλὴς καὶ θεοῖς συνδίαιτος εὐδαιμονία.   For the language and
rites used in the mysteries, see also Plut. *de Is.* c. 78; *id. Demetr.* 26; Clem.
Al. *Strom.* v. p. 689; Rohde *Psyche* II. 284; and the designs from a cinerary
urn reproduced in Harrison, *Proleg.* p. 547.

ὧν ἕνεκα.   "The final cause": cp. 210 E, *Charm.* 165 A.

ταῦτα.   Repeating ταῦτα...τὰ ἐρωτικά: see the recapitulation in 211 C.

οἷός τ᾽ ἂν εἴης.   Sc. μυηθῆναι: this, as Thompson observes, shows that
μύησις includes ἐποπτεία.   Notice the emphasis laid, here at the start and
throughout, on educational *method*, τὸ ὀρθῶς μετιέναι.

προθυμίας...ἀπολείψω.   Cp. *Rep.* 533 A τό γ᾽ ἐμὸν οὐδὲν ἂν προθυμίας
ἀπολείποι.

πειρῶ δὲ ⟨καὶ σὺ⟩ ἔπεσθαι.   I have added καὶ σὺ from the Papyrus; it serves

ἂν οἷός τε ᾖς. δεῖ γάρ, ἔφη, τὸν ὀρθῶς ἰόντα ἐπὶ τοῦτο τὸ πρᾶγμα
ἄρχεσθαι μὲν νέον ὄντα ἰέναι ἐπὶ τὰ καλὰ σώματα, καὶ πρῶτον
μέν, ἐὰν ὀρθῶς ἡγῆται ὁ ἡγούμενος, ἑνὸς αὐτὸν σώματος ἐρᾶν καὶ
ἐνταῦθα γεννᾶν λόγους καλούς, ἔπειτά δὲ αὐτὸν κατανοῆσαι, ὅτι τὸ
κάλλος τὸ ἐπὶ ὁτῳοῦν σώματι τῷ ἐπὶ ἑτέρῳ σώματι ἀδελφόν ἐστι, Β
καὶ εἰ δεῖ διώκειν τὸ ἐπ' εἴδει καλόν, πολλὴ ἄνοια μὴ οὐχ ἕν τε
καὶ ταὐτὸν ἡγεῖσθαι τὸ ἐπὶ πᾶσι τοῖς σώμασι κάλλος· τοῦτο δ'
ἐννοήσαντα καταστῆναι πάντων τῶν καλῶν σωμάτων ἐραστήν,
ἑνὸς δὲ τὸ σφόδρα τοῦτο χαλάσαι καταφρονήσαντα καὶ σμικρὸν

210 A ἂν: εαν O.-P.   αὐτὸν TW O.-P.: αὐτῶν B, Sz. Bt.: αὖ του Verm.
σώματος secl. (Rückert) Voeg. J.-U. Hug   ἔπειτα δὲ libri, O.-P.: ἔπειτα καὶ
Themist.: ἔπειτα Usener   αὐτὸν: fort. αὖ   B κάλλος τὸ ἐπὶ BT O.-P.:
κ. τῷ ἐπὶ W   σώματι τῷ TW O.-P.: σ. τὸ B   ἐπὶ ἑτέρῳ B O.-P.: ἑτέρῳ T
εἰ ⟨δὴ⟩ δεῖ cj. Jn.   τοῦτο δ' BW O.-P.: τούτῳ δ' T

to lay an appropriate stress on the personal effort required on the part
of the disciple, the incapacity of whose "natural man" is so persistently
emphasized.

δεῖ γάρ κτλ. The sentence runs on without a full stop till we reach the
close of 210 D: Rettig sees in this straggling style a parody of the style of
Pausanias. The passage following was a favourite with the neo-Platonists;
see the reff. in Alcinous *isag.* 5; Plut. *quaest. Plat.* 3. 2. 1002 E; Themist. *or.*
13, p. 168 C; Plotin. *Enn.* I. 6. 1, p. 50; Procl. *in Alcib. I.* p. 330.

ὁ ἡγούμενος. The educational "conductor" is represented as a μυσταγωγός.
So we have ἀγαγεῖν 210 C, παιδαγωγηθῇ 210 E, ἄγεσθαι 211 C.

ἑνὸς αὐτὸν σώματος. If we retain σώματος—and emphasis requires its
retention,—it is difficult to justify the Bodleian αὐτῶν: and αὐτὸν, which
has the support of the Papyrus, although rather otiose, is preferable to
such substitutes as Hommel's αὖ τῶν (σωμάτων) or Vermehren's αὖ του, since
αὖ is hardly in place here. Voegelin's objection to αὐτὸν, endorsed by Rettig,
that it should involve the repetition of δεῖ, does not strike one as fatal; and
I follow Rückert and Stallb. in adopting it.

210 B **τὸ ἐπὶ...σώματι.** Cp. 186 A.
τὸ ἐπ' εἴδει καλόν. This has been interpreted in three ways: (1) "das in
der Idee Schöne"(Schleierm.), "das Schöne der Gesammtgattung"(Schulthess);
so too Zeller and F. Horn; (2) "quod in specie (opp. to 'summo genere')
pulchrum est" (Stallb., after Wyttenbach), so too Hommel; (3) "das in der
Gestalt Schöne" (Ruge), "pulcritudo quae in forma est atque sensibus per-
cipitur" (Rückert). The last of these is undoubtedly right, and has the
support also of Vermehren, Rettig and Hug; for εἴδος of physical "form"
or "outward appearance," cp. 196 A, 215 B.

μὴ οὐχ...ἡγεῖσθαι. See Goodwin *G. M. T.* § 817.
ἐννοήσαντα καταστῆναι. Sc. αὐτὸν δεῖ, resuming the oblique construction.
τὸ σφόδρα τοῦτο. "Idem est quod τοῦτο τὸ σφόδρα ἐρᾶν vel τὸν σφοδρὸν
τοῦτον ἔρωτα" (Stallb.). We have had a description of this σφοδρότης already,
in 183 A ff.

ἡγησάμενον· μετὰ δὲ ταῦτα τὸ ἐν ταῖς ψυχαῖς κάλλος τιμιώτερον
ἡγήσασθαι τοῦ ἐν τῷ σώματι, ὥστε καὶ ἐὰν ἐπιεικὴς ὢν τὴν
C ψυχήν τις κἂν σμικρὸν ἄνθος ἔχῃ, ἐξαρκεῖν αὐτῷ καὶ ἐρᾶν καὶ
κήδεσθαι καὶ τίκτειν λόγους τοιούτους [καὶ ζητεῖν] οἵτινες ποιήσουσι βελτίους τοὺς νέους, ἵνα ἀναγκασθῇ αὖ θεάσασθαι τὸ ἐν
τοῖς ἐπιτηδεύμασι καὶ τοῖς νόμοις καλὸν καὶ τοῦτ᾽ ἰδεῖν ὅτι πᾶν
αὐτὸ αὑτῷ ξυγγενές ἐστιν, ἵνα τὸ περὶ τὸ σῶμα καλὸν σμικρόν τι
ἡγήσηται εἶναι· μετὰ δὲ τὰ ἐπιτηδεύματα ἐπὶ τὰς ἐπιστήμας
ἀγαγεῖν, ἵνα ἴδῃ αὖ ἐπιστημῶν κάλλος, καὶ βλέπων πρὸς πολὺ ἤδη
D τὸ καλὸν μηκέτι τῷ παρ᾽ ἑνί, ὥσπερ οἰκέτης, ἀγαπῶν παιδαρίου

210 C κἂν Herm. Bdhm. Bt.: καὶ ἐὰν BT O.-P.: καὶ ἂν W: καὶ Ast Sz.
καὶ ζητεῖν secl. Ast (fort. transp. post αὑτῷ): καὶ secl. Bdhm. Mdvg. Sz. Bt.
εἴ τινες W   ἀναγκασθεὶς Ast   ἵνα...εἶναι secl. Hug: ἵνα del. Ast   ἵνα
ἴδῃι T: ινα ειδηι O.-P.: ἵν᾽ αιδηι B: fort. ἵνα διίδῃ   αὖ ⟨τὸ τῶν⟩ Hirschig
D τῷ Schleierm. Sz. Bt.: τὸ libri, O.-P.   οἰκέτης: ὁ ἱκέτης Hommel
παιδαρίου del. Ast

ὥστε καὶ ἐὰν κτλ.   The uncontracted form καὶ ἐάν is very rare in Plato, see
Schanz *nov. comm.* p. 95.   For ἄνθος, cp. 183 E.

210 C [καὶ ζητεῖν].   Ast rightly condemned these words as "ineptum
glossema."   To excise καὶ only (as Badham) is unsatisfactory, since as Hug
justly observes τίκτειν ζητεῖν λόγους "ist unerträglich matt."   Stallb. attempts
to justify the words thus: "Diotima hoc dicit, talem amatorem non modo
ipsum parere quasi et ex se procreare, sed etiam aliunde quaerere et in-
vestigare eiusmodi sermones, qui iuvenes reddant meliores"; so too Rettig.
But this is futile.

ἐν τοῖς ἐπιτηδεύμασι.   "In Morals" (Stewart): cp. *Laws* 793 D ὅσα νόμους
ἢ ἔθη τις ἢ ἐπιτηδεύματα καλεῖ: *Rep.* 444 E: *Gorg.* 474 E.

ἵνα τὸ...εἶναι.   This clause is subordinate to, rather than coordinate with,
the preceding ἵνα clause (like the ἕως ἂν clause in D *infra*),—a juxtaposition
which sounds awkward.   Hence it is tempting either to excise this clause
with Hug, or with Ast to read ἀναγκασθεὶς for ἀναγκασθῇ, and delete the
second ἵνα.   Against Hug's method it may be urged that the words are
wanted to correspond to ἑνὸς...σμικρὸν ἡγησάμενον in 210 B above, and to
emphasize the "littleness" of corporeal beauty even when taken in the mass.
For this belittling of things of the earth, cp. *Theaet.* 173 E ἡ δὲ διάνοια, ταῦτα
πάντα ἡγησαμένη σμικρὰ καὶ οὐδέν, ἀτιμάσασα...φέρεται κτλ.   Observe how πᾶν
...ξυγγενές here balances (πᾶν) κάλλος...ἀδελφόν in 210 B.

ἀγαγεῖν.   The construction is still dependent upon δεῖ, but the subject to
be supplied (*viz.* τὸν ἡγούμενον) is changed.

210 D μηκέτι τῷ παρ᾽ ἑνί κτλ.   τῷ, *sc.* καλῷ, is governed by δουλεύων, and
the phrase contains a clear reference to the language of Pausanias in 183 A ff.
ὥσπερ οἰκέτης, "like a lackey," is of course contemptuous, as in *Theaet.* 172 D
κινδυνεύουσιν...ὡς οἰκέται πρὸς ἐλευθέρους τεθράφθαι.   For ἀγαπῶν, "contented
with," cp. *Menex.* 240 C.   If we retain the MSS.' τὸ παρ᾽ ἑνί the construction is

κάλλος ἢ ἀνθρώπου τινὸς ἢ ἐπιτηδεύματος ἑνός, δουλεύων φαῦλος
ᾖ καὶ σμικρολόγος, ἀλλ᾽ ἐπὶ τὸ πολὺ πέλαγος τετραμμένος τοῦ
καλοῦ καὶ θεωρῶν πολλοὺς καὶ καλοὺς λόγους καὶ μεγαλοπρεπεῖς
τίκτῃ καὶ διανοήματα ἐν φιλοσοφίᾳ ἀφθόνῳ, ἕως ἂν ἐνταῦθα ῥωσθεὶς καὶ αὐξηθεὶς κατίδῃ τινὰ ἐπιστήμην μίαν τοιαύτην, ἥ ἐστι
καλοῦ τοιοῦδε. πειρῶ δέ μοι, ἔφη, τὸν νοῦν προσέχειν ὡς οἷόν τε E
μάλιστα.

210 D κάλλος del. Bdhm.   ἢ ἀνθρώπου del. Schirlitz: fort. ἄνου
ἑνός: τινος O.-P.[1]   δουλεύων del. Bast   τίκτῃ Coisl. corr.: τίκτει BT
καὶ διανοήματα del. Bdhm.: ante τίκτῃ transp. Hommel   ἄφθονα Ast
ῥωθεὶς W

awkward, as Stallb.[2] admits—"quod olim accusativum defendendum susce-
pimus, videtur nunc interpretatio loci quam proposuimus, quamvis Rückerto
et Hommelio probata, nimis contorta nec satis simplex esse." I am inclined
to suspect the phrase ἢ ἀνθρώπου τινὸς. Schirlitz proposed to excise ἢ ἀνθρώπου: I suggest παιδαρίου κάλλος [ἢ] ἄνου τινὸς, "of some witless urchin," and
suppose a reference to what Pausanias said in 181 B ἐρῶσι...ὡς ἂν δύνωνται
ἀνοητοτάτων: 181 D οὐ γὰρ ἐρῶσι παίδων, ἀλλ᾽ ἐπειδὰν ἤδη ἄρχωνται νοῦν ἴσχειν
(cp. next n.).

φαῦλος...σμικρολόγος. Cp. 181 B, where those who follow Aphrodite Pandemos (loving women and boys) are described as οἱ φαῦλοι τῶν ἀνθρώπων.

ἐπὶ τὸ πολὺ πέλαγος. πέλαγος of itself connotes vastness; cp. Rep. 453 D
εἰς τὸ μέγιστον πέλαγος μέσον (ἄν τις ἐμπέσῃ): Prot. 338 A φεύγειν εἰς τὸ πέλαγος
τῶν λόγων. The phrase is alluded to in Clem. Al. protrept. 69 A; Plut. quaest.
Plat. 1001 E; Themist. or. XIII. p. 177 C.

θεωρῶν. This should be taken closely (supplying αὐτό) with what precedes,
not with πολλοὺς...λόγους (as Ast's Dict. s.v. implies). The parable suggests
that the spectator, having reached the hill-top, turns himself about and
gazes, wonder-struck, at the mighty ocean of beauty which lies spread before
him, till the spectacle quickens his soul and moves it to deliver itself of many
a deep-lying thought.

καλοὺς...μεγαλοπρεπεῖς. Cp. Menex. 247 B: ib. 234 C: Rep. 503 C νεανικοί τε
καὶ μ. τὰς διανοίας: ib. 486 A, 496 A γεννᾶν διανοήματά τε καὶ δόξας. Cp. for the
sense Plotin. de pulcr. 8 C (Cr.).

ἀφθόνῳ. ἄφθονος is used alike of fruits (Polit. 272 A) and of soils (Soph.
222 A), thus meaning both "abundant" and "bountiful"—"unstinted" and
"unstinting."

ῥωσθεὶς. Cp. Phaedr. 238 C; 176 B supra.

ἐπιστήμην μίαν. This unitary science—ἐπιστήμη in the strict Platonic
sense, called also (211 C) μάθημα—is dialectic: cp. Phaedr. 247 B τὴν ἐν τῷ ὅ
ἐστιν ὂν ὄντως ἐπιστήμην οὖσαν. See parallels in Plotin. de pulcr. 2 A (Cr.);
Procl. in I. Alc. p. 246.

210 E πειρῶ δέ μοι κτλ. Here again, as at 210 A (πειρῶ δὲ ἔπεσθαι κτλ.),
a climax in the exposition is marked.

XXIX. Ὃς γὰρ ἂν μέχρι ἐνταῦθα πρὸς τὰ ἐρωτικὰ παιδαγωγηθῇ, θεώμενος ἐφεξῆς τε καὶ ὀρθῶς τὰ καλά, πρὸς τέλος ἤδη
ἰὼν τῶν ἐρωτικῶν ἐξαίφνης κατόψεταί τι θαυμαστὸν τὴν φύσιν
καλόν, τοῦτο ἐκεῖνο, ὦ Σώκρατες, οὗ δὴ ἕνεκεν καὶ οἱ ἔμπροσθεν
211 πάντες πόνοι ἦσαν, πρῶτον μὲν ἀεὶ ὂν καὶ οὔτε γιγνόμενον οὔτε
ἀπολλύμενον, οὔτε αὐξανόμενον οὔτε φθῖνον, ἔπειτα οὐ τῇ μὲν
καλόν, τῇ δὲ αἰσχρόν, οὐδὲ τοτὲ μέν, τοτὲ δὲ οὔ, οὐδὲ πρὸς μὲν τὸ
καλόν, πρὸς δὲ τὸ αἰσχρόν, οὐδ᾽ ἔνθα μὲν καλόν, ἔνθα δὲ αἰσχρόν

211 A   τοδε δε O.-P.

___

ἐφεξῆς τε καὶ ὀρθῶς. "In correct and orderly succession"; see 211 B ad fin.
τοῦτο γὰρ δή ἐστι τὸ ὀρθῶς...ἰέναι κτλ., and 210 A where the right order of
procedure (πρῶτον...ἔπειτα, etc.) is specially emphasized.

πρὸς τέλος ἤδη ἰών. "πρὸς τέλος ἰέναι dicebantur ii, qui superatis gradibus
tandem ad spectanda arcana admittebantur" (Hommel). Cp. the use of τέλεα
in 210 A, τέλεον 204 C, τέλος 205 A.

ἐξαίφνης. "On a sudden": this suggests the final stage in the mystery-
rites, when out of darkness there blazed forth suddenly the mystical φέγγος,
and ἐν αὐγῇ καθαρᾷ the φάσματα (Phaedr. 250 c) or ἱερὰ μυστικά—consisting
probably of images of Demeter, Iacchus and Persephone, and other sacred
emblems—were displayed to the awe-struck worshipper (μακαρία ὄψις τε καὶ
θέα). Cp. Plotin. Enn. 43. 17 ὅταν ἡ ψυχὴ ἐξαίφνης φῶς λάβῃ κτλ.; Plato Ep.
vii. 341 C ἐξαίφνης, οἷον ἀπὸ πυρὸς πηδήσαντος ἐξαφθὲν φῶς, ἐν τῇ ψυχῇ γενό-
μενον (sc. the highest μάθημα). See further Rohde, Psyche II. 284.

κατόψεται. Cp. 210 D supra, and Phaedr. 247 D (καθορᾷ μὲν αὐτὴν δικαιοσύνην κτλ.), which suggest that καθορᾶν was a vox propria for viewing ritual
displays.

θαυμαστὸν...καλόν. Similarly Phaedr. 250 B κάλλος δὲ τότ᾽ ἦν ἰδεῖν λαμπρόν.
For θαυμαστόν cp. 219 B: it often connotes the supernatural, e.g. Rep. 398 A
προσκυνοῖμεν ἂν αὐτὸν ὡς ἱερὸν καὶ θ. καὶ ἡδύν.

οὗ δὴ ἕνεκεν κτλ. "The goal to which all our efforts have been directed":
cp. 210 A; Phaedr. 248 B οὗ δ᾽ ἕνεχ᾽ ἡ πολλὴ σπουδή κτλ. See the parallel in
Plotin. de pulcr. 42 C, D (Cr.).

211 A πρῶτον μὲν...ἔπειτα...οὐδ᾽ αὖ κτλ. The Ideal object is distinguished
by three leading characteristics, viz. (1) eternity and immutability; (2) abso-
luteness, or freedom from relativity; (3) self-existence. Compare the accounts
of Ideal being given in Phaedo 78 c ff., Phaedr. 247 c ff., Cratyl. 386 D, 439 c ff.,
Rep. 476 A, 479 A ff., Soph. 249 B ff., Phileb. 15 B, 58 A, Tim. 51 D ff. The
description has, necessarily, to be conveyed by means of negative propositions,
i.e. by way of contrast with phenomenal objects. See also the parallels in
Plotin. Enn. v. viii. 546 C, VI. vii. 727 C.

τῇ μὲν...τῇ δὲ. "In part...in part": so Theaet. 158 E, Polit. 274 E, Laws
635 D.

πρὸς μὲν τό...τό. This denotes varying "relation," as in the Aristotelian
τὸ πρός τι.

[ὡς τισὶ μὲν ὂν καλόν, τισὶ δὲ αἰσχρόν]· οὐδ' αὖ φαντασθήσεται
αὐτῷ τὸ καλὸν οἷον πρόσωπόν τι οὐδὲ χεῖρες οὐδὲ ἄλλο οὐδὲν ὧν
σῶμα μετέχει, οὐδέ τις λόγος οὐδέ τις ἐπιστήμη, οὐδέ που ὂν ἐν
ἑτέρῳ τινί, οἷον ἐν ζώῳ ἢ ἐν γῇ ἢ ἐν οὐρανῷ ἢ ἔν τῳ ἄλλῳ, ἀλλὰ Β
αὐτὸ καθ' αὑτὸ μεθ' αὑτοῦ μονοειδὲς ἀεὶ ὄν, τὰ δὲ ἄλλα πάντα καλὰ
ἐκείνου μετέχοντα τρόπον τινὰ τοιοῦτον, οἷον γιγνομένων τε τῶν

211 A ὡς...αἰσχρόν secl. Voeg. J.-U. Hug Sz. Bt.   ὂν om. W   αὖ BT
O.-P.: αὐτὸ W   αὐτῷ BT O.-P.: αὐτὸ W   οὐδὲν ὧν libri, edd.: ουδε εν O.-P.
B μετ αυτου O.-P.: del. Naber   τρόπον τινὰ B O.-P.: τινα τρόπον TW

ὥς τισὶ...αἰσχρόν. Rettig defends this clause, quoting Wolf's note, "τισί
(geht) auf alle vier (vorher genannten) Ideen, Theile, Zeit, Verhältniss, Ort."
Teuffel argues that "ausser Platon selbst hätte nicht leicht Jemand einen
Anlass gehalt einen Beisatz zu machen." None the less, I believe we have
here another "ineptum glossema."

φαντασθήσεται αὐτῷ. Sc. τῷ θεωμένῳ. φαντάζεσθαι often connotes illusive
semblance; cp. *Phaedo* 110 D, *Rep.* 572 B.

οὐδέ τις λόγος. It is difficult to be sure of the sense in which λόγος is
used here. (1) It is most natural to refer it, and ἐπιστήμη following, to the
λόγοι and ἐπιστῆμαι of 210 C, and to render by "discourse," "argument" (with
Gomperz, Stewart and Zeller). This rendering has in its favour the fact that
this is the usual sense of λόγος (λόγοι) throughout this dialogue. (2) Or
λόγος may mean "concept"; so Rettig, who comments: "Die Ideen sind
nicht blosse Begriffe, sie sind vielmehr Existenzen, χωρισταί, wie Aristoteles
sich ausdrückt, und Bedingungen des Seins und Werdens der Dinge der
Sinnenwelt." Cp. *Phaedr.* 245 E, *Laws* 895 E, *Phaedo* 78 C, in which places
(to quote Thompson) "λόγος is equivalent to ὅρος or ὁρισμός, of which οὐσία
is the objective counterpart." This more technical sense is, perhaps, less
probable in the present context; but, after all, the difference between the
two renderings is not of vital importance. The essence of the statement,
in either case, is that the Idea is not dependent upon either corporeal or
mental realization, *i.e.* that it is not subjective, as a quality or product of
body or mind, but an objective, self-conditioned entity. A third possible
sense of λόγος is "ratio," or mathematical relation. Perhaps "formula" would
best render the word here.

οὐδέ που ὄν. που is probably used in a local sense: cp. Arist. *Phys.* III. 4.
203ᵃ 7 Πλάτων δὲ ἔξω μὲν οὐδὲν εἶναι σῶμα, οὐδὲ τὰς ἰδέας, διὰ τὸ μηδέ που
εἶναι αὐτάς. But though the Ideas are extra-spatial, it is Platonic (as Aristotle
implies, *de An.* III. 4. 429ᵃ 27) to say τὴν ψυχὴν εἶναι τόπον εἰδῶν.

211 B μονοειδές. Cp. *Phaedo* 78 D μ. ὂν αὐτὸ καθ' αὑτό: *ib.* 80 B μονοειδεῖ
καὶ ἀδιαλύτῳ: *Theaet.* 205 D: *Tim.* 59 B: *Rep.* 612 A εἴτε πολυειδὴς εἴτε μονοει-
δὴς (ἡ ἀληθὴς φύσις). Stewart renders "of one Form," but the full force may
be rather "specifically unique," implying that it is the sole member of its class.

μετέχοντα. For the doctrine of "participation," see esp. *Phaedo* 100 C ff.,
Parmen. 130 B ff.

τοιοῦτον, οἷον. Equiv. to τοιοῦτον ὥστε (see Madv. *Gr. S.* § 166 c).

ἄλλων καὶ ἀπολλυμένων μηδὲν ἐκεῖνο μήτε τι πλέον μήτε ἔλαττον
γίγνεσθαι μηδὲ πάσχειν μηδέν. ὅταν δή τις ἀπὸ τῶνδε διὰ τὸ
ὀρθῶς παιδεραστεῖν ἐπανιὼν ἐκεῖνο τὸ καλὸν ἄρχηται καθορᾶν,
σχεδὸν ἄν τι ἅπτοιτο τοῦ τέλους. τοῦτο γὰρ δή ἐστι τὸ ὀρθῶς ἐπὶ
C τὰ ἐρωτικὰ ἰέναι ἢ ὑπ᾽ ἄλλου ἄγεσθαι, ἀρχόμενον ἀπὸ τῶνδε τῶν
καλῶν ἐκείνου ἕνεκα τοῦ καλοῦ ἀεὶ ἐπανιέναι, ὥσπερ ἐπαναβαθμοῖς
χρώμενον, ἀπὸ ἑνὸς ἐπὶ δύο καὶ ἀπὸ δυοῖν ἐπὶ πάντα τὰ καλὰ
σώματα, καὶ ἀπὸ τῶν καλῶν σωμάτων ἐπὶ τὰ καλὰ ἐπιτηδεύματα,
καὶ ἀπὸ τῶν ἐπιτηδευμάτων ἐπὶ τὰ καλὰ μαθήματα, καὶ ἀπὸ
τῶν μαθημάτων ἐπ᾽ ἐκεῖνο τὸ μάθημα τελευτῆσαι, ὅ ἐστιν οὐκ

211 B ἐκεῖνο Β Ο.-Ρ.: ἐκείνῳ TW   μήτε τι BTW: μήτε Vind. 31 Paris
1642 Ο.-Ρ.   ὅταν δή Β Ο.-Ρ.: ὅταν δὲ δή TW   C ἐπαναβαθμοῖς W: ἐπ᾽
ἀναβαθμοῖς Β: ἐπαναβασμοῖς T Ο.-Ρ.   σωμάτων ⟨ἐπὶ τὰς καλὰς ψυχάς, καὶ ἀπὸ
τῶν καλῶν ψυχῶν⟩ ἐπὶ Sydenham   ἀπὸ τῶν ⟨καλῶν⟩ ἐπιτ. vulg.   μαθήματα,
καὶ libri Ο.-Ρ., Bdhm. Usener Hug: μαθ., ὡς Sz. Bt.: μαθ., ἔστ᾽ ἂν vulg.: μ.,
ἕως ἂν Stallb.: μ. ἕως Herm.: μ., ἵνα Sauppe: μ., ἵνα καὶ Winckelmann   τὸ
μάθημα τελευτήσῃ del. Bdhm.   τελευτῆσαι Usener Hug: τελευτήσῃ libri, Sz.
Bt.: ante τελευτήσῃ lacunam statuit Voeg.

ἐκεῖνο. *Sc.* (αὐτὸ) τὸ καλόν. So frequently "ἐκεῖνο et ἐκεῖνα das Ueber-
sinnliche significat, τάδε vero vel ταῦτα das Sinnliche" (Ast): cp. *Phaedr.*
250 A, *Phaedo* 74 B, etc.

μηδὲ πάσχειν μηδέν. As to the ἀπάθεια of the Idea, see *Soph.* 248 A ff.,
251 c ff., and my article on "The Later Platonism" in *Journal of Philol.*
XXIII. pp. 189 ff.

ἐπανιών. Cp. *Rep.* 521 C τοῦ ὄντος οὖσαν ἐπάνοδον, ἣν δὴ φιλοσοφίαν ἀληθῆ
φήσομεν εἶναι: *ib.* 532 B, C.

τοῦ τέλους. This combines the senses "goal" and "sacred symbol": cf.
210 A; Soph. *fr.* 753 N. ὡς τρὶς ὄλβιοι | κεῖνοι βροτῶν, οἳ ταῦτα δερχθέντες τέλη |
μόλωσ᾽ ἐς Ἅιδου.

τοῦτο γὰρ δή κτλ. Here commences a recapitulation of "the Ascent of
Love" as described in 210 A—211 B; cp. *Rep.* VI., VII. for both language and
thought.

211 C ὑπ᾽ ἄλλου ἄγεσθαι. This refers to the παιδαγωγός or μυσταγωγός
of 210 E, not (as Wolf thought) to the operation of a δαίμων.

ἐπαναβαθμοῖς. For the notion of a ladder of ascent cp. *Rep.* 510 B ff., 511 B
τὰς ὑποθέσεις ποιούμενος οὐκ ἀρχὰς ἀλλὰ...οἷον ἐπιβάσεις τε καὶ ὁρμὰς ἵνα μέχρι
τοῦ ἀνυποθέτου ἐπὶ τὴν τοῦ παντὸς ἀρχὴν ἰὼν...οὕτως ἐπὶ τελευτὴν καταβαίνῃ κτλ.
Cp. Tennyson's "the great world's altar-stairs"; the dream-ladder at Bethel;
and the Titanic heaven-scaling of 190 B. Possibly a contrast is intended
between the futile attempt of the Earth-born εἰς τὸν οὐρανὸν ἀνάβασιν ποιεῖν,
and the successful efforts of the Heaven-born lover ἐπὶ τὸ καλὸν ἐπανιέναι.
For later parallels, see Plotin. *de pulcr.* 60 B (Cr.); Clem. Al. *Strom.* v.
p. 611 D.

καὶ ἀπὸ τῶν μαθημάτων κτλ. The reading and construction of this passage

ἄλλου ἢ αὐτοῦ ἐκείνου τοῦ καλοῦ μάθημα, <ἵνα> καὶ γνῷ αὐτὸ
τελευτῶν ὃ ἔστι καλόν. ἐνταῦθα τοῦ βίου, ὦ φίλε Σώκρατες, ἔφη D
ἡ Μαντινικὴ ξένη, εἴπερ που ἄλλοθι, βιωτὸν ἀνθρώπῳ, θεωμένῳ
αὐτὸ τὸ καλόν. ὃ ἐάν ποτε ἴδῃς, οὐ κατὰ χρυσίον τε καὶ ἐσθῆτα
καὶ τοὺς καλοὺς παῖδάς τε καὶ νεανίσκους δόξει σοι εἶναι, οὓς νῦν
ὁρῶν ἐκπέπληξαι καὶ ἕτοιμος εἶ καὶ σὺ καὶ ἄλλοι πολλοί, ὁρῶντες
τὰ παιδικὰ καὶ ξυνόντες ἀεὶ αὐτοῖς, εἴ πως οἷόν τ' ἦν, μήτε ἐσθίειν
μήτε πίνειν, ἀλλὰ θεᾶσθαι μόνον καὶ ξυνεῖναι. τί δῆτα, ἔφη,
οἰόμεθα, εἴ τῳ γένοιτο αὐτὸ τὸ καλὸν ἰδεῖν εἰλικρινές, καθαρόν, E
ἄμικτον, ἀλλὰ μὴ ἀνάπλεων σαρκῶν τε ἀνθρωπίνων καὶ χρωμάτων

211 C ⟨ἵνα⟩ καὶ scripsi: καὶ libri: ἵνα Usener: κἂν Bdhm.: καὶ γνῷ...καλόν
secl. Hug   αὐτὸ: αυτω O.-P.   D μαντικὴ vulg., Themistius   ποτε ιδης
O.-P.: ποτ' εἴδης B: ποτ' εἴδῃς T: ποτ' ἴδῃς apographa, Sz.   χρυσίον: χρυσον
O.-P.   ἀεὶ post μόνον καὶ transp. Ast   θεᾶσθαι μόνον TW: θεάσασθαι
μόνον B: μονον θεασασθαι O.-P.   E ἄμικτον post θνητῆς, ἀλλ' transp.
Liebhold   ἀλλὰ del. Ast Liebhold   αναπλεω O.-P.

---

are uncertain. I follow Usener in changing τελευτήσῃ to the infinitive and in
inserting ἵνα after μάθημα (retaining, however, καὶ before γνῷ which he needlessly deletes). The objection to Schanz's ὡς (for καὶ) ἀπὸ τῶν μ. is that ὡς,
in the final use, occurs but once elsewhere in Plato, according to Weber's
statistics (see Goodwin, G. M. T. p. 398), being very rare in all good prose-
writers except Xenophon. Another possible expedient would be to read
γνῶναι in place of γνῷ. ἔστ' ἄν is a non-Platonic form.

τελευτῆσαι...τελευτῶν. The repetition serves to emphasize the finality of
the Idea.

αὐτὸ...ὃ ἔστι. For this formula to express ideality, cp. Phaedo 74 B,
75 B οἷς ἐπισφραγιζόμεθα τοῦτο ὃ ἔστι : Theaet. 146 E.

211 D ἐνταῦθα...εἴπερ που ἄλλοθι. "There above all places"; so Phaedo
67 B ἐκεῖ...εἴπερ που ἄλλοθι: cp. 212 A εἴπερ τῳ ἄλλῳ...ἐκείνῳ. For ἐνταῦθα
c. gen. cp. Theaet. 177 C, Rep. 328 E. For βίος βιωτός, cp. Apol. 38 A, Eur.
Alc. 802.

οὐ κατὰ χρυσίον κτλ. Similar is Proverbs viii. 11 "Wisdom is better than
rubies; and all the things that may be desired are not to be compared to it."
That Socr. held this view is shown in 216 D, E. For κατά c. acc., of comparison,
cp. Gorg. 512 B, Rep. 466 B.

ξυνόντες...μήτε πίνειν. Cp. 191 A ff.; also Sappho 2, Archil. 103, Soph. fr.
161 N. (ὀμμάτειος πόθος): Rel. Med. "There are wonders in true affection—
when I am from him I am dead till I be with him," etc.

τί δῆτα...οἰόμεθα. Sc. γενέσθαι αὐτῷ, or the like.

211 E εἰλικρινές κτλ. Cp. Phileb. 52 D τὸ καθαρόν τε καὶ εἰλικρινές: Phaedo
66 A, Rep. 478 E.

μὴ ἀνάπλεων. Tim. ἀνάπλεως· ἀναπεπλησμένος· χρῆται δὲ ἐπὶ τοῦ μεμο-
λυσμένου: cp. Phaedo 83 D and the use of the verb in Phaedo 67 A μηδὲ

9—2

132 ΠΛΑΤΩΝΟΣ [211 E

καὶ ἄλλης πολλῆς φλυαρίας θνητῆς, ἀλλ' αὐτὸ τὸ θεῖον καλὸν
δύναιτο μονοειδὲς κατιδεῖν; ἆρ' οἴει, ἔφη, φαῦλον βίον γίγνεσθαι
212 ἐκεῖσε βλέποντος ἀνθρώπου καὶ ἐκεῖνο ᾧ δεῖ θεωμένου καὶ
ξυνόντος αὐτῷ; ἢ οὐκ ἐνθυμῇ, ἔφη, ὅτι ἐνταῦθα αὐτῷ μοναχοῦ
γενήσεται, ὁρῶντι ᾧ ὁρατὸν τὸ καλόν, τίκτειν οὐκ εἴδωλα ἀρετῆς, ἅτε οὐκ εἰδώλου ἐφαπτομένῳ, ἀλλ' ἀληθῆ, ἅτε τοῦ ἀληθοῦς
ἐφαπτομένῳ· τέκοντι δὲ ἀρετὴν ἀληθῆ καὶ θρεψαμένῳ ὑπάρχει

211 E θνητῆς del. Bdhm. ἀλλ'...κατιδεῖν del. Bdhm. ἔφη om. T
212 A ᾧ δεῖ Ast: ὧ δεῖ B: ὡδὶ b: ὁ δεῖ T: δὴ Schleierm.: ἀεὶ Rohde Sz.
ἐφαπτομένῳ del. Voeg.

ἀναπιμπλώμεθα τῆς τούτου (sc. τοῦ σώματος) φύσεως, ἀλλὰ καθαρεύωμεν ἀπ'
αὐτοῦ. Also *Rep.* 516 E, *Theaet.* 196 E. This passage is cited by Plotin. *Enn.*
I. vi. 7, p. 56.

χρωμάτων. For the Idea as ἀχρώματος οὐσία, see *Phaedr.* 247 C.

φλυαρίας θνητῆς. "Lumber of mortality": cp. *Phaedo* 66 C ἐρώτων δὲ καὶ
ἐπιθυμιῶν καὶ φόβων καὶ εἰδώλων παντοδαπῶν καὶ φλυαρίας ἐμπίπλησιν ἡμᾶς
πολλῆς (sc. τὸ σῶμα); *Gorg.* 490 C; *Rep.* 581 D.

φαῦλον βίον. For the sense, cp. Soph. *fr.* 753 N., Eur. *fr.* 965 D. ὄλβιος ὅστις
...ἀθανάτου καθορῶν φύσεως | κόσμον ἀγήρω κτλ.

212 A ἐκεῖνο ᾧ δεῖ. "With the proper organ," sc. τῷ νῷ: cp. *Phaedr.*
247 C ἡ γὰρ...ἀναφὴς οὐσία, ὄντως οὖσα, ψυχῆς κυβερνήτῃ μόνῳ θεατὴ νῷ κτλ. :
Phaedo 65 E; *Rep.* 490 B αὐτοῦ ὃ ἔστιν ἑκάστου τῆς φύσεως ἅψασθαι ᾧ προσήκει
ψυχῆς ἐφάπτεσθαι τοῦ τοιούτου: *ib.* 532 A πρὶν ἂν αὐτὸ ὃ ἔστιν ἀγαθὸν αὐτῇ
νοήσει λάβῃ. For the organ of intellectual vision (τὸ ὄργανον ᾧ καταμανθάνει
ἕκαστος...οἷον εἰ ὄμμα), see *Rep.* 518 C: cp. *S. Matth.* vi. 22 ff. So Browne
Hydriot. "Let intellectual tubes give thee a glance of things which visive
organs reach not": cp. Plotin. *de pulcr.* 60 B (Cr.).

οὐκ εἴδωλα...ἀλλ' ἀληθῆ. Rettig writes, "εἴδωλον ist hier nicht *Trugbild*,
sondern *Abbild*. εἴδωλα ἀρετῆς sind...Tugenden zweiten Grades. Vgl. Pol. VII.
516 A, 534 C, X. 596 A, 598 B...Commentar zu unserer Stelle ist Symp. 206 D."
On the other hand, cp. *Theaet.* 150 A εἴδωλα τίκτειν, with 150 C πότερον εἴδωλον
καὶ ψεῦδος ἀποτίκτει τοῦ νέου ἡ διάνοια ἢ γόνιμόν τε καὶ ἀληθές. Evidently here
the point of εἴδωλα lies in the inferiority rather than the similarity of the
objects when compared with ὄντως ὄντα. But it is scarcely probable that an
allusion is intended, as Zeller suggests, to the myth of Ixion "der seine
frevelnden Wünsche zu Here erhob, aber statt ihrer ein Wolkenbild umarmte
und mit ihm die Centauren erzeugte."

ἐφαπτομένῳ. Of mental action, cp. *Rep.* 490 B (quoted above). Voegelin
proposed to omit the second ἐφαπτομένῳ, but Plato never omits the participle
with ἅτε. For parallels, see *Phaedo* 67 B, *Rep.* 534 C; Plotin. *de pulcr.*
46 E (Cr.).

θρεψαμένῳ. Cp. 209 C.

θεοφιλεῖ γενέσθαι, καὶ εἴπερ τῳ ἄλλῳ ἀνθρώπων ἀθανάτῳ καὶ
ἐκείνῳ;
  Ταῦτα δή, ὦ Φαῖδρέ τε καὶ οἱ ἄλλοι, ἔφη μὲν Διοτίμα, πέπεισμαι B
δ᾽ ἐγώ· πεπεισμένος δὲ πειρῶμαι καὶ τοὺς ἄλλους πείθειν ὅτι τούτου τοῦ κτήματος τῇ ἀνθρωπείᾳ φύσει συνεργὸν ἀμείνω Ἔρωτος
οὐκ ἄν τις ῥᾳδίως λάβοι. διὸ δὴ ἔγωγέ φημι χρῆναι πάντα ἄνδρα
τὸν Ἔρωτα τιμᾶν καὶ αὐτὸς τιμῶ, <καὶ> τὰ ἐρωτικὰ καὶ διαφερόντως ἀσκῶ καὶ τοῖς ἄλλοις παρακελεύομαι, καὶ νῦν τε καὶ ἀεὶ
ἐγκωμιάζω τὴν δύναμιν καὶ ἀνδρείαν τοῦ Ἔρωτος καθ᾽ ὅσον οἷός τ᾽

212 A θεοφιλεῖ rec. t O.-P., vulg.: θεοφιλῆ BTW   B ὦ om. O.-P.
ἐγὼ χρῆναί φημι Method.   〈καὶ〉 τὰ ἐρωτικὰ καὶ Sz. : καὶ τὰ ἐρωτικὰ Usener:
τὰ δ᾽ ἐρωτικὰ καὶ Bdhm.   ἀσκῶν Vahlen   τον ερωτα post ἐγκωμιάζω add.
O.-P.¹   καὶ ἀνδρείαν secl. Hug: τε καὶ χρείαν Bdhm.

θεοφιλεῖ. Cp. *Rep.* 612 E, *Phil.* 39 E.
εἴπερ τῳ ἄλλῳ. Cp. *Phaedo* 58 E, 66 A; and 211 D *supra* (*ad init.*).
ἀθανάτῳ. Cp. Soph. *fr.* 864 N. οὐκ ἔστι γήρας τῶν σοφῶν, ἐν οἷς ὁ νοῦς |
θείᾳ ξύνεστιν ἡμέρᾳ τεθραμμένος. A passage such as this might have evoked
the remark in Isocr. *c. Soph.* 291 E μόνον οὐκ ἀθανάτους ὑπισχνοῦνται τοὺς
συνόντας ποιήσειν.
  212 B πέπεισμαι κτλ. "Beachte man das Spiel mit πέπεισμαι, πεπεισμένος, πειρῶμαι, πείθειν" (Rettig). Cp. 189 D ἐγὼ οὖν πειράσομαι κτλ.
κτήματος. *I.e.* αὐτοῦ τοῦ καλοῦ. Cp. *Phil.* 19 C τί τῶν ἀνθρωπίνων κτημάτων
ἄριστον : *ib.* 66 A.
συνεργὸν. Cp. 180 E; and 218 D τούτου δὲ οἶμαί μου συλλήπτορα οὐδένα
κυριώτερον εἶναι σοῦ.
διὸ δὴ...τιμᾶν. This echoes both Phaedrus's οὕτω δὴ ἔγωγέ φημι Ἔρωτα
θεῶν...τιμιώτατον (180 B) and Agathon's ᾧ χρὴ ἔπεσθαι πάντ᾽ ἄνδρα (197 E).
Probably τιμᾶν here implies practical veneration ; cp. the Homeric use of
τιμή (P 251, λ 304, ω 30, etc.), and Hes. *Theog.* 142.
τὰ ἐρωτικὰ...ἀσκῶ. For Socrates' devotion to "erotics," see 177 D οὐδέν
φημι ἄλλο ἐπίστασθαι ἢ τὰ ἐρωτικά, 198 D *ad init.* Probably ἀσκῶ (like τιμῶ)
has a religious connotation here, "I am a devotee of"; cp. Hesych. ἄσκεια·
θρήσκεια, εὐσέβεια : Pind. *Nem.* IX. 9 (with J. B. Bury's *note*). In spite of
Rettig's objection that Usener's conj. (see *crit. n.*) "bewirkt eine Tautologie
mit dem Folgenden καὶ νῦν...Ἔρωτος," it seems to me—as to Hug—an improvement, and (as modified by Schanz) I adopt it: a certain amount of
tautology is inevitable, unless we resort to excision. For καὶ (intensive)
διαφερόντως cp. *Phaedo* 59 A, *Rep.* 528 D. Vahlen, reading ἀσκῶν, construes
καὶ αὐτὸς τ. and καὶ τ. ἄ. παρακ. as parallel : but in this case I should expect
αὐτός 〈τε〉. Most edd. (Bekk., Bt., etc.) put commas after τιμᾶν and ἀσκῶ.
τὴν δύναμιν καὶ ἀνδρείαν. For the δύναμις of Eros cp. 188 D (Eryx.) πᾶσαν
δύναμιν ἔχει...ὁ πᾶς Ἔρως: and for his ἀνδρεία, 179 A (Phaedr.), 196 C ff.
(Agathon) εἷς γε ἀνδρείαν κτλ., 203 D (Socr.) ἀνδρεῖος ὤν (cp. 219 D ff.). The
intention here may be (as I find suggested also by Schirlitz) that the long

C εἰμί. τοῦτον οὖν τὸν λόγον, ὦ Φαῖδρε, εἰ μὲν βούλει, ὡς ἐγκώμιον εἰς Ἔρωτα νόμισον εἰρῆσθαι, εἰ δέ, ὅ τι καὶ ὅπῃ χαίρεις ὀνομάζων, τοῦτο ὀνόμαζε. XXX. Εἰπόντος δὲ ταῦτα τοῦ Σωκράτους τοὺς μὲν ἐπαινεῖν, τὸν δὲ Ἀριστοφάνη λέγειν τι ἐπιχειρεῖν, ὅτι ἐμνήσθη αὐτοῦ λέγων ὁ Σωκράτης περὶ τοῦ λόγου· καὶ ἐξαίφνης τὴν αὔλειον θύραν κρουομένην πολὺν ψόφον παρασχεῖν ὡς κωμαστῶν, καὶ αὐλητρίδος D φωνὴν ἀκούειν. τὸν οὖν Ἀγάθωνα, Παῖδες, φάναι, οὐ σκέψεσθε; καὶ ἐὰν μέν τις τῶν ἐπιτηδείων ᾖ, καλεῖτε· εἰ δὲ μή, λέγετε ὅτι οὐ

212 C επιχειρειν λεγειν τι O.-P.   αὔλειον rec. t O.-P., vulg.: αὔλιον BT
κροτουμένην T   ⟨καὶ⟩ ὡς Bdhm.: ὡς ⟨ὑπὸ⟩ Naber: καὶ Ast   D κεψεσθε
O.-P.   ἐὰν : αν O.-P.

course of παιδαγωγία described above requires ἀνδρεία in the learner who is to attain πρὸς τὸ τέλος: cp. *Meno* 81 D ἐάν τις ἀνδρεῖος ᾖ καὶ μὴ ἀποκάμῃ ζητῶν. Neither Badham's χρείαν (cp. 204 c) nor Hug's athetesis of ἀνδρείαν is probable.

212 C εἰ μὲν βούλει...εἰ δέ. Cp. *Euthyd.* 285 c (with Gifford's *n.*); Goodwin *G. M. T.* § 478.

ὅ τι...χαίρεις ὀνομάζων. Cp. *Prot.* 358 A; *Phaedr.* 273 c; Eur. *fr.* 967 D. σοὶ... Ζεὺς εἴτ' Ἀίδης | ὀνομαζόμενος στέργεις.

τοὺς μὲν ἐπαινεῖν. Observe that Socr. is not so enthusiastically applauded as Agathon (πάντας ἀναθορυβῆσαι, 198 A): Socrates appealed rather τῷ ἔχοντι ὦτα ἀκούειν.

λέγων...περὶ τοῦ λόγου. See 205 D ff. καὶ λέγεται...λόγος κτλ.

τὴν αὔλειον θύραν. For this "street-door," which generally opened inwards and gave admittance to a narrow passage (θυρωρεῖον), see Smith *D. A.* I. 661 *b*.

κρουομένην. As the Porter in *Macbeth* would say, "there was old knocking at the door." For κρούειν cp. *Prot.* 310 A, 314 D ; but the usual Attic word is κόπτειν (Moeris κόπτει τὴν θύραν ἔξωθεν...Ἀττικῶς, κροτεῖ δὲ Ἑλληνικῶς: Schol. ad Ar. *Nub.* 132 ἐπὶ μὲν τῶν ἔξωθεν κρουόντων κόπτειν λέγουσιν, ἐπὶ δὲ τῶν ἔσωθεν ψοφεῖν), or πατάσσειν Ar. *Ran.* 38. Cp. Smith *D. A.* I. 990 *b*.

ὡς κωμαστῶν. "Ut comissatorum, h. e. quasi comissatores eum (*sc.* strepitum) excitarent" (Stallb.). Stallb. rightly removed the comma placed after παρασχεῖν in Bekker's text. κωμασταί, "flown with insolence and wine," would naturally be in a noisy mood. For Alcib. as a reveller, see Plut. *Alcib.* 193 D.

αὐλητρίδος φωνὴν. Not "tibicinae vocem," as Wolf, but rather "sonum tibiae, quam illa inflavit," as Stallb. For φωνή thus (poetically) applied to instrumental music, cp. *Rep.* 397 A πάντων ὀργάνων φωνάς: similarly Xen. *Symp.* VI. 3 ὅταν ὁ αὐλὸς φθέγγηται. For the αὐλητρίς as a regular accessory of κῶμοι, cp. 176 E, *Theaet.* 173 D : similar are the ἑταῖραι of *Rep.* 373 A, 573 D : cp. Catullus's "cenam non sine candida puella."

212 D καλεῖτε. "Invite him in"; cp. 174 D, E, 175 B.

πίνομεν ἀλλὰ ἀναπαυόμεθα ἤδη. καὶ οὐ πολὺ ὕστερον Ἀλκιβιάδου τὴν φωνὴν ἀκούειν ἐν τῇ αὐλῇ σφόδρα μεθύοντος καὶ μέγα
βοῶντος, ἐρωτῶντος ὅπου Ἀγάθων καὶ κελεύοντος ἄγειν παρ᾽
Ἀγάθωνα. ἄγειν οὖν αὐτὸν παρὰ σφᾶς τήν τε αὐλητρίδα ὑπολαβοῦσαν καὶ ἄλλους τινὰς τῶν ἀκολούθων, καὶ ἐπιστῆναι ἐπὶ τὰς
θύρας ἐστεφανωμένον αὐτὸν κιττοῦ τέ τινι στεφάνῳ δασεῖ καὶ ἴων, E
καὶ ταινίας ἔχοντα ἐπὶ τῆς κεφαλῆς πάνυ πολλάς, καὶ εἰπεῖν·
Ἄνδρες, χαίρετε· μεθύοντα ἄνδρα πάνυ σφόδρα δέξεσθε συμπότην,

212 D   αλλα παυομεθα O.-P.   σφόδρα μ. καὶ del. Hartmann   ⟨καὶ⟩
ἐρωτῶντος vulg. Hirschig: del. Hommel Hartmann   κελεύοντος ⟨ἐ⟩ Hirschig
Sz.   E   ταινίας T O.-P.: τενίας B (et mox)   ὦνδρες Sz.: ὦ ᾽νδρες Usener
δέξεσθε B O.-P. corr.: δέξασθε T: δεξεσθαι O.-P.[1]

ἀναπαυόμεθα ἤδη.   "We are retiring already," rather than "the drinking
is over" (Jowett): cp. *Prot.* 310 C ἐπειδὴ...δεδειπνηκότες ἦμεν καὶ ἐμέλλομεν
ἀναπαύεσθαι κτλ.   The statement here would be a social fiction (see 174 D *n.*).

σφόδρα μεθύοντος κτλ.   Hommel and Hartman may be right in regarding
ἐρωτῶντος as a gloss: for βοᾶν followed directly by a question the former
quotes Asclep. *Epigr.* XIX. 5 τῇ δὲ τοσοῦτ᾽ ἐβόησα βεβρεγμένος· ἄχρι τίνος,
Ζεῦ;

ἄγειν οὖν.   Evidently the subject of this infin. is not Agathon's παῖδες, as
implied in Schleierm.'s transl., but Alcib.'s own attendants.

ὑπολαβοῦσαν.   For ὑπολαβεῖν in this physical sense, "casurum sustentare,"
cp. *Rep.* 453 D (the only other ex. in Plato), and Hdt. I. 24 of the dolphin
"supporting" by "getting under" Arion (L. and S.'s "take by the hand" is
probably wrong).

ἐπὶ τὰς θύρας.   "Intellige fores ipsius domus, in qua convivae erant, sive
τὴν μέταυλον θύραν" (Stallb.).

212 E   αὐτὸν...ἴων.   "More Graecorum abundat αὐτόν propter oppositio-
nem taeniarum quas gestabat in capite" (Wolf).   Violets were specially in
fashion at Athens, as implied in the epithet ἰοστέφανοι (Pind. *fr.* 46).   Other
favourite materials for wreaths were myrtle and roses: cp. Stesich. 29 πολλὰ
δὲ μύρσινα φύλλα | καὶ ῥοδίνους στεφάνους ἴων τε κορωνίδας οὔλας.

ταινίας.   Cp. Thuc. IV. 121 δημοσίᾳ μὲν χρυσῷ στεφάνῳ ἀνέδησαν...ἰδίᾳ δὲ
ἐταινίουν κτλ. : Pind. *Pyth.* IV. 240; Hor. *Carm.* IV. 11. 2.   See Holden on
Plut. *Timol.* p. 266: "ταινία, taenia, lemniscus, a sort of fillet or riband, given
as a reward of honour, either by itself, or more commonly as a decoration to
be fastened upon other prizes, such as crowns, wreaths, which were considered
more honourable when accompanied with a *lemniscus* than when they were
simply given by themselves.   Originally it was made of linden-bark or of wool,
but afterwards of gold and silver tinsel (Plin. *N. H.* 21. 4)."

μεθύοντα...πάνυ σφόδρα.   The peculiar order—"a drunken fellow right
royally (drunk)"—seems intended to indicate that the speaker is, or feigns
to be, considerably mixed.

ἢ ἀπίωμεν ἀναδήσαντες μόνον Ἀγάθωνα, ἐφ᾽ ᾧπερ ἤλθομεν; ἐγὼ
γάρ τοι, φάναι, χθὲς μὲν οὐχ οἷός τ᾽ ἐγενόμην ἀφικέσθαι, νῦν δὲ
ἥκω ἐπὶ τῇ κεφαλῇ ἔχων τὰς ταινίας, ἵνα ἀπὸ τῆς ἐμῆς κεφαλῆς
τὴν τοῦ σοφωτάτου καὶ καλλίστου κεφαλὴν †ἐὰν εἴπω† οὑτωσὶ
ἀναδήσω. ἆρα καταγελάσεσθέ μου ὡς μεθύοντος; ἐγὼ δέ, κἂν
213 ὑμεῖς γελᾶτε, ὅμως εὖ οἶδ᾽ ὅτι ἀληθῆ λέγω. ἀλλά μοι λέγετε
αὐτόθεν, ἐπὶ ῥητοῖς εἰσίω ἢ μή; συμπίεσθε ἢ οὔ;
Πάντας· οὖν ἀναθορυβῆσαι καὶ κελεύειν εἰσιέναι καὶ κατακλίνεσθαι, καὶ τὸν Ἀγάθωνα καλεῖν αὐτόν. καὶ τὸν ἰέναι ἀγόμενον
ὑπὸ τῶν ἀνθρώπων, καὶ περιαιρούμενον ἅμα τὰς ταινίας ὡς ἀναδή-
σοντα, ἐπίπροσθε τῶν ὀφθαλμῶν ἔχοντα οὐ κατιδεῖν τὸν Σωκράτη,
ἀλλὰ καθίζεσθαι παρὰ τὸν Ἀγάθωνα ἐν μέσῳ Σωκράτους τε καὶ

212 E ᾧπερ B: ὅπερ TW O.-P.   ἤλθομεν TW O.-P.: ἤχθομεν B
ἐχθές O.-P.   οἷός τ᾽ T O.-P.: οἷς τ᾽ B   ἐπὶ...ταινίας del. Naber   ἐὰν εἴπω
οὑτωσὶ BT: κεφαλὴν add. W: post ἀναδήσω transp. cj. Steph., post ἆρα Ast:
secl. Wolf J.-U. Bt.: ἀνειπὼν (vel ἐὰν ἀνείπω) οὑτωσὶ Winckelmann: ὧν εἶδον
οὔτ. Usener: ἐὰν εἰσίω οὔτ. Bergk: ἐὰν ἔτι οἷός τ᾽ ὦ, οὔτ. temptabam   κατα-
γελάσασθαι W   213 A   κελεύειν T: κελεύει B

χθὲς. *I.e.* at the main celebration of Agathon's victory, cp. 174 A.

ἐὰν εἴπω οὑτωσὶ. Since Wolf most edd. agree in obelizing these words as
a (misplaced) gloss on the following clause. Hommel's conj. is ingenious,
though far-fetched—ἐὰν εἶπον (addressed to his attendants) "dixi iam saepius,
mitti me velle liberum a vestris manibus." I have proposed ἐὰν ἔτι οἷός τ᾽ ὦ,
οὑτωσὶ ἀναδήσω, "if I am still capable of doing so," in jesting allusion to his
own incapable condition: or perhaps the original had νεανίσκου. The scenic
effectiveness of οὑτωσὶ, used δεικτικῶς, I should be loth to use. Jowett's "as
I may be allowed to call him" cannot be got out of the Greek.

213 A   αὐτόθεν. *Statim, illico* (Stallb.); cp. Thuc. VI. 21. 2.

ἐπὶ ῥητοῖς. "On the terms stated" (cp. *Laws* 850 A), *i.e.* as a συμπότης.
This is made clear by the following clause, συμπίεσθε ἢ οὔ; which repeats the
condition already stated in 212 E (μεθύοντα...δέξεσθε συμπότην): Rückert, as
Stallb. observes, is wrong in saying "at nullam (conditionem) dixit adhuc."
That Alcibiades meant his "conditions" to be taken seriously is shown by
the sequel, 213 E ff.

ἀναθορυβῆσαι. Cp. 198 A. For καλεῖν, see 212 D *ad init.*

ὑπὸ τῶν ἀνθρώπων. Including, we may suppose, the αὐλητρίς, see 212 D.

ἐπίπροσθε...Σωκράτη. "Und da er sie sich vor die Augen hielt, bemerkte
er Sokrates nicht" (Zeller). Ficinus, followed by Wolf and Schleierm., wrongly
renders "Socratem, licet e conspectu adstantem, non vidit"; so too Hommel
writes "ante oculos habuit et vidit Socratem, sed eum non agnovit." For
ἐπίπροσθεν ἔχειν, cp. *Critias* 108 C.

παρὰ τὸν Ἀγάθωνα. *I.e.* on the ἐσχάτη κλίνη: for the disposition of the
company see 175 C.

ἐκείνου· παραχωρῆσαι γὰρ τὸν Σωκράτη ὡς ἐκεῖνον κατεῖδεν. Β
παρακαθεζόμενον δὲ αὐτὸν ἀσπάζεσθαί τε τὸν Ἀγάθωνα καὶ
ἀναδεῖν. εἰπεῖν οὖν τὸν Ἀγάθωνα Ὑπολύετε, παῖδες, Ἀλκιβιάδην,
ἵνα ἐκ τρίτων κατακέηται. Πάνυ γε, εἰπεῖν τὸν Ἀλκιβιάδην·
ἀλλὰ τίς ἡμῖν ὅδε τρίτος συμπότης; καὶ ἅμα μεταστρεφόμενον
αὐτὸν ὁρᾶν τὸν Σωκράτη, ἰδόντα δὲ ἀναπηδῆσαι καὶ εἰπεῖν Ὦ
Ἡράκλεις, τουτὶ τί ἦν; Σωκράτης οὗτος; ἐλλοχῶν αὖ με ἐνταῦθα
κατέκεισο, ὥσπερ εἰώθεις ἐξαίφνης ἀναφαίνεσθαι ὅπου ἐγὼ ᾤμην C
ἥκιστά σε ἔσεσθαι. καὶ νῦν τί ἥκεις; καὶ τί αὖ ἐνταῦθα κατεκλίνης, καὶ οὐ παρὰ Ἀριστοφάνει οὐδὲ εἴ τις ἄλλος γελοῖος ἔστι

213 B κατεῖδεν scripsi: κατιδε[ν] O.-P.: καθίζειν libri: ὡς...καθίζειν secl.
Bdhm. Sz. Bt. ὅδε τρίτος W O.-P., Sz. Bt.: ᾧδε τρίτος B, J.-U.: τρίτος ὅδε T
ὁρᾶν T O.-P.: ὁρᾷ B τουτὶ τί ἦν TW O.-P.: τοῦτ' εἰπεῖν B Wmg. Σωκράτης
del. Naber ἐνλοχῶν B C εἰώθης vulg. καὶ οὐ Herm. Sz. Bt.: ὡς οὐ B:
πῶς οὐ Hug οὐδὲ B: οὔτε T

---

213 B παραχωρῆσαι. "Locum dedisse": cp. Prot. 336 B.
ὡς ἐκεῖνον κατεῖδεν. The adoption of this reading from the Papyrus obviates
the necessity of bracketing the words (see crit. n.). Adam on Rep. 365 D
writes "ὡς for ὥστε...is a curious archaism, tolerably frequent in Xenophon...
but almost unexampled in Plato," citing as instances Prot. 330 E, Phaedo
108 E, II. Alc. 141 B, and our passage: Goodwin, however (G. M. T. § 609),
recognizes only one instance of ὡς=ὥστε c. infin. in Plato (viz. Rep. l.c.).
Certainly this is no fit context for the introduction of a "curious archaism."
Ὑπολύετε. "Calceos solvite": see Smith D. A. I. 393 b. The opposite
process is ὑποδεῖν (174 A).
ἐκ τρίτων. Cp. Gorg. 500 A, Tim. 54 A; Eur. Or. 1178.
τουτὶ τί ἦν; "Mirandi formula, qua utuntur, quibus aliquid subito et
praeter exspectationem accidit" (Stallb.). The idiom is common in Aristophanes, e.g. Vesp. 183, 1509, Ran. 39, etc. The words Σ. οὗτος are, as
Rettig observes, "nicht Ausruf, sondern an sich selbst gerichtete Frage des
Alcibiades."
ἐλλοχῶν. Cp. Prot. 309 A ἀπὸ κυνηγεσίου τοῦ περὶ τὴν Ἀλκιβιάδου ὥραν;
I. Alc. 104 C. See also the description of Eros in 203 D (ἐπίβουλος κτλ.).
213 C ἐξαίφνης ἀναφαίνεσθαι. Cp. 210 E; Theaet. 162 C εἰ ἐξαίφνης οὕτως
ἀναφανήσει κτλ.
καὶ οὐ παρὰ κτλ. I adopt Hermann's καὶ for the ὡς of the mss. Stallb.
explains ὡς by "quippe, nam, ut mox in verbis ὡς ἐμοὶ...γέγονεν": Hommel,
putting a question-mark after βούλεται, renders "warum setzest du dich grade
dahin, als zum Beispiel nicht neben A." etc.: but, if ὡς be kept, it would be
best to mark a question after κατεκλίνης.
γελοῖος...βούλεται. With βούλεται, supply γελοῖος εἶναι. For Aristoph. as
γελοῖος, cp. 189 B. The sense is, as Rettig puts it, "Was hast du γελοῖος und

τε καὶ βούλεται, ἀλλὰ διεμηχανήσω ὅπως παρὰ τῷ καλλίστῳ τῶν
ἔνδον κατακείσῃ; καὶ τὸν Σωκράτη, Ἀγάθων, φάναι, ὅρα εἴ μοι
ἐπαμύνεις· ὡς ἐμοὶ ὁ τούτου ἔρως τοῦ ἀνθρώπου οὐ φαῦλον
πρᾶγμα γέγονεν. ἀπ᾽ ἐκείνου γὰρ τοῦ χρόνου, ἀφ᾽ οὗ τούτου
D ἠράσθην, οὐκέτι ἔξεστί μοι οὔτε προσβλέψαι οὔτε διαλεχθῆναι
καλῷ οὐδ᾽ ἑνί, ἢ οὑτοσὶ ζηλοτυπῶν με καὶ φθονῶν θαυμαστὰ
ἐργάζεται καὶ λοιδορεῖταί τε καὶ τὼ χεῖρε μόγις ἀπέχεται. ὅρα
οὖν μή τι καὶ νῦν ἐργάσηται, ἀλλὰ διάλλαξον ἡμᾶς, ἢ ἐὰν
ἐπιχειρῇ βιάζεσθαι, ἐπάμυνε, ὡς ἐγὼ τὴν τούτου μανίαν τε καὶ
φιλεραστίαν πάνυ ὀρρωδῶ. Ἀλλ᾽ οὐκ ἔστι, φάναι τὸν Ἀλκιβιάδην,
ἐμοὶ καὶ σοὶ διαλλαγή. ἀλλὰ τούτων μὲν εἰσαῦθίς σε τιμωρή-

213 C βούλεται ⟨εἶναι⟩ Bdhm.   διεμηχανήσω : τι εμηχανησω O.-P.   ⟨ὢ⟩
Ἀγάθων vulg. Jn.   ἐπαμύνεις libri, Bt.: ἐπαμυνεῖς Steph. J.-U. Sz.   οὐ T :
οὗ B   D οὑτοσὶ ₓₓₓ T : οὑτοσί πως Coisl.   θαυμαστὰ B O.-P.: θαυμάσια
TW   ἐπάμυνε T : ἐπάμυναι B

ὑβριστής bei dem liebenswürdigen Tragiker zu thun, du gehörst zu dem Spott-
vogel Aristophanes": "birds of a feather should flock together." Rückert
suggests that the antithesis γελοῖος)(κάλλιστος may imply a reflection on
"Aristophanis forma."

διεμηχανήσω. For erotic scheming, cp. 203 D ff.

ἐπαμύνεις. "In animated language the present often refers to the future,
to express *likelihood, intention*, or *danger*" (Goodwin, *G. M. T.* § 32).

213 D προσβλέψαι. This may have been the *vox propria* for a lover's
glance, cp. Ar. *Plut.* 1014 (quoted below).

ἢ οὑτοσί. This (elliptical) use of ἤ, *alioquin*, "but that," is "regular with
δεῖ, προσήκει, and the like, in the preceding clause" (Adam on *Prot.* 323 A).

ζηλοτυπῶν. This is a ἅπ. εἰρ. in Plato : cp. Ar. *Plut.* 1014 ff. ὅτι προσέβλεψέν
μέ τις, | ἐτυπτόμην διὰ τοῦθ᾽ ὅλην τὴν ἡμέραν. | οὕτω σφόδρα ζηλότυπος ὁ
νεανίσκος ἦν.

θαυμαστὰ ἐργάζεται. Cp. *Laws* 686 C θ. ἐργασάμενον; *Theaet.* 151 A θ.
δρῶντες; 182 E *supra* θ. ἔργα ἐργαζομένῳ: similarly 218 A ποιοῦσι δρᾶν τε καὶ
λέγειν ὁτιοῦν.

τὼ χεῖρε. This and 214 D *infra* are the only exx. in Plato of ἀπέχεσθαι in
the sense *continere* (*manum*): elsewhere it occurs mainly in poetry (*Od.* XXII.
316, etc.).

μανίαν. Cp. *Laws* 839 A λύττης...ἐρωτικῆς καὶ μανίας: Soph. *fr.* 162 νόσημ᾽
ἔρωτος τοῦτ᾽ ἐφίμερον κακόν : and 173 D *supra*.

φιλεραστίαν. "Amor quo quis amatorem amplectitur" (Ast); equivalent
to ἀντέρως (*Phaedr.* 255 D): cp. 192 B.

ὀρρωδῶ. *Horresco*, a strong word for "quaking with fear."

διαλλαγή. Alcib. catches up Socrates' word διάλλαξον and negatives it
with a "What hast thou to do with peace?" "But," he proceeds, "I'll have

σομαι· νῦν δέ μοι, Ἀγάθων, φάναι, μετάδος τῶν ταινιῶν, ἵνα
ἀναδήσω καὶ τὴν τούτου ταυτηνὶ τὴν θαυμαστὴν κεφαλήν, καὶ μή Ε
μοι μέμφηται ὅτι σὲ μὲν ἀνέδησα, αὐτὸν δὲ νικῶντα ἐν λόγοις
πάντας ἀνθρώπους, οὐ μόνον πρῴην ὥσπερ σύ, ἀλλ᾽ ἀεί, ἔπειτα
οὐκ ἀνέδησα. καὶ ἅμ᾽ αὐτὸν λαβόντα τῶν ταινιῶν ἀναδεῖν τὸν
Σωκράτη καὶ κατακλίνεσθαι. XXXI. Ἐπειδὴ δὲ κατεκλίνη, εἰπεῖν· Εἶεν δή, ἄνδρες·
δοκεῖτε γάρ μοι νήφειν· οὐκ ἐπιτρεπτέον οὖν ὑμῖν, ἀλλὰ ποτέον·
ὡμολόγηται γὰρ ταῦθ᾽ ἡμῖν. ἄρχοντα οὖν αἱροῦμαι τῆς πόσεως,
ἕως ἂν ὑμεῖς ἱκανῶς πίητε, ἐμαυτόν. ἀλλὰ φερέτω, Ἀγάθων, εἴ τι
ἔστιν ἔκπωμα μέγα. μᾶλλον δὲ οὐδὲν δεῖ, ἀλλὰ φέρε, παῖ, φάναι,

213 D ⟨ὦ⟩ Ἀγάθων Sauppe Jn. Sz.: ὦ 'γάθων J.-U.   Ε ἀναδήσω καὶ
TW O.-P., Sz. Bt.: ἀναδησώμεθα Β: ἀναδήσωμεν καὶ Herm. J.-U.   τὴν τούτου
secl. Jn.   ἄνδρες: ὦνδρες Sz. J.-U.   οὖν ὑμῖν T, Winckelmann Bt.: ὑμῖν Β,
J.-U. Sz.   φερέτω, Ἀγάθων Bt.: φερέτω Ἀγ. libri: φέρετ᾽, ὦ Ἀγ. Cobet
J.-U.: φερέτω, ὦ Ἀγ. Naber: Ἀγάθων secl. Sz.   ἔκπωμα T: ἔκπομα Β

---

that out with you by-and-bye!" (see 214 c *ad fin.* ff.). Then, with a sudden
change of tone from bullying and banter to affectionate earnestness, he begins
νῦν δέ μοι κτλ.

213 E τὴν τούτου...κεφαλήν. "Incipit Alc. dicere τὴν τούτου κεφαλήν,
quod priusquam elocutus est, sentit nimis languidum esse; inde revertitur
quasi ac denuo progreditur, positis verbis ταυτηνὶ τὴν θ. κ." (Rückert). Perhaps as Alc. says these words (notice the deictic ταυτηνί) he playfully strokes
the head of Socr. τούτου is expanded by Jowett into "of this universal
despot."

νικῶντα. The present symposium was part of Agathon's *epinikian* celebration (see 174 A), and his victory also was gained by λόγοι (cp. 194 B).

ἔπειτα. *Tamen,* "yet after all," *i.e.* in spite of the fact of his perpetual
victoriousness. Cp. *Prot.* 319 D, 343 D.

κατακλίνεσθαι. Ever since he first discovered Socrates, Alcibiades had
been standing (see 213 B *ad fin.* ἀναπηδῆσαι).

Εἶεν δή. "Come now": "die Worte enthalten hier eine Aufforderung"
(Rettig). Cp. 204 c, *Phaedo* 95 A. The question to drink or not to drink is
now resumed from 213 A *ad init.*

οὐκ ἐπιτρεπτέον. "This can't be allowed": cp. *Rep.* 379 A and 219 c *infra.*

ὡμολόγηται κτλ. See 212 E f.

ἄρχοντα...τῆς πόσεως. "As symposiarch": cp. the Latin *arbiter* (*magister*)
bibendi Hor. *C.* I. 4. 17, II. 7. 25. For the qualifications proper in such
"archons," see *Laws* 640 c ff.; and for other details, Smith *D. A.* II. 740 *b* ff.
The emphatic position of ἐμαυτόν is to be noticed.

φερέτω, Ἀγάθων. Sc. ὁ παῖς: I adopt Burnet's improved punctuation,
which renders further change needless.

214 τὸν ψυκτῆρα ἐκεῖνον, ἰδόντα αὐτὸν πλέον ἢ ὀκτὼ κοτύλας χωροῦντα.
τοῦτον ἐμπλησάμενον πρῶτον μὲν αὐτὸν ἐκπιεῖν, ἔπειτα τῷ Σωκράτει κελεύειν ἐγχεῖν καὶ ἅμα εἰπεῖν· Πρὸς μὲν Σωκράτη, ὦ
ἄνδρες, τὸ σόφισμά μοι οὐδέν· ὁπόσον γὰρ ἂν κελεύῃ τις, τοσοῦτον
ἐκπιὼν οὐδὲν μᾶλλον μή ποτε μεθυσθῇ. τὸν μὲν οὖν Σωκράτη
ἐγχέαντος τοῦ παιδὸς πίνειν· τὸν δ' Ἐρυξίμαχον Πῶς οὖν, φάναι,
ὦ Ἀλκιβιάδη, ποιοῦμεν; οὕτως οὔτε τι λέγομεν ἐπὶ τῇ κύλικι
B οὔτε τι ᾄδομεν, ἀλλ' ἀτεχνῶς ὥσπερ οἱ διψῶντες πιόμεθα; τὸν οὖν

214 A πλέον : πλεῖν J.-U.   τοῦτον ⟨οὖν⟩ Athenaeus   κελεύῃ B :
κελεύσῃ T   ποιῶμεν apogr. Laur. IX. 85, Hirschig Naber (ποιῶμεν—λέγωμεν—
ᾄδωμεν Sommer)   B οὔτε τι ᾄδομεν T, Bt.: οὔτ' ἐπᾴδομεν B, J.-U. Sz.

214 A τὸν ψυκτῆρα. "Yonder wine-cooler." Suid. ψυκτῆρα· κάδδον ἢ ποτή-
ριον μέγα, ἀπὸ τοῦ θᾶττον ψύχεσθαι ἐν αὐτῷ τὴν κρᾶσιν : Poll. VI. 99 ὁ δὲ ψυκτήρ
πολυθρύλητος, ὃν καὶ δῖνον ἐκάλουν, ἐν ᾧ ἦν ὁ ἄκρατος· οἱ πολλοὶ δὲ ἀκρατοφόρον
αὐτὸν καλοῦσιν. οὐ μὴν ἔχει πυθμένα ἀλλ' ἀστραγαλίσκους. Other names for
it were πρόχυμα (Moeris, Schol. Ar. Vesp. 617) and κάλαθος (Hesych. s.v.):
for details see Smith D. A. s.v. Psycter; cp. Xen. Mem. II. i. 30 ἵνα δὲ ἡδέως
πίῃς,...τοῦ θέρους χιόνα περιθέουσα ζητεῖς : Xen. Symp. II. 23 ff.

ὀκτὼ κοτύλας. The κοτύλη or ἡμίνα (=6 κύαθοι) was ·48 of a pint, so
that 8 κοτύλαι are nearly equal to 2 quarts. For a ψυκτήρ this seems to
have been a small size, since Athenaeus (v. 199) mentions ψυκτῆρες holding
18 to 54 gallons. Alcib. was not alone in his taste for an ἔκπωμα μέγα:
cp. Anacr. 32 τρικύαθον κελέβην ἔχουσα: Alcaeus 41. 2 καδ' δ' ἄειρε κυλίχναις
μεγάλαις : Xen. Symp. l.c. ὁ παῖς ἐγχεάτω μοι τὴν μεγάλην φιάλην : Gouffé (Le
Verre) "Nous devons aux petites gens Laisser les petits verres."

ἐμπλησάμενον. "Ast: implevisse. Immo implendum curasse" (Rückert).

ἐγχεῖν. Cp. Soph. fr. 149 D φορεῖτε, μασσέτω τις, ἐγχείτω βαθὺν κρητῆρα:
Alcaeus 31. 4 ἔγχεε κίρναις ἕνα καὶ δύο κτλ.: Theogn. 487 σὺ δ' ἔγχεε τοῦτο
μάταιον | κωτίλλεις ἀεί· τοὔνεκά τοι μεθύεις. Notice that Alcib. adopts the
order ἐπὶ δεξιά, see 175 E.

τὸ σόφισμά μοι οὐδέν. "My trick avails nothing." For σόφισμα, "a witty
invention," cp. Lach. 183 D, Rep. 496 A; Aesch. P. V. 470. Alcib., with his
σόφισμα, recals Eros the σοφιστής (203 D).

οὐδὲν...μεθυσθῇ. See Goodwin G.M.T. § 295. For Socrates' invincible head
for wine, see also 176 C, 220 B, 223 C.

Πῶς οὖν...ποιοῦμεν. The present indic. differs from the subjunctive, "quod
dicitur de eo quod revera iam fit, neque adhuc suscipiendum est" (Stallb.):
contrast ἀλλὰ τί ποιῶμεν (deliberative) just below. For the indignant οὕτω
cp. Hom. Il. II. 158 οὕτω δὴ οἴκόνδε...φεύξονται.

214 B οὔτε τι ᾄδομεν. This lection is preferable to B.'s οὔτ' ἐπᾴδομεν
which is accepted by most later editors. Eryx. would not propose to "chant
spells," the only sense in which the compound word is used by Plato. For
the idea of trolling a catch over one's cups, cp. Gouffé (Couplets) "On boit

Ἀλκιβιάδην εἰπεῖν Ὦ Ἐρυξίμαχε, βέλτιστε βελτίστου πατρὸς
καὶ σωφρονεστάτου, χαῖρε. Καὶ γὰρ σύ, φάναι τὸν Ἐρυξίμαχον·
ἀλλὰ τί ποιῶμεν; Ὅ τι δᾶν σὺ κελεύῃς. δεῖ γάρ σοι πείθεσθαι·
ἰητρὸς γὰρ ἀνὴρ πολλῶν ἀντάξιος ἄλλων·
ἐπίτατte οὖν ὅ τι βούλει. Ἄκουσον δή, εἰπεῖν τὸν Ἐρυξίμαχον.
ἡμῖν πρὶν σὲ εἰσελθεῖν ἔδοξε χρῆναι ἐπὶ δεξιὰ ἕκαστον ἐν μέρει
λόγον περὶ Ἔρωτος εἰπεῖν ὡς δύναιτο κάλλιστον, καὶ ἐγκωμιάσαι. C
οἱ μὲν οὖν ἄλλοι πάντες ἡμεῖς εἰρήκαμεν· σὺ δ' ἐπειδὴ οὐκ εἴρηκας
καὶ ἐκπέπωκας, δίκαιος εἶ εἰπεῖν, εἰπὼν δ' ἐπιτάξαι Σωκράτει ὅ τι
ἂν βούλῃ, καὶ τοῦτον τῷ ἐπὶ δεξιὰ καὶ οὕτω τοὺς ἄλλους. Ἀλλά,
φάναι, ὦ Ἐρυξίμαχε, τὸν Ἀλκιβιάδην, καλῶς μὲν λέγεις, μεθύοντα
δὲ ἄνδρα παρὰ νηφόντων λόγους παραβάλλειν μὴ οὐκ ἐξ ἴσου ᾖ.

214 B Ἐρυξίμαχε del. Naber   δᾶν Bt.: δ' ἂν T: ἂν B, J.-U.   πιθέσθαι
Bdhm. ἰητρὸς T, Sz. Bt.: ἰατρὸς B   C ὡς ⟨ἂν⟩ Sauppe   ⟨τοὺς⟩ νηφόντων
vel νήφοντας cj. Steph.   λόγους ⟨λόγον⟩ Bast

chez eux, on boit beaucoup Et de bourgogne et de champagne; Mais rien ne
vaut un petit coup Qu'un petit couplet accompagne."
For λόγοι ἐπικυλίκειοι, cp. Athen. 2 A; Lucian *Timon*, c. 55.
Ὦ Ἐρυξίμαχε κτλ. Alcibiades—as if to show how ready he is ᾄδειν τι—
replies with an iambic trimeter—"A noble sire's most noble, sober son!"
The superlatives are not without irony, cp. 177 B, Xen. *Mem.* III. 13. 2.
χαῖρε. "All hail!" Alcibiades pretends to have noticed the doctor
before.
ἰητρὸς γὰρ...ἄλλων. From *Il.* XI. 514: "Surely one learnèd leech is a
match for an army of laymen." Pope's rendering—"the wise physician skilled
our wounds to heal"—hardly deserves the name, although Jowett paid it the
compliment of borrowing it.
ἐπίτατte. "Prescribe": the techn. term for a medical prescription, cp.
Rep. 347 A κατὰ τὴν τέχνην ἐπιτάττων : *Polit.* 294 D, *Laws* 722 E.
ἔδοξε κτλ. See 177 D.
214 C ὡς δύναιτο κάλλιστον. Cp. Thuc. VII. 21 ναῦς ὡς δύνανται πλείστας
πληροῦσιν (Madv. *Gr. S.* § 96): there is no need to insert ἄν, as Sauppe
suggested.
καὶ ἐκπέπωκας. "But have finished your draught."
μεθύοντα...παραβάλλειν. "μεθύοντα negligentius dictum est pro λόγον
ἀνδρὸς μεθύοντος" (Wolf). For the brachylogy cp. 180 C μετὰ δὲ Φαῖδρον
κτλ. (see *note ad loc.*); 217 D ἐν τῇ ἐχομένῃ ἐμοῦ κλίνῃ. With παραβάλλειν
we must supply as subject τινα (with Rettig) rather than σε, i.e. Ἐρυξίμαχον
(with Wolf). Of conjectures Bast's is the most plausible. Cp. Theogn. 627
αἰσχρόν τοι μεθύοντα παρ' ἀνδράσι νηφόσι μεῖναι.
For a stricture on ἔπαινοι μεθύοντος, see *Phaedr.* 240 E.

142 ΠΛΑΤΩΝΟΣ [214 c

D καὶ ἅμα, ὦ μακάριε, πείθει τί σε Σωκράτης ὧν ἄρτι εἶπεν; ἢ
οἶσθα ὅτι τοὐναντίον ἐστὶ πᾶν ἢ ὃ ἔλεγεν; οὗτος γάρ, ἐάν τινα ἐγὼ
ἐπαινέσω τούτου παρόντος ἢ θεὸν ἢ ἄνθρωπον ἄλλον ἢ τοῦτον, οὐκ
ἀφέξεταί μου τὼ χεῖρε. Οὐκ εὐφημήσεις; φάναι τὸν Σωκράτη.
Μὰ τὸν Ποσειδῶ, εἰπεῖν τὸν Ἀλκιβιάδην, μηδὲν λέγε πρὸς ταῦτα,
ὡς ἐγὼ οὐδ' ἂν ἕνα ἄλλον ἐπαινέσαιμι σοῦ παρόντος. Ἀλλ' οὕτω
ποίει, φάναι τὸν Ἐρυξίμαχον, εἰ βούλει· Σωκράτη ἐπαίνεσον.
E Πῶς λέγεις; εἰπεῖν τὸν Ἀλκιβιάδην· δοκεῖ χρῆναι, ὦ Ἐρυξίμαχε;
ἐπιθῶμαι τῷ ἀνδρὶ καὶ τιμωρήσωμαι ὑμῶν ἐναντίον; Οὗτος, φάναι
τὸν Σωκράτη, τί ἐν νῷ ἔχεις; ἐπὶ τὰ γελοιότερά με ἐπαινέσει; ἢ τί
ποιήσεις; Τἀληθῆ ἐρῶ. ἀλλ' ὅρα εἰ παρίης. Ἀλλὰ μέντοι, φάναι,
τά γε ἀληθῆ παρίημι καὶ κελεύω λέγειν. Οὐκ ἂν φθάνοιμι, εἰπεῖν
τὸν Ἀλκιβιάδην. καὶ μέντοι οὑτωσὶ ποίησον. ἐάν τι μὴ ἀληθὲς
λέγω, μεταξὺ ἐπιλαβοῦ, ἂν βούλῃ, καὶ εἰπὲ ὅτι τοῦτο ψεύδομαι·

214 D ἢ οἶσθ' J.-U.   E τιμωρήσομαι W   ἐπαινέσει Bekk. Sz.:
ἐπαινέσεις BTW : ἐπαινέσαι Bt.   παριεῖς Schanz

214 D ὦ μακάριε. "Gutmuthig-ironisch" (Rettig): cp. 219 A.
πείθει...εἶπεν; "H. e. πείθει σέ τι τούτων ἃ Σ. ἄρτι εἶπεν;...h. e. noli
quidquam eorum credere quae modo dixit S." (Stallb.). A. is alluding to
213 C—D (ἀπ' ἐκείνου γὰρ τοῦ χρόνου κτλ.).
οὐκ ἀφέξεται κτλ. "Satis lepide iisdem fere verbis hic utitur Alcib. quae
Socr. l. l. exhibuit" (Hommel) ; A. is turning the tables on S.
Μὰ τὸν Ποσειδῶ. This form of oath is rare in Plato, see Schanz nov. comm.
Plat. p. 23. The main reason why A. chooses Poseidon to swear by is, no
doubt, because P. was the special deity of the ancient aristocracy of Athens
(see R. A. Neile's ed. of Ar. Knights, p. 83) ; but A. may also be punning on
πόσις, as if Ποσειδῶν meant "drink-giver," and invoking a "deus madidus"
as appropriate to his own "madid" condition. Cp. Euthyd. 301 E, 303 A.
214 E τιμωρήσωμαι. This echoes the τιμωρήσομαι of 213 D.
Οὗτος. "Ho, there!" Cp. 172 A.
ἐπὶ τὰ γελοιότερα. "To make fun of me": cp. Phileb. 40 C (ἡδοναὶ) μεμι-
μημέναι τὰς ἀληθεῖς ἐπὶ τὰ γελοιότερα ("caricatures"): so ἐπὶ τὰ αἰσχίονα Polit.
293 E, 297 C.
ἐπαινέσει. Plato always uses the middle form of the future, with the
doubtful exception of Laws 719 E (where Burnet, after Bekker, corrects ἐπαι-
νέσοι to ἐπαινέσαι), see Veitch Gk. Verbs s.v.
Οὐκ ἂν φθάνοιμι. Sc. τἀληθῆ λέγων : iamiam dicam. Cp. 185 E, Phaedo
100 C, Euthyd. 272 D (in all which places the participle is expressed).
καὶ...ποίησον. Hommel rashly proposes to read ποιήσων for ποίησον and
remove the stop after the word. For καὶ μέντοι, see Madv. Gr. S. § 254.
ἐπιλαβοῦ. "Pull me up," "call me to order." Cp. Gorg. 469 C, 506 B
ἐπιλαμβάνου ἐάν τί σοι δοκῶ μὴ καλῶς λέγειν.

ἐκὼν γὰρ εἶναι οὐδὲν ψεύσομαι. ἐὰν μέντοι ἀναμιμνῃσκόμενος 215
ἄλλο ἄλλοθεν λέγω, μηδὲν θαυμάσῃς· οὐ γάρ τι ῥᾴδιον τὴν σὴν
ἀτοπίαν ὧδ' ἔχοντι εὐπόρως καὶ ἐφεξῆς καταριθμῆσαι.
XXXII. Σωκράτη δ' ἐγὼ ἐπαινεῖν, ὦ ἄνδρες, οὕτως ἐπιχειρήσω,
δι' εἰκόνων. οὗτος μὲν οὖν ἴσως οἰήσεται ἐπὶ τὰ γελοιότερα, ἔσται
δ' ἡ εἰκὼν τοῦ ἀληθοῦς ἕνεκα, οὐ τοῦ γελοίου. φημὶ γὰρ δὴ ὁμοιό-
τατον αὐτὸν εἶναι τοῖς σιληνοῖς τούτοις τοῖς ἐν τοῖς ἑρμογλυφείοις

215 A   τι : τοι vulg. Hirschig   ἑρμογλυφίοις T

215 A **ἄλλο ἄλλοθεν.** "In a wrong order," or "in promiscuous fashion":
cp. *Il.* II. 75, Aesch. *Ag.* 92, etc. Alcib. forestalls criticism by this apology for
the "mixed" style of his reminiscences, on the ground of what he calls his
"present condition" (ὧδ' ἔχοντι=μεθύοντι, *crapula laboranti*).
οὐ γάρ τι ῥᾴδιον. For οὔτι, *handquaquam*, cp. 189 B.
ἀτοπίαν. Cp. *Gorg.* 494 D ; 221 c *infra.* That Socrates is an "out-of-the-
way" character, a walking conundrum, is, in fact, the main theme of Alc.'s
speech : it is a mistake to limit this ἀτοπία to the contradiction between his
outer and inner man, as Susemihl does.
οὕτως...δι' εἰκόνων. For οὕτως with an epexegetic phrase, cp. 193 c, *Laws*
633 D, *Rep.* 551 c οὕτω...ἀπὸ τιμημάτων. For εἰκόνες, "similes," see Ar. *Rhet.*
III. 4, where they are described as a kind of μεταφοραί ("A simile is a metaphor
writ large, with the details filled in," Cope *ad loc.*). εἰκασίαι ("conundrums")
were also "a fashionable amusement at Greek social gatherings" (Thompson
on *Meno* 80 c), see for exx. Ar. *Vesp.* 1308 ff., *Av.* 804 ff. : cp. *Rep.* 487 E, *Phaedo*
87 B ; Xen. *Symp.* VI. 8 ff.
ἐπὶ τὰ γελοιότερα. *Sc.* οὕτως ποιήσειν, or the like : cp. 214 E.
τοῖς σιληνοῖς κτλ. These were statuettes representing a Silenus playing a
flute or pipe ; the interiors were hollow and served as caskets to hold little
figures of gods wrought in gold or other precious materials. But the precise
fashion of their construction and how they opened (διχάδε διοιχθέντες) is by no
means clear. (1) Hug thinks they were made with a double door (δικλίδες):
similarly Stallb. and Hommel ("in contrariis Silenorum lateribus duobus duo
foramina erant, quae epistomio quodam claudi poterant"). (2) Schulthess
supposes that one section telescoped into the other ("Schiebt man sie aus-
einander, so erblickt man inwendig Götterbilder"). (3) Panofka, with
Schleiermacher, supposes that the top came off like a lid. (4) Lastly,
Rettig "denkt an ein Auseinandernehmen in zwei Hälfte," though exactly
how this differs from (3) he does not clearly explain. But—as Rettig himself
observes—"mag es verschiedene Arten solche Gehäuse gegeben haben," and
in the absence of further evidence it would be rash to decide which of the
possible patterns is here intended: the language (διχάδε διοιχθέντες) rather
favours the idea that the figures split into two, either horizontally or
vertically—possibly, also, with a hinge. Cp. Synes. *Ep.* 153, p. 292 B ὥσπερ
ἐποίουν Ἀθήνησιν οἱ δημιουργοὶ Ἀφροδίτην καὶ Χάριτας καὶ τοιαῦτα κάλλη θεῶν
ἀγάλμασι σιληνῶν καὶ σατύρων ἀμπίσχοντες : Maximus *comm. in Dion. Areop.*
de div. nom. c. ix. t. II. p. 201 f. (ed. Cord.) ἐκεῖνοι γὰρ οἶά τινας ἀνδριάντας

Β καθημένοις, οὕς τινας ἐργάζονται οἱ δημιουργοὶ σύριγγας ἢ αὐλοὺς
ἔχοντας, οἳ διχάδε διοιχθέντες φαίνονται ἔνδοθεν ἀγάλματα ἔχοντες
θεῶν. καὶ φημὶ αὖ ἐοικέναι αὐτὸν τῷ σατύρῳ τῷ Μαρσύᾳ. ὅτι
μὲν οὖν τό γε εἶδος ὅμοιος εἶ τούτοις, ὦ Σώκρατες, οὐδ' <ἂν> αὐτὸς
δή που ἀμφισβητήσαις· ὡς δὲ καὶ τἄλλα ἔοικας, μετὰ τοῦτο
ἄκουε. ὑβριστὴς εἶ· ἢ οὔ; ἐὰν γὰρ μὴ ὁμολογῇς, μάρτυρας
παρέξομαι. ἀλλ' οὐκ αὐλητής; πολύ γε θαυμασιώτερος ἐκείνου.

C ὁ μέν γε δι' ὀργάνων ἐκήλει τοὺς ἀνθρώπους τῇ ἀπὸ τοῦ στόματος
δυνάμει, καὶ ἔτι νυνὶ ὃς ἂν τὰ ἐκείνου αὐλῇ· ἃ γὰρ Ὄλυμπος ηὔλει,

215 B διχάδε : δίχα Steph. Ast   οὐδ' ⟨ἂν⟩ αὐτὸς Stallb.   δήπου BT,
vulg.: ἂν δήπου Sauppe: ἄν που Baiter Sz. Bt.: om. Stallb.   ἀμφισβητήσεις
vulg.

ἐποίουν μήτε χεῖρας μήτε πόδας ἔχοντας, οὓς ἑρμᾶς ἐκάλουν· ἐποίουν δὲ αὐτοὺς
διακένους, θύρας ἔχοντας, καθάπερ τοιχοπυργίσκους· ἔσωθεν οὖν αὐτῶν ἐτίθεσαν
ἀγάλματα ὧν ἔσεβον θεῶν κτλ. (cp. Etym. Magn. s.v. ἀρμάριον): Xen. Symp.
IV. 19; Julian Or. VI. p. 187 A.

τοῖς ἑρμογλυφείοις. "The statuaries' shops," apparently a ἅπαξ εἰρ.:
cp. Luc. Somn. 2. 7.

215 B ἀγάλματα...θεῶν. Cp. 222 A, Phaedr. 251 A.

φημὶ αὖ κτλ. This second comparison arises out of the first, since the
Satyr is himself akin to the Sileni: on the connexion between the two (as
both originally horse-demons) see Harrison, Proleg. p. 388. Schol. : Μαρσύας
δὲ αὐλητής, 'Ολύμπου υἱός, ὅς...ἤρισεν 'Απόλλωνι περὶ μουσικῆς καὶ ἡττήθη, καὶ
ποινὴν δέδωκε τὸ δέρμα δαρείς, κτλ.

τό γε εἶδος. For the Satyr-like ugliness of Socr., cp. Schol. ad Ar. Nub. 223
ἐλέγετο δὲ ὁ Σωκράτης τὴν ὄψιν Σειλήνῳ παρεμφαίνειν· σιμός τε γὰρ καὶ φαλακρὸς
ἦν : Theaet. 143 E προσέοικε δὲ σοὶ τήν τε σιμότητα καὶ τὸ ἔξω τῶν ὀμμάτων : ib.
209 B, Meno 80 A f.; Xen. Symp. IV. 19, V. 7.—δήπου ⟨ἂν⟩ ἀμφισβ. (cp.
Meno 72 c) is another possible order of words.

ὑβριστὴς εἶ. "You are a mocker" or "a bully" (Jowett): so too Agathon
had said, in 175 E. For the present Alcib. forbears to enlarge on this Satyr-like
quality, but he resumes the subject in 216 c ff., see esp. 219 c, 222 A. Observe
also that Alcib. is here turning the tables on Socr., who had brought practically
the same charge against A. in 213 c, D. Schleierm.'s rendering, "Bist du über-
müthig, oder nicht?", is based on a wrong punctuation.

οὐκ αὐλητής. I.e. (as Schol. B puts it) ἐν ἤθει. ἐκείνου, sc. Μαρσύου.

215 C Ὄλυμπος. For Ὄλυμπος ὁ Φρὺξ as τὰ παιδικά of Marsyas, cp. Minos
318 B; Paus. X. 30; also Laws 677 D, 790 D ff.; Arist. Pol. V. 5. 1340ᵃ 8 ff.;
Clem. Al. Strom. I. p. 307 c.

For κατέχεσθαι of "possession" (by supernal or infernal powers), cp. Meno
99 D, Phaedr. 244 E; Ion 533 E ff. (Rohde Psyche II. pp. 11, 18 ff., 48¹, 88).
The orgiastic flute-music (having a cathartic effect parallel to that of tragedy)
provided, as Aristotle teaches, a kind of homoeopathic remedy for the fit of
ἐνθουσιασμός.

Μαρσύου λέγω που, τοῦ διδάξαντος· τὰ οὖν ἐκείνου ἐάν τε ἀγαθὸς
αὐλητὴς αὐλῇ ἐάν τε φαύλη αὐλητρίς, μόνα κατέχεσθαι ποιεῖ καὶ
δηλοῖ τοὺς τῶν θεῶν τε καὶ τελετῶν δεομένους ¦ διὰ τὸ θεῖα εἶναι.
σὺ δ᾽ ἐκείνου τοσοῦτον μόνον διαφέρεις, ὅτι ἄνευ ὀργάνων ψιλοῖς
λόγοις ταὐτὸν τοῦτο ποιεῖς. ἡμεῖς γοῦν ὅταν μέν του ἄλλου ἀκού- **D**
ωμεν λέγοντος καὶ πάνυ ἀγαθοῦ ῥήτορος ἄλλους λόγους, οὐδὲν
μέλει ὡς ἔπος εἰπεῖν οὐδενί· ἐπειδὰν δὲ σοῦ τις ἀκούῃ ἢ τῶν σῶν
λόγων ἄλλου λέγοντος, κἂν πάνυ φαῦλος ᾖ ὁ λέγων, ἐάν τε γυνὴ
ἀκούῃ ἐάν τε ἀνὴρ ἐάν τε μειράκιον, ἐκπεπληγμένοι ἐσμὲν καὶ
κατεχόμεθα. ἐγὼ γοῦν, ὦ ἄνδρες, εἰ μὴ ἔμελλον κομιδῇ δόξειν
μεθύειν, εἶπον ὀμόσας ἂν ὑμῖν, οἷα δὴ πέπονθα αὐτὸς ὑπὸ τῶν
τούτου λόγων καὶ πάσχω ἔτι καὶ νυνί. ὅταν γὰρ ἀκούω, πολύ μοι **E**
μᾶλλον ἢ τῶν κορυβαντιώντων ἥ τε καρδία πηδᾷ καὶ δάκρυα

215 **C** που, τοῦ scripsi : τούτου BT, Bt.: τοῦ τοῦτον Voeg.: τοῦ Bdhm. Sz.:
τοῦτον Sommer : αὐτοῦ Liebhold　　　μόνους olim Orelli : μανία Winckelmann
δηλοῖ τοὺς: δ. θνητοὺς Hommel : κηλεῖ τοὺς Orelli　　**D** τις ἀκούῃ del. Hirschig
ἔγωγ᾽ οὖν T　　κομιδὴ B　　ἐπομόσας cj. Naber　　**E** νῦν T

M. λέγω που, τοῦ δ. I venture on this slight innovation : otherwise it
were best, with Badham, to cut down the τούτου to τοῦ.

δηλοῖ...δεομένους. Cp. the imitative passage in *Minos* 318 B καὶ μόνα κινεῖ
καὶ ἐκφαίνει τοὺς τῶν θεῶν ἐν χρείᾳ ὄντας. θεῶν δεόμενοι is virtually equiv. to
κορυβαντιῶντες (215 E) ; cp. Rohde *Psyche* II. 48[1]. "μόνα = vorzugsweise. Vgl.
Symp. 222 A" (Rettig).

ψιλοῖς λόγοις. *I.e.* "in prose," devoid of metrical form as well as of
musical accompaniment (ἄνευ ὀργάνων). Cp. *Laws* 669 D λόγους ψ. εἰς μέτρα
τιθέντες : *Menex.* 239 C.

215 D ὅταν μέν κτλ. Observe the antitheses σοῦ)(του ἄλλου—τῶν σῶν
λόγων)(ἄλλους λόγους—πάνυ φαῦλος...λέγων)(πανὺ ἀγαθοῦ ῥήτορος.

ἢ...ἄλλου λέγοντος. A case in point is the *Symposium* itself, where Socrates'
λόγοι are reported at second-hand.

ἐάν τε γυνὴ κτλ. "No sex or age is impervious to the impression"—in
antithesis to the preceding universal negative οὐδενί. For ἔκπληξις as a
love-symptom, cp. *Charm.* 154 C.

κομιδῇ...μεθύειν. Schol. κομιδῇ· ἰσοδυναμεῖ...τῷ σφόδρα καὶ τελέως. Cp. 212 E.

εἶπον ὀμόσας ἄν. "I would have stated on my oath," *i.e.* I would not
merely have described the facts, as I am about to do, but would have called
Heaven to witness by a ὅρκος (cp. 183 A). Hommel supposes that Alcib.
"rem silentio praeterire apud se constituit"; but this is confuted by the
context. For a ref. to this passage, see Procl. *in I. Alc.* p. 89.

215 E τῶν κορυβαντιώντων. Tim. κορυβαντιᾶν· παρεμμαίνεσθαι καὶ ἐνθου-
σιαστικῶς κινεῖσθαι : Schol. ad Ar. *Vesp.* 9 κορυβαντιᾶν· τὸ κορύβασι κατέχεσθαι.
Cp. *Crito* 54 D ταῦτα...ἐγὼ δοκῶ ἀκούειν, ὥσπερ οἱ κορυβαντιῶντες τῶν αὐλῶν

ἐκχεῖται ὑπὸ τῶν λόγων τῶν τούτου· ὁρῶ δὲ καὶ ἄλλους παμπόλλους τὰ αὐτὰ πάσχοντας. Περικλέους δὲ ἀκούων καὶ ἄλλων ἀγαθῶν ῥητόρων εὖ μὲν ἡγούμην λέγειν, τοιοῦτον δ' οὐδὲν ἔπασχον, οὐδ' ἐτεθορύβητό μου ἡ ψυχὴ οὐδ' ἠγανάκτει ὡς ἀνδραποδωδῶς διακειμένου· ἀλλ' ὑπὸ τουτουὶ τοῦ Μαρσύου πολλάκις δὴ οὕτω
216 διετέθην, ὥστε μοι δόξαι μὴ βιωτὸν εἶναι ἔχοντι ὡς ἔχω. καὶ ταῦτα, Σώκρατες, οὐκ ἐρεῖς ὡς οὐκ ἀληθῆ. καὶ ἔτι γε νῦν ξύνοιδ' ἐμαυτῷ ὅτι εἰ ἐθέλοιμι παρέχειν τὰ ὦτα, οὐκ ἂν καρτερήσαιμι ἀλλὰ ταὐτὰ ἂν πάσχοιμι. ἀναγκάζει γάρ με ὁμολογεῖν ὅτι πολλοῦ ἐνδεὴς ὢν αὐτὸς ἔτι ἐμαυτοῦ μὲν ἀμελῶ, τὰ δ' Ἀθηναίων

215 E ὑπὸ...τούτου secl. Voeg. Hug   τῶν τούτου TW : τούτου B : τούτου
secl. J.-U.   ταὐτὰ ⟨ταῦτα⟩ π. Naber   216 A   Σώκρατες B, J.-U.: ὦ Σ. T,
Jn. Bt. (cf. 217 B)   ταὐτὰ : ταῦτα BT   ἔτι T : τι B

δοκοῦσιν ἀκούειν : *Ion* 533 E, 536 C. Among the symptoms of κορυβαντιασμός were the hearing of faery flute-notes, visions, hypnotic dreams, dance-motions etc. (see Rohde *Psyche* II. 47 ff.): cp. also Plut. *adv. Colot.* 1123 D.

ἥ τε καρδία πηδᾷ. Cp. *Ion* 535 C, *Phaedr.* 251 C; Sappho 2. 5 τό μοι μάν | καρδίαν ἐν στήθεσιν ἐπτόασεν : Ar. *Nub.* 1393 οἶμαί γε τῶν νεωτέρων τὰς καρδίας | πηδᾶν ὅτι λέξει.

ὑπὸ τῶν λ. τ. τούτου. Rettig seems right in arguing that a Glossator would be unlikely to write thus; and repetitions of this kind are characteristic of Alc.'s speech (cp. 221 D).

Περικλέους δὲ ἀκούων. For the oratorical powers of Pericles, cp. *Phaedr.* 269 E, *Meno* 94 A, *Menex.* 235 E; Thuc. II. 65; Ar. *Ach.* 530 ff.; Cic. *Brut.* XI. 44, *de or.* III. 34; and esp. Eupolis Δῆμοι (*fr.* 6. 34) κράτιστος οὗτος (*sc.* Περικλῆς) ἐγένετ' ἀνθρώπων λέγειν | ...πειθώ τις ἐπεκάθιζεν ἐπὶ τοῖς χείλεσιν | οὕτως ἐκήλει, καὶ μόνος τῶν ῥητόρων τὸ κέντρον ἐγκατέλειπε τοῖς ἀκροωμένοις. Comparing this with our passage,—taken in conjunction with 213 D (νικῶντα ἐν λόγοις πάντας ἀνθρώπους), 215 B (ἐκήλει τοὺς ἀνθρώπους), 218 A (πληγείς τε καὶ δηχθεὶς ὑπὸ τῶν...λόγων), 221 C (οἷος αὖ Περικλῆς κτλ.),—it seems probable that Plato has this passage of Eupolis in mind, and represents Alcib. as confuting Eupolis— as a return for the raillery he had suffered at the hands of E. in his Βαπταί : cp. the story told in Cic. *Att.* VI. 1 that Alcib. got Eupolis drowned.

μου ἡ ψυχή. For this position of the genitive of the pronoun, which gives it nearly the force of an ethic dat., cp. *Rep.* 518 C, *Phaedo* 117 B (cp. Vahlen *op. Acad.* I. 440 ff.).

ὡς ἀνδραποδωδῶς δ. Cp. Xen. *Mem.* IV. 2. 39: 210 D ὥσπερ οἰκέτης... δουλεύων.

216 A μὴ βιωτὸν. This echoes, by way of contrast, 211 D ἐνταῦθα... βιωτόν.

ἔχοντι ὡς ἔχω. Cp. ὧδ' ἔχοντι, 215 A.

οὐκ...ἀληθῆ. Notice these repeated protestations of veracity : cp. 214 E, 215 B (and see *Introd.* § II. A).

οὐκ ἂν καρτερήσαιμι. Contrast with this the καρτερία of Socr., 219 D, 220 A.

πράττω. βίᾳ οὖν ὥσπερ ἀπὸ τῶν Σειρήνων ἐπισχόμενος τὰ ὦτα οἴχομαι φεύγων, ἵνα μὴ αὐτοῦ καθήμενος παρὰ τούτῳ καταγηράσω. πέπονθα δὲ πρὸς τοῦτον μόνον ἀνθρώπων, ὃ οὐκ ἄν τις οἴοιτο ἐν B ἐμοὶ ἐνεῖναι, τὸ αἰσχύνεσθαι ὁντινοῦν· ἐγὼ δὲ τοῦτον μόνον αἰσχύνομαι. σύνοιδα γὰρ ἐμαυτῷ ἀντιλέγειν μὲν οὐ δυναμένῳ, ὡς οὐ δεῖ ποιεῖν ἃ οὗτος κελεύει, ἐπειδὰν δὲ ἀπέλθω, ἡττημένῳ τῆς τιμῆς τῆς ὑπὸ τῶν πολλῶν. / δραπετεύω οὖν αὐτὸν καὶ φεύγω, καὶ ὅταν ἴδω, αἰσχύνομαι τὰ ὡμολογημένα. καὶ πολλάκις μὲν ἡδέως ἂν ἴδοιμι αὐτὸν μὴ ὄντα ἐν ἀνθρώποις· εἰ δ' αὖ τοῦτο γένοιτο, εὖ οἶδα ὅτι C πολὺ μεῖζον ἂν ἀχθοίμην, ὥστε οὐκ ἔχω ὅ τι χρήσωμαι τούτῳ τῷ ἀνθρώπῳ.

216 A βίᾳ: βύων Abresch J.-U. ἐπισχόμενος secl. J.-U. C ἂν μεῖζον Sauppe χρήσωμαι corr. Ven. 185, Bekk.: χρήσομαι BT

βίᾳ...φεύγων. "Invitus mihique ipsi vim inferens aufugio" (Rückert). Hommel wrongly takes βίᾳ with ἐπισχόμενος. βύων, the conjecture of Abresch, based on Hesych. (βύων τὰ ὦτα· ἐπιφράττων) makes the order awkward and produces tautology. ἐπισχόμενος τὰ ὦτα is the opposite of the foregoing παρέχειν τὰ ὦτα: cp. Plut. Pomp. 55; Hor. Ep. II. 2. 105 obturem patulas impune legentibus aures; Acts vii. 57 συνέσχον τὰ ὦτα αὐτῶν: Ps. lviii. 4, 5 (A.V.) "they are like the deaf adder that stoppeth her ear; which will not hearken to the voice of charmers, charming never so wisely." For the Σειρῆνες, cp. Hom. Od. XII. 39 ff., and see Harrison Proleg. pp. 197 ff.

αὐτοῦ...παρὰ τούτῳ. αὐτοῦ is not really "redundant" (as Ast)—"sitting still here beside him," i.e. "müssig und entfernt von Staatsgeschaften" etc. (Rettig); cp. Ar. Ran. 1490 ff.; Apol. 31 c ff.

καταγηράσω. Perhaps a double entendre—A. implying that S.'s moralizings ("rumores senum severiorum") would soon make an old man of him.

216 B ὃ οὐκ...ἐνεῖναι. This is a specimen of the naive candour which characterizes Alcib. throughout. For Alcib.'s self-assurance, cp. Xen. Mem. I. 2. 47.

ἡττημένῳ...πολλῶν. "Me honori, quo me ornet populi multitudo, succumbere" (Stallb.). Cp. Rep. 359 A: Xen. Cyrop. III. 3. 2 ἥδεσθαι τῇ ὑπὸ πάντων τιμῇ: Thuc. I. 130. 1. For the thought, cp. Rep. 491 c ff.

δραπετεύω. "I take to my heels," like a runaway slave (δραπέτης, Meno 97 E).

τὰ ὡμολογημένα. I.e. the conclusions as to his own ἔνδεια forced upon him by S.; cp. 216 A ἀναγκάζει...ὁμολογεῖν.

216 C πολὺ μεῖζον. So μέγα κήδεται Il. II. 26.

οὐκ ἔχω ὅ τι χρήσωμαι. Since Alcib. is here generalizing, the (dubitative) subj. seems preferable to the more definite fut., as Hommel argues against Stallb.

Alcib. is in the position of a "Dipsychus," "halting between two opinions"

10—2

XXXIII. Καὶ ὑπὸ μὲν δὴ τῶν αὐλημάτων καὶ ἐγὼ καὶ ἄλλοι
πολλοὶ τοιαῦτα πεπόνθασιν ὑπὸ τοῦδε τοῦ σατύρου· ἄλλα δὲ ἐμοῦ
ἀκούσατε ὡς ὅμοιός τ᾽ ἐστὶν οἷς ἐγὼ ἤκασα αὐτὸν καὶ τὴν δύναμιν
ὡς θαυμασίαν ἔχει. εὖ γὰρ ἴστε ὅτι οὐδεὶς ὑμῶν τοῦτον γιγνώσκει·
D ἀλλὰ ἐγὼ δηλώσω, ἐπείπερ ἠρξάμην. ὁρᾶτε γὰρ ὅτι Σωκράτης
ἐρωτικῶς διάκειται τῶν καλῶν καὶ ἀεὶ περὶ τούτους ἐστὶ καὶ
ἐκπέπληκται, καὶ αὖ ἀγνοεῖ πάντα καὶ οὐδὲν οἶδεν, ὡς τὸ σχῆμα

216 C ἤκασα Fischer: εἴκασα libri   D καὶ αὖ...οἶδεν secl. Jn. Bdhm.
Sz. αὖ B: om. TW   ἀγνοεῖ πάντη (καὶ...οἶδεν deletis) Bast   οἶδεν. ὡς
distinxit Bt.   ὡς: πῶς Ast: ἦ Usener

or rather two instincts. Cp. Soph. *fr.* 162. 8 οὕτω γε τοὺς ἐρῶντας αὐτὸς ἵμερος |
δρᾶν καὶ τὸ μὴ δρᾶν πολλάκις προίεται: Anacr. *fr.* 89 ἐρῶ τε δηῦτε κοὐκ ἐρῶ | καὶ
μαίνομαι κοὐ μαίνομαι.
οἷς ἐγὼ ἤκασα αὐτόν. *Sc.* τοῖς σιληνοῖς. ἤκασα recalls the δι᾽ εἰκόνων of 215 A.
οὐδείς...γιγνώσκει. Plato may mean by this, as Hug suggests, that the
majority of the admirers and followers of Socr. possessed a very dim insight
into the sources of his real greatness—ἀλλ᾽ ἐγὼ (Plato, behind the mask of
Alcib.) δηλώσω.
216 D ἐρωτικῶς διάκειται κτλ. For Socrates as (professing to be) subject
to intense erotic emotion, see the vivid description in *Charm.* 155 c ff. ἐγὼ
ἤδη ἠπόρουν, καί μου ἡ πρόσθεν θρασύτης ἐξεκέκοπτο...καὶ ἐφλεγόμην καὶ οὐκέτ᾽
ἐν ἐμαυτοῦ ἦν κτλ.
καὶ αὖ...οἶδεν. Most of the later critics (including Voeg., Teuffel, Hug)
agree in ejecting this clause. Rettig, who defends it, writes: "die Worte
gehen auf den vermeintlichen Stumpfsinn des S., wie er so häufig mit roher
Sinnlichkeit verbunden ist...Die Worte εἰρωνευόμενος...διατελεῖ den obigen
καὶ αὖ...οἶδεν gegensätzlich gegenüberstanden...Da nicht blos die Silene ἐρωτικῶς διάκεινται κτλ., so würde ohne unsere Worte die folgende Frage ὡς τὸ
σχῆμα...οὐ σιληνῶδες; kaum motivirt sein." But (as generally interpreted)
the clause seems hardly pertinent to the main argument, which is the contrast
between the outward appearance of eroticism and the inner σωφροσύνη of
Socr.: the clause εἰρωνευόμενος κτλ. does nothing to strengthen the case for
the reference to γνῶσις here; while there is no reason to suppose that
professions of ignorance were specially characteristic of Sileni (in spite of
the story of Midas and Silenus in Plut. *ad Ap. de consol.* 115 c (Σειλ.) οὐδὲν
ἔθελεν εἰπεῖν ἀλλὰ σιωπᾶν ἀρρήτως). If retained as it stands the clause is
best taken closely with the previous words, as expressing an erotic symptom.
[Possibly, however, for πάντα we should read πάντας and for οὐδὲν, οὐδέν᾽,
taking the words as masc. (*sc.* τοὺς καλούς).] This implies of course that οἶδεν
bears the sense "agnoscit" (and ἀγνοεῖ the opposite), for which cp. Eur. *H. F.*
1105 ff. ἔκ τοι πέπληγμαι...τίς...δύσγνοιαν ὅστις τὴν ἐμὴν ἰάσεται; σαφῶς γὰρ
οὐδὲν οἶδα τῶν εἰωθότων: *id. El.* 767 ἔκ τοι δείματος δυσγνωσίαν | εἶχον προσώ-
που· νῦν δὲ γιγνώσκω σε δή. (Cp. for this sense, Vahlen *op. Ac.* II. 63 f.)
ὡς τὸ σχῆμα αὐτοῦ. "Which is the rôle he affects." For this use of σχῆμα

αὐτοῦ. τοῦτο οὐ σιληνῶδες; σφόδρα γε. τοῦτο γὰρ οὗτος ἔξωθεν περιβέβληται, ὥσπερ ὁ γεγλυμμένος σιληνός· ἔνδοθεν δὲ ἀνοιχθεὶς πόσης οἴεσθε γέμει, ὦ ἄνδρες συμπόται, σωφροσύνης; ἴστε ὅτι οὔτ᾽ εἴ τις καλός ἐστι μέλει αὐτῷ οὐδέν, ἀλλὰ καταφρονεῖ τοσοῦτον ὅσον οὐδ᾽ ἂν εἷς οἰηθείη, οὔτ᾽ εἴ τις πλούσιος, οὔτ᾽ εἰ ἄλλην τινὰ τιμὴν ἔχων τῶν ὑπὸ πλήθους μακαριζομένων· ἡγεῖται δὲ πάντα ταῦτα τὰ κτήματα οὐδενὸς ἄξια καὶ ἡμᾶς οὐδὲν εἶναι—

216 D αὐτοῦ. τοῦτο disting. vulg. Schleierm. Sz.   τοῦτο· οὐ distinxit
Bernhardy   ἐγλυμμένος J. U.   ⟨εὖ⟩ ἴστε cj. Bdhm.   E ἡμᾶς: τιμῆς
Heusde

of an acted part, cp. *I. Alc.* 135 D, *Rep.* 576 A : similarly σχηματίζω, *simulo*, *Phaedr.* 255 A οὐχ ὑπὸ σχηματιζομένου τοῦ ἐρῶντος, ἀλλ᾽ ἀληθῶς τοῦτο πεπονθότος. This is preferable to rendering by "forma et habitus," as Stallb. The punctuation of the passage has been disputed : "vulgo enim legebatur καὶ οὐδὲν οἶδεν, ὡς τὸ σχῆμα αὐτοῦ τοῦτο οὐ σειληνῶδες σφόδρα γε, quod Stephanus ita corrigebat ut pro οὐ σειληνῶδες scriberet ὃν σειλ." (Stallb.) : Stallb., Rückert, Badham, Schanz and Hug follow Bekk. and Schleierm. in putting a comma after οἶδεν and a full stop after αὐτοῦ (so too Hommel, but proposing οὐδέ for οὐδέν) : Rettig follows Bernhardy in putting the full stop after τοῦτο, with a comma at οἶδεν : Burnet puts a full stop at οἶδεν, and no further stop before σιληνῶδες; : Ast proposed πῶς for ὡς. Bast, reading πάντη for πάντα and ejecting καὶ οὐδὲν οἶδεν, construed ὡς...σφόδρα γέ as dependent on ἀγνοεῖ : and Stephens's οὐδέ involves a similar construction.

περιβέβληται. "Has donned" as it were a "cloak" of dissimulation : cp. Xen. *Oec.* II. 5 εἰς δὲ τὸ σὸν σχῆμα ὁ σὺ περιβέβλησαι : *Ps.* cix. 18 "he clothed himself with cursing like as with his garment."

ἔνδοθεν δὲ ἀνοιχθείς. Cp. 215 B : Soph. *Antig.* 709. The word ἔνδοθεν recals Socrates' prayer in *Phaedr.* 279 B ὦ...θεοί, δοίητέ μοι καλῷ γενέσθαι τἀνδόθεν.

ἴστε ὅτι κτλ. For the general sense, cp. *Charm.* 154 B.

216 E ὅσον οὐδ᾽ ἂν εἷς. Cp. 214 D.

πλούσιος...τιμὴν ἔχων. Stallb. renders "aut praeterea honore aliquo ornatus," distinguishing τιμή from κάλλος and πλοῦτος; whereas Rückert states that "τιμή dicta est h. l. de re, quae honorem habet efficitque τιμίᾳ, ita ut κάλλος et πλοῦτος etiam τιμαί esse possint." Rettig supports Stallb., but probably the other two ἀγαθά are also classed in A.'s mind as τίμια. Cp. 178 C, 216 B : Pind. *fr. inc.* 25.

τῶν...μακαριζομένων. Sc. τιμῶν.

καὶ ἡμᾶς οὐδὲν εἶναι. "h. e. atque nos, qui talia magni faciamus nullo in numero habendos censet" (Stallb.). This,—or Rückert's "nos ipsos qui pulcri, qui divites sumus,"—seems to bring out rightly the point of the personal reference; in spite of Rettig, who writes "vollig fremd ist der Platonischen Stelle der Zusatz, welchen Stallb. hier macht." For this use of οὐδὲν (= οὐδενὸς ἀξίους) cp. 219 A, 220 A. The attitude here ascribed to Socr. is very like that ascribed to his admirer Apollodorus in 173 C, D.

λέγω ὑμῖν,—εἰρωνευόμενος δὲ καὶ παίζων πάντα τὸν βίον πρὸς
τοὺς ἀνθρώπους διατελεῖ. σπουδάσαντος δὲ αὐτοῦ καὶ ἀνοιχθέντος
οὐκ οἶδα εἴ τις ἑώρακε τὰ ἐντὸς ἀγάλματα· ἀλλ' ἐγὼ ἤδη ποτ'
217 εἶδον, καί μοι ἔδοξεν οὕτω θεῖα καὶ χρυσᾶ εἶναι καὶ πάγκαλα καὶ
θαυμαστά, ὥστε ποιητέον εἶναι ἐμβραχὺ ὅ τι κελεύοι Σωκράτης.
ἡγούμενος δὲ αὐτὸν ἐσπουδακέναι ἐπὶ τῇ ἐμῇ ὥρᾳ ἕρμαιον ἡγη-
σάμην εἶναι καὶ εὐτύχημα ἐμὸν θαυμαστόν, ὡς ὑπάρχον μοι
χαρισαμένῳ Σωκράτει πάντ' ἀκοῦσαι ὅσαπερ οὗτος ᾔδει· ἐφρόνουν
γὰρ δὴ ἐπὶ τῇ ὥρᾳ θαυμάσιον-ὅσον. ταῦτα οὖν διανοηθείς, πρὸ τοῦ

216 E λέγω ὑμῖν ΒΤ: λέγων μὲν οὖ Herm.: ἡγούμενος Bdhm.: ἵνα λέγω
ὑμῖν Sz.: ἀλλ' ἐρῶ ὑμῖν Usener: del. Voeg.: fort. transp. post ἀλλὰ infra
τε καὶ Usener   217 A καί μοι Τ, J.-U. Bt.: καὶ ἐμοὶ Β: κἀμοὶ Hirschig Sz.
ἔμβραχυ Cobet Sz. Bt.: ἐν βραχεῖ ΒΤ   ὅ τι ⟨ἂν⟩ Sauppe Jn.   οὗτος: αὐτὸς
Bdhm.   δὴ Β: ἤδη TW: ἔτι cj. Wolf

λέγω ὑμῖν. There is no objection, at least in A.'s speech, to this kind of
parenthetic interjection (cp. οἴεσθε, D *supra*); cp. *Apol.* 30 A, Thuc. VI. 37. 2,
Eur. *Med.* 226.   Similarly in *Gorg.* 464 C, 526 C "asseverandi causa orator ad
ea quae maxime attendi vult addit illa φημί, λέγω" (see Vahlen *op. Acad.* I.
479).   I am, however, inclined to suspect that the words are misplaced, and
originally stood after ἀλλά, three lines lower down; if so, we should read ἀλλά—
λέγω ὑμῖν—ἐγὼ κτλ., or perhaps ἀλλὰ ἃ λέγω ὑμῖν ἐγώ: this would serve to echo
the ἀλλ' ἐγὼ δηλώσω of D *ad init.*   Cp. also 222 B ἃ δὴ καὶ σοὶ λέγω.

εἰρωνευόμενος. Schol. εἴρων.: ὑποκρινόμενος, χλευάζων.   Cp. 218 D; *Rep.*
337 A αὕτη ἐκείνη ἡ εἰωθυῖα εἰρωνεία Σωκράτους.

τὰ ἐντὸς ἀγάλματα. See 215 A *n.*: ἄγαλμα, as ἐφ' ᾧ τις ἀγάλλεται, can fitly
be applied to spiritual as well as material treasures: cp. the use of ἱερόν in Eur.
Hel. 1002.   This passage is cited in Procl. *in Alc. I.* p. 89; Clem. Alex. *Strom.*
VII. 5, p. 846 P.: cp. Cic. *de Legg.* I. 22 "ingeniumque in se suum sicut
simulacrum aliquod dedicatum putabit."

217 A χρυσᾶ. "Nur ein poetischer mit καλός synonymer Ausdruck"
(Rettig); no doubt the material ἀγάλματα referred to were of gold or gilt,
cp. *Critias* 116 D χρυσᾶ...ἀγάλματα ἐνέστησαν.   For the metaph. use, cp. *Hipp.
Mai.* 301 A, *Phaedr.* 235 E φίλτατος εἰ καὶ ὡς ἀληθῶς χρυσοῦς: *Gorg.* 486 D
χρυσῆν ἔχων...τὴν ψυχήν: and Shakspere's "Golden lads and lasses."

ἔμβραχυ. "In short," used to qualify a universal statement expressed
by a relative such as ὅστις: cp. *Gorg.* 457 A (with Heindorf *ad loc.*), *Hipp.
Min.* 365 D; Ar. *Vesp.* 1120.

ἐσπουδακέναι ἐπὶ κτλ. Observe how this contrasts with the παίζειν of 216 E:
A., we are to infer, had not as yet (at the date of the incident following) learnt the
"irony" of Socr.   With the attitude of Alcib. here cp. what Pausanias says in
184 B ff.

ὥρᾳ. ὥρα as *flos aetatis* is nearly equiv. to ἄνθος (183 E, 210 C): cp. 219 C,
Phaedr. 234 A, I. *Alc.* 131 E τὰ...σὰ λήγει ὥρας, σὺ δ' ἄρχει ἀνθεῖν.

ἐφρόνουν κτλ. For Alc.'s vanity, cp. I. *Alc.* 104 A.

οὐκ εἰωθὼς ἄνευ ἀκολούθου μόνος μετ᾽ αὐτοῦ γίγνεσθαι, τότε ἀπο-
πέμπων τὸν ἀκόλουθον μόνος συνεγιγνόμην· δεῖ γὰρ πρὸς ὑμᾶς B
πάντα τἀληθῆ εἰπεῖν· ἀλλὰ προσέχετε τὸν νοῦν, καὶ εἰ ψεύδομαι,
Σώκρατες, ἐξέλεγχε· συνεγιγνόμην γάρ, ὦ ἄνδρες, μόνος μόνῳ, καὶ
ᾤμην αὐτίκα διαλέξεσθαι αὐτόν μοι ἅπερ ἂν ἐραστὴς παιδικοῖς ἐν
ἐρημίᾳ διαλεχθείη, καὶ ἔχαιρον. τούτων δ᾽ οὐ μάλα ἐγίγνετο οὐδέν,
ἀλλ᾽ ὥσπερ εἰώθει διαλεχθεὶς ἄν μοι καὶ συνημερεύσας ᾤχετο
ἀπιών. μετὰ ταῦτα, ξυγγυμνάζεσθαι προυκαλούμην αὐτὸν καὶ
συνεγυμναζόμην, ὥς τι ἐνταῦθα περανῶν. συνεγυμνάζετο οὖν μοι C
καὶ προσεπάλαιε πολλάκις οὐδενὸς παρόντος· καὶ τί δεῖ λέγειν;
οὐδὲν γάρ μοι πλέον ἦν. ἐπειδὴ δὲ οὐδαμῇ ταύτῃ ἤνυτον, ἔδοξέ
μοι ἐπιθετέον εἶναι τῷ ἀνδρὶ κατὰ τὸ καρτερὸν καὶ οὐκ ἀνετέον,
ἐπειδήπερ ἐνεκεχειρήκη, ἀλλὰ ἰστέον ἤδη τί ἐστι τὸ πρᾶγμα.
προκαλοῦμαι δὴ αὐτὸν πρὸς τὸ συνδειπνεῖν, ἀτεχνῶς ὥσπερ

217 **A** μόνος secl. Hirschig J.-U. Hug   **B** ⟨ὦ⟩ Σώκρατες Sz.   δ᾽ οὐ·
δὴ O.-P.   ἄν BT: αὖ Wolf: δὴ Sauppe Sz.: ἅττα Ast: ἄλλα Rettig: del.
Hommel Hirschig : fort. ἀεί   καὶ συνεγυμναζόμην secl. Sauppe Sz. Hug
C ἐνταῦθά ⟨γε⟩ Naber   ἀνετέον : ανεταιον O.-P.[1]   ἰτέον ἤδη ἐπὶ τὸ πρ.
Wyttenbach

217 **B** τἀληθῆ...ψεύδομαι. Cp. 216A, 214 E for similar protestations. Observe
the effectiveness of this pause in the narration, and of the challenge to contradiction, as marking an approaching climax : cp. Phaedo 85 D.

ἐν ἐρημίᾳ. "Tête-à-tête": cp. Rep. 604 A, Phaedr. 236 c ἐσμὲν...μόνω ἐν
ἐρημίᾳ.

ἄν...ᾤχετο. If ἄν is right we must take it to denote repeated action,
"solebat identidem discedere" (Stallb.): cp. Apol. 22 B (Madv. Gr. S.
§ 117 b, R. 3; L. and S. s.v. ἄν c).

συνημερεύσας. The only other ex. in Plato is Phaedr. 240 c παιδικοῖς...
ἐραστὴς...εἰς τὸ συνημερεύειν πάντων ἀηδέστατον.

ξυγγυμνάζεσθαι. For this practice, cp. 182 C, Menex. 236 D, Rep. 452 A ff. ;
and Xen. Symp. II. 16 ff., where Socr. treats of public and private gymnastics.

217 **C** οὐδὲν...πλέον ἦν. "Nihil enim proficiebam" (Stallb.): cp. 222 D.

ἐπειδὴ δὲ κτλ. Rettig supposes an allusion to Eur. Hipp. 390 ff. ἐπειδὴ
τοιόσδ᾽ οὐκ ἐξήνυτον Κύπριν | κρατῆσαι, κατθανεῖν ἔδοξέ μοι. For other reff. to
Eurip., see 177 A, 189 C, 196 E.

ἰστέον...πρᾶγμα. Reynders is alone in approving of Wyttenbach's "restoration," ἰτέον ἤδη ἐπὶ τὸ πρᾶγμα: for, as Rückert argues, this must imply either
that A. had as yet made no "conamen alliciendi S.," which is untrue, or that
he had not as yet begun his narration, which is equally untrue. The sense of
the text is "I must get to the bottom of the matter without more ado,"
i.e. discover the real ground of Socrates' indifference. Cp. Apol. 20 c τὸ σὸν
τί ἐστι πρᾶγμα;

προκαλοῦμαι δὴ κτλ. Here comes the third and most desperate expedient,

D ἐραστὴς παιδικοῖς ἐπιβουλεύων. καί μοι οὐδὲ τοῦτο ταχὺ ὑπήκουσεν, ὅμως δ' οὖν χρόνῳ ἐπείσθη. ἐπειδὴ δὲ ἀφίκετο τὸ πρῶτον, δειπνήσας ἀπιέναι ἐβούλετο. καὶ τότε μὲν αἰσχυνόμενος ἀφῆκα αὐτόν· αὖθις δὲ ἐπιβουλεύσας, ἐπειδὴ ἐδεδειπνήκεμεν, διελεγόμην ἀεὶ πόρρω τῶν νυκτῶν, καὶ ἐπειδὴ ἐβούλετο ἀπιέναι, σκηπτόμενός ὅτι ὀψὲ εἴη, προσηνάγκασα αὐτὸν μένειν. ἀνεπαύετο οὖν ἐν τῇ ἐχομένῃ ἐμοῦ κλίνῃ, ἐν ᾗπερ ἐδείπνει, καὶ οὐδεὶς ἐν τῷ οἰκήματι E ἄλλος καθηῦδεν ἢ ἡμεῖς. μέχρι μὲν οὖν δὴ δεῦρο τοῦ λόγου καλῶς ἂν ἔχοι καὶ πρὸς ὁντινοῦν λέγειν· τὸ δ' ἐντεῦθεν οὐκ ἄν μου ἠκούσατε λέγοντος, εἰ μὴ πρῶτον μέν, τὸ λεγόμενον, οἶνος—ἄνευ

217 D ἐδεδειπνήκεμεν Bt.: 'δεδειπνήκειμεν Usener: δεδειπνήκαμεν Bekk. anecd.: ἐδεδειπνήκει BT O.-P. ἀεὶ add. Bekk. anecd.: om. BT O.-P. ⟨γε⟩ O.-P. αὐτὸν: αὐτοῦ Sauppe μένειν: μονον O.-P.[1] E οὖν δὴ B O.-P. Tmg.: οὖν TW καὶ ⟨ἐξείη⟩ πρὸς cj. Liebhold

in which Alcib. reverses their respective rôles and acts towards Socr. no longer as παιδικά but as ἐραστής (cp. 213 c, 222 b, and see *Introd.* § vi. 3). For *three* as a climacteric number cp. *Phil.* 66 D, *Euthyd.* 277 c, *Rep.* 472 A. For ἐπιβουλεύων, cp. 203 B, 203 D.

217 D ἀεί...νυκτῶν. "Usque ad multam noctem" (Stallb.). For this force of ἀεί, cp. ἀεὶ διὰ τοῦ βίου *Phaedo* 75 B, etc.; so with πόρρω, *Gorg.* 486 A τοὺς πόρρω ἀεὶ φιλοσοφίας ἐλαύνοντας. For the plural νύκτες, "night-watches," cp. 223 c, *Prot.* 310 c πόρρω τῶν νυκτῶν: *Phil.* 50 D.

ἐν τῇ...κλίνῃ. ἐμοῦ is short for τῆς ἐμῆς (or ἐμοῦ) κλίνης: cp. the similar brachylogy in 214 c: Hom. *Od.* vi. 308.

οἰκήματι. "Room": cp. *Prot.* 315 D, *Phaedo* 116 A.

217 E μέχρι...δεῦρο. So *Laws* 814 D τῆς...δυνάμεως τὸ μέχρι δεῦρο ἡμῖν εἰρήσθω.

καὶ πρὸς ὁντινοῦν λέγειν. This reminds one of Diotima's language in 209 E ff. (ταῦτα μὲν οὖν κτλ.).

τὸ λεγόμενον κτλ. Photius explains thus: οἶνος ἄνευ παίδων δύο παροιμίαι· ἡ μὲν οἶνος καὶ ἀλήθεια, ἡ δὲ οἶνος καὶ παῖδες ἀληθεῖς. For the first of these, cp. Alcaeus *fr.* 57 B, Theocr. *Id.* xxix. 1. We might render "In wine and wean is candour seen." Cp. Schol. *ad h. l.*; Athen. ii. 37 E Φιλόχορος δέ φησιν ὅτι οἱ πίνοντες οὐ μόνον ἑαυτοὺς ἐμφανίζουσιν οἵτινές εἰσιν, ἀλλὰ καὶ τῶν ἄλλων ἕκαστον ἀνακαλύπτουσι, παρρησίαν ἄγοντες. ὅθεν "οἶνος καὶ ἀλήθεια" λέγεται: Alcaeus *fr.* 53 οἶνος γὰρ ἀνθρώποις δίοπτρον: Hor. *Sat.* I. 4. 89 condita cum verax aperit praecordia Liber. Similar sayings about the effects of wine are Ar. *Plut.* 1048 μεθύων ὀξύτερον βλέπει: Theogn. 479 ff. οἶνος...κοῦφον ἔθηκε νόον. The explanations of H. Müller ("Trunkene sagten die Wahrheit, mochten Diener zugegen sein oder nicht") and of Hommel ("si proverbio illo vinum, quod neque praesentiam neque absentiam servorum curat (alluding to the ἀκόλουθος of 217 A), non esset veridicum") are clearly wrong. Cp. Xen. *Symp.* viii. 24.

τε παίδων καὶ μετὰ παίδων—ἦν ἀληθής, ἔπειτά ἀφανίσαι Σωκράτους ἔργον ὑπερήφανον εἰς ἔπαινον ἐλθόντα ἄδικόν μοι φαίνεται.
ἔτι δὲ τὸ τοῦ δηχθέντος ὑπὸ τοῦ ἔχεως πάθος κἀμὲ ἔχει. φασὶ
γάρ πού τινα τοῦτο παθόντα οὐκ ἐθέλειν λέγειν οἷον ἦν πλὴν τοῖς
δεδηγμένοις, ὡς μόνοις γνωσομένοις τε καὶ συγγνωσομένοις, εἰ πᾶν 218
ἐτόλμα δρᾶν τε καὶ λέγειν ὑπὸ τῆς ὀδύνης. ἐγὼ οὖν δεδηγμένος τε
ὑπὸ ἀλγεινοτέρου καὶ τὸ ἀλγεινότατόν ὧν ἄν τις δηχθείη—τὴν
καρδίαν ἢ ψυχὴν [γὰρ] ἢ ὅ τι δεῖ αὐτὸ ὀνομάσαι, πληγείς τε καὶ

218 A　τε καὶ ὑπὸ W　ἀλγεινοτάτου Steph.　δηχθείη Τ Ο.-Ρ.: δειχθῇ Β
ἢ ψυχὴν γὰρ Β : γὰρ ἢ ψ. ΤW Ο.-Ρ.: ἢ ψ. non legit Schol. Β, secl. Usener Sz.
Βt.: ἢ ψ. γὰρ secl. Christ: γὰρ seclusi : fort. ἢ ψ. τἄρα

ἀφανίσαι. "To keep dark": notice the play ἀφανίσαι...φαίνεται, which
Lehrs represents by "eine helle That des S. ins Dunkle zu setzen."　φαίνεται
after the impf. ἦν is one of Alc.'s anacolutha.

ὑπερήφανον. The adj. here, though *prima facie* eulogistic, evidently contains
(as Rückert notes) "grata quaedam ambiguitas," as alluding to the ὕβρις of
Socr., cp. the use of ὑπερηφανία to denote "superbia cum contemtione
coniuncta" (Ast) in 219 C. For the good sense of the word, cp. *Phaedo*
96 A, *Gorg.* 511 D.

τὸ τοῦ δηχθέντος κτλ.　For this proverbial case, cp. Aristides *or.* 15, I.
p. 234 ὥσπερ τὸν ὑπὸ τῆς ἐχίδνης φασὶ πληγέντα μὴ ἐθέλειν ἑτέρῳ λέγειν ἀλλ᾽ ἢ
ὅστις πεπείραται: *id. or.* 49, II. p. 395: Xen. *Symp.* IV. 28 ὥσπερ ὑπὸ θηρίου
τινὸς δεδηγμένος...ἐν τῇ καρδίᾳ ὥσπερ κνῆσμά τι ἐδόκουν ἔχειν : *id. Mem.* I. 3.
12 ff. ἐνίησι γάρ τι τὰ φαλάγγια κατὰ τὸ δῆγμα...ὥστε μαίνεσθαι ποιεῖν. This
last passage refers to the "bite of love," for which cp. Soph. *fr.* 721 ἔρωτος
δῆγμα : Socrates (Bergk *P. L. G.* II. p. 288) πόθῳ δηχθείς. Rückert is no doubt
right in holding that there is allusion here "ad certam fabellam, nobis licet
ignotam." Cp. also Aesch. *Cho.* 996.

218 A　πᾶν...λέγειν.　"Alii de remediis totoque curationis genere (haec)
verba intelligunt, alii de motibus, gestibus furibundis, dictisque quae doloris
magnitudo elicuerit, sanis hominibus nil nisi risum moturis" (Rückert).　The
former of these views is adopted by Stallb. and Rettig (who takes the phrase
to refer to the superstitious use of charms, amulets, etc.), the latter by Hommel.
The phrase recals 182 E θαυμαστὰ ἔργα...τολμᾷ ποιεῖν : 208 D πάντα ποιοῦσιν :
cp. *Rep.* 576 A.　It seems best here to interpret it broadly of the results of the
δῆγμα, whether or not directly aiming at a cure : *i.e.* as covering both the
senses indicated above.

τὸ ἀλγεινότατον.　"In my most sensitive part."

τὴν καρδίαν.　Schol. Β, ὅτι τὴν καρδίαν (καρδίαν τὴν Herm.) ψυχὴν καλεῖ.
This implies—as Usener inferred—that the words ἢ ψυχὴν were absent from
the Scholiast's text: none the less, in view of the context, I think it rash to
expunge the words, and content myself with obelizing γάρ. For ἢ ὅτι κτλ.,
cp. 212 C.

δηχθεὶς ὑπὸ τῶν ἐν φιλοσοφία λόγων, οἳ ἔχονται ἐχίδνης ἀγριώ-
τερον, νέου ψυχῆς μὴ ἀφυοῦς ὅταν λάβωνται, καὶ ποιοῦσι δρᾶν τε
καὶ λέγειν ὁτιοῦν—καὶ ὁρῶν αὖ Φαίδρους, Ἀγάθωνας, Ἐρυξι-
B μάχους, Παυσανίας, Ἀριστοδήμους τε καὶ Ἀριστοφάνας· Σωκράτη
δὲ αὐτὸν τί δεῖ λέγειν, καὶ ὅσοι ἄλλοι; πάντες γὰρ κεκοινωνήκατε τῆς φιλοσόφου μανίας τε καὶ βακχείας· διὸ πάντες ἀκούσεσθε·
συγγνώσεσθε γὰρ τοῖς τε τότε πραχθεῖσι καὶ τοῖς νῦν λεγομένοις·
οἱ δὲ οἰκέται, καὶ εἴ τις ἄλλος ἐστὶ βέβηλός τε καὶ ἄγροικος, πύλας
παμμεγάλας τοῖς ὠσὶν ἐπίθεσθε.

XXXIV. Ἐπειδὴ γὰρ οὖν, ὦ ἄνδρες, ὅ τε λύχνος ἀπεσβήκει
C καὶ οἱ παῖδες ἔξω ἦσαν, ἔδοξέ μοι χρῆναι μηδὲν ποικίλλειν πρὸς
αὐτόν, ἀλλ' ἐλευθέρως εἰπεῖν ἅ μοι ἐδόκει· καὶ εἶπον κινήσας

218 A   μὴ B O.-P.: καὶ μὴ T, Bt.   B δεῖ καὶ vulg.   τοῖς τε B (?):
τοῖς T (?)   εἴ τις T O.-P.: εἴ τι B   παμμεγάλας Naber J.-U.: πάνυ μεγάλας
libri, Sz. Bt.   C ⟨καὶ⟩ κινήσας O.-P.

ὑπὸ τῶν...λόγων. Cp. 210 D λόγους...ἐν φιλοσοφία ἀφθόνῳ. For πληγείς, cp.
Euthyd. 303 A ὥσπερ πληγεὶς ὑπὸ τοῦ λόγου ἄφωνος ἐκείμην : Epist. vii. 347 D.
νέου ψυχῆς. Rost, removing the comma before νέου, connected ν. ψυχῆς
with ἔχονται, wrongly : for ἔχεσθαι without a genitive, cp. Gorg. 494 E.
Observe the word-play ἔχ-ονται ἐχ-ίδνης.
μὴ ἀφυοῦς. Cp. 209 B ψυχῇ...εὐφυεῖ.
Φαίδρους κτλ. For a similar (generalizing) use of the plural of proper
names, cp. Menex. 245 D, Ar. Ran. 1040 ff., Av. 558 f.
218 B συγγνώσεσθε. This echoes the συγγνωσομένοις of 218 A supra.
οἱ δὲ οἰκέται. This echoes Diotima's ὥσπερ οἰκέτης, 210 D ad init. : cp. Ar.
Ach. 242, Ran. 41 for the nomin. of address.
βέβηλός. Cp. Schol. Aristid. III. p. 471 ἔστι δὲ κήρυγμα μυστικὸν τὸ "θύρας...
βέβηλοι," ὥς που καὶ Ὀρφεὺς δηλοῖ "φθέγξομαι οἷς θέμις ἐστί· θύρας δ' ἐπίθεσθε
βέβηλοι": Tim. βέβηλοι· ἀμύητοι. Alcib.'s language, like Diotima's, is suggestive of mystery-lore: cp. Theaet. 155 E; Eur. Bacch. 70 ff., 472; Horace's "odi
profanum volgus et arceo."
πύλας...τοῖς ὠσίν. Cp. Theogn. 421 πολλοῖς ἀνθρώπων γλώσσῃ θύραι οὐκ
ἐπίκεινται | ἁρμόδιαι.
ὅ τε λύχνος ἀπεσβήκει. Cp. Ar. Plut. 668 ὡς δὲ τοὺς λύχνους ἀποσβέσας...
ἐγκαθεύδειν: Juv. IX. 104, Hor. C. III. 6. 28.
218 C ποικίλλειν. "Artificiose, h. e. obscure vel ambigue loqui" (Ast):
"to beat about the bush." Cp. the use of ποικίλος in 182 B: Laws 863 E τό
τε δίκαιον καὶ τὸ ἄδικον...σαφῶς ἂν διορισαίμην οὐδὲν ποικίλλων: Soph. Trach.
421, 1121.
ἐλευθέρως εἰπεῖν. Cp. Pind. Nem. IX. 49 θαρσαλέα δὲ παρὰ κρατῆρι φωνὰ
γίνεται. Notice the word-play ἔδοξε...ἐδόκει. For κινήσας, cp. Rep. 329 D
βουλόμενος ἔτι λέγειν αὐτὸν ἐκίνουν καὶ εἶπον κτλ.

αὐτόν, Σώκρατες, καθεύδεις; Οὐ δῆτα, ἦ δ' ὅς. Οἶσθα οὖν ἅ μοι
δέδοκται; Τί μάλιστα; ἔφη. Σὺ ἐμοὶ δοκεῖς, ἦν δ' ἐγώ, ἐμοῦ
ἐραστὴς ἄξιος γεγονέναι μόνος, καί μοι φαίνῃ ὀκνεῖν μνησθῆναι
πρός με. ἐγὼ δὲ οὑτωσὶ ἔχω· πάνυ ἀνόητον ἡγοῦμαι εἶναι σοὶ μὴ
οὐ καὶ τοῦτο χαρίζεσθαι καὶ εἴ τι ἄλλο ἢ τῆς οὐσίας τῆς ἐμῆς δέοιο
ἢ τῶν φίλων τῶν ἐμῶν. ἐμοὶ μὲν γὰρ οὐδέν ἐστι πρεσβύτερον D
τοῦ ὡς ὅ τι βέλτιστον ἐμὲ γενέσθαι, τούτου δὲ οἶμαί μοι συλλήπτορα οὐδένα κυριώτερον εἶναι σοῦ. ἐγὼ δὴ τοιούτῳ ἀνδρὶ
πολὺ μᾶλλον ἂν μὴ χαριζόμενος αἰσχυνοίμην τοὺς φρονίμους,
ἢ χαριζόμενος τούς τε πολλοὺς καὶ ἄφρονας. καὶ οὗτος ἀκούσας
μάλα εἰρωνικῶς καὶ σφόδρα ἑαυτοῦ τε καὶ εἰωθότως ἔλεξεν Ὦ φίλε
Ἀλκιβιάδη, κινδυνεύεις τῷ ὄντι οὐ φαῦλος εἶναι, εἴπερ ἀληθῆ

218 C ἔχω Β O.-P.: ἔχων TW   χαρισασθαι O.-P.   εἴ τι Β O.-P.: ἔτι
TW   D ὡς ὅ τι TW O.-P.: ὅσῳ τι Β   μοι Vind. 21 O.-P. (prob.), vulg.:
μου BTW   ⟨παρ'⟩ ἑαυτοῦ Stallb.: ⟨πρὸς⟩ ἑαυτοῦ Herwerden   ἑαυτῷ εἰωθότως
vulg.   φίλε om. O.-P.[1]   κινδυνεύει...φαῦλ' εἶναι Bdhm.

ἐμοῦ...ἄξιος. Whether ἐμοῦ goes closely with ἐραστὴς or with ἄξιος is open
to doubt: Jowett renders "the only one who is worthy of me," whereas Rettig
writes "ἄξιος absolut = würdig, beachtenswerth."

ὀκνεῖν κτλ. "To be shy of mentioning (your love) to me": cp. I. Alc.
103 A οἶμαί σε θαυμάζειν ὅτι πρῶτος ἐραστής σου γενόμενος...τοσούτων ἐτῶν
οὐδὲ προσεῖπον.

τῆς οὐσίας...τῶν φίλων. Cp. 183 A ἢ χρήματα...ὑπὸ φίλων. For ἢ τῶν φίλων
= ἢ τῆς τῶν φίλων, cp. the brachylogy in 217 D (ἐμοῦ).

218 D πρεσβύτερον. Poll. II. 12 καὶ πρεσβεύειν τὸ τιμᾶν παρὰ Πλάτωνι καὶ
τὸ "οὐδέν ἐστι πρεσβύτερον" ἀντὶ τοῦ "οὐδὲν τιμιώτερον": 186 B, 188 C supra.

συλλήπτορα. For the ἐραστής as an aid to ἀρετή, see 185 A; cp. Socrates'
description of Eros as συνεργός, 212 B. μοι was taken by Stallb. with συλλήπτορα, by Rückert with εἶναι, but it is better to say with Hommel that, as an
ethic dat., "ad totum verborum complexum refertur."

κυριώτερον. "More competent": cp. Theaet. 161 D.

τοὺς φρονίμους...ἄφρονας. Compare the similar aristocratic sentiment of
Agathon, 194 B. It is worth noticing that whereas Pausanias had spoken of
those who disapprove of χαρίζεσθαι as τινές, here they are termed οἱ πολλοί.
Cp. Xen. Mem. I. 6. 13. Similarly Browne, Rel. Med. "This noble affection
falls not on vulgar and common constitutions."

σφόδρα ἑαυτοῦ. "Very characteristically": cp. "suum illud est" Cic. Tusc.
I. 42. 99.

οὐ φαῦλος. "Kein Dummkopf" (Hug); cp. 174 C, 175 E. Socr. means
that if Alcib. proposes to make such a profitable bargain, bartering his own
cheap κάλλος for the rare κάλλος of Socr., he evidently is a "cute" man of

E τυγχάνει ὄντα ἃ λέγεις περὶ ἐμοῦ, καί τις ἔστ᾽ ἐν ἐμοὶ δύναμις, δι᾽ ἧς ἂν σὺ γένοιο ἀμείνων· ἀμήχανόν τοι κάλλος ὁρῴης ἂν ἐν ἐμοὶ καὶ τῆς παρὰ σοὶ εὐμορφίας πάμπολυ διαφέρον. εἰ δὴ καθορῶν αὐτὸ κοινώσασθαί τέ μοι ἐπιχειρεῖς καὶ ἀλλάξασθαι κάλλος ἀντὶ κάλλους, οὐκ ὀλίγῳ μου πλεονεκτεῖν διανοῇ, ἀλλ᾽ ἀντὶ δόξης 219 ἀλήθειαν καλῶν κτᾶσθαι ἐπιχειρεῖς καὶ τῷ ὄντι "χρύσεα χαλκείων" διαμείβεσθαι νοεῖς. ἀλλ᾽, ὦ μακάριε, ἄμεινον σκόπει, μή σε λανθάνω οὐδὲν ὤν. ἤ τοι τῆς διανοίας ὄψις ἄρχεται ὀξὺ βλέπειν ὅταν ἡ τῶν ὀμμάτων τῆς ἀκμῆς λήγειν ἐπιχειρῇ· σὺ δὲ τούτων ἔτι πόρρω. κἀγὼ ἀκούσας, Τὰ μὲν παρ᾽ ἐμοῦ, ἔφην, ταῦτ᾽ ἐστίν, ὧν οὐδὲν ἄλλως εἴρηται ἢ ὡς διανοοῦμαι· σὺ δὲ αὐτὸς οὕτω βουλεύου ὅ τι σοί τε ἄριστον καὶ ἐμοὶ ἡγεῖ. Ἀλλ᾽, ἔφη, τοῦτό γε εὖ λέγεις· B ἐν γὰρ τῷ ἐπιόντι χρόνῳ βουλευόμενοι πράξομεν ὃ ἂν φαίνηται νῶν περί τε τούτων καὶ περὶ τῶν ἄλλων ἄριστον.

218 E τοι BTW O.-P.: τι al., Bekk.: τε vulg.   τέ μοι BT O.-P.: μοι W
219 A καλῶν del. Bdhm.   νοεῖς secl. Voeg., J.-U.   ἤ τοι W, Steph.: ἤτοι
BT   ὄψις ἄρχεται om. Stob.   ἐμοῦ TW O.-P.: ἐμοί B   [σοι τε] οτι O.-P.

---

business. Cp. Diog. L. III. 63 ὁ γοῦν φαῦλος λέγεται παρ᾽ αὐτῷ (sc. Platoni) καὶ ἐπὶ τοῦ ἁπλοῦ, ὡς καὶ παρ᾽ Εὐριπίδῃ ἐν Λικυμνίῳ κτλ. (see Eurip. fr. 476 N. φαῦλον, ἄκομψον, τὰ μέγιστ᾽ ἀγαθόν κτλ.).

218 E ἀμήχανόν κτλ. Supply from the context, with Stallb., "nam hoc ita si sit." Rückert, after Schleierm., wrongly connects this clause with the preceding, "qua fiat, ut tu melior evadas, atque exinde immensam in me pulcritudinem cernas"; while Hommel makes it depend upon εἴπερ. Cp. Rep. 509 B, 608 D; Charm. 155 D.

εὐμορφίας. For the notion of a beauty-competition here suggested, cp. Xen. Symp. v. 1. Cp. also the σοφία-match of 175 E.

ἀντὶ δόξης ἀλήθειαν κ. "Real for sham beauties": ἀλήθειαν καλῶν = ἀλήθινα καλά. Cp. Phil. 36 C ff.; and for the antithesis, cp. 198 E, 212 A supra.

219 A χρύσεα χαλκείων. A "familiar quotation" from Il. VI. 235—6 (Γλαῦκος) ὃς πρὸς Τυδείδην Διομήδεα τεύχε᾽ ἄμειβεν | χρύσεα χαλκείων, ἑκατόμβοι᾽ ἐννεαβοίων. Later reff. to the proverb are frequent, e.g. Plut. adv. Stoic. 1063 E; Clem. Alex. Cohort. ad Gent. 71 C. Cp. Winter's Tale I. 2 "take eggs for money." In χρύσεα there is an obvious allusion to the ἀγάλματα χρυσᾶ of 216 E.

ἤ τοι...ὄψις. For this idea of the inverse development of vision, cp. Laws 715 D, II. Alc. 150 D. Rettig thinks that in this passage there may lie a ref. to Phaedr. 253 D ff., and an indication that the views there put forward are crude and the book itself "eine jugendliche Schrift."

219 B ἐν γὰρ τῷ κτλ. Thus Socr. practically defers the consideration of the matter to "the Greek Kalends." Rettig calls attention to the catalectic hexameter in ἐν γὰρ...βουλευόμενοι, which gives a touch of jocular liveliness.

Ἐγὼ μὲν δὴ ταῦτα ἀκούσας τε καὶ εἰπών, καὶ ἀφεὶς ὥσπερ
βέλη, τετρῶσθαι αὐτὸν ᾠμην· καὶ ἀναστάς γε, οὐδὲ ἐπιτρέψας
τούτῳ εἰπεῖν οὐδὲν ἔτι, ἀμφιέσας τὸ ἱμάτιον τὸ ἐμαυτοῦ τοῦτον—
καὶ γὰρ ἦν χειμών—ὑπὸ τὸν τρίβωνα κατακλινεὶς τὸν τουτουί,
περιβαλὼν τὼ χεῖρε τούτῳ τῷ δαιμονίῳ ὡς ἀληθῶς καὶ θαυμαστῷ, C
κατεκείμην τὴν νύκτα ὅλην. καὶ οὐδὲ ταῦτα αὖ, ὦ Σώκρατες, ἐρεῖς
ὅτι ψεύδομαι. ποιήσαντος δὲ δὴ ταῦτα ἐμοῦ οὗτος τοσοῦτον περιεγένετό τε καὶ κατεφρόνησε καὶ κατεγέλασε τῆς ἐμῆς ὥρας καὶ
ὕβρισε καὶ περὶ ἐκεῖνο <ὅ> γε ᾠμην τι εἶναι, ὦ ἄνδρες δικασταί—

219 B βέλει TW O.-P.   τούτῳ T, Thiersch: τοῦτο B: τοῦτον W
τουτουί TW O.-P. (prob.), Bt.: τούτου B, J.-U. Sz.   C αὖ B: om. TW
καὶ περὶ ἐκεῖνο ⟨ὅ⟩ γε scripsi: [καὶ] περι εκεινο γε O.-P.: καίπερ ἐκεῖνό γε TW:
καίπερ κεῖνό γε B: καὶ 'κεῖνό γε Sz.: καίτοι 'κεῖνό γε Bt.: καίπερ...εἶναι secl. Hug

ἀφεὶς ὥσπερ βέλη. Sc. τοὺς λόγους. For this image applied to "winged
words," cp. the use of βαλών 189 B; Phileb. 23 B βέλη ἔχειν ἕτερα τῶν ἔμπροσθεν λόγων: Theaet. 180 A; Pind. Ol. I. 112.
τετρῶσθαι. "I thought I had winged him." Cp. Theogn. 1287 ἀλλά
σ' ἐγὼ τρώσω φεύγοντά περ: and the description of Eros as θηρευτὴς δεινός,
203 D.
τρίβωνα. Cp. Prot. 335 D; Ar. Ach. 184, etc. The vogue of the "philosopher's
cloak" (pallium) seems to date from Socrates: cp. Plut. de disc. ad. 56 C. For
the incident, see also Lysias in Alcib. XIV. 25 (Teichmüller Litt. F. II. 267 ff.);
Theocr. Id. XVIII. 19; cp. Theogn. 1063 ff. ἐν δ' ἥβῃ πάρα μὲν ξὺν ὁμήλικι καλ
λίθ' εὕδειν | ἱμερτῶν ἔργων ἐξ ἔρον ἱέμενον. Notice the stylistic effect produced
both by the row of successive participles, mostly asyndetic ("der Sturmlauf
ist vergeblich" Rettig); and by the repetition of the pronoun (τούτῳ, -τον,
-τουί, -τῳ, οὗτος). "Forsan haec illustrat Soph. Trach. 944. Respexit
Alciphron I. 38" (Wyttenb.).
219 C δαιμονίῳ. Cp. 202 D.
καὶ οὐδὲ ταῦτα κτλ. Alcib.'s fourth appeal to Socr. for confirmation, cp.
217 B.
τοσοῦτον. "Dictum est δεικτικῶς et per quandam exclamationem ut signi-
ficet: mirum quantum me vicit" (Stallb.): Rückert and Hommel, on the other
hand, suppose that "sequi debebat ὥστε" so as to give the sense "ut non aliter
ab eo surrexerim," etc. (Rückert), or ὥστε καὶ καταφρονῆσαι κτλ. (Hommel).
Rückert's view, which explains the change of construction as due to the
intervening parenthesis, seems the most probable.
περιεγένετό κτλ. Alcib. is fond of piling up synonyms by way of emphasis;
cp. 207 A, 219 D, 221 E.
ὕβρισε. ὕβρις is a vox propria in erotic literature for the "spretae iniuria
formae"; cp. Anthol. Pal. V. 213 οὐκ οἴσω τὰν ἀπάλαιστρον ὕβριν.
Anacreon fr. 129 ὑβρισταὶ καὶ ἀτάσθαλοι (Ἀνακρέων ἀπειλεῖ τοῖς Ἔρωσιν...
ἐπειδήπερ ἑώρα τὸν ἔφηβον ὀλίγον αὐτοῦ φροντίζοντα...εἰ μὴ αὐτῷ τιτρώσκοιεν

δικασταὶ γάρ ἐστε τῆς Σωκράτους ὑπερηφανίας. εὖ γὰρ ἴστε μὰ
θεούς, μὰ θεάς, οὐδὲν περιττότερον καταδεδαρθηκὼς ἀνέστην μετὰ
D Σωκράτους, ἢ εἰ μετὰ πατρὸς καθηῦδον ἢ ἀδελφοῦ πρεσβυτέρου.

XXXV. Τὸ δὴ μετὰ τοῦτο τίνα οἴεσθέ με διάνοιαν ἔχειν, ἡγούμενον μὲν ἠτιμάσθαι, ἀγάμενον δὲ τὴν τούτου φύσιν τε καὶ σωφροσύνην καὶ ἀνδρείαν, ἐντετυχηκότα ἀνθρώπῳ τοιούτῳ οἵῳ ἐγὼ οὐκ

219 D ἢ εἰ B O.-P.: ἢ TW

αὐτίκα τὸν ἔφηβον κτλ.). Cp. Spenser's, "Thou hast enfrosen her disdainefull
brest," and "Whilst thou tyrant Love doest laugh and scorne At their com-
plaints, making their paine thy play, Whylest they lie languishing like thrals
forlorne" (cp. καταδεδουλωμένος 219 E infra).

καὶ περὶ ἐκεῖνο ⟨ο⟩ γε κτλ. So I have ventured to write on the strength of the
evidence of the Papyrus.

Rettig keeps the Bodleian κεῖνο, as tolerable "in hac Alcibiadis oratione
singularia amantis," and refers to Poppo ad Thuc. VIII. 86, Lob. ad Phryn. p. 7,
and other authorities : but to bolster up the double anomaly "vain is the
strength of man" : if κεῖνο be retained we must assume prodelision ('κεῖνο).

τί εἶναι. "Magni quid esse" (Rückert): cp. Gorg. 472 A : it is the opposite
of οὐδὲν εἶναι, 216 E, 219 A.

δικασταί. Alcib. appeals to the audience to try the case, the notion of a
lawsuit (γραφὴ ὕβρεως) having been suggested by the word ὕβρισεν. We have
already had, in this speech, terms suggestive of legal proceedings, viz. 214 D
τιμωρήσωμαι ὑμῶν ἐναντίον : 215 B μάρτυρας παρέξομαι : and δικαστής itself was
already used by Agathon in 175 E.

μὰ θεούς, μὰ θεάς. Such an invocation of the whole pantheon is unusual,
but cp. Tim. 27 C.

οὐδὲν περιττότερον. Haud aliter, cp. Isocr. III. 43.

καταδεδαρθηκώς. Cp. 223 C, Apol. 40 D. For the incident cp. Petron. 128
non tam intactus Alcibiades in praeceptoris sui lecto iacuit : Lucian vit. auct.
15 ; Corn. Nep. Alcib. c. ii.

219 D τίνα...διάνοιαν. A.'s feelings were a blend of chagrin and veneration : cp. the perplexity described in 216 C; Theogn. 1091 ff. ἀργαλέως μοι
θυμὸς ἔχει περὶ σῆς φιλότητος· | οὔτε γὰρ ἐχθαίρειν οὔτε φιλεῖν δύναμαι, κτλ.

ἠτιμάσθαι. Cp. Theogn. 1313 ἐμὴν δὲ μεθῆκας ἀτίμητον φιλότητα.

ἀγάμενον. This is an echo, both of Phaedrus's language in 179 C, 180 A,
and of ἀγαστός applied to Eros (197 D). Observe the assonance ἡγούμενον...
ἀγάμενον. Cp. Xen. Symp. VIII. 8.

τὴν τούτου φύσιν κτλ. Hommel renders "des Mannes ganzem Wesen
besonders seiner Besonnenheit und Charakterfestigkeit" etc. ; Rettig explains
φύσις as "die geistige Naturanlage des S., seine theoretische und spekulative
Begabung, ingenium, σοφία (vgl. Theaet. 144 A)." The former seems the more
natural interpretation ; φύσις may be intended also as an echo of Aristophanes'
use of the word (189 D etc.).

ἂν ᾤμην ποτὲ ἐντυχεῖν εἰς φρόνησιν καὶ εἰς καρτερίαν; ὥστε οὔθ'
ὅπως οὖν ὀργιζοίμην εἶχον καὶ ἀποστερηθείην τῆς τούτου συνουσίας, οὔθ' ὅπῃ προσαγαγοίμην αὐτὸν ηὐπόρουν. εὖ γὰρ ἤδη ὅτι Ε
χρήμασί γε πολὺ μᾶλλον ἄτρωτος ἦν πανταχῇ ἢ σιδήρῳ ὁ Αἴας,
ᾧ τε ᾤμην αὐτὸν μόνῳ ἁλώσεσθαι, διεπεφεύγει με. ἠπόρουν δή,
καταδεδουλωμένος τε ὑπὸ τοῦ ἀνθρώπου ὡς οὐδεὶς ὑπ' οὐδενὸς
ἄλλου περιῇα. ταῦτά τε γάρ μοι ἅπαντα προυγεγόνει, καὶ μετὰ
ταῦτα στρατεία ἡμῖν εἰς Ποτίδαιαν ἐγένετο κοινῇ καὶ συνεσιτοῦμεν
ἐκεῖ. πρῶτον μὲν οὖν τοῖς πόνοις οὐ μόνον ἐμοῦ περιῆν, ἀλλὰ καὶ
τῶν ἄλλων ἁπάντων· ὁπότ' ἀναγκασθείημεν ἀποληφθέντες που,

219 D   ωομην O.-P. corr.   καρτερίαν : ἐγκρατειαν O.-P.   οὔθ' : ουδ
O.-P. corr.   ει και O.-P.   συνηθειας O.-P.¹   Ε ὅποι vulg.   ἤδη B :
ἤδειν W O.-P.   γε TW O.-P., Jn.: τε B, J.-U. Sz. Bt.   δή BT O.-P. :
τε W   ταῦτά τ' ἄρα Bdhm.   κοινῇ vulg. J.-U. Naber : κοινὴ BT O.-P.,
Sz. Bt.   οὖν libri, Bt.: οὖν ⟨ἐν⟩ Winckelmann J.-U. Sz.   ὁπότ' W, Herm.:
ὁπόταν BT O.-P. : ὁπόταν γοῦν vulg.: ὁπότε δ' Sauppe Jn.: ὁπότ' αὖ Rohde :
οἷον ὁπότ' cj. Usener   ἀποληφθέντες Cornarius, Sz. Bt.: ἀπολειφθέντες libri,
O.-P.: ἀπολειφθέντες σίτου, οἷα Heusde

φρόνησιν...καρτερίαν. "φρόνησις verbunden mit καρτερία ist doch nichts
Anderes als die Auflösung des Begriffs der σωφροσύνη in seine beiden Bestand-
theile. Vgl. Pol. IV. 430 E, Phädr. 237 E, Krat. 411 E" (Rettig).

οὔθ'...εἶχον. Of moral impossibility, as in 190 C, *Phaedr.* 241 A.

219 E ἄτρωτος. "Invulnerable on all sides": cp. τετρῶσθαι 219 B. For
the incorruptibility of Socr., shown by his sending back Alcib.'s presents, see
Stob. *Flor.* XVII. 17, Ael. *v. h.* IX. 29.

σιδήρῳ ὁ Αἴας. For the impregnable seven-fold shield of Ajax, see Pind.
Isthm. v. 45; Soph. *Aj.* 576; Welcker *Kl. Schr.* II. p. 267.

ᾧ τε ᾤμην. Sc. τῇ ὥρᾳ (cp. 219 C): the antecedent, κατὰ τοῦτο (διαπεφ.), has
to be supplied.

καταδεδουλωμένος. Cp. *Euthyd.* 303 C. Above, 215 E, we had ἀνδραποδωδῶς
διακείμενος.

περιῇα. "I wandered about," suggestive of aimless despair: cp. *Prot.*
348 D, *Rep.* 620 C: so περιτρέχων 173 A.

στρατεία...κοινῇ. Potidaea revolted from Athens in 435 B.C. and after
5 years of war was reduced in 430 (see Bury's *Hist. Gr.* pp. 392—3): Socr.'s
part in the campaign is alluded to also in *Apol.* 28 E, *Charm.* 153 A, C: cp.
Plut. *adv. Colot.* p. 1117 E.

συνεσιτοῦμεν. "We were mess-mates" (σύσσιτοι). This implies personal
friendship rather than proximity of origin; for Socr. and Alcib. belonged to
different φυλαί and to different τάξεις.

τοῖς πόνοις. Cp. 197 E (Ἔρως) ἐν πόνῳ...ἄριστος.

ἀποληφθέντες. "Cut off," "a commeatu intercepti et prohibiti" (Stallb.):
cp. Hdt. II. 115. 2; Thuc. VI. 22; *Gorg.* 522 A.

220 οἷα δὴ ἐπὶ στρατείας, ἀσιτεῖν, οὐδὲν ἦσαν οἱ ἄλλοι πρὸς τὸ καρτερεῖν. ἔν τ' αὖ ταῖς εὐωχίαις μόνος ἀπολαύειν οἷός τ' ἦν τά τ' ἄλλα καὶ πίνειν οὐκ ἐθέλων, ὁπότε ἀναγκασθείη, πάντας ἐκράτει, καὶ ὃ πάντων θαυμαστότατον, Σωκράτη μεθύοντα οὐδεὶς πώποτε ἑώρακεν ἀνθρώπων. τούτου μὲν οὖν μοι δοκεῖ καὶ αὐτίκα ὁ ἔλεγχος ἔσεσθαι. πρὸς δὲ αὖ τὰς τοῦ χειμῶνος καρτερήσεις—δεινοὶ γὰρ αὐτόθι χειμῶνες—θαυμάσια εἰργάζετο τά τε ἄλλα, καί ποτε ὄντος B πάγου οἵου δεινοτάτου, καὶ πάντων ἢ οὐκ ἐξιόντων ἔνδοθεν ἢ εἴ τις ἐξίοι ἠμφιεσμένων τε θαυμαστὰ δὴ ὅσα καὶ ὑποδεδεμένων καὶ ἐνειλιγμένων τοὺς πόδας εἰς πίλους καὶ ἀρνακίδας, οὗτος δ' ἐν

220 A   πρὸς τὸ: πρὸς αὐτὸν εἰς τὸ Sauppe: πρὸς αὐτὸν τῷ Bdhm.   ἐν δ'
αὖ Wolf   ἀπολλύειν O.-P.¹   οἷός τ' ἦν del. Bdhm.   τε τἆλλα Bdhm.
πίνων Usener   πάντας: πάντων Hirschig   ὃ πάντων TW O.-P.: ὁπόταν B
θαυμασιωτατον O.-P. Vind. 21   ἑώρακεν TW O.-P.: ἑωράκει B   χειμῶνες
del. Naber   B   πάγου B O.-P.: τοῦ πάγου TW   ἢ οὐκ B O.-P.: οὐκ TW
δὴ TW O.-P.: ἢ B   οὗτος δ' BTW: οὗτος O.-P. Vind. 21

220 A   οἷα δὴ κτλ.   Sc. φιλεῖ γίγνεσθαι, or the like; cp. Rep. 467 B οἷα
δὴ ἐν πολέμῳ φιλεῖ (sc. γίγνεσθαι); Euthyd. 272 A.
οὐδὲν ἦσαν...πρὸς κτλ.   Cp. 195 D οἷος ἦν...πρὸς κτλ., and 216 E οὐδὲν
εἶναι.
εὐωχίαις.   Cp. Laws 666 B ἐν τοῖς συσσιτίοις εὐωχηθέντα: 203 B supra.
τά τ' ἄλλα κτλ.   The construction is loose; we may either explain it (with
Stallb.) as a brachylogy for τά τ' ἄλλα καὶ δὴ καὶ τοῦτο ὅτι...ἐκράτει, or say (with
Wolf) that ἐκράτει is carelessly put for κρατῶν.   Hug construes πίνειν closely
with ἀναγκασθείη, marking οὐκ ἐθέλων as a parenthesis; but it is simpler to
regard πίνειν as a kind of accus. of respect ("at drinking") with ἐκράτει.   For
the ἀνάγκη of the "symposiarch's" ruling cp. 176 A, 223 B.
ἑώρακεν.   The plpf. ἑωράκει (in spite of Rettig, etc.) is inconsistent with
πώποτε.   For Socr.'s invincibility in carousals, see 176 C, 214 A, 223 C; and
cp. Theogn. 491 ἀνίκητος δέ τοι οὗτος | ὃς πολλὰς πίνων μή τι μάταιον ἐρεῖ.
αὐτίκα...ἔσεσθαι.   I.e. we shall have proof, before the night is over, of Socr.'s
καρτερία in this regard.
δεινοί...χειμῶνες.   Cp. Thuc. II. 70 ὁρῶντες μὲν τῆς στρατιᾶς τὴν ταλαιπωρίαν
ἐν χωρίῳ χειμερινῷ: Aesch. Pers. 495 ff.
θαυμάσια εἰργάζετο.   An echo of 182 E and 213 D.
220 B   οἵου δεινοτάτου.   I.e. τοιούτου οἷος δεινότατός ἐστιν: cp. Apol. 23 A
(Madv. Gr. S. § 96. 1).
πίλους.   Schol. πῖλος· ἱμάτιον ἐξ ἐρίου πιλήσεως γινόμενον, εἰς ὑετῶν καὶ
χειμώνων ἄμυναν.   Cp. Laws 942 D; Hes. Op. 541 ff.   "Had their feet swathed
in felt and fleeces" (Jowett).
ἀρνακίδας.   Schol. ἀρνακίδες δὲ ἀρνῶν κῴδια: Suid. ἀρνακίς· τὸ τοῦ ἀρνὸς
κῴδιον, τὸ μετὰ τῶν ἐρίων δέρμα.   Cp. Themist. or. IV. 50 B.

τούτοις ἐξῄει ἔχων ἱμάτιον μὲν τοιοῦτον οἷόνπερ καὶ πρότερον
εἰώθει φορεῖν, ἀνυπόδητος δὲ διὰ τοῦ κρυστάλλου ῥᾷον ἐπορεύετο
ἢ οἱ ἄλλοι ὑποδεδεμένοι.   οἱ δὲ στρατιῶται ὑπέβλεπον αὐτὸν ὡς
καταφρονοῦντα σφῶν.

XXXVI. Καὶ ταῦτα μὲν δὴ ταῦτα·   C
     οἷον δ' αὖ τόδ' ἔρεξε καὶ ἔτλη καρτερὸς ἀνὴρ
ἐκεῖ ποτὲ ἐπὶ στρατιᾶς, ἄξιον ἀκοῦσαι. ξυννοήσας γὰρ αὐτόθι
ἕωθέν τι εἱστήκει σκοπῶν, καὶ ἐπειδὴ οὐ προυχώρει αὐτῷ, οὐκ
ἀνίει ἀλλὰ εἱστήκει ζητῶν. καὶ ἤδη ἦν μεσημβρία, καὶ ἄνθρωποι
ᾐσθάνοντο, καὶ θαυμάζοντες ἄλλος ἄλλῳ ἔλεγον ὅτι Σωκράτης ἐξ
ἑωθινοῦ φροντίζων τι ἕστηκε. τελευτῶντες δέ τινες τῶν Ἰώνων,

220 B οἷόνπερ B O.-P.: οἷον TW   C αὖ τόδ' W O.-P., Cornarius :
αὐτὸ BT   ἔρρεξε B   στρατιᾶς O.-P., Cobet Sz. Bt.: στρατείας libri, J.-U.
εἱστήκει vulg. O.-P.: ἑστήκει libri   προχώρει B   ἀνίει : ανειη O.-P.   ἄνθρωποι
Mehler Cobet Sz. Bt.: ἄνθρωποι libri   ἔλεγον Mehler Cobet Sz.: ἔλεγεν
libri, O.-P., Bt.   ἐξ : ως εξ O.-P.   καὶ ante τελευτῶντες add. W   Ἰώνων
libri, O.-P.: νέων Mehler Hug Sz.: ἰδόντων Schmidt: Παιόνων Rettig

ἱμάτιον...φορεῖν. Cp. 220 A n.; Xen. Mem. I. 2. 1, 6. 2 καὶ ἱμάτιον ἠμφίεσαι
οὐ μόνον φαῦλον ἀλλὰ τὸ αὐτὸ θέρους τε καὶ χειμῶνος, ἀνυπόδητος δὲ καὶ ἀχίτων
διατελεῖς. For ἀνυπόδητος, see also 174 A, 203 D.

ὑπέβλεπον. "Looked askance (suspiciously) at him," i.e. "quippe quem
ipsos despicere opinarentur" (Stallb.). Cp. Eryx. 395 A ὑποβλέψας...ὥσπερ
τι ἀδικούμενος : Crito 53 B ὑποβλέψονταί σε διαφθορέα ἡγούμενοι τῶν νόμων.

220 C Καὶ ταῦτα...ταῦτα. For this formula of transition, dismissing the
subject, cp. Laws 676 A.

οἷον δ' αὖ...ἀνήρ. From Hom. Od. IV. 242, with the slight alteration οἷον
δ' αὖ for ἀλλ' οἷον : there it is spoken by Helen in describing Odysseus.

ξυννοήσας. Rettig holds that the following section is an illustration of the
"spekulative Begabung" (φύσις 219 D) of Socr.; but it describes, primarily,
another phase of his καρτερία. For S.'s habit of thought-immersion, cp.
174 E ff., Gell. N. A. II. 1; similarly, in Indian gymnosophists, Plin. H. N.
VII. 2. 22. The similar incident in 174 E ff. is there construed by Agathon
as a symptom of σοφία (see 175 C—D).

Ἰώνων. Rückert comments "Iones illo tempore sub Atheniensium ditione
erant, unaque militabant"; but most recent editors suspect corruption after
Mehler (ad Xen. Symp. p. 75) "Neque fuere eorum in ordinibus, neque
Platonis haec sunt verba." To Mehler's restoration, τῶν νεῶν, Rettig
objects that "den Athenern gleichviel ob jung oder alt diese Weise des
Sokrates kaum auffallend war, da man ihn genugsam kannte"; while in
favour of his own conj. Παιόνων, he cites Thuc. I. 59, 61, etc. But I agree
with Usener (Rhein. Mus. LIII. p. 372) that Ἰώνων may well be genuine.

D ἐπειδὴ ἑσπέρα ἦν, δειπνήσαντες—καὶ γὰρ θέρος τότε γ᾽ ἦν—χαμεύνια ἐξενεγκάμενοι ἅμα μὲν ἐν τῷ ψύχει καθηῦδον, ἅμα δὲ
ἐφύλαττον αὐτὸν εἰ καὶ τὴν νύκτα ἑστήξοι. ὁ δὲ εἱστήκει μέχρι
ἕως ἐγένετο καὶ ἥλιος ἀνέσχεν· ἔπειτα ᾤχετ᾽ ἀπιὼν προσευξάμενος
τῷ ἡλίῳ.

Εἰ δὲ βούλεσθε ἐν ταῖς μάχαις· τοῦτο γὰρ δὴ δίκαιόν γε αὐτῷ
ἀποδοῦναι· ὅτε γὰρ ἡ μάχη ἦν, ἐξ ἧς ἐμοὶ καὶ τἀριστεῖα ἔδοσαν οἱ
στρατηγοί, οὐδεὶς ἄλλος ἐμὲ ἔσωσεν ἀνθρώπων ἢ οὗτος, τετρω-
E μένον οὐκ ἐθέλων ἀπολιπεῖν, ἀλλὰ συνδιέσωσε καὶ τὰ ὅπλα καὶ
αὐτὸν ἐμέ. καὶ ἐγὼ μέν, ὦ Σώκρατες, καὶ τότε ἐκέλευον σοὶ
διδόναι τἀριστεῖα τοὺς στρατηγούς, καὶ τοῦτό γέ μοι οὔτε μέμψῃ

220 D προσευξόμενος b   ἐν ταῖς : και εν ταις O.-P.   οὐκ ἐθέλων
τετρώμενον T   E Σωκρατην O.-P.

220 D **χαμεύνια.** ταπεινὰ κλινίδια (Schol.); τὰ ἐπὶ τῆς γῆς στρωννύμενα
(Tim.): cp. (Eros) χαμαιπετής, 203 D: Hipponax 67 ἐν σταθμίῳ τε καὶ χαμευνίῳ
γυμνόν.

προσευξάμενος τῷ ἡλίῳ. Hesiod (*Op.* 339) prescribes prayer at sunrise and
sunset; cp. *Laws* 887 E, 966 D; Soph. *O. C.* 477; Ar. *Plut.* 771 καὶ προσκυνῶ
γε πρῶτα μὲν τὸν ἥλιον. The suggestion here may be that the Sun-god
(*Phoebus*, the revealer, "the light of the world") brings mental illumination,
and that Socr.'s εὐχή was in part a thanksgiving therefor. As a parallel to
Socr., we may refer to "the devotion of Orpheus to Helios" as pointed out in
Harrison *Proleg.* p. 462. Moreover, Socr. regarded Apollo as his special
patron-god, see *Apol.* 39 D ff., *Phaedo* 85 B, *Tim.* 40 A (Adam, *R. T. G.*
pp. 325, 434 ff.): and the sun is the symbol of ideal Good, see *Rep.* 530 A,
Phileb. 28 D. For the content of a Socratic prayer, see *Phaedr.* 279 B—C ;
Xen. *Mem.* I. 3. 2 ηὔχετο δὲ πρὸς τοὺς θεοὺς ἁπλῶς τἀγαθὰ διδόναι. Of prayers
to Helios we have exx. in Soph. *Aj.* 845 ff.; *id. fr.* 772 Ἥλιος οἰκτείρειέ με | ὃν
σοφοὶ λέγουσι γεννητὴν θεῶν | καὶ πατέρα πάντων.

Εἰ δὲ βούλεσθε. Sc. ἀκοῦσαι οἷος ἦν, or the like; cp. 177 B. Alcib. here
passes on to treat of the ἀνδρεία of Socr.

ἀποδοῦναι. "Tanquam debitum persolvere" (Stallb.).

ἡ μάχη. "Illa pugna (omnibus nota)" (Rückert); *i.e.* the fight (in
432 B.C.) which preceded the blockade of Potidaea, cp. 219 E *n.*, Thuc. I.
62 ff., II. 2.

ἔσωσεν. With this, and συνδιέσωσεν below, cp. Eros as σωτὴρ ἄριστος,
197 E.

220 E **οὐκ ἐθέλων ἀπολιπεῖν.** This passage echoes the language of
Phaedrus in 179 A: ἐγκαταλιπεῖν γε τὰ παιδικὰ κτλ., and ὅπλα ἀποβαλών. To
rescue a man's arms was to save him from the disgrace attaching to ὅπλων
ἀποβολή.

οὔτε μέμψῃ. Here for the fifth time Alcib. challenges Socr. to contradict
him (cf. 219 c): for μέμφομαι, cp. 213 E.

οὔτε ἐρεῖς ὅτι ψεύδομαι· ἀλλὰ γὰρ τῶν στρατηγῶν πρὸς τὸ ἐμὸν
ἀξίωμα ἀποβλεπόντων καὶ βουλομένων ἐμοὶ διδόναι τἀριστεῖα,
αὐτὸς προθυμότερος ἐγένου τῶν στρατηγῶν ἐμὲ λαβεῖν ἢ σαυτόν.
ἔτι τοίνυν, ὦ ἄνδρες, ἄξιον ἦν θεάσασθαι Σωκράτη, ὅτε ἀπὸ Δηλίου 221
φυγῇ ἀνεχώρει τὸ στρατόπεδον· ἔτυχον γὰρ παραγενόμενος ἵππον
ἔχων, οὗτος δὲ ὅπλα. ἀνεχώρει οὖν ἐσκεδασμένων ἤδη τῶν ἀνθρώπων οὗτός τε ἅμα καὶ Λάχης· καὶ ἐγὼ περιτυγχάνω, καὶ ἰδὼν
εὐθὺς παρακελεύομαί τε αὐτοῖν θαρρεῖν, καὶ ἔλεγον ὅτι οὐκ ἀπολείψω αὐτώ. ἐνταῦθα δὴ καὶ κάλλιον ἐθεασάμην Σωκράτη ἢ ἐν
Ποτιδαίᾳ—αὐτὸς γὰρ ἧττον ἐν φόβῳ ἢ διὰ τὸ ἐφ' ἵππου εἶναι—
πρῶτον μὲν ὅσον περιῆν Λάχητος τῷ ἔμφρων εἶναι· ἔπειτα ἔμοιγε B
ἐδόκει, ὦ Ἀριστόφανες, τὸ σὸν δὴ τοῦτο, καὶ ἐκεῖ διαπορεύεσθαι
ὥσπερ καὶ ἐνθάδε, "βρενθυόμενος καὶ τὠφθαλμὼ παραβάλλων,"

221 A σωκράτην T   ἤ B: ἤ TW: η O.-P.: ἤν vulg.   B ὥσπερ καὶ
ἐνθάδε secl. Jn. J.-U.   τὼ ὀφθαλμὼ T O.-P.: τῶ φθαλμῶ B: τ' ὀφθαλμὼ W

ἀξίωμα. "Social standing": "erat genere Alcmaeonida...ipse Periclis in
tutela erat" (Rückert). Cp. *I. Alc.* 104 B; Thuc. II. 37, v. 43, etc.
ἢ σαυτόν. We should expect μᾶλλον ἢ αὐτός, but the accus. is put in order
to balance ἐμὲ, "propter oppositionis gravitatem" (Stallb.). For the omission
of μᾶλλον after words "denoting a wish or choice," see Madv. *Gr. S.* § 93 c.
221 A ἀπὸ Δηλίου. For this famous battle in Boeotia (424 B.C.), when
the Athenians under Hippocrates were routed by the Thebans under Pagondas,
see Thuc. IV. 76 ff., Bury's *Hist. Gr.* pp. 442—3.
καὶ Λάχης. Cp. *Lach.* 181 B. Athenaeus (v. 329 E.) perversely contends
that Socr. took part in no battle.
περιτυγχάνω. Cp. Hermann on Ar. *Nub.* 196, "ἐπιτυγχάνειν dicitur qui
quaerit, περιτυγχ. qui non quaerens in aliquid incidit."
κάλλιον ἐθεασάμην. "I got a finer view of": cp. *Rep.* 467 E ἐφ' ἵππων...
κάλλιστά τε θεάσονται...καὶ ἀσφαλέστατα κτλ.
ἐν φόβῳ. Cp. 197 D.
ἔμφρων. "Cool," "collected"; cp. *Ion* 535 B πότερον ἔμφρων εἶ, ἢ ἔξω
σαυτοῦ γίγνει; *Laws* 791 B ἀντὶ μανικῶν...ἕξεις ἔμφρονας ἔχειν.
221 B τὸ σὸν δὴ τοῦτο. An accus. absol., like τὸ λεγόμενον : "ut tuo illo
utar" (Stallb.). Cp. *Soph.* 233 B, *Euthyd.* 284 C (with Schanz, *nov. comm.*
pp. 76 f.). The ref. is to Ar. *Nub.* 362 ὅτι βρενθύει τ' ἐν ταῖσιν ὁδοῖς καὶ
τὠφθάλμω παραβάλλεις. The *Clouds* was not produced until the year after
the battle of Delium, viz. 423 B.C.
βρενθυόμενος. "Stalking like a pelican" (Jowett): Schol. *ad Nub.* 362
βρενθύει· ἀποσεμνύνεις σεαυτὸν ἐν τῷ σχήματι καὶ ταυρηδὸν ὁρᾷς· κομπάζεις καὶ
ὑπεροπτικῶς βαδίζεις: cp. Schol. *ad Pax* 25, *ad Lysist.* 887. "Nimirum
ductum est verbum a βρένθος, quod significat avem aquaticam, frequenter ad
paludes commorantem altisque pedibus incedentem" (Stallb.).
τὠφθαλμὼ παραβάλλων. "H. e. torvo vultu oculos in obliquum vertens"

11—2

ἠρέμα παρασκοπῶν καὶ τοὺς φιλίους καὶ τοὺς πολεμίους, δῆλος ὢν παντὶ καὶ πάνυ πόρρωθεν, ὅτι εἴ τις ἅψεται τούτου τοῦ ἀνδρός, μάλα ἐρρωμένως ἀμυνεῖται. διὸ καὶ ἀσφαλῶς ἀπῄει καὶ οὗτος καὶ ὁ ἑταῖρος· σχεδὸν γάρ τι τῶν οὕτω διακειμένων ἐν τῷ C πολέμῳ οὐδὲ ἅπτονται, ἀλλὰ τοὺς προτροπάδην φεύγοντας διώκουσι.

Πολλὰ μὲν οὖν ἄν τις καὶ ἄλλα ἔχοι Σωκράτη ἐπαινέσαι καὶ θαυμάσια· ἀλλὰ τῶν μὲν ἄλλων ἐπιτηδευμάτων τάχ' ἄν τις καὶ περὶ ἄλλου τοιαῦτα εἴποι, τὸ δὲ μηδενὶ ἀνθρώπων ὅμοιον εἶναι, μήτε τῶν παλαιῶν μήτε τῶν νῦν ὄντων, τοῦτο ἄξιον παντὸς θαύματος. οἷος γὰρ Ἀχιλλεὺς ἐγένετο, ἀπεικάσειεν ἄν τις καὶ Βρασίδαν καὶ

221 B περισκοπῶν Ast Bekk. Sz.   φιλίους BTW : φίλους al., O.-P.,
Steph.   αψαιτο O.-P.   ἀμύνηται B   διὸ...διώκουσιν secl. Hartmann
διὸ δὴ καὶ Arist.   οὗτος : αυτος O.-P.   ἑταῖρος Arist., Sz. Bt.: ἕτερος libri,
O.-P., J.-U.   ἐν τῷ πολέμῳ ante ἀλλὰ ponit Arist.   C μᾶλλον post φεύγοντας addit Arist.   θαυμάσαι Hirschig   τῶν μὲν : των O.-P. (ut videtur)
δὲ : δε δη O.-P.   εἶναι μήτε TW. O.-P.: εἶναί με B

(Stallb.). Rettig objects that this rendering is inconsistent with ἠρέμα φιλίους, and explains by "oculis prope admotis intueri, also scharf ansehen," cp. *Phaedo* 103 A, *Rep.* 531 A. Ast gives "oculos in aliquid immotos habere intentos": Reynders, τὸ βλέμμα ἄνω καὶ κάτω κινεῖν : Jowett, "rolling his eyes."

ἠρέμα παρασκοπῶν. This verb is ἅπ. εἰρ. in Plato, and perhaps conveys a literary allusion: Rückert explains it to mean "oculis quasi comitari, observare, ut omnes motus lento oculorum motu notare videaris."

δῆλος...πόρρωθεν. "Similiter Apollodorus, qui Socratis incessum imitatus est, τῶν οὖν...πόρρωθεν ἐκάλεσεν κτλ." (Hommel).

ὁ ἑταῖρος. So Jahn, after Aristides t. II. p. 72: the more definite term is preferable, as Rettig argues against Teuffel. For confusion of the two words in the codd., cp. 183 C (*crit. n.*), and see Schanz, *nov. comm.* p. 59.

221 C προτροπάδην. "In headless rout"—an Epic (*Il.* XVI. 304) word, ἅπ. εἰρ. in Plato. For the sense, cp. Tyrt. 11. 11—13 οἱ μὲν γὰρ τολμῶσι... παυρότεροι θνήσκουσι κτλ. : Seneca, *Ep.* 94 audentes fortuna iuvat (see Bergk, ad Simon. *fr.* 227): *Il.* V. 531 f. αἰδομένων δ' ἀνδρῶν πλέονες σόοι ἠὲ πέφανται | φευγόντων δ' οὔτ' ἄρ κλέος ὄρνυται οὔτε τις ἀλκή : *ib.* XV. 561 ff.

Πολλά...καὶ ἄλλα κτλ. Cp. 195 B, 201 D. Hirschig's θαυμάσαι gives us (as Rettig argues) "einen matten Gedanken."

θαύματος. "Of wonder" (the subjective feeling), cp. *Phil.* 36 D, *Laws* 967 A: elsewhere in Plato θαῦμα means "quod mirum est."

οἷος γὰρ κτλ. For Achilles, see *Od.* IV. 267 ff. ; and cp. 179 E f.

Βρασίδαν. For this famous Spartan leader, who fell fighting at Amphipolis in 422 B.C., see Thuc. II. 25, 85 ff., v. 6; Bury, *Hist. Gr.* pp. 445 ff.

ἄλλους, καὶ οἷος αὖ Περικλῆς, καὶ Νέστορα καὶ Ἀντήνορα, εἰσὶ δὲ
καὶ ἕτεροι· καὶ τοὺς ἄλλους κατὰ ταῦτ' ἄν τις ἀπεικάζοι· οἷος D
δὲ οὑτοσὶ γέγονε τὴν ἀτοπίαν ἄνθρωπος, καὶ αὐτὸς καὶ οἱ λόγοι
αὐτοῦ, οὐδ' ἐγγὺς ἂν εὕροι τις ζητῶν, οὔτε τῶν νῦν οὔτε τῶν
παλαιῶν, εἰ μὴ ἄρα εἰ οἷς ἐγὼ λέγω ἀπεικάζοι τις αὐτόν, ἀνθρώπων μὲν μηδενί, τοῖς δὲ σιληνοῖς καὶ σατύροις, αὐτὸν καὶ τοὺς
λόγους.

XXXVII. Καὶ γὰρ οὖν καὶ τοῦτο ἐν τοῖς πρώτοις παρέλιπον,
ὅτι καὶ οἱ λόγοι αὐτοῦ ὁμοιότατοί εἰσι τοῖς σιληνοῖς τοῖς διοιγο-
μένοις. εἰ γὰρ ἐθέλοι τις τῶν Σωκράτους ἀκούειν λόγων, φανεῖεν E
ἂν πάγγελοιοι τὸ πρῶτον· τοιαῦτα καὶ ὀνόματα καὶ ῥήματα ἔξωθεν
περιαμπέχονται, σατύρου [ἂν] τινὰ ὑβριστοῦ δοράν. ὄνους γὰρ

221 C εἰσὶ...ἕτεροι secl. Jn. J.-U.   εἰσὶ: οἷοι Bdhm.   D τοὺς del.
Bdhm.: τοὺς ⟨μὲν⟩ Hirschig   ταῦτ': ταῦτ' B: τοῦτ' W   ἄνθρωπος Sauppe
Sz. Bt.: ἄνθρωπος BT   οὔτε τῶν νῦν...παλαιῶν del. (Hommel) Hirschig Jn.
ἄρα εἰ B: ἄρα TW O.-P.   λέγω TW O.-P.: λέγων B   αὐτόν τε καὶ vulg.
E ἐθέλοι B: ἐθέλει T   τῶν...λόγων TW O.-P.: τὸν...λόγον B   παγγέλοιοι
scripsi: πάνυ γελοῖοι TW O.-P., vulg. Bt.: γελοῖοι B, J.-U. Sz.   τινὰ B O.-P.,
J.-U. Sz.: ἄν τινα TW: δή τινα Baiter Cobet Bt.: αὖ τινα Rückert

---

Περικλῆς.   Sco 215 E n., Gorg. 515 c ff., 519 A.

Νέστορα καὶ Ἀντήνορα.   Comparable to Pericles on the ground of eloquence
(cp. 215 E, Pericles as ἀγαθὸς ῥήτωρ)· For Nestor, see Hom. Il. I. 247 ff. ; for
Antenor, Il. VII. 347 ff. ; Hor. Ep. I. 2. 9.

221 D τὴν ἀτοπίαν.   "Originalität" (Wolf): see 215 A n.

ἀνθρώπων μὲν κτλ.   See 215 A, B, 216 E.

221 E παγγέλοιοι.   Cp. 189 B, 215 A ; the context shows that -γέλοιος here
is nearly equiv. to καταγέλαστος. Of Socr., as of S. Paul, it was said that "his
speech was contemptible."

ὀνόματα καὶ ῥήματα.   See 198 B n.

ἔξωθεν περιαμπέχονται.   Cp. 216 B ἔξωθεν περιβέβληται.

σατύρου [ἂν] τινά.   Stallb. vainly argues in a long note that "ἂν tenendum et
per ellipsin verbi (i.e. οὖσαν) explicandum esse."

ὑβριστοῦ.   Cp. 215 B, 175 E.   In δοράν, the satyr's "hide," there is an
allusion, no doubt, to the flaying of Marsyas by Apollo.

ὄνους γὰρ κτλ.   "His talk is of pack-asses and smiths and cobblers and
curriers" (Jowett).   Schol. κανθηλίους· τοὺς βραδεῖς νοῆσαι ἢ ἀφυεῖς. ἀπὸ κάν-
θωνος, ὅς ἐστιν ὄνος, εἰρημένοι, κτλ. : cp.Ar. Vesp. 170 ff., 177 ff.   For ὄνοι in Plato,
cp. Gorg. 516 A, Rep. 563 c ; for χαλκεῖς, Prot. 319 D, Crat. 388 D, 389 E. Cp.
Gorg. 490 c ff., where Callicles objects ἀτεχνῶς γε ἀεὶ σκυτέας τε καὶ κναφέας
καὶ μαγείρους λέγων καὶ ἰατροὺς οὐδὲν παύει κτλ.: Xen. Mem. I. 2. 37 ὁ δὲ
Κριτίας, Ἀλλὰ τῶνδέ τοί σε ἀπέχεσθαι, ἔφη, δεήσει, ὦ Σώκρατες, τῶν σκυτέων καὶ
τῶν τεκτόνων καὶ τῶν χαλκέων : ib. IV. 4. 5—6: Max. Tyr. diss. IX. 1.

κανθηλίους λέγει καὶ χαλκέας τινὰς καὶ σκυτοτόμους καὶ βυρ-
σοδέψας, καὶ ἀεὶ διὰ τῶν αὐτῶν τὰ αὐτὰ φαίνεται λέγειν, ὥστε
ἄπειρος καὶ ἀνόητος ἄνθρωπος πᾶς ἂν τῶν λόγων καταγελάσειεν.

222 διοιγομένους δὲ ἰδὼν αὖ τις καὶ ἐντὸς αὐτῶν γιγνόμενος πρῶτον μὲν
νοῦν ἔχοντας ἔνδον μόνους εὑρήσει τῶν λόγων, ἔπειτα θειοτάτους
καὶ πλεῖστ' ἀγάλματ' ἀρετῆς ἐν αὑτοῖς ἔχοντας καὶ ἐπὶ πλεῖστον
τείνοντας, μᾶλλον δὲ ἐπὶ πᾶν ὅσον προσήκει σκοπεῖν τῷ μέλλοντι
καλῷ κἀγαθῷ ἔσεσθαι.

Ταῦτ' ἐστίν, ὦ ἄνδρες, ἃ ἐγὼ Σωκράτη ἐπαινῶ· καὶ αὖ ἃ μέμφομαι συμμίξας ὑμῖν εἶπον ἅ με ὕβρισεν. καὶ μέντοι οὐκ ἐμὲ
B μόνον ταῦτα πεποίηκεν, ἀλλὰ καὶ Χαρμίδην τὸν Γλαύκωνος καὶ
Εὐθύδημον τὸν Διοκλέους καὶ ἄλλους πάνυ πολλούς, οὓς οὗτος
ἐξαπατῶν ὡς ἐραστὴς παιδικὰ μᾶλλον αὐτὸς καθίσταται ἀντ'

221 E κανθηλινους O.-P. 222 A διοιγουμένους B αὖ Bekk. Hug Bt.:
ἄν libri, O.-P.: δὴ Sz. ἐγγὺς αὐτῶν γε Hommel εὑρήσειε Usener τῶν
λόγων TW O.-P.: τὸν λόγον B: del. Wagner Voeg. τείνοντας TW: τινοντας
O.-P.: τείναντας B ἐπὶ TW O.-P.: ἔτι B B πάνυ om. O.-P.

222 A ἰδὼν αὖ τις. "ἄν cum participio cohaeret hoc sensu, ἐάν τις ἴδῃ...
si quis forte viderit" (Rückert); Stallb., too, defends ἄν, citing Rep. 589 E,
Phaedo 61 C, Euthyd. 287 D; the objection of Rückert and Rettig, that αὖ
ought to stand after διοιγομένους rather than after ἰδών, is not fatal.

μόνους...τῶν λόγων. For the contrast implied, cp. Homer's οἶος πέπνυται,
ταὶ δὲ σκιαὶ ἀίσσουσιν (Meno 100 A). A similar ascription of life to λόγοι is to
be found in Phaedr. 276 A.

θειοτάτους κτλ. Cp. 216 D—E. The whole of this account of Socrates'
λόγοι is virtually an encomium of his σοφία.

τείνοντας...ἐπὶ πᾶν. Cp. 188 B ἐπὶ πᾶν ὁ θεὸς τείνει: Rep. 581 B. For
echoes of phrases in the previous speeches here, and throughout Alcib.'s
speech, see Introd. § vi (3).

ἃ μέμφομαι κτλ. "Verba ita connectenda sunt: καὶ συμμίξας αὖ ἃ μέμφομαι εἶπον ὑμῖν ἅ με ὕβρισε" (Stallb.). Stephens erroneously put a comma,
Wolf a full stop, after μέμφομαι. Rückert, agreeing with Stallb., put a comma
after συμμίξας, and Hommel added another after αὖ. Jowett's transl.,—"I
have added my blame of him for his ill-treatment of me"—seems to imply
a different view of the construction. The points alluded to are those mentioned in 217 B ff., 219 C.

222 B Χαρμίδην. For Charmides, Plato's avunculus, see Charm. 154, 157;
Xen. Mem. III. 7, Symp. III. 9 etc.

Εὐθύδημον. This Euthydemus, son of Diocles (see Xen. Mem. IV. 2. 40), is
not to be confounded with his namesake the sophist, who appears in the
dialogue Euthyd.

παιδικὰ...ἀντ' ἐραστοῦ. "The object rather than the subject of love."
This may fairly be construed, with Rettig, as an indication that Socr., the

ἐραστοῦ. ἃ δὴ καὶ σοὶ λέγω, ὦ 'Αγάθων, μὴ ἐξαπατᾶσθαι ὑπὸ τούτου, ἀλλ' ἀπὸ τῶν ἡμετέρων παθημάτων γνόντα εὐλαβηθῆναι, καὶ μὴ κατὰ τὴν παροιμίαν ὥσπερ νήπιον παθόντα γνῶναι. XXXVIII. Εἰπόντος δὴ ταῦτα τοῦ 'Αλκιβιάδου γέλωτα C γενέσθαι ἐπὶ τῇ παρρησίᾳ αὐτοῦ, ὅτι ἐδόκει ἔτι ἐρωτικῶς ἔχειν τοῦ Σωκράτους. τὸν οὖν Σωκράτη, Νήφειν μοι δοκεῖς, φάναι, ὦ 'Αλκιβιάδη. οὐ γὰρ ἄν ποθ' οὕτω κομψῶς κύκλῳ περιβαλλόμενος ἀφανίσαι ἐνεχείρεις οὗ ἕνεκα ταῦτα πάντα εἴρηκας, καὶ ὡς ἐν παρέργῳ δὴ λέγων ἐπὶ τελευτῆς αὐτὸ ἔθηκας, ὡς οὐ πάντα τούτου

222 B ἐξαπατᾶσθε B   ἀλλ' υπο O.-P.¹   γνῶντα B   C παρησια O.-P. εδοκε τ[ι] O.-P.¹   ομψῶς pr. B   οὗ ἕνεκα TW: οὐδ' ἕνεκα B: ουνεκα O.-P. (ν e δ corr.): οὗ δὴ ἕνεκα Usener

embodiment of the ideal κάλλος, is exalted above Eros (cp. 201 A): contrast 180 B θειότερον ἐραστὴς παιδικῶν. For the reversal of the rôles of Alc. and Socr., cp. *I. Alc.* 135 D κινδυνεύσομεν μεταβαλεῖν τὸ σχῆμα, ὦ Σώκρατες, τὸ μὲν σὸν ἐγώ, σὺ δὲ τοὐμόν. οὐ γὰρ ἔστιν ὅπως οὐ παιδαγωγήσω σε κτλ. Cp. also Xen. *Symp.* VIII. 5; and see *Introd.* § VI. 3.

ἃ δὴ...ἐξαπατᾶσθαι. Hommel and Rettig, after Stallb., take the infin. clause to be epexegetic of ἅ: Rückert construes ἐξαπ. as a second accus. depending on λέγω: Hug makes the infin. depend on ἃ λέγω (equiv. to "I give you this warning") as on a "verbum voluntatis." It may be simply an oblique imperative.

κατὰ τὴν παροιμίαν. Cp. Hom. *Il.* XVII. 33 ῥεχθὲν δέ τε νήπιος ἔγνω: *ib.* XX. 198 : Hes. *Op.* 218 παθὼν δέ τε νήπιος ἔγνω: Hdt. I. 207 παθήματα μαθήματα: Aesch. *Ag.* 177, *Cho.* 313 : Soph. *O. C.* 143: and our English proverb "a burnt child dreads the fire." Schol. ῥεχθὲν...ἔγνω· ἐπὶ τῶν μετὰ τὸ παθεῖν συνιέντων τὸ ἁμάρτημα. ἐπὶ τὸ αὐτὸ ἑτέρα παροιμία· ὁ ἁλιεὺς πληγεὶς νοῦν φύσει· κτλ.

222 C παρρησίᾳ. "Naivetät" (Wolf); see A.'s excuses for it in 217 E.

Νήφειν μοι δοκεῖς. Echoing the phrase previously used by Alcib. (δοκεῖτε γάρ μοι νήφειν 213 E), Socr. jocosely derides his repeated plea of intoxication 212 E, 214 C, etc.), saying in effect: "It's sober you are, not drunk; otherwise you could never have excogitated so deep a scheme."

κομψῶς. Of a "pretty" trick; cp. *Theaet.* 202 D, *Soph.* 236 D.

κύκλῳ περιβαλλόμενος. See Ast *ad Phaedr.* 272 D "imago desumta est ab amictu, quem rhetores, priusquam perorarent, componere solebant: V. Quintil. XI. 3. 116": Cic. *de or.* III. 39. 138 se circumvestit dictis. For κύκλῳ cp. Ar. *Rhet.* I. 9. 33 (with Cope's note), III. 14. 10, and Virgil's "per ambages" (*G.* II. 45).

ἐπὶ τελευτῆς. *I.e.* as if it were an after-thought only: cp. 198 B, *Phaedr.* 267 D.

168 ΠΛΑΤΩΝΟΣ [222 C

D ἕνεκα εἰρηκώς, τοῦ ἐμὲ καὶ 'Αγάθωνα διαβάλλειν, οἰόμενος δεῖν ἐμὲ
μὲν σοῦ ἐρᾶν καὶ μηδενὸς ἄλλου, 'Αγάθωνα δὲ ὑπὸ σοῦ ἐρᾶσθαι
καὶ μηδ' ὑφ' ἑνὸς ἄλλου. ἀλλ' οὐκ ἔλαθες, ἀλλὰ τὸ σατυρικόν
σου δρᾶμα τοῦτο καὶ σιληνικὸν κατάδηλον ἐγένετο. ἀλλ', ὦ φίλε
'Αγάθων, μηδὲν πλέον αὐτῷ γένηται, ἀλλὰ παρασκευάζου ὅπως
ἐμὲ καὶ σὲ μηδεὶς διαβαλεῖ. τὸν οὖν 'Αγάθωνα εἰπεῖν, Καὶ μήν,
E ὦ Σώκρατες, κινδυνεύεις ἀληθῆ λέγειν. τεκμαίρομαι δὲ καὶ ὡς
κατεκλίνη ἐν μέσῳ ἐμοῦ τε καὶ σοῦ, ἵνα χωρὶς ἡμᾶς διαλάβῃ.
οὐδὲν οὖν πλέον αὐτῷ ἔσται, ἀλλ' ἐγὼ παρὰ σὲ ἐλθὼν κατακλινή-
σομαι. Πάνυ γε, φάναι τὸν Σωκράτη, δεῦρο ὑποκάτω ἐμοῦ κατα-

222 D διαβαλεῖ Hirschig Cobet Sz. Bt. : διαβαλει O.-P. : διαβάλῃ BTW

---

222 D ἐμὲ...διαβάλλειν. "To set us at variance": cp. 222 D, *Rep.* 498 c.
οἰόμενος δεῖν κτλ. *I.e.* thinking that you must at once monopolise Socr. as
your ἐραστής and Agathon as your παιδικά. For δεῖν, cp. 222 E.
ἀλλ' οὐκ ἔλαθες κτλ. For the conversational carelessness of the repeated
ἀλλά, cp. 175 B (four times).
τὸ σατυρικόν σου δρᾶμα κτλ. A playful allusion to the εἰκόνες employed
by Alcib. in his encomium (see 215 B). For "satyric drama" see Smith,
D. A. II. 860 b: "The satyr-drama was so-called because the Chorus consisted
of satyrs attendant on Dionysus...it was aptly described as παίζουσα τρα-
γῳδία": Jevons, *Hist. Gk. Lit.* p. 186.
μηδὲν πλέον κτλ. An echo of the language of Alcib. in 217 c.
222 E χωρὶς διαλάβῃ. "Dictum hoc eleganter cum amphibolia quadam,
ut et de spatio possit cogitari et de animorum disiunctione" (Stallb.): cp.
Phil. 55 D.
ὑποκάτω ἐμοῦ. The original order of the places on this (ἐσχάτη) κλίνη was
(1) Agathon, Socrates (see 175 C—D): then Alcibiades on his entrance had
seated himself in the middle (213 B *ad init.*), thus making the order
(2) Agathon, Alcib., Socr.: now Socrates invites Agathon to shift his position
so as to change the order to (3) Alcib., Socr., Agathon: presently, in the
sentence following, Alcibiades suggests that, instead of this, Agathon should
take the middle place (ἐν μέσῳ ἡμῶν) which would result in the order
(4) Alcib., Agathon, Socrates. But the adoption of this last order is, as
Socr. hastens to point out, impossible, inasmuch as it would cause serious
dislocation in the series of λόγοι which are bound to proceed in order from left
to right (see 214 c), each speaker taking for his theme his next neighbour on
the right. If the order (4) were adopted, it would be the duty of the next
speaker, Agathon, to eulogize Socrates, a task already performed by Alcib.
himself; whereas by adopting the order (3), the next speech would fall to
Socr., and he would have for his theme Agathon, an arrangement unobjectionable in itself and well-pleasing to Socr. (πάνυ ἐπιθυμῶ αὐτὸν ἐγκωμιάσαι, 223 A)
as well as to Agathon (ἰοῦ ἰοῦ κτλ., 223 A).

κλίνου. Ὦ Ζεῦ, εἰπεῖν τὸν Ἀλκιβιάδην, οἷα αὖ πάσχω ὑπὸ τοῦ ἀνθρώπου. οἴεταί μου δεῖν πανταχῇ περιεῖναι. ἀλλ᾽ εἰ μή τι ἄλλο, ὦ θαυμάσιε, ἐν μέσῳ ἡμῶν ἔα Ἀγάθωνα κατακεῖσθαι. Ἀλλ᾽ ἀδύνατον, φάναι τὸν Σωκράτη. σὺ μὲν γὰρ ἐμὲ ἐπῄνεσας, δεῖ δ᾽ ἐμὲ αὖ τὸν ἐπὶ δεξί᾽ ἐπαινεῖν. ἐὰν οὖν ὑπὸ σοὶ κατακλινῇ Ἀγάθων—οὐ δή που ἐμὲ πάλιν ἐπαινέσεται, πρὶν ὑπ᾽ ἐμοῦ μᾶλλον ἐπαινεθῆναι; ἀλλ᾽ ἔασον, ὦ δαιμόνιε, καὶ μὴ φθονήσῃς τῷ 223 μειρακίῳ ὑπ᾽ ἐμοῦ ἐπαινεθῆναι· καὶ γὰρ πάνυ ἐπιθυμῶ αὐτὸν ἐγκωμιάσαι. Ἰοῦ ἰοῦ, φάναι τὸν Ἀγάθωνα, Ἀλκιβιάδη, οὐκ ἔσθ᾽ ὅπως ἂν ἐνθάδε μείναιμι, ἀλλὰ παντὸς μᾶλλον μεταναστήσομαι, ἵνα ὑπὸ Σωκράτους ἐπαινεθῶ. Ταῦτα ἐκεῖνα, φάναι τὸν Ἀλκιβιάδην, τὰ εἰωθότα· Σωκράτους παρόντος τῶν καλῶν μεταλαβεῖν ἀδύνατον ἄλλῳ. καὶ νῦν ὡς εὐπόρως καὶ πιθανὸν λόγον ηὗρεν, ὥστε παρ᾽ ἑαυτῷ τουτονὶ κατακεῖσθαι.

222 E περιεῖναι: περιϊέναι O.-P.   γὰρ ἐμὲ B O.-P.: γάρ με TW   αὖ τὸν Bekk.: αυ τον B O.-P.: αὐτὸν T: αὖ τόνδ᾽ Ast   κατακλιθη O.-P.   οὐ δή που: οὕτω δήπου Bdhm.: fort. οὐ δεῖ που   ἐπαινέσεται: fort. ἐπαινέσαι vel ἐπαινεῖσθαι   πρὶν: δεῖν Usener Hug: παρὸν (vel παρεὶς...ἄλλον) Bdhm.   223 A μᾶλλον B O.-P.: ₓₓₓ μᾶλλον T: om. Vind. 21: ἄλλον Mdvg. ἐπαινεθῆναι; distinxit Ast   ἰού ἰού T   παντὸς: παντοσ[ᾳ] O.-P.   εὐπορω O.-P.

οἷα αὖ πάσχω. "How I am fooled" (Jowett). This echoes 215 D οἷα δὴ πέπονθα κτλ.: cp. 184 B κακῶς πάσχων (sc. ὁ ἐρώμενος).

ὑπὸ σοί. ὁ ὑπό τινι (or ὑποκάτω τινος) is equiv. to ὁ ἐπὶ δεξιά (cp. 175 C n.).

οὐ δή που κτλ. If we retain the MS. reading, this clause is best printed as interrogative (so Bt. and Lehrs)—taking the place of a regular apodosis, such as δεήσει αὐτὸν ἐμὲ πάλιν ἐπαινεῖν. Against Badh.,—who wrote "monstri vero simile est, πρὶν ὑπ᾽ ἐμοῦ μᾶλλον ἐπαινεθῆναι,"—Rettig attempts to defend the text thus: "Statt der Worte: 'er wird eher wollen von mir gelobt werden, als mich loben,' setze man: es wird nicht verlangt werden können, dass er mich lobe, bevor ich vielmehr ihn gelobt habe"; i.e. οὐ δήπου ἐπαινέσεται is equiv. to οὐ δήπου ἐπαινεῖν ἐθελήσει. This, however, is awkward; and some corruption must, I believe, be assumed: if so, the changes I have proposed seem the most plausible.

223 A Ἰοῦ ἰοῦ. For a distinction between ἰοῦ, as a cry of joy, and ἰού, of pain, see Schol. on Ar. Nub. 1170. Here it denotes jubilation, not commiseration as Hommel suggests ("Wehe, wehe, armer Alkibiades" etc.).

Ταῦτα ἐκεῖνα. Cp. 210 E, Charm. 166 B (Schanz nov. comm. p. 16).

εὐπόρως. This echoes phrases in the description of Eros, son of Πόρος, see 203 D (πόριμος), 203 E (εὐπορήσῃ), 204 B (πατρὸς...εὐπόρου). Similarly πιθανὸν suggests the plausible tongue of the γόης and σοφιστής of 203 D.

πιθανὸν λόγον ηὗρεν. For this "inventiveness of plausible argument" as belonging to the art of the sophistical rhetor, cp. Gorg. 457 A ff., Phaedr. 269 D.

B XXXIX. Τὸν μὲν οὖν Ἀγάθωνα ὡς κατακεισόμενον παρὰ τῷ
Σωκράτει ἀνίστασθαι· ἐξαίφνης δὲ κωμαστὰς ἥκειν παμπόλλους
ἐπὶ τὰς θύρας, καὶ ἐπιτυχόντας ἀνεῳγμέναις ἐξιόντος τινὸς εἰς τὸ
ἄντικρυς πορεύεσθαι παρὰ σφᾶς καὶ κατακλίνεσθαι, καὶ θορύβου
μεστὰ πάντα εἶναι, καὶ οὐκέτι ἐν κόσμῳ οὐδενὶ, ἀναγκάζεσθαι
πίνειν πάμπολυν οἶνον. τὸν μὲν οὖν Ἐρυξίμαχον καὶ τὸν Φαῖδρον
καὶ ἄλλους τινὰς ἔφη ὁ Ἀριστόδημος οἴχεσθαι ἀπιόντας, ἒ δὲ
C ὕπνον λαβεῖν, καὶ καταδαρθεῖν πάνυ πολύ, ἅτε μακρῶν τῶν νυκτῶν
οὐσῶν, ἐξεγρέσθαι δὲ πρὸς ἡμέραν ἤδη ἀλεκτρυόνων ᾀδόντων,
ἐξεγρόμενος δὲ ἰδεῖν τοὺς μὲν ἄλλους καθεύδοντας καὶ οἰχομένους,
Ἀγάθωνα δὲ καὶ Ἀριστοφάνη καὶ Σωκράτη ἔτι μόνους ἐγρηγορέναι
καὶ πίνειν ἐκ φιάλης μεγάλης ἐπὶ δεξιά. τὸν οὖν Σωκράτη αὐτοῖς

223 B αναιωγμεναις O.-P.[1]   εἰς τὸ : εισω O.-P.   ⟨τους⟩ αλλους O.-P.
ἒ δὲ BW : ἔαδε T : εαυτον δε O.-P.   C καταδάρθειν Rettig   πάνυ : ατε
O.-P.[1]   Σωκρατη και Αριστοφανη O.-P. Ven. 184 Vind. 21   μεγαλης
φι[λ]αλης O.-P. Paris 1642 Vat. 229

223 B **ἐξαίφνης δὲ** κτλ. Cp. the "sudden" tumultuous entrance of
Alcibiades (212 C καὶ ἐξαίφνης κτλ.). The incursion here is devised in order
to save the situation. For the sake of artistic effect, the series of λόγοι must
now stop: the climax having been reached in the encomium of Socr. by
Alcib., to add a eulogy of any lesser personage would be bathos.

ἐξιόντος τινὸς κτλ. Hommel comments : "imaginem proponit comissatorum
contra nitente eo, qui iam exiturus erat, aditum vi expugnantium." But, as
Rettig remarks, there is no hint in the text of *vis* or of *nisus*. The words
ἐξιόντος τινὸς are merely put in to explain how it was that they found the
doors open. εἰς τὸ ἄντικρυς is connected by Hommel and Stallb.[2] with ἐξιόντος,
but by Rückert, Ast and Stallb.[1] with πορεύεσθαι: the former view is
preferable.

Ἐρυξίμαχον. Eryx. and Phaedrus are represented throughout as "hunting
in couples"; and it is characteristic of the former, as an authority on health,
and of the latter, as a valetudinarian, that they should be the first to escape
from the scene of θόρυβος and παμπολὺς οἶνος: cp. 176 B ff., 214 A ff.

223 C **μακρῶν τῶν νυκτῶν.** This indication of date would suit either the
Lenaea in January or the *Great Dionysia* in March, though rather favouring
the former (cp. *Introd.* § VIII a).

ἀλεκτρυόνων ᾀδόντων. Cp. *Theaet.* 164 C ἀλεκτρυόνος ἀγεννοῦς δίκην...ᾄδειν.
The hour of cock-crow was, theoretically, the 3rd watch (12—3 a.m.): cp. *Ev.
Mc.* xiii. 35. Jowett's "he was awakened by a crowing of cocks" misses ἤδη,
which goes with ᾀδόντων.

καὶ οἰχομένους. We should expect ἤ rather than καί: but (as Rückert
observes) οἱ μὲν ἄλλοι fall into two subdivisions,—those absent in spirit
(καθεύδ.), and those absent in body (οἴχομ.).

ἐγρηγορέναι κτλ. Cp. Athen. v. 192 A Σωκράτης...ἐγρήγορε...καὶ πίνει ἐξ
ἀργυροῦ φρέατος· καλῶς γάρ τις τὰ μεγάλα ποτήρια οὕτως ὠνόμασε κτλ.

διαλέγεσθαι· καὶ τὰ μὲν ἄλλα ὁ Ἀριστόδημος οὐκ ἔφη μεμνῆσθαι
τῶν λόγων—οὔτε γὰρ ἐξ ἀρχῆς παραγενέσθαι ὑπονυστάζειν τε· τὸ D
μέντοι κεφάλαιον, ἔφη, προσαναγκάζειν τὸν Σωκράτη ὁμολογεῖν
αὐτοὺς τοῦ αὐτοῦ ἀνδρὸς εἶναι κωμῳδίαν καὶ τραγῳδίαν ἐπίστασθαι
ποιεῖν, καὶ τὸν τέχνῃ τραγῳδοποιὸν ὄντα <καὶ> κωμῳδοποιὸν
εἶναι. ταῦτα δὴ ἀναγκαζομένους αὐτοὺς καὶ οὐ σφόδρα ἑπομένους
νυστάζειν, καὶ πρῶτον μὲν καταδαρθεῖν τὸν Ἀριστοφάνη, ἤδη δὲ
ἡμέρας γιγνομένης τὸν Ἀγάθωνα. τὸν οὖν Σωκράτη, κατακοιμίσαντ' ἐκείνους, ἀναστάντα ἀπιέναι, καὶ <ἓ> ὥσπερ εἰώθει ἕπεσθαι,
καὶ ἐλθόντα εἰς Λύκειον, ἀπονιψάμενον, ὥσπερ ἄλλοτε τὴν ἄλλην

223 D　καὶ κωμωδοποιὸν Vind. 21, vulg. Sz. Bt.: κωμῳδοποιὸν BTW O.-P.
πρῶτον B: πρότερον TW O.-P.　　Ἀριστοφαν[ους] O.-P.　　γενομένης vulg.
Hirschig　κατακοιμίσαντ' BW O.-P.: κατακοιμήσαντ' T　　καὶ ἓ Herm. Sz.
Bt.: καὶ libri, O.-P.: καὶ ἱ Bekker　　ἄλλην: ὅλην Ficinus

τὰ μὲν ἄλλα κτλ.　This is artistic selection disguised under the cloke of
imperfect recollection, cp. 178 A, 180 C.
223 D τὸ μέντοι κεφάλαιον. "The gist of it was...": cp. 205 D ad init.
τοῦ αὐτοῦ ἀνδρὸς κτλ. Cp. Ion 534 B τέχνῃ ποιοῦντες. Here both τέχνῃ
and ἐπίστασθαι are emphatic, with no distinction between them implied.
The point of Socrates' argument is that the scientific poet must be master of
the art of poetry in its universal, generic aspect, and therefore of both its
included species, tragedy and comedy. This thought, if developed, might be
shown to mean that full knowledge both of λόγοι and of ψυχαί, and of the
effects of the one on the other, is requisite to form a master-poet. Which is
equivalent to saying that, just as the ideal State requires the philosopher-
king, so ideal Art is impossible without the φιλόσοφος-ποιητής. The thesis
here maintained by Socrates finds in the supreme instance of Shakspere
both illustration and confirmation: "The Merry Wives" came from the
same hand as "Othello" and "Lear."
The statement in Schol. ad Ar. Ran. 214 and Philostr. (vit. soph. I. 9,
p. 439) that Agathon wrote comedies as well as tragedies is probably due to a
blunder: see Bentley, opusc. phil. p. 613.
οὐ σφόδρα ἑπομένους. "Erant enim vino languidi. Ad ἑπομένους in-
telligi potest τοῖς λεγομένοις Euthyphr. p. 12 A οὐχ ἕπομαι τοῖς λεγομένοις"
(Stallb.).
κατακοιμίσαντα. An allusion, perhaps, to Agathon's κοίτην ὕπνον τ' ἐνὶ
κήδει, 197 C. Cp. Laws 790 D κατακοιμίζειν τὰ δυσυπνοῦντα τῶν παιδίων.
<ἓ>. I.e. Aristodemus, the narrator: for his practice (εἰώθει) of dogging
the footsteps of the Master, cp. 173 B, 174 B (ἕπου).
Λύκειον. This was a gymnasium, sacred to Apollo Lyceus, situated in the
eastern suburbs of Athens, though the exact site—whether S.E. or N. of the

ἡμέραν διατρίβειν, καὶ οὕτω διατρίψαντα εἰς ἑσπέραν οἴκοι ἀναπαύεσθαι.

223 D   και κ[α]ι ουτω O.-P.

Cynosarges—is uncertain.   The Lyceum is mentioned also in the beginning
of the *Lysis* and of the *Euthyphro*; cp. Xen. *Mem.* I. 1. 10, Paus. I. 19. 4.
"Ibi Socr. versabatur propterea quod sophistae in eo scholas habebant,
quorum inscitiam solebat convincere, et quod plurimos illic adolescentes
nanciscebatur, quibus cum sermones instituere posset" (Stallb.).

INDEX I. GREEK.

INDEX II. ENGLISH.

.

Printed in Great Britain
by Amazon

18140986R00154